CHILD WELFARE AND FAMILY SERVICES

POLICIES AND PRACTICE

SIXTH EDITION

SUSAN WHITELAW DOWNS

Wayne State University

ERNESTINE MOORE

Wayne State University

EMILY JEAN MCFADDEN

Grand Valley State University

LELA B. COSTIN

Professor Emeritus
University of Illinois at Urbana-Champaign

ALLYN AND BACON

Boston • London • Toronto • Sydney • Tokyo • Singapore

To the memory of John Moreland Whitelaw and Alvis Love Whitelaw
S. W. D.
To my mom and the children we serve
E. M.
To my grandchildren, Robin, Justice, Africa, Danny, and Sarah
E. J. M.
To the memory of Laura Kerr Brown
L. B. C.

Senior Editor, Social Work and Family Therapy: Judy Fifer
Vice President, Social Sciences: Karen Hanson
Editorial Assistant: Julianna Cancio
Marketing Manager: Lisa Kimball
Editorial-Production Administrator: Annette Joseph

Composition Buyer: Linda Cox
Electronic Composition: Omegatype Typography, Inc.
Manufacturing Buyer: Julie McNeill
Cover Administrator: Linda Knowles
Cover Designer: Brian Gogolin

Copyright © 2000, 1996, 1991 by Allyn & Bacon
A Pearson Education Company
160 Gould St.
Needham Heights, MA 02494

Internet: www.abacon.com

Between the time Website information is gathered and then published, it is not unusual for some sites to have closed. Also, the transcription of URLs can result in unintended typographical errors. The publisher would appreciate notification where these occur so that they may be corrected in subsequent editions. Thank you.

Library of Congress Cataloging-in-Publication
Child welfare and family services : policies and practice / Susan
    Whitelaw Downs ... [et al.]. — 6th ed.
        p.   cm.
    Rev. ed. of Child welfare / Susan Whitelaw Downs, c1996.
    Includes bibliographical references and index.
    ISBN 0-8013-3046-7 (HC)
    1. Child welfare—United States. 2. Family services—United
States. I. Downs, Susan. II. Downs, Susan. Child welfare and
family services.
    HV741.C664 1999
    362.7'0973–dc21   99-34364
                                                   CIP

Printed in the United States of America
10 9 8 7 6 5 4 3 2 1   04 03 02 01 00 99

CONTENTS

Child Welfare and Family Services: Policies and Practice, Sixth Edition, presents concepts, policies, and practice in the broad field of family and child services. Material has been drawn from research findings, legislation, judicial decisions, professional literature, reports of social work practice, and interviews with practitioners. These sources inform the major subjects of the book: the needs of families and children, the major policies and programs of social services designed for them, and the policy issues that emerge for future planning. Our intent is to provide the student—undergraduate or graduate—with a substantive base of knowledge about policies and practice in family and child services.

The place of family and child services in the curricula of schools of social work is changing in response to broadened concepts of services for families and children within the human service community. In earlier years of social work education, child welfare was narrowly defined as a field of practice dealing mainly with children in foster care, in institutions, or in the process of adoption, with some emphasis on protective services. Correspondingly, child welfare courses were self-contained entities in a school's curriculum, combining policy and background knowledge with a large component of practice methods in this specialized field. Today, child welfare services have been redefined as family and child services and include knowledge of the traditional child welfare services as well as a wide range of programs to support families and children and to prevent the need for children's out-of-home care. Because this book addresses policies and programs directed at all families and children, the conceptual framework is appropriate not only for traditionally defined child welfare courses where the instructor may choose to use the content selectively; it is also especially suitable in the curricula of schools of social work that now offer "concentrations" or "specializations" more broadly defined as "services to families, children, and youth." Students in these concentrations are exposed to a range of social services to families and children, organized in a continuum from universal services, through preventive services of various kinds, to the traditional child welfare services. They may be assigned field placements in a variety of agencies serving families and children, including family service agencies, public and private child welfare agencies, child guidance clinics, the courts, and the schools. Students in related concentrations—for example, health and mental health services—for whom knowledge of public policy with respect to families is essential, often elect to enroll in family, child, and youth courses.

The text is designed for use in collaborative educational arrangements between state public child welfare agencies and schools of social work. These partnerships emerged and evolved in the 1980s and 1990s, supported by state and federal funds to promote the reintegration of public agency practice into BSW and MSW programs. The appendix contains curriculum competencies of the state of Michigan, developed by a consortium of six schools of social work in the state and administrators, practitioners, and union representatives of the Michigan Department of Social Services, as a foundation for the education of current and future public agency employees.

Child Welfare and Family Practice is useful as a reliable reference for new personnel entering employment in family and child social agencies and as a tool for planned staff development programs. In some instances, it can be helpful to citizens in our highly technological society who want to influence the environment in which social services are carried out.

Our major objectives are to help the reader do the following:

1. Develop a vital concern for families and children and their potentialities, their cultural diversity, and their experiences in neighborhood, school, and community.
2. Develop an overall orientation to the family as a unit of attention, and to the emerging service concerns of family support, family preservation, kinship care, the continuity of family relationships, and culturally competent approaches.
3. Identify problems necessitating family and child services, see how these problems are related to institutional gaps in the provision of appropriate services, and develop an appreciation for the need for collaboration and integration among service systems.
4. Become familiar with the policies, practices, and goals of current family and child welfare programs and acquire a basis for evaluating them.
5. Learn how services to families and children interact with the larger social and political structures and American cultural values and the profound way these affect the goals and implementation of social policies.
6. Identify some of the salient aspects of social work history that arose in response to rather narrowly conceived social and family/child problems and that still influence family and child welfare programs in this country.
7. Distinguish between family and child welfare practices based on verified knowledge and those based mainly on custom and belief.

This book reflects our conviction that to be effective in today's turbulent world, it is essential that we avoid an overly narrow, categorical view of the welfare of children and their families. This conviction is reflected in the modifications of the book's title for the fifth and sixth editions—from *Child Welfare: Policies and Practice* of earlier editions to *Child Welfare and Family Services: Policies and Practice.* Services for families and children must be broadly defined. It would be inaccurate to portray child welfare as a narrow band of traditional services quite apart from the larger societal context in which it finds its energy, focus, and niche. It would be irresponsible to ignore the impact of public welfare and the courts as major influences on the status of families and children.

Full consideration is given to the basic core of child welfare services: services to protect children from neglect and abuse, family preservation services, foster care, adoption, and child advocacy. These topics are discussed with particular attention to continuity of family relationships and to kinship care. In this edition and the last, we have expanded the scope to include discussion of the rapidly developing family support movement, the most significant advance in preventive services to families in recent decades. We also address emerging issues in public welfare, juvenile delinquency, day care, child development programs, and services to teenage parents.

With an increased focus on the family, we have also striven to highlight the cultural context within which families operate. We have been attentive to the need for cultural understanding and for the culturally competent organization of services. We have, thus, infused content on cultural and ethnic issues throughout the text.

In addition, the text includes the legal framework that governs the affairs of children and young persons (an aspect of the family and child welfare system whose importance has burgeoned) as reflected in laws of guardianship and recent United States Supreme Court decisions, the organization and functioning of the juvenile court and family courts, and the sociolegal issues that emerge in matters of poverty, unwed parenting, delinquency, child neglect and abuse, foster care, and adoption.

This book contains two new chapters: "Family Income Security" and "Juvenile Delinquents: The Community's Dilemma." These chapters reflect the national developments in welfare reform and major changes in society's response to the troubling issue of juvenile crime. To make room for them and for new research findings and other significant aspects of family and child services that have emerged since the fifth edition was published, as well as to avoid having an overly long book, the chapters from the fifth edition entitled "Early Childbearing and the Family" and "The Regulation of Children's Out-of-Home Care" have been omitted from this edition. Content on these topics has been integrated into appropriate chapters, particularly those on family support, day care, and foster care.

All the chapters in the sixth edition of *Child Welfare and Family Services: Policies and Practice* have been carefully revised and updated to include more case material illustrating family-centered approaches. The case material is drawn generally from our own experience and that of other practitioners, but as presented here it is entirely fictitious. The chapters also include findings from recent research, important new court decisions and legislation affecting the child and the family, and innovative demonstrations in recent practice with families and children, which reflect the renewed commitment to preserve a child's own home and to offer services early to prevent serious family breakdown.

The order of chapters reflects our preference for providing the student with a beginning understanding of families and of services to families, since this is the primary focus of the book. The first two chapters provide a foundation for the study of family and child welfare, presenting the historical background, an overview of services, and the legal framework for the relationship among children, parents, and the state. The following three chapters emphasize the importance of basic services to families, including material on family support services, services to teenage parents, welfare reform, day care, and child development programs. The last half of the book covers traditional child welfare services, including child protective services, family preservation services, foster care, adoption, and juvenile delinquency. A chapter on juvenile and family courts provides a legal framework for this material. The last chapter addresses the role of social workers in child advocacy and also professional issues in child welfare practice.

The chapters have also been written to stand alone so they can be ordered in a number of different ways to reflect the individual instructor's personal preferences in constructing a family and child services course and teaching outline. In our teaching, we have presented the chapters in differing order for different groups of students. This book is highly adaptable in organization.

At the end of each chapter are questions for individual study and for class discussions as well as selected sources that the instructor can use for lecture-discussion material or that the student can use for further independent study. For this edition, we have added two new sections at the end of each chapter: a chapter summary and a list of relevant Internet sites, reflecting the rapid increase in use of the World Wide Web. For additional exploration of ideas, the references at the end of each chapter provide a substantial bibliography of family and child services.

In the course of preparing six editions of *Child Welfare and Family Services: Policies and Practice,* we have incurred many debts to numerous colleagues and academicians in other disciplines, and to administrators and staff members of public child welfare agencies and professional social workers in other settings, who carry out the demanding work in family and child services. They have directed us to new material and offered criticism and new insights that have been invaluable. We are also heavily indebted to our students, who are keen critics, providing sometimes unexpected enlightenment, and who represent for us the future of family and child services as an essential field of social work practice. We also owe thanks to colleagues who reviewed the text in preparation for both the fifth and sixth editions: Mary Ellen Elwell, Salisbury State University; Edward J. Gumz, Loyola University; Karen V. Harper, West Virginia University; John M. Herrick, Michigan State University; Vanessa G. Hodges, University of North Carolina–Chapel Hill; Dorinda N. Noble, Louisiana State University; Ruth Pellow, University of Arkansas at Monticello; Elizabeth M. Tracy, Case Western Reserve University; Maha N. Younes, University of Nebraska–Kearney.

We express appreciation to the late Cynthia J. Bell and to Charles A. Rapp, who, as coauthors of earlier editions of this book, supplied new ideas and keen analysis of social problems and practices. We also thank our universities, Wayne State University and Grand Valley State University, for encouragement, resources, and support.

CHAPTER 1

An Introduction to Family and Child Services

In the green years of childhood the young begin their irreversible march into the future with the resolution and sweet calmness of innocence. The march of childhood goes on as long as the human race endures, an affirmation of new hope and the freshness of life that comes with every generation. The message proclaims another chance for mankind.
—United Nations Children's Fund

Child and family welfare services reflect society's organized conviction about the worth of the child and the family, and the child's rights as a developing person and future citizen. Within the wide range of social welfare and social work, child welfare has a dual role: providing direct services to children and families where serious problems of children and youth are identified, and influencing public policy to improve the lives of all children. To strengthen family life for children is regarded as the primary purpose of child welfare.

The field of practice traditionally known as child welfare has been a dominant and influential force in the development of the social work profession. However, child welfare today as a specialized field of social work practice is coming to be known as *family and child services.* It is vastly more complex than it was in the nineteenth and early twentieth centuries when our ancestors confidently responded to problems of family functioning by "rescuing" children of poor or neglectful parents and placing them in institutions of one kind or another. Since then, for at least half a century, social changes have impelled child and family agencies to adapt and innovate services. Today's high public concern about the family, traditionally regarded as society's best institution for promoting stability, is showing more clearly the impact of social, industrial, and economic dislocation. Child and family welfare, as a specialized field of social work practice, is now facing challenges to its gradual but respected evolutionary growth as it confronts demands to move beyond the residual, outworn classification of child welfare services and to respond to new, complex family problems.

Some of the effects of rapid social change over the past decades are manifested in alternative family forms and child-rearing patterns, in the greatly accelerated entry of women with very young children into the labor force, in the unprecedented growth of female-headed families and of unmarried teenage parenting, and in increased official reporting of child abuse and neglect. Other developments have heightened concern among the public and professionals in the child welfare system—the phenomenon of children with acquired immune deficiency syndrome (AIDS); children and families who are homeless; the violence perpetrated by a small number of young people which goes beyond the activities usually labeled as "delinquent"; and the heavy damage to parents, children, and adolescents caused by highly increased rates of drug use.

Despite continuing reform efforts to preserve families and reduce the need for out-of-home placement for children, the number of children in foster care is increasing. The public has become incensed at the shocking newspaper and television accounts of children who have been terribly abused sexually and physically, or neglected to the point of serious impairment or death, and the apparent inability of the child welfare system to prevent maltreatment or to protect children either in their own families or in substitute care. The anger at maltreating parents and apparent agency unresponsiveness has led to myriad calls for change, including congressional debate on bringing back orphanages for children of substance-abusing parents, class action and civil liability suits against agencies, and grassroots reform efforts to give children more legal standing in court to separate themselves from their parents. All these developments, as well as new federal and state legislation and judicial decisions, have served to give a new face to much of child welfare practice, and to make more urgent the need for competent personnel in the system of child and family social services.

This book, then, is about children. It is about their needs and their problems. It is about our society and its influence on children, and therefore it is also a book about families, governments, agencies, and professionals. It is about what we do *for* children and what we do *to* children. It is also a book about how we can do better for the nation's children.

The welfare of children is dependent on the interaction between them and their environments. It is this focus that places the family at center stage because the family is the most dominant part of a child's environment. The family is the major instrument for providing for the welfare of children. It is the primary social institution in meeting social, education, and health care needs. It is the family that negotiates with a larger environment to see that the child's needs are met. A larger society becomes involved when families are judged incapable of ensuring the child's welfare. This can occur because of the extraordinary needs of a special group of children, such as handicapped children, which can easily overwhelm family resources. Or it can occur because families, owing to lack of resources or major dysfunction, cannot meet even minimal standards of child care, as in the case of neglected or abused children.

Social work has had a uniquely important role in the connection between children, families, and organized social welfare. The earliest efforts of the profession were devoted to children and families. As Ann Hartman has described it:

> The profession has supported, replaced, taught, rehabilitated, treated, dismantled, abandoned, and embraced the family. To Mary Richmond [practitioner, teacher, and social work theoretician], the family was the central focus of social work's concern. The first professional practice journal was titled The Family. . . . The early child guidance workers focused their efforts on helping parents to be better parents, and the child-saving movement sought to rescue children by placing them with families. (1981, p. 7)

Traditionally, child welfare has been at the center of the social work profession. Today, that partnership between child welfare and social work is reflected in the philosophy that the best way to help children is to support, strengthen, and supplement the efforts of families. Laird (1985) has offered this precept for child and family welfare:

> Ecologically oriented child welfare practice attends to, nurtures, and supports the biological family. Further, when it is necessary to substitute for the biological family, such practice dictates that every effort be made to preserve and protect important kinship ties. Intervention in families must be done with great care to avoid actions which could weaken the natural family, sap its vitality and strength, or force it to make difficult costly adjustments. (p. 177)

THE CHANGING AMERICAN FAMILY

Many observers have claimed that more changes have occurred in the American family over recent decades than ever before in our history. The changes have led some to pronounce that the American family is breaking down, losing its preeminent position in American society. The more prevalent belief is that the American family is merely adapting to a very different world from the one it experienced earlier. As one commentator has stated, "Current family changes indicate American pluralism rather than family breakdown" (*Listening*, 1980, p. 160). Regardless of the conclusions, few would argue that the last four decades have witnessed major changes in the family.

The U.S. Department of Commerce, Bureau of the Census, has reported that in 1998 there were 70.2 million children under the age of 18, making this the first year that the population of children in the United States has risen above the peak of the baby boom in 1966, when the nation had 69.9 million children. The population of children declined during the 1970s and 1980s, but began to rise again in the 1990s.

The "Millennium Generation," as the new baby boom is called, looks very different from the previous one, which was fueled by the large number of births following World War II. The current boom was created by immigration as much as by an increase in births to those born in the United States. The Millennium Generation is more ethnically diverse than the earlier one; 14 percent of today's children are Hispanic, compared to 9 percent in 1980. The current generation of children is 66 percent white, compared to 74 percent in 1980. Children of African-American descent comprise 15 percent of the population, a percentage which has remained stable since 1980. The percentage of Asian children has doubled since 1980, from 2 percent to 4 percent (Russakoff, 1998).

Even though the number of children is increasing, the number of children as a percentage of the total population continues to decline, from 36 percent in 1966 to 26 percent in 1996, as other age segments of the population increase more rapidly than does the under-18 age group. There are fewer households with children at the same time that the number of children is increasing overall. This decreasing proportion may result in a loss to children of the government-provided services they need, such as schools, day care, and health care, because there will be fewer households advocating for the needs of children (Russakoff, 1998).

Divorce statistics suggest that America's families may be stabilizing to some extent, although divorce rates remain high. The divorce rate in 1990 was 20.9 divorces per 1,000 married women over age 14; this represents a decline from a rate of 22.8 in 1979 (*Monthly vital statistics report, 1995*). About 1 in every 12 two-parent families that exist at the beginning of a typical two-year period no longer exist two years later. Family breakup is strongly related to unemployment and poverty (U.S. Department of Commerce, 1992b).

Another change within American families is the unprecedented increase in the number of single-parent families. In 1970, 89 percent of families with children had both parents in the household, 10 percent had mothers only, and 1 percent had fathers only. Since then, the proportion of single-parent families has risen significantly to 23 percent for mother-only families and 5 percent for father-only families. The largest increase in single-parent families occurred during the 1970s and 1980s; since 1990 the increase has been slight (Bryson & Casper, 1998). Today, about 20 million children live with one parent. See Chapter 3.

Related to the increase in single-parent families is the decision by increasing numbers of young people to delay marriage. Young men and women are much less likely to marry in their teens and early twenties than they were in the 1960s. Today, the median age at first marriage is 27 for men and 25 for women. One result of this has been an increase in the proportion of children born to unmarried parents. Between 1980 and 1991, the number of births to unmarried women rose by 82 percent. In 1991, there were 1.2 million births to unmarried mothers, representing three out of every ten births. The comparable figures for 1980 were 0.7 million births, fewer than two out of ten births (Saluter, 1994).

Many young, single parents choose to live with their own parents, so the trend toward three-generation households is increasing. Today, about 5 percent of all children live in the home of their grandparent(s), up from 3 percent in 1970. African-American children are more likely than other children to live with a grandparent: In 1993, 12 percent of African-American children were in three-generation households (Saluter, 1994).

The increased participation of mothers in the labor force is another distinguishing feature of family life today. Impelled by the trend toward single parenthood, the women's rights movement, and the state of the economy, more women, especially women with children, entered or reentered the labor force in the 1970s than ever before in U.S. history. The trend has continued. Today, 53 percent of mothers who gave birth in the last year are in the labor force, up from 31 percent in 1976 (U.S. Department of Commerce, 1992b). The percentages for mothers with older children are much higher: 65 percent of mothers with children under age 6, and 78 percent of mothers with children ages 6 to 13 are in the labor force. Very troubling is the fact that only a minority of these children have safe, affordable, quality child care (*CDF facts about child care in America, 1998*). See Chapter 5.

The last three decades have witnessed a large migration of people from Northern urban areas to the South and West. There has also been a shift of people from large cities to medium- and small-sized areas. Even with these trends however, most children and youth continue to live in or near a city. Further, the majority of urban nonwhite children live in central cities, while the majority of white children live in suburbs. Yet larger numbers of white than nonwhite children live in central cities. This latter statement illustrates the paradox of numbers versus proportions, which sometimes obscures other facts such as this: The majority of nonwhite children are poor, yet the majority of poor children are white.

PROBLEMS OF CHILDREN AND YOUNG PERSONS

Among the nation's children are millions who are living and growing up under economic, social, or psychological conditions that hinder their development and their prospects for future success. Their problems result from the interaction among their individual characteristics and those of their parents, factors associated with their particular family composition or situations, conditions within the neighborhood and community in which they live, and national issues and influences.

Being Poor Means Being at Risk

Poverty is a condition that affects about a fifth of American families with children (Zill & Nord, 1994). This poverty may grow out of parents' mental or physical illness or disability, low educational levels and lack of marketable skills, or a lack of access to employment because the parents are not sufficiently mobile, which in turn is a condition that may be due to lack of housing near employment or lack of transportation to it. Other factors in a technological economy over which an individual parent has no control contribute to high levels of unemployment. Some families remain poor because they are headed by women with low-level work skills who have young children at home to care for and whose only recourse is to an inadequate system of public assistance.

Regardless of cause, for children being poor means that the odds are stacked against them developmentally. Poor children face a higher risk of death; they have a higher risk of infant mortality; and they are more likely to die from disease, accident, drowning, or fire. Poor children are more likely to have stunted physical and intellectual growth. These risks are caused in part by inadequate housing and insufficient health care services. The environments in which many poor children live include toxic waste contamination and high levels of lead poisoning caused by drinking water from contaminated pipes and breathing lead-filled paint dust in the air. Lead poisoning in children can cause brain damage and behavior problems, which lead to school failure, and eventually delinquency and dropping out of school (Children's Defense Fund, 1994; Bearer, 1995). Poverty and unemployment are strongly related to child maltreatment (all forms of abuse and neglect combined), which Garbarino (1992) calls "certainly the bottom line when it comes to indicators of child welfare and family functioning" (p. 227).

In some areas, the poor have been clustered together in public housing complexes or inner-city neighborhoods where a variety of factors, including racism, lack of jobs, poor schools, and lack of social and community services, have combined to exacerbate the physical effects of poverty with a systematic pattern of deprivation. Children in crowded inner cities usually have only the street as a place for play, where they are often at the mercy of hostilities and violence. Safe areas to play may be similarly lacking in isolated rural areas. Growing up in such communities, these children may never be able to overcome their developmental disadvantages to become successful in the competitive American economy.

He's scared and crying bad; stopped wanting to go to school 'cause of the shooting. (A mother in a dangerous neighborhood—The Ounce of Prevention Fund, 1993)

Because of larger social and economic changes, the condition of childhood poverty today is often experienced as a state of deprivation in the midst of material affluence. During the past two decades, society has become increasingly polarized; while the top 20 percent of American families have grown richer, the bottom 20 percent have experienced a decline in income. Social isolation, alienation, low self-esteem, and other social and psychosocial problems are exacerbated by the condition of deprivation and feeling excluded from mainstream society. See Chapter 4.

Homelessness.   Homelessness is a devastating experience for parents and children. By the time they have lost their home and entered a shelter, family members have already experienced stressful events they could not control. A family's homeless status brings a clear risk for child development, not unlike the plight of millions of children who have long lived in severe poverty. Family life is disrupted, children's schooling is interfered with, physical and emotional health may be damaged, and family members could be separated (Ziesemer, Marcoux, & Marwell, 1994).

Attempting to assess the magnitude of homeless families and children, census takers have been confronted with numerous definitional and methodological issues. However, a 1996 survey of mayors in twenty-nine cities found that families with children make up 38 percent of the homeless population. Particularly alarming was the finding that families with children make up the fastest-growing homeless group (Masten, 1992; Bernstine, 1997).

Negative Peer Influence, Violence, and Substance Abuse

As children age, they become susceptible to a variety of developmental risks to their health and to their social and intellectual development. Millions of youth confront a lack of opportunity to develop useful skills and find satisfying employment. Noting this situation and its consequence, Currie (1982) wrote: "As long as we continue to trap many young people in a low wage, unstable and generally unrewarding sector of the economy, increasing their stake in 'straight life' will be impossible" (p. 25).

Many of these problems in large part reflect the failure of communities and the public schools to educate young people in ways that are relevant to the complexity of life today and that generate a level of competence vital to successful social functioning and individual well-being. For many school children and youth, the result is a diminishing desire to learn, an inability to adapt to change, confusion about life goals, alienation from school and community, and antagonistic attitudes toward a society that has not solved its problems of war, poverty, unemployment, drugs, and racism.

As children get older, peer influences become more important, and friends can influence each other in a positive or negative way. Peers are more influential for today's youth than in the past for a variety of reasons. Adult authority today is weaker, and there is less consensus on the core values and behaviors that should be transmitted to youth. Young people are spending greater amounts of time with each other as society in general becomes more age-segregated and they have more freedom in directing their own lives. The mass media and the entertainment industry expose youth to a broader range of experiences and behavior than formerly, and youth fads are often amplified and glorified in the media (Zill & Nord, 1994).

Parents, teachers, social workers, and other professionals have had to face a lack of knowledge about how to help youth with the growing problem of alcohol and drug usage. Young people throughout the population experiment with all kinds of available drugs. The problems have appeared most noticeably among suburban upper-middle-class youth and among lower-class young people of various racial and ethnic backgrounds. The growth in the numbers of young addicts and the increase in numbers of teenagers who die as a result illustrate the widespread danger of drug use.

A particularly poignant result of the drug epidemic is evidenced in the rising number of infants born addicted to drugs. The babies' most common symptoms are associated with withdrawal from drugs—prematurity, underweight (birth weight of two or three pounds), muscle rigidity, inability to sleep, poor appetite, jerking convulsions, and peculiarly high-pitched and constant crying.

The AIDS Epidemic. Another tragic risk for children and families is illustrated in the AIDS epidemic. The numbers of children with AIDS is growing; each year there are approximately 2,000 new cases of AIDS among infants. The problem is particularly acute in African-American and Latino communities; 94 percent of HIV-infected children are members of these ethnic groups. Women are especially vulnerable to infection, either through sexual contact with an infected person or through intravenous injection of drugs. It is estimated that between 125,000 and 150,000 children will be orphaned by the AIDS epidemic by the turn of the century (Stein, 1998). See Chapter 9.

Youth Violence. The drug epidemic has brought in its wake a wave of violence that engulfs children, young people, and residents of entire communities, as victims or as offenders, or both. Although media accounts of youth violence have fanned fears of a coming wave of juvenile "superpredators," the truth is that young people are ten times more likely to be the victims of violence than to be arrested for it. In 1994, almost 3,000 children were homicide victims and 1.6 million youths reported that they had been victims of a violent crime (Children's Defense Fund, 1997).

After a decade of large increases in youth violence, juvenile arrests for violent crimes have fallen, although the rate is still quite high. In one national survey, 20 percent of adolescents reported having engaged in one violent incident by the time they were 18 years of age. Although no community or ethnic group is immune, youth violence is particularly prevalent in urban neighborhoods characterized by high levels of male unemployment, extreme poverty, social disorganization, poor schools, gang activity, and families who have engaged in criminal activity and who engage in violent acts with each other (Earls, 1994). See Chapter 11. Most of the increase in violent crime affecting juveniles as either victims or perpetrators involves guns. As the Children's Defense Fund points out:

Because juveniles have increasingly easy access to guns, what formerly would have been a fist fight or knife fight, or a serious act of delinquency, now too often involves a gun and is far more likely to result in death or a homicide arrest. (Children's Defense Fund, 1997)

Children of Vulnerable Families

For many families who seek help in behalf of their children, the presenting problem centers on functioning within the family and conflict in the parent-child relationship or between husband and wife. Some parents are immature and overwhelmed with new or over-demanding responsibilities; others are poorly equipped with the knowledge they need to give good care to children and maintain family balance. Despite greater availability of birth control, many parents lack the help they want to plan the size of their families and to use contraception effectively.

Some children's problems stem from their birth to teenage parents who are themselves immature, highly vulnerable to discontinued schooling, and lacking the knowledge of how to care for their children as well as the financial means to do so. See Chapter 3.

Children are frequently brought to the attention of social agencies because of complaints that they are neglected or abused by their parents or other caretakers. The incidence of these reports has increased greatly since the reporting laws were established in the 1970s, currently reaching a level of about 3 million a year (Petit & Curtis, 1997). Federal funding and leadership have been inadequate to address the need for child protection. The solution to the problem of how to protect these children, yet maintain the family, continues to be elusive in too many cases. Some of these children must be enabled to live away from their own parents in foster homes or institutions, though many others can re-

main at home safely if sufficient supportive services are available to their families. See Chapters 7, 8, and 9.

The experience of out-of-home placement exposes children to the wrenching emotional trauma of separation from familiar family members, home, school, and neighborhood. In addition, they may be vulnerable to confusion over guardianship. The juvenile court, the public child welfare agency, the foster parents, and the parents all have legally sanctioned rights and responsibilities to the child, but these interests may be conflicting, overlapping, and not well defined. Children are often left with the powerless feeling that those who decide where they will live and other important life issues are remote strangers. See Chapters 2 and 6.

The approximately 18,000 children whose parental rights have been severed but who have not been placed in an adoptive home face special vulnerabilities and the disregard of their individual rights (Tatara, 1992). They are without an adult protector, guide, or advocate. Their duly appointed guardian is an officer of the state or an administrator of a large child-care agency. This practice fixes responsibility for the child but denies the child an opportunity for an ongoing personal relationship with his or her guardian. Adoption has been shown to be a successful solution for children who need new homes and loving, responsible parents, but there are thousands who grow older as children of the state, waiting for adoptive parents who do not materialize. See Chapter 10.

All these problems directly affect the well-being of the nation's children and are appropriate for attention by family and child agencies. Child welfare as a field of social work practice deals with only a small portion of the nation's children; the wider range of family and child service agencies addresses a larger segment, mainly through offering various preventive and supportive services. In spite of these services, many children and families need help that is not available at all or that is insufficient to improve their situation.

HISTORICAL HIGHLIGHTS OF SERVICES TO FAMILIES AND CHILDREN

The history of family and child welfare policy shows distinct, although sometimes overlapping, organized efforts to improve the welfare of children and the development of social services for them and their parents.

Indenture and "Outdoor Relief"

In the early years of this nation, individuals who could not maintain themselves or their families were considered the responsibility of the local township. Some children were mentally retarded; some were physically handicapped. Some were orphaned by epidemics and other disasters. Some showed incorrigible behavior. The methods of treatment within a community, however, were simple. The youngest children who required support by the town were "farmed out" to the lowest bidder—a family that agreed to give care to the child for a small, regular sum of money or goods. Others were often sent to live in the dreary, unsanitary almshouses with the adult misfits of the town—the mentally ill, the mentally deficient, lawbreakers, and the aged and infirm.

Able-bodied, older children were usually indentured, that is, placed under contract with a citizen of the town who agreed to maintain the child and teach him or her a trade or other gainful occupation in return for the profit from the child's labor. This was a favored practice, as everyone's labor was needed during the development of the new country. With the beginning of the Industrial Revolution, indenture became less feasible and by 1875 had almost completely disappeared (Folks, 1911). Despite some cases of cruel masters, indentured children, on the whole, were more fortunate than were children in almshouses. In that sense, indenture was seen as a forward step in child care (Thurston, 1930).

Another choice, termed *outdoor relief* and managed by the local poor law authority, was to give meager aid to dependent children in their own homes. This approach was poorly administered and the least-accepted form of care (Abbott, 1938). Nevertheless, public outdoor relief provided aid to more dependent children than all other special forms of protecting children. (A current form of outdoor relief is seen in today's Temporary Assistance to Needy Families program.)

Children's Institutions and the Growth of Voluntary Agencies

Gradually, society realized that children need a different type of care from adults and more "security"

than was provided by a master under a contract of indenture. Many of the earliest institutions for children were sponsored not by government but by private child-caring agencies. To a large extent, these private or voluntary agencies had their beginnings in the desire of people to fulfill neighborly obligations. Orphanages were a response of the community to disasters that left children without parents (Downs & Sherraden, 1983). Concerned citizens would then undertake to organize a group of people to care for the children in need. Examples include the Ursuline Convent in New Orleans, which in 1729 undertook the care of ten girls who had been orphaned by Indian wars; an asylum for the care and education of destitute girls, established in Baltimore in 1799 by St. Paul's Church; and institutions in various states called Protestant Orphan Asylums, which came into being to care for children orphaned in the cholera epidemics of the 1830s. Many of these institutions later became child-placing agencies, extending their care of children into foster homes in the communities or taking on other community activities.

The latter half of the nineteenth century brought an era of "child-saving" activities. The intent was to save children from conditions of crime, vice, and poverty found in urban areas where slums were crowded with poor, European immigrants. The Children's Aid Societies, found first in the cities of the eastern seaboard, took many children into care and placed them in free foster homes (Nelson, 1995; Cook, 1995). An example is the Children's Aid Society of New York City, founded in 1853 by the Reverend Charles Loring Brace, who organized a massive program that resettled nearly 100,000 children from eastern cities in free foster homes in midwestern and southern states.

In addition to the intent of the new voluntary agencies to protect harmless children orphaned by disaster or to save others from a life of crime and moral degradation, a third concern was protection of children from neglect and cruelty. Where laws existed for the protection of children from cruelty and abuse, they were poorly enforced. The New York Society for the Prevention of Cruelty to Children (NYSPCC)—the first of its sort—was formed in 1875 to rescue children from cruelty and inhumane treatment and to bring about enforcement of existing laws and passage of new laws.

Still another kind of voluntary agency established in the nineteenth century pioneered in many kinds of service to families and children. Settlement houses such as Jane Addams's famous Hull House in Chicago and Lillian Wald's Henry Street Settlement in New York were notable examples. Founded with broad aims and open to all the inhabitants of the neighborhood, they focused on the needs of families and the preservation and enhancement of human dignity, skill, and values. They were attuned to the social forces that buffeted poor people, most of whom were immigrants of various nationalities and religions. These early settlement houses demonstrated new services for families and children and worked steadfastly for social reform and for strengthening local communities as environments for families.

African-American Children. Slavery is a shocking and terrible part of American history. According to some estimates, between 1686 and 1786 approximately 2 million African people were forcibly taken from their homes; about 250,000 of them became slaves in America. Slavery as an institution was established to meet the need for cheap labor, particularly in the South. The economy of the North was also deeply implicated through its involvement in transporting slaves in its shipping industry. In addition to slaves, some Africans came to America during earliest colonial days as explorers and servants.

During the time of slavery and beyond, the family was the major and often only system of child welfare for African-American children. In the North, African-American children were excluded from most orphanages. A notable exception was the Philadelphia Association for the Care of Colored Children, a Quaker shelter for African-American children founded in 1822. It was burned down by a white mob in 1838.

After the Civil War, limited progress was made in providing for needy African-American children through the efforts of African Americans. They worked though mutual aid groups such as churches and benevolent organizations, some of which formed cooperative arrangements with white philanthropists and governmental sponsors. For example, the Virginia Industrial School for Colored Girls, founded in 1915, was maintained by the Virginian Federation of Colored Women's Clubs with an arrangement for interracial cooperation (Peebles-Wilkins, 1995). African-American children were not fully integrated into the public child welfare system until after World War II (Billingsley & Giovannoni, 1972).

State Boards of Charities

During the latter part of the nineteenth century, states had begun to assume responsibility for certain classes of the poor—those the towns, parishes, and other local units of government were unwilling or unable to care for. Children, too, began to benefit from this assumption of responsibility by the state. Specialized state institutions were established: "reform" schools and training schools for children who were blind, deaf, or mentally deficient (Sherraden & Downs, 1984). This increased activity underscored the need for a central agency at the state level to coordinate the administration of the welfare programs that local governments had been unable to finance or administer. Massachusetts, in 1863, was the first state to establish such a central agency, the State Board of Charities, for the supervision of all state charities.

Federal Government Involvement

The federal government was long reluctant to become involved with child and family welfare because of concern that it would violate *states'* rights, as social welfare is considered primarily the domain of state and local government. Even more significant in the opposition to federal action was the fear of invasion of *family* rights. Traditionally, the right and the responsibility for raising children had been held by parents; the government's role was confined to local matters and protection. As one senator in 1919 framed the situation, "The homes of the country are best protected through the local government" and not by a "federal nursery that shall pass upon the wisdom of the mothers and fathers of the land" (Heyburn, 1919, p. 189). This emphasis on family rights, conceived as the essential, basic civil right to conceive and raise one's children without governmental interference, has continued to influence development of federal policy (Garwood et al., 1989).

Federal Policy on Native American Families.   An exception to the general principle of nonintervention into family life was the role of the federal government in breaking up Native American families. As described in Chapters 3 and 6, during the early twentieth century, federal policy toward Native Americans was to encourage the dissolution of Indian culture and the incorporation of Indians into mainstream American life. As part of this policy, Native American children were removed from their families and placed in Indian boarding schools, where they were required to give up their language and culture, and where they lost ties to their families, who were far away on reservations. The Indian Child Welfare Act of 1978 has put safeguards in place to prevent the loss of Indian children to their culture.

Growth of Federal Programs.   Despite the opposition to federal involvement in families, inequities among the states and the lives of children were apparent. Initial steps to address the problems nationally were indirect—the founding of the U.S. Children's Bureau and the first White House Conference of 1912. Significantly, each endeavor was oriented toward wide dissemination of information, not the delivery of much-needed services to families. The Great Depression of the 1930s made it clear that government intervention was essential to help many persons and families cope with various overwhelming problems. Under the Social Security Act of 1935, the federal government established the financial assistance program known as Aid to Families with Dependent Children (AFDC), which served far more families and children than any other federal program. Since 1996, that program has become Temporary Assistance to Needy Families (TANF) and has changed substantially. See Chapter 4. The act also established a federal role in child welfare services through Title IV-B.

The social climate of the 1960s fostered a significant expansion of the federal role in numerous facets of life for children and families; an array of programs

was created. Federal and state joint efforts produced extensive legislation on such crucial problems as public assistance, civil rights, housing, and employment. In the 1970s, dissatisfaction began to be heard about the size of the federal government and some of its decisions. A more conservative view of the role of federal government prevailed. Since then, there have been fewer new services for children, and overall federal spending for children's programs has eroded from budget cuts and inflation (Garwood et al., 1989).

Public policy toward families and children during the last quarter of the twentieth century has been characterized by conflicting ideological trends. The perceived worsening of the condition of children and families has led to calls for a comprehensive, concerted national effort on their behalf. However, concerns about the suitability and feasibility of expanded governmental involvement have prevented a consensus from forming to support such a comprehensive vision. Currently, most family policy is directed toward only one aspect of family life: economic security. Public policy in relation to the family as a unit has been neglected because of the lack of agreement about the scope of governmental involvement with families and a reluctance to interfere with their "privacy."

PUBLIC POLICIES FOR FAMILIES AND CHILDREN

Social policy has received enormous public attention in recent years. Books and television debate such social policy issues as the future of Social Security and Medicare, the need to change the financial structure of health care insurance, including public insurance such as Medicare and Medicaid, and the changes to public welfare known as welfare reform. Furthermore, there is a vigorous debate on which level of government is best suited to implement public policy, as responsibility is shifting from the federal to the state levels of government, and from public to nonprofit and for-profit agencies and organizations (Ewalt, Freeman, Kirk, & Poole, 1997).

In the study of family and child welfare, we are primarily concerned with the impact of *public social policy* on the child and on family life developed by government through its judicial, legislative, and executive branches. Figure 1.1 shows these branches of government, and the names of the governmental bodies in each branch at the federal, state, and local levels. Together these entities make and implement most of the public social policy in the United States.

As used here, social policy refers to official decisions about social issues or a broad principle of operation for carrying out a specific aspect of the social welfare system. Policies define such matters as the nature of the services or aid, who shall receive service, what the standards of practice shall be, and specific principles and procedures for carrying out a social welfare program.

Three broad areas of current debate in family policy concern the scope of governmental services: the residual versus the developmental view of social welfare programs; the balancing of responsibilities for the well-being of children between government and families; and the devolution of power from the federal to the state and local levels of government.

Residual Versus Developmental View of Social Welfare

The residual conception of social welfare emphasizes the provision of programs and services for people only after the primary group that usually functions has broken down. Services are provided in relation to an underlying assumption (although often denied or unacknowledged) that normal families—adequate and competent families—do not need help. Such an assumption influences legislative and administrative decisions. As a result, the policy directions for a particular service often reflect restrictive and inconsistent attitudes, and negative views of people and their circumstances. Frequently services have been provided only after the family has endured hardship and trouble and the community has stood by while the family in crisis disintegrates.

By contrast, an "institutional" or "developmental" conception of social welfare holds that many "normal" and adequate families in today's complex, technological society have common human needs and require help at various times; therefore services for children and families, in addition to being protective and therapeutic, should also be preventive and supportive, easily available without stigma. They should provide social supports necessary to help families meet the social realities of the present patterns of family and community living. This conception includes social inventions to support, reinforce, and enhance family functioning, available to *all* people, not only

FIGURE 1.1 Sources of Policy by Level and Branch of Government

BRANCH / LEVEL	LEGISLATIVE	EXECUTIVE	JUDICIAL
FEDERAL	U.S. Congress	President Department of Health and Human Services Other Departments	U.S. Supreme Court
STATE	State Legislature	Governor Department of Social Services Other Departments	State Supreme Court
LOCAL	City Council County Board of Commissioners School Board	Mayor County Executive School Superintendent	Family Court Juvenile Court District Circuit Court

those who are in some way a casualty of modern life and in need of protective or therapeutic services. Kahn (1965) has termed these kinds of social services "social utilities" to emphasize the notion of the user as citizen rather than client or patient.

In the field of family and child welfare, the distinction between residual and developmental services is seen in the contrast between preventive services and traditional child welfare services. Preventive services, including family support programs and day care, are developmental services offered widely in the community on a voluntary basis. Traditional child welfare services, such as child protective services and foster care, are interventions offered only after the family system has broken down, and are therefore classified as residual services. See Classification of Services.

Families and Government

Traditionally, the family has been viewed in America as an inappropriate target for government planning and intervention except under the most compelling circumstances. Family policy issues raise fears, unresolved reluctance, and serious division within a population that has been wary of change in the relations of the family and the state. To some extent, the reluctance of government to intervene in family life has given way to a perspective that encourages public involvement under certain conditions. When family dysfunction touches enough families, public or quasi-public efforts are initiated to fulfill the economic, physical, or emotional needs of the individuals affected.

There are at least two reasons for this changing perspective. First, the changes taking place in American families, noted earlier in this chapter, have brought to many a growing fear that the family as an institution is breaking down. The declining role of the parent and the inevitably increasing role of the state have led to expectations in some quarters that the essential concerns of the family will be reflected in effective public social policy. Proponents for a more visible family policy believe that the importance of parental affection and a full parent-child relationship is not to be minimized, but neither is a positive role for government in the welfare of the child and his or her family.

A second reason for the change in perspective has been the realization that virtually all governmental actions directly or indirectly affect families. Varying state and federal programs have an impact on family life even though family concerns were not a reason for the intervention or directly considered in the formulation of the policies. For example, the globalization of the economy can affect drastically the ability of workers to find good paying manufacturing jobs in the United States, and therefore also affects the well-being of families who depend for their livelihood on those workers. Similarly, if the government acts ineffectively to prevent the pollution of lake waters by the discharge of industrial waste, already scarce recreational areas that are important to family life are lost. Some urban renewal programs have cleared unsightly and overcrowded areas of a city and constructed modern buildings, but in doing so they have ignored the established patterns of neighborhood life that had lifelong importance to some families. This more comprehensive view of the relationship between government actions and the family has led to interest in evaluating new government laws and regulations before passage for their effects on family well-being.

America needs the best adults we can make: individuals who are caring, resourceful, moral, healthy, literate, and able to lead this nation into the twenty-first century. We must develop a common focus and purpose to change the conditions that jeopardize the health and well-being of so many of our youngest citizens. Failure only defers to the next generation the rising social, moral, and financial costs of our neglect. We can and must be better masters of our nation's destiny. (National Commission on Children, 1991, p. 390)

This is not to say that government can replace families or do what good families can do in nurturing and socializing children into useful adulthood. But by testing its policies of taxation, energy, trade, transportation, housing, education, and income security for their effects on family life, government can add to the stability of the family—the unit of society this country still depends on for its basic child-rearing tasks.

The debate over government involvement with families has shifted from whether it should occur to how and when it should occur. The debate becomes most intense when it is focused, not in the abstract, but on a specific problem or proposal. For example, abortion and contraception, public policies regarding same-sex domestic partners, and the rights and responsibilities of unmarried fathers have developed proponents and opponents who can be equally vociferous. The lack of unanimity has contributed to the fragmented and erratic nature of American policy toward families and reflects, in part, the impossibility of mandating a comprehensive family policy in our pluralistic society.

The struggle to find a balance between governmental and family responsibility in promoting the welfare of children is evident in the debates over welfare reform, day care, and health care for children. The 1996 welfare reform law, called the Personal Responsibility and Work Opportunity Reconciliation Act, changed the program known as Aid to Families with Dependent Children to Temporary Assistance for Needy Families. As the name of the act implies, the emphasis has shifted from a program of governmental aid to an emphasis on parental work as a means to support children. Linked to this new emphasis is increased federal responsibility for the enforcement of child support laws and for financing day care and health care for the children of poor working parents, though it is not clear that governmental support in these areas will be even minimally adequate (Hagen & Davis, 1997). See Chapters 4 and 5.

Behind much of the new emphasis on family responsibility is a changing assumption about the causes of poverty. Since the New Deal, the assumption was that large economic changes, outside the control of individuals, were the main cause of poverty. However, that view has now changed to one that places primary responsibility for poverty on behavioral choices that are in the control of individuals. As Kamerman (1997) observed:

> In a process that has been under way for several decades, the problem of poverty has been largely redefined by some groups in Congress and elsewhere in society from an unfortunate condition resulting from external social and economic factors to a problem that results mostly from the immoral and irresponsible behavior of individuals. And the solution has been transformed, for those who hold such views, from a search for effective social policies to an emphasis on individual change. (pp. 167–168)

Devolution

Federal spending on social policy increased during the three decades after World War II, as did federal regulation of these funds that would be spent at the state and local level. Federal involvement increased at least in part because of growing skepticism that the states would allocate federal funds fairly and effectively. There was particular concern that the southern states would discriminate against African-Americans. However, it would be a mistake to overestimate the extent of federal power in social welfare policy during these decades. Most federal funds continued to be administered through state and local agencies.

During the 1990s, there has been a movement to return more authority for social policy to the states, where it rested during the nineteenth century and in the twentieth century until the New Deal of the 1930s. The hope is that smaller units of government, closer to those the programs are designed to serve, will offer more flexible, efficient, and targeted programs. It is further expected that state and local governments can form partnerships with nonprofit agencies and community organizations to better tailor programs to the needs and cultural values of local families (Weil, 1997). Those who remember the discriminatory, erratic, and extremely meager condition of many state welfare programs before the federal government became involved are concerned that any "devolution" to state-level units of government will result in a major setback to the well-being of children and families (Kamerman, 1997). See Chapter 4.

CLASSIFICATION OF SERVICES

Services to families and children traditionally have been classified into four major groups: supportive, protective, foster care, and adoption services. These categories reflect the historical development of child and family services and their varying legal mandates.

- *Supportive services* are available to families to support and strengthen family life, to promote the healthy development of children and adults, and to help families maintain connections with community institutions such as schools, welfare, and the workplace. Depending on the type of service offered, these services may be called therapeutic, preventive, or supportive. See Chapters 3, 4, and 5.
- *Protective services* are for families who have fallen below a minimally sufficient level of child rearing and whose children therefore suffer from abuse or neglect. Services include investigation of the family's situation and help in improving family life so that the children can remain safely in the home. See Chapters 7 and 8.
- *Foster care services* are for families who temporarily cannot maintain a minimally sufficient child-rearing environment in the home. While children are in foster care, the focus is on helping parents to improve their life situation so that children can be returned to them safely. Children may be placed with relatives, called "kinship care," in a foster family, in a group home, or in a children's institution. They are helped to cope with the separation and to adjust to their new living situation. Arranging visitation to help family members maintain connection with one another and planning for reunifcation as early as possible are important aspects of foster care services. See Chapter 9.
- *Adoption services* are available to children in need of a new, permanent family because their biological parents have relinquished them for adoption or had their parental rights permanently terminated in court. Helping the child (if older) grieve for the loss of his or her biological family and adjust to the new family are key adoption services. Adoption services provide support to the adoptive family and the biological family. See Chapter 10.

Supportive services differ from the other three service categories—protective services, foster care, and adoption—in a number of ways. Protective services, foster care, and adoption are traditionally considered the elements making up the domain of child welfare services. Government, through regulation,

funding, and the legal system, defines much of the framework within which these services are offered. Families usually do not seek out protective services and foster care services voluntarily; the agencies, through their legally established mandates, require the family's participation when its ability to maintain a minimally sufficient environment for children is in serious question. The families in these service systems come disproportionately from the poorest and most vulnerable segments of the population.

Supportive services, in contrast, are a loosely grouped category comprising a number of disparate programs and approaches offered in a variety of community settings. Family counseling, individual therapy for adults and children, and group work may all be used. Services are offered in mental health and family service agencies as well as in such community settings as schools, community centers, and other neighborhood-based programs. They are available to families on a voluntary basis, to help them improve the quality of family life, weather a crisis, or find and use community resources. Traditionally, these services have fallen outside the child welfare system and were not closely linked to it. See Chapter 3.

Characteristics of Services

Although each of these service categories has a distinct mission and role in the service system, they all share an overarching goal: to ensure an adequate environment in which children can grow and develop. Because the overall focus is on the family, certain themes and treatment approaches cut across all the service categories (McFadden & Downs, 1995).

Focus on Continuity of Family Relationships.   A basic principle of family and child services is that all efforts to support families are attentive to the needs of children for continuity of family relationships. Particularly with families in the child welfare system, it is important to remember that the focus needs to be on maintaining continuity of the child's emotional attachments. Kinship networks can play an important part in maintaining this continuity. Children who need to be placed temporarily away from biological parents are likely to feel more comfortable about the move if they are going to relatives they know, if they are moving with their siblings, or if they are remaining in their neighborhoods where they can stay in touch with friends and relatives. For children who must be permanently separated from their parents, planning must focus on maintaining continuity of the child's attachments—for example, through permanent placement with relatives or foster parents already known to the child, or through maintaining a connection to the biological parents in an "open adoption" arrangement.

Array of Services.   Families participate in similar social work approaches that cut across all service categories. Supportive counseling, parent education, referrals to community resources, individual and family therapy, and group work approaches are offered to families based on the needs and wishes of the family and availability of services, whether the family is voluntarily seeking help, is receiving child protective services, or has children in foster care. The American Public Welfare Association (1991) has presented the image of an "array of services" that can be "wrapped around" a family to prevent placement or promote reunification. The term *wraparound services* refers to the effort to provide families with whatever community services they need to prevent separate placement of their children or promote reunification. Thus, a family with a child in foster care may receive parent education, supportive counseling, help with housing and employment, drug treatment, and other services, depending on the needs of the family. Figure 1.2

FIGURE 1.2   Circle of Caring: A Holistic View of Family Continuity Services

Source: E. J. McFadden & S. W. Downs. (1995). Family continuity: The new paradigm in permanence planning. *Community Alternatives: International Journal of Family Care,* 7(1), 51. Reprinted with permission.

shows the array of services available in family and child services.

Continuity of Professional Services. Social workers and families have learned from experience that services to families are likely to be most fruitful if offered in a context of service integration and continuity of relationships between the social workers and the families. The four service categories—supportive, protective, foster care, and adoption—should not be offered as isolated service systems, with families required to make stressful transitions between them. Rather, the focus should be on maintaining continuity between the worker and the family, allowing them the opportunity to form a relationship that will sustain the family through whatever transitions they are required to make.

Pyramid of Services

The Children's Defense Fund has developed a framework called the Pyramid of Services, which places services in a continuum of increasing intensity, reflecting the needs of the family (see Figure 1.3). Services needed by all families, such as

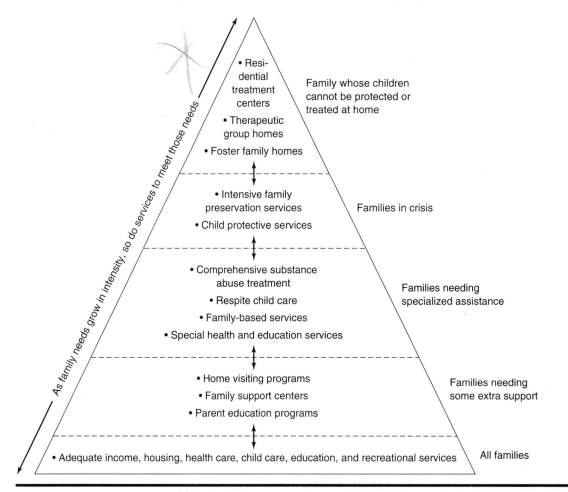

FIGURE 1.3 Building a Pyramid of Services

Source: Children's Defense Fund. (1993, December). Family support. *CDF Reports, 15,* p. 7. Reprinted with permission of Children's Defense Fund.

schools, health care, and recreational facilities are at the base of the pyramid, reflecting their status as widely available services. Families needing some extra support from time to time, often during family transitions such as divorce, birth, or death, or during other periods of stress, may need such services as a home visitor or parent education programs. Other families may also need a more specialized level of assistance, for such serious threats to family functioning as substance abuse, the physical or intellectual impairment of family members, or domestic violence. All of these services at the lower half of the pyramid are included in the category described earlier of supportive services and should be widely available in the community on a voluntary basis to families.

Services at the upper end of the pyramid include the traditional child welfare services of child protection and foster care, for families who are in crisis and for families whose children cannot be protected and treated at home. They are needed by a relatively small number of families. They are of high intensity, in that the parents are expected to be highly involved in the treatment process, and require more professional time and other resources than do less intensive services.

CULTURALLY COMPETENT FAMILY AND CHILD SERVICES

The majority of the families involved with the formal child welfare system (protective, foster care, and adoption services) and the juvenile justice systems are members of cultural groups of color, particularly African Americans, Native Americans, and Hispanics or Latino Americans (the fourth major group, Asian/Pacific Islanders, is not overrepresented in these systems) (Leashore, Chipungu, & Everett, 1991). Yet the majority of workers and administrators are white, and the agencies and organizations within the child welfare system are based on models formulated by various European cultures. In past decades, service systems to families and children often were not culturally responsive and sometimes were actually destructive to the cultural values of various ethnic groups (McPhatter, 1997).

Examples of inattention to cultural issues in child welfare include setting standards for foster and adoptive families that have the effect of excluding poor families, including many families of color; directing youth of color into the juvenile justice system while generally referring white youth to the mental health system; misinterpreting parents' behavior and therefore erroneously assuming that they wish to harm or neglect their children; and failing to reach out in a cooperative and mutually respectful spirit to communities of color, leaving them excluded from planning and decision-making processes regarding agency policies and structures.

Cultural groups of color are over-represented in the child welfare system for a number of historical and continuing social and economic reasons. The long history of oppression of African Americans through slavery and the Jim Crow laws created enormous strains on family life, prevented parents from earning a decent living, withheld education, and left entire communities in terror of organized, systematic violence against them. Native Americans suffered enormous losses during the conquest of North America by European cultures and underwent further cultural destruction by forced assimilation policies. Hispanic or Latino Americans have, like the other groups, suffered overt as well as covert discrimination and racism, and have been hampered by language barriers. The difficulties these groups have faced in the United States have caused disruptions in family life that result in disproportionate numbers of their children needing child welfare services. Unfortunately, the children and families have suffered from discrimination and insensitive treatment in this service system as well, leading to further family and community problems.

Today, many groups, including community organizations, associations of professionals of various ethnicities, and university researchers are exploring new ways for child welfare to become more responsive to the needs and cultural values of various ethnic groups (Family Resource Coalition, 1994–1995; Jackson & Brissett-Chapman, 1997; Ortega, Guillean, & Najera, 1996; Schiele, 1996; Uehara et al., 1996; Weaver, 1998; Williams & Ellison, 1996). One approach that has received wide attention is the Cultural Competence Continuum, described here.

The Cultural Competence Continuum

Cultural competence has been defined as "a set of congruent behaviors, attitudes, policies, and structures which come together in a system, agency, or among professionals and enables that system, agency, or those professionals to work effectively in the context of cultural differences (Cross, 1988, pp. 1–4). Acknowledging that children and families of color have a history of being treated unfairly is an important first step in creating a culturally competent service system. Terry Cross, director of the Northwest Indian Child Welfare Institute, recognized that becoming culturally competent is a developmental process for human service workers and for agencies. He has developed a continuum that ranges from cultural destructiveness, at the negative pole, to cultural proficiency, at the positive pole. Box 1.1 describes six points along the continuum.

Children of color account for an increasing percentage of the nation's children. Family and child service systems are challenged to develop ways to serve these children effectively and to use their cultural background as an asset in program planning. Culturally competent models of service delivery are concerned with more than ensuring that workers understand and value cultural differences. The approach addresses organizational attitudes, policies, and structures. Mason (1994) recommends that agencies wishing to become more effective in working with cultures of color should undertake self-assessment and planning activities in a "spirit of collaboration utilizing as many culturally- or community-based resources as possible" (p. 7).

Program Example: Organizing Urban Families for Children's Mental Health

The Federation of Families for Children's Mental Health is an association of local organizations for parent empowerment and advocacy in the nation's mental health system. Wishing to expand its organization into minority communities, the federation is developing materials for families of color who have a child with serious mental health problems. The goals are to introduce members of diverse communities to the services available from a variety of national, state, and local resources and to "build the necessary trust of people of color involved in local organizations with the hope that they might choose to affiliate themselves formally with the Federation as a local chapter" (Huff & Telesford, 1994, p. 10). The federation organized focus groups in various communities in order to obtain the advice of families of color on the types of materials they would like the federation to develop. Initially, federation planners "were shocked to learn how little we actually knew about the difficulties families experience—difficulties that limit their opportunities to access and participate in the activities of organizations such as the Federation" (Huff & Telesford, 1994, p. 10).

The federation identified community leaders through churches, schools, public housing resident councils, Head Start programs, and other centers. Working with these leaders, they learned to respect the geographical boundaries of the neighborhood as understood by the residents. Meetings were held within those boundaries in locations accessible to the target participants by walking or public transportation; meeting times were scheduled for late afternoon, because families, apprehensive about criminal activity, were afraid to be out after dark. Transportation was provided as needed. The federation publicized the meetings by telephone and mail delivery, and also posted flyers announcing meetings in laundromats, clinics, churches, grocery stores, public transportation stops, and day care centers. "We have learned not to ask people, 'What's your address?' or 'What's your phone number?' Instead, we ask, 'Do you have an address or telephone number?' 'Are there ways we can get in touch with you?' " (Huff & Telesford, 1994, p. 10). Federation members sent flyers home with children after school and made public service announcements on the local radio. As incentives, the flyers announced that child care and food would be provided at the meetings. Follow-up meetings were held less than a month apart in order to sustain momentum.

The federation members learned not to be discouraged by the difficulties in organizing parents in some very poor neighborhoods. Only after the challenges of reaching families and reducing barriers to attending meetings were addressed could the work

Box 1.1 _____

Cultural Competence Continuum for Agencies

CULTURAL DESTRUCTIVENESS

Assumes one race is superior and should eradicate "lesser" cultures; combines bigotry with vast power differentials.

Examples: boarding schools for Native Americans whose purpose was to destroy their culture; purposefully denying people of color access to their natural helpers or healers; removing children from their families on the basis of race; purposely involving minority individuals in social or medical experiments without their knowledge or consent.

CULTURAL INCAPACITY

Not intentionally destructive but lacks capacity to help minority persons or communities; characterized by ignorance and fear of people of color; paternalistic attitude toward "lesser" races.

Examples: discriminatory hiring practices; subtle messages to people of color that they are not valued or welcome; and generally lower expectations of minority persons. May act as agents of oppression by enforcing racist policies and maintaining stereotypes.

CULTURAL BLINDNESS

The belief that color and culture make no difference and that we are all the same; that the helping approaches traditionally used by the dominant culture are universally applicable; that if the system worked as it should, all people, regardless of race or culture, would be served with equal effectiveness. Reflects a well-intentioned liberal philosophy, but such services ignore cultural strengths, encourage assimilation, and blame the victims for their problems.

Examples: foster care licensing standards that restrict licensure of extended family systems occupying one home or of families lacking material resources; pretending not to notice the race of a client.

CULTURAL PRE-COMPETENCE

Realizes shortcomings in serving minority persons and attempts to improve; desires to deliver quality services and has a commitment to civil rights; has begun the process of becoming culturally competent but may lack information on how to proceed.

Examples: hiring minority staff, exploring how to reach people of color in the service area, entering into needs assessments concerning minority communities, recruiting minority persons for agency boards of directors and advisory committees. Ask "What can we do?" Danger is in "tokenism" or in stopping short after undertaking only one or a few activities.

CULTURAL COMPETENCE

Accepts and respects differences; holds culture in high esteem; conducts continuous self-assessment regarding culture; pays careful attention to the dynamics of difference; seeks to expand knowledge of cultures and their resources.

Examples: hires staff who are specialists in culturally competent practice; advocates improved relations among cultures; adds to the knowledge base of culturally competent practice by conducting research and developing new therapeutic approaches based on culture; advocates cultural competence throughout the system.

Source: Adapted from Terry L. Cross. (1988). Cultural competence continuum. *Focal Point, 3*(1). [The Bulletin of the Research and Training Center to Improve Services for Seriously Emotionally Handicapped Children and Their Families. Regional Research Institute for Human Services, School of Social Work, Portland State University, Portland, Oregon].

begin of empowering parents to be advocates for their children's mental health needs.

THE ORGANIZATION OF SERVICES

Family and child services usually are provided under the auspices of a social welfare agency—a formal organization existing to serve children and their families and sanctioned by society. Some of the agencies offer a variety of services to families and children; others are specialized in that they offer fewer services, or even only one.

Social welfare agencies providing services to children and their families are identified by various names, usually "child welfare agencies" or "family service agencies." Until recently, child welfare services and family services were conceptually and organizationally separate despite their common professional knowledge and principles. According to Meyer (1985), the separation resulted in "a dysfunctional structure of services for both families and children" (p. 109). To understand how this separation came about, she cites the late nineteenth-century child-saving history of child welfare with its focus, not on maintaining intact families, but rather on child placement as a way to protect children from their parents, who were perceived by child-savers as inadequate or harmful. Another factor reinforcing separateness was the founding of two national organizations in the early twentieth century—the Child Welfare League of America and the Family Service Association of America—two bodies that traditionally have not found ways to join forces effectively. In addition, the fragmentation of federal funding in family and children's legislation worked to keep the fields of child welfare and family services apart. The current focus on family support to prevent abuse and neglect, and family preservation services to prevent foster care, now are resulting in a long-needed integration of child welfare services and family services. However, the transition to a fully integrated service system is not complete, and, in many communities, the work of family service agencies remains quite separate from that of child welfare agencies.

The organization offering the social services may be a "public" agency, or the services may be given under private auspices by a "voluntary" (nonprofit) agency or as a "proprietary" (for-profit) venture. While both public and voluntary agencies are committed to broad, common goals in behalf of children, there are significant differences between the two forms of organization. Each has its separate legal base and means of financing its work; there are also differences in the underlying philosophy and in the groups of children served. Proprietary services for children differ considerably from both public and voluntary child welfare services.

Child welfare agencies come in all shapes and sizes. Some agencies may employ only two to five people and provide a specialized service, such as family treatment or adoption home placements. Some of the smaller agencies will have a few professionals and many volunteers or paraprofessionals, like those in homemaker programs or in big brother and big sister programs. These small agencies are usually highly specialized or are located in sparsely populated rural areas where demand is small, and are usually privately operated.

Mental health centers, child guidance clinics, family service agencies, and youth service bureaus may all be mid-size agencies. These types of agencies are more likely to provide several child welfare services. For example, mental health centers may provide psychological assessment, family therapy, individual counseling, group work, and perhaps consultation to schools and the juvenile court. Family service agencies may provide homemakers, parenting education, and a variety of treatment options. These agencies would typically employ between eight and fifty people.

At the most complex end of the continuum are the large state child welfare agencies. They may employ thousands of people responsible for providing a wide range of services, geographically dispersed throughout the state. The budgets of such organizations can reach hundreds of millions of dollars a year. These state agencies have been delegated public responsibility for the protection and care of children and authority over life-determining decisions for children and families who come under their mandate.

Public Child Welfare Services

The public child welfare agency is established by the passage of law—a particular statute that defines the agency's responsibilities for providing a welfare service for children and their families. Public welfare services for children and families are financed by taxation—federal, state, or local, or some combination of these sources. Most federal expenditures for children are made by or channeled through some unit of the Department of Health and Human Services (DHHS). Federal funds provide a significant proportion of the total expenditures for children's programs, particularly in such programs as public assistance, Medicaid, Head Start, foster care, and maternal and child health services.

The primary responsibility for administering public child welfare services rests on the states and their regional and local subdivisions. The principle of local responsibility is well entrenched in the history of social welfare. Local and state influences have always been strong in child welfare programs because children and their families are closely linked to other concerns that traditionally have been regarded as the responsibility of the various states. For example, marriage, divorce, guardianship, custody, adoption, juvenile delinquency, and treatment of the mentally ill are all principally matters for legislation by the separate states.

Voluntary Family and Child Agencies

A voluntary (nonprofit) child and family welfare agency receives its authorization from a group of responsible citizens who undertake to assume responsibility for a defined and limited part of a community's social services for families and children. They may form a corporate body and obtain a legal charter by showing that a need for a particular service exists and that a group of citizens is ready to support the activity. Some of these interested citizens are selected to serve as members of a board of directors with certain policy-making and advisory responsibilities in relation to a professional social work staff. A voluntary agency frequently has a cooperative relationship with a local, federated, fund-raising corporation (for example, the United Fund) and a community council of social agencies that plans and coordinates social work activities in a community. The voluntary agency that provides out-of-home care of children is usually subject to the regulatory authority of the state and must establish its eligibility for a license certifying that it meets certain standards of child care.

In theory, voluntary welfare agencies are financed completely by voluntary contributions from citizens. However, the practice of channeling public tax monies to voluntary agencies has a long history, going back to the early 1800s and increasing in the latter quarter of the nineteenth century when a variety of voluntary agencies were established for pur-

poses of "child-saving" and "child rescue." Many such agencies depended on public money for a considerable part of their annual income. During the twentieth century the practice of a public agency paying a private group for services to a particular family or child has grown. The author of a comprehensive study of thirty child and family agencies was led to assert that "the growing use of purchase-of-service contracts between government and nonprofit child welfare agencies" was perhaps "the most critical development within child welfare policy during the last 25 years affecting the response of child welfare service organizations to children in need." The danger cited was that the increase in public contracting with voluntary agencies for services "is restructuring the relationship between government and nonprofit child welfare agencies, leading to greater government intervention and influence in nonprofit agencies" (Smith, 1989, pp. 289, 290).

The pattern of shared financing presents a complicated issue. The public authority has the broad responsibility for services required to meet the needs of children and their families and is guided by "norms of equity," that is, fairness reflected in "equivalent services across geographic regions, services to the neediest clients, and nondiscrimination in the provision of services." Voluntary agencies, in contrast, are responsive to "clients who are deemed to be consistent with the basic mission of their organizations" (Smith, 1989, p. 291). If that level of appropriateness for services is established, then a child may receive a variety of intensive and beneficial services. Public agencies sometimes claim that a pattern of selecting children to help who fit the organizational mission results in unnecessarily long treatment that deprives other waiting children of services. The voluntary agency in turn sees this treatment as representing their commitment to make the utmost efforts in behalf of the child and the family accepted for access to their services (Smith, 1989).

In any case, if purchase of care is employed as one means of financing a community's social services for children, it should be carried out within a framework of community planning if it is to further the welfare of children and their families.

Proprietary Child Welfare Services

Purchase of child welfare services is sometimes contracted between a public agency and a *proprietary for-profit* agency. For-profit contracting occurs mainly in the provision of child care for working parents (Smith, 1989, p. 297). Very large numbers of other children have care arranged and carried out for them independent of any social welfare agency. Some families have found their own homemaker to bring into the home during periods of crisis and the mothers' absence. Some parents find a foster home and make arrangements for others to care for their children. Many children are placed in adoptive homes without the planning or supervision of a social welfare agency; this is very often arranged by an attorney for a fee or by other intermediaries.

Not enough is known about the quality of care and the experiences of children through these various independent arrangements. Some such children suffer poor quality of care, instability, and even abuse. However, some parents, particularly those with initiative, sound judgment, and financial resources, have been able to make satisfactory, independent arrangements for some aspects of their children's care.

Further systematic study of existing forms of independent care of children is needed, with attention paid not only to the hazards of these care systems but also to the factors contributing to a successful experience for children and families. Such a study could provide a basis for new experimentation in the development of independent care as well as give direction to parents who want to use independent forms of care. This research could also provide important information to state licensing authorities in the reformulation of mandatory licensing standards for child care facilities.

Interagency Partnerships

A major barrier to more effective services to vulnerable families and children has been the way that social services are compartmentalized into separate organizations, each one responsible for providing only one service. For example, child welfare agencies traditionally have been responsible for investigating abuse and neglect and for placing children in out-of-home care; mental health agencies have provided inpatient and outpatient services to children with identified mental health problems; the juvenile justice system has provided correctional facilities and services; and the schools and the health care system have offered specific educational or health care services. Yet these organizations tend to serve the same children and families. The fragmentation of services is confusing for families, causes many to "fall through the cracks" and not get the service they need from any source, and is wasteful of resources. The following case shows a family in need of coordinated services.

> Mike is a fifth-grade boy, eleven years of age. He does not have a father at home. As far as is known, he has no contact with his father. Mike's mother is sickly and is generally homebound. He has an older sister who stays with him along with her boyfriend and a baby. Mike's older brother is in reform school. At the beginning of the year he was identified as a child who "gets into trouble and seldom finishes or does his homework." Mike responded by saying, "I don't care about school and my work is too hard." Mike follows peers who delight in disrupting classroom activities; he never smiles, and when things get too stressful, breaks into tears with no sound. (Bruner, 1991, p. 4)

Mike's family needs economic assistance, social support, and psychological assistance as well as educational help for Mike. However, our current service delivery system is structured into separate services with specific eligibility guidelines and bureaucratic regulations about what kinds of services it can offer and to whom. Mike and his family may get help but it is likely to be offered by different service providers working for different agencies and to be confusing for the family. Fragmented services to families like Mike's can also be very expensive: reform school, psychological assessment and counseling for the brother, welfare assistance, and Medicaid for the family may cost the state tens of thousands of dollars annually but not result in an integrated plan to help the family move toward self-sufficiency.

Recognizing the problems caused by uncoordinated service systems, state governments and local communities are making efforts to increase the level of cooperation and collaboration among agencies. Interagency partnerships may take place at the service delivery level or the system level. Melaville and Blank (1991) describe these two levels as follows:

> At the service delivery level, *interagency initiatives focus on meeting the needs of individual children and families. Initiatives are designed to improve access, availability, and the quality of services that participating organizations provide to their clients.*
>
> At the system level, *initiatives are focused on creating a set of policies and practices that can help to build a community-wide network of comprehensive service delivery. Broad-based system-level efforts involving a cross-section of human service, education, government, business, and civic organizations identify gaps in service systems across the community and recommend ways in which they could be filled. (p. 15)*

Forging partnerships at the service-delivery level is often easier than at the systems level because such relationships do not attempt to reorganize agencies' administrative structures. However, they can improve services to families substantially by convincing service providers of the need to cooperate, getting them to agree on common goals, and by creating an administrative structure to implement changes (U.S. General Accounting Office, 1992).

Program Example: Child Welfare and Community Mental Health

One area where closer collaboration is greatly needed is between the child welfare and mental health systems. According to a report by Knitzer and Yelton (1990), the children and families served by these systems are virtually indistinguishable. A further reason to cooperate is that both systems have complementary policy agendas: In child welfare, the Adoption Assistance and Child Welfare Act of 1980 (P.L. 96–272) encourages states to offer services to families to avoid the need for foster care or to shorten the time that children need to remain out of the home. In the mental health system, the Child and Adolescent Service System Program (CASSP), a new federal pro-

gram now operating in most states, encourages states to create a range of mental health services for children in their own homes and communities to avoid more restrictive forms of care. The mental health reforms expand a set of community-based services, including respite care for parents, day treatment programs, intensive case management, and therapeutic foster care. "Taken together, P.L. 96–272 and CASSP define mutually supportive strategies, the one focusing on protections for individual children designed to ensure access to appropriate services, the other on broadening the array of services" (Knitzer & Yelton, 1990, p. 26).

Knitzer and Yelton (1990) describe one highly successful collaboration as follows:

> The potentially most significant new efforts to help troubled children and adolescents involve comprehensive reforms that bring the philosophy behind the CASSP program to the overall service delivery system. Perhaps the best example of this approach was developed in Ventura County, California. The Ventura County Board of Supervisors decided in 1985 to target an all-out effort on children who were likely to be placed out of home through child welfare, mental health, juvenile justice, or special education agencies. The county has used a $2 million state grant to supplement existing services with a day treatment program, therapeutic foster homes, and most recently a family preservation program. A strong case management program was also developed with mental health as the lead agency, and a series of inter-agency agreements was promulgated. Data suggest that county juvenile justice recidivism rates are down, the number of children in psychiatric hospitals has decreased, and Aid to Families with Dependent Children (AFDC) group home costs have been reduced by 13 percent. (pp. 29, 30)

Interagency partnerships can begin at different levels and through different procedures. A key to successful cooperation is strong leadership. "Someone, either by mandate or by predilection, must want collaboration to happen—and must have the clout to engage other agencies" (Knitzer & Yelton, 1990, p. 32). At the same time that administrative arrangements are made to promote cooperation, workers at the direct service level must also be committed to building bridges to workers in other agencies. Ultimately, integration of funding streams, though challenging to accomplish, would link services to families more holistically.

Changing the ways agencies work with one another takes time and can be seen as a threat to existing ways of doing things. The "inertia of the system" may prevent people at all levels of the organization from working to identify and overcome obstacles to closer cooperation. An important step to fostering a climate of opinion within the organization that favors change is to undertake agency-wide assessment activities that promote a common understanding of how the goals of the organization can be better met through partnerships with other agencies. Box 1.2, Seven Key Points to Remember, provides an overview of the issues involved in interagency collaboration.

Box 1.2

Seven Key Points to Remember

1. *Collaboration is not a quick fix for many of the vexing problems society faces.* It will not build affordable housing, create sufficient Head Start slots for all eligible children, end poverty, or stop the tragedy of abuse and neglect.

2. *Collaboration is a means to an end, not an end in itself.* Policy makers must ask what problems collaboration is designed to solve, prior to proposing collaboration as the means to solve them. The end goal is more successful, productive lives for children and families.

3. *Developing interagency collaboration is extremely time-consuming and process-intensive.* Policy makers must recognize that the substantial resources that go into establishing interagency collaborative ventures should be expended only when the benefits of collaboration are correspondingly large. While some initiatives may leverage new resources and deploy existing ones more efficiently, collaboration will not create resources. Collaboration is not *always* the best investment of resources; depending on local needs and circumstances, some services may be better provided without multiple agency involvement.

4. *Interagency collaboration does not guarantee the development of a client-centered service system nor the establishment of a trusting relationship between an at risk child or family and a helping adult.* If that is the goal of policy makers, they must make collaboration at the worker–client level a central part of their initiatives and not trust it to occur because agencies are required to coordinate with one another at the administrative/management level.

5. *Collaboration occurs among people—not among institutions. Workers must be supported at each level of organization where collaboration is expected to take place.* Time for collaboration must be built into the work day, and workers must be rewarded for their efforts. Interagency agreements—important institutional mechanisms to clarify, formalize, and spell out relationships and to avoid misunderstandings among agencies—must be structured to support workers' interactions with colleagues within the agency, with those in other agencies, and with the families being served.

6. *Creative problem-solving skills must be developed and nurtured in those expected to collaborate. Among these skills are the ability to deal with the ambiguity and stress that increased discretion brings.* Policy makers must recognize that, if workers are expected to share responsibility and make decisions based on family needs and flexible guidelines rather than rigid protocols, they must be provided with back-up support and guidance to assure that this autonomy is widely employed. The interpersonal, problem-solving skills required in collaboration will be skills many collaborators have not previously been called upon to use in their work.

7. *Collaboration is too important a concept to be trivialized.* It must represent more than the shifting of boxes on an agency organizational chart. If the very real needs of children and families are to be met, service providers must find ways to meet these needs more comprehensively, and more holistically. Ultimately, this will require more careful, considered, and extensive collaborative activity.

Source: C. Bruner. (1991). *Thinking collaboratively: Ten questions and answers to help policy makers improve children's services.* Washington, DC: Education and Human Services Consortium.

TRENDS AND ISSUES

The Increasing Complexity of Family and Child Welfare Practice

As a specialized field of social work practice, child welfare is now being challenged to move beyond the residual, outworn classification of child welfare services and to respond to new, complex family problems. New forces are impelling change. Society's expectations for child welfare have increased. It is no longer enough to rescue children from unsuitable home situations; the child welfare system is expected to provide a relatively high level of care and to plan appropriately for the children's future. A number of legal reforms over the past two decades have increased accountability and reduced autonomy in agencies. Workers are required to work within a clear legal and policy framework. The sometimes competing goals of protecting children and preserving families have resulted in widely publicized reviews of agency decisions that have been proven by subsequent events to be bad judgments.

At the same time that child welfare has fallen under closer public scrutiny, the deteriorating condition of many children and families has presented new challenges to the system. The poverty, isolation, violence, and fractured family life experienced by many children have increased demands on the child welfare system. The disease of HIV/AIDS, in particular, has created a new group of orphans who need care and planning assistance from the child welfare system.

It is no longer possible for child welfare to remain a relatively small service system addressing the needs of a limited number of children who require out-of-home care or protective services. The problems of families and children demand that the child welfare system broaden its scope and diversify its practice approaches into a wider arena of family and child services. The child welfare system must forge new relationships with families, with neighborhoods and communities, and with other organizations in the service delivery system. These linkages are essential to meaningful prevention efforts, but they also provide new opportunities for foster care and adoption. Maintaining children within kin networks and within neighborhoods allows children continuity of relationships while addressing their needs for safe home environments. In 1990, the National Commission on Child Welfare and Family Preservation expressed commitment to an expanded framework for family and children services:

> We contend all families need help at some time, and our recommendations represent a commitment to families throughout their lifecycles. It is critical that we marshal community resources in support of families and that we establish accountability measures that assure our interventions genuinely improve the quality of life of the families served. Our policies must successfully promote family stability, the physical and mental health of children and families, the safety of children, and educational attainment for children. (National Commission on Child Welfare and Family Preservation, 1990, p. v)

In tandem with the increasing array of problems in child welfare and the services to address them, professional responsibilities also have become more complex in the past few decades. Issues of professional malpractice and liability and concerns about the scope and limits of confidentiality have influenced practice both directly and indirectly. New mandates increasingly require social workers to understand complicated protocols for risk management, to warn others of threats made about them, to conduct forensic investigations, and to testify competently in judicial proceedings. These heavy responsibilities and expectations have not been matched by sufficient training, leaving workers exposed to legal and other difficulties. See Chapter 12.

Managed Care

The emergence of managed care in child welfare services is creating a new service and professional environment, requiring workers to understand complicated funding streams and resolve ethical dilemmas posed by the sometimes competing mandates of cost efficiency and human needs. Managed care in health care is a strategy for controlling costs while improving service delivery. The child welfare field, after a decade of escalating costs and fragmented services, is currently borrowing the managed care strategy in an effort to improve efficiency and control costs. Managed care has two basic elements. It has a "capitated" system, whereby agencies are paid a preset price for offering a range of services; the agency must manage its resources to provide all necessary services within that price. Thus the agency takes some financial risk of having more demands for service than the preset fee will cover. The second basic element of managed care is the coordination of services through a single entity. This entity can provide services itself or contract with other providers.

A major concern about adapting the health care model of managed care to child welfare is that, unlike health care, child welfare has legal responsibility to serve all children who are experiencing abuse or neglect, as well as their families. The child welfare system cannot legally choose to deny services to any of these children, on the grounds of cost-saving or efficiency.

In a recent study, the Government Accounting Office has found that managed care is a growing strategy in the public child welfare system. Currently thirteen states have projects using managed care, and twenty other states are planning such projects. Most of these involve foster care, which is a complex and costly child welfare service. The most popular model is one in which the state public agency incorporates some elements of managed care into its traditional practice of purchasing services from voluntary agencies. Other states have contracted with a private agency that coordinates the services for a defined population of children. The lead agency functions as a contractor for services from other providers, with case-management responsibilities. The study reports that little is known about the effects of managed care on the children and families in the service system (U.S. General Accounting Office, 1998).

Child advocates are concerned that managed care, with its focus on controlling costs, may reduce needed services. The Child Welfare League of America, among other advocacy groups, is actively studying the implementation of managed care and attempting to identify its effects on service provision. See Chapter 9, the section Trends and Issues, for a discussion of managed care in foster care services.

Community Approaches to Family and Child Welfare

It is widely recognized that the communities in which children are raised influence their development. Fam-

ilies do not raise their children in isolation but in communities which, for better or worse, also affect how the child grows to maturity. Some of the ways that communities affect children are through the quality of their schools, parks, and recreation facilities, their provisions for public safety, the economic opportunities that exist, the availability of positive adult role models and mentors, and the residents' values of citizenship and norms of socialized behavior. The importance of the community in children's development is captured in the phrase, "It takes a village to raise a child." The profession of social work, recognizing that the functioning of families depends on their social environment, has a long history of working to improve community life. The settlement houses at the turn of the century are only one example of organized efforts to increase community cohesion, to provide more resources for families in a community setting, and to organize focused advocacy efforts to improve neighborhood conditions.

It is also recognized that the failures of children are concentrated geographically and ethnically. Many of the children in the United States who are not prepared for successful, productive adult lives inhabit highly distressed and socially deprived neighborhoods. Recently, there has been renewed interest in community-level interventions in order to make these communities a more positive environment for children. Bruner (1996) has identified several interventions that would strengthen communities: increased family support services, including frontline practice; restructuring public systems to involve more interagency partnerships, which can respond to families holistically and deliver services locally; establishment of additional programs such as youth recreation leagues either through outside resources or through mobilizing the community; connecting with and strengthening the "social capital" in the community, such as faith communities and neighborhood leaders; and creating economic hope and opportunity.

Bruner calls for a comprehensive vision of family and child welfare which would recreate the current fragmented service system into a holistic, dynamic program of renewal functioning at the neighborhood level. In the long run, he contends, improving neighborhoods will be a more effective and less expensive way to improve outcomes for children than our current system of categorical services for different types of child and family problems.

Another approach to connecting child welfare more closely with communities is the effort to involve residents and grass roots organizations more directly with the child welfare service system. Federal and state funding, as well as philanthropic foundations, have encouraged child welfare agencies to develop more permeable boundaries and to establish community partnerships. These efforts have borne fruit in the form of family support programs and intensive family preservation services, which attempt to strengthen families by coordinating an array of local services.

Recently, the concept of partnership between child welfare and community services has been expanded to include the idea of community responsibility for child safety, involving child protective service collaborations with local entities. The rationale for this initiative is that remote bureaucracies such as child protective services cannot do the whole job of keeping children safe. Ultimately, families and communities must also be mobilized in cooperative arrangements with child protective services to achieve this goal. Public child welfare agencies are just beginning to experiment with ways to share responsibility for child protection with communities. Farrow (1998) has identified some early demonstration efforts. One approach is to outstation child protection staff in schools or other neighborhood settings, as part of teams with other community workers. CPS workers may "walk the streets, get to know neighborhood residents before problems occur, and are familiar with each neighborhood's assets and resources" (Farrow, 1998, p. 12). Another approach is to organize neighborhood networks that include both formal service systems, such as health care and schools, and informal supports, such as neighborhood leaders. "Network members identify risk of maltreatment earlier, and assign responsibilities among their many members to respond preventively as well as after abuse or neglect has occurred" (Farrow, 1998, p. 12).

The idea that communities themselves have resources that have been insufficiently mobilized is an appealing one, and the new approaches described in the preceding paragraph show promise for strength-

ening child protective services through partnerships. However, there are reasons to be cautious about the ability of communities harrowed by substance abuse, poverty, unemployment, and violence to solve seemingly intractable child welfare problems. Wattenberg (1998) points out that "the conflicting views of the community as the source of problems or the location of solutions have not been reconciled" (p. 15) and that some communities lack the capacity to deliver social services. She notes that in some neighborhoods, there is reluctance to intervene directly to "confront, chastise or even offer help to a child" for fear of retribution from parents. In these areas, an anonymous call to child protective services may be the limit of what can be expected in neighborly responsibility for children's welfare. Another barrier is the belief of some community-based organizations that they will be tainted and stigmatized if it becomes known that they are cooperating with child protective services, a governmental agency that is viewed with suspicion by many residents in inner-city neighborhoods.

The community partnership concept is a work in progress. At this early stage, it is important to assess neighborhoods individually and carefully for their capacity to be hospitable environments for young families. So far, we have had the most experience with community-based programs whose focus is on promoting family strengths and preventing maltreatment. Much less is known about the potential for community collaborations with child protective services.

Partnerships Between Social Work Education and Family and Child Services

The social work profession and the field of practice known as child welfare have a long, shared history. Social work has been the predominant discipline in child welfare. More than all other fields of social work practice, child welfare is the most familiar to the public and to social work recruits. For many years, child welfare was the only field of practice in which social workers were in control of their own programs (Meyer, 1984).

Starting in the 1970s, however, child welfare and social work as a profession diverged. Kamerman and Kahn (1989) have identified some of the conditions within the child welfare system that weakened its status and the effectiveness of its services: (1) growth in the numbers of very difficult cases, along with a decline in the numbers of professional staff; (2) a perception of deprofessionalization on the part of staff emanating from a decline in autonomy and flexibility, which in turn stems from accountability for tasks imposed by child abuse requirements; (3) a downgrading of positions by reclassifying many from professional to nonprofessional, accompanied by further declining salaries, making the positions less attractive to the professional staff; and (4) a loss in the availability of social work professionals for child welfare positions in some communities (Kamerman & Kahn, 1989, pp. 24–25). By 1988, only 22 percent of child welfare workers had master's degrees (Lieberman, Russell, & Hornby, 1989).

At the same time that child welfare was being perceived as less professional than other social work fields, the work was becoming increasingly complex, requiring higher levels of skill than ever before, as discussed in the earlier section, The Increasing Complexity of Family and Child Welfare Practice. In response to these new demands, during the 1980s public agencies again sought professionally trained staff but had difficulty recruiting them (U.S. General Accounting Office, 1993). There was also concern that the curricula in many schools of social work did not prepare students adequately for public child welfare practice.

These developments encouraged renewed collaboration between public child welfare and social work education. In 1986 the Administration for Children, Youth, and Families and the National Association of Social Workers issued an agenda for action for upgrading the skills of staff in public child welfare with recommendations for schools of social work to adapt their programs to the needs of public child welfare employees. Significant efforts have been made to reverse the earlier trend of increasing divergence between the social work profession and child welfare (Terpstra, 1993). In 1992 the Council on Social Work Education identified three principal reasons for renewed collaboration:

- A widespread, growing concern on the part of the helping professions for the declining socioeconomic conditions of children and their families;

- A recommitment of social work education to its mission of preparing workers to meet the needs of vulnerable and oppressed children and their families;

- A renewed interest on behalf of public agencies in collaborating with social work education programs, to ensure that workers have the skills and knowledge necessary for public human service practice (Council on Social Work Education, 1992).

In the past few years, the connections between public child welfare and social work education have been strengthened, through collaborative training and educational programs using federal entitlement programs to help fund partnership efforts at little or no cost to state child welfare agencies. Currently many states have responded to this opportunity (Briar, Hansen & Harris, 1992; McFadden, Berns & Downs, 1995; Zlotnick, 1997). According to the Council on Social Work Education, increased educational emphasis must be given to promoting interprofessional, collaborative, practice methodologies, to understanding the complex funding streams and mandates for service in managed care, and to increasing curriculum offerings in strengths-oriented, family-centered, community-focused service modalities (Zlotnick, 1997).

CHAPTER SUMMARY

The profession of social work, throughout its history, has been closely linked to the field of child welfare. During the last half of the twentieth century, child welfare services have become more complex, as they respond to the demands of society that they expand protection to all vulnerable children and provide a high level of service to them and to their families. Today the emphasis is on maintaining continuity of family relationships through all phases of the child welfare system, to ensure that the child retains emotional attachments that are crucial to his or her development. The field of child welfare is changing into a comprehensive service system for families and children, reflecting the recognition that the well-being of children is inextricably linked to the welfare of their families.

American families are changing, as more children than ever before are being raised by parents, many of them single, who are working outside the home. The nation's families are becoming more ethnically diverse, a trend which is expected to continue into the twenty-first century. Children today face a number of serious threats to their healthy development. In spite of the increased work effort of parents, about one-fifth of the children in the United States live in poverty, which increases their risks for entry into the child welfare and delinquency systems and reduces their chances of achieving success in adulthood. Many children are affected by the substance abuse epidemic, which has devastated families and created a large number of orphans. Reports of child abuse and neglect are increasing, leading to large numbers of children who are in foster care or awaiting adoption.

The United States has been reluctant to involve government in policies directly affecting families, due to a long-standing tradition of respect for the privacy of family life. Governmental policy has developed piecemeal, in response to particular problems of children and families. A comprehensive plan for governmental support for families and children, which would be supportive, preventive, and developmental,

has not emerged. A growing emphasis on shared responsibility between the federal and state governments and families is reflected in the 1996 welfare reform legislation, which returned much of the authority for welfare to the states and requires parents to work in order to be eligible for benefits.

Family and child services are classified as supportive, protective, foster care and adoption. There is increased awareness of the importance of "culturally competent" services, which means including members of all ethnic groups in the planning and delivery of services. Services may be provided by public child welfare agencies, voluntary nonprofit agencies, or proprietary for-profit agencies.

There is a great need for increased collaboration among agencies, to counter the fragmentation which limits the effectiveness of the entire social welfare system. Other reforms of the family and child service system include the trend toward managed care and increased involvement with local communities. A promising development is the increasing linkage between the public child welfare system and social work education, reflecting the increased complexity of child welfare practice and the need for a more highly trained, professional work force to address the serious problems of families and children.

FOR STUDY AND DISCUSSION

1. Identify forces in today's world affecting families and children. What new approaches are needed to address changing demands for service?

2. Learn something of the background of a social agency in your area. When was it founded? Is it public or private? What are its funding sources? What is its service mission today, and has that mission changed over time?

3. Delineate services that should be included in a comprehensive system of services for families and children.

4. What is meant by *family continuity* and how can this be achieved in practice and program?

5. Assess an agency with which you are familiar on the Cultural Competence Continuum. What steps

could the agency take to move further along the continuum?

6. Undertake a planning process to develop a partnership with a professional in another agency and/or a partnership whereby your agency establishes a more formal relationship with another organization. Identify obstacles and how you would overcome them.

7. For a socially deprived neighborhood with which you are familiar, consider the extent to which it provides a hostile or benevolent environment for families with young children. What possibilities do you see for partnerships between child welfare services and grass roots organizations to strengthen families and increase child safety? What would be the obstacles?

FOR ADDITIONAL STUDY

The Annie E. Casey Foundation. (1997). *Kids count data book: State profiles of child well-being.* Greenwich, CT: Author. Published annually.

Ewalt, P. L., Freeman, E. M., Kirk, S. A., & Poole, D. L. (1997). *Social policy: Reform, research, and practice.* Washington, DC: NASW Press.

Haveman, R., & Wolfe, B. (1994). *Succeeding generations: On the effects of investments in children.* New York: Russell Sage Foundation.

Jackson, S., & Brissett-Chapman, S. (Eds.). (1997, January/February). *Child Welfare Special Issue: Perspectives on Serving African-American Children, Youth, and Families, 76*(1).

Kamerman, S. B., & Kahn, A. J. (1997). *Child welfare in the context of welfare reform.* New York: Columbia University School of Social Work.

Lindsey, D. (1994). *The welfare of children.* New York: Oxford University Press.

National Commission on Child Welfare and Family Preservation. (1990). *A commitment to change.* Washington, DC: American Public Welfare Association.

Ortega, R. M., Guillean, C., & Najera, L. G. (1996). *Latinos and child welfare/Latinos y et bienestar del Nino, voces de la communidad.* Ann Arbor: The University of Michigan School of Social Work.

Schorr, L. (1997). *Common purpose.* New York: Doubleday.

Stein, T. J. (1998) *The social welfare of women and children with HIV and AIDS.* New York: Oxford University Press.

Zlotnick, J. L. (1997). *Preparing the workforce for family-centered practice: Social work education and public human services partnerships.* Alexandria, VA: Council on Social Work Education.

INTERNET SITES: INTRODUCTION

The Administration for Children and Families (ACF), within the Department of Health and Human Services (HHS) is responsible for federal programs that promote the economic and social well-being of families, children, and communities. The Web site includes press releases, organizational information, fact sheets on ACF programs, and links to other, related federal government sites. Programs described at this Web site include welfare, foster care, adoption, family preservation, child protection, Head Start, child care, child support enforcement, services to youth, programs to strengthen communities, and special programs for such populations as the developmentally disabled, refugees, and Native Americans. **www.acf.dhhs.gov**

Bureau of the Census has a Web site with sources of data on children and on children's programs, such as child care and child support enforcement. It lists current reports on children produced by the Census Bureau and provides links to census demographic data at the federal and local levels. It also gives links to other federal sources of data on children, such as the National Center for Health Statistics. **http://www. census.gov/population/www/socdemo/children. html**

Child Welfare League of America is the nation's oldest and largest membership-based child welfare organization. It is an association of almost 1,000 public and private nonprofit child welfare agencies. The Web site lists the services offered to members and provides advocacy information concerning current policy proposals of the federal government. **www.cwla.org**

Children's Defense Fund is an advocacy organization for children in America who cannot vote, lobby, or speak for themselves. It pays particular attention to the needs of poor and minority children and those with disabilities. The Web site offers current information on federal policy initiatives and encourages citizen involvement in the policy process. **www.childrensdefense.org**

Handsnet is a Web site offering information, training, and technical assistance to nonprofit agencies, using the resources of the World Wide Web. It provides bulletins and summaries of recent federal policy initiatives of interest to the human service community. **www.handsnet.org**

KIDS COUNT, a project of the Annie E. Casey Foundation, is a national and state-by-state effort to track the status of children in the United States. By providing policymakers and citizens with benchmarks of child well-being, KIDS COUNT seeks to secure better futures for all children. The annual *KIDS COUNT Data Book* uses the best available data to measure the educational, social, economic, and physical well-being of children. The Web site provides the information from the KIDS COUNT reports. www.aecf.org/aeckids.htm

Welfare Information Network is a foundation-funded project to help states and communities obtain the information, policy analysis, and technical assistance they need to develop and implement welfare reforms. It has a clearinghouse of welfare reform–related information, including special Web sites on teenage parenting, child support, and all aspects of child welfare. The site includes summaries of federal legislation concerning families and children and a calendar of welfare-related events. It provides links to related organizations, policy analysis research centers, state agencies, and technical assistance resources, including "best practices" projects www.welfareinfo.org. The site devoted specifically to child welfare issues is http://www.welfareinfo.org/childwelf.htm

REFERENCES: AN INTRODUCTION TO FAMILY AND CHILD SERVICES

Abbott, C. (1938). *The child and the state, vol. 1.* Chicago: University of Chicago Press.

Barbaro, F. (1979). The case against family policy. *Social Work, 24*(6), 447–456.

Bearer, C. F. (1995). Environmental health hazards: How children are different from adults. *The Future of Children, 5*(2), 11–26.

Bernstine, N. (1997). Housing and homelessness. *The state of America's children: Yearbook, 1997.* Washington, DC: Children's Defense Fund.

Billingsley, A., & Giovannoni, J. M. (1972). *Children of the storm: Black children and American child welfare.* New York: Harcourt Brace Jovanovich.

Briar, K. H., Hansen, V. H., & Harris, N. (Eds.). (1992). *New partnerships: Proceedings from the National Public Child Welfare Training Symposium, 1991.* Miami: Florida International University.

Bruner, C. (1991). *Thinking collaboratively: Ten questions and answers to help policy makers improve children's services.* Washington, DC: Education and Human Services Consortium.

Bruner, C. (1996). *Realizing a vision for children, families, and neighborhoods.* Des Moines, IA: National Center for Service Integration.

Bryson, K., & Casper, L. M. (1998, April). *Household and family characteristics: March, 1997.* (Current Population Reports, P20–509, U.S. Department of Commerce, Census Bureau). Washington, DC: U.S. Government Printing Office.

CDF facts about child care in America (1998, March 10). Available on-line at: www.childrensdefense.org/cc_facts.html. [May, 1998]

Children's Defense Fund. (1997). *The state of America's children: Yearbook, 1997.* Washington, DC: Children's Defense Fund.

Cook, J. F. (1995). A history of placing-out: The orphan trains. *Child Welfare, 74*(1), 181–200.

Council on Social Work Education. (1992). *Social work education and public human services: Developing partnerships.* Washington, DC: Council on Social Work Education.

Cross, T. L. (1988). Services to minority population: Cultural competence continuum. *Focal point, 3*(1), 1–4. [Bulletin of the Research and Training Center on Family Support and Children's Mental Health, Portland State University, Regional Research Institute for Human Services, Portland, OR].

Currie, E. (1982). Fighting crime. *Working Papers, 9*(4).

Downs, S. W. & Sherraden, M. (1983). The orphan asylum in the nineteenth century. *Social Service Review, 57*(2), 272–290.

Earls, F. E. (1994). Violence and today's youth. *The Future of Children, 4*(3), 4–24.

Ewalt, P. L., Freeman, E. M., Kirk, S. A., & Poole, D. L. (1997). *Social policy: Reform, research, and practice.* Washington, DC: NASW Press.

Family Resource Coalition (1994–1995). *Report: Empowerment and Latino Families, 13*(3 & 4).

Farrow, F. (1998). Community responsibility for protecting children: What does it mean now, what can it mean in the future? *The Prevention Report, 1998*(1), 11–13.

Folks, H. (1911). *The care of destitute, neglected, and delinquent children.* New York: Macmillan.

Garbarino, J. (1992). The meaning of poverty in the world of children. *American Behavioral Scientist, 35*(2), 220–237.

Garwood, S. G., Phillips, D., Hartman, A., & Zigler, E. G. (1989). As the pendulum swings: Federal policy programs for children. *American Psychologist* (February), 434–440.

Hagen, J. L. & Davis, L. V. (1997). Mothers' views on child care under the JOBS program and implications for welfare reform. In P. L. Ewalt, E. M. Freeman, S. A. Kirk, & D. L. Poole (Eds.), *Social policy: Reform, research and practice* (pp. 280–296). Washington, DC: NASW Press.

Hartman, A. (1981). The family: A central focus for practice. *Social Work, 26*(1).

Heyburn, I. (1919). *The congressional record* (Senate). Washington, DC: U.S. Government Printing Office: 189.

Huff, B., & Telesford, M. C. (1994). Outreach efforts to involve families of color in the Federation of Families for Children's Mental Health. *Focal Point, 8*(2), 10–12. [Bulletin of the Research and Training Center to Improve Services for Seriously Emotionally Handicapped Children and Their Families, Portland State University, Regional Research Institute for Human Services, Portland, OR].

Jackson, S., & Brissett-Chapman, S. (Eds.) (1997). *Child Welfare Special Issue: Perspectives on Serving African-American Children, Youth, and Families, 76*(1).

Kadushin, A. (1987). Child welfare services. In *Encyclopedia of social work* (18th ed.). Washington, DC: National Association of Social Workers: 265–275.

Kahn, A. J. (1965). The societal context of social work practice. *Social Work, 10*(4), 145–155.

Kamerman, S. B. (1997). The new politics of child and family policies. In P. L. Ewalt, E. M. Freeman, S. A. Kirk, & D. L. Poole (Eds.), *Social policy: Reform, research and practice* (pp. 167–183). Washington, DC: NASW Press.

Kamerman, S. B., & Kahn, A. J. (1989). *Social services for children, youth and families in the United States.* New York: Columbia University School of Social Work, Annie E. Casey Foundation.

Knitzer, J., & Yelton, S. (1990). Collaborations between child welfare and mental health. *Public Welfare, 48*(2), 24–33.

Laird, J. (1985). An ecological approach to child welfare. In C. Germaine (Ed.). *Social work practice: People and environments.* New York: Columbia University Press.

Leashore, B. R., Chipungu, S. S., & Everett, J. E. (1991). *Child welfare: An afrocentric perspective.* New Brunswick, NJ: Rutgers University Press.

Lieberman, A., Russell, M., & Hornby, H. (1989). *National survey of child welfare workers.* Portland, ME: University of Southern Maine, National Resource Center for Management and Administration.

Listening to America's families: Action for the 80's. The report to the President, Congress, and families of the nation. (1980). Washington, DC: U.S. Government Printing Office.

Mason, J. L. (1994). Developing culturally competent organizations. *Focal Point, 8*(2), 1–8. [Bulletin of the Research and Training Center to Improve Services for Seriously Emotionally Handicapped Children and Their Families, Portland State University, Regional Research Institute for Human Services, Portland, OR].

Masten, A. S. (1992). Homeless children in the United States: Mark of a nation at risk. *Current Directions in Psychological Science, 1*(2), 41–44.

McFadden, E. J., Berns, D. A., & Downs, S. W. (1995). *Partnerships in developing graduate curriculum competencies: The Michigan experience.* Unpublished manuscript.

McFadden, E. J., & Downs, S. W. (1995). Family continuity: The new paradigm in permanence planning. *Community Alternatives: International Journal of Family Care, 7*(1), 44.

McPhatter, A. R. (1997). Cultural competence in child welfare: What is it? How do we achieve it? What happens without it? *Child Welfare, 76*(1), 255–278.

Melaville, A. I., & Blank, M. J. (1991). *What it takes: Structuring interagency partnerships to connect children and families with comprehensive services.* Washington, DC: Education and Human Services Consortium.

Meyer, C. H. (1984). Can foster care be saved? *Social Work, 29*(6), 499.

Meyer, C. H. (1985). The institutional context of child welfare. In J. Laird & A. Hartman (Eds.), *Handbook of child welfare.* New York: Macmillan.

Monthly vital statistics report (1995, March 22), *43*(9).

National Commission on Child Welfare and Family Preservation (1990). *A commitment to change.* Washington, DC: American Public Welfare Association.

Nelson, K. (1995). The child welfare response to youth violence and homelessness in the nineteenth century. *Child Welfare, 74*(1), 56–70.

Ortega, R. M., Guillean, C., & Najera, L. G. (1996). *Latinos and child welfare/Latinos y et bienestar del Nino, voces de la communidad.* Ann Arbor: The University of Michigan School of Social Work.

Ounce of Prevention Fund. (1993). *Beethoven's Fifth: The first five years of the center for successful child development.* Chicago: Ounce of Prevention Fund.

Peebles-Wilkins, W. (1995). Janie Porter Barrett and the Virginia Industrial School for Colored Girls: Community response to the needs of African-American children. *Child Welfare, 74*(1), 143–161.

Petit, M. R., & Curtis, P. A. (1997). *Child abuse and neglect: A look at the states.* Washington, DC: CWLA Press.

Russakoff, D. (1998, September 28). Birth of a new boom. *Washington Post, National Weekly Edition:* 6.

Saluter, A. F. (1994). *Marital and living arrangements: March, 1993.* (Current Population Reports, P20-478, U.S. Department of Commerce, Bureau of the Census). Washington, DC: U.S. Government Printing Office.

Schiele, J. H. (1996). Afrocentricity: An emerging paradigm in social work practice. *Social Work, 41*(3), 284–295.

Sherraden, M., & Downs, S. W. (1984). Institutions for juvenile delinquency in historical perspective. *Children and Youth Services Review, 6*(3), 155–173.

Smith, S. R. (1989). The changing politics of child welfare services: New roles for the government and the nonprofit sectors. *Child Welfare, 68*(3), 289–299.

Stein, T. J. (1998). *The social welfare of women and children with HIV and AIDS.* New York: Oxford University Press.

Steiner, G. Y. (1981). *The futility of family policy.* Washington, DC: The Brookings Institution.

Tatara, T. (1992, September). Substitute care population trends, FY 82 through FY 91—A summary. *VCIS Research Notes, 6,* 1–5.

Terpstra, J. (1993). *Reprofessionalizing child welfare.* Concept paper circulated from the U.S. Children's Bureau.

Thurston, H. W. (1930). *The dependent child.* New York: Columbia University Press.

Uehara, E. S., et al. (1996). Toward a values-based approach to multicultual social work research. *Social Work, 41*(6), 613–623.

U.S. Department of Commerce, Bureau of the Census. (1989). *Statistical abstract of the United States (109th ed.)* Washington, DC: U.S. Government Printing Office.

U.S. Department of Commerce (1992a). *Household type and presence and age of children: Summary of tape file 3A, 1990* (CD 90-3A-29) (CD-Rom). Washington, DC: U.S. Government Printing Office.

U.S. Department of Commerce (1992b). *How we're changing: Demographic state of the nation, 1992.* (Current Population Reports, Series P-23, No. 177). Washington, DC: U.S. Government Printing Office.

U.S. General Accounting Office. (1992). *Integrating human services: Linking at-risk families with services more successful than system reform efforts.* (GAO/HRD-92-108). Washington, DC: U.S. Government Printing Office.

U.S. General Accounting Office. (1993). *Foster care: Federal policy on Title IV-E share of training costs.* Washington, DC: U.S. Government Printing Office.

U.S. General Accounting Office. (1998, October). *Child welfare: Early experiences implementing a managed care approach.* [GAO/HEHS–99-8)] Washington, DC: U.S. Government Printing Office.

Wattenberg, E. (1998). Are communities the problem or the solution for high-risk families and children? *The Prevention Report, 1998*(1), 14–17.

Weaver, H. N. (1998). Indigenous people in a multicultural society: Unique issues for human services. *Social Work, 43*(3), 203–212.

Weil, M. (1997). Community building: Community practice. In P. L. Ewalt, E. M. Freeman, S. A. Kirk, & D. L. Poole (Eds.) *Social policy: Reform, research, and practice.* (pp. 35–61). Washington, DC: NASW Press.

Williams, E. E., & Ellison, F. (1996). Culturally informed social work practice with American Indian clients: Guidelines for Non-Indian social workers. *Social Work, 41*(2), 147–152.

Ziesemer, C., Marcoux, L., & Marwell, B. E. (1994). Homeless children: Are they different from other low-income children? *Social Work, 39*(6), 658–668.

Zill, N., & Nord, C. W. (1994). *Running in place: How American families are faring in a changing economy and an individualistic society.* Washington, DC: Child Trends, Inc.

Zlotnick, J. L. (1997). *Preparing the workforce for family-centered practice: Social work education and public human services partnerships.* Alexandria, VA: Council on Social Work Education.

CHAPTER 2

Rights and Responsibilities of Parents, Children, and Government

The child is not the mere creature of the State; those who nurture him and direct his destiny have the right, coupled with the high duty, to recognize and prepare him for additional obligations.
—*Pierce v. Society of Sisters*, 1925, p. 535

CHAPTER OUTLINE

CASE EXAMPLE

Joshua DeShaney was born in 1979. His parents divorced in 1980 and his father was granted custody. In January 1982 the father's second wife reported that the father had hit the child causing marks. The Winnebago County Department of Social Services (DSS) inter-viewed the father, who denied the charges. DSS closed the case. In January 1983 Joshua was admitted to a local hospital with multiple bruises and abrasions. The examining physician filed a suspected child abuse report with DSS. DSS obtained a court order to keep Joshua hospitalized until a multidisciplinary team could review the case. Three days later, the team decided that there was insufficient evidence of child abuse to pursue continuing court jurisdiction. They recommended some measures to protect Joshua, which his father voluntarily agreed to. Joshua was returned to his father. A month later, Joshua was treated in an emergency room for "suspicious injuries." A report to DSS was made. The caseworker investigated, concluded that there was no basis for court action, and continued to make monthly visits under the voluntary arrangement; she documented these visits and her suspicions that someone in the home was physically abusing Joshua. Nothing else was done. In November 1983, Joshua was treated again for suspicious injuries. The caseworker visited the home, but did not see Joshua because the father told her he was too sick to see her. In March 1984, Joshua was badly beaten and fell into a life-threatening coma. Joshua suffered brain injuries so severe that he was expected to spend the rest of his life confined to an institution. His father was tried and convicted of child abuse.

Joshua's mother and guardian ad litem brought a suit against DSS, alleging that DSS violated his constitutional rights (Fourteenth Amendment: deprivation of liberty without due process) "by failing to intervene to protect him against a risk of violence at his father's hands of which they knew or should have known" (*DeShaney v. Winnebago County DSS*, 1989, p. 193). The Court concluded that the state had not violated Joshua DeShaney's constitutional rights in failing to protect him from his father's abuse. The Court stated:

nothing in the language of the Due Process Clause itself requires the State to protect the life, liberty, and property of its citizens against invasion by private actors. The Clause is phrased as a limitation on the State's power to act, not as a guarantee of certain minimal levels of safety and security. It forbids the State itself to deprive individuals of life, liberty, or property without "due process of law," but its language cannot fairly be extended to impose an affirmative obligation on the State to ensure that those interests do not come to harm through other means. (Id., p. 195)

While finding that there was no constitutional violation, the Court held open the possibility of liability of the state under state law. It concluded:

It may well be that, by voluntarily undertaking to protect Joshua against a danger it concededly played no

part in creating, the State acquired a duty under state tort law to provide him with adequate protection against that danger. . . . A State may, through its courts and legislatures, impose such affirmative duties of care and protection upon its agents as it wishes. (DeShaney v. Winnebago County DSS, 1989, p. 201)

INTRODUCTION

Child welfare practice is rooted in a legal environment that seeks to balance the interests of child, parents, and the government (federal and state). It is an area that requires understanding the interplay of the federal and state legislative, executive, and judicial systems. This chapter provides a basic overview of that legal environment.

Historical Context

A discussion of the historical context of the three entities whose interests are to be balanced—parent, child, and government—is necessary to understanding how we got to where we are now and to projecting where we might go in the future. In our society, historically and presently, the primary right and responsibility of caring for children rests with their parents.

Until the onset of the nineteenth century, parents were afforded almost absolute autonomy, privacy, and independence in carrying out their parental responsibilities unless they committed some criminal act against the child. During the nineteenth century, the government began to impose certain restrictions on parental rights related to child labor and education. Religious organizations and other reformers began to take an interest in the basic care, or lack thereof, of children and to establish orphanages and boarding homes for children found to be destitute, abandoned, or wayward. In 1899, the first juvenile court was established in Illinois to address the abuse, neglect, and delinquency of children (Kramer, 1994).

The early twentieth century saw the beginning of federal involvement, with the first White House Conference on Children in 1909 and establishment of the Children's Bureau in 1912. These actions signaled the beginning of federal leadership in developing legislation and programs to promote the general well-being and protection of children throughout the country.

Policy and Legal Context

Legal ramifications of the parent-child relationship are demanding more and more attention from social workers engaged in the spectrum of child protection services: prevention, protection, family preservation, foster care, guardianship, custody, adoption, and juvenile justice. Various public constituencies, often with different values and philosophies, want to and do participate in the development of public social policy that is generally codified, that is, written down, in federal or state laws that form the basis of administrative rules and policies for agencies delegated the responsibilities to carry out the requirements of the laws. Some advocates for the family favor policy reaffirming the traditional presumption that parents will act in their child's best interests, and support legislation that safeguards the rights of parents by imposing stringent legal procedures to justify governmental intrusion into the family's autonomy. Other child and family advocates place greater emphasis on policy that advocates the legal rights of children as distinct from those of their parents. Most child and family advocates prefer an approach to intervention to remedy or alleviate family problems that represents the least intrusive intervention necessary to ensure that the harm or threatened harm to the child is removed. Chapter 12 provides more detail on the role of advocacy in the development of social policy. Chapters 1, 3, 4, 6, 7, 8, 9, 10, and 11 provide detailed reviews of specific federal legislation impacting child welfare policy and practice.

The legal framework for child welfare practice is rooted in federal and state laws (constitutions, statutes, ordinances) that regulate parent, child, and government interrelationships; the administrative rules and agency policies promulgated to carry out these laws; and the judicial and administrative decisions applying the laws to specific cases. Every state now has laws covering the basic areas of child welfare practice, protecting children from the certain acts of commission or omission by their parents, guardians, or caretakers; addressing the status offender and the juvenile offender/delinquent; establishing the conditions and procedures for legal guardianship; establishing conditions and procedures for emancipation; and establishing the procedures for adoption. In addition, every state has laws that regulate matters that the child welfare professional frequently encounters, such as education, medical treatment, consent for abortion, treatment for sexually transmitted diseases, mental health treatment, and substance abuse treatment. The scope of this text is such that each cannot be discussed in detail. You are encouraged to obtain and review copies of the applicable statutes within the state where you practice. It is important to note that not every state law on a similar matter is the same. Subsequent chapters highlight some of these statutory variances and expound on the practice implications.

Constitutional Overlay

The states and the federal government, under the police powers, have the right and responsibility to enact laws to promote public safety, peace, morals, and general societal welfare which regulate the behaviors of its citizenry, but the scope of authority of those police powers are limited by the constitutional privileges afforded to the citizenry. A basic principle of U.S. law (broadly speaking, "law" includes constitutions, statutes, ordinances, rules, regulations, and policies) is that actions of the legislative or executive branches at the state and federal level must not violate rights and privileges provided under the Constitution of the United States (*Lawton v. Steele, 1893*). Coupled with that basic principle is another; namely, the courts do not "case find." Someone (an aggrieved person, that is, a person who thinks their rights have been violated, or a person acting on behalf of them) must present a "controversy" to the court via the method prescribed in court rules, usually a petition or complaint. Once presented with a petition or complaint, the courts can determine whether or not the facts in the case are such that a violation of the law, including the Constitution, has occurred. In the area of parent, child, and government interrelations, the interpretation of the constitutional rights of parents and children vis-à-vis one another, independently and in relation to the state and federal government, is unfolding. Since the Supreme Court of the United States, the Court, has the final decision as to whether or not a particular law (federal, state, or local), as applied to a specific set of facts, is constitutional or not, several decisions of that Court with respect to parents, children, and governmental interests and rights within the context of child welfare practice are discussed here and in subsequent chapters. This gives us a framework for understanding the decisional climate in which states must operate as they enact laws affecting child welfare.

Before beginning that discussion, however, a brief overview of the mechanics of the Supreme Court, its decision-making process, and the usual mechanism by which cases come before the Supreme Court may help you understand the case decisions. The **nine justices** are appointed for life by the president with the consent of the Senate. The **decision** (also known as the **holding or ruling,** depending on the nature of the decision) of the majority is the decision of the Court. The **majority opinion** has the greatest weight and the more justices included in the majority the stronger the decision. Where there is agreement on the decision but differences in the reasoning—that is, the legal explanation—one or more **minority opinions** or **concurring opinions** are written. Any justice who disagrees with the court's decision writes a **dissenting opinion.** While this opinion holds no authority, it frequently provides food for thought for legislators and lawyers (Pratt, 1993).

The process by which the Supreme Court usually comes to hear cases involving parent, child, and state interests is as an appeal of a federal court decision that claims the action (that is, a particular statute or administrative rule, policy, or practice) of the state agent violated the constitutional rights of the person. Constitutional protections against states' actions are granted under the due process or equal protection clauses of the Fourteenth Amendment of the Constitution of the United States. Section 1 of the Fourteenth Amendment states:

All persons born or naturalized in the United States and subject to the jurisdiction thereof, are citizens of the United States and of the State wherein they reside. No State shall make or enforce any law which shall abridge the privileges or immunities of citizens of the United States; nor shall any State deprive any person of life, liberty, or property, without due process of law; nor deny to any person within its jurisdiction the equal protection of the laws.

The Supreme Court Justices, by vote, determine which cases will be heard by the Court, a process known as *writ of certiorari.*

The decisions and reasoning of the Supreme Court in the area of parent, child, and state rights, responsibilities, and interests are complex and at first glance contradictory. However, with careful review and analyses of the difference in the legal questions being asked, the laws or rules being applied, and the facts of the specific cases, the decisions become more cogent. A fundamental reason for the variances is that Supreme Court decisions interpret the public policy that frames the often conflicting needs and goals of parents, children, and society. Some of these cases are weighted in the direction of reinforcing the rights of parents in the upbringing of their children. Some clearly extend legal rights to minors; others limit rights they would have but for their status as minors. In all cases the influences and interests of society are apparent.

The justices have clearly said that the child, merely on account of his or her minority status, is not beyond the protection of the Constitution: "Whatever may be their precise impact, neither the Fourteenth Amendment nor the Bill of Rights is for adults alone" (*In re Gault,* 1967, p. 13). In some cases the Court has concluded that the child's right to due process is the same as that of an adult, particularly in matters of threat to liberty or property interests (*In re Gault,* 1967; *Tinker v. Des Moines School District,* 1969). But also it has rejected "the uncritical assumption that the constitutional rights of children are indistinguishable from those of adults," or that under the law children can never be treated differently from adults (*Bellotti v. Baird,* 1979, p. 633). The challenge facing the Court is one of achieving a just and workable balance in parent-child-society conflicts.

U.S. Supreme Court cases not only reveal the rights of parents and their offspring but also the Court's view of children—their needs, protections, and capabilities. The justices have offered three principles that guide their reasoning and justify the conclusion that the constitutional rights of children cannot be unequivocally equated with those of adults: "the peculiar vulnerability of children; their inability to make critical decisions in an informed, mature manner; and the importance of the parental role in child-rearing" (*Bellotti v. Baird,* 1979, p. 623). In the words of former Justice Felix Frankfurter, "Children have a very special place in life which law should reflect. Legal theories and their phrasing in other cases readily leads to fallacious reasoning if uncritically transferred to determination of a State's duty toward children" (*May v. Anderson,* 1953, p. 536).

It follows that although children are generally protected by the same constitutional guarantees as adults, the state is allowed to adjust its legal system to accord with children's vulnerability and the unique role of the family; constitutional principles must be applied flexibly and sensitively to the special needs of children and parents. Given this framework for legal reasoning in relation to child rights, the ambivalence perceived by child advocates (that is, a dichotomy of rights bestowed and rights denied) becomes more understandable, if not fully acceptable, to proponents of expanded and inclusive constitutional protections for children.

RIGHTS AND RESPONSIBILITIES OF PARENTS

In our society the primary right and responsibility of caring for children rests with their parents. Differences are accepted and valued as part of our way of life. Parents have the right of natural guardianship by the fact that the child was born to or legally adopted by them. In situations where a child is born to unwed parents, the mother automatically assumes natural guardianship rights and responsibilities. The unwed (also known as putative) father must follow the law and procedures legislated by each state to establish paternity and acquire care, custody, support, and visitation rights. Parents determine the living pattern and the standards of everyday conduct that influence the developing personality of the child. They can determine religion and may affect basic ethical values of the child. They influence the kind and extent of the child's education, the decision as to vocation, and the level of adult achievement. The quality of health care the child receives depends not only on the availability of health services in a particular community but also on the extent of the parents' knowledge and the choices made by them when medical care is needed.

The responsibilities of parenthood include (1) financial support—meeting the child's money needs in a society that looks with disfavor on economic dependency and the inability of parents to keep the family economically self-supporting; (2) the provision of physical care—keeping the child safe from harm and injury and giving attention to his or her physical condition and health needs; (3) emotional care—for many parents a nebulous and poorly defined concept, carrying connotations of responsibility without knowledge of ways to meet it; and (4) a range of other parental duties, such as giving guidance and supervision to the young child as well as to the adolescent, promoting the growth of self-discipline, and setting forth clear parental and societal expectations that are adapted to the individual child's pace and ability. In addition, the right of parents to make certain major decisions for the child—for example, consent to medical care, to enlistment in the armed forces, and to marriage—is also a serious responsibility.

Decisions Reinforcing Parental Rights

Parental rights to make decisions about various aspects of their children's lives have been reinforced in several Supreme Court decisions. The following discussion summarizes the most relevant decisions. The format used in this discussion is to summarize the state law being challenged; to then state the issue before the court, that is, the alleged constitutional violation(s); and to state the relevant facts, the rule of law as applied to the case facts and the holding of the Court. Further, in each instance, specific quotations from the decisions are given to show the rationale for the Court's decision.

Pierce v. Society of Sisters, 1925.   The Oregon Compulsory Education Act required parents of children between the ages of 8 and 16 years to send them

to public schools. Two private schools brought action on behalf of themselves and the parents of children attending their schools claiming that this act deprived them of property interests and deprived the parents of their right to direct the religious upbringing of their children. The Court held that a state could not require parents to send their children to public schools only. The Court stated:

> Under the doctrine of Meyer v. Nebraska, 262 U.S. 390, we think it entirely plain that the Act of 1922 unreasonably interferes with the liberty of parents and guardians to direct the upbringing and education of children under their control. As often heretofore pointed out, rights guaranteed by the Constitution may not be abridged by legislation which has no reasonable relation to some purpose within the competence of the State. The fundamental theory of liberty upon which all governments in this Union repose excludes any general power of the State to standardize its children by forcing them to accept instruction from public teachers only. The child is not the mere creature of the State; those who nurture him and direct his destiny have the right, coupled with the high duty, to recognize and prepare him for additional obligations. (Pierce v. Society of Sisters, 1925, pp. 534–535)

Wisconsin v. Yoder, 1972. Wisconsin required parents to send their children to either public or private school until the age of 16 years. Amish parents refused to send their 14- and 15-year-old children to school after completion of the eighth grade because they believed it to be contrary to their religion. The Court stated:

> The record strongly indicates that accommodating the religious objections of the Amish by forgoing one, or at most two, additional years of compulsory education will not impair the physical and mental health of the child, or result in an inability to be self-supporting or to discharge the duties and responsibilities of citizenship, or in any other way materially distract from the welfare of society. (Wisconsin v. Yoder, 1972, p. 234)

Justice Douglas stated *in dissent:*

> On this important and vital matter of education, I think the children should be entitled to be heard. While the parents, absent dissent, normally speak for the entire family, the education of the child is a matter on which the child will often have decided views. . . . It is the student's judgment, not his parents, that is essential if we are to give full meaning to what we have said about the Bill of Rights and of the rights of students to be masters of their own destiny. (Id., pp. 244–245)

Palmore v. Sidoti, 1984. This case involved a child-custody decision. These types of cases are extremely rare before the Supreme Court. Two Caucasian parents divorced when their child was three years old. Custody was given to the mother. She subsequently cohabitated with and married a Negro. The father petitioned for custody on the basis of "changed conditions." A Florida court awarded custody to the father based on a counselor's recommendation for the change in custody because "the wife has chosen for herself and for her child, a life-style unacceptable to the father and to society. . . . The child is, or at school age, will be subject to environmental pressures not of her choice" (Palmore v. Sidoti, 1984, p. 431).

The Supreme Court stated:

> It would ignore reality to suggest that racial and ethnic prejudices do not exist or that all manifestations of those prejudices have been eliminated. . . . The question, however, is whether the reality of private biases and the possible injury they might inflict are permissible considerations for removal of an infant child from the custody of its natural mother. We have little difficulty in concluding that they are not. The Constitution cannot control such prejudices but neither can it tolerate them. (Id., p. 433)

The Supreme Court repeatedly has emphasized the guiding role of parents in the upbringing of their children and the responsibility of parents to "inculcate and pass down many of our most cherished values, moral and cultural" (Wisconsin v. Yoder, 1972, p. 233). This "unique role" of the family, the Court has said, entitles biological parents to substantive due process protections and, although not without disagreement among the Justices, justifies limitations on the freedom of minors.

Parham v. J. R., 1979. A long-awaited Supreme Court decision was made in this case challenging the rights of parents to institutionalize their children for mental health treatment and of the state to institutionalize its wards (that is, children under its supervision and/or in its custody) without due process procedures in behalf of the child. Georgia's law, in relevant part, stated:

> *The superintendent of any facility may receive for observation and diagnosis any individual under 18 years of age for whom such application is made by his parent or guardian. If found to show evidence of mental illness and to be suitable for treatment, such person may be given care and treatment at such facility and such person may be detained by such facility for such period and under such conditions as may be authorized by law. (Ga. Code Section 88-503.1)*
>
> *The superintendent of the facility shall discharge any voluntary patient who has recovered from his mental illness or who has sufficiently improved that the superintendent determines that hospitalization of the patient is no longer desirable. (Ga. Code Section 88-503.2)*

J. R. was a neglected child who was removed from his natural parents at 3 months and placed in seven different foster homes prior to admission to the state hospital at 7 years of age on request of the Department of Family and Children Services. He was assessed to be borderline retarded with an unsocialized, aggressive reaction of childhood and suitable for admission and treatment. His case was reviewed periodically. Unsuccessful efforts were made to place him in foster homes during the hospitalization.

On these facts, the Supreme Court concluded that the traditional presumption that natural bonds of affection lead parents to act in the best interests of their children should apply. Parents should retain a substantial if not the dominant role in the decision to voluntarily commit their children to an institution. Furthermore, Georgia law provided for informal medical review 30 days after admission to state hospitals, and the Court underscored as protection to the child the authority of doctors to make medical judgments. Thus the decision reinforced not only the authority of parents and agents of the state over children, but also the authority of the medical profession in confining children for medical treatment.

Justice Brennan, concurring in part and dissenting in part, noted that even under ideal circumstances, psychiatric diagnosis and decisions about therapy are uncertain; that when a child is institutionalized by his or her parents, there has already been a break in family autonomy; and that parental authority should not stand in the way of a child's constitutional rights. Further, children held in mental hospitals are "not only deprived of physical liberty; they are also deprived of friends, family, and community, and at risk of stigma as well. They live in unnatural surroundings under the continuous and detailed control of strangers" (*Parham v. J. R.,* 1979, p. 632). Brennan questioned the traditional presumption that parents will act in their child's best interests when making commitment decisions and said "a child who has been ousted from his family has even greater need for an independent advocate" (Id., p. 631).

Santosky v. Kramer, 1982. The New York law provided that a child could be declared permanently neglected using a "fair preponderance of the evidence" standard and, on the basis of that declaration, the court could permanently terminate parental rights.

The Santoskys had lost custody of three children on petitions filed by the local Department of Social Services alleging neglect of the oldest child, physical abuse of the second child, and "immediate removal necessary to avoid imminent danger to his life or health" of the third child within three days of birth. The children were placed in foster care, where they remained for about five years before the petition to terminate parental rights.

While the Santosky children were in foster care, the Department of Social Services offered the parents training by a mother's aide, a nutritional aide, and a public health nurse and counseling at a family planning clinic. In addition, psychiatric treatment and vocational training were offered to the father and counseling at a family service center to the mother. Eventually the department filed a termination petition stating that the parents' response to their efforts was "marginal at best": they wholly disregarded some of the available services and used others only sporadically. Infrequent visits between parents and children had been "at best superficial and devoid of any real emotional content"

(*Santosky v. Kramer*, 1982, p. 751). The New York Family Court terminated parental rights. The parents appealed, alleging that the New York statute under which the termination of their rights occurred violated the due process clause of the Fourteenth Amendment. Without expressing any opinion on the merits, the Court held that the appropriate question before them was "What is the standard of proof that should be used in termination of parental rights proceedings?" The justices, in a five-to-four decision, ruled that the due process clause of the Fourteenth Amendment demands more than "a fair preponderance of the evidence" before terminating irrevocably the parent-child relationship. Allegations must be supported by at least "clear and convincing evidence."

The Court stated:

> *A majority of the States has concluded that a "clear and convincing evidence" standard of proof strikes a fair balance between the rights of the natural parents and the States' legitimate concerns. We hold that such a standard adequately conveys to the factfinder the level of subjective certainty about his factual conclusions necessary to satisfy due process. We further hold that determination of the precise burden equal to or greater than that standard is a matter of state law left to state legislatures and state courts. (Santosky v. Kramer, 1982, p. 769)*

In summary, the Supreme Court decisions have established that parents have full right to choose to send their child to a public or a private school; to refuse to adhere to compulsory school attendance statutes where they can show that compliance is in violation of their religious beliefs; to institutionalize their child for mental health treatment provided there is appropriate assessment, evaluation, and periodic reviews that support the need for the institutionalization; and to have a clear and convincing standard of proof applied in proceedings to terminate their parental rights.

Parental Rights of the Unwed Father

Within recent decades the unwed father has gained legal recognition of some aspects of parental rights to his nonmarital child. A chain of U.S. Supreme Court cases has established that the father must have developed a significant and personal relationship with his nonmarital child to warrant constitutional protection in adoption proceedings. To date, the fact of biological relationship alone between father and nonmarital child does not merit protection. Unwed fathers must "grasp the opportunity" of their biological connection to their child to form an actual parenting relationship. What is protected, then, is a "liberty interest" in a "developed parent-child relationship resulting from the father's shouldering significant responsibility with respect to daily supervision, education, protection and care of his child that has been recognized as an interest with due process safeguard" (Gitlin, 1987, p. 2).

Stanley v. Illinois, 1972. Illinois law provided that the state could assume custody of children of married parents, divorced parents, and unmarried mothers only after a hearing and proof of neglect. The children of unmarried fathers, however, are declared dependent children, that is, children who have no surviving parent or guardian. Furthermore, Illinois law stated "parent means the father and mother of a legitimate child, or the survivor of them, or the natural mother of an illegitimate child, and includes any adoptive parent" (*Stanley v. Illinois*, 1972, p. 650). Under a dependency proceeding, the state is only required to show that the father was not married to the mother and need not prove unfitness, as required for married mothers and fathers or unmarried mothers.

Stanley was an unwed father who had lived with the mother of his children, provided some financial support, and served in the parental role. After the death of the mother, the children were declared dependent and made wards of the state without any hearing to determine Stanley's fitness. Stanley was excluded from a voice in the state's effort to place his children in adoptive homes. He appealed, alleging that the Illinois law deprived him and other unwed fathers of due process and equal protection rights granted by the Fourteenth Amendment.

The Court stated:

> *The private interest here, that of a man in the children he has sired and raised, undeniably warrants deference and, absent a powerful countervailing interest, protection. It is plain that the interest of the parent in*

the companionship, care, custody, and management of his or her children comes to this Court with a momentum for respect lacking when appeal is made to liberties which derive merely from shifting economic arrangements.

But we are here not asked to evaluate the legitimacy of the state ends, rather, to determine whether the means used to achieve these ends are constitutionally defensible. What is the State interest in separating children from fathers without a hearing designed to determine if the father is unfit in a particular disputed case? We observe that the State registers no gain toward its declared goals when it separates children from the custody of fit parents. Indeed if Stanley is a fit father, the State spites its own articulated goals when it needlessly separates him from his family.

The State's interest in caring for Stanley's children is de minimis *if Stanley is shown to be a fit father. It insists on presuming rather than proving Stanley's unfitness solely because it is more convenient to presume than to prove. Under the Due Process Clause that advantage is insufficient to justify refusing a father a hearing when the issue at stake is the dismemberment of his family. . . . We have concluded that all Illinois parents are constitutionally entitled to a hearing on their fitness before their children are removed from their custody. It follows that denying such a hearing to Stanley and those like him while granting it to other Illinois parents is inescapably contrary to the Equal Protection Clause. (Id., pp. 652–658)*

Quilloin v. Walcott, 1978. Georgia law provided both parents' consent to the adoption of a child born in wedlock, whereas only the mother's consent was required for the adoption of an illegitimate child, that is, a child born out of wedlock. The law further provided that the father could acquire veto rights over the adoption if he had legitimated the child through marriage to the child's mother or acknowledgment of paternity.

Quilloin, the father, had never exercised custody over his child nor assumed any significant responsibility for the child's daily care, protection, supervision, or education. For eleven years he had not availed himself of the opportunity under Georgia law to legitimate his nonmarital child and thus gain full parental rights. He petitioned to block the adoption of the child by the mother's husband after the mother had consented and the husband filed a petition to

adopt. He did not seek custody or object to the child continuing to live with the mother and her husband. The child had resided with and been parented by the mother's husband for almost nine years. The Georgia courts conducted a trial on his petitions stating "these matters are being tried . . . to allow the biological father . . . a right to be heard with respect to any issue or other thing upon which he desire(s) to be heard, including his fitness as a parent . . ." (Id., p. 250). Based on the findings at the trial, the Georgia courts concluded that the adoption was "in the child's best interests" and that granting either legitimation or visitation rights would not be in the child's best interests. On that basis it found that Quilloin had no right to object to the adoption. Quilloin appealed, alleging that the Georgia law as applied violated the equal protection and due process clauses of the Fourteenth Amendment. He contended that he should be entitled to the same power to veto the adoption as the unwed mother and married or divorced parents.

The Court stated, "*Stanley* left unresolved the degree of protection a State must afford to the rights of an unwed father in a situation, such as that presented here, in which the countervailing interests are more substantial" (Id., p. 248). It further determined the issue before it to be "Whether, in the circumstances of this case and in light of the authority granted by Georgia law to married fathers, appellant's (Quilloin's) interests were adequately protected by a 'best interests of the child' standard" (Id., p. 254).

The Court responded:

We have little doubt that the Due Process Clause would be offended if a State were to attempt to force the breakup of a natural family, over the objections of the parents and their children, without some showing of unfitness and for the sole reason that to do so was thought to be in the children's best interest. . . . But this is not a case in which the unwed father at any time had, or sought, actual or legal custody of his child. Nor is this a case in which the proposed adoption would place the child with a new set of parents with whom the child had never before lived. Rather, the result of the adoption in this case is to give full recognition to a family unit already in existence, a result desired by all concerned, except appellant. Whatever might be required in other situations, we cannot say that the State was re-

quired in this situation to find anything more than that the adoption, and denial of legitimation, were in the 'best interests of the child' (Id., p. 255).

The Court found no violation of the equal protection clause. It stated:

We think appellant's interests are readily distinguishable from those of a separated or divorced father, and accordingly believe that the State could permissibly give appellant less veto authority than it provides to a married father. . . . He has never exercised actual or legal custody over his child, and thus has never shouldered any significant responsibility with respect to the daily supervision, education, protection, or care of the child. Appellant does not complain of his exemption from these responsibilities and, indeed, he does not even now seek custody of his child. In contrast, legal custody of children is, of course, a central aspect of the marital relationship, and even a father whose marriage has broken apart will have borne full responsibility for the rearing of his children during the period of the marriage. (Quilloin v. Walcott, 1978, p. 256)

Caban v. Mohammed, 1979. New York law provided that an unwed mother, but not an unwed father, could block the adoption of a child by withholding consent.

Caban lived with the mother and their two children, his name appeared on the birth certificates of the children, he had contributed to their support, and, even after the mother left with the children to marry another man, he continued to see them frequently. The mother's new husband subsequently sought to adopt the children with the mother's consent but without the consent of the biological father.

Caban petitioned to block the adoption on the basis that the New York law violated the equal protection clause of the Fourteenth Amendment because it bore no substantial relation to an important state interest. The Court stated:

The State's interest in providing for the well being of illegitimate children is an important one. We do not question that the best interests of such children often may require their adoption into new families who will give them the stability of a normal, two-parent home. Moreover, adoption will remove the stigma under which illegitimate children suffer. But the unquestioned

right of the State to further these desirable ends by legislation is not in itself sufficient to justify the gender-based distinction of § 111. Rather, under the relevant cases applying the Equal Protection Clause it must be shown that the distinction is structured reasonable to further these ends. . . . Such a statutory classification must be reasonable, not arbitrary, and must rest upon some ground of difference having a fair and substantial relation to the object of the legislation, so that all persons similarly circumstanced shall be treated alike. . . . We find that the distinction in § 111 between unmarried mothers and unmarried fathers, as illustrated by this case, does not bear a substantial relation to the State's interest in providing adoptive homes for its illegitimate children. (Caban v. Mohammed, 1979, p. 391)

The effect of New York's classification is to discriminate against unwed fathers even when their identity is known and they have manifested a significant paternal interest in the child. The facts of this case illustrated the harshness of classifying unwed fathers as being invariably less qualified and entitled than mothers to exercise a concerned judgment as to the fate of their children. . . . We conclude that this undifferentiated distinction between unwed mothers and unwed fathers, applicable in all circumstances where adoption of a child of theirs is at issue, does not bear a substantial relationship to the State's asserted interests. (Id., p. 394)

In summary, uncertainty still persists as to the scope of constitutional protections of the rights of the unwed father with respect to his nonmarital children. However, the Supreme Court decisions have established that unwed fathers have the right to be notified and to be heard when the matter of termination of parental rights and adoption of their illegitimate child is concerned, and, if they have had a substantial relationship with their child, they have a right to a "determination of fitness" equal to that afforded married parents or unmarried mothers before their children can be taken from them. Many states have statutes and procedural rules which further clarify the rights of unwed fathers. As long as these laws and rules afford the unwed father the protections of notice and opportunity to be heard, and they support a legitimate state interest without discrimination on the basis of race or gender, they will most likely pass constitutional challenges.

Decisions Limiting Parental Rights

The Supreme Court has also issued decisions in which the rights of parents in the choices affecting their children were limited. For the most part, this line of cases recognizes that children have rights separate from their parents and that the states have interests in protecting those rights.

Prince v. Massachusetts, 1944. Massachusetts law prohibited children under 12 years of age from selling newspapers, magazines, and periodicals in public places. Further, it was unlawful for any parent or guardian to permit a minor to engage in such behavior. The aunt of a 9-year-old girl gave her Jehovah's Witness magazines to distribute on the streets at 5 cents per copy. The aunt was convicted of violating the law. Her appeal alleged that the Massachusetts law violated the free exercise of religion provision in the First Amendment. The Supreme Court stated:

> The state's authority over children's activities is broader than over like adult activities. . . . What may be wholly permissible for adults therefore may not be so for children, either with or without their parents' presence. . . . Parents may be free to become martyrs themselves. But it does not follow that they are free, in identical circumstances, to make martyrs of their children before they have reached the age of full and legal discretion when they can make that choice for themselves. . . . We think that with reference to the public proclaiming of religion, upon the streets and in other similar public places, the power of the state to control the conduct of children reaches beyond the scope of its authority over adults, as is true in the case of other freedoms, and the rightful boundary of its power has not been crossed in this case. (Prince v. Massachusetts, 1944, pp. 168–170)

Baltimore City Department of Social Services v. Bouknight, 1990. The Fifth Amendment of the Constitution provides, in part, that "no person shall be compelled in any criminal case to be a witness against himself, nor be deprived of life, liberty, or property, without due process of law." Bouknight was the mother of an adjudicated abused child who was in her custody under the supervision of Baltimore City Department of Social Services (BCDSS). A petition was filed to return the child to foster care based on the mother's failure to follow the court-ordered treatment plan. She refused to produce the child. The court held her in contempt and ordered her imprisoned until she produced the child or revealed to the court his whereabouts. She appealed this order claiming that it violated her Fifth Amendment rights. The Court of Appeals of Maryland found "that the contempt order unconstitutionally compelled Bouknight to admit through the act of production "a measure of continuing control and dominion over Maurice's person" in circumstances in which "Bouknight had a reasonable apprehension that she will be prosecuted." BCDSS appealed. The Supreme Court reversed the judgment of the Maryland Court of Appeals, stating:

> Once Maurice was adjudicated a child in need of assistance, his care and safety became the particular object of the State's regulatory interests. . . . By accepting care of Maurice subject to the custodial order's conditions . . . Bouknight submitted to the routine operation of the regulatory system and agreed to hold Maurice in a manner consonant with the State's regulatory interests and subject to inspection by BCDSS. (Baltimore City Department of Social Services v. Bouknight, 1990, p. 559)

In summary, the Supreme Court has supported the states, allowing them greater authority than parents in the regulation and enforcement of child labor (the age at which children can work, the types of jobs or labor they can perform, the hours they can work, etc.) and child protection.

Parental Authority and the Reproductive Rights of Minors

No issue of child, parent, and society rights and responsibilities has attracted and sustained more controversy than the question of the minor's right to control his or her own reproductive capacities by access to contraception or abortion.

Roe v. Wade, 1973. This well-known case gave constitutional protection to the right of women to choose abortion early in pregnancy and the right of the state to regulate the termination of pregnancy after "viability of the fetus," that is, "when the life of the unborn child may be continued indefinitely outside the womb by natural or artificial life supportive systems" (*Roe v. Wade,* 1973, p. 163).

Planned Parenthood of Central Missouri v. Danforth, 1976.

A Missouri statute required the written consent of a parent or person *in loco parentis* for an abortion during the first 12 weeks of pregnancy of an unmarried woman under the age of 18 years unless there was a certification by a physician that abortion was necessary to preserve the life of the mother. The Court found the statute unconstitutional and stated:

> . . . the State may not impose a blanket provision, such as § 3 (4), requiring the consent of a parent or person in loco parentis *as a condition for abortion of an unmarried minor during the first 12 weeks of her pregnancy. Just as with the requirement of consent from the spouse, so here, the State does not have the constitutional authority to give a third party an absolute, and possibly arbitrary, veto over the decision of the physician and his patient to terminate the patient's pregnancy, regardless of the reason for withholding the consent. Constitutional rights do not mature and come into being magically only when one attains the state-defined age of majority. Minors, as well as adults, are protected by the Constitution and possess constitutional rights. . . . The Court indeed, however, long has recognized that the State has somewhat broader authority to regulate the activities of children than of adults. . . . It remains, then, to examine whether there is any significant state interest in conditioning an abortion on the consent of a parent or person in loco parentis that is not present in the case of an adult. (Planned Parenthood of Missouri v. Danforth, 1976, pp. 74–75)*

The Court went on to discuss the argument that the state's interest was in safeguarding the family unit and parent's authority. It concluded that an absolute veto power did nothing to safeguard the family unit or the parent's authority. The Court stated clearly that this opinion did not preclude state regulation of abortion decision making for minors; rather it precluded a state statute that provided absolute veto power over that decision to a parent or person *in loco parentis*.

Bellotti v. Baird, 1979.

A Massachusetts's statute required a pregnant unmarried minor to have the con-

sent of her parent or the permission of a judge of a state court of general jurisdiction before she could obtain an abortion. Massachusetts passed this statute after the *Danforth* decision and provided an alternative procedure—that is, the permission of a judge—to ensure that the parent did not have absolute veto authority over the unmarried minor's abortion decision. The Court affirmed the desirability of fostering parental involvement in a minor's large decisions and noted that deference to parents may be appropriate with respect to a range of choices facing a minor. However, the Court stated:

> Although it satisfies constitutional standards in large part, § 12S falls short of them in two respects: First, it permits judicial authorization for an abortion to be withheld from a minor who is found by the superior court to be mature and fully competent to make this decision independently. Second, it requires parental consultation or notification in every instance, without affording the pregnant minor an opportunity to receive an independent judicial determination that she is mature enough to consent or that an abortion would be in her best interests. (Bellotti v. Baird, 1979, p. 651)

After the Court decisions discussed above, some states sought to maintain parental involvement in unmarried minors' abortion decisions by enacting legislation that mandated *notice* to parents, rather than consent.

H. L. v. Matheson, 1981.

A Utah law required a physician to notify, if possible, the parents or guardians of a minor upon whom the physician intended to perform an abortion. Neither parents nor judges had veto power over the minor's abortion decision. Her physician had advised a 15-year-old pregnant girl, living with her parents, that an abortion would be in her best medical interests. Because of the criminal liability involved, he refused to perform the abortion without notifying her parents. The girl argued that this notification requirement restricted her right to privacy to obtain an abortion and to enter into a doctor-patient relationship. The Court upheld the law and stated:

> That the requirement of notice to parents may inhibit some minors from seeking abortions is not a valid basis to void the statute as applied to appellant and

the class properly before us. The Constitution does not compel a state to fine-tune its statutes so as to encourage or facilitate abortions. To the contrary, state action "encouraging childbirth except in the most urgent circumstances" is "rationally related to the legitimate governmental objective of protecting potential life." . . . As applied to the class properly before us, the statute plainly serves important state interests, is narrowly drawn to protect only those interests, and does not violate any guarantees of the Constitution. (H. L. v. Matheson, 1981, p. 413)

Ohio v. Akron Center for Reproductive Health, 1990.

An Ohio law required a physician or other person contemplating performing an abortion on a pregnant unmarried person under the age of 18 to notify at least one parent or to have a judge's order permitting the minor to consent to the abortion (a judicial bypass). To secure a judicial bypass order, the minor was required to present "clear and convincing proof that she has sufficient maturity and information to make the abortion decision herself, that one of her parents has engaged in a pattern of physical, emotional, or sexual abuse against her, or that notice is not in her best interests" (*Ohio v. Akron Center for Reproductive Health,* 1990, p. 502). The Court, after much discussion of the compatibility of the Ohio statute with the requirements imposed by the prior decisions of the Court on the issues of parental consent and parental notification, stated "It would deny all dignity to the family to say that the State cannot take this reasonable step in regulating its health professions to ensure that, in most cases, a young woman will receive guidance and understanding from a parent" (Id., p. 520).

Hodgson v. Minnesota, 1990.

The Court held unconstitutional the section of Minnesota law requiring physicians or their agent to notify both parents of an unmarried person under the age of 18 years of the intent to perform an abortion and to wait 48 hours before carrying out the procedure, while holding constitutional that section of the law which provided for judicial bypass to two-parent notification where the minor could establish that she was mature and capable of giving informed consent, that she was the victim of parental abuse or neglect, or that it was in her best interests to have an abortion without notice to one or both of her parents and the judge authorized the physician to perform the abortion. In holding the two-parent notification provision unconstitutional, the Court stated:

It is equally clear that the requirement that both parents be notified, whether or not both wish to be notified or have assumed responsibility for the upbringing of the child, does not reasonably further any legitimate state interest. The usual justification for a parental consent or notification provision is that it supports the authority of a parent who is presumed to act in the minor's best interest and thereby assures that the minor's decision to terminate her pregnancy is knowing, intelligent, and deliberate. To the extent that such an interest is legitimate, it would be fully served by a requirement the minor notify one parent who can then seek the counsel of his or her mate or any other party, when such advice and support is deemed necessary to help the child make a difficult decision. . . . Not only does the two-parent notification fail to serve any state interest with respect to functioning families, it disserves the state interest in protecting and assisting the minor with respect to dysfunctional families. (Hodgson v. Minnesota, 1990, p. 450)

Carey v. Population Services, 1977.

A New York statute prohibited the sale and distribution of nonprescription contraceptives to minors under the age of 16 years. In its decision to strike down the statute, the Court stated that "the right to privacy in connection with decisions affecting procreation extends to minors as well as to adults" and that inhibiting minors' privacy rights was valid only to serve "a significant state interest," one that would not be present in the case of an adult. There was substantial doubt, the Court said, that limiting access to contraception would in fact act as a meaningful deterrent to sexual activity among the young, as had been contended (*Carey v. Population Services International,* 1977, pp. 693–694).

The decision did not abate the controversy. Congress subsequently amended Title X of the Public Health Service Act that governed the federal funding of family planning services. The statutory amendment required that such federally funded programs encourage "family participation" in the provision of contraceptive services "to the extent practical." The Reagan administration, through the secretary of Health and Human Services, stated its intent to implement the amendment by requiring federally funded family planning programs to notify the parents of "unemancipated minors" who sought contraceptive services. Criticism and support for the proposed regulations came from many sides. The rules were amended to provide that

> *A project is not required to comply with paragraph (a)(12)(i)(A) [the parental notification provision] of this section where the project director or clinic head (when specifically so designated by the project director) determines that notification will result in physical harm to the minor by a parent or guardian. 42 CFR 59.5 (a)(12)(i)(B).*

Several lawsuits were filed even after this amendment to the rules. The Court of Appeals of the District of Columbia enjoined the implementation of these rules in *Planned Parenthood of America, Inc. v. Heckler,* 719 F.2d 650 (1983). Thus the parental notification provisions never went into effect.

The area of parental authority over the reproductive rights of minors has been and continues to be surrounded in controversial debate. The Supreme Court decisions have established that minors have the right to receive contraceptive services without parental permission; that they have a right to abortions; that their parents or persons acting *in loco parentis* may not have an absolute veto power over their decision to have an abortion; and that they have a right to an independent judicial determination that they are mature enough to make a decision to have an abortion or that an abortion is in their best interests. However, the Court has not precluded states from enacting legislation requiring or permitting notification to a parent of the minor's decision to have an abortion by the medical professional who will perform the abortion.

RIGHTS AND RESPONSIBILITIES OF CHILDREN

Constitutional Rights

An essential question in any formulation of family social policy is the extent to which children have their own rights and interests independent of their parents,

with a claim to their recognition and enforcement. The common law, upon which the American legal system is based, provided limited freedom to children because "they needed to be protected against their own actions, while society, in addition, needs to be protected from their 'untutored' behavior" (Nurcombe & Partlett, 1994). The evolution of children's rights in America is divided into four periods: pre–nineteenth century, 1800 to 1900, 1900 to 1967, and 1967 forward. Prior to the nineteenth century, children were considered their parents' property to do with as they saw fit. In the nineteenth century, with industrialization and urbanization leading to neglect, abandonment, and exploitation of children, benevolent laws and institutions were established to offer protection to children. In the early years of the twentieth century, juvenile courts and the attitude of benevolent oversight of orphaned, abandoned, neglected, abused, and delinquent children predominated. *In re Gault* and *Kent v. United States,* decided by the U.S. Supreme Court in 1966, marked the beginning of the children's legal rights era (Kramer, 1994).

While the U.S. Constitution makes no reference to children per se, U.S. Supreme Court decisions have afforded children the protections enumerated in the First, Fourth, Fifth, Sixth, Eighth, and Fourteenth Amendments (Jacobs, 1995). The reproductive rights cases, presented in the Rights of Parents section, provide a framework for understanding the Court's perspectives on balancing the interests of children's privacy rights and parents' rights to decide matters affecting their children within the constitutional context. In this section, we present those case decisions that focus specifically on children's due process and equal protection rights within the scope of child welfare practice areas, through discussions of Supreme Court decisions.

Brieland and Lemmon (1985) observed that "laws dealing with youths are characterized by paradoxes and inconsistencies" (p. 15). These paradoxes and inconsistencies are explained by the balancing of interests present in all legislation and case decisions involving children's rights: The interests of the family (privacy and autonomy), the child (self-determination, privacy, and autonomy), and the state (*parens patriae*) must be addressed in every case brought before the Court. Each decision rests on how the Court resolves the fundamental interests being attacked.

The juvenile court system's procedures for handling delinquency matters sparked the children's rights under the Constitution era. What had been designed as a benevolent system to handle child abuse, neglect, and delinquency so as to protect children from the trauma of the adult legal system was found to be constitutionally deficient.

Kent v. United States, 1966.   A District of Columbia law provided that a person 16 years of age or older charged with an offense that would be a felony if committed by an adult could be waived to the adult court for trial after a full investigation by the juvenile judge. Kent was charged with robbery, rape, and breaking and entering. He was waived. He challenged the waiver on the grounds that he was not afforded a hearing, no reasons for the waiver were provided to him, and his lawyer was denied access to his records. The Court held that under the due process clause, a juvenile was entitled to a hearing, full access to records and reports used by the court in arriving at its decision, and a statement of the reason for the juvenile court's decision.

In re Gault, 1967.   Gault was a 15-year-old charged with making a lewd telephone call to a neighbor. He was on probation at the time of the call. He was arrested without notification to his parents, detained, not provided counsel, and never afforded a formal hearing. He was found delinquent and committed to the state training school until the age of majority. He challenged the proceedings. The Court, in reversing the decision of the Arizona Supreme Court, established the due process requirements for juvenile delinquency hearings: (1) notice of sufficient detail to mount a defense; (2) right to be represented by counsel and, if necessary, right to court-appointed and -paid counsel if child and parents could not afford counsel; (3) privilege against self-incrimination; and (4) right to review evidence and cross-examine witnesses. Justice Fortas made two statements in this decision that challenged the basic foundation of the

juvenile court system and signaled the scope of constitutional protections for juveniles:

> . . . *neither the Fourteenth Amendment nor the Bill of Rights is for adults alone.* (In re Gault, p. 13)
>
> . . . *juvenile court history has again demonstrated that unbridled discretion, however benevolently motivated, is frequently a poor substitute for principle and procedure.* (Id., p. 18)

In re Winship, 1970.   Winship was a 12-year-old charged with stealing. He was adjudicated delinquent. The Court held that the standard of proof in a delinquency case is "beyond a reasonable doubt," the same standard required in adult criminal proceedings. The Court stated:

> *The constitutional safeguard of proof beyond a reasonable doubt is as much required during the adjudicatory stage of a delinquency proceeding as are those constitutional safeguards applied in Gault.* (Id., p. 363)

McKeiver v. Pennsylvania, 1971.   McKeiver was a 16-year-old charged with robbery, larceny, and receiving stolen property. He was denied a jury trial, adjudicated, and placed on probation. He challenged the denial of a jury trial. The Court held that the fundamental fairness standard in fact-finding procedures for juvenile proceedings as developed by *Gault* and *Winship* did not require a jury trial: "One cannot say that in our legal system the jury is a necessary component of accurate fact-finding" (*McKeiver v. Pennsylvania*, 1971, p. 543). A signal of the willingness of the Court to maintain some of the informalities of the juvenile court system is found in the words of Justice Blackmun:

> *If the formalities of the criminal adjudicative process are to be superimposed upon the juvenile court system there is little need for its separate existence. Perhaps that ultimate disillusionment will come one day, but for the moment we are disinclined to give impetus to it.* (Id., p. 551)

Breed v. Jones, 1975.   Jones was a 17-year-old charged with armed robbery. The juvenile court found that he had committed the crime and then determined that he was not suitable for treatment in the juvenile system. They turned him over for prosecution in the adult system. Jones appealed, claiming that this was a violation of the double jeopardy clause of the Fifth Amendment and the due process and equal protection clauses of the Fourteenth Amendment. The double jeopardy clause provides that a state may not bring a person charged with a criminal offense to trial more than once for the same crime. The issue before the Supreme Court was whether the prosecution of Jones as an adult, after the juvenile court had found he had committed the crime, violated the Fifth and Fourteenth Amendments. The Court held that a transfer to adult court for prosecution after an adjudication of delinquency in the juvenile court violates the Fifth Amendment protection against double jeopardy.

> We conclude that respondent was put in jeopardy at the adjudicatory hearing. Jeopardy attached when respondent was "put to trial before the trier of the facts" . . . that is, when the Juvenile Court, as the trier of the facts, began to hear evidence. (Breed v. Jones, 1975, p. 531)

In addressing the issue of juvenile court waivers—that is, transfer of its jurisdictional authority in a particular case to the adult system—the Court held that the state must determine whether to handle the case in the juvenile or the adult system prior to engaging in any proceedings that might result in an adjudication. In essence, where the state's statute required the juvenile court to determine if a case is to be waived or not, it must utilize a process to make that determination without requiring evidence sufficient for an adjudication.

Fare v. Michael C., 1979. Michael was a 16-year-old charged with murder. He was taken into custody and advised of his rights under *Miranda* (specifically, the right to an attorney and the right to remain silent). He asked to see his probation officer. The request was denied. He provided information about the murder. When he was charged with the murder, he sought to have the information he provided to police suppressed because it had been obtained in violation of his *Miranda* rights in that his request to see his probation officer constituted a request to remain silent. The Court held that a juvenile's request to speak with his

probation officer does not constitute a per se request to remain silent nor is it tantamount to a request for an attorney, since the probation officer "does not fulfill the important role in protecting the rights of the accused juvenile that an attorney plays" (*Fare v. Michael C.*, 1979, pp. 723–724).

Eddings v. Oklahoma, 1982. Eddings was a 16-year-old youth tried as an adult for first-degree murder. He was convicted and sentenced to death. Oklahoma law provided for presentation of evidence of "mitigating circumstances." Eddings offered that he had a history of beatings by his father and of serious emotional disturbance. The judge refused to consider this evidence in mitigation. The Court vacated the death sentence and held that the Eighth and Fourteenth Amendments required individualized consideration of mitigating circumstances in capital cases. It is important to note that the Court did not say that a death penalty could not be imposed, only that the trial judge must consider and weigh all mitigating evidence.

Schall v. Martin, 1984. New York law authorizes pretrial detention of an accused juvenile delinquent upon a finding that there is a serious risk that the youth might commit another offense if not detained pending trial. Martin, a 14-year-old, was arrested for first-degree robbery, second-degree assault, and criminal possession of a weapon. He was detained overnight after lying about where he lived. A hearing was held the following day upon a delinquency petition. He was ordered detained pending trial. Five days later a probable cause hearing was held and probable cause was found to exist for all charges. Within fifteen days of the original detention, Martin was adjudicated delinquent and placed on two years' probation. Martin, as well as other juveniles similarly detained, challenged the New York law as violative of the due process and equal protection clauses of the Fourteenth Amendment. The Court's balancing dilemma is quite evident in this discussion from the opinion:

> There is no doubt that the Due process Clause is applicable in juvenile proceedings. "The problem," we have stressed "is to ascertain the precise impact of the due process requirement upon such proceedings."

*. . . We have held that certain basic constitutional pro-
tections enjoyed by adults accused of crimes also
apply to juveniles. . . . But the Constitution does not
mandate elimination of all differences in the treatment
of juveniles. . . . The State has "a parens patriae interest in preserving and promoting the welfare of the
child," . . . which makes a juvenile proceeding fundamentally different from an adult criminal trial. We
have tried, therefore, to strike a balance—to respect
the "informality" and "flexibility" that characterize
juvenile proceedings . . . and yet ensure that such proceedings comport with the "fundamental fairness" demanded by the due process clause.*

*. . . The question before us is whether preventive de-
tention of juveniles pursuant to §320.5(3)(b) is compatible with the "fundamental fairness" required by
due process. (Schall v. Martin, 1984, p. 263)*

The Court held that the referenced statute was
not invalid under the due process clause of the Fourteenth Amendment "given the regulatory purpose for
the detention and the procedural protections that precede its imposition" (Id., p. 281).

Thompson v. Oklahoma, 1988.

Oklahoma law pro-
vided that juveniles charged with serious offenses
could be tried and sentenced as adults. Thompson was
a 15-year-old charged with murder. He was tried as
an adult, convicted, and sentenced to death. The question addressed by the Court was whether the "execution of that sentence would violate the constitutional
prohibition against the infliction of 'cruel and unusual
punishments' because petitioner was only 15 years
old at the time of his offense" (Thompson v. Oklahoma, 1988, pp. 818–819). The Court, in holding that
it would violate the Constitution, stated:

*The authors of the Eighth Amendment drafted a cate-
gorical prohibition against the infliction of cruel and
unusual punishments, but they made no attempt to define the contours of that category. They delegated that
task to future generations of judges who have been
guided by the "evolving standards of decency that
mark the progress of a maturing society." . . . In performing that task the Court has reviewed the work
product of state legislatures and sentencing juries, and
has carefully considered the reasons why a civilized
society may accept or reject the death penalty in certain types of cases. Thus, in confronting the question*

*whether the youth of the defendant—more specifically,
the fact that he was less than 16 years old at the time
of his offense—is sufficient reason for denying the
State the power to sentence him to death, we first review relevant legislative enactments, then refer to jury
determinations, and finally explain why these indicators of contemporary standards of decency confirm
our judgment that such a young person is not capable
of acting with the degree of culpability that can justify
the ultimate penalty. (Id., pp. 821–823)*

Stanford v. Kentucky, 1989 and Wilkins v. Missouri, 1989.

Stanford was 17 years and 4 months old when
he committed a murder in Kentucky. The juvenile court
transferred him for trial as an adult under Kentucky
law. He was convicted and sentenced to death. Wilkins
was 16 years and 6 months old when he committed
murder in Missouri. He was also tried as an adult, convicted, and sentenced to death. The issue before the
Court in both cases was whether the imposition of the
death sentence for a 16- or 17-year-old constituted
cruel and unusual punishment under the Eighth
Amendment. The Court held that it did not. It distinguished this decision from that in *Thompson* by finding
that, in reviewing state legislative actions and jury decisions as objective indicia of the evolving standards
of what constitutes cruel and unusual punishment,

*we discern neither a historical nor a modern societal
consensus forbidding the imposition of capital punishment on any person who murders at 16 or 17 years
of age. Accordingly, we conclude that such punishment
does not offend the Eighth Amendment's prohibition
against cruel and unusual punishment. (Id., p. 380)*

In summary, then, for juveniles charged with
delinquent/criminal offenses, the Court has clearly established that they must be afforded due process
rights equal to those afforded adults, and that the
states can, provided the fundamental fairness tests are
met, maintain some flexibility and informality in its
juvenile court processes to ensure the benevolent
treatment of juveniles. We discuss these decisions in
more detail in Chapter 11.

Most states extended by legislation or court rules
the principles of fundamental fairness developed by
the line of delinquency case decisions to child abuse
and neglect matters (*Saltzman & Proch*, 1990).

State Interventions to Protect Children's Independent Rights

The states, acknowledging that children's rights and interests might be different from those of parents, have provided for appointment of a guardian *ad litem* or emancipation process.

Guardian *ad litem*.   Recognizing the particular vulnerabilities of children and the potential for conflicting interests between the child's interests and the parent's interests, all states provide for appointment of a guardian *ad litem* to serve in a particular litigation to which a minor is a party for the purpose of representing and protecting that child's interests. See Chapter 6 for specific situations where assignment of a guardian *ad litem* is appropriate.

A 1992 Florida circuit court ruling, which attracted nationwide interest, concerned the rights of children to bring legal actions without the assistance of a guardian *ad litem,* or "next friend." While the news media promoted the story as "child divorces his own parents," this was a termination of parental rights under Florida's law for such actions. It was the first widely reported case in the United States in which parental rights were ended as the result of a legal action brought by a child rather than by a state agency or an adult. The circumstances were these: Gregory K. had lived in foster homes most of his life. In the last eight years he had lived with his birth mother for only seven months. At the time of the trial, Gregory was living with foster parents who hoped to adopt him, as Gregory also wished to happen. In asking the court to end the parental rights of his biological mother, Gregory took the stand and, in more than an hour of questioning, described how she had long neglected, abused, and abandoned him. He asked the juvenile court to allow him to be adopted by his current foster parents, who had cared for him for the last year.

Gregory's birth father was ready to relinquish his parental rights if the foster parents were allowed to adopt Gregory. His mother had a long history of serious behavioral problems that made it highly improbable she could provide the care Gregory needed. Her claim for Gregory was based on the rights of natural families over any other interest. When the foster parents had made known their desire to adopt, the state was planning to return Gregory to his mother, a factor that led Gregory's foster father to talk with him about the possibility of Gregory himself taking legal action that would free him to choose adoption by his foster parents. As Gregory's situation became clearer, the state changed its position and favored Gregory's adoption by his foster parents. The judge terminated the mother's parental rights and allowed Gregory's foster parents to adopt him.

It is generally agreed that Gregory K.'s case established a significant legal precedent: that a child has the same constitutional rights as adults to due process, equal protection, privacy, access to the courts, and the right to life, liberty, and the pursuit of happiness. In 1993, a Florida appellate court held that Gregory did not have the capacity to bring the action independently (Russ, 1993, p. 366). The Florida Supreme Court declined to review the appellate decision. The present state of the law was that children, through guardians *ad litem* or next friend, had long had the right to bring legal actions, including action to terminate parental rights. Thus, a child, whose child welfare agent is not pursuing or who refuses to file a petition for termination of parental rights, must request that an adult do so for him or her.

Emancipation.   Partial or complete "emancipation" is a means by which in some instances a young person can be legally released from parental custody and control and thereafter be considered an adult for most purposes. Although state statutes vary, criteria used frequently to justify an action of emancipation are that the youth is living separately from parents, is self-supporting, has joined the military, or is married. Emancipation empowers a minor to transact business such as buying or selling property, suing or being sued, enlisting in the military, and consenting to medical, psychological, or social work services (Horowitz & Davidson, 1984, p. 152).

The doctrine of emancipation is not new; it existed in common law times. Traditionally, however, the courts declared a minor emancipated only in particular cases involving individual circumstances distinct from those that might be more generally found among youth. To the extent that emancipation cases commonly involved minors in the 18 to 21 age group, the overall significance of the emancipation doctrine was diminished by the adoption of 18 rather than 21, as the age of majority. In more recent years, legislation in some states has allowed persons under 18 years of age to petition the court for a determination of emancipation. A typical example appears in the California Civil Code, which permits "a child fourteen or older to petition the court for emancipation on a showing that the child lives separately and apart from the parents with the parents' consent and is self-supporting. . . . The petition is granted if the court finds the information contained in it to be true and that emancipation would not be adverse to the child's best interest" (Davis & Schwartz, 1987, p. 40).

RIGHTS AND RESPONSIBILITIES OF GOVERNMENT

Recognition of the government's role in intervening in the autonomy of the family was slow to develop. This role is being further defined and limited by the decisional law (that is, the Court decisions discussed above) involving the balancing of interests cases. Many of the Court cases served to clarify the permissible scope of governmental intrusion and the procedures requisite to ensuring that those intrusions did not violate the rights of parent or child or both. While the cases have been discussed in the context of parent or child rights, it is important to note that the cases were before the Court because of a challenge that a specific state law or procedure violated a protection granted under the U.S. Constitution. In other words, the state, via its laws, was attempting to balance the rights of child, parent, and state. The aggrieved party challenged the state's conclusion as to what the balance should be and asked the Supreme Court, the final voice on the constitutionality of a specific law, to review the state's conclusion. Thus each case discussed above is in fact an exploration of the permissible scope of governmental action under its police powers and *parens patriae* authority (Myers, 1992, p. 26).

Federal and State Government Interests

The government's interest in protecting children from harm and protecting society from the delinquent acts of children is rooted in the principle of *parens patriae,* which translated literally, means "father of the country." Under this principle, the state is required to ensure that children (and other persons under disability) receive proper care from their parents or guardians and, if a child is deprived of appropriate parental care, control, and oversight, to exercise its police powers and assume parental authority over the child (Nurcombe, Partlett, 1994; *Chapsky v. Wood,* 1902; *Prince v. Massachusetts,* 1944). In *New York v. Ferber,* 1982 the Court stated that the state's interest in protecting children from abuse and neglect is "an objective of surpassing importance" (Id., p. 757).

This authority is the basis for all governmental legislation regulating the parent-child relationship, the scope of the child's independent rights and responsibilities, and the relationship of society to the child. For example, the government, through state and federal laws, plays significant roles in altering the parenting relationships:

- if the parents are unwed, state laws are invoked to establish paternity;
- if the parents separate or divorce, state child custody laws are invoked to determine custody, parenting time (visitation), and support;
- if the parents are temporarily unable to care for the child, state guardianship laws are invoked to provide for voluntary transfer of guardianship or state child abuse and neglect or juvenile delinquency laws are invoked to provide for court wardship due to dependency, abuse, neglect, or delinquency (involuntary action);
- if parents are found to be unable or unwilling to remedy the situation which necessitated involuntary action, then state termination of parental rights of child emancipation laws are invoked to permanently terminate their rights and responsibilities (emancipation or termination of parental rights); and
- if new parents are found, state adoption laws are invoked to legally establish a new parenting re-

lationship with all the rights, privileges, and duties afforded biological parents.

The specifics of the legislation impacting these areas of family life are discussed in more detail in subsequent chapters.

In addition, state and federal legislation regulates the rights of minors in many areas: child labor (hours and types of jobs a child can work), mandatory education (ages for school attendance, discipline in public schools, search and seizure guidelines), medical treatment consent (age at which a child can give consent or types/duration of treatments to which a child can consent without parental notification), sexual exploitation/child pornography, marriage (minimum age, permissions required, prerequisites to receiving license), freedom of movement (curfews, access to shopping centers), and alcohol and drug use (age for sale and purchase).

What are the state's responsibilities once it has undertaken to provide a service or offer a protection? In *DeShaney,* the case discussed at the beginning of this chapter, the Court, while holding that there was no constitutional right to protection from the abusive acts of the parent (a private party), did state that there may be basis for action under the state statute governing child abuse and neglect. Thus the question to be asked is not, "Were Joshua's constitutional rights violated when the state failed to protect him from continuing abusive acts by his father?" but "Did the State fail to follow its own laws, regulations, policies, and procedures, and, if so, did this failure lead to Joshua's harm?" This is the fundamental question for any examination of the broader question, "Once the state has undertaken a responsibility, what is its liability when it fails to carry out that responsibility in the manner proscribed by it?"

In *Suter v. Artist M.* (1992), the Court held that private parties could not bring a case to enforce the "reasonable efforts" provisions of the Adoption Assistance and Child Welfare Act of 1980. This decision is discussed in detail in Chapter 9. It is interesting to note that the Court let stand the lower court opinion. That opinion permitted private parties to seek and receive enforcement of the procedural requirements (completion and periodic review of case plans) of the Act while stating that there was no right to force agencies to provide specific services as part of the case plans (*Suter v. Artist M.,* 1992).

Native Americans. The government has a special relationship with Native Americans because of the sovereignty granted to tribes through many treaties and agreements. The specific protections depend on the legal issues involved and the unique legal relationships created by treaties, agreements, and special legislation (Getches, Rosenfelt & Wilkinson, 1979). The Indian Child Welfare Act of 1978 (ICWA) frames child welfare practice for an "Indian child." "Indian child" is defined as "any unmarried person who is under age eighteen and is either (a) a member of an Indian tribe or (b) is eligible for membership in an Indian tribe and is the biological child of a member of an Indian tribe" (25 USC 1606). ICWA provides that the tribe has first right to address—that is, exclusive jurisdiction—child welfare issues for children meeting the definition and provides specific procedures to ensure compliance by the states with U.S. policy as stated in the Act "to protect the best interests of Indian children and to promote the stability and security of Indian tribes and families." Specifics of the Act are discussed in subsequent chapters.

The Supreme Court has decided one case involving ICWA. In *Mississippi Band of Choctaw Indians v. Holyfield,* the Court held that ICWA clearly intended that the tribes would have exclusive jurisdiction over custody proceedings involving an Indian child who resides or is domiciled within a tribe's reservation. Two babies were born 200 miles from the reservation to parents who were enrolled members of the Mississippi Band of Choctaw Indians. The parents voluntarily released the children for adoption. The tribe challenged the jurisdiction of the state courts. The Court found that the mother was domiciled on the reservation; the children's domicile is determined by that of the parents or, in this case, by the mother since the children were born of unwed parents. The intent of ICWA was to preserve the integrity of the tribes by reducing the number of unnecessary removals of Indian children; thus "Congress could not have intended to enact a rule of domicile that would permit individual reservation-domiciled tribal members to defeat the tribe's exclusive jurisdiction by the simple expedient of giving birth and placing the child for adoption off the reservation" (Id., p. 35).

TRENDS AND ISSUES

States' Responsibility to Children with Whom It Has Entered into a Special Relationship

The *DeShaney* decision raised the issue of what state actions constitute violations of the constitutional rights of children whom it has undertaken to protect. While that decision addressed the state's protective role for children remaining in their own homes and found no constitutional rights were violated, there is growing interest in defining the scope of the state's responsibility for protecting children placed in out-of-home care under the supervision of the state. The Supreme Court has yet to hear a case on this issue. However, several U.S. Court of Appeals decisions have been issued. These essentially find the state has entered into a special relationship with these children and therefore there are constitutional rights issues and responsibility for abuse or neglect of children by foster parents, residential facility staff, and others with whom it has placed children (*Walker v. Ledbetter,* 1987; *Doe v. New York City Department of Social Services,* 1982). Each such infraction requires a careful examination of the individual state's law—including agency policies and procedures—to determine the actual lapse in care required before liability ensues.

While *Suter* appears to have foreclosed states' responsibility to provide comprehensive services to meet the "reasonable efforts" requirements, advocates are attempting to utilize the procedural requirements to challenge states' inadequacies in service provisions. Thus as time passes, we may see greater legal responsibility imposed on the state once it has entered into special relationships with children, neither to do further harm nor to permit those under its authority to perform their duties inadequately.

Children with Emotional Disabilities

A problem that continues to exist in many states concerns children with serious emotional disabilities that require costly and intensive special treatment at residential centers. In many instances, states refuse to provide for the expensive treatment of these children unless the parents agree to relinquish legal custody, a practice that reportedly exists in 60 percent of states responding to a 1990 survey (Cohen et al., 1991, p. 527).

These children's parents are not necessarily characteristic of those who come to the attention of child protective agencies following reports of child neglect and abuse. "They may be birth parents or adoptive parents—unquestionably involved in providing the best for [their children] but who most often seek a foster home or a special treatment facility when they reach the limits of their physical endurance and financial resources. They are no less a family because of the special needs of their children and wish to maintain their legal responsibility as well as the embrace of their love and concern" (Stubbee, 1990, p. 1).

The parents face a choice—"either surrender their children into the custody of the state and thereby receive necessary services, or retain custody and concomitantly deny their children the services they require." If they accept the first option, "they lose both the right and the responsibility to make important decisions on behalf of their children. . . . They may be denied access to medical records, information on planned educational activities, and the opportunity to participate in treatment planning. Their children may be moved from one location to another and parents may not even be notified of the change. The possibility of family reunification may be seriously compromised" (McManus & Friesen, 1989, p. 5).

Prominent among the reasons why many states require parents to give up custody of their child in order to receive financial help for the needed intensive services is a mistaken interpretation of Title IV-E of the Social Security Act (the Federal Adoption Assistance and Foster Care Act of 1980, PL 96–272), even though the law makes specific reference to the acceptability of a voluntary placement agreement (Cohen et al., 1991, p. 526; McManus & Friesen, 1989, p. 1). Some states resist voluntary placement agreements on the grounds that time-limited voluntary placement agreements are inconvenient and potentially disruptive to treatment. Residential staff frequently prefer that agencies have custody to protect against parents' early removal of the child from the program. These points of view are clearly not consistent with goals of involving parents in decision making and treatment planning while retaining legal custody of their children as long as the out-of-home services are needed.

The issue of inadequate mental health treatment services for children (and their parents) already in out-of-home care due to neglect, abuse, or delinquency also continues to pose great challenges for most states as they debate whether their child welfare, juvenile justice, or mental health service agencies are primarily responsible for providing the necessary services. Meanwhile, the children remain inappropriately serviced and, some might say, suffer greater harm at the hands of the systems which ostensibly are designed to protect them from harm.

Custody in Same-Sex Relationships

The awarding of custody where one parent is engaged in a same-sex relationship or the approval for foster care or adoption by gay and lesbian persons engaged in same-sex relationships continues to be hotly debated. Judicial prejudice against homosexual parents in child custody cases remains despite the fact that the child's best interests standard is the overriding one for all states. Most of the contested cases have involved actions by fathers to obtain custody from their former spouses who are now living in lesbian relationships. The contemporary trend is to "assess, case by case, whether parental eccentricities preclude adequate child care" (Nurcombe & Partlett, 1994, p. 108); but even so, the courts do not seem to stray far from considerations of "the stigma"; "the influence on the child's own sexuality"; "the effect on the child's morals"; and "the homosexual parent as criminal for violating state sodomy laws" analyses (Seidel, 1994).

Foster care and adoption agencies appear to favor a "don't ask, don't tell" approach. When confronted openly with the issue, they are hesitant to place foster children in these homes but less hesitant to complete adoption placements. Some suggest the former is out of fear of potential suits from birth parents or the children placed with these parents (Jacobs, 1995).

CHAPTER SUMMARY

This chapter focused on the current state of U.S. Supreme Court decisional law with respect to balancing the interests of child, parent, and state within the context of the U.S. Constitution. The Court's decisions result from challenges to state actions (legislation or administrative rules), which the aggrieved parties contend go beyond legitimate state interest in regulating the conduct of its citizens and/or substantially impede a constitutional guarantee without compelling state interest. The Court's decisions appear somewhat contradictory at first glance; however, with careful analysis, they become less so.

The current balance says that the state has the right and responsibility to regulate the behavior of parents regarding their children where that parental behavior causes harm or potential harm, interferes with the privacy rights of mature minors as related to medical treatments including abortion, and to promote the general welfare of its citizens. While great deference in the responsibility of raising children remains with the parents and while children have not been granted the full, absolute protections of the Constitution granted to adults, the Court clearly acknowledges that children are citizens entitled to the protections of the Constitution in their own right, but those protections need to be tempered on the basis of developmental capacities and childhood status within the family context.

FOR STUDY AND DISCUSSION

1. Reconcile the Supreme Court's decisions on duties, rights, and limitations on parents' rights of care, custody, and control of their children.

2. Read in its entirety one of the U.S. Supreme Court decisions discussed in the text. Then, with other students, analyze the line of reasoning used by the majority and minority justices. How does such reasoning square with your own conception of a just balance in parent, child, and society rights and responsibilities?

3. Why is it important that the juvenile court system provides due process in delinquency and child abuse and neglect matters?

4. Should age be a factor in determining whether or not the death penalty is cruel and unusual punishment? Why or why not?

5. What are the requirements in your state for parents to obtain needed treatment for their emotionally impaired children? Are there circumstances under which they need to relinquish custody solely for the purpose of getting access to treatment?

FOR ADDITIONAL STUDY

Friedman, S. E. (1992). *The law of parent-child relationships: A handbook*. Chicago: American Bar Association.

Humm, S. R., Ort, B. A., Anbari, M. M., Lader, W. S., & Biel, W. S. (Eds.) (1994). *Child, parent and state law and policy reader*. Philadelphia: Temple University Press.

Ziegler, E. F., Kagan, & Hall, N. W. (Eds.) (1996). *Children, families and government: preparing for the twenty-first century*. Cambridge: Cambridge University Press.

INTERNET SITES

The following sites provide a range of information and access to statutes, case decisions, and agency regulations.

United States Supreme Court—http://www.uscourts.gov

United States Congress—http://thomas.loc.gov

U.S. Department of Health and Human Services—http://www.os.dhhs.gov

National Center on Child Abuse and Neglect Clearinghouse—http://www.calib.com/nccanch

Office of Juvenile Justice and Delinquency Prevention—http://www.ncjrs.org/ojjhome.html

The Juvenile Justice Clearinghouse—http://www.fsu.edu/~crimdo/jjclearinghouse/jjclearinghouse.html

REFERENCES

Cases

Baltimore City Department of Social Services v. Bouknight, 493 U.S. (1990)

Bellotti v. Baird, 428 U.S. 132 (1979)

Breed v. Jones, 421 U.S. 519 (1975)

Caban v. Mohammed, 441 U.S. 380 (1979)

Carey v. Population Services International, 431 U.S. 678 (1977)

DeShaney v. Winnebago County Department of Social Services, 489 U.S. 189 (1989)

Doe v. New York City Department of Social Services, 670 F.Supp. 1145 (S.D.N.Y. 1987)

Eddings v. Oklahoma, 455 U.S. 104 (1982)

Fare v. Michael C., 442 U.S. 707 (1979)

H. L. v. Matheson, 450 U.S. 398 (1981)

Hodgson V. Minnesota, 497 U.S. 417 (1990)

In re Gault, 387 U.S. 1 (1967)

In re Winship, 397 U.S. 358 (1970)

Kent v. United States, 383 U.S. 541 (1966)

Lawton v. Steele, 1893

May v. Anderson, 345 U.S. 528 (1953)

McKeiver v. Pennsylvania, 403 U.S. 528 (1971)

Meyer v. Nebraska, 262 U.S. 390 (1923)

Mississippi Band of Choctaw Indians v. Holyfield, 490 U.S. 30 (1989)

New York v. Ferber, 458 U.S. 747 (1982)

Ohio v. Akron Center for Reproductive Health, 497 U.S. 502 (1990)

Palmore v. Sidoti, 466 U.S. 429 (1984)

Parham v. J. R., 442 U.S. 584 (1979)

Pierce v. Society of Sisters, 268 U.S. 510 (1925)

Planned Parenthood of America, Inc. v. Heckler, 719 F.2d 650 (1983)

Planned Parenthood of Central Missouri v. Danforth, 428 U.S. 52 (1976)

Prince v. Massachusetts, 321 U.S. 158 (1944)

Quilloin v. Walcott, 434 U.S. 246 (1978)

Roe v. Wade, 410 U.S. 160 (1973)

Santosky v. Kramer, 455 U.S. 745 (1982)

Schall v. Martin, 467 U.S. 253 (1984)

Stanford v. Kentucky, 492 U.S. 361 (1989)

Stanley v. Illinois, 405 U.S. 645 (1972)

Suter v. Artist M., 1992

Thompson v. Oklahoma, 487 U.S. 815 (1988)

Tinker v. Des Moines Independent Community School District, 393 U.S. 503 (1969)

Walker v. Ledbetter, 818 F.2d 791 (11th C.R. 1987)

Wilkins v. Missouri, 492 U.S. 361 (1989)

Wisconsin v. Yoder, 406 U.S. 205 (1972)

Constitution and Statutes

U.S. Constitution

Child Abuse Prevention and Treatment Act, 42 U.S.C. § 5101 (1974)

Indian Child Welfare Act, 25 U.S.C. § 1901 (1978)

The Federal Adoption Assistance and Foster Care Act of 1980, PL 96-272

Books, Chapters and Articles

Brieland, D., & Lemmon, J. A. (1985). *Social work and the law* (4th ed.). St. Paul: West Publishing.

Cohen, R., Preiser, L., Gottlieb, S., Harris, R., Baker, J., & Sonenklar, N. (1990). *Relinquishing custody as a requisite for receiving services for children with serious emotional disorders: A review.* Richmond: Commonwealth Institute for Child and Family Studies, Virginia Treatment Center for Children.

Davis, S. M., & Schwartz, M. D. (1987). *Children's rights and the law.* Lexington, MA: Lexington Books/D.C. Heath.

Getches, D. H., Rosenfelt, D. M., Wilkinson, C. F. (1979). *Cases and materials on federal Indian law.* St. Paul: West Publishing.

Gitlin, H. J. (1987, November 3). The rights of fathers of illegitimate children. *Chicago Daily Bulletin,* pp. 2, 20.

Horowitz, R. M., & Davidson, H. A. (Eds.). (1984). *Legal rights of children.* Colorado Springs: Shepard's/McGraw-Hill.

Jacobs, T. A. (1995, supp. 1997). *Children and the law: Rights and obligations.* St. Paul: West Publishing.

Kramer, D. T. (1994). *Legal rights of children* (2nd ed.). Colorado Springs: Shepard's/McGraw-Hill.

McManus, M. C., & Friesen, B. C. (1989). Barriers to accessing services: Relinquishing legal custody as a means of obtaining services for children with serious emotional disabilities. *Focal Point, 3*(3), 1–5.

Myers, J. E. B. (1992). *Legal issues in child abuse and neglect.* Newbury Park, CA: Sage Publications.

Nurcombe, B., & Partlett, D. F. (1994). *Child mental health and the law.* New York: The Free Press.

Pratt, D. V. (1993). *Legal writing: A systemic approach,* 2nd ed. St. Paul: West Publishing.

Russ, G. H. (Fall 1993). Through the eyes of a child, "Gregory K.": A child's right to be heard. *Family Law Quarterly, 27*(3).

Saltzman, A., & Proch, K. (1990). *Law in social work practice.* Chicago: Nelson-Hall.

Seidel, A. I. (1994). Custody denials to parents in same-sex relationships: an equal protection analysis. In S. R. Humm, B. A. Ort, M. M. Anbari, W. S. Lader, & W. S. Biel, eds., *Child, parent & state law and policy reader* (pp. 51–67). Philadelphia: Temple University Press.

Stubbee, B. (1990). Relinquishing custody: Continuing the dialogue. *Focal Point 4*(2), 1–2.

CHAPTER 3

Family Support

The little world of childhood with its familiar surroundings is a model of the greater world. The more intensively the family has stamped its character upon the child, the more it will tend to feel and see its earlier miniature world again in the bigger world of adult life.
—Carl Gustav Jung

Mitakuye oyasin. (We are all related.)
—Oglala Lakota Sioux

CHAPTER OUTLINE

CASE EXAMPLE: REACHING OUT TO A FAMILY AT RISK FOR CHILD MALTREATMENT

This case shows a family support worker in Hawaii's Healthy Start program reaching out to an overburdened mother just home from the hospital with a new baby.

Jane is a poor Hawaiian woman in her early thirties who lives in a community where the disparities between rich and poor are extreme. When the Healthy Start program first came into contact with Jane, she had just given birth to twins, leaving Jane with four children under the age of three. Since Jane had no phone, Healthy Start home visitor Evelyn went to Jane's home to meet Jane, an introduction that took three months to complete.

Each week for twelve weeks, Evelyn stood outside Jane's door hoping to speak to her. While Evelyn waited patiently, a typical scene would ensue: Jane and her partner could be heard shouting and yelling, the older children sobbing, and the twin babies screaming, looking for attention amid the confusion. When the older children stared out the window at Evelyn, the fighting seemed to escalate. Evelyn worried about what to do, but stuck with a gut feeling that if she persisted with the family she could make contact.

When Jane finally did let Evelyn in, Evelyn learned something that surprised her about her earlier visits. Jane told her that although she was afraid to let this strange woman into her commotion-filled home, she also felt soothed by her presence.

This was the start of trust-building between Evelyn and Jane, which was necessary to begin work on Jane's many needs. Jane's family had no family doctor and no concept of preventive medicine. Evelyn soon discovered that Jane had used the drug "ice" (methamphetamine) while pregnant with her first two children and that extended family members sold the drug on the streets. Two months after giving birth to the twins, Jane was pregnant with a fifth child. In another ten months, she would become pregnant again.

Over a period of months, Evelyn and Jane set some initial goals for their work together: finding an acceptable means of birth control, developing an understanding and commitment to well-care (i.e., preventive health care) for her children, finding programs to help her become drug-free, and establishing a stable home.

In three years of work and weekly visits with Jane, Evelyn feels that the family has made important headway. The older children have been enrolled in kindergarten and Head Start respectively; the twins have started in a special program for children with developmental delays; and the newest baby has received consistent medical care since birth and shows no signs of delay. Most importantly, Jane's approach to her children's health and development has changed. No longer are emergencies the only time her children come into contact with a doctor. All six of her children receive regular health check-ups from a local physician. Jane actively seeks out programs and activities for them as well. Instead of sending her children to school alone, Jane now walks them there and even volunteers at her son's Head Start program.

Jane's attitude toward Evelyn has transformed as well. Jane calls Evelyn every other day from a pay phone and talks openly about her daily problems. Although Jane's situation isn't altogether rosy—she has recently lost her housing and lives in a hut on the beach—Jane and Evelyn continue to work at the problem one step at a time. Jane thinks differently now about what she can do to help her children get off to the right start. (Adapted from Charles Bruner and Judy Langford Carter, *Family Support and Education: A Holistic Approach to School Readiness,* Denver and Washington, DC: National Conference of State Legislatures, 1991. Reprinted with the permission of National Conference of State Legislators.)

Twenty years ago this family might have been sent home from the hospital with no follow-up services, until, as seems likely, the parents' care of the children deteriorated to the point that someone made a referral to child protective services. The children probably would have been placed in foster care. The family support services described in this chapter are an effort to intervene early in the lives of families, before the home situation becomes untenable, so that children can safely remain with their parents.

A description of the Hawaiian Healthy Start Program is located in this chapter, in the Programs to Enhance Parenting Skills and Family Functioning section.

NEW INTEREST IN SERVICES TO FAMILIES

For most of the twentieth century, professionals in the human services have recognized the importance of a child's own home. Yet efforts to conceptualize and develop social services to preserve, strengthen, and enhance family life and the quality of the child's environment have lagged. Society's reliance on the family for essential nurturance and guidance of the nation's children has not been accompanied by necessary changes in social and economic policies and preventive social provisions. As a result, social agencies tend to be overwhelmed with demands from families and children in crisis.

If you care about children, then care about families. (Emlen, 1978, p. 1)

In recent decades much of the general public has voiced alarm about what it perceives as increasing breakdown of the family system. Professionals have responded with keener awareness of the important meaning to the child of his or her own home and the need for more and better support services to families. Their efforts were first visible in the movement within the foster care system to get children out of foster care and into permanent homes, and later in the numerous social service projects, known as family preservation services, that are aimed at providing timely services to families before breakdown occurs (see Chapter 8). During the past two decades interest has increased in services to help maintain and strengthen families who were not at imminent risk of foster care placement but who needed outside support to improve their ability to raise children and to cope with the stresses of employment and other difficulties. These services are the subject of this chapter.

Concern about the absence of fathers from the lives of their children has reached national levels of attention. A consensus is emerging that a key to strengthening families is increased involvement of fathers. This consensus includes the entire political spectrum, from liberal to conservative, as well as leaders in science, religion, and civil rights. In the political arena, Vice President Al Gore has called for a "nationwide father-to-father movement" to bring together young, struggling fathers with older adult mentors. The prestigious National Academy of Sciences has spearheaded research on fatherhood and public policy. Promise Keepers, a fundamentalist religious group, has called on men to renew their commitment to their families. The Million Man March, a gathering of African-American men brought together in Washington, D.C. to renew their commitment to family and community, brought widespread national attention to the role of fathers. These events are challenging social workers to reevaluate their own practices to develop more father-inclusive models for serving families and children.

The gradual trend toward the need for more support services to families reflects such factors as these:

1. Serious social problems arising from an urban culture in which many families, even normal, self-supporting ones, cannot cope unaided with the demands and strains of daily life.
2. Modified patterns of family life seen in changing lifestyles and norms governing male-female relationships, teenage parenting, divorce, and expectations that children will be accorded rights that were formerly denied them.
3. New awareness of violence in marriage, particularly among couples with inadequate means, heavy stresses, and dependent children.
4. Difficulties experienced in attempting to return children successfully from foster care to their own families, or in finding other homes for them, and an awareness that some children in foster care could have remained at home if their parents had had access to supportive services.
5. Changes in other fields of practice that have influenced the nature of family situations and child welfare concerns. For example, community mental health care makes long absences of mentally ill parents from home less likely than in the past. However, their behavior and the treatment process may still generate considerable stress for family members, which social services could help to alleviate.
6. Legislated amendments to the Social Security Act that have emphasized social services to low-income families and legally defined "support services" and other family-based legislation such as the Indian Child Welfare Act, the Adoption Assistance and Child Welfare Act, and the Family Preservation and Support Services Act.

PROBLEMS TOWARD WHICH SERVICES ARE DIRECTED

Many parents cannot provide an environment conducive to the positive functioning of their children. The kinds of problems they face are numerous and may vary widely in their characteristics, duration, and degree of gravity. Their causes and symptoms are interrelated and frequently overlapping.

Naturally Occurring Stress in Family Life

Many "normal" events in the course of family life can become problems that create tensions and demand an extraordinary output of physical or emotional energy on the part of one or more family members. Whether these events produce growth or generate more serious problems depends not only on the capacities of family members but also on the extent of available outside resources and opportunities.

Hazardous life events that may produce such stress include the following:

1. Separation, divorce, and the forming of stepfamilies all require that family members adjust to loss and changed personal and economic circumstances, and develop new ways of relating within the family.
2. Early childbirth, especially combined with insufficient education of the parents, frequently results in a lowered standard of living, overwhelming pressure to postpone personal gratification, and risks to the infants.
3. A long season of contagious and confining illness among young children in a family without

outside help may burden a mother excessively and create or intensify marital tensions.

4. The death of a child, learning of an unwanted pregnancy, the birth of a handicapped child, or the death of a parent's own mother or father usually requires a particular and demanding adjustment.

5. Specific events, such as the youngest child entering school, the oldest child leaving home, a mother entering the labor market, or the addition of a grandparent or other relative into the household, may thrust the family into a changed pattern of living.

Continuing Constraints on Parental Capabilities

Many children are denied constructive experiences and opportunities because of inadequate parental care.

1. For many parents, the overriding problem is *poverty* and all its accompaniments (see Chapter 4): poor health; low educational levels; unemployment or underemployment; substandard housing; discrimination; lack of playgrounds, libraries, and other public facilities; loneliness; alienation from the mainstream of society; and individual depression and lack of hope.

2. Families with *only one parent* may be handicapped in providing a suitable child-rearing environment and normal family relationships. The parent may be overwhelmed with total responsibility for home management and rearing of children. There may be lack of adequate adult models of both sexes, insufficient financial and emotional support, difficulties in visiting arrangements by the absent parent, or trauma to other members if the parent's absence is due to death.

3. *Mental deficiency, mental or physical illness of parents, or drug or alcohol dependency* may sharply limit their capacity to care for their children. For example, parents suffering from depression may provide an insufficient level of care and developmental opportunities to children.

4. In some families the problems are exemplified by *interpersonal conflicts between family members.* Marital conflict may threaten family unity or endanger a child's emotional balance. In other instances, there is conflict or a lack of satisfying relationships between a parent and a particular child, or among siblings.

5. *Parents with serious behavior problems* may cause deleterious conditions within a family and impair a child's chance to develop normally. At all socioeconomic levels a parent may steal or lie, have destructive attitudes that affect success in employment, be addicted to drugs or alcohol, or be sexually exploitive or aggressively hostile. In recent years a long-standing pattern has been documented—violence in marriage—that has proved difficult to interrupt and modify. Some parents are struggling with unresolved issues from their own childhoods, such as sexual abuse, which impede their functioning as parents.

6. Many persons have been poorly prepared for parental responsibilities and show *family management problems*—for example, inability to handle income efficiently, to obtain and keep appropriate housing, to organize and execute housekeeping tasks, to get children to school regularly and on time, or to protect them from health hazards. Parents frequently have not learned successful methods of child rearing, and their ignorance is reflected in damaging methods of discipline or supervision. They may be unprepared for the responsibility of planning and controlling family size, and may have difficulty in seeking or using contraceptive methods. Inadequate preparation for parenthood, resulting in dissatisfactions in the parental role, may stem from psychological problems of adjustment to the requirements, rewards, and penalties of parenthood.

Behaviors Centered in Children

Physical and mental conditions and behavior in children often constitute a problem toward which services are directed:

1. Some children have *special needs* as a result of mental handicaps, physically disabling conditions, severe emotional disturbances, or chronic illness. They often experience parental rejection, feelings of inferiority, isolation from other children, lack

of normal play, or separation from parents in order to receive treatment or education. A lack of appropriate treatment resources and social services compounds their problems and generates new ones for them, their parents, and the community.

2. Some children who are without easily observable or serious physical or mental impairment nevertheless show symptoms of *disturbed functioning or development.* These symptoms may reflect trouble in parent-child relationships or in other aspects of home or community life. In turn, the disturbed behavior and other troublesome symptoms may produce new inabilities to function successfully on the part of both the children and their parents. These symptoms and exacerbated behaviors may take the form of temper tantrums, moodiness, jealousy, or simply a general aura of unhappiness. Some children have no friends or interest in school; they often do not acquire the basic competencies needed in today's world. Young people who have come to feel alienated from their families, schools, or communities may resist supervision, get into trouble with the authorities in their communities, engage in irresponsible or deviant sexual behavior, or use harmful drugs. A considerable number of them run away from their parents' homes.

freely roam the neighborhood. The loss of traditional neighborhood and extended family supports has increased the pressure on the nuclear family to meet the needs of all family members and has deprived them of the companionship, help, and comfort that all families need to raise children effectively.

Formal social services are often far removed from the day-to-day needs of families. Many are available only after a crisis occurs, reflecting the historical trend toward offering *residual* rather than *developmental* services (see Chapter 1). Examples of residual services include public assistance, available only when a family is totally destitute; child protective services, triggered when parental care has deteriorated to the point that children are seriously abused or neglected; and some mental health services, for which only those with diagnosable conditions are eligible. Overlapping and restrictive eligibility regulations and bureaucratic procedures also limit access of families to traditional social services. The mismatch between public social service requirements and the needs of families has given impetus to the "family support" movement, which attempts to fill the gap between the everyday needs of families and the requirements of formal social services by offering flexible, easily accessible services with a holistic service approach, close to the family's home.

Community Characteristics

Many of the supports traditionally available to families from extended family systems and neighborhood or village life are lacking in modern society. Today, conditions within a community, a state, or the nation often are unfavorable to family life and infringe on the needs and rights of children and youth. The mobility of many families, precipitated by the vagaries of the job market, have placed them far from close relatives and friends who would otherwise be available to them at times of family stress. The increasing employment of women has left some neighborhoods nearly empty of adults during the day. In some inner-city neighborhoods, families feel they must remain behind locked doors to be safe. Neighbors distrust rather than help one another, and children cannot

THE MANY FACES OF FAMILY LIFE

The "traditional" family form—two married parents caring for children born within their marriage, with the father as the essential wage earner and the mother the chief child caretaker in the home—has never been the majority family form in the United States, but for many years it was considered the norm. In 1950, only 43 percent of all families with children under age 18 fit the "traditional family" criteria. The rapid rise in divorce and in out-of-wedlock births and the large-scale entrance of mothers into the labor force have changed the composition of families so that now even fewer are "traditional." The 1990 census shows that only 18 percent, or less than one-fifth of all families, now fit the "traditional" category (U.S. Bureau of the Census, 1993). See Figure 3.1.

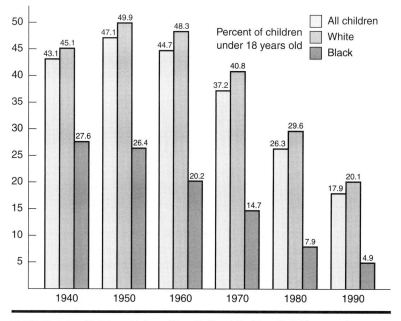

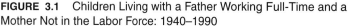

FIGURE 3.1 Children Living with a Father Working Full-Time and a Mother Not in the Labor Force: 1940–1990

Source: D. Hernandez, A. Saluter, & C. O'Brien. (1993). *We the American Children.* Washington, DC: Bureau of the Census.

Today children live in a variety of family types. About 48 million children (68 percent) live with two parents, 20 million (28 percent) live with one parent, and 3 million (4 percent) live with no parent, but may live with grandparents or other relatives (U.S. Bureau of the Census, 1997). All family forms have parenting and child care needs in common, whether that family is an intact family with two working parents, a single-parent family, a stepparent family, a lesbian or gay-parent family, or a teenage parent family. However, the "new" forms of family life usually carry additional demands or have needs and problems that become intensified, making access to supportive social services even more essential.

SINGLE-PARENT FAMILIES

One of the most remarkable demographic trends is the large increase in the number of American children living with one parent, usually the mother. Families headed by women do not constitute a new phenome-

non, having been present throughout history. Nevertheless, the recent acceleration in the number of such families and awareness of the problems that many of them face have attracted national concern.

In contrast with the 20 million children living with one parent today, in 1970 only 8.2 million children (12 percent) lived with a single parent (Saluter, 1994). Recent evidence suggests that during the 1990s the trend of the previous two decades toward more single-parent families may be stabilizing, as the rapid increase of earlier decades has slowed (U.S. Bureau of the Census, 1998).

Another change over the past 30 years is in the increase in single parents who have never married. The percentage of children living in single-parent homes whose parents had never married rose from 7 percent in 1970 to 35 percent in 1995. Although the percentage of never-married single parents is rising, marital instability still remains the main cause of fatherless households. Today about 38 percent of children in single-parent households live with a divorced parent, and another 19 percent have parents who have separated (U.S. Bureau of the Census, 1997).

Ethnic groups vary in the percentage of families headed by a single parent. In 1996, about 22 percent of white families, 57 percent of black families, and 32 percent of Hispanic families were headed by a single parent, mainly the mother (Saluter & Lugalla, 1998). See Figure 3.2.

The needs of single-parent families are not markedly different from those of all other families. At the same time, because of the responsibility of single parents to carry out the duties of child care and family decision making without a marital partner, and because of the higher probability that family income will be limited, normal needs and problems may become harder to deal with.

Single parenthood has pervasive and negative effects on the income and employment of the family head, usually a woman. Limited economic resources—not enough money—and the continuing pressure to balance one financial need against another are especially troublesome aspects of daily life for most single parents. Over half of all mother-only families are poor. They have high poverty rates for several reasons: (1) many noncustodial parents do not pay child support or do not pay much; (2) wage rates for women lag behind those of men; and (3) if parents must rely on welfare, the benefits are not enough to pull them out of poverty (Garfinkel & McLanahan, 1986, p. 23) and are now, with recent welfare reform, time-limited. The combined trends of an increase in the number of mother-only families and the decline in their living standards relative to other kinds of families are captured in the phrase, the "feminization of poverty." See Chapter 4.

The growing but still relatively small number of fathers who become single parents of families often also face economic problems (Meyer & Garasky, 1993). Although they usually have higher earnings than their divorced wives, have been employed longer, and have more opportunity for upward career mobility, they too must cope with combining child care and work. A 1982 survey of a national, nonrandom sample of 1,136 fathers who had custody of their minor children found that combining work with child rearing was difficult for nearly four out of five fathers. "Job mobility, earning power, freedom to work late, job performance, and job advancement are all negatively affected. Some fathers had to quit or were fired" (Greif, 1985, p. 181).

Children's Adjustment to Divorce and Single-Parent Family Life

Children and adults in single-parent families face a number of special challenges. Research on children of divorce has found that they may suffer from depression and emotional distress, may exhibit behavioral

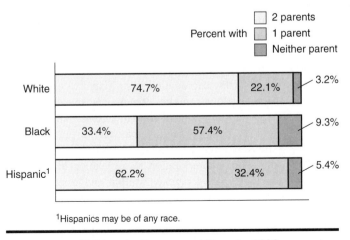

¹Hispanics may be of any race.

FIGURE 3.2 Children by Presence of Parents: 1996
Source: U.S. Bureau of the Census (1996).

and learning difficulties in school, and may suffer low self-esteem (Fields & Smith, 1998; Amato, 1993; Hetherington, Cox, & Cox, 1985; Wallerstein & Kelly, 1980). When they reach adulthood, children of divorce continue to have psychological tasks for adapting to the divorce, lower socioeconomic attainment, and greater marital instability than do children who grew up in intact families (Amato & Keith, 1991). A recent study by McLanahan and Sandefur (1995) found that, other things being equal, teenagers who spent part of their childhood apart from their biological father were twice as likely to drop out of high school, twice as likely to become parents themselves before age 20, and one and a half times as likely to be idle in their late teens and early twenties. The research also shows, however, that the differences found in adjustment between children of divorce and children of intact families are not great, and that many children of single-mother families fare very well (Amato, 1993).

One explanation for the difficulties of children of divorce has already been mentioned—the great drop in income that many custodial mothers and their children experience following divorce. Families may have to move to a new and less desirable neighborhood, thereby losing their old neighborhood supports at a time when the family is already under stress from the divorce. Less income may mean that the parent lowers her aspirations for expensive higher education for her children.

Children may find that their parents have less time for them during the divorce and afterwards. Although many fathers do remain involved with their children, the reality for a growing number of families is a "disappearing father," one who absents himself from his children, emotionally and financially. A recent national survey showed that most children have little or no contact with their father following divorce, and only about one-sixth see their father once a week or more (Furstenberg & Harris, 1990, p. 4).

The remaining parent, the mother, though physically present, may have difficulty shouldering all the responsibilities of single parenthood. Mothers typically speak of task overload.

In this day and age of child rearing it sure would be nice to be sharing the responsibility with someone else.

I get tired of being a full-time policeman and everything else. (A divorced mother of three teenagers— Richards & Schmiege, 1993)

The custodial parent, usually the mother, often finds herself alone with arranging day care and with housekeeping and home maintenance tasks, chores that before her divorce she shared to some extent and in various ways with her spouse. Single fathers have some advantage as their average larger incomes make it more feasible for them to hire housework and babysitting services. Relatives tend to provide such help to men more readily than to women (Kurdek, 1988; Lindblad-Goldberg, 1987). Perhaps most hazardous for the single parent is loneliness and a feeling of isolation in the absence of emotional support from a partner who shares responsibility for the family and its well-being (Wallerstein, 1986).

Children of divorced parents often have experienced parental conflict, and numerous studies have shown that conflict between parents affects children negatively. Children may react with fear or anger and other negative emotions. They may find themselves taking sides against a parent. They may learn a number of negative behaviors, such as physical or verbal aggression. Finally, it is not uncommon for children to blame themselves for the deterioration in their parents' relationship and the deterioration of family life (Amato, 1993). Many researchers now believe that the conflict itself, rather than the divorce, may be the primary cause of children's adjustment problems. Families in which parents are fighting cause unhappiness in children regardless of whether the marriage ends in divorce.

No one explanation is sufficient to explain the various adjustments children may make following divorce, and it seems likely that a combination of factors is at play. Children may face a pileup of the stressors already mentioned—loss of the noncustodial parent, deterioration of the relationship with the custodial parent, parental conflict, and loss of income, which may involve other stressful events such as moving and changing schools. Amato (1993) suggests that the concepts of *stressors* and *resources* may be useful in understanding children's adjustment following divorce. In this view, divorce may make children vulnerable to adjustment problems because it creates stressors, such as moving and parental conflict, at the same time that it may reduce the resources children have available, such as loss of parental attention. It is the total configuration of resources and stressors that matter, not the presence or absence of any particular factor.

Child Abduction: A Special Risk of Single-Parent Children

Unfortunately, sometimes children become pawns in bitter quarrels between divorcing parents and are caught in their parent's unresolved problems. The kidnapping of a child or children by noncustodial parents in divorce is now recognized as a widespread national problem. The numbers of abductions are increasing, influenced by the higher rate of divorce and the greater ease of cross-country travel. The practice is pervasive, found among all social classes and racial groups. The incidence of child snatching is hard to estimate; the most recent federal government survey indicates that over 350,000 family abductions occur each year in the United States (U.S. Department of Justice, 1990).

The problem, so detrimental to the affected children, has been a difficult one to bring under control because of inadequacies in the law. Because lawmakers eschewed the use of criminal procedures to solve what were perceived as domestic disputes, the Federal Kidnapping Act passed in 1932 excluded parents who abducted their own children, leaving the FBI an unempowered source of help to aggrieved parents. Noncustodial parents who were angry at their state court's custody decision, could abduct their children and move to a state that would grant custody without examining too closely prior custody determinations in another state. To address this growing problem, between 1968 and 1983 all states adopted the Uniform Child Custody Jurisdiction Act (UCCJA), which mandates that one state honor a court custody decision made in another state and which assigns court costs, attorney fees, and travel expenses against the kidnapping parent. Several states have attacked the problem further by making child abduction by parents a felony. The federal government responded by enacting the Parental Kidnapping Prevention Act in 1980, the Missing Children's Assistance Act in 1984, and the National Child Search Assistance Act of 1990. These acts have extended use of federal investigative resources to local authorities and have established the National Center for Missing and Exploited Children, which offers assistance to parents and local law enforcement agencies. However, locating abducted children and prosecuting their kidnappers remains primarily a state and local responsibility, and states vary widely in the effectiveness with which they respond to these cases (Steidel, 1994).

The experience of abduction has profound effects on children. A child abducted without his or her consent at best has had personal liberty interfered with and is apt to feel like a piece of property to be quarreled over. Some children seen by clinicians are reported to have become deeply confused and distrustful of parent figures, with the trauma they endured during the conflict between their parents in a contested custody action intensified. Some children, as they may do in other situations, take on feelings of guilt for their parents' troubled and objectionable behavior. The risks are even greater when the snatching involves violence toward the person attempting to protect the child, and sometimes toward the children themselves (Greif & Hegar, 1992).

The need is very great for more professional services to parents considering divorce to help them understand the consequences and reach a custody decision that each can accept, one that is the best alternative for the child. In recent years social workers in some family and child social agencies and in court services have been providing such help.

FAMILIES WITH LESBIAN OR GAY PARENTS

Homosexuality, though it has always existed, has until recently been an unacknowledged phenomenon. With increasing openness about sexual orientation, lesbian and gay families are slowly becoming more visible in the community. Social workers in child welfare are being called on more frequently than in the past for advice and guidance in relation to families headed by lesbian or gay parents, particularly in matters of child custody, and in planning services for these families. Thus social workers are challenged to learn about homosexuality and parenthood and its implications for the lives of children.

It is not known precisely how many lesbian and gay families exist in the United States. Many parents conceal their sexual orientation for fear of discrimination. Despite these difficulties, estimates have been made of about 1 to 5 million lesbian mothers in the United States (Patterson, 1992). These numbers include a wide range of family forms. Many lesbian and gay families are formed when a parent has children in a heterosexual relationship and then, often as a result of recognizing her or his orientation, leaves the marriage. Artificial insemination, adoption, and heterosexual sexual intercourse outside a committed relationship are other ways in which homosexual families with children are formed. Once formed, homosexual families may be headed by a single parent, or by a parent living with a same-sex partner. The partner may or may not have a stepparent relationship to the children. If the partner also has children, the children in the household may have stepsibling relationships with one another (Weston, 1991).

Community Attitudes

In a more socially tolerant climate brought about by changes in sex mores and in the rights of women, homosexuals' need for secrecy about themselves has been reduced, particularly in urban areas. Homosexual parents, as well as homosexuals without children, now find more support for their sexual identification. However, this support is often elusive. Adults who seek to provide foster care or adoption as a route to parenthood have a sharply reduced chance of doing so if the decision maker in an agency knows that the applicant is homosexual. Lesbian and gay parents in the process of divorce are at high risk of losing their children in custody contests. Some states now have laws stating that homosexuality cannot be used as a basis for custody decisions, but in other states parents who openly identify themselves as lesbian or gay are presumed to be unfit as parents (Patterson, 1992). Regulations governing foster care and adoption may create barriers for lesbian and gay adults interested in becoming adoptive or foster parents.

Underlying these attitudes is a series of largely untested stereotyped beliefs: (1) The child reared in a homosexual home will lack traditional role models and will be more likely than others to become gay or lesbian; (2) the child will be harmed by the stigma that attaches to the parent and inevitably extends to the child; (3) the child is at risk of sexual abuse by the parent or her or his friends; and (4) homosexuality will compete with and undermine the provision of parental care, thus impairing the child's overall growth and development (Lewin, 1981; Patterson, 1992).

Behind these fears is a view of homosexuality as indicative of an inherent pathology that would dominate all other aspects of family interaction. In the past fifteen years, the results of systematic research on children of lesbian mothers and gay fathers has accumulated, providing new information that challenges the older assumptions of the detrimental effects of lesbian and gay families on children.

Studies of Families with Gay or Lesbian Parents

In a review of recent research on children of gay and lesbian parents, Patterson (1992) looked at areas of child development, including sexual identity, personality, and social relationships. In light of concerns that children of gay or lesbian parents would grow up with confused sexual identity, a number of studies have examined this aspect of development through its components of gender identity, gender role behavior, and sexual orientation. *Gender identity* concerns a person's self-identification as male or female. *Gender role behavior* describes the extent to which a person's activities, occupations, and the like are regarded by the culture as masculine, feminine, or both. *Sexual orientation* refers to a person's choice of sexual partner. Patterson's review of research on these aspects of sexual identity, using 12 different samples with a total of 300 children of gay or lesbian parents, found that in every study, the sexual orientation of the children fell "within normal bounds. . . . No evidence has been found for significant disturbances of any kind in the development of sexual identity among these individuals" (p. 1032).

Regarding social relationships, there has been concern that children of gay or lesbian parents would be stigmatized by other children. Research on this question has shown that, like their peers, children of homosexual parents tend to have same-sex friends during their grade school years.

Research on the contact that children have with men and particularly with their fathers has revealed that "children in custody of divorced lesbian mothers have more frequent contact with their fathers than do children in custody of divorced heterosexual mothers" (Patterson, 1992, p. 1034). Lesbian mothers expressed more concern than heterosexual mothers that their children have ongoing contact with their fathers and with other adult men, such as the mother's relatives.

Although the weight of evidence is reassuring that children are not harmed by being raised by lesbian or gay parents, Patterson also points out that some questions remain unanswered. One limitation of recent research is that most studies have compared children living with lesbian mothers, many of whom are living with lesbian partners, with children in families headed by divorced, heterosexual mothers who are living without partners. Future research should focus on the difference having a partner in the home makes to the well-being of the mother and the children. Another limitation is that those studied to date have been mainly Caucasian, well-educated, middle- to upper-class families, so less is known about lesbian and gay families in other socioeconomic and ethnic groups.

Special Issues in Lesbian and Gay Parenting

Difficulties that lesbian and gay families face are not caused by homosexuality per se but rather by the stigma associated with homosexuality in American society. This widespread view is that "it is good to be a mother, but it is bad to be a lesbian" (Levy, 1992, p. 23). One area of concern is the issue of disclosure of the parent's sexual orientation to the children. It is generally agreed that it is preferable to tell children at a young age of their parent's homosexuality (Patterson, 1992). It is better for the child to hear the disclo-

sure from a parent, who can explain the situation to the child in a caring and loving way, than for the child to hear of it first from relatives, neighbors, or schoolmates, who may have prejudicial interpretations.

Although it is neither desirable nor practically feasible for the parent not to tell the child but remain in hiding to the world at large, there are potential negative consequences to leading an open lesbian or gay existence, including discrimination in jobs, housing, and child custody decisions. As one mother explained:

> I am . . . mindful of the tremendous additional responsibility my partner and I have as parents because we are lesbians. It is a constant "take a deep breath and come out/stay out again!" We are absolutely committed to being out—the only time we would not be would be if it were a clear danger for the kids. We are an extremely happy family. My partner and I know why we chose our two daughters (not them specifically but children!) and we really do enjoy and love our family. Of course we have "blips," but we work stuff through with our focus on both individual and family needs.
>
> Every step of the way we've had stuff to deal with since becoming parents—but invisibility of our relationship as a couple or "dancing around" our family make-up just isn't part of the consideration. We believe open honesty will serve us all the best and certainly we would rather step forward first and not have our kids in front. Mostly it works—my choices, were I to begin again, would be the same. (Lott-Whitehead & Tully, 1993, p. 276)

Another area of possible concern for lesbian and gay families is to ensure adequate social support. All parents need other caring adults around them to help them meet the difficult responsibilities of parenthood. Research on lesbian families emphasizes the role of social support networks in reducing stress (Levy, 1992). Unfortunately, lesbian families may find that they are often cut off from these sources. Straight families with children may not be very available as a source of sharing and mutual support. Homosexual communities have, until recently, not organized around parenthood and may not be responsive to the needs parents have for support. The lesbian or gay parent's own family of origin may or may not be helpful, depending on their attitudes toward their child's orientation. As with the issue of disclosure to the children, the problem of social isolation is not inherent to the condition of homosexuality, but rather is an outcome of the prejudice and homophobia of society (Weston, 1991).

The Role of Social Work

Social workers traditionally see their role as improving the transactions between people and their environments, to help people adapt more successfully to their surroundings, and also to change environments to make them more compatible with the needs of individuals and families. This perspective is particularly useful in considering the social worker's role with lesbian and gay families (Berkman & Zinberg, 1997). Levy (1992) suggests several ways in which social workers can intervene effectively with lesbian and gay families. (1) She suggests that they first "examine their biases and attitudes toward lesbians and gay men in general and lesbian families in particular. If these professionals are not comfortable working with lesbian families, they can either refer these clients to another practitioner or make use of supervision to resolve their discomfort" (p. 29). (2) Social workers can play a significant role in helping gay and lesbian parents decide to come out, as they weigh the value of coming out as it relates to their own self-identity with concerns about possible adverse effects on child custody. (3) Social workers also can help these parents devise strategies for disclosing their sexual orientation to their children, their families of origin, and other significant people. (4) Forming support groups for lesbian and gay parents can provide a way of building self-esteem and of creating mutual-aid networks. (5) Support groups for the children, particularly as they reach adolescence and face issues of self-identity, can be helpful, as many children report that they do not know any other children of lesbian or gay parents (O'Connell, 1993). (6) Advocacy for all family members may be necessary with schools, the legal system, and other traditional service systems. In summary, social workers can help lesbian families by providing sensitive interventions, by offering guidance or support, and by advocating social change.

STEPPARENT FAMILIES

The current high rates of divorce followed by new marriage has resulted in a major and no longer unusual phenomenon: the family made up of children and one or two stepparents. These families are variously termed *remarried, reconstituted,* or *blended* families. Their composition varies and can include a stepmother with no children married to a man with children, a stepfather with no children married to a woman with children, or a man with children married to a woman with children.

Accurate demographic data about stepparent families in the United States are not available. However, we do know that the number of such families has sharply increased in recent decades. Based on Census Bureau estimates, about one-quarter of children today will live with a stepparent before they are grown. Stepchildren make up about 15 percent of all children who live in married-couple families (Miller & Moorman, 1989).

Distinctive Aspects

While many of the characteristics and problems of family life in the stepparent family are the same as those found in other family forms, certain factors within it are distinctive (Sager, Steer, Crohn, Rodstein, & Walker, 1980).

1. The family is created without the usual pattern of evolutionary growth.
2. Commonly there is an ex-spouse, and often ex-grandparents, who, although "outsiders," seek to influence the new family system.
3. Children often have mixed loyalties to old and new parents; parents in turn often feel guilt and ambivalence toward the children or ex-spouse—feelings that complicate family life.
4. Children are at risk of residual problems from marital conflict or desertion by a parent.
5. Children, who usually are not given a choice, may not want to be a part of the newly formed family.
6. Children who move back and forth between households carry many kinds of messages, some

of which accentuate differences in value systems between the different households with which the child is connected.

7. Role confusion for all family members is characteristic of the newly formed stepfamily.

Characteristics of Successful Stepfamilies

Although stepfamilies undoubtedly have unique challenges, many researchers and practitioners today no longer view these units as inherently problematic. The prevailing perception is that they represent a normative family form. Visher and Visher (1990) have identified the challenges and tasks of creating a successful stepfamily. These tasks are of two types: the "in-house tasks" involve "the challenge of moving from an absence of emotional connections between people, now living under the same roof, to a sense of belonging to a group of individuals who feel connected to one another" (p. 4); there are also "supra-family relationships," where the challenge is to maintain meaningful connections between the newly formed stepfamily and the households of the children's other parents and close relatives. Successful stepfamilies are those that have dealt successfully with these challenges. Visher and Visher (1990) identify the following characteristics of these families.

Losses Have Been Mourned. All members of the newly formed stepfamily may have losses to mourn. Children have experienced the loss of living with the other parent and of their hopes for their family of origin to reunify. Adults have lost the hopes of success with which they entered the previous marriage.

Expectations Are Realistic. Successful stepfamilies do not attempt to duplicate nuclear families; they respect the distinctive aspects and the complexity of their newly formed family. The period of adjusting and forming new family relationships takes a long time, according to researchers, possibly one to two years if the children are young, and five to six years for stepfamilies with older children.

There Is a Strong, Unified Couple. Newly married couples forming stepfamilies are trying to "have a

honeymoon in the midst of a crowd." Parents may feel that they should devote more time to helping their children adjust to the new family, or they may be hesitant to put trust in an intimate relationship again. However, in successful stepfamilies, the parents have given the nurturing of their relationship a high priority, as "parents realize that, while their children continue to need them, they also need the sense of security that comes from a stable couple and the assurance that the stepfamily unit will continue" (Visher & Visher, 1990, p. 8).

Constructive Rituals Are Established. Shared memories and family rituals foster the sense of belonging to a strong family group. For stepfamilies, rituals must be blended or new ones established. Adjusting day-to-day schedules requires humor and flexibility, particularly in juggling the visits of children to their other parent while maintaining a strong sense of family routines.

Stick out the hard times and don't underestimate your personal strength. Talk a lot—try to listen, but keep on talking. (A stepparent—Dahl, Cowgill, & Asmundsson, 1987, p. 3)

Satisfactory Step-Relationships Have Formed. Successful stepfamilies recognize that a number of relationships are possible for stepparents and their stepchildren besides the traditional role of "parent." Stepparents must move into the family slowly, particularly in the area of discipline. At the same time, the birth parent must not abdicate responsibility for enforcing household rules. "Helping a stepparent back off and a parent remain or become active in a limit-setting role is an important therapeutic task which needs to be clarified as an active, not passive, decision on the part of both adults" (Visher & Visher, 1990, p. 9).

The Separate Households Cooperate. Successful stepfamilies form workable "parenting coalitions" with the adults from both households involved in raising the children. Too frequently, these relationships are marked by competition rather than cooperation, a situation that can lead children to feel caught in the crossfire. As one child said, "They're shooting arrows at each other and the arrows go right through me" (p. 10). On the other hand, when parents, including stepparents, in both households cooperate, "permeable boundaries are established and children go between households more easily" (p. 10). A strength of successful stepfamilies is that they increase the number of caring adults around the child. "There is an appreciation of the richness and diversity of relationships, some of them 'given' through birth, others created through mutual effort and caring. It is proving to be a viable and productive family form with the potential for satisfaction and happiness for its members" (p. 11).

The Need for Stepparent Family Services

The stepparent family is an established and viable family form that serves many children well in their growing years. Viewing this unit much as it did the single-parent family earlier, society has been slow to recognize the importance of stepparent families and the need to develop supportive services in their behalf.

Stepparents are required to cope with complicated and emotionally demanding situations. When there are not others with whom to share these challenges, tensions persist for stepparent family members. Sometimes the primary service need is for marital counseling with individual couples. In numerous instances, however, the primary need of stepparents and their children is an opportunity to share their feelings and experiences with other stepparents and stepchildren (Dahl et al., 1987).

FAMILIES OF COLOR

The effectiveness of family support services depends in large measure on the extent to which the services have been planned and offered within the context of a family's own cultural, racial, and ethnic identity. Family and child services focus on family functioning and child-rearing practices. Any group's cultural or ethnic identity is most clearly reflected within the family. Whether the services offered are based on an understanding of ethnically determined behaviors and

cultural differences will be a potent influence on whether they are used. Ethnicity is significant in determining how different groups define normality and social competence. The way in which a family addresses a particular situation reveals the practical strategies it has developed over time to manage many aspects of daily life. However, the usefulness of these strategies may not be readily understood by a social worker who is charged with assessing family functioning but is unfamiliar with the culture (Cross, 1996; Schiele, 1996).

As suggested by the cultural competence continuum presented in Chapter 1, family support programs must address cultural issues at all levels of the organization. Individuals of the same race or ethnicity as the families being served should be included among the professional, paraprofessional, and volunteer participants in a family support program. This practice is essential to an accurate interpretation of community norms and of the ways ethnicity affects a family's lifestyle and child-rearing practices. Having members of the service team who share the family's culture facilitates recruitment and empathetic communication and understanding, and gives credibility to the services being offered. Program materials such as flyers, handouts, crafts, and videos should reflect the ethnic background of participants. Decisions about the kinds of services to offer, scheduling, and overall approach will be more successful if they are made using knowledge from those closely connected to the community.

African-American Families

Among the 11 percent of American families that are African American, great diversity exists. Country of origin, level of acculturation, religion, and socioeconomic status combine to create families that differ in lifestyle and values (Black, 1996). However, all black families in America share the experience of color discrimination. Racism and oppression too often have prevented African Americans from moving into the mainstream of American life. The strengths of black families are credited with helping those of African-American descent to advance in education, income, and employment, despite the almost overwhelming obstacle of discrimination. As a group, African-American families value kinship ties and mutual help, work, and educational attainment (Nobles, 1988; Billingsley, 1992; Hill, 1997).

If we are going to serve Black children and families, we have to understand how Blacks are simultaneously like every family in this country, like some other families, and like no other family at all. The professional helping person has to be able to assess at what point they are dealing with universalities and at what point they are dealing with unique issues. (Solomon, 1985, p. 10)

Three aspects of black family and community life that have helped African Americans survive in America are role flexibility of family members, the extended family support system, and the church. Black parents are able to take on a range of roles within the family, regardless of gender; fathers and mothers both expect to work outside the home and to care for children and the home, although women do seem to assume more responsibility for child rearing (Hall & King, 1982). This flexibility has enabled black families to survive the undermining of the male role as family provider, caused by discriminatory employment practices (Pinderhughes, 1982; Hines & Boyd-Franklin, 1996).

The concept of role sharing extends to children as well as grandparents and other extended family members, who may take instrumental and affective roles in the family. Freeman (1990) cites the advantages and potential difficulties for children of role sharing in the family. "Such patterns tend to broaden each child's role network and teach him or her responsibility for others in the 'group'—those within the same cultural context. In assessment, however, distinctions must be made between these normative cultural expectations within black families, and dysfunctional circumstances involving child neglect" (Freeman, 1990, p. 58).

Social workers and other professionals especially need an understanding of the extended family ties found in black communities. Here, the definition of "family" includes extended family members and per-

haps also close family friends. Extended family networks operate informal exchange systems of mutual help, sharing resources of various kinds, such as material goods, transportation, and child care. Relatives often live near each other and help raise their nieces, nephews, and grandchildren. "Informal adoption" is not unusual, in which children are raised by close family members other than their parents (Billingsley, 1992). These arrangements take place outside the formal child welfare system; usually, the family turns to the public child protection system only after the resources of the extended family have attempted to resolve the problem. The child welfare system is a "last resort" for the family, if extended family strengths are insufficient to maintain an adequate level of protection for the child.

African-American families are complex and power in the family may reside with relatives, such as grandparents, who are key decision makers in issues affecting their children and grandchildren (Hunter, 1997). Social workers may find that these significant family members do not necessarily present themselves to the agency, yet ignoring them risks jeopardizing the planned interventions with the family. These influential family members are usually best identified and included in the treatment plan if sessions with the social worker are held in the family home.

African-American families take many forms besides the traditional two-parent type. Single-parent families and multigenerational families are common. These family forms are often highly functional; however, family members may experience a blurring of boundaries and ambiguous family roles (Hines & Boyd-Franklin, 1996).

The black church has been the predominant cultural institution of Americans of African descent. During slavery and the Jim Crow era the church was a source of strength, consolation, and community solidarity. In today's world, the church continues to be a strong source of cohesiveness in African-American communities. Churches offer social support in times of family crisis and offer age-related activities for all family members. Groups for the enhancement of personal and family development, day care centers, and support groups for people suffering from various physical and psychological difficulties are offered through the churches. With the continuing decay of inner-city neighborhoods, black churches have renewed their commitment to residents in these areas by expanding the range of social services they provide (Lewin, 1988). After-school programs, food pantries, clothing exchanges, and tutorial services for school children are common. Innovative programs are being developed in many churches to help adolescent boys make the transition to manhood, through sports, recreation, opportunities for exchanges with adult role models, and group sessions devoted to health, spirituality, family life, and the special problems of black men (Haight, 1998). A Chicago church established the "One Church, One Child" program to encourage black families to adopt black children. Churches in thirty-one states have replicated the program (Lewin, 1988). The philosophy of this program is that the shortage of African-American adoptive families was a problem "that could not be solved by the state. The people in the Black community themselves had to do it and the churches are the life blood of the Black community" ("One Church, One Child," 1984, p. 23). Social workers may find that churches and religious leaders are important allies in their work with black families (Davis & Proctor, 1989, p. 78).

Hispanic/Latino Families

The diverse groups in the United States who are known as "Hispanic" or "Latino" share a common link to Latin America, the Spanish language, and certain religious and cultural values. Within this unity of background, there is great variation. About 60 percent are of Mexican or Chicano origin, most of whom are not immigrants but original settlers in lands later conquered by the United States and now comprising the southwestern portion of the nation. Fifteen percent of Hispanic persons in America are immigrants from Puerto Rico, and a quarter consist of Cubans and Central and South Americans. Besides the southwest, Hispanic families reside mainly in Florida or in cities along the eastern seaboard (Hernandez, 1987).

Hispanic Americans are the fastest growing ethnic group in the United States. About 21 million Americans, or 9 percent of the population, claim Hispanic identity, according to the U.S. Census (del Pinal, 1992). Between 1980 and 1990, the Latino population grew by 53 percent, compared to 9 percent for the population as a whole (Gutierrez, 1994–95), and it is expected to be the largest ethnic "minority group" by the turn of the century (Orrego, 1994–95). The great increase in population is due largely to immigration, particularly from Mexico and among Central Americans fleeing economic and political turmoil (Ortiz, 1995).

Hispanic/Latino groups share a history of exploitation and oppression, conquest and defeat. In Latin America as in the United States, white European groups held power and gained control of the land while oppressing indigenous populations. Although liberation movements have been successful in some parts of Latin America, the social and economic effects of civil war and ongoing oppression have caused many people from these countries to look to the United States as a place to achieve security and economic stability (Garcia-Preto, 1996).

However, once in the United States, Latin American immigrants frequently encounter prejudice and oppression based on their language, traditions, and color. They may see themselves as placed at the bottom of the social ladder. Recent proposed and enacted legislation penalizing illegal and, in some cases, legal immigrants have increased the sense of alienation among Hispanic groups. They may perceive the dominant Anglo culture as cold, competitive, and hostile to their own culture, which they see as warmer, more family-oriented, and more respectful of individual dignity (Padilla, 1997).

Poverty is a way of life for many persons of Hispanic background. Forty percent of Hispanic children live in families below the poverty line, although most Hispanic families have an adult who is working or looking for work. A major factor in the pervasive poverty of Hispanic families, in spite of high levels of work, is the low level of educational attainment: Only 54 percent of Hispanic children have a parent who graduated from high school. Other factors are recent immigration and the lack of English language ability (Zambrana, Silva-Palacios, & Powell, 1992).

Social workers involved with Hispanic families need to learn about the specific cultural attributes of those families, since much diversity exists among those who are identified as Hispanic or Latino, depending on the country of origin. However, some commonalties have been identified for Hispanic/Latino families in general. Familism is a characteristic strongly emphasized in discussions of Latino family life—the family as a central source of emotional support through close bonds not only with immediate family members but also with grandparents, aunts, uncles, cousins, and family friends (Rothman, Gant, & Hnat, 1985; Vega, 1990). Grandparents are influential in the lives of children, less as authority figures than as sources of love and nurturance. Extended family networks offer much needed social support to Hispanic families, especially those who are recent immigrants and have left other supports behind. Many Hispanic families prefer to live close to extended family members. Support may take the form of economic or other instrumental help, and also of socioemotional interaction.

Extended family systems include not only blood relatives but also other persons close to the family such as *compadres* (godparents) and *hijos de crianza* (adopted children, whose adoption may not have been legalized), as described by Garcia-Preto (1996). *Compadrazco* (godparenthood) is a system of ritual kinship with binding, mutual obligations for economic assistance, encouragement, and even personal correction. *Hijos de crianza* refers to the practice of transferring children from one nuclear family to another within the extended system in times of crisis. Relatives assume responsibility as if the children were their own and "do not view the practice as neglectful" (p. 151).

Although the concepts of *machismo* and *marianismo,* terms describing prescribed sex roles for men and women, may reflect a general organizing framework for relations between the sexes, the reality is much more complicated than these terms suggest. The mother in Mexican-American family life is critically important in intrafamily relationships despite the common characterization of the father as the unquestioned authority in the family. Family decision making is often either a joint process of both parents or primarily the job of the mother. Vega (1990) points to the flexibility and adaptability of Hispanic families to meet changing social conditions, with the result that families may differ greatly on how closely they adhere to traditional gender roles.

For Hispanic women, joining the labor force is not necessarily a sign of personal autonomy or liberation from the family. If the family is poor, the mother may work out of economic necessity and quit when the family has achieved economic stability. Thus the status of being employed may reflect positively on men, but for women, it may reflect the family's vulnerability (Vega, 1990).

Hispanic families seen by social workers usually want help in improving their lives. They may have special concerns for the safety of their children, as the poor neighborhoods in which they often live are plagued by violence, disease, and low educational attainment. They may be grieving for losses associated with immigration, and, if here illegally, may have extremely serious problems in accessing needed health and social services. Adolescents may feel a conflict between values and expectations at home and the allure of popular culture. Garcia-Preto recommends that social workers help Hispanic families reflect on cultural contrasts and on the positives and negatives of each culture. "The metaphor of building bridges to connect the world they come from to the world they live in now helps them to take what is needed from both. Validating the positives in their culture is essential to help Latinos rid themselves of shame, regain their dignity, make connections, and have a sense of community" (Garcia-Preto, 1996, p. 153).

We are bilingual, bicultural, and by ourselves. How do we retain our assets, how do we contribute to society at large in a synergy that makes us all more? (Mario J. Aranda)

Native American Families

After centuries of decline, the population of Native Americans in the United States is again increasing. In 1993, the Census reported almost two million Indians

(Sutton & Broken Nose, 1996). The introduction of modern medical services in rural areas has helped lower infant mortality rates, and improved adaptations to modern living have increased somewhat the longevity of adults (Attneave, 1982). With these population changes, it is likely that the stresses and problems of young families will become of increasing interest to agencies involved with Native Americans.

The term "Indian" can be defined in many ways, such as having a certain percentage of Indian blood as established by the Federal Register of the United States, enrollment in a recognized tribe, community recognition, and self-declaration, the method used by the Census Bureau. Each Indian nation sets its own criteria for membership. The Census reports 500 different tribes and 314 reservations. Over half of those declaring themselves to be Indian live in urban areas. There is a wide range of cultural identification; at one end of the spectrum are those who claim Indian heritage because of an Indian ancestor; at the other end are those born on reservations who speak native languages as well as English (Sutton & Broken Nose, 1996). Native Americans differ from other ethnic "minority" groups in that the federal government and some state governments have specific legal rights and responsibilities toward them, including tribal recognition and issues of tribal sovereignty (Weaver, 1998).

Traditional Indian culture was diverse, with an estimated 200 different nations at the time of first European contact in the 1600s (Spicer, 1980). In spite of much variation, it is broadly true that each nation provided natural systems to safeguard children and promote their healthy development. Children were raised in an extended family environment that included three or more generations; separate households of cousins, aunts, and uncles; and nonrelatives who became incorporated into the family (Red Horse, 1980). Aunts, uncles, and grandparents had specific roles and responsibilities in regard to the family's children, and were also ready to help if the parents became overburdened, incapacitated, or died. Children could form bonds to several parental figures who offered affection, education in proper behavior, and various role models (Attneave, 1982; Sutton & Broken Nose, 1996). Spiritual beliefs reinforced the value of children as a special gift from the Creator (Cross, 1986).

The conquest of America by Western immigrants drastically altered tribal life. The loss of land separated families so that the extended family system could no longer provide a nurturing environment for children. Adults lost their traditional occupations and their ability to be role models as competent providers. Women's domestic skills made it easier for them than for Indian men to find work in the economy of the dominant culture, both on and off the reservation. The massive unemployment of Indian men has resulted in an increase of single-mother families (Attneave, 1982). Alcohol, introduced by early explorers to Native American cultures with no social context to control its use, has plagued Indian families. Sixty deaths due to alcoholism per 100,000 individuals is reported for Indians; the comparable number for the general population in the United States is nine (Lamarine, 1988). For Indian and non-Indian families alike, alcoholism is associated with higher rates of family problems, child maltreatment, and developmental disabilities. Native Americans have a shared background of being a people subject to policies that had the effect of genocide, resulting in the devastation of an entire people and their civilization.

Native American families historically have been at great risk of family breakup because of government programs and policies. Indian boarding schools, established in the late nineteenth century by the Bureau of Indian Affairs, were designed to "separate a child from his reservation and family, strip him of his tribal lore and mores, force the complete abandonment of his native language, and prepare him in such a way that he would never return to his people" (*Indian Education,* 1969). Consequently, Indian children were often forcibly removed from their homes, given English names, required to speak English, and in many instances not allowed to return home. A devastating effect of this program was that young people grew up with no experience of family life and no parental role models to guide their own efforts to establish families after they were grown and had left the schools (Tafoya & Del Vecchio, 1996). Some children suffered abuse in these institutions, which offered them only negative patterns of child-rearing.

Through the years, Indian children continued to be at highest risk of out-of-home placement of children in any racial or cultural group in the country, with placement rates reported to be 20 times higher than that of white children (Johnson, 1981). Little regard was given to the unique character of the Indian family and sociocultural aspects of life on the reservation, and children were removed from their families often because of poverty, poor housing, and problems that could have been resolved had adequate family services been available. The foster and adoptive homes were mainly non-Indian, at least partly because Indian families often could not meet the housing and income requirements to qualify as substitute homes. Many non-Indian foster and adoptive families provided loving and caring homes, but the children were inevitably deprived of the opportunities needed to incorporate their cultural heritage into their personal identity. By the 1970s, it is estimated that a quarter of all Indian children were not living with their families but were in boarding schools, or foster or adoptive homes (Johnson, 1981). This great loss of Indian children to their cultural heritage gave impetus to the passage of the Indian Child Welfare Act of 1978, federal legislation intended to restore and preserve Indian families.

In spite of adversity, Indian culture and Indian families endure. Present-day Indians are survivors who have learned to adapt to an alien culture. Many urban Indian families are coping and managing successfully. These families tend to be open to learning and using the technology and social norms of white culture. Significantly, maintaining interest in tribal folkways, language, and values is also associated with successful adaptation to urban life (Attneave, 1982). A study of Indian women in rural North Dakota who were affiliated with Head Start found that their family and personal relationships were characterized by mutual respect and helpfulness. The women were optimistic and courageous, and were "certain they could make plans work" (Light & Martin, 1986).

In recent years, the interest of government and industry has focused on certain tribes that own land rich in energy and other natural resources. Resource development and other entrepreneurial activity such as the development of casinos on Indian lands is changing social and economic conditions of life on reservations, and may result in greater economic and political power for Native American groups in relation to the dominant society (Snipp, 1986).

CHARACTERISTICS OF FAMILY SUPPORT SERVICES

"Family support services" is a term covering a wide range of programs aimed at preventing abuse and neglect and strengthening family functioning. These programs are intended for all types of families, but may be particularly useful for those who face special challenges in family life due to single parenthood, racial oppression, or other difficulties. Some programs offer a comprehensive array of services, including health care, employment, education, housing, and other services, in addition to family education and support, while others offer a more limited program focused on parent–child relationships, child management, and other aspects of family life. Services may be delivered through home visiting or through center programs, including formal groups for parents and for children, or they may combine both in home and center activities. Auspices of family support programs are human service agencies, schools, hospitals, community centers, and others, or the program may stand alone. Staff may include volunteers, paraprofessionals, and professionals with credentials in social work, education, early childhood development, community planning, or health care.

Principles of Family Support Services

Although different programs may have different auspices, scope of service, target population, and strategies of service, they share a common set of principles as identified by The Family Resource Coalition (1996, p. 6).

1. Staff and families work together in relationships based on equality and respect.
2. Staff enhance families' capacity to support the growth and development of all family members—adults, youth, and children.
3. Families are resources to their own members, to other families, to programs, and to communities.

4. Programs affirm and strengthen families' cultural, racial, and linguistic identities and enhance their ability to function in a multicultural society.
5. Programs are embedded in their communities and contribute to the community-building process.
6. Programs advocate with families for services and systems that are fair, responsive, and accountable to the families served.
7. Practitioners work with families to mobilize formal and informal resources to support family development.
8. Programs are flexible and continually responsive to emerging family and community issues.
9. Principles of family support are modeled in all program activities, including planning, governance, and administration.

Theoretical Base

Family support programs are based on the premise that the primary responsibility for the well-being of children rests with families, and that all segments of society should support families so that they can successfully rear their children (Family Resource Coalition, 1996). They integrate a number of theoretical perspectives to form a common conceptual framework for realizing this fundamental premise. Family support services use an *ecological approach* to service delivery, which views parents and children as embedded in their environments. Thus they are affected by the cultural and socio-economic characteristics of the communities in which they live. Families' ability to function successfully depends, to some extent, on the quality of the surrounding environment, including the agencies, schools, and other community services and the state and federal policies affecting them (Gaudin, Wodarski, Arkinson, & Avery, 1990–91; Tracy & Whittaker, 1987). Thus family support services often focus on increasing the social supports available to families and to creating safer, more supportive neighborhoods and communities (Cochran, 1991).

Family support services use a helping philosophy emphasizing *empowerment,* which refers to a process of personal development in which individuals become increasingly aware of their strengths and abilities, build competency and self-esteem, and take steps to make positive changes in their family relationships and other immediate environments. Programs with an empowerment perspective are based on the fundamental idea that all persons have strengths but may need a supportive environment to unlock them. These programs differ markedly from deficit models of helping, in which the deficiencies of clients are first identified and then a treatment, therapy, or educational program is supplied to address the defined area of weakness in the client's functioning (Bronfenbrenner, 1987; Cochran, 1993).

Empowerment can take place at the group and community levels as well as within individuals and families. Using traditional social work concepts of community organization, family support programs may work with neighborhood groups to advocate changes such as better bus service or the development of a teen recreation center.

Family support services operate on the belief that *prevention* of problems is more humane and more effective than offering services after a crisis has occurred. Research studies to date suggest that supportive interventions with parents, especially with families in which the mother is pregnant and those with infants or preschoolers, can contribute to preventing such problems as child neglect and abuse (Gaudin et al., 1990–91; Wolfe, 1993; Powell, 1994; Olds et al., 1998).

I learned to listen to what my children were trying to tell me. I'm more involved with their activities. I hug them more than before. (A mother in a family support program—The Ounce of Prevention Fund, 1993)

Family support programs attempt not only to prevent negative outcomes but also to enhance participants' quality of life (Weissbourd & Kagan, 1989) by taking a *developmental approach* to service delivery. Developmentally enriched preschool programs for children, recreational and tutorial programs for school-age children and adolescents, and adult education and other personal development programs for adults can improve the quality of life for all family members.

The philosophy of family support programs is that services should be *universally available* (Class,

1968; Family Resource Coalition, 1996). As it is impossible to know in advance which families may experience problems later on, these preventive, developmental services should be available to all. They should also be accessible to families at any point in the family's developmental course. Young children and their families need a chance to get a good start developmentally, and families with older children often need help in maintaining positive family interaction while teenagers are in the process of separating from home. Currently family support services are not universally available to families. They are insufficient in number, usually have an uncertain or time-limited financial base, and have served for the most part as experiments or demonstrations.

Historical Development of Family Support Programs

Recognizing that traditional supports for families, such as extended kinship networks and close-knit communities, may have become attenuated or disappeared altogether in present-day American cities and rural areas, family support programs attempt to recreate the benefits of these traditional forms of caring. A key characteristic of the family support movement is the development of programs at the grassroots level. During the 1980s, when federal funds for social services decreased, local citizens' groups, community-based agencies, charitable foundations, faith communities, and local governments created local programs in response to local needs.

Family support programs are both old and new: old, because they have antecedents in the history of social services, education, and health and mental health services; new, because they are influenced strongly by current conditions of American life, new research findings on child, adult, and family development, and recent changes in funding patterns for social services to families (Weiss & Halpern, 1990; Weissbourd, 1994).

Settlement Houses.   Settlement houses were founded in the late nineteenth century to address an emerging problem: the dislocation and lack of support felt by families who had recently immigrated to U.S. cities

from their rural homes in America or Europe. These families lacked the extended family and neighborly supports that had been available to guide and assist them in their previous communities. Immigrants from Europe were vulnerable to exploitation by landlords and employers, and lacking political power, they were often ignored by local politicians.

A major function of the settlement houses was to work toward better living conditions for urban slum dwellers through political activities at the city, state, and federal levels. Settlement house workers, together with local residents, were effective in securing better street lighting, garbage pickup, and police protection. In addition to advocacy, settlement houses offered a range of programs to help children, adults, and families adapt to their new life situation and to create a sense of community and mutual support. English language classes, political discussion groups, sewing and child care classes, and recreational and arts programs for youth were among the programs commonly offered.

The settlement house model has contributed substantially to the development of family support programs. Settlement houses were among the first social service programs to recognize that the neighborhood influenced the way families functioned in raising their children and to develop methods of intervention at the neighborhood level. Settlement houses were also a model for organizing and delivering services to all members of a community, not targeting service only to those previously identified as needing special help. Thus they pioneered in offering preventive services to families. They also showed how professionals could work with local residents in community advocacy and create conditions under which those residents would be empowered to take action on their own behalf (Addams, 1909; Husock, 1992; Wald, 1915).

Head Start.   Head Start was founded in the 1960s to help children develop their potential, so they could take advantage of opportunities created by advances in civil rights for those who had been discriminated against. Although the focus of Head Start was initially on the child, its scope was gradually expanded to include parents. The idea of offering services to parents as well as their preschool children appeared in other programs, including the Parent-Child Development Centers of the 1970s, the Child and Family Resource Programs, and Home Start. These programs developed innovative ways to offer services to parents as well as to children and began to identify themselves as child development and family support programs (Weiss & Halpern, 1990). See Chapter 5.

The Self-Help Movement.   Beginning in the 1940s and 1950s, people started to form associations focused on a life issue, such as having a severely mentally retarded or mentally ill family member at home, or personal problems such as alcoholism or divorce. These associations tended to exclude professionals, relying instead on the support and advice of members of the group to help one another cope with difficult life situations. The self-help movement provided a model for programs that could grow locally, on shoestring budgets, and without government involvement, relying on the interest and capabilities of local citizens. These groups had an empowerment orientation, looking to themselves for the answers to their problems rather than to professionals. They lobbied government and other larger systems for policy changes to ameliorate their situations; they also focused on learning how to adapt at an individual and family level (Weissbourd, 1994).

Parent Education.   Throughout the early 1960s, parent education programs served the middle class almost exclusively. They offered an early model of a preventive, voluntary program for families who might not be experiencing great difficulty in child rearing but wished to parent more competently and with less anxiety. Research on these programs in the 1970s and early 1980s pointed to modest but measurable and positive program effects on children's development, parental competency, and parental attitude (Powell, 1986). Adapting parent education approaches to make them effective with families outside the suburban middle class has been a major thrust of the family support movement.

Federal and State Involvement in Family Support

In 1993, the federal government took a major step forward in addressing the need for family support ser-

vices with passage of the Family Preservation and Support Services Act, an amendment to Title IV-B of the Social Security Act. This legislation continued funding for family preservation services and authorized new funding for family support services offered through state child welfare agencies.

The act defined family support services and family preservation services.

> Family support services *are primarily community-based preventive activities designed to alleviate stress and promote parental competencies and behaviors that will increase the ability of families to successfully nurture their children; enable families to use other resources and opportunities available in the community; and create supportive networks to enhance child-rearing abilities of parents and help compensate for the increased social isolation and vulnerability of families.*
>
> Family preservation services *typically are services designed to help families alleviate crises that might lead to out-of-home placement of children; maintain the safety of children in their own homes; support families preparing to reunify or adopt; and assist families in obtaining services and other supports necessary to address their multiple needs in a culturally sensitive manner. (If a child cannot be protected from harm without placement or the family does not have adequate strengths on which to build, family preservation services are not appropriate.) (Highlights, 1994, p. 1)*

Note that family *support* services are preventive services available on a voluntary basis to a wide range of families, whereas family *preservation* services are intended for a smaller number of families who have been found to be abusive or neglectful and who need more intensive services in order to preserve their families and prevent foster care. Family preservation services are the subject of Chapter 8 in this text.

Funding for this legislation was authorized at nearly a billion dollars over a five-year period, of which 25 percent must be spent on family support, rather than family preservation, services. This federal funding was important because until it was authorized, family support programs survived on grants from foundations and other local funding. While crucial to the development of these programs, such limited, unstable funding could not provide a solid foundation to expand and improve family support programs throughout the country.

Two recent studies indicate that the institutionalization of family support is occurring, as states use the federal dollars made available by the 1993 legislation and supplement it with state, local, and foundation funding and voluntary contributions. The U.S. General Accounting Office (1997) and The Family Resource Coalition (1996) found that the increased funding authorized by the 1993 legislation was helping states expand their family support services. States were allocating about 44 percent of the federal dollars received under this act to family support services and 56 percent to family preservation services. Since most states already had family preservation services in place, they used the money to expand their family support services. Currently, evaluations are underway of these new programs.

FAMILY SUPPORT PROGRAMS

Most family support programs fall into one of the following categories: neighborhood-based programs that provide comprehensive, collaborative services; or more narrowly focused programs that seek to enhance parenting skills and family functioning. In addition, family support programs may exist as a component of other services, such as substance abuse or violence prevention, services to families with children with special needs, or child-care programs. Further, some school systems have developed family support programs to link parents to the schools and promote their involvement in the education of their children.

Neighborhood-Based Programs

These programs typically offer a range of services to families in a specific geographic area. They often are reminiscent of the early settlement houses in that they strive to create a friendly, nonstigmatizing atmosphere, inviting drop-ins and informal exchanges among staff and local visitors. They may develop programs in response to local need, and like the settlements, they see their mission as improving community life and neighborhood conditions as well as helping individuals and families.

Among the more common program components are nursery schools, parent education programs, after-school care and tutorial services, job counseling, chemical addiction treatment and prevention groups, and youth sports and recreational programs. Centers also frequently administer clothing and food banks, and offer emergency housing and fuel assistance to community residents. Staff may act as advocates and mediators for residents with schools, the welfare department, the employment office, and other complex service organizations.

An innovative center in Brooklyn, New York, is the Center for Family Life, sponsored by St. Christopher-Ottilie, a voluntary child welfare agency. It is in a low-income neighborhood, with many recent immigrants from Puerto Rico, Palestine, Asia, and South and Central America (Sheffer, 1992). The center is somewhat unusual among neighborhood-based programs in the emphasis it gives to counseling and psychotherapy as important services for families. The counseling and education program is well-developed, consisting of individual and group programs for parents, young children, and adolescents. Counseling occurs at the center or in the family's home, on evenings and weekends as well as weekdays. Referrals come from the schools, the public child welfare agency, and word of mouth. Families seek help for a number of reasons, including abuse and neglect, mental health problems, and drug abuse.

The Center for Family Life, under a contract with the Department of Employment to provide employment counseling, places a large number of neighborhood residents in jobs; the participants are mainly Puerto Rican, with limited reading skills. The focus of the program is not on training for specific job skills but on helping participants resolve personal and family issues that interfere with their ability to work and to help them make the transition to the world of work. Participants receive considerable individualized attention and follow-up.

The center runs extensive after-school and teen recreation programs at three elementary schools and one junior high school. These programs provide a safe place for children after school while their parents work and offer supplementary, developmental opportunities for children outside their normal school experiences.

Program elements include efforts to involve parents in helping their children do homework, group activities, art, music and theater activities, newsletters, and youth leadership programs. The success of these programs has depended on the staff's forming close working alliances with the principals of the schools and the school bureaucracy, a task that requires ongoing effort. Close alliances of staff with school social workers and guidance personnel have helped the program provide individualized assistance to children with special needs.

A special feature of this center is that it combines a spectrum of traditional supportive services, including those listed above, with specialized, intensive child welfare services. The center offers child protective services, intensive family counseling, foster care, and family preservation and reunification services to the subgroup of neighborhood residents with serious problems of family functioning (McGowan, 1989).

Combining the services traditionally offered by a community center with those of a child welfare agency has important advantages for families who need child welfare services. These families are offered a continuum of services, from occasional socializing events to intensive counseling and substitute care, in one easily accessible setting. This broad spectrum allows center staff to adjust the intensity and mix of services to meet the changing needs of the family over time. For the children who must go into temporary foster care, the center provides foster families in the child's own neighborhood; this placement lessens the disruption of leaving home, permits the child to remain with her school and friends, and eases arrangements for visiting with parents. Intensive services to parents are initiated immediately, with the goal of rapid reunification, in order to normalize and abbreviate the disruption of foster care (McGowan, 1989).

An evaluation of the center's impact on the neighborhood revealed that it has been a unifying force in the community, which is somewhat fractionalized by ethnic and organizational rivalries. The center's programs have helped to assimilate new immigrant groups, such as Asians, into the existing social structure. Residents are enthusiastic about the center; they particularly point out the way the program fills gaps by

serving entire families, and the value of the extensive after-school and youth programs. The directors believe that "long-range, developmental preventive services in a community, combined with many different kinds of informal practical assistance, are the best prescription for the long-term health of the community" (Sheffer, 1992, p. 66).

Programs to Enhance Parenting Skills and Family Functioning

These programs may be located in free-standing drop-in centers, in health or mental health centers, or in other human service organizations. Services may include home visiting as well as center-based activities. Parents using these programs come from a broad range of backgrounds, including those who wish to learn the latest information so that they can provide the highest level of care to their children and those who are mandated by the courts to attend parenting classes (Family Resource Coalition, 1996). The program may have as a major goal the enhancement of family life, or be targeted more specifically to an at-risk population and have the purpose of preventing child abuse and neglect.

One such program is the Healthy Start Program on the island of Oahu, Hawaii. Work with a family in this program is highlighted in the case example at the beginning of this chapter, "Reaching out to a family at risk of maltreatment." The Healthy Start Program, which began in 1985 as a demonstration project, was expanded to a statewide, publicly-funded family support services program in 1988. Healthy Start has been replicated in several other states as well.

Families are first identified at the hospital when the mother gives birth. They are screened for risk factors, such as a history of unstable housing, substance abuse background, depression, parent's abuse as a child, late or no prenatal care, less than high school education, poverty, and unemployment. Because the program has resources for a limited number of families, only families with several risk factors are accepted. Families identified as needing services are offered a place in the program.

The support workers are members of the community. They are close to the families served in social and cultural background and can approach the families in the helpful, nonthreatening way of a concerned neighbor or extended family member. Workers carry caseloads of twenty-five families and initially visit families weekly.

At the beginning, the workers and families often must cope with crises in housing, employment, or substance abuse. During this early period, workers also try to get the families established in using the medical system for preventive health care, encouraging them to keep regularly scheduled well-baby and immunization appointments rather than waiting for medical emergencies.

Over time, as the family's situation stabilizes, the family begins to set goals and define its own level of participation. After a trusting relationship has been established with the worker, the focus may turn to parent-child relationships, child development, parenting skills, family planning, and relationships between the adult partners. A child development specialist is available to visit the family concerning developmental issues of children. A male worker may visit the father to discuss the male role in the family. Gradually, the home visitor may decrease the visits to once a month.

Group activities are also available to families and participation is encouraged. Groups meet at local neighborhood shopping centers to discuss issues of common concern. The groups also have special activities and field trips.

Families may remain in the program until the youngest child is five and ready to enter school. About 40 percent of the families remain that long.

The program cost about $2,100 per family in 1992 (Allen, Brown, & Finlay, 1992). The State Health Department provides 98 percent of the funding (about three and a half million dollars annually), with other funding coming from foundations and community fund raisers (Bruner & Carter, 1991).

An evaluation of the initial three-year demonstration project found that the project was successful at identifying families at high risk for child maltreatment and at preventing abuse and neglect. Of the 241 families served, abuse was halted in 100 percent of the cases, and child neglect occurred in only four cases, resulting in referrals to child protective services. In comparison, families identified as high risk but not included in the program because of lack of space had abuse and neglect rates three times that of the general population (Allen, Brown, & Finlay, 1992).

THE PRACTICE OF FAMILY SUPPORT SERVICES

Skills in working with individuals, families, groups, and communities of diverse cultures and ethnicities are needed by those planning and implementing family support programs. Important elements of family support practice include

- recruitment and outreach,
- relationship building,
- enhancing family capacity,
- building community cohesiveness, and
- advocacy.

Family support work can be difficult and demanding; programs may lack resources and stable funding, and families may find it difficult to accept the need to change. The following examples are not intended to provide a complete overview of the challenges of family support practice, but do show the skills needed and how family support workers have used these skills in the past. For a more complete treatment of family support practice, see publications of the Family Resource Coalition.

Recruitment and Outreach

Recruitment, start-up, and outreach are important aspects of program development. Too frequently, new programs are not allowed enough time to get established before funders and evaluators start addressing the question of whether the program works. Ironically, the low-income, socially isolated neighborhoods where family support programs are most needed are also the places where they will take the longest to become established. Experience has shown that programs need at least a year to become fully operational and may take longer under some conditions, such as insufficient funding, complicated organizational and collaborative arrangements, or particularly challenging neighborhood environments.

Residents in poor communities often have attitudinal and other barriers to participation. They may have learned to distrust new programs because they have seen so many come and go over the years, after having raised expectations for improvements that never materialized. In many low-income areas, the only parenting programs known to residents are those that abusive and neglectful parents are mandated to attend, so family programs have become stigmatized as punishment for "bad" parents (Downs & Nahan, 1990). Another problem is that people who have experienced multiple failures in school, work, and personal relationships may feel that they cannot be helped. A further barrier to participation is the lack of knowledge families may have about support programs and how they can be beneficial. Many people do not think of parenting as a skill that can be learned, nor have they thought that receiving information and social support could help them strengthen their family life. For all these reasons, recruitment of families requires careful strategizing and expenditure of program resources.

Program experience has identified several potentially helpful recruitment and retention strategies (Downs, 1994):

- Different recruitment strategies recruit different types of people. Flyers, posters, and other broad-brush efforts will attract people who already know the value of family support programs and are not intimidated by the prospect of contact with strangers. Such strategies will not attract people who are unaware that these programs can benefit them and who are apprehensive about interacting with strangers (Powell, 1987).
- Personal contact with other local service providers, the leadership councils in nearby housing projects, school personnel, faith community leaders, police, and welfare and other government workers is helpful, as is direct recruiting in public social and health service waiting rooms (Downs & Walker, 1996).
- Placing the program in a host setting that is already established in the community can be helpful; such a setting could be a mental health clinic or a community center.

- Door-to-door recruiting is an essential component of recruitment in low-income communities where people have not heard of and do not understand the value of family support programs.
- Offering small incentives, such as snacks or food coupons, gives tangible evidence that the program cares about the participants. Community baby showers have also been used as recruiting devices; for these, area merchants and charitable organizations donate baby supplies. Day care and transportation are very helpful and may be necessary in some cases.
- Once a program is established, word-of-mouth information from participants to their family and friends is a potent recruitment strategy. Participants are the ideal recruiters because they already have a relationship of trust with those they are likely to recruit and because they can speak with conviction about the benefits of the program. Further, they are likely to know the individuals among their relatives and neighbors who are motivated to improve the interactions of family life and therefore are ready to benefit from program involvement.

Assertive Outreach.   It is a mistake to believe that if families who know about the program won't come, then nothing more can be done unless the situation warrants a report to child protective services. There is room to maneuver between totally voluntary participation and forced participation through the child protection system. *Assertive outreach* is the term given to focused, persistent, yet respectful recruitment efforts targeted to needy but reluctant families. In general, if the program offers the family a tangible benefit and does not label them *dysfunctional,* they can eventually be recruited.

Relationship Building

Family support programs attempt to create a homelike atmosphere, with plenty of toys, comfortable chairs, and the provision of food and drink. Cultural and ethnic preferences are respected through celebration of holidays such as Cinco de Mayo and Kwanzaa. Staff should be from the community and able to relate in a comfortable, egalitarian way with the families. Families should not be viewed as "clients" with "problems" to be solved by professionals, but as partners in the joint effort to explore new ways for the family to work together. Families are encouraged to contribute ideas for center activities and be involved in carrying them out.

Highly deprived families may live in a state of perpetual crisis, faced with seemingly unsolvable problems and vast unmet needs for such basics as decent housing, food, clothing, and a reasonably safe environment. Programs need to be able to respond to concrete and emergency needs. Families who feel that they have been helped in tangible ways are more likely to be open to hearing information about improving family interaction and to trusting the program to help them with interpersonal problems and parenting issues.

Building trust can take a long time. A number of strategies can help the staff and families develop a relationship so that together they can begin the work of helping families to improve their functioning.

Start with the Parent's Concerns.   This may involve addressing the immediate, concrete needs of the adults as a first step, even if the ultimate goal of the intervention is to improve the ability of the adults to parent. Following is an example of how this can be accomplished.

A family support worker in a program to prevent child abuse and neglect, Mr. Soumah, was approached by Mrs. McIntyre at an agency open house. She started crying and said she had no job, her family was angry at her and not helpful, and she was soon going to be evicted from her apartment. Further inquiry revealed that the woman also feared that her mother was going to make a referral to child protective services as Mrs. McIntyre admitted leaving her children unattended for long periods because she "got involved in things and forgot the time." Mr. Soumah helped her negotiate with her landlord for an extension of one week while she looked for a job. Mrs. McIntyre could barely write and asked for help filling out job applications. She also asked Mr. Soumah to help her negotiate with her mother, and together they arranged for the mother to

provide child care for her grandchildren while her daughter was at work. Mrs. McIntyre was able to find a job and her situation stabilized. Mr. Soumah's role was to offer comfort and practical help, and to coach Mrs. McIntyre through negotiations with the landlord, prospective employers, and her mother. With stressors reduced, she was able to begin to address the needs of her children.

Let the Family Set the Pace.   Sometimes parents need a long time to develop trust both in the family support workers and in themselves before they can confront the need for major change.

Mrs. Benson, nine-months pregnant, came to the Family Resource Center at a community-based health clinic on the last day of work before Christmas with her 6-year-old daughter. She told Mrs. Draper, the family support worker, that she had no food and no presents for her daughter. Family members with whom she was staying were beginning to insist she leave. Mrs. Draper gave the child a new ski jacket and a game and gave Mrs. Benson a referral for emergency food. After Christmas, Mrs. Benson came back for an appointment for her baby, who had been born over the holiday. She made a point of stopping by Mrs. Draper's office to thank her. For a year, she would stop by irregularly and talk while standing in the doorway. She attended parenting workshops irregularly, explaining to Mrs. Draper that she was very slow to make friends. Mrs. Draper noticed that she seemed to be going downhill; she again was complaining about being kicked out of the relatives' house. Finally, Mrs. Draper asked if she were using drugs and Mrs. Benson admitted she was. Mrs. Draper suggested a treatment program and Mrs. Benson agreed, but only on an outpatient basis. After three days of the program, Mrs. Benson called Mrs. Draper to say she had enrolled in a one-year inpatient program where she could have the children with her and learn new job skills. Mrs. Draper's availability and willingness to let Mrs. Benson set the pace for her involvement in the program appear to have been key to the success of the intervention.

Create Opportunities for Families to Feel Successful.   At the local family center, the worker used crafts as an enjoyable, nonthreatening way of helping parents get involved in the program, and as an easy basis for conversations to develop about family life and parenting.

> One very quiet mother concentrated on creating a scrapbook cover that was pleasing to her. The next week she told the worker that her abusive, live-in boyfriend belittled her project just as he belittled her. She said that she knew what she had made was beautiful, and that made her believe that she deserved better from the person close to her. With further support from the worker, she was able eventually to leave this abusive relationship.

Enhancing Family Capacity

Family support workers often work with families in groups, using psychoeducational approaches to sharing ideas about ways to improve family life. They may also work individually with parents, using a problem-solving approach. It is common for programs to use both individual and group approaches with the families.

Meet with Parents in Groups to Share Information and Provide Social Support.

Although some family support programs, particularly those focused on mothers with infants, see their families only on an individual basis, many programs incorporate parent groups into the mix of services. Groups provide an opportunity to process information on parenting, such as basic information on child development, reasonable expectations, and child behavior management techniques other than physical discipline. Groups also give parents a chance to get to know one another, share information, and offer and receive social support.

In the following example, the social worker narrates an experience with a group of parents, most of whom were previous or current users of illegal drugs. All had voluntarily joined the group to learn new ways of managing their children and creating strong families.

> During my parenting workshop, one of the parents, Ms. Robinson, who has been coming regularly, asked if 6-year-olds should be able to have their own opinions and make their own decisions. After a little discussion, the general feeling was that of course it was all right to learn to make decisions and think for oneself. Ms. Robinson then asked, "Should a 6-year-old be allowed to go to the store by herself four long blocks away from home?" The group said "No" in unison, but then one member asked why it was a concern. Ms. Robinson said that she used drugs in the past and now she wanted desperately to learn how to be a good mother to her daughter, Lenora. She explained that when she was doing drugs she used to send her daughter to the store alone, just to get her out of the house. Now she wonders if that is the right thing to do with a small child. The group assured her that the streets are too dangerous for a girl that age, and that it would be terrific if she could now show her a different kind of mothering by walking as a family to the store, while still allowing Lenora some choice about what to buy. They went on to explain that a little child wants to feel taken care of and that knowing that her mother wanted her to be safe would make Lenora feel secure. Ms. Robinson explained that she thought it would be hard to take away the freedom her daughter had had for over a year, and the group reassured her that Lenora would probably like the fact that she is now taking charge and being the parent. Several went on to say that she could explain that she had problems before and sometimes that meant Lenora had to do things that little girls shouldn't have to do. Now that she is better, she wants to be with Lenora and keep her safe. I reflected that sometimes it is better to just listen, not to be the "specialist," and just let the parents teach. When they do, everyone learns and is empowered. (Lee, 1992, p. 4)

Use a Problem-Solving Approach.

Family support workers often use a systematic, problem-solving approach with families, who may be overwhelmed and immobilized with multiple problems. Parents are encouraged to identify and prioritize problems and suggest resources available to them to resolve those problems. The worker also contributes suggestions for resources, helps devise strategies of action, and helps the parents monitor progress toward resolution. The following case shows how a family support worker used this approach with an overwhelmed mother from Central America.

> The worker, Isabel, saw a pregnant woman on the street at a pay phone. It was the middle of winter and the

woman had two children with her, who looked about ages 5 and 4. Isabel thought that the mother looked like she was in trouble, so she stopped the car and approached the woman. She introduced herself and asked if she could help. The woman gave her name, Maria, and explained that she was on the phone to her sister. She was trying to leave home because her husband was having an affair with an American woman whom he had also gotten pregnant. Isabel invited her and the children to come to the family support center with her. After offering coffee and food to her and the children, and finding books and toys for the children, Isabel listened to Maria's story. Maria was afraid to go to a shelter because of her lack of English. She had been in this country for eight years and, fortunately, was here legally. Together they devised a plan. The first step was to find temporary housing for Maria. She was able to reach her sister, who was willing to keep her and the children for a few nights. However, the sister had five children of her own and lived in very crowded conditions, so this could not be a permanent arrangement.

The next step was to get medical care. To get Medicaid, Maria needed a note from a doctor saying she was pregnant. Isabel took her to the health clinic and got her signed up for prenatal care. The following week, Maria talked with her pastor about housing, and he found an apartment for her near the church, owned by another parishioner.

Maria began coming to the parents' group once a week. She was quite depressed but found some comfort in the interaction with other parents. Since child care was provided, the weekly sessions also gave her a needed break from caring for her children. She was able to get a part-time job cleaning motel rooms, to supplement her husband's child support.

In weekly sessions with the family support worker, Maria began to try to plan for the future, after the baby was born. Trained as a trailer mechanic, she hoped to return to work and was using the time of her pregnancy to explore options for child care. At the worker's suggestion, she is on the waiting list of the mental health center for counselling on her depression and on her marital problems.

Building Community Cohesiveness

The following example shows how a community program improved the neighborhood as an environment for families and children (Chappelle & Robinson, 1993). The Family Resource Partnership, located in Tucson, Arizona, was created by the Tucson Urban League and the Tucson Community Foundation to help residents in one community meet their goals for neighborhood improvement.

> *The [initial neighborhood assessment] interviews found that a significant degree of isolation and mistrust exists within neighborhoods. People who didn't know their neighbors expressed longing for the "good old days" when families knew everyone on the block and could count on their neighbors for support. The Partnership families have tried to recreate that feeling of community through Family Nights. Once each month, on a Friday evening, families gather at the Family Resource Partnership Center to share food, play games, and make friends. Parents and children play together. New neighborhood families are invited to join in. The positive consequences of these gatherings are reflected in parents' comments. "I feel that my neighborhood is safer. My children know where the other Partnership families live and know they can go there if they are in trouble or if they need a safe place." These opportunities to relax are treasured. As one parent put it, "This is a time when we can come be together, and laugh. I can get away from my problems." (Chappelle & Robinson, 1993, pp. 7–8)*

Advocacy

A key skill for family support workers is the ability to advocate on behalf of the families in the program and to teach the families how to be more effective at finding and using resources. Parents may need help in negotiating with schools and health care bureaucracies, and in locating employment, transportation, day care, and emergency services. Family support workers may act as mediators and negotiators for families in getting needed resources.

As family support programs become more established in their community, staff become involved in area-wide organizations to coordinate services. Because they work closely with neighborhood families, staff are aware of the unmet needs and community problems that hinder parents from managing their families, and can become effective advocates for community improvement.

ASSESSMENT OF FAMILY SUPPORT

Family support programs have grown rapidly, outpacing the development of research and evaluation studies that could guide and shape them. An increasing number of process and outcome evaluations have been conducted, however, and have produced some results useful to program planners and policy makers.

The reported experiences of many participants and staff of family support programs provide testamentary evidence of the effectiveness of family support programs. Parents typically report that they felt "listened to," perhaps for the first time in their dealings with the human service system, that they learned new ways to interact with family members, and that they received assistance with problem solving or obtaining basic services. They may also have learned that they are entitled to have positive relationships with others and to take time for their own development. Staff report that parents seem to "soften" appreciably in their interactions with their children. They are more relaxed, seem to enjoy their children more, and speak of them more positively. They make more sensitive responses to their children (Cooke, 1992; Powell, 1986).

In addition to testimonials from families and workers, there is some evidence from formal, outcome-based research. Family support programs present challenges to rigorous evaluation designs. The development of instruments suitable for measuring changes in parenting has lagged. Rigid designs requiring pre- and posttests and comparison groups are difficult to implement without disrupting the voluntary, empowering qualities of the programs and are financially beyond the reach of most programs.

In spite of these difficulties, several recent reviews of research have pointed to modest but measurable effects of family support programs (Powell, 1994; Weiss & Halpern, 1990). Regarding parental competency, parents have been shown to increase their knowledge of child development and their skills in managing their children's behavior. They have ex-

hibited more realistic expectations of their children and more ability to use play and other interactions to support their children's development. Studies of comprehensive programs have shown effects on parents' general coping ability and personal development, such as returning to school or taking other steps toward economic self-sufficiency.

Studies of the effects of programs on infants and young children have shown short-term improvements in developmental tests. So far, it has been difficult to assess long-term effects, given the small number of longitudinal studies.

Studies of home-visiting programs have found that the health and well-being of the parents and children improved compared with families not receiving services. Specific benefits identified by research include fewer low-birth-weight babies, fewer reported cases of child abuse and neglect, higher rates of childhood immunizations, and more age-appropriate development in children (Olds et al., 1998).

Because of the wide range of program designs, generalizing about overall program effects is difficult. However, there is enough evidence from research to conclude that family support programs can have a positive impact on parents, children, and the quality of family life.

EARLY CHILDBEARING AND THE FAMILY

Historically, teenage pregnancy was a problem left to parents, schools, faith communities, and social service agencies. But starting in the 1970s, the old concern about unwed mothers expanded into an explosive controversy about teenage sexuality and teenage parenting. The issues involved—adolescent sexual intercourse, contraception, abortion, adoption, race, family structure, child support, and welfare dependency—evoke impassioned conflicts of value and ideology.

The enormous increase in systematic study on the subject since the 1970s is an outgrowth of a highly publicized belief that the nation is confronted with a dangerous "epidemic" of teenage pregnancies. It is curious that during most of the past 40 years, while interest in the problem increased dramatically, births to teenagers were actually declining. A major cause for the increased public attention has been the *great increase in the percentage of teenage births to parents who are not married.*

There have been both positive and negative outcomes from this concern about a teenage pregnancy epidemic. Positively, it has increased public awareness and acceptance of the need for contraceptive services and education about sexuality for adolescents, and has stimulated federal funds for such services and for research. Negatively, however, the "crisis" approach has been sexist in its focus on the problem-laden, sexually active female; it has clouded the realities of birthrate statistics; and it has directed attention away from the more fundamental social and economic problems that warp the lives of so many teenagers, especially if they are black or come from low-income backgrounds.

Americans hold complicated beliefs about teen pregnancy. A recent survey showed that most Americans believe that high school students should not be sexually active, and that society has a responsibility to strongly promote abstinence to teenagers. At the same time, survey respondents also believe that sexually active teens should have access to contraception (Princeton Survey Research Associates, 1997). Thus, they support the view that a variety of approaches are needed in addressing teen sexuality; programs should take a multi-pronged approach, incorporating abstinence as a value and also information on contraception.

Trends in Teenage Childbearing

The rate of teenage childbearing is almost 50 percent lower than it was in the 1950s. Explanations for this reduction include better access to sex education, contraceptives, and abortion. Overall, young people are waiting longer to marry, probably in part because it takes longer to achieve financial independence. Young women from middle-class backgrounds have many life options besides motherhood; if they do become pregnant, they may terminate the pregnancy or choose adoption. On the other hand, young women from poverty-stricken backgrounds are more apt to see parenthood as an achievable path to adulthood.

They are more likely than middle-class young women to become pregnant and to keep the child.

The 1980s saw an increase in the rate of teen pregnancy, although this trend appears to have been reversed, and rates are once again decreasing. Between 1991 and 1996 teen birth rates declined in all fifty states and the District of Columbia, and have declined for white, African-American, Native American, Asian, and Hispanic women aged 15 to 19. The rate for African-American teens, previously the highest of all races, declined the most, down 21 percent from 1991 to reach the lowest rate ever for this ethnic group. The 1996 rate for all races was 54.7 live births per 1,000 women aged 15 to 19, down 12 percent from 1991 when the rate was 62.1 (Teen Birth Rates Down, 1998). About 500,000 women aged 15 to 19 gave birth in 1996. These changes in the birth rate to teenagers are reflected in Figure 3.3.

This decline reflects changes in sexual behavior since the 1980s. The amount of sexual activity among teenagers has leveled off or declined, particularly among suburban youth. Contraceptive use has increased dramatically among African-American teenage females, and among males of all races. Use of oral contraceptives has declined, having been replaced by new methods of contraception like Norplant and DepoProvera (Abma & Sonenstein, 1998). These trends indicating behavioral change are recent and for the most part small; therefore it is not clear whether they will be sustained. They are of great interest, however, because they are the first indicators that the decades-long trend toward increased sexual activity among teenagers could be reversed. Although the trends are encouraging, sexual activity among teenagers is still high; by their seventeenth birthday, 52 percent of girls and 58 percent of boys have had sex (Busting Myths, 1996).

In contrast to earlier decades, when many unmarried mothers relinquished their children for adoption, today only about 5 percent do so. To a large extent, this trend reflects a change among white teenagers; relinquishment for adoption has never been a common practice among blacks.

Although the overall rate of births to teenagers has declined since the 1950s, the percentage of those

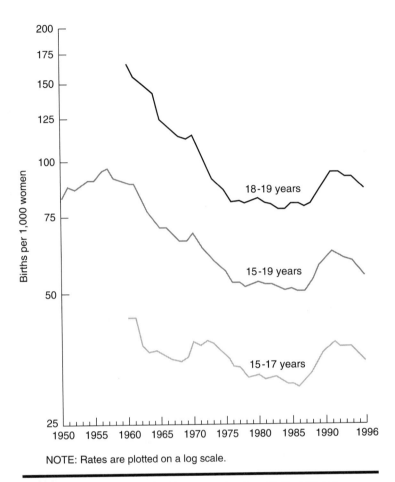

NOTE: Rates are plotted on a log scale.

FIGURE 3.3 Birth Rates for Teenagers by Age: United States, 1950–1996

Source: S. Ventura, S. Curtin, & T. Mathews. (1998). *Teenage births in the United States: National and state trends, 1960–96.* Washington, DC: U.S. Department of Health and Human Services, National Center for Health Statistics.

births to parents who are unmarried has increased greatly. Today, most teen births are to unmarried parents. This is a matter of great concern, because many of these young people may not be ready financially or emotionally to undertake the care of a child. Early childbearing increases the chances that the family will remain poor, which also carries risks to the child. Figure 3.4 illustrates the large increase in the percentage of births to teenagers who are unmarried.

The National Campaign to Prevent Teen Pregnancy (1997) points out the following reasons why teen pregnancy is a problem requiring national attention:

- The United States has the highest rate of teen pregnancy and births in the western, industrialized world.
- More than four out of ten young women become pregnant at least once before they reach the age

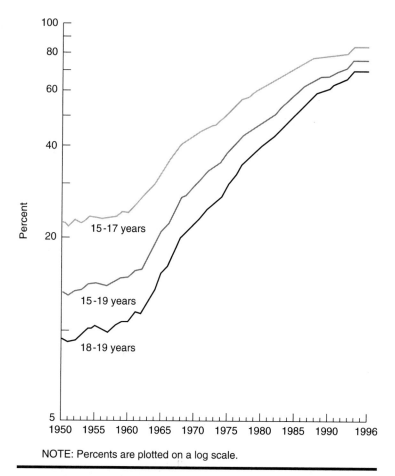

NOTE: Percents are plotted on a log scale.

FIGURE 3.4   Percent of Births to Unmarried Teenagers by Age: United States, 1950–1996

Source: S. Ventura, S. Curtin, & T. Mathews. (1998). *Teenage Births in the United States: National and state trends, 1960–96.* Washington, DC: U.S. Department of Health and Human Services, National Center for Health Statistics.

of 20—nearly one million a year. Most of these pregnancies are unintended and most are to unmarried teens.

- The younger a teenager becomes sexually active, the more likely she is to have had unwanted or involuntary sex. Close to four in ten girls who had first intercourse at 13 or 14 report it was either nonvoluntary or unwanted (Moore & Driscoll, 1997).

- Research indicates that early childbearing may have negative consequences for the parent and for the child.

Public Welfare and Teenage Childbearing

A frequently heard explanation for adolescent childbearing is that some girls become pregnant in order to receive welfare. Supporting this view is the fact that nearly half of all teen mothers, and nearly three-quarters of unmarried teen mothers, receive welfare within four years of giving birth (Ooms & Herendeen, 1990). The interest of policy makers in the issue of teen pregnancy stems partly from the associated financial burden; estimates of the combined costs of welfare, food stamps, and Medicaid attributable to adolescent childbearing range from $7 billion to $25 billion a year (Center for Population Options, 1992; The National Campaign to Prevent Teen Pregnancy, 1997). Plotnick (1993) and Wilcox, Robbennolt, O'Keefe, & Pynchon (1996) reviewed research findings on the relationship between welfare and teenage pregnancy and found that the evidence is inconclusive on whether the availability of welfare encourages teenagers to become pregnant. Other considerations, particularly the vision the adolescent has of her future, are much more influential. However, once a teen is pregnant, the availability of financial assistance tends to increase her alternatives for decision making because it lessens the pressure to marry, have an abortion, or place the child for adoption (Allen & Pittman, 1986).

The new welfare law, the Personal Responsibility and Work Opportunity Reconciliation Act of 1996, contains several provisions intended to discourage out-of-wedlock births and adolescent childbearing. Minor teen parents are required to live in an adult-supervised setting and to stay in school in order to receive benefits. States are required to submit plans for establishing pregnancy-prevention programs and for educating the public on statutory rape. Bonuses are available to states that reduce out-of-wedlock births and abortion among the general population, and states may also get grants to provide abstinence education. States are encouraged to develop special voluntary paternity procedures for teens (Barkan, 1996; Mayden & Brooks, 1996).

Decision-Making Patterns

Research indicates that few teenagers set out to become pregnant. Rather, pregnancy results from the teen's lack of attention to the consequences of his or her behavior (Furstenberg, Brooks-Gunn, & Chase-Lansdale, 1989). If teens had to take a pill to become pregnant, probably very few would do so. However, once pregnant, teenagers may become increasingly committed to the pregnancy as it proceeds. Parents may be initially hostile or upset, but usually end up being supportive. Thus parenthood is the end result of a complex series of choices the teenager makes, either intentionally or by default: the decision to be sexually active; the decision to use contraceptives effectively; the decision to have an abortion or carry to term; and finally, the decision to keep or release the baby for adoption.

As adolescents move from childhood to adulthood, they gradually develop adult patterns of decision making. Mature decision making is a "strategic process of making choices" (Kaufman, 1985) and requires the ability to think logically. Teenagers vary widely in their ability to apply logical reasoning to such emotional areas of life as sexuality and romance. Strauss and Clarke (1992) have identified patterns of thought characteristic of adolescence that may lead to poor sexuality choices. *Egocentrism* is the thought process in which the adolescent sees herself as unique, someone to whom the ordinary rules of the game do not apply. Adolescents with this thought pattern may consider themselves invincible; they mean it and aren't just making lame excuses when they say, "I didn't think it could happen to me." *Risk taking* is another characteristic of adolescence, because their immature problem-solving skills make them unaware of consequences. They may have factual information but may not apply it to themselves. Immediate concerns are more real than possible future consequences, an attitude that explains why they sometimes discontinue contraceptives because of the inconvenience. Then they are genuinely surprised when pregnancy occurs. Their inability to think realistically about the future may leave them unable to develop goals that would provide a framework for making choices in the present.

We must turn all of our educational efforts to training our children for the choices which will confront them. (Margaret Mead)

Teenagers may have very *limited coping skills,* relying mainly on denial and avoidance. They may not have learned yet to reflect on how they characteristically solve problems or on possible alternative choices. They may believe that "things just happen."

Socially, adolescence is a time of separation from parents, which may manifest itself in rebellion against the standards of the older generation, including standards of sexual responsibility. Increased *dependence on a peer group* may replace dependence on parents, leading to an over-susceptibility to peer pressure.

The tendency of teenagers to dramatize their lives may lead to *unrealistically romantic visions* of their relationships; they may see unprotected intercourse as an affirmation of love and commitment. Some young people believe that planning in advance for intercourse reduces the spontaneity; they want to be swept away with passion. This may reduce their sense of personal responsibility for their actions ("I couldn't help it; I was overwhelmed with emotion"). Some peer groups condemn girls who are prepared for intercourse, believing that preparation means that they are too experienced.

Associated Conditions and Causes

As parenting by teenagers has become more publicly visible, its causal patterns, the conditions associated with it, and its consequences have become matters of keen concern in America. One of the methodological limitations of much of the research on teenage parenting is that confounding variables are often confused with causes of adolescent childbearing. Low achievement at school, race, social class, intrafamilial relationships, and other conditions that were characteristic of these young people or were in their environment prior to their becoming pregnant may be moderately or highly correlated with teenage pregnancy, but are not necessarily "causes" of it (Abrahamse, Morrison, & Waite, 1988).

Teenagers from poor families are much more likely than other teenagers to become parents. As family income rises, the proportion of teens who become parents declines. Another strong predictor of teenage pregnancy is academic skills; doing poorly at school and scoring low on tests of basic skills are associated with teen parenthood (Children's Defense Fund, 1994).

The limited number of studies on characteristics of adolescents and use of abortion have found that those who use abortion tend to come from intact, non-Catholic, and nonwelfare families and are more likely to be white than black or Hispanic. They are doing well in school before the pregnancy, have relatively high educational goals, are self-confident, and come from white-collar or skilled working-class families. In general, young women in favorable economic circumstances are substantially more likely than others to abort a pregnancy (Chilman, 1980; King, Myers, & Byrne, 1992).

The vision a teenager has of her future influences the decisions she makes in the present, and research has shown that young women who do not feel successful in school, who do not expect to have satisfying careers, go to college, or marry are more likely to become parents at a young age (Cervera, 1993; Manlove, 1995). Factors that tend to impede a young person's chances, such as low socioeconomic status and membership in an historically oppressed racial or ethnic group, may influence their decisions on sexual activity and early parenthood in this way. "Research reveals that poverty status often breeds attitudes of fatalism, powerlessness, alienation, a sense of personal incompetence and hopelessness in respect to striving for high educational and occupational goals. This is especially apt to be true when racism combines with poverty to reduce one's life chances" (Chilman, 1980, p. 797).

Race and Ethnicity

In 1996, the number of births per 1,000 females aged 15 to 19 was 25.4 for Asian and Pacific Islanders, 48.1 among whites, 75.1 among Native Americans, 91.7 among African Americans, and 101.6 among Hispanics, who have now surpassed African Americans in having the highest birth rate (Ventura, Curtin, & Mathews, 1998). The higher rates for some ethnicities are related to differences in poverty rates, education, and employment and earnings potential. Research also indicates that differences exist among ethnic groups in rates of premarital sexual activity and contraceptive use (Furstenberg, 1987; Children's Defense Fund, 1994; Smith, 1997). Reflecting the overall trend of a decline in the number of teenage births, the birth rate for various ethnic groups in the United States has also declined in the 1990s. Figure 3.5 shows the changes in birth rates for teens of various ethnic groups over time.

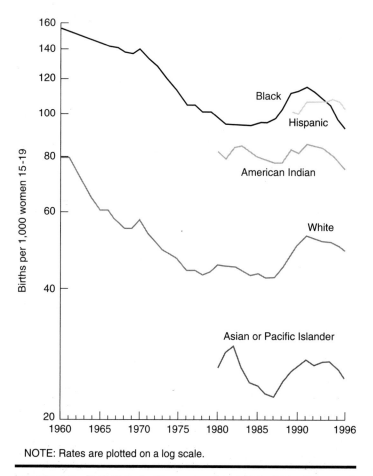

NOTE: Rates are plotted on a log scale.

FIGURE 3.5 Birth Rate for Teenagers Aged 15 to 19 by Race and Hispanic Origin: United States, 1960–1996

Source: S. Ventura, S. Curtin, & T. Mathews. (1998). *Teenage births in the United States: National and state trends, 1960–96.* Washington, DC: U.S. Department of Health and Human Services, National Center for Health Statistics.

Black teen births are of special concern to the black community and all advocates of black children because a large number occur to mothers who are not married (90 percent) and because nearly half (45 percent) the mothers are in the younger end of the age spectrum, age 17 or younger. These factors exacerbate the health, economic, social, and educational consequences of teen pregnancy (Furstenberg, Brooks-Gunn, & Chase-Lansdale, 1989).

Traditionally, black families have provided supportive and nurturing environments for young mothers and their babies, whether or not the birth occurred within a marriage. Informal adoption has been a common community practice, "reflecting the cultural value of the inherent worth of each child no matter what the birth circumstances" (Dore & Dumois, 1990, p. 94; Stack, 1974). Ladner (1985) points out that the black grandmother traditionally assumed some of the responsibility for the care of grandchildren born outside marriage. However, the declining age of black unmarried mothers has resulted in a generation of very young black grandmothers who are likely to be in the workforce and are not home with the grand-children. The consequence of the changing role of grandparents is that teenage mothers "are growing up more isolated than any generation before them. . . . Without the support of their parents, without the continued nurturance teenage mothers received from their own mothers in the past as they nurtured their babies, these girls today are physically isolated and emotionally deprived of the continued socialization they so desperately need" (Ladner, 1985, p. 19).

Among Hispanics, the profile of teenage parent-hood varies according to subgroup. Puerto Ricans have a high rate of unmarried, teenage parenthood (Children's Defense Fund, 1988). Informal fostering of children within the kinship network is common among Puerto Rican families, who often send way-ward teenagers to relatives on the island or back to the mainland. Gutierrez (1987) states that in Puerto Rico the cultural norm is for teen pregnancies to lead quickly to marriage, and this norm survives among many who have emigrated to the mainland. For these families, the pregnancy of an unwed daughter is apt to create a crisis. Ortiz and Vazquez-Nuttall (1987), on the other hand, believe that a young woman who becomes pregnant outside of marriage is seldom ostra-cized anymore and can usually be assured of a home for herself and her child.

Among Mexican Americans, teenage parenthood is not uncommon; however, over half of teenage mothers are married. Cuban and South and Central American groups have smaller proportions of births to unmarried teenage mothers than do other Hispanic groups or whites (Children's Defense Fund, 1988).

Consequences of Early Childbearing

In considering the consequences of teenage parent-ing, it must be kept in mind that underlying factors that were present in the lives of these new parents prior to pregnancy and childbirth may also be present afterwards. Thus behavior and conditions, such as the variables discussed above as correlates of becoming pregnant and giving birth, may later be observed and assumed to be outcomes of teenage parenting instead of simply being later manifestations of patterns present or in formation much earlier. Nevertheless,

the teenager who becomes a parent is vulnerable to a range of new high-risk factors, risks to herself and to her child as well.

Teen mothers are more likely than other mothers to receive late or no prenatal care. Only three in five re-ceive prenatal care during the first trimester, and one in ten receive no prenatal care or obtain it only in the last trimester (Children's Defense Fund, 1994). The reasons include the teenager's denial of or wish to con-ceal the pregnancy; lack of initiative; lack of informa-tion about the importance of prenatal care or of how to obtain it; fear or distrust of the health system; and, for teenagers in poverty, lack of access to quality care. Many of the tasks of pregnancy are burdensome to adolescents, leading them to ignore critical elements of care. The need to maintain a consistent nutritious diet is a significant example. Lack of timely prenatal care is a primary factor in maternal complications of birth, such as prematurity, toxemia, hypertension, and syphilis.

Young women who become pregnant are more likely to drop out of school (Butler, 1992). With lim-ited educational backgrounds, teenage mothers are more likely to have lower incomes and earning po-tential during their future years than are young women of similar backgrounds who put off child-bearing until they are older.

Those who become parents as teenagers are more likely to have more children, to experience more mar-ital instability, and to be the sole adult in the house-hold, than are those who postpone childbearing (Butler, 1992). These conditions exacerbate their eco-nomic vulnerability, as married couples are much less likely to be poor than are single-parent families. As a result of the pattern of divorce and separation, it is es-timated that 70 percent of children born to teenage mothers have spent part of their childhood in a single-parent household by the time the children are 8 years old. Young mothers are far less likely than older mothers to receive financial help from absent fathers (Danziger & Nichols-Casebolt, 1987–1988).

Furstenberg and his colleagues, in a follow-up study of Baltimore women 17 years after they became first-time parents, found that in the long run many women who became mothers as teenagers were able to make up for lost ground in later life. Educational achievement, fertility control, and marriage were routes to improved circumstances in later life, and women who accomplished success in these areas largely caught up with those who started their families when they were older (Furstenberg, Brooks-Gunn, & Morgan, 1987). Although this research shows that becoming a teenage parent does not consign the parent to a hopeless future, nonetheless the weight of evidence is that becoming a parent in the teenage years adversely affects one's future prospects for economic comfort and marital stability.

Developmental Risks to the Children of Teenagers

Partly because of the failure to receive prenatal care, teenagers are more likely than others to have low-birth-weight babies (under 5.5 pounds at birth). Low-birth-weight babies are at higher risk of dying during infancy; those who survive are at risk of lifelong developmental disabilities such as mental retardation, blindness, deafness, cerebral palsy, and other health problems (Children's Defense Fund, 1994).

Chilman (1980), Furstenberg, Brooks-Gunn, and Chase-Lansdale (1989) and Dubow & Luster (1990) show consistent correlations between adolescent childbearing and developmental outcomes of the resulting children. Children of teenage parents have significantly lower scores in cognitive development, are more likely to repeat a grade at school, and have higher rates of behavioral problems than do children born to older parents. Sons are affected more negatively than daughters; they tend to have lower reading scores and are rated in larger proportions as having learning disabilities. School adjustment problems of the children of teenage mothers are likely to increase, with more serious behavior and school problems being apparent by adolescence. In the Baltimore study, Furstenberg, Brooks-Gunn, and Morgan (1987) found that, "even with the mothers' best intentions, many [of the children] seemed destined to repeat [their mothers' struggle] based on the startlingly high rates of high school failure, juvenile delinquency in males, and fertility in females" (p. 105). Furstenberg, et al. (1987) noted that the mother's pattern of unstable relation-

ships with adult men was repeated by the children. Few of the children's fathers took an active role in their upbringing or paid child support. Lack of consistent relationships with men may have contributed to the problems noted in the children of teen mothers.

Services to Pregnant and Parenting Teenagers

Working with adolescent mothers is characterized by the special aspects of their teenage status that seem incongruous with motherhood. Most adolescents are in a stage of personality development that, with its rapid contrasts in maturity and immaturity and varying degrees of rebellion against adult authority, confronts the social worker with special problems in understanding which of the young mother's reactions are normal responses for an adolescent and which are unduly distorted by the early pregnancy. The stress the teenage mother feels is apt to be intensified by her having to adapt herself to disharmonious roles—that of young adolescent and that of mother (Bucholz & Gol, 1986).

Sexual Abuse and Teen Pregnancy. It is usually assumed that teen pregnancies are the result of liaisons between the teen mother and a boyfriend. However, evidence is mounting that for some pregnant teenagers, particularly younger ones, the pregnancy may be the result of sexual abuse. The perpetrator is usually a family member or known to the family. Legal, health, and social work professionals working with teen parents must be aware of the possibility that the pregnancy may have been the result of forced intercourse, and provide services for survivors of sexual abuse as well as family support services (Mayden, 1997; Moore & Driscoll, 1997). See Chapter 7.

The Decision to Parent or to Choose Adoption

The number of infants relinquished by their mothers for adoption has sharply declined in the past 25 years. Currently, only about 5 percent of children of teenage mothers are released, in contrast to 19 percent in the early 1970s (Bachrach, 1986; Lewin, 1992). Changes in society's acceptance of single mothers and increased employment opportunities for women make the decision to be a single parent more feasible than in earlier times.

Young women who "place" tend to have the most to lose by teenage parenthood. They are likely to be in school, to have parents who went to college, and to have aspirations for college or other personal achievement goals. In contrast, characteristics associated with parenting include living in poverty, having a family on public assistance, and dropping out of high school (Bachrach, 1986).

Family members, particularly the teenager's mother, peers, and the baby's father, may have a strong influence on the teenager's decision to relinquish or keep the infant. Unmarried mothers who decide to parent the child usually receive emotional support and practical help from family members; a pregnant teenager's anticipation of help from her family may influence her decision to place or parent (Cervera, 1993).

The ability of the mother to weigh alternatives wisely and think through the consequences may also affect her decision to place or parent. In the past, some agencies and caseworkers have been reluctant to broach the subject of adoption with pregnant teenagers under the principle of client self-determination or because they were unprepared to counsel teenagers on the difficult issues of grief and loss inherent in a plan of relinquishment. Social workers can help pregnant teenagers weigh the burdens and benefits of keeping or placing the child, and imagine the future for themselves and the child given different decisions about adoption (Cervera, 1993). See Chapter 10.

Research indicates that teenagers believe that if they choose adoption, they would always wonder about their child in the future; the prospect of never knowing how their child was faring is a powerful influence on their decision not to pursue adoption (Barth, 1987). The concept of open adoption, in which the relinquishing mother retains some connection to the developing child, appeals to some of the mothers as a way of reducing uncertainty about their child's future. (See Chapter 10).

The extent to which adolescents are informed about adoption and would be more receptive to adoption if they were given a more accurate understanding of it was of interest in another study (Mech, 1988). In a part of this study, data were collected from fifty-seven health facilities claiming to offer pregnancy counseling services. About 14,400 pregnant teenagers came to these facilities during a one-year period for pregnancy testing and prenatal care. Because most health facilities do not emphasize adoption as an alternative, these facilities offered a unique opportunity to devise a model for communicating balanced information to pregnant adolescents about choices: keeping the baby, placing for adoption, or seeking abortion. Predemonstration study had shown that many of the health facility counselors had little conviction that adolescent parenting was a desirable decision, although, paradoxically, they asserted firm support to teenagers who decided to parent. They tended to believe that few pregnant teenagers wanted information about adoption. Many of the counselors were uninformed about adoption procedures and unable to make a clear distinction between agency adoptions and those arranged privately.

A counseling model for communicating adoption information to pregnant adolescents was developed to identify those adolescents who appeared interested and were willing to consider an adoption plan. They were provided with information about adoption, access to an adoption agency, and support for their interest in adoption. These pregnant teenagers were encouraged to discuss adoption with birthparents who had chosen to place their child, with adoptive parents, and with an agency social worker. Group sessions were provided with a focus on decision making during pregnancy. Findings showed that the adoption screening procedures, in conjunction with the counseling supports, were associated with low but important increases in adoption placement rates. The program was most effective with white adolescents who recorded a placement rate of 15.7 percent. For nonwhite adolescents (52 percent of the sample) the overall relinquishment rate was only 2.1 percent. The combination of limited availability of adoptive homes for black infants coupled with a shortage of black staff to provide adoption counseling posed barriers for minority adolescents who might have wanted to place children for adoption in nonrelative homes.

Family Support Programs and Teen Parents

Family support programs for teen parents are needed because of the documented deficits in development that often occur in the teen parents and in their children (see above). Teen parents may need help in developing knowledge of child development, a positive, realistic attitude toward parenting, and an appreciation for appropriate parenting techniques. Research has shown that teen mothers are less cognitively prepared for parenthood than are older mothers (Sommer et al., 1993; Karraker & Evans, 1996). Early intervention is key, since the longer the teen parent takes to learn adequate parenting skills and to create a supportive environment, the greater the risk to her child. Although family support programs for teen parents are very similar to the family support programs described earlier in this chapter, the Family Resource Coalition (no date) has identified certain essential qualities reflective of the parent's adolescent status:

- Emphasis on strong teen-staff relationships which are accepting yet firm and which foster high levels of trust
- Awareness of and sensitivity to the cultural milieu in which teens live, including understanding of kinship and extended family systems and of community norms
- Focus on teens' visions of the future, while working incrementally to attain skills needed for current goals and an improved sense of control
- Provision of long-term support, which starts, ideally, during the pregnancy and remains intact throughout the first several years of the child's life
- Coordination of services to ensure linkages to health, education, and economic resources
- Involvement of fathers and extended families in supporting teen mothers and their children
- Opportunities for teen peers to share and validate their experiences (p. 4).

Family support programs for teen parents, like other family support programs, usually offer a range of services, including home visits before and after the birth, groups with educational and supportive components, outreach to the extended family, and coordi-

nation with health care. In addition, they generally emphasize educational and vocational goals for the mother, and include a component on preventing second pregnancies through improved contraceptive use and setting future goals.

Recruitment and retention are particularly important considerations in programs for teenage mothers. Because teenagers are likely to be in the developmental process of separating from their family of origin and achieving independence, accepting services can seem like a threatening regression to dependency. Pregnancy, with its physiological changes, important decision making, and impending unknowns of delivery and subsequent parenting, can overwhelm the teenager. Under stress, the pregnant adolescent may resort to denial in order to maintain psychological equilibrium. Teenagers of color or from disadvantaged communities may distrust social services, which they may have experienced in the past as coercive, intrusive, authoritarian, and not helpful. Young persons with these attitudes are not likely to find the program on their own; the program must go to them. Building a reputation in the community for helpfulness while respecting participants is essential for recruitment and retention and is a process that may take several months or even years.

The Clinical Infant Development Program in Baltimore, Maryland, serving a largely African-American population, developed a strategy of "persistent outreach" to engage pregnant teenagers. Although workers remain respectful of the participant's right to refuse services, they rarely accept the adolescent's "no" as a final refusal or a severing of the therapeutic connection. They learn "to walk the thin line of persisting in outreach with sensitivity and without intrusion" (O'Leary, Shore, & Wieder, 1984, p. 300). They recognize that spotty attendance, missed appointments, and lackluster participation in group sessions are to be expected, and that teenagers benefit from the program in spite of these behaviors. Many reluctant participants become much more involved in the program after the stress of pregnancy and birth are over, and their attitude toward their worker becomes much more positive. The teenager is then more likely to express the need for help and to form a positive relationship with the worker.

Evaluations of family support programs for teen parents indicate that the best results occur for prenatal medical services; it is well known that teenagers who get regular prenatal care are more likely than those who do not to have healthy pregnancies that result in healthy babies (Brooks-Gunn, McCormick, & Heagarty, 1988). Programs that encourage teenagers to continue their education and to become economically self-sufficient appear to help those who maintain their participation, but irregular attendance and attrition are common (Furstenberg, Brooks-Gunn, & Chase-Lansdale, 1989). During the past two decades, evidence has mounted that follow-up services after delivery can reduce the likelihood that a teenager will get pregnant again (Seitz & Apfel, 1993).

A supportive extended family can ameliorate many of the risks to children born to teenage parents. The family is the most significant refuge for adolescent childbearers immediately following birth (Furstenberg & Crawford, 1988). Staying with the family facilitates a division of labor in child care through collaborative arrangements that provide care for the infant and at the same time protect the young mother from the full impact of premature parental responsibilities. Such families serve as a system of apprenticeship to early childbearers. A major task for members of the household is to decide just how to integrate the child, and possibly also the infant's father, into the family (Cooley & Unger, 1991; Thompson & Peebles-Wilkins, 1992).

SERVICES TO FATHERS

The high level of interest in services to fathers reflects research showing that children whose fathers are positively involved with them tend to do better and that fathers who do not live with their children are more likely to provide financial support if they also nurture and care for their children (National Center for Children in Poverty, 1997). These findings increase concern about estimates that over half of all children will spend all or part of their childhood separated from one of their parents, usually their father (McLanahan & Sandefur, 1994). The trend toward fatherless families is increasing and is likely to be repeated by subsequent generations of children growing up in fatherless households. Although fatherless families live in all parts of the United States, they are particularly concentrated in some neighborhoods; three million children, or one in twenty, live in a neighborhood made up almost entirely of mother-only households (Levine & Pitt, 1995). Additionally, an increasing number of fathers (currently about two million) are raising children alone (National Center for Children in Poverty, 1997).

Social services, often explicitly or implicitly directed mainly at women and children, are challenged to find ways of reconnecting fathers to their families (Miller, 1997). The Fatherhood Project of New York City, a practice-based research initiative, has identified that defining and articulating clear expectations for fatherhood is a first step toward changing paternal behavior and the practices of social agencies that have the effect of discouraging father participation. According to the Fatherhood Project,

> . . . a man who behaves responsibly toward his family does the following:
>
> * He waits to make a baby until he is prepared emotionally and financially to support his child.
> * He establishes his legal paternity if and when he does make a baby.
> * He actively shares with the child's mother in the continuing emotional and physical care of their child, from pregnancy onwards.
> * He shares with the child's mother in the continuing financial support of their child, from pregnancy onwards. (Levine & Pitt, 1995, p. 5)

Fathers of Children Born to Teenage Mothers

Fewer adolescent boys than girls become parents, since teenage females tend to be several years younger than their male partners. Among fathers of children born to teenage mothers, fewer than half are under 20 years of age. Some older men are predatory in seeking out young teenagers. Those fathers who are teenagers tend to share the same characteristics as teenage mothers: they are often from poor, unstable households, have low educational levels, and little or no sense of future possibilities (Levine & Pitt, 1995).

Establishing Paternity

Important benefits accrue to children for whom paternity has been established. These benefits include financial support, such as Social Security payments, dependent allowance and educational benefits from the armed services, health insurance, benefits from worker's compensation, and child support. Although young unmarried fathers may have little income to contribute to their newborn children, their ability to contribute increases with time. There are also extremely important, intangible benefits from knowing one's parentage. Children who know the identity of their fathers can get valuable genetic information and medical history. Psychologically, paternity establishment gives children a stronger sense of their identity and the security that comes from having been "claimed" by both parents. Early establishment of paternity can strengthen the bond the father has to the child and encourage a pattern of responsible parenting.

Concerns about the poverty and dependency of never-married mothers have revealed that the child support enforcement system is at its weakest in establishing child support for children of unmarried parents. Until the father is legally identified, child support procedures cannot be activated, and the father has no legal responsibility to support. No national data are collected on the number of children for whom paternity is established or the number who remain in need of legal paternity action, but estimates are that only about a third of children born out of wedlock have had paternity established legally (Wattenberg, Brewer, & Resnick, 1991).

In spite of the importance of establishing paternity, many barriers, both attitudinal and systemic, to doing so exist. The Fatherhood Project has identified the following "barriers and biases":

- The underground economy, in which decisions about the father's contributions are tied to considerations of the mother's welfare eligibility
- Lack of knowledge by fathers that children could benefit through Social Security or the military if paternity were established
- Peer pressure, which in some neighborhoods promotes a cultural norm of making babies to establish masculinity but not of claiming them legally

- Resistance from the mother's family, particularly if the father has few employment prospects. The family may not realize that paternity establishment offers benefits to the child even if the parents are not married.
- Lack of knowledge by professionals who may not know the benefits of paternity establishment or what procedures are needed. Some professionals help create a self-fulfilling prophecy by assuming unmarried fathers are irresponsible and by ignoring or "disrespecting" them. (Summarized from Levine & Pitt, 1995, pp. 101–102)

Primary responsibility for establishing paternity rests with the states, which vary widely in established procedures. The federal government now requires each state to develop a simple process for voluntarily establishing paternity and to create hospital-based programs so that parents can establish legal paternity in the hospital.

Growing evidence suggests that the best time to establish paternity is at birth. Offering parents an opportunity to complete paternity procedures in a simple, voluntary way at the hospital capitalizes on the "glow of the moment." Most fathers are present at the birth of their child or visit the hospital during this time and find it a moving experience. One young man said, "It straightened my life out a lot. It gave me a look out on how life really is . . . puts you in the pictures instead of seeing it through glass" (Wattenberg, Brewer, & Resnick, 1991, p. 7).

Demonstration programs in hospital-based paternity establishment have produced the following "lessons learned" (Levine & Pitt, 1995; Pearson & Thoennes, 1996):

- Simplify the state's paternity establishment procedures, eliminating the need for court appearances, notarized signatures, copies of previous divorce decrees and other documents, requirements that forms be registered in government offices, and all fees. Replace these procedures with simple forms that can be signed and witnessed at the hospital.
- Train key hospital staff to educate parents on the importance of paternity establishment to the child. Experience has shown that hospital per-

sonnel respond best if the emphasis in training is on the benefits to the child and the father. Linkage to child support enforcement should be discussed but not the main focus of training. Help hospital personnel to examine and overcome negative feelings about unmarried fathers and remind them that not all are "deadbeat dads."

- The focus of paternity workers should be on *educating* parents about the benefits of paternity establishment and the procedures for accomplishing it. The main reason parents do not establish paternity is that they are not *educated*.
- Give the father a copy of the paternity papers. One program administrator observed, "Everybody tells me that dads appreciate it. When dad gets his affidavit, he takes it as an outward sign of his psychological bonding" (Levine & Pitt, 1995, p. 106).

Support Programs for Young Fathers

Family support programs emphasize the interdependence and importance of all family members, and should be attuned to giving both mothers and fathers the benefit of program services. Programs can promote father involvement by including both parents in activities, providing opportunities for fathers to network and learn from each other, offering services outside of working hours, and being sensitive to the shame fathers may feel if unemployed, emphasizing their role as emotional nurturers as well as financial providers.

Some programs have developed a special emphasis or focus on young fathers, such as the Institute for Responsible Fatherhood and Family Revitalization in Cleveland, Ohio. The innovative leader, Mr. Charles Augustus Ballard, was an unmarried teenage parent who declared paternity after being released from jail. He started the project in 1982 in one of Cleveland's community health centers, serving African-American and other inner city fathers. He and his outreach workers began doing home visits to encourage fathers to bring their children in for immunizations and to get the fathers involved in the lives of their children through such activities as reading, changing diapers, and going to school conferences. Although the program had originally been thought of as a drug and violence prevention program for chil-

dren, Mr. Ballard soon realized that it was meeting the needs not only of children but also of fathers. "We discovered that men need children. Fathers need their children. The more we can nurture the father part, the healthier he will become. When you connect the father with his child from an emotional standpoint, other things change—he changes his thinking and his environment" (Levine & Pitt, 1995, p. 111).

An important component of the project is intensive mentoring. The young person is called a "protege," meaning one under the protection of an older adult, with the implication that he is being groomed for a future role. Staff mentors have a potent role in modeling adult behavior. " 'The thing I learned from this program was the importance of marriage,' said a young father. 'Well, do they teach you about that?' 'No, but I've been to the worker's home. I've been on picnics with him and his family,' said the protégé" (Levine & Pitt, 1995, p. 111). The program has shown that talking about behavior is not nearly so effective as modeling it.

The key to the success of this program is the positive, respectful relationships that staff establish with the youth. Most of the young men did not have fathers or adult men as significant role models while they were growing up. The program founder believes that they need to have a personal relationship with an older man who is functioning well in work and family life. In this way, the young person can see for himself what the expectations are and get personalized help along the path to responsible fatherhood and competency in adult life.

[W]hat drives them to be good fathers is the nurturing piece. . . . [I]f a man understands his child's needs and that his future is in his child, he will change his behavior. Charles Augustus Ballard, Director of a support program for young fathers. (Levine & Pitt, 1995, p. 115)

PREGNANCY PREVENTION PROGRAMS

In contrast to earlier decades, when teenage pregnancy was seen as a manifestation of maternal pathology, today services related to teenage pregnancy usually take an ecological approach to understanding early parenthood. Teenage pregnancy is seen as a complex phenomenon with multiple causes, including social and economic conditions, cultural attitudes about early parenthood, family, school and peer influences, and developmental and psychological issues related to individual teenagers.

Public concern about the costs and consequences of teenage pregnancy have led to increased interest in developing effective programs to prevent teenagers from becoming parents. Originally it was thought that if teenagers had access to birth control and information on how to prevent pregnancy, pregnancy rates would fall. Experience has shown that this approach is too simplistic. During the past 25 years, extensive research on teenage pregnancy has indicated that this phenomenon is complex and has many causes. Therefore, prevention programs have also gained in complexity. Ooms and Herendeen (1990) have summarized research on these programs.

Abstinence Programs

Abstinence programs operate from the framework of social learning theory, which holds that people's behavior is influenced by the norms and behavior of the people around them. The programs communicate that it is desirable to postpone sexual intercourse and, failing that goal, that unprotected sex should be avoided. The programs may take place in schools or in community settings such as hospitals. They usually combine information on human sexuality with specific, concrete skill-building sessions on how to resist influences encouraging sexual activity. Some programs also work to increase parent-child communication on sexuality and sexual choices. Evaluations suggest that they may encourage virgins to continue abstaining from sex and help those who are sexually active to use contraceptives more effectively (Barth, Leland, Kirby, & Fetro, 1992; Howard & McCabe, 1992). The 1996 welfare reform law provided funding to states to expand programs based on communicating the desirability of abstention from sex until marriage (Haskins & Bevan, 1997).

Family Planning Programs

The goal of family planning programs is to improve access to contraceptives through such agencies as family planning or school-based clinics, with the ultimate aim of more effective use of contraceptives. Teenagers often prefer such clinics to the family physician because of their lower cost and privacy, as teenagers may fear that the family doctor will tell their parents. Clinics have demonstrated their effectiveness in reducing unwanted births through both increased contraceptive use and increased abortion. Critics of these clinics believe that their presence encourages youth to engage in sexual activity that they would not do if the services were unavailable. To date there is no research to show conclusively that the presence of family planning clinics increases sexual activity. It is an area that needs further research (Ooms & Herendeen, 1990).

Life Options Programs

Studies have shown linkages among dropping out of school, delinquency, substance abuse, and teen pregnancy, indicating that unprotected sexual activity is part of a cluster of high-risk behaviors. Life options programs try to reduce risky behavior through discussion groups of possible careers, remedial education, and job counseling. The effectiveness of these programs in preventing pregnancy has not yet been determined because they are still relatively new and few in number. They vary greatly in intensity, program content, and sponsorship. Early results indicate that such programs can reduce pregnancy, and much is being learned about how to establish and implement them. Successful programs have built strong neighborhood coalitions in which the entire community communicates the message that young people have many options and should not settle for too-early childbearing (Ooms & Herendeen, 1990, p. 13).

Parental and Community Involvement

A challenging area for pregnancy prevention is the involvement of parents. Parental attitudes and behavior and the quality of parent-teen communication are important factors in teenage sexual behavior, a fact which argues for involving parents in pregnancy prevention programs. However, controversy and confusion surround the question of how parents should become involved. Parents and teenagers can feel confused about parents' role in guiding their teenager because sexual behavior is essentially private, and the onset of sexual relationships marks a stage in the separation of the young person from the family. Prevention programs may involve parents in the planning process, which ensures broad community support for sex education or school clinic programs, and in developing a curriculum directed at parents, particularly on communication with teenagers.

The community in which young people live can reinforce norms of sexual responsibility and of concerned and committed parenting. A number of efforts to mobilize community involvement are under way. For example, the Male Responsibility Project of the National Urban League is a community education program to make more visible the important role African-American fathers play in the lives of their children. This message is reinforced with posters, such as one depicting a father tenderly holding his young child, captioned by the lyrics of a Billie Holliday song: "God bless the child who's got his own" (Battle, 1990). The program also involves African-American fathers as role models and mentors for young men.

Faith communities have also begun developing programs to influence the behavior of adolescents. These may include discussion groups on values and abstinence; explorations of life options, including tutoring and mentoring; and public information efforts to reinforce the value of family commitment.

Ooms and Herendeen (1990) reviewed evaluation studies of pregnancy prevention programs and identified several general conclusions from research on teenage pregnancy:

- Because of the wide array of socioeconomic, cultural, ethnic, religious, and social factors associated with early teenage sexual activity, "preventive remedies need to be complex and multi-levelled and different strategies will be more effective with different subgroups of the population" (p. 2).
- While teenagers at every socioeconomic level are at risk, those from severely disadvantaged backgrounds are at much higher risk of pregnancy.
- Research is beginning to show that pregnancy is related to other forms of adolescent risk-taking

behavior, such as drug use. This suggests that pregnancy prevention programs should not be planned and executed in isolation from other preventive initiatives.
- Research has documented that teenagers are greatly influenced in their sexual behavior by the attitudes, values, and behavior of those close to and important to them, such as parents, peers, and romantic partners. This finding suggests that preventive programs should broaden their target beyond teenage girls to include young men, parents, community and religious leaders, and community institutions.
- So far, little is known about how to mount effective prevention programs for a subpopulation of great concern and at high risk: young women and their partners who begin sexual activity at a very young age and who have repeated pregnancies. Their behavior is deeply rooted in family and cultural experiences and has proved resistant to preventive strategies. For them, successful preventive efforts must be far-reaching, involving their parents and neighborhoods, and must mobilize broad cultural and economic change in disadvantaged communities.

HISTORICAL ASPECTS OF SERVICES TO TEENAGE PARENTS

Services relating to adolescent pregnancy have changed greatly during the twentieth century. In view of the high degree of concern engendered by the incidence of out-of-wedlock births and in view of the many unanswered questions about causation and appropriate societal responses to the phenomenon, it is enlightening to examine some of the earlier views about unmarried parents and the professional response to the problem.

Treatment of the unwed mother early in this century was based on these principles, laid down by the founder of the National Florence Crittenton Mission: (1) Isolation of the unwed girl from the immoral influences of the outside world is an important element in her rehabilitation; (2) the experience of motherhood itself "is often the means of regeneration; hence the mother must be kept with the child *for the influence it will have upon her*" [italics added]; and (3) the child born outside of marriage should remain with its mother because it needs the maternal care that "only a mother can give" (Barrett, 1929, pp. 49–50).

Maternity homes developed policies and practices providing for authoritative supervision of the mother and child. In order to breast-feed a baby, a practice important to the infant's health in the days before sanitized milk, the mother might stay in a maternity home or in a protected family setting with the child for the first six months. After the nursing period, agencies usually expected that the mother might seek suitable employment and a new living arrangement. The most approved arrangement was for the mother to live with her baby in her family's home, or with relatives or friends, or even in a boarding home, so long as the baby was with her.

Adoption was least favored; rather, the best ultimate solution was considered to be the mother's marriage to a man who would accept her child. One part of agency supervision was an attempt to secure financial support for the mother. Because support from the father was considered part of the child's "rightful status," and agency funds to help the mother and child were limited, agencies usually participated actively in efforts to secure paternal support.

Interest in Adoption

During the 1930s, agencies began to respond to an increasing interest in adoption and to the requests for infants from would-be adoptive parents. With adoption as an increasingly acceptable solution, another change was reflected in an increasing emphasis on secrecy about the pregnancy. While earlier maternity homes had favored isolation of the unmarried mother as a means of furthering her rehabilitation through separation from her former life, this practice had not ensured secrecy about her pregnancy. Indeed, it could not, since the goal was to have her resume life in the community with her child. The practice of secrecy had certain disadvantageous effects. It encouraged an unwillingness on the part of agencies to initiate or even allow the unmarried mother to initiate paternity actions because of the likelihood of publicity. It led some agencies to a policy of regarding the alleged fa-

ther as of no importance to the situation, or at least to a policy of nonrecognition of the father as a means of "helping the girl to forget a disagreeable experience." It led in some instances to an agency's usurpation of parental duties, as when a young unwed mother was deliberately separated from her own parents to shield her from severe parental blame or from some other manifestation of disturbance in her relationship with her own parents (Reed, 1934, pp. 48–51, 157).

The Psychological Nature of Unwed Parenthood

Social work literature of the 1940s began to reflect a heavy emphasis on the psychological nature of unmarried parenthood. Social factors were seen as unimportant or at least secondary. Psychiatrists reinforced a growing conviction that unmarried mothers were almost always neurotic and incapable of providing good care for their children. Their problems and motivations were deeply embedded in the powerful emotions of their own early childhood. The best treatment, then, was psychotherapy for the mother and adoption for the child.

By the 1950s, the social work profession was heavily committed to an application of psychoanalytic principles in its casework method and thus looked less at social forces that might be contributing to out-of-wedlock pregnancy. The literature is replete with references to the serious emotional maladjustment of the unmarried mother, the pregnancy as a result of psychic pressures with which she cannot deal, and giving up the baby as a positive solution.

Underserved Ethnic Groups

During the 1960s, the social work profession began to be criticized because its involvement with most unwed mothers, particularly among the voluntary agencies, was limited to only one subset of the unwed mother population: white adolescents (Bernstein, 1963). Many voluntary child-placing agencies had tended to define their function in terms of adoption, and maternity homes increasingly had given priority to service for unwed clients who planned to relinquish their babies for adoption. Since the decision to keep a child is related to low socioeconomic (and thereby racial) factors, black and other nonwhite unwed mothers received less than their share of community services. Most social workers assumed that black children of unwed parents were accepted in a matter-of-fact way, that they were not faced with social ostracism, and that the black community's readiness to care for its children should be seen as a positive innate characteristic rather than as a response to a lack of social services. Some social workers questioned these broad generalizations, however. Davis (1948), at the United States Children's Bureau, warned that the common assumption that blacks accept unwed pregnancies leads to the premise that no action needs to be taken in behalf of black children.

Today we see a renewed interest in some of these earlier solutions to the problem of unwed parenthood. There are calls for maternity homes and other approaches that would reinstate a form of the "authoritative supervision" of the early decades of this century. The new welfare reform law of 1996 requires unmarried teen mothers to live in a supervised setting if they cannot live at home, in order to receive assistance. States are encouraged to provide group homes or other arrangements that offer the unmarried teen parent and her child the necessities of life in return for the mother's participation in a planned educational and social program.

There is also renewed interest in adoption as a resolution to teenage pregnancy. New efforts are being made to form partnerships between social workers and members of ethnically identified communities to devise culturally congruent approaches to teenage sexual behavior and parenthood. As social workers, policy makers, and advocacy groups propose "new" solutions to the old problem of teenage pregnancy, it is instructive to see how these solutions worked in the past, and how we can learn from these earlier efforts.

OTHER APPROACHES TO STRENGTHENING FAMILIES

Besides family support programs, a range of social services is available to support family life: homemaker services, counseling, crisis centers, support groups, and other services.

Therapeutic services stem from the identification of a serious problem, the development of an assessment, and the engagement of an individual or group in a course of social treatment whose goal is to stimulate change from maladaptive functioning to more adaptive behavior. People may seek these therapeutic services on their own initiative or be strongly encouraged to seek help; in any case, in varying ways and degrees they acknowledge a problem and choose to engage themselves in the treatment process. Typical examples are the casework treatment of a seriously emotionally disturbed boy or girl, the group work treatment of a number of children with similar handicapping behavior problems, the treatment of a mentally ill parent in an outpatient facility or hospital setting, and therapy based on the interaction of family members as a vital part of both the cause and the treatment of the family problems. Therapeutic services are essential for the deeply troubled family or the seriously upset young person. These services are specialized and relatively well developed among the agencies offering family and child services; however, such services are too frequently not available in communities where children and families most need them.

Auspices and Settings

Services for families and children may be offered by public or private agencies, whether profit or nonprofit, and in a variety of settings. Their purpose may be to help children with their own problems or to strengthen their family life. Services may be given by child welfare or family service units of public welfare departments, by voluntary family service agencies, by neighborhood service centers, by settlement houses, by child guidance clinics or other mental health agencies, and by courts, hospitals, and schools.

Casework with Individual Parents

A principal method in family and child services is work with individual parents. A commonly used approach is one that is strength-based and solution-focused. In this approach, the social worker and parent together usually arrive at an assessment early in the intervention process, emphasizing the issues the parent wishes to address and identifying strengths the parent brings to the plan for resolving them. Through helping the parent identify the problem causing stress in the family, understand some of its roots, and recognize the feelings and behaviors the problem produces, the social worker hopes to enable the parent (and indirectly other family members) to act more effectively. Social workers may lend strong emotional support to parents. They may attempt to clarify a situation by identifying troublesome components of the unhappy family situation and the alternative actions the parents may take. They may offer interpretations of the parents' feelings and behaviors to help them gain insight into the behaviors that affect all family members.

From their knowledge of the community and its resources, social workers may also offer information and suggestions about opportunities that can benefit parents or other family members. They may refer the parents to another social agency for a specialized service, prepare written summaries of the family situation and the basis for referral, and sometimes continue as a liaison between the family and the new agency until service gets underway. They may act directly on behalf of the parents by accompanying them in stressful situations, such as when they must ask for supplementary financial assistance or confront a negligent landlord about repairs. They may teach effective ways of getting attention to legitimate requests for service in the community, or they may act on the parents' behalf by speaking for them and actively pressing for attention to their rights and needs.

Social workers may perform other tasks or employ other innovative techniques, but at all stages of the service they seek to involve parents in an assumption of responsibility for the solution to family problems.

Crisis Intervention.   A crisis intervention approach looks for the source of the client's difficulty in the social situation rather than in personal pathology (Lufton, 1982). Proponents believe that effective professional intervention at crisis points can help clients resolve the immediate problem and prevent more serious problems from arising later on. Because family members are often more motivated to use help at a point of crisis, when their usual coping patterns have

proved inadequate, a social worker may help family members improve their performance of social roles and strengthen their ability to solve problems.

In one program, for example, crisis workers are teamed with police to respond to calls of spouse abuse. The workers may be able to help the parties resolve the immediate domestic problem, or they may help the victim find safe emergency housing. Over the long run, they support and encourage victims through legal processes if the assailant is being criminally prosecuted. The workers also can help abused wives make permanent changes in their living situation when they feel ready to do so (Fein & Knaut, 1986). This program illustrates that preventive intervention at a point of crisis not only capitalizes on people's readiness to use help but can also mobilize and coordinate community and agency resources on behalf of families with multiple needs.

Treatment for the Individual Child

Children are often interviewed or observed by social workers outside the presence of their parents for the purpose of making a social study and evaluation as a basis for recommending certain actions in their behalf. But many children can best be helped by participating directly in the modification of their troubling behavior, in which case a social worker may give therapy to the individual child. Therapy is offered on the assumption that the child is a person in his or her own right, that the child's behavior is not just a reflection of the parents' problems, and that the child is an important actor in the situation, one capable of significant self-expression in words or deeds.

Social-Cognitive Treatment.   The term "social-cognitive" refers to a set of techniques for promoting sociobehavioral and cognitive changes in children. The therapist, or child helper, supports the child's efforts to increase his or her social and cognitive skills. Social skills include accepting the influence of adults and others in authority, engaging in reciprocally enjoyable social exchanges with friends, and resolving conflict appropriately. The child helper may teach the child cognitive strategies such as anger-management training, social problem solving, and self-instruction. The latter includes the ability to set goals, make commitments to reach those goals, evaluate one's own progress, and manage one's wishes and desires. This approach recognizes the significance of the social environment and of the attitudes and coping skills that children have learned (Barth, 1986).

The helping process is structured as a sequence of tasks, from initial contact through identifying the problems, developing a treatment plan, completing a plan, evaluation, and termination (Barth, 1986). The intervention will have both social and cognitive aspects. If, for example, a teenager has a habit of skipping school, the child helper might involve the family, the school, and the community in establishing a coordinated strategy, with consistent reinforcers for the desired behavior. Parents, attendance officers, and proprietors of popular teenage hangouts can all help the child to decide to go to school rather than spend the day elsewhere.

> In designing cognitive interventions, the child helper understands that students may believe that school success will not accrue to them regardless of their effort or skill. Older youth especially often judge themselves to be victims of teachers' arbitrariness or prejudice. These beliefs are stubborn. Antidotes to such belief systems are not always successful, but some cognitive strategies have promise. . . . The child helper can encourage students to identify students similar to themselves—that is, those of the same race, with similarly cut hair, or with a history of trouble—who are achieving success. This may help make success seem more possible and advance a discussion of the coping strategies that others use to manage in a sometimes hostile environment. Cognitive rehearsal of successful interactions in such environments may also forward reentry into the classroom. (Barth, 1986, p. 246)

Other Work with Children. Social workers blend theories and techniques in various ways to help children reach certain developmental goals, learn about themselves and the world around them, utilize opportunities, meet an unexpected crisis, or resolve a conflict that impairs their social functioning.

They may apply principles of ego psychology to provide a supportive casework service to a child to help him or her during a stressful ordeal, such as a period of extended and frightening medical care. In such an instance the goal may be to modify the child's disabling feelings and behavior and strengthen the ego's capacity to endure and adapt to frustration.

Social workers act as casefinders in the early detection of children's problems. They seek to discover or develop opportunities for children in the community. They refer them for a variety of community services, for recreational programs, music and art activities, or health services. Sometimes they seek a relatively simple service, such as the assignment of a volunteer who offers a child companionable friendship and new experiences. Sometimes the need is complex, and social workers must bring together a combination of resources and professional personnel to collaborate in behalf of a child. In a variety of ways they seek to discover children's strengths and reinforce these in their daily lives.

Group work is an increasingly common approach used in working with children. Groups may take place at schools or social service agencies, and have been used successfully with children as young as four or five. Groups are commonly organized around an experience the children share, such as having a substance-affected family member, living in a divorced family, suffering abuse or neglect, or having adjustment difficulties at school. Many groups for children have both an educational and a therapeutic purpose, encouraging children to learn new ways of coping and also to explore feelings in a safe environment.

Family Therapy

Sometimes distress revolving around a particular child in a family or some problem that a family encounters lends itself most effectively to a form of family therapy, or family unit treatment.

The varying forms of family therapy are based on the view that family life is a system of relationships between people. The goals are directly related to the well-being of children and the enhancement of their learning and growth opportunities. For example, the goals may be to open communication between family members, educate them as to how to get along within the family and the community, help parents to take on sound child-rearing practices, and clarify and stabilize family roles.

Family therapy may provide several advantages: attention to each individual member as well as the family as a whole; an opportunity for the reenactment of crucial themes within a family and a broader and more balanced diagnostic view of the strengths and weaknesses in the family; a reduction of the pressure on a single family member, particularly a child who may have been singled out by other family members as their special problem; and an increase in the probability that improvement in a child's behavior and direction of growth will be sustained by changes and adaptations within the total family pattern of interaction (Hartman & Laird, 1983).

Adaptations in family therapy have been made in order to bring services to some families with urgent problems who generally do not use existing services. For example, the Mental Hygiene Clinic of the Henry Street Settlement in New York City undertook an experimental approach to bringing mental health services to low-income families in ways they could use. Because persons from this social class appeared to need mental health services keenly but had often not followed through with service offered in traditional ways—for example, appointments in the office and formal interviews—treatment was shifted from the clinic to the home in a series of regularly scheduled, nonthreatening visits.

The social worker's role was either to act as a catalyst to dramatize the particular conflict or to break into the destructive pattern as it occurred. Then the social worker demonstrated ways and means of settling differences, with family members testing out and talking about the new methods. This excerpt from a case record is illustrative (Levine, 1964, pp. 24–25):

The Cs are a Chinese family living in a crowded, four-room slum tenement. Mr. C. is fifteen years older than his wife and there are four school-age children, the oldest 12 and the youngest 6. . . . Tom, the 9-year-old, . . . had violent, uncontrollable temper outbursts, during which he would run out of the school building. His 10-year-old brother Danny was released a few months ago from a state hospital and, except for his

readmission to school, there was little follow-up by the after-care clinic in assessing his problems or needs in readjustment to the family and community. . . .

Typical forms of discipline used by the parents were to isolate the children when they got into fights, beat them in explosive fits of anger, or tell them that Danny was crazy and should be left alone. . . .

The worker's visits were planned at a time when all family members were present, which was before the evening meal. The children were always around the kitchen table ready to begin a game or to work with clay. In the first few sessions Mr. C. would sit nearby but not participate except to criticize or correct the children, and Mrs. C. would continue preparing the evening meal, with one eye on the table to see what was going on. During this period, too, considerable attention was diverted toward Danny, who, in keeping with the parental discipline of isolating him, hung back and would not come into the room. He finally came in after some tentative moves.

In the games or other activities Danny did quite well in learning to share materials and adult attention while the worker was present. Yet, as the time approached to terminate the session, he would invariably provoke one of the other children. During one session he claimed he won a game of cards, although Tom was the real winner. Mrs. C. immediately pushed the winning cards to Danny in order to avert the tantrum she anticipated. Tom, furious, ran off in tears. Enlisting the parents' help, the worker brought Tom back, gently but firmly, and the issue was discussed before everybody. As this was clarified, other grievances between the brothers were brought out. Danny had broken a table that Tom had made in the settlement workshop and proudly taken home. The parents claimed it was beyond repair. The worker had the table brought in, looked over, and repaired then and there, with Danny's help.

In succeeding weeks, incidents such as these and others typical in the lives of children who are in rivalry and angry with each other were either observed or reported during the activity sessions. Each time the worker would encourage each to tell his version and bring out his feelings, and each time the grievance or dispute would either be settled to everybody's satisfaction or it would be evident that angry feelings were in better control.

This approach of "treatment in the home" had parallels with more traditional family casework and family therapy in that it included the provision of concrete services, focused on the whole family, and attempted to build on whatever family strengths could be detected. However, these clients could not be viewed as "motivated" in the usual sense; modification of behavior patterns through some level of insight therapy was not attempted. The Henry Street experiment is illustrative of the origins of in-home services, which are now proliferating.

Group Work Approaches

Some parents and children have needs that lend themselves to social group work. Social workers may bring together a number of parents or children who can be expected to profit from an association together under social work or other trained guidance. Group work may be the only service offered, or it may be used as a supplement to casework with individuals or to community work.

In selecting group members, the intent is to make possible a climate of acceptance and support as an aid to learning, and the emergence of a process of meaningful interaction within the group. For some, the group provides security. Groups may be formed of parents who share common problems or demands, such as parents of mentally retarded children, mothers of one-parent families, and parents who are facing difficulties with their children's adolescent behavior.

Some group work carries a strong component of counseling or therapy and is directed primarily toward problems in a participant's personality and interpersonal relationships. Other work with groups may be termed *family life education,* which focuses more directly on imparting to parents knowledge that can be expected to have a positive effect on family life. Some groups are fused with elements of both education and counseling (Berry, 1988).

Services for Families with a Handicapped Member

Families whose members have disabilities face the same stresses as other families: single parenthood, ge-

ographic mobility, and attenuated extended family ties. In addition, families with a disabled member face other stresses; they must find special services needed by the disabled person and deal with a range of service professionals; and they often must direct special attention to the tasks of balancing their lives and supporting the needs of *all* family members. Too often service professionals assume that families with a disabled member are dysfunctional and inadequate. Particularly if the disability is severe emotional illness, professionals may assume that the family is the source of the problem. This assumption adds to the family's already considerable burdens (Will, 1988).

For many years, children with serious mental or physical disorders were institutionalized. Their disabilities were thought to require expert treatment in a highly specialized environment. Treatment plans often excluded parents either purposely or by default. Since the 1960s, public policy changes have caused a shift away from institutional care and toward community-based supports for families. This change recognizes that families with a disabled member can sustain satisfying family life with the right kind of external supports (Friesen, Griesbach, Jacobs, Katz-Leavy, & Olson, 1988).

The National Institute of Mental Health is sponsoring projects to help states design and try out family-centered services for families with a severely emotionally disturbed child. These projects value individualized service plans, in which the needs of the child and family dictate the mix of services provided. They also value the personal dignity of the children and families served, respecting their wishes and goals, and involving them as vital partners in all aspects of the service plan (Stroul & Friedman, 1988). Services may include child care, crisis intervention, legal assistance, housing, recreation, homemaker services, parent education, counseling, transportation, therapeutic camping, respite care, educational programs, and vocational counseling. With the help of these projects, families organize themselves and meet together for social support, information sharing, and advocacy efforts directed toward local and state governing bodies. Through informal parent-to-parent interaction and more formalized self-help organizations, parents benefit from knowing they are not alone and can make positive changes in their lives.

Homemaker Service

Homemaker service in behalf of children is provided by a governmental or nonprofit health or welfare agency to enable children to receive care in their own homes when their mother for any number of reasons cannot fully meet her maternal and homemaking responsibilities. In such instances, the agency provides a homemaker (sometimes called a home-health aide), a woman trained in child care and in home management who comes into the home for a few hours or more a day to perform a variety of tasks to help the family maintain itself. In addition to the help provided by the homemaker, the sponsoring agency tries to facilitate use of other social or health services by family members as may be needed. Homemaker service was originally conceived of as a short-term emergency service to hold families together during a crisis. While it still serves this purpose, the present-day conception of this service permits its application to a broader range of situations and to all socioeconomic groups.

Homemaker service can be helpful in a variety of situations. In some the mother is absent from the home. In others she is present but unable to meet her responsibilities fully. In either case, the homemaker's function is to help the family maintain itself and improve its level of functioning. Homemaker service is also a useful resource in homes when a mother needs to learn better household practices or child care. She may lack the knowledge or motivation needed to meet her responsibilities; an accepting and competent homemaker can demonstrate ways of fulfilling her role more effectively and, in so doing, provide support and encouragement that nourish her motivation. Sometimes a mother's excessively poor housekeeping threatens the family with eviction; a homemaker can stave off this action while she teaches the mother to perform more adequately.

The usefulness of homemaker service has been demonstrated in a variety of socioeconomic groups and problem situations. It has kept families together during a period of crisis and avoided unhappy alternatives—haphazard care of children by neighbors, children scattered among relatives, or children left alone and unsupervised. Homemaker service can be provided at less cost in terms of both money and human stress than can foster care, particularly when there are several children in the family.

TRENDS AND ISSUES

Institutionalizing Family Support

In the 1990s, family support and parent education have been high on the national agenda. These programs are part of reform efforts in public welfare, public education, child welfare, and health care. The Family Preservation and Support Services Act of 1993 put substantial federal funds into state child welfare programs specifically targeted for prevention. In addition, several pioneering states have initiated state-supported family programs. Government interest in family support represents a shift in focus from crisis intervention centered on child protection to family-oriented preventive services.

Weiss (1990) has pointed out that family support programs have a value base that is consistent with both conservative and liberal ends of the political spectrum. From the conservative point of view, these programs are valuable because they promote self-supporting families and the development of children into independent adults. Conservatives also are attuned to the self-help, nonbureaucratic aspects of the programs. Liberals endorse the programs, which acknowledge the need of families for external support from communities and government. Thus, Weiss concludes, these programs "are important nationally, not least because they are helping to establish and demonstrate a new middle ground for family policy, and because they can provide the conceptual framework necessary for integrating disparate initiatives—from welfare reform to abuse and neglect prevention—into community-based systems to strengthen families" (Ibid., p. 4).

The increasing role of government represents a new stage in the development of family support programs. Many began as grassroots, local efforts, supported as demonstrations by private foundations and can now expect increased and more stable funding as they become linked to government (Koser, 1996). The linkage of family support programs with government, while it holds the promise of more stable funding over time, also creates the risk that the programs, in order to qualify for funds, will have to compromise their approach and lose those aspects that make them effective. Schorr (1991) has identified points of possible conflict between the attributes of effective services and the ways of large service bureaucracies:

- Comprehensiveness, a characteristic of family support, is at odds with the categorical funding of most government programs.
- Flexibility and front-line worker discretion are at odds with the traditional training of professionals and managers and with conventional approaches to assuring accountability.
- Intensiveness and individualization are at odds with pressures to assure equity despite insufficient funds.
- A long-term preventive orientation is at odds with pressures for immediate payoffs.
- A program's ability to evolve over time is at odds with the pervasiveness of short-term and often unpredictable funding. (p. 8)

Schorr recommends creative funding approaches such as the decategorization of certain categorical funds and automatic waivers. These mechanisms could be targeted to geographic areas that are at risk. Eligibility for services would be linked to residency in the area, not to identified individual failure or need. The neighborhood focus, by channeling money from various governmental agencies to a small geographical area would, Schorr argues, make possible the establishment of a "critical mass" of services that would be sufficient to make a difference at a relatively low cost.

In summary, the increased involvement of state and federal governments in family support is a promising development because it offers the promise of sustainable funding and wider implementation. However, the planning process needs to be attentive to the risks that government involvement may destroy the characteristics that make the programs effective.

CHAPTER SUMMARY

Family support services are based on the principle that all families need help from time to time in order to fill their societal function of promoting the healthy development of all family members. Families may require services at times of crisis, such as after the death of a family member. Some families face special stresses to healthy functioning because of social and economic discrimination or other hardships. Single-parent families, gay and lesbian families, and families of color are particularly likely to need family support services because of the special challenges they face.

The United States has lagged behind other nations in developing a comprehensive array of supportive services to help families on a voluntary basis before child maltreatment or other symptoms of family breakdown occur. During the 1980s and 1990s, preventive services to families have expanded, first as a result of numerous efforts at the local level and later through linkages to federal and state funding. Today a wide range of family support services exist, financed through combinations of government and private sources, and offered in a variety of settings, including social service agencies, schools, welfare offices, and health departments. These programs take an empowerment focus, working in partnership with families to help them improve their level of functioning. Typical services include home-visiting programs, particularly to new mothers, parent education, drop-in and other center-based activities, and neighborhood organization. Family support services also advocate for families—individually, to help a family locate services, and on the political level—to identify gaps in services and work to fill them.

Services to pregnant and parenting teens are a particular focus of many family support services. Children and their parents in these families are often at risk for poor developmental outcomes. In addition to health, education, and social services for the mother and her child, the fathers of children born to teenage mothers also require a focused service approach. Fathers need help particularly with understanding their state's procedures for establishing paternity, and learning how to function appropriately in the paternal role. Services to prevent pregnancy are also needed and may be directed at young people, often in a school setting, or at changing attitudes about out-of-wedlock parenthood of entire communities.

Family support services have promised to strengthen families, to prevent family breakdown, and to promote positive personal development and family interaction. To date, however, they remain without a strong, stable funding base and are often not well coordinated with other services in the community.

FOR STUDY AND DISCUSSION

1. For an ethnic or racial group with which you are familiar, consider the group's definition of family, child-rearing patterns, and family roles. How have adaptations to dominant American society affected family functioning of this ethnic or racial group? How would you design a culturally competent family support program for this group?

2. Visit a family planning clinic. Ask the personnel to explain the services and procedures. How well are the alternatives presented: becoming sexually active; using contraception, having an abortion; choosing adoption?

3. Find out whether there is a family support program in your community. If so, learn the auspices under which it operates, funding sources, program goals, the number of families it serves, the range of services it offers, and eligibility requirements, if any. Discover whether the program has had any evaluation. Make an assessment of the benefits you see of the program and ways the program could improve. If possible, interview staff, participating families, and other service providers who know the program.

4. Review the development of settlement houses. What themes have reemerged in the family support movement?

5. What are the arrangements for establishing paternity in your state? Which agencies or courts are responsible? Are parents routinely counseled on paternity establishment at the hospital? Do procedures and practices work to encourage or discourage voluntary avowal of paternity?

6. At the present time, family support programs often are not linked with child welfare services such as child protective services, family preservation services, foster care, or adoption. In what ways could such a linkage be developed?

FOR ADDITIONAL STUDY

Dunst, C., Trivette, C., & Deal, A. (Eds.). (1994). *Supporting and strengthening families, Vol. I: Methods, strategies, and practices.* Cambridge, Mass: Brookline Books.

Family Resource Coalition. (1996). *Guidelines for family support practice.* Chicago: Author.

Kagan, S. L., & Weissbourd, B. (Eds.). (1994). *Putting families first: America's family support movement and the challenge of change.* San Francisco: Jossey-Bass.

Levine, J. A., & Pitt, E. W. (1995). *New expectations: Community strategies for responsible fatherhood.* New York: Families and Work Institute.

McGoldrick, M., Giordano, J., & Pearce, J. K. (1996). *Ethnicity and family therapy* (2nd ed.) New York: The Guilford Press.

McLanahan, S., & Sandefur, G. (1994). *Growing up with a single parent: What hurts, what helps.* Cambridge, MA: Harvard University Press.

INTERNET SITES

Family Education Network. An educationally focused Web site for parents, with resources, an on-line community, and links to other sites. Education partners include the PTA and the American Association of School Administrators. Internet address: http://www.familyeducation.com

Family Resource Coalition of America. This organization offers a range of services designed to assist states, tribal organizations, and local programs to develop community-based family resource programs and networks. The Web site describes the organization and provides numerous links to demonstration programs and sources of information and support. Internet address: http://www.frca.org

Father & Family Link. Produced by the National Center of Fathers and Families at the University of Pennsylvania, this comprehensive Web site provides current, reliable information on research, practice, policy, and programs related to fathers in families. Internet address: http://www.ncoff.gse.upenn.edu/fatherlink/index.htm

National Parent Information Network.   This Web site offers resources from ERIC Clearinghouse on Elementary and Early Childhood Education and the ERIC Clearinghouse on Urban Education, provides information to parents and those who work with parents, and fosters the exchange of parenting materials. Includes information for urban/minority families. Internet address: http://www.ericeece.org

National Campaign to Prevent Teen Pregnancy. This national advocacy organization works to prevent teen pregnancy by supporting values and stimulating actions that are consistent with a pregnancy-free adolescence. The Web site includes information for parents, teenagers, advocates, and scholars. Internet address: http://www.teenpregnancy.org

National Center for Missing and Exploited Children.   This organization spearheads national efforts to locate and recover missing children and raises public awareness about ways to prevent child abduction, molestation, and sexual exploitation. Established in 1984, NCMEC operates under a Congressional mandate and works in conjunction with the U.S. Department of Justice's Office of Juvenile Justice and Delinquency Prevention. The Web site includes child photos and other child search services for use by parents and law enforcement agencies, as well as educational materials to prevent abduction. Internet address: http://www.missingkids.org

National Indian Child Welfare Association.   This organization serves tribes in the United States and helps them enhance their capacity to deliver quality child welfare services. The site contains information on community development, public policy, and information exchange. Internet address: http://www.nicwa.org

NativeWeb.   This Web site of a collective project provides a cyber-community for Earth's indigenous peoples, with an extensive search capacity and links to other sites. Internet address: http://www.nativeweb.org

Parents' Place.   This Web site run by and for parents contains parenting information on a wide range of subjects, shopping information, an extensive search facility, and numerous chat rooms. http://www.parentsplace.com.

U.S. Bureau of the Census: Children.   This Web site describes and provides links to U.S. government census data and recent reports on children. Internet address: http://www.census.gov/population/www/socdemo/children.html

Welfare Information Network: Teen Parents.   The Welfare Information Network offers up-to-date policy information on issues relating to public welfare. A special section of their Web site is devoted to policies concerning teen pregnancy. Internet address: http://www.welfareinfo.org/teen.htm

REFERENCES

Abma, J., & Sonenstein, F. L. (1998, April). *Teenage sexual behavior and contraceptive use: An update.* Available: http://www.welfare-reform-academy.org/ [April, 1998].

Abrahamse, A. F., Morrison, P. A., & Waite, L. J. (1988). *Beyond stereotypes: Who becomes a teenage mother?* Santa Monica, CA: Rand Corporation.

Addams, J. (1909). *The spirit of youth and the city streets.* New York: Macmillan.

Allen, M., Brown, P., & Finlay, B. (1992). *Helping children by strengthening families: A look at family support programs.* Washington, DC: Children's Defense Fund.

Allen, M., & Pittman, K. (1986). *Welfare and teen pregnancy: What do we know? What do we do?* Washington, DC: Children's Defense Fund, Adolescent Pregnancy Prevention Clearinghouse.

Amato, P. R. (1993). Children's adjustment to divorce: Theories, hypotheses, and empirical support. *Journal of Marriage and the Family, 55*(1), 23–28.

Amato, R. R., & Keith, B. (1991). Parental divorce and adult well-being: A meta-analysis. *Journal of Marriage and the Family, 53*(1), 43–58.

Attneave, C. (1982). American Indian and Alaska native families: Emigrants in their own homeland. In M. McGoldrick, J. Pearce, & J. Giordano (Eds.), *Ethnicity and family therapy* (pp. 55–83). New York: Guilford Press.

Bachrach, C. A. (1986). Adoption plans, adopted children and adoptive mothers. *Journal of Marriage and the Family, 48,* 243–253.

Barkan, S. (1996, December). *Teen parent provisions in the new law.* Washington, DC: Center for Law and Social Policy. Available: www.handsnet.org/handsnet2/welfarereform/Articles/art.849902466.html [September, 1997].

Barrett, R. S. (1929). *The care of the unmarried mother.* Alexandria, VA: National Florence Crittenton Mission.

Barth, R. P. (1986). *Social and cognitive treatment of children and adolescents.* San Francisco: Jossey-Bass.

Barth, R. P. (1987). Adolescent mothers' beliefs about open adoption. *Social Casework, 68*(6), 323–331.

Barth, R. P., Leland, N., Kirby, D., & Fetro, J. V. (1992). Enhancing social and cognitive skills. In B. C. Miller, J. Card, R. L. Paikoff, & J. L. Peterson (Eds.), *Preventing adolescent pregnancy.* Newbury Park, CA: Sage.

Battle, S. F. (1990). African-American male responsibility in teenage pregnancy: The role of education. In D. J. Jones & S. F. Battle (Eds.), *Teenage pregnancy: Developing strategies for change in the twenty-first century.* New Brunswick, NJ: Transaction Publishers.

Berkman, C. & Zinberg, G. (1997). Homophobia and heterosexism in social workers. *Social Work, 42*(4), 313–332.

Bernstein, R. (1963, March–April). Gaps in services to unmarried mothers. *Children, 10,* 50–51.

Berry, M. (1988). A review of parent training programs in child welfare. *Social Service Review, 62*(2), 302–322.

Billingsley, A. (1992). *Climbing Jacob's ladder: The enduring legacy of African-American families.* New York: Simon & Schuster.

Black, L. (1996). Families of African origin: An overview. In M. McGoldrick, J. Giordano, & J. Pearce (Eds.), *Ethnicity and family therapy* (2nd ed.), (pp. 57–65). New York: The Guilford Press.

Bronfenbrenner, U. (1987). Foreword. In S. L. Kagan, D. R. Powell, B. Weissbourd, & E. F. Zigler (Eds.), *America's family support programs: Perspectives and prospects.* New Haven, CT: Yale University Press.

Brooks-Gunn, J., McCormick, M. C., & Heagerty, M. C. (1988). Preventing infant mortality and morbidity: Developmental perspectives. *American Journal of Orthopsychiatry, 58,* 288–296.

Bruner, C., & Carter, J. L. (1991, November). Family support and education: A holistic approach to school readiness. *Network Briefs.* Denver and Washington, DC: National Conference of State Legislatures.

Bucholz, E. S., & Gol, B. (1986). More than playing house: A developmental perspective on the strengths of teenage motherhood. *American Journal of Orthopsychiatry, 56,* 347–359.

Busting myths about teenage childbearing (1996, Winter). *Casey Journalism Center Newsletter.* Available: http://www.inform.umd.edu:8080/EdREs/Colleges?JOUR/Casey/w962.html [July, 1998].

Butler, A. C. (1992, March). The changing economic consequences of teenage childbearing. *Social Service Review,* 1–31.

Center for Population Options. (1992). *Teenage pregnancy and too-early childbearing: Public costs, personal consequences.* Washington, DC: Author.

Cervera, N. J. (1993). Decision making for pregnant adolescents: Applying reasoned action theory to research and treatment. *Families in Society: The Journal of Contemporary Human Services, 74*(6), 355–365.

Chappelle, J., & Robinson, M. (1993, Summer). Creating family support programs: Mobilizing communities in Tucson. *Family Resource Coalition Report, 12,* 7–8.

Children's Defense Fund. (1994). Births to teens. *CDF Reports, 16*(8).

Children's Defense Fund. (1988). *Teenage pregnancy: An advocate's guide to the numbers.* Washington, DC: Children's Defense Fund, Adolescent Pregnancy Prevention Clearinghouse.

Child Welfare League of America. (1993). *Cultural competence self-assessment instrument.* Washington, DC: Child Welfare League of America.

Chilman, C. S. (1980). Social and psychological research concerning adolescent childbearing: 1970–1980. *Journal of Marriage and the Family, 42*(4), 794–805.

Class, N. E. (1968, September–October). Licensing for child care—A preventive welfare service. *Children, 15,* 188–192.

Cochran, M. (1991). Personal social networks as a focus of support. In D. G. Unger & D. R. Powell (Eds.), *Families as nurturing systems: Support across the lifespan* (pp. 45–48). New York: Haworth Press.

Cochran, M. (1993). Parent empowerment: Developing a conceptual framework. *Family Science Review, 5*(1 & 2), 81–92.

Cooke, B. (1992). *Changing times, changing families: Minnesota Early Childhood Family Education parent outcome interview study.* Minneapolis: Minnesota Department of Education.

Cooley, M. L., & Unger, D. G. (1991). The role of family support in determining developmental outcomes in children of teen mothers. *Child Psychiatry and Human Development, 21*(3, Spring), 217.

Cross, T. L. (1986). Drawing on cultural tradition in Indian child welfare practice. *Social Casework, 67,* 283–289.

Cross, T. L. (1996, Spring). Developing a knowledge base to support cultural competence. *The Prevention Report,* 2–5.

Dahl, A. S., Cowgill, K. M., & Asmundsson, R. (1987). Life in remarriage families. *Social Work, 32*(1), 40–49.

Danziger, S., & Nichols-Casebolt, A. (1987–1988). Teen parents and child support: Eligibility, participation, and payment. *Journal of Social Service Research, 11*(2/3), 1–20.

Davis, A. L. (1948, December). Attitudes toward minority groups: Their effect on social services for unmarried mothers. *The Child, 13,* 82–85.

Davis, L. E., & Proctor, E. K. (1989). *Race, gender, and class: Guidelines for practice with individuals, families and groups.* Englewood Cliffs, NJ: Prentice-Hall.

del Pinal, J. H. (1992). *Exploring alternative race-ethnic comparison groups in current population surveys* (Current Population Reports, Series P23–182). Washington, DC: U.S. Bureau of the Census.

Dore, M. M., & Dumois, A. O. (1990, February). Cultural differences in the meaning of adolescent pregnancy. *Families in Society: The Journal of Contemporary Human Services, 71,* 93–101.

Downs, S. W. (1994). *Neighborhood-based family support.* Detroit: Skillman Center for Children, Wayne State University.

Downs, S. W. & Nahan, N. (1990, Fall). Mixing clients and other neighborhood families: Neighborhood family support centers offer services plus peer support. *Public Welfare 48*(4), 26–33.

Downs, S. W., & Walker, D. (June/July, 1996). Family support while you wait: The waiting room approach. *Zero to Three, 16*(6), 25–32.

Dubow, E. F., & Luster, T. (1990). Adjustment of children born to teenage mothers: The contribution of risk and protective factors. *Journal of Marriage and the Family, 52*(2), 393–404.

Emlen, A. C. (1978). *Overcoming barriers to planning for children in foster care.* Washington, DC: U.S. Government Printing Office.

Family Resource Coalition (no date.) *Family support programs and teen parents.* [Online] Available: http://www.ericeece.org [July, 1998].

Family Resource Coalition. (1996). *Guidelines for family support practice.* Chicago: Family Resource Coalition.

Fein, E., & Knaut, S. A. (1986). Crisis intervention and support: Working with the police. *Social Casework, 67*(5), 276–282.

Fields, J. M., & Smith, K. E. (1998). Poverty, family structure, and child well-being: Indicators from the SIPP. (Population Division Working Paper No. 23). Washington, DC: U.S. Bureau of the Census. Available: http://www.census.gov/population/www/documentation/twps0023.html. [July 2, 1998].

Freeman, E. M. (1990). The black family's life cycle: Operationalizing a strengths perspective. In S. M. L. Logan, E. M. Freeman, & R. G. McRoy (Eds.), *Social work practice with black families* (pp. 55–72). White Plains, NY: Longman.

Friesen, B., Griesbach, J., Jacobs, J., Katz-Leavy, J., & Olson, D. (1988). Improving services for families. *Children Today, 17*(4), 18–22.

Furstenberg, F. F. (1987). Race differences in teenage sexuality, pregnancy, and adolescent childbearing. *The Milbank Quarterly, 65* (Suppl. 2), 381.

Furstenberg, F. F., Brooks-Gunn, J., & Chase-Lansdale, L. (1989, February). Teenaged pregnancy and childbearing. *American Psychologist, 44,* 313–381.

Furstenberg, F. F., Brooks-Gunn, J., & Morgan, S. P. (1987). *Adolescent mothers in later life.* New York: Cambridge University Press.

Furstenberg, F. F., & Crawford, A. G. (1988). Family support: Helping teenage mothers to cope. *Family Planning Perspectives, 10*(6).

Furstenberg, F. F., & Harris, K. M. (1990, April). *The disappearing father? Divorce and the waning significance of biological parenthood.* Paper presented at the Albany Conference on Demographic Perspectives on the American Family: Patterns and Prospects.

Garcia-Preto, N. (1996). Latino families: An overview. In M. McGoldrick, J. Giordano, & J. Pearce (Eds.), *Ethnicity and family therapy* (2nd ed.), (pp. 141–154). New York: The Guilford Press.

Garfinkel, I., & McLanahan, S. S. (1986). *Single mothers and their children.* Washington, DC: Urban Institute Press.

Gaudin, J., Wodarski, J. S., Arkinson, M. K., & Avery, L. S. (1990–1991). Remedying child neglect: Effectiveness of social network interventions. *Journal of Applied Social Sciences, 15*(1), 97–123.

Greif, G. L. (1985). *Single fathers.* Lexington, MA: Lexington Books.

Greif, G. L., & Hegar, R. L. (1992). Impact on children of abduction by a parent: A review of the literature. *American Journal of Orthopsychiatry, 62*(4), 599–604.

Gutierrez, M. J. (1987). Teenage pregnancy and the Puerto Rican family. In M. Lindblad-Goldberg (Ed.), *Clinical issues in single-parent households* (pp. 73–84). Rockville, MD: Aspen.

Gutierrez, L. (1994–1995). Empowerment and Latinos: Implications for practice. *Family Resource Coalition Report, 13*(3 & 4), 5–8.

Haight, W. L. (1998). "Gathering the spirit" at First Baptist Church: Spirituality as a protective factor in the lives of African-American children, *Social Work (43)*3, 213–221.

Hall, E. H., & King, G. C. (1982). Working with the strengths of black families. *Child Welfare, 61*(8), 536–544.

Hartman, A., & Laird, J. (1983). *Family centered social work practice.* New York: Free Press.

Haskins, R., & Bevan, C. S. (1997). *Abstinence education under welfare reform.* Available: http://www. welfare-reform-academy.org

Hernandez, J. (1987). Some facts in understanding Latino families. *Family Resource Coalition Report, 6*(2), 2.

Hetherington, E. M., Cox, M., & Cox, R. (1985). Long-term effects of divorce and remarriage on the adjustment of children. *Journal of the American Academy of Child Psychiatry, 24,* 518–530.

Highlights from the family preservation and support services program instruction. (1994, January). Washington, DC: U.S. Department of Health and Human Services.

Hill, R. B. (1997, Spring). Supporting African-American families: Dispelling myths, building on strengths. *Children's Voice, 2*(3), 4–7.

Hines, P. M., & Boyd-Franklin, N. (1996). African-American families. In M. McGoldrick, J. Giordano, & J. Pearce (Eds.), *Ethnicity and family therapy* (2nd ed.), (pp. 66–84). New York: The Guilford Press.

Howard, M., & McCabe, J. A. (1992). An information and skills approach for younger teens: Postponing sexual involvement program. In B. C. Miller, J. Card, R. L. Paikoff & J. L. Peterson (Eds.), *Preventing adolescent pregnancy.* Newbury Park, CA: Sage.

Hunter, A. G. (1997). Counting on grandmothers: Black mothers' and fathers' reliance on grandmothers for parenting support. *Journal of Family Issues, 18*(3), 251–269.

Husock, H. (1992, Fall.). Bring back the settlement house. *The Public Interest, 109,* 53–72.

Indian education: A national tragedy: A national challenge. (1969). Washington, DC: Committee on Labor and Public Welfare, Special Subcommittee on Indian Education; U.S. Senate, 91st Cong., 1st Sess.

Johnson, B. B. (1981). The Indian Child Welfare Act of 1978: Implications for practice. *Child Welfare, 60*(7), 435–446.

Karraker, K. H., & Evans, S. L. (1996). Adolescent mothers' knowledge of child development and expectations of their own infants. *Journal of Youth and Adolescence, 25*(5), 651–666.

Kaufman, D. J. (1985). An interview guide for helping children make health-care decisions. *Pediatric Nursing, 11,* 365–367.

King, R. H., Myers, S. C., & Byrne, D. M. (1992). The demand for abortion by unmarried teenagers: Economic factors, age, ethnicity and religiosity matter. *American Journal of Economics and Sociology, 51*(2), 223–235.

Koser, G. (Ed.). (1996). *From communities to capitols: State experiences with family support.* Chicago: Family Resource Coalition.

Kurdek, L. A. (1988). Social support of divorced single mothers and their children. *Journal of Divorce, 11*(3/4), 167–188.

Ladner, J. (1985). Adolescent pregnancy: A national problem. *New Directions, 12,* 16–21.

Lamarine, R. J. (1988). Alcohol abuse among Native Americans. *Journal of Community Health, 13*(3), 143–155.

Lee, B. (1992). *Monthly narratives of a family support program.* Unpublished manuscript. Detroit: Wayne State University, Urban Family Program.

Levine, R. (1964). Treatment in the home. *Social Work, 9*(1), 19–28.

Levine, J. A., & Pitt, E. W. (1995). *New expectations: Community strategies for responsible fatherhood.* New York: Families and Work Institute.

Levy, E. F. (1992). Strengthening the coping resources of lesbian families. *Families in Society: The Journal of Contemporary Human Services, 23*–31.

Lewin, E. (1981). Lesbianism and motherhood: Implications for child custody. *Human Organization, 40*(1), 6–14.

Lewin, T. (1988, August 24). Black churches: New mission on family. *New York Times,* pp. 1, 9.

Lewin, T. (1992, February 27). Sharp decline found in number of children up for adoption. *New York Times,* p. 10.

Light, H. K., & Martin, R. E. (1986). American Indian families. *Journal of American Indian Education, 26*(1), 1–5.

Lindblad-Goldberg, M. (1987). The assessment of social networks in black, low-income single-parent families. In M. Lindblad-Goldberg (Ed.), *Clinical issues in single-parent households* (pp. 39–46). Rockville, MD: Aspen.

Lott-Whitehead, L., & Tully, C. T. (1993). The family lives of lesbian mothers. *Smith College Studies in Social Work, 63*(3), 265–280.

Lufton, R. C. (1982). Myths and realities of crisis intervention. *Social Casework, 63,* 276–285.

Manlove, J. (1995). *Breaking the cycle of disadvantage: Ties between educational attainments, dropping out and school-age motherhood.* Washington, DC: Child Trends, Inc.

Mayden, B. (1997). Child sexual abuse: Teen pregnancy's silent partner. In *Adolescent sexuality, pregnancy, and parenting: Selected readings* (pp. 57–60). Washington, DC: Child Welfare League of America.

Mayden, B., & Brooks, T. R. (1996). *Welfare reform and teen parents.* Washington, DC: Child Welfare League of America.

McGowan, B. (1989). A neighborhood-based, comprehensive, child and family service. In S. Kamerman & A. J. Kahn (Eds.), *Social services for children, youth and families in the United States* (pp. 248–254). New York: Columbia University School of Social Work/Annie E. Casey Foundation.

McLanahan, S., & Sandefur, G. (1994). *Growing up with a single parent: What hurts, what helps.* Cambridge, MA: Harvard University Press.

Mech, E. V. (1988). *Final report summary for an inventory-based counseling model for communicating adoption to pregnant adolescents.* (Grant #APH00018). Washington, DC: Office of Adolescent Pregnancy Programs, Public Health Service, Department of Health and Human Services.

Meyer, D. R., & Garasky, S. (1993, February). Custodial fathers: Myths, realities, and child support policy. *Journal of Marriage and the Family, 55,* 73–89.

Miller, D. B. (1997). Adolescent fathers: What we know and what we need to know. *Child and Adolescent Social Work Journal, 14*(1), 55–69.

Miller, L. F., & Moorman, J. E. (1989). Married couple families with children. *Studies in Marriage and the Family, Current Population Reports* (Special Studies Series P-23, No. 162.) Washington, DC: U.S. Government Printing Office.

Moore, K. A., & Driscoll, A. (1997). Partners, predators, peers, protectors: Males and teen pregnancy. In *Not just for girls: The roles of boys and men in teen pregnancy* (pp. 5–10). Washington, DC: The National Campaign to Prevent Teen Pregnancy.

National Campaign to Prevent Teen Pregnancy (1997). *Whatever happened to childhood? The problem of teen pregnancy in the United States.* Washington, DC: National Campaign to Prevent Teen Pregnancy.

National Center for Children in Poverty. (1997, Summer). Study maps state strategies to spur responsible fatherhood. *News and Issues, 7*(1), 1–2.

Nobles, W. G. (1988). American family life: An instrument of culture. In H. P. McAdoo (Ed.), *Black Families* (2nd ed.), (pp. 44–53). Beverly Hills, CA: Sage.

O'Connell, A. (1993). Voices from the heart: The developmental impact of a mother's lesbianism on her adolescent children. *Smith College Studies in Social Work, 63*(3), 281–299.

Olds, D., Perritt, L. M., Robinson, J., Henderson, C., Ekenrode, J., Kitzman, H., Cole, B., & Powers, J. (1998). Reducing risks for antisocial behavior with a program of prenatal and early childhood home visitation. *Journal of Community Psychology, 26*(1), 65–83.

O'Leary, K. M., Shore, M. F., & Wieder, S. (1984). Contacting pregnant adolescents: Are we missing cues? *Social Casework: The Journal of Contemporary Social Work, 65*(5), 297–306.

"One Church, One Child" plan by Chicago cleric boosts black adoptions. (1984, October 15). *Jet,* p. 22.

Ooms, T., & Herendeen, L. (1990). Teenage pregnancy programs: What have we learned? *Background briefing report and meeting highlights: Family Impact Seminar.* Washington, DC: American Association for Marriage and the Family.

Orrego, M. E. (1994–1995). Introduction to this issue. *Family Resource Coalition Report, 13*(3 & 4), 3–4.

Ortiz, V. (1995). The diversity of Latino families. In R. E. Zambrana, (Ed.), *Understanding Latino families,* (pp. 18–39). Thousand Oaks: Sage.

Ortiz, C. G., & Vazquez-Nuttall, E. (1987). Adolescent pregnancy: Effects of family support, education, and religion on the decision to carry or terminate among Puerto Rican teenagers. *Adolescence, 22*(8), 897–917.

Padilla, Y. C. (1997). Immigrant policy: Issues for social work practice. *Social Work, 42*(6), 595–606.

Patterson, C. J. (1992). Children of lesbian and gay parents. *Child Development, 63,* 1025–1042.

Pearson, J., & Thoennes, N. (1996). Acknowledging paternity in hospital settings. *Public Welfare, 54* (Summer), 44–51.

Pinderhughes, E. (1982). Afro-American families and the victim system. In M. McGoldrick, J. Pearce, & J. Giordano (Eds.), *Ethnicity and family therapy* (pp. 109–122). New York: Guilford Press.

Plotnick, R. D. (1993). The effect of social policies on teenage pregnancy and childbearing. *Families in Society: The Journal of Contemporary Human Services, 74*(6), 324–328.

Powell, D. R. (1986). Parent education and support programs. *Young Children, 41*(3), 47–52.

Powell, D. R. (1994). Evaluating family support programs: Are we making progress? In S. L. Kagan & B. Weissbourd (Eds.), *Putting families first: America's family support movement and the challenge of change* (pp. 441–470). San Francisco: Jossey-Bass.

Princeton Survey Research Associates. (1997, May). *A summary of the findings from National Omnibus Survey Questions about teen pregnancy.* Available: http://www.welfare-ref_g/cont/past/brown3.htm [April, 1998].

Red Horse, J. G. (1980). Family structure and value orientation in American Indians. *Social Casework, 61,* 462–467.

Reed, R. (1934). *The illegitimate family in New York City.* New York: Columbia University Press.

Richards, L. N., & Schmiege, C. J. (1993). Problems and strengths of single-parent families: Implications for practice and policy. *Family Relations, 42,* 227–285.

Rothman, J., Gant, L. M., & Hnat, S. A. (1985). Mexican-American family culture. *Social Service Review, 59*(2), 197–215.

Sager, C. J., Steer, H., Crohn, H., Rodstein, E., & Walker, E. (1980). Remarriage revisited. *Family and Child Mental Health Journal, 6*(1).

Saluter, A. F. (1994). Singleness in America. In U.S. Department of Commerce, Bureau of the Census, *Studies in marriage and the family: Current population reports* (Special Studies Series P-23, No. 162, pp. 1–10). Washington, DC: U.S. Government Printing Office.

Saluter, A. F. & Lugalla, T. A. (1998, March). *Marital status and living arrangements: March 1996.* (Current Population Reports P20–496). Washington, DC: U.S. Bureau of the Census.

Schiele, J. H. (1996). Afrocentricity: An emerging paradigm in social work practice. *Social Work, 41*(3), 284–294.

Schorr, L. (1991). *Successful programs and the bureaucratic dilemma: Current deliberations.* New York: National Center for Children in Poverty.

Seitz, V., & Apfel, N. H. (1993). Adolescent mothers and repeated childbearing: Effects of a school-based intervention program. *American Journal of Orthopsychiatry, 63*(4), 572–580.

Sheffer, E. (1992). *The center for family life and the Sunset Park community.* New York: Surdna Foundation and the Foundation for Child Development.

Smith, C. A. (1997). Factors associated with early sexual activity among urban adolescents. *Social Work, 42*(4), 334–346.

Snipp, C. M. (1986). The changing political and economic status of the American Indians: From captive nations to internal colonies. *Journal of Economics and Sociology, 45*(2), 145–157.

Solomon, B. B. (1985). Assessment, service, and black families. In S. S. Gray, A. Hartman, & E. S. Saalberg (Eds.), *Empowering the black family* (pp. 9–20). Ann Arbor: University of Michigan, National Child Welfare Training Center.

Sommer, K., Whitman, T. L., Borkowsk, J. G., Schellenbach, C., Maxwell, S., & Keogh, D. (1993). Cognitive readiness and adolescent parenting. *Developmental Psychology, 29,* 389–398.

Spicer, E. (1980). American Indians. In S. Thernstrom, A. Orlov, & O. Handlin (Eds.), *Harvard encyclopedia of American ethnic groups.* Cambridge, MA: Harvard University Press.

Stack, C. (1974). *All our kin: Strategies for survival in a black community.* New York: Harper & Row.

Steidel, S. E. (Ed.) (1994). *Missing and abducted children: A law enforcement guide to case investigation and program management.* Arlington, VA: National Center for Missing and Exploited Children.

Strauss, S. S., & Clarke, B. A. (1992). Decision-making patterns in adolescent mothers. *Image: Journal of Nursing Scholarship, 24*(1), 69–74.

Stroul, B. A., & Friedman, R. M. (1988). Principles for a system of care. *Children Today, 17*(4), 11–15.

Sutton, C. T., & Broken Nose, M. A. (1996). American Indian families: An overview. In M. McGoldrick, J. Giordano, & J. Pearce (Eds.), *Ethnicity and family therapy* (2nd ed.), (pp. 57–65). New York: The Guilford Press.

Swigonski, M. E. (1996). Challenging privilege through Africentric social work practice. *Social Work, 41*(2), 153–161.

Tafoya, N., & Del Vecchio, A. (1996). Back to the future: An examination of the Native American holocaust experience. In M. McGoldrick, J. Giordano, & J. Pearce (Eds.), *Ethnicity and family therapy,* 2nd ed. (pp. 45–54). New York: The Guilford Press.

Teen Birth Rates Down in All States. (1998, April). *HHS News.* Available: http://www.cdc.gov/nchswww/releases/98news/98news/teenrel.htm [July, 1998].

Thompson, M. S., & Peebles-Wilkins, W. (1992). The impact of formal, informal, and societal support networks on the psychological well-being of Black adolescent mothers. *Social Work, 37*(4), 322.

Tracy, E. M., & Whittaker, J. K. (1987). The evidence base for social support interventions in child and family practice: Emerginng issues for research and practice. *Children and Youth Services Review, 9,* 249–270.

U.S. Bureau of the Census. (1998, May). *Family composition begins to stabilize in the 1990s, Census Bureau reports.* Available: http://www.census.gov/Press-Release/cb98-88.html. [July, 1998].

U.S. Bureau of the Census. (1997, Sept.). *Children of single parents: How they fare.* (Census Brief 197-1). Washington, DC: U.S. Bureau of the Census.

U.S. Bureau of the Census. (1993, September). *We the American children.* Washington, DC: U.S. Bureau of the Census.

U.S. Department of Justice, Office of Juvenile Justice and Delinquency Prevention (1990). *National incidence studies of missing, abducted, runaway, and thrown-away children in America.* Washington, DC: U.S. Government Printing Office.

U.S. General Accounting Office. (1997, February). *Child welfare: States' progress in implementing family preservation and support services.* [GAO/HEHS-97-34]. Washington, DC: U.S. General Accounting Office.

Vega, W. A. (1990). Hispanic families in the 1980s: A decade of research. *Journal of Marriage and the Family, 52*(1), 1015–1024.

Ventura, S. J., Curtin, S. C., & Mathews, T. J. (1998). *Teenage births in the United States: National and state trends, 1990–1996.* National Vital Statistics System. Hyattville, MD: National Center for Health Statistics.

Visher, E. B., & Visher, J. S. (1990). Dynamics of successful stepfamilies. *Journal of Divorce & Remarriage, 14*(1), 3–12.

Wald, L. D. (1915). *The house on Henry Street.* New York: Henry Holt.

Wallerstein, J. S. (1986). Women after divorce: Preliminary report from a ten-year follow-up. *American Journal of Orthopsychiatry, 56*(1), 65–77.

Wallerstein, J. S., & Kelly, J. B. (1980). *Surviving the breakup: How children and parents cope with divorce.* London: Grant McIntyre.

Wattenberg, E., Brewer, R., & Resnick, M. (1991). Executive summary of a study of paternity decisions: Perspectives from young mothers and young fathers. Minneapolis: Center for Urban and Regional Affairs, University of Minnesota.

Weaver, H. (1998). Indigenous people in a multicultural society: Unique issues for human services. *Social Work, 43*(3), 203–211.

Weiss, H. (1990). *Innovative models to guide family support and education policy in the 1990s: An analsyis of four pioneering state programs.* Cambridge, MA: Harvard Family Research Project, Harvard Graduate School of Education.

Weiss, H., & Halpern, R. (1990). *Community-based family support and education programs: Something old or something new?* New York: National Center for Children in Poverty, Columbia University.

Weissbourd, B. (1994). The evolution of the family resource movement. In S. L. Kagan & B. Weissbourd (Eds.), *Putting families first: America's family support movement and the challenge of change* (pp. 28–47). San Francisco: Jossey-Bass.

Weissbourd, B., & Kagan, S. (1989). Family support programs: Catalyst for change. *American Journal of Orthopsychiatry, 59*(1), 20–31.

Weston, K. (1991). *Families we choose: Lesbians, gays, kinship.* New York: Columbia University Press.

Wilcox, B. L., Robbennolt, J. K., O'Keefe, J. E., & Pynchon, M. E. (1996). Teen nonmarital childbearing and welfare: The gap between research and political discourse. *Journal of Social Issues, 52*(3), pp. 71–90.

Will, M. (1988). Family support: Perspectives on the provision of family support services. *Focal Point 2*(3), 1–2. (Bulletin of the Research and Training Cetner to Improve Services for Seriously Emotionally Handicapped Children and Their Families, Regional Research Institute for Human Services, Portland, OR)

Wolfe, D. A. (1993). Prevention of child neglect: Emerging issues. *Criminal Justice and Behavior, 20*(1), 90–111.

Zambrana, R. E., Silva-Palacios, V., & Powell, D. (1992). Parenting concerns, family support systems, and life problems in Mexican-origin women: A comparison by nativity. *Journal of Community Psychology, 20*(4), 276–288.

CHAPTER 4

Family Income Security*

A caring society is one where people need not lose their dignity if they fall ill or fall on hard times or simply grow old; where each child is encouraged to fulfill his or her talents; and where people can live like human beings . . .

—John R. Short, as cited in Mulroy (1995)

CASE EXAMPLE: WELFARE REFORM CREATES HARD CHOICES FOR MOTHERS

Denise Jordan, a 34-year-old mother of three children, is a former welfare recipient who now has a govern-

*By Dr. Alma H. Young, Coleman A. Young Professor of Urban Affairs, and Interim Dean, College of Urban, Labor and Metropolitan Affairs (CULMA), Wayne State University. Dr. Young was educated at Radcliffe College (B.A. 1969), Columbia University (M.S. 1970), and the Massachusetts Institute of Technology (Ph.D. 1978). Her areas of research include women and children in poverty and the political economy of urban development.

ment job in Washington, D.C., which she likes. Her oldest daughter is childless and in the Army. Her middle daughter, Kyisha, is 15 years old, with a sickly nine-month-old son, and pregnant again. Her youngest child is Kimberly, a bright 7-year-old, with an optimistic view of her future.

Denise Jordan is now faced with several major decisions, made more poignant given the recent changes in the federal welfare system. Before 1996, if a teenage girl became pregnant, she could establish her own household and begin collecting welfare benefits. Under the 1996 law, to collect welfare benefits, a teenage girl must live with her parents or guardians. If the family has too much income, then the girl gets no benefits. Denise Jordan makes too much for her family to receive benefits. Thus Denise Jordan is faced with a dilemma—how to get child care assistance for Kyisha's babies.

Does she leave her full-time job, which she has gotten after years of being on welfare and working part-time jobs? If she does, then her family would be back on public assistance and qualify for benefits, including child care assistance for Kyisha's babies. Does she keep her job, but ask Kyisha to drop out of school and take care of her babies, thus saving the child care cost of about $800 a month, which would be half of Denise's take-home monthly salary?

Does Denise take a second job in the evenings in order to make the additional money necessary to cover child-care costs? If she does, then she will not be available to help Kyisha take care of her babies in the evenings, or help her 7-year-old when she comes home from school. In the neighborhood where Denise lives, she knows that keeping children occupied after school is extremely important.

"I have felt myself a strong woman, but now I feel my spirit breaking." (Denise Jordan, in Boo, 1997)

After not being able to talk Kyisha into an abortion or into putting the baby, once born, up for adoption or in foster care, Denise ponders other options for Kyisha. She could put her out on the street, but the child is too "slow" to make it on her own. She could encourage Kyisha and her boyfriend to marry, but she knows that is not likely given his limited resources. Even so, the boyfriend maintains an occasional presence in the family. In the end, after the second baby is born, Denise decides to keep her government job, not look for an additional evening job because the children need her presence more than the extra earnings, and ask Kyisha to drop out of school to take care of her babies. Denise hates to see Kyisha so trapped, but she hopes that life will be better for 7-year-old Kimberly (Boo, 1997).

This case study, taken from a *Washington Post* article, conveys some of the private costs borne by those who leave welfare for work, and the dilemmas faced by the poor and the near-poor in the United States. This country has a history of dividing the poor into the deserving and the undeserving (Katz, 1986), with the undeserving seen as not worthy of assistance, whether from public or private sources. To be considered deserving, the poor must prove their worthiness, generally through the kinds of behaviors that they exhibit (e.g., being willing to work, being capable of maintaining strong families, and being willing to make short-term sacrifices for long-term gains).

Much of the current debate about welfare reform centers on how to get the poor to exhibit "proper" behaviors, with the assumption being that if they do so, they will no longer be poor. The federal welfare reform legislation passed in 1996, the Personal Responsibility and Work Opportunity Reconciliation Act (PRWORA), linked personal responsibility with work, and ended the country's sixty-year program that entitled poor people to public assistance.

POVERTY IN THE UNITED STATES

What Is Poverty?

Although many families in the United States feel financial pressure, some families experience serious difficulties in providing basic needs to their family members. These families are considered poor. The federal government measures the extent of poverty in the United States and regularly issues reports through the U.S. Census Bureau. The basis for measuring poverty in this country is the government's Poverty Line Index, which attempts to classify families as being above or below an income level required to maintain a minimally adequate standard of living for families of different sizes. Poverty, then, refers to those families with cash incomes falling below the official U.S. poverty line. In 1996, the poverty line for a family with two parents and two children was $15,911, and for a family with one parent and two children it was $12,641 (U.S. Census, 1998). Based on the government's definition, a total of 35.6 million people lived in poor families in 1997, which represents 13.3 percent of the population (U.S. Census, 1998). The poverty rate for the nation as a whole has been declining slightly in recent years (see Figure 4.1). A little more than one in seven American families is considered poor, down from one in six in 1992.

There are a number of points that need to be kept in mind when using the Poverty Line Index (Blank, 1997). First, the poverty line is not one number, but a series of numbers developed for families of different sizes. The calculations were devised in the mid-1960s and have not been adjusted for changes in spending patterns over the past thirty years. Second, poverty is based on the income of the family, not the individual. An individual is poor if the income of his or her family (those with whom he or she resides) is below the official poverty line for that size family. Third, there are no provisions for noncash assistance programs such as food stamps and Medicaid, which have grown in size since the 1960s. Fourth, there is no adjustment for differences in the cost of living across regions of the United States or between rural and urban areas. Finally, the poverty numbers do not give

any indication of the intensity of poverty; people are considered as either poor or not poor.

Who Are the Poor?

Many of our conceptions of who is poor in the United States are based on stereotypes. The truth is, the poor are a heterogeneous group of individuals. Some of the poor are more visible than others, especially the poor who live in concentrated areas of central cities, in places of deteriorating housing and stagnant economies. Others are almost invisible, like the children of the working poor.

Who is poor changes over time. In the 1960s, the concern was with the high rate of poverty among the elderly. As a result of federal programs, their rate of poverty has dropped sharply, from approximately 30 percent in 1965 to about 11 percent in 1997. (See Figure 4.2.) However, poverty among children under 18 declined from a high of 27 percent in 1960 to about 14 percent in 1969, but then began an upward spiral in the 1970s to almost 20 percent today. Children represent 40 percent of the poor population. The re-

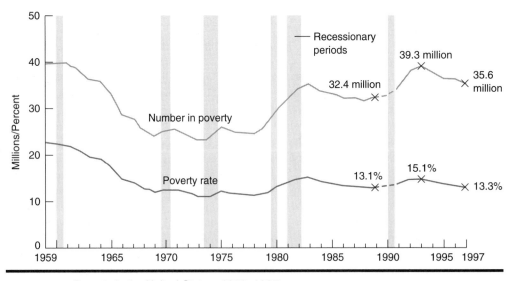

FIGURE 4.1 Poverty in the United States, 1959–1997
Source: U.S. Bureau of the Census (1998).

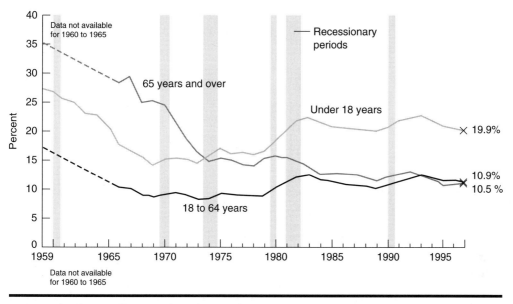

FIGURE 4.2   Poverty Rates by Age, 1959–1997
Source: U.S. Bureau of the Census (1998).

mainder of the population, those between 18 to 64 years old, experienced a poverty rate in single digits from 1965 to 1980; since then that group has experienced a slight but perceptible rise.

If we look at the distribution of poverty among families in the United States, we see a disproportionate number of poor families among people of color. (See Figure 4.3.) Among white families in 1997, 9 percent were poor, but among African Americans and Hispanics the numbers were almost triple that figure, (25.5 percent for African Americans and 26 percent for Hispanics). The same differences hold for families, whether we look at married couple families or single heads of household. Figure 4.4 shows poverty among married couples at about 7 percent for white families, 11 percent for African-American families, and 22 percent for Hispanic families. Thus even married couples experience a significant amount of poverty in this country.

Figure 4.5 shows that while the differences among racial groups hold for single heads of households, poverty rates among females are higher than among males for each group. Poverty rates are highest among African-American female heads of house-

holds (51 percent) and among Hispanic female heads (59.7 percent). Finally, Figure 4.6 shows that the percent of children under 18 who live in poverty is high: 15 percent for white children and close to 40 percent for African-American and Hispanic children. Poverty figures are highest—60 percent—for children under six who live in female-headed households.

How long someone has lived in poverty is another concern. Those who have been poor for a relatively short period of time might face fewer disadvantages than those who have been poor for longer periods of time. Based on a random sample of Americans whose income was surveyed annually over the years 1979 to 1991, Blank (1997) found that two-thirds of those in the sample were never in a poor family during those years. Of those who were poor, about half experienced poverty for less than three years. However, about 7 percent were poor for ten or more years. Compared to whites, African Americans are more likely to experience long-term poverty. Long-term poverty is especially detrimental to children and their physical and social development. Blank (1997) reports that, if we look only at younger children in the random sample

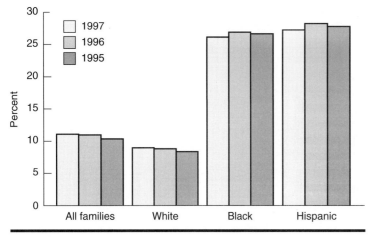

FIGURE 4.3 Poverty of Families by Race, 1995–1997
Source: U.S. Bureau of the Census (1998).

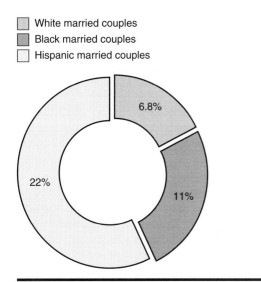

FIGURE 4.4 Poverty Among Married Couples by Race,1995–1997
Source: U.S. Bureau of the Census (1998).

studied, less than 3 percent of white children are poor for ten or more years, while over 30 percent of the African-American children were poor for that period of time.

What Causes Poverty?

The link between poverty and work seems clear: Those who work experience less poverty than those who do not (Blank, 1997). Full-time employment seems the most likely way to move out of poverty, yet many poor adults do not work full-time. There are a number of explanations offered as to why they do not. According to some, the poor do not work because they are not motivated to do so (Murray, 1984). Thus one motivation for the Personal Responsibility and Work Opportunity Reconciliation Act (PRWORA) of 1996 was to encourage people to work and penalize those who do not. Others believe that the poor do not work because of structural constraints—either because of the changing nature of work, the location of jobs, or domestic responsibilities (Wilson, 1987; Mulroy, 1995).

Blank (1997) reminds us, though, that we must be careful in suggesting that people are poor simply because they do not work. More than 60 percent of all poor families contain at least one worker. About 75 percent of male-headed families, and about 50 percent of female-headed households include one worker. The poor who do work are less likely to work full-time than the nonpoor. This is increasingly true among men in married-couple families. Still, at least 20 percent of poor families contain one adult who works full-time,

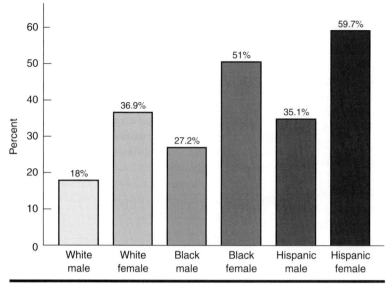

FIGURE 4.5 Poverty Among Single Heads of Household by Race and Gender, 1996

Source: U.S. Bureau of the Census (1998).

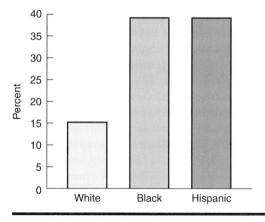

FIGURE 4.6 Poverty Among Children Under 18 Years, by Race

Source: U.S. Bureau of the Census (1998).

year-round. Even full-time work does not always ensure that a family can escape poverty (Blank, 1997). Some suggest that the changing economy and the structural impediments to work explain why families enter poverty and, for increasing numbers, stay poor.

In the past thirty years, a number of changes have occurred in the U.S. economy that make it difficult for many families to maintain a decent standard of living. One of the major changes has been the stagnation in wages; in contrast to the quarter century following World War II, when wages increased rapidly, during the past ten years (from 1985 to 1995) the median weekly earnings of full-time workers increased by only $136 (from $343 to $479). Hardest hit have been young men, aged 16 to 24. In recent years, as the economy has expanded (and with it, the number of jobs created), wages have still declined. This is especially troubling because of the long-held assumption that economic growth leads to a reduction in poverty. These wage losses are related to fundamental changes in the American economy:

- Loss of manufacturing jobs due to foreign competition, automation, and the transfer of jobs by U.S. companies to overseas factories
- Growth of jobs in the service industry, which tend to pay less than manufacturing jobs, have fewer fringe benefits, and are less secure

- Recent technological changes that affect the skill level needed by American workers and the stability of American firms

A compounding factor is the eroded value of the minimum wage. The minimum wage held constant between 1981 and 1989, despite the continuing rise in the cost of living. The minimum wage was raised in 1990, from $3.35 to $3.80, and again in 1991 to $4.25. Congress raised the minimum wage again, to $4.75, in 1996, and then to $5.15 in 1997 (Stout, 1996).

These changes in the U.S. economy have been most detrimental to low-skilled, poorly-educated workers, especially young men. As their wages have declined, young men have also worked fewer hours. In response to the stagnation of male wage rates, women have entered the labor force in larger numbers, to supplement the family income. Women seem to have been less affected by declining wages. For many women, wages have risen dramatically, at least partly due to increasing job opportunities for women. The exception is among women who have dropped out of high school; they experienced a 6 percent decline in wages between 1979 and 1993 (Blank, 1997) and their earnings remain far below those of similarly skilled men. Nor have job opportunities increased for poorly skilled women, as they have for most other women. These women continue to face a narrow range of jobs, with low wages and few job-related benefits, just as they have in the past (Blank, 1997). Many women also continue to work in part-time jobs: a little under 30 percent of all women workers have part-time jobs, a figure that has been constant for a number of years. Many of these women choose to work part-time in order to be able to fulfill their child-care and other domestic responsibilities (Edin & Lein, 1997).

Women with limited education and skills continue to have "access to bad jobs at bad wages" (Blank, 1997, p. 64)

Even though in most American families with children both parents now work outside the home, their standard of living has not improved. Although family incomes are higher in two-earner than in one-earner

families, the larger economic changes described above have limited sharply the financial gains to working parents. To make matters worse, the effort to maintain a stable income through increasing work has added stressors at home, as parents try to meet both work and family commitments. With less time for family life, parents are hard-pressed to provide the level of nurturing and supervision of children that they would prefer to do. This juggling of child care and paid work becomes especially difficult for single mothers who are poor.

HISTORY OF WELFARE POLICY IN THE UNITED STATES

Background to Federal Involvement

In the early years of this nation, the able-bodied poor (whether adult or child, male or female) were usually indentured, that is, placed under contract with a citizen of the town who agreed to maintain them in return for the profit from their labor. This was a favored practice, as everyone's labor was needed in the development of the new country. Those who were infirmed and could not work were sent to dreary almshouses where they mingled with others considered misfits by the townspeople—the mentally ill, lawbreakers, and the aged. A less preferred choice, termed "outdoor relief" and managed by the local poor law authority, was to give meager aid to dependent children in their own homes. This approach was suspect, since it seemed to be giving aid to those who had not earned it. Nonetheless, public outdoor relief proved a helpful way of providing for many children.

With the beginning of the Industrial Revolution, indenture became less feasible and by 1875 had almost disappeared. Taking its place was waged labor, which was needed in abundance during the heyday of industrialization. During this period, single women and poor youth were seen as cheap and necessary sources of labor. However, as women entered the paid labor force in larger numbers, they were characterized as having defied the "cult of domesticity," which since the early nineteenth century had defined women's place as being in the home, where they could fulfill their "natural" roles as wives and mothers. Thus poor women who were compelled to seek work as a means of economic survival were now socially condemned as "lacking in virtue" for doing so (Abramovitz, 1988, as cited in Mink, 1998). Ways were sought to keep mothers at home with their children.

As a result of this concern, in 1911 forty states established mothers' pensions, which provided small amounts of cash to women without the protection of a male breadwinner in order that they might be able to stay at home with their children. This program was never fully implemented, perhaps because some thought that the mothers' pensions compromised the need for paid labor and the role of the male breadwinner. But the program did shift the focus to the needs of children. "Child-saving" activities were popular during the latter part of the nineteenth century, when institutions and programs were created to rescue children from poverty, neglect, and abuse. As long as the mother was seen as "morally upright," attempts were made to help her provide for her children. The focus on children, and on mothers as "conduits for care and the indoctrination of appropriate values and behaviors (particularly work habits), is a theme that runs from mothers' pensions through Aid to Dependent Children" (Mink, 1998, p. 18).

Aid to Families with Dependent Children

When the Social Security Act was passed in 1935, mothers' pensions were replaced by Aid to Dependent Children (ADC). The Act required that all states implement the program. As is clear from its name, ADC did not provide for mothers directly but only for their children. Coverage for mothers was introduced in 1950. In 1962 ADC was renamed Aid to Families with Dependent Children (AFDC) to reflect its new purpose of strengthening families. Initially the program was limited to single parents, but in 1961 the program was expanded in approximately half the states to include unemployed parents (AFDC-UP), thus providing aid to families with an unemployed male head. The 1988 Family Support Act required that AFDC-UP be implemented in all states by 1994 (Mink, 1998).

ADC and later AFDC established a federal role in child and family welfare. The federal government had long been reluctant to become involved with these matters out of concern that this would violate the rights of states and families. However, inequities among the states were apparent, and the Great Depression of the 1930s made it clear that the intervention of the federal government was essential to ameliorate the severe poverty in which many families lived. Thus, under the Social Security Act of 1935, the federal government established a cooperative program between itself and the states. The intent of the program was to provide financial assistance when a family had no income or insufficient income and to do so in ways that would enable children to remain in their own homes, where they could be reared by at least one of their parents or by relatives.

In 1995, AFDC served 4,873,398 families a year (U.S. Department of Health and Human Services, 1998). Even with the large numbers aided by AFDC, not all poor children were in families receiving public assistance. Furthermore, most families who were aided by AFDC payments were provided with income still well below the poverty level. The great bulk of the AFDC caseload was made up of families headed by a woman, always among the most vulnerable to poverty. Since the 1930s, the federal government has used two principal approaches to assure individuals and families of income security—social insurance and public assistance. Social insurance is based on the notion of an earned right and is more generous and popular; Social Security is a form of social insurance. Public assistance is less generous and more stigmatizing; AFDC was a form of public assistance.

AFDC was never envisioned as a right that the poor could claim. Instead, AFDC was a means-tested program, which required applicants to meet federal and state criteria of eligibility in order to receive benefits. Once an applicant was deemed eligible for aid, he or she was enrolled in the program and began to receive a monthly grant. Recipients would have to prove their eligibility periodically. Individual grant levels fluctuated to reflect changes in the recipient's other sources of income. The grant was reduced dollar-for-dollar by the amount received from other sources, not including food stamps and Medicaid.

The public increasingly viewed AFDC with suspicion and disappointment, and from time to time it came under bitter attack. As the federal government under the Reagan administration moved away from social policy development, many states began to experiment with requiring AFDC recipients to find jobs or engage in job-readiness programs. Concern was high that the existing AFDC program had an unintentional consequence of discouraging work by enabling recipients to subsist on welfare payments. Although at least half of all AFDC recipients remain on welfare only temporarily, others were caught in a pattern of continuing dependency, and the public perception was that their children too would grow up without the ability to become self-sufficient workers.

In their efforts to find a means to break this "cycle of dependency," several states created demonstration work programs. The common element among these demonstration programs was large-scale education and job training among targeted groups of teenage mothers, young families, and others vulnerable to long-term welfare dependence. Studies of several state programs carried out by the Demonstration Research Corporation showed a promising level of success, leading to a belief that such demonstration programs benefited welfare recipients and that the programs could eventually pay for themselves.

Compelling economic factors also influenced the efforts toward welfare reform. Welfare costs had long been deplored as a heavy drain on tax resources. Furthermore, projections of serious labor shortages led to the conviction that the economy would require all available trained workers by the end of the 1990s. A social factor that contributed heavily to the new consensus on welfare was that, women having for some time been entering the work force in large numbers, a new norm of family life was in place, and welfare mothers who stayed home with their children seemed to be out of step with reality.

Family Support Act of 1988

In 1988 Congress passed the Family Support Act, the intent of which was to enable the states to help poor families leave welfare and become self-sufficient. The Act required AFDC recipients to participate in education, job training, and work programs. The major provisions of the act were as follows:

- Improved mechanisms for child support and establishment of paternity
- The Jobs Opportunities and Basic Skills (JOBS) program, which replaced earlier work incentive programs. Under the Act, most welfare recipients had to participate in the JOBS program if they were to continue to receive financial assistance. Participants were offered a range of educational activities (such as literacy or proficiency in English, job training, and job placement services).
- Guaranteed child care for AFDC parents who were working or participating in education or training and the provision of transitional child care and Medicaid for twelve months after an AFDC recipient left the rolls because of employment and increased earnings
- A requirement that all states provide coverage of two-parent families where the primary earner was unemployed (AFDC-UP) for at least six months of the year. Until that time, only twenty-six states had offered AFDC to poor families in which the second parent (usually the father) was at home and unemployed. For families in this program, at least one parent had to participate for at least sixteen hours per week in unpaid community work experience programs or other forms of work supplementation or on-the-job training.

One early and innovative JOBS program concluded that "while states can save significant amounts of money by requiring welfare recipients to work, the incomes and living standards of the poor may not improve" (Mathews, 1990, p. A4). The study of a San Diego JOBS program found that for each dollar spent on the JOBS program, the government saved $3. For AFDC participants, however, the outcomes were less positive; those who moved into part-time or full-time jobs earned no more than their welfare checks and benefits had brought, and, in some cases, less. This led to criticism that the program simply replaced one source of poverty-level income with another (Mathews, 1990). How one judged the program's success appeared to depend on whether one took the perspective of the taxpayer or the welfare recipient.

"The political climate is not a friendly one for poor women on relief" (Kingfisher, 1996, p. 22).

The Family Support Act of 1988 reflected the country's shifting views of welfare and work. The Act incorporated the principle of parental responsibility by strengthening child support enforcement and by emphasizing work and employment training for parents. It also made AFDC available for two-parent families so that families would not have to separate in order to become eligible for aid. It increased the commitment of the state to the goal of family self-sufficiency through the guarantee of child care and Medicaid for twelve months after the parent left welfare for work.

TEMPORARY ASSISTANCE FOR NEEDY FAMILIES

In the years after the passage of the Family Support Act, momentum increased for further welfare reforms to link welfare benefits to approved parental behaviors of work and family responsibility. Donna Shalala, secretary of the Department of Health and Human Services (HHS), described the welfare reform strategy of the Clinton administration as being "based on a simple point: welfare must be a temporary, transitional program that builds on core American values—work, family, opportunity, and responsibility" (Shalala, 1993, p. 5).

The nation's governors also lobbied to have more power devolved to the states, a move that was endorsed by the Republicans when they became the majority in the House of Representatives in 1994. By then devolution had become a favored policy choice. Devolution reflects the changing federal-state relationship in which the federal government gives greater flexibility to the states to determine the social agenda, and the states in turn assume more responsibility for the design and administration of social programs. Congress incorporated this idea when it dramatically transformed the social safety net for low-income fam-

ilies with the 1996 passage of the Personal Responsibility and Work Opportunity Reconciliation Act (PRWORA). PRWORA eliminated the 61-year-old AFDC program and replaced it with a block grant to states to establish the Temporary Assistance for Needy Families (TANF) program.

Emphasis on Work

TANF emphasizes short-term, employment-related assistance (Pavetti, 1997). Families are eligible to receive TANF assistance for only sixty months in their lifetime. TANF recipients are also required to perform community service after receiving assistance for two months. They must work once they are determined to be job ready or after receiving assistance for twenty-four months. States can set shorter time limits for work participation. TANF requires states to sanction those who refuse to work. That is, states may reduce the family's TANF grant or completely terminate assistance. Medicaid coverage can also be terminated for an adult who refuses to work, although Medicaid coverage for children must remain intact. To ensure that state TANF programs emphasize work, PRWORA requires states to meet steadily increasing work participation rates in order to receive their full TANF allocation (see Table 4.1). Because TANF is so prescriptive in the area of work

TABLE 4.1   TANF Work Participation Rate Requirements for All Families

FISCAL YEAR	PARTICIPATION RATE	REQUIRED HOURS PER WEEK
1997	25%	20
1998	30	20
1999	35	25
2000	40	30
2001	45	30
2002	50	30

Source: L. Pavetti. (1997). *How much more can they work? Setting realistic expectations for welfare mothers.* Washington, DC: The Urban Institute. A report to the Annie E. Casey Foundation.

participation, families must quickly find employment or other sources of support.

In comparing the TANF program with its precursor, JOBS, Pavetti (1997) found some significant differences. First, the required TANF work participation rates are substantially higher than those required under the JOBS training program. Second, due to numerous exemptions from program participation, only about 10 percent of the AFDC caseload was required to participate in JOBS activities, but there are fewer exemptions possible under TANF, and by 2002, at least 50 percent of all TANF families must be in work-related activities. Third, what counts as participation is also substantially different under TANF than under the JOBS program. Under TANF, activities that count toward the participation rate focus primarily on employment; under JOBS, they focused more on employment preparation activities such as assessment or education and training. Fourth, TANF includes a caseload reduction credit to reward states for lowering their welfare caseload, presumably by moving recipients into private-sector jobs that would make them ineligible for program benefits. Because TANF does not require states to show that their caseload reductions have resulted from increased employment, many advocates of families are concerned that the states will increase their work participation rates by making it more difficult for families to qualify for assistance. In a study of about three dozen states across the country, Vobejda and Haveman (1998) found that welfare officials are working hard to keep families from ever getting on the rolls:

> *Welfare offices are urging applicants to ask for help from relatives instead of signing up for government assistance, writing one-time emergency checks in place of monthly benefits, or requiring applicants to spend weeks searching for work before they receive their first welfare payment. (Vobejda & Haveman, 1998, p. A1)*

Approaches Differ by State

Under PRWORA, there is no longer one national model of welfare provision. Within very general guidelines, as stated above, states have now been given the flexibility to design welfare programs that

respond to their political and economic needs. Even before TANF was passed, thirty-seven states, through waivers from the Department of Health and Human Services, had enacted major welfare reforms. Since TANF, every state has passed a comprehensive welfare program that is work-based. Almost every state has adopted time limits, although there is some variation in the limits set. (See Table 4.2.) The majority of states have adopted lifetime limits, most sixty months; six states have set shorter lifetime limits. A few states have set "periodic time limits" that allow recipients to return to the welfare rolls after being off for a certain period of time. For instance, in Ohio a family can receive a total of 36 cumulative months of benefits and then, unless it gets a hardship exemption, it must wait 24 months to reapply (Tweedle, 1998).

Most states have expanded their income disregards; that is, they have increased the amount of money that recipients can earn without losing eligibility for some benefits. Connecticut and Indiana, for example, allow recipients to earn up to the federal poverty threshold before they lose benefits. Other states have increased the percentage of earnings that are disregarded from determining the family's benefits. In Massachusetts, families can keep more than half their earnings and still get benefits (Tweedle, 1998). Many states allow recipients to build assets and still be eligible for assistance. These assets include the value of a car, or monies in individual development accounts, which recipients can open in order to save for education, starting a business, or buying a home.

More than twenty states have enacted family caps, which limit the amount of increase in benefits that families that have additional children while on welfare can receive. South Carolina allows the increase only in vouchers for the child's expense or the mother's education and training expenses. Florida provides half the regular increase for the first child born on welfare (Tweedle, 1998). About 40 percent of the states provide diversion payments. These are lump sums to prospective recipients to cover expenses that would prevent them from working (e.g., buying a car so that they have transportation to work, or for emergency shelter). Finally, fourteen states provide lower benefits for recipients who moved into the state

TABLE 4.2   Comparison of State Welfare Reform Programs, by Selected Criteria

STATE	LIFETIME LIMITS	EXPAND INCOME DISREGARDS	INCREASE ASSET VALUE ON CAR	FAMILY CAP	DIVERSION PAYMENT	LOWER BENEFITS FOR NEW STATE RESIDENTS
Alabama	No provision					
Alaska	60 months	•			•	
Arizona	60 months	•	•	•	•	
Arkansas	24 months	(A)	•	•		
California	60 months	•	•	•	•	•
Colorado	60 months	•	•		•	
Connecticut		•	•	•		•
Delaware		•	•	•		
D.C.		•		•		
Florida	48 months	•	•	•	•	
Georgia	48 months	(A)	•	•		•
Hawaii	60 months	•	•			
Idaho	(A)				•	
Illinois	60 months	•		•		•
Indiana	24 months	•		•		
Iowa	Individual*	(A)	(A)			•
Kansas	(A)	•	•			
Kentucky					•	
Louisiana	60 months	(A)	(A)			
Maine		•			•	
Maryland	60 months	•	•	•	•	
Massachusetts	60 months	•	•	•		
Michigan		•	•			
Minnesota	60 months	•	•		•	•
Mississippi	60 months	•		•		
Missouri		•	•			
Montana	60 months	•	•		•	
Nebraska		•	•	•		
Nevada	60 months					
New Hampshire		•	•			•
New Jersey	60 months	•		•		
New Mexico						
New York	60 months	•			•	•
North Carolina	24 months					
North Dakota	60 months	•	•	•		•
Ohio	60 months	•	•			
Oklahoma	60 months	•	•	•	•	•
Oregon		•	•			
Pennsylvania		•	•			•
Rhode Island	60 months	•	•		•	•
South Carolina	60 months	•	•	•		
South Dakota	(A)		•		•	

continued

TABLE 4.2   Continued

STATE	LIFETIME LIMITS	EXPAND INCOME DISREGARDS	INCREASE ASSET VALUE ON CAR	FAMILY CAP	DIVERSION PAYMENT	LOWER BENEFITS FOR NEW STATE RESIDENTS
Tennessee	60 months		•	•		
Texas			•		•	
Utah	36 months	•	•		•	
Vermont		•	•			
Virginia		•	•	•	•	
Washington	60 months	•	•		•	•
West Virginia	60 months				•	
Wisconsin	60 months		•	•	•	•
Wyoming	60 months	•	•	•		

(A) = Agency discretion

Source: J. Tweedle. (1998, January). Building a foundation for change in welfare. Reprinted with permission. *State Legislatures,* 26–35.

during the preceding year. In most of these states, applicants receive the benefit level from their former state for twelve months if it is lower (Tweedle, 1998).

Leaving Welfare for Work

It is still too early to determine the impact of the new welfare laws on American families. We know that in the short period since TANF became operative the results seem quite positive in terms of the number of families leaving the welfare rolls. By 1997, caseloads had fallen by roughly 1.4 million families since the caseloads peaked in March 1994, with almost half of that drop in caseloads occurring in 1996 and 1997 alone (DeParle, 1997; Vobejda & Jeter, 1997). While these results allow for some optimism, research suggests that our assessment of welfare reform should be guarded. We are currently in an economic boom, with a great need for low-skilled jobs. If the economy enters a recession, the number of available jobs will likely decrease and we may see an increase in welfare applications. Most recipients who have left the welfare rolls for work have been the easiest to place—that is, they have been better educated, with work experience, and often have older children. Now

states must deal with the hard-to-place. A recent review of welfare cases in New York City found that those still on the welfare rolls were disproportionately African American and Hispanic, outnumbering whites by about two to one. The remaining caseload is increasingly concentrated in large cities (DeParle, 1998).

Among those who have left welfare for work, a significant number are unable to remain off welfare for long. A Maryland study found that about 20 percent of those who left welfare returned within three to six months, that about 50 percent of those who left the rolls reported earnings in the first three months, and that, of those working, about 75 percent had found minimum-wage jobs in the retail or service industry (Tweedle, 1998). The Maryland findings parallel the results of earlier studies suggesting that work among welfare recipients is common (Edin & Lein, 1997). However, much of that work was short-term and relatively unreliable. In addition, few studies showed more than half of the AFDC caseload working, even over an extended period of time (Pavetti, 1997).

Earlier studies on who is likely to leave welfare for work found that a woman's transition to work is significantly affected by four factors:

1. *The amount of education she has and whether or not she is in school. Women who have not completed high school are more likely to lose jobs once they become employed.*
2. *The presence of young children. Having a child under the age of five significantly reduces the likelihood that a woman who is jobless will make the transition to employment. Having a child under the age of one significantly increases the likelihood that a woman with a job will return to joblessness.*
3. *The structure and condition of the local labor market. Women living in areas of lower unemployment are more likely to find jobs than women living in areas with higher levels of unemployment. Employment outcomes are somewhat better for women living in urban areas.*
4. *The length of time a woman has been jobless and her previous work history. The longer a woman stays unemployed, the less likely she is to find a job. (Pavetti, 1997)*

Although there is great diversity among the welfare population, on average the women who turn to welfare at some point in their lives tend to have substantially lower levels of education and basic skills, have more children to care for, and are more likely to be members of a racial or ethnic minority than women who do not turn to welfare. The majority of welfare recipients are white, but minorities are overrepresented among welfare mothers. These are often the same women who have had limited work experience and are likely to have considerable difficulty finding jobs.

> *It is hard to imagine a scenario where states could meet the work participation rates required under TANF without increasing employment among the most disadvantaged recipients and/or increasing the length of employment spells among recipients who have already managed to find employment on their own. Unfortunately, states have had limited experience and/or limited success with accomplishing either of these tasks. . . . Even if recipients with the lowest skills were to follow the same employment paths as nonrecipients, fewer than half of them would be steadily employed by the time they reach their late twenties, suggesting that during periods of joblessness these families may continue to need access to a safety net over an extended period of time. (Pavetti, 1997, p. 12)*

OTHER INCOME PROGRAMS FOR FAMILIES WITH CHILDREN

TANF, like AFDC before it, provides cash income to poor families. The federal government also provides other kinds of assistance to families in need. These noncash resources include tax credits, food stamps, medical benefits, and child care subsidies. When PRWORA was passed in 1996, it affected the way some of these noncash resources would be dispensed.

SSI and Social Security

Enacted in 1972, Supplemental Security Income (SSI) provides assistance to elderly or disabled persons who are below certain income levels. For the elderly, it supplements Social Security and pension income if the amount they receive in retirement benefits is insufficient. For those who are medically certified as physically or mentally unable to work, it provides a source of income. Because SSI is strict in its certification guidelines, only those with considerable physical or mental disabilities can qualify for the program.

Unlike AFDC and now TANF, SSI is a federally designed program with a standard set of national benefits. A single individual living alone with no other income can receive a maximum of $446 per month, no matter where that person lives in the United States (Blank, 1997). Support decreases for those who live with others. Benefit amounts in SSI are calculated in the same way that AFDC benefits were: Maximum benefits go to those with no other source of income. Those with other sources of income receive fewer benefits as their other income rises. "SSI recipients have their benefits taxed away at a lower rate than AFDC recipients as their earnings increase. Thus, those we largely expect not to work have access to a program with greater work incentives than the parents on AFDC whom we increasingly expect to be employed" (Blank, 1997, p. 104).

The 1996 Welfare Reform Act toughens the definition of disability and requires reviews of children's disabilities every three years. The 1996 legislation also made legal immigrants ineligible for SSI and food stamps until they become citizens. Those legal immigrants who have worked for at least ten years were exempted from all benefit restrictions. The Balanced Budget Act of 1997 restored SSI and derivative Medicaid benefits to all elderly and disabled immigrants receiving SSI at the time PRWORA was enacted, and to all legal immigrants who were in the United States on the date of enactment and who become disabled in the future. The budget also restores additional benefits to refugees and expands the group of immigrants treated as refugees for the purposes of welfare assistance. The Welfare Reform Act draws lines more sharply than before among classes of immigrants in the United States and devolves more of immigration policy to the states. For instance, states must now police benefit programs to ensure that unauthorized immigrants do not receive benefits (Fix & Tumlin, 1997).

Earned Income Tax Credit

The Earned Income Tax Credit (EITC) was passed by Congress in 1975 to offset the Social Security taxes paid by low-income families. The credit is available only to working poor people and is intended to encourage work by supplementing the income of low-wage earners. EITC is the fastest growing antipoverty program in the country and has wide bipartisan support. It was a relatively small program until it was expanded in 1993 under the Clinton administration. In 1994, more than 18 million families received benefits, for a total cost of nearly $10 billion.

The EITC operates in a way that is almost the opposite of a cash grant program like AFDC. The EITC pays nothing if an individual does not work. As an individual earns income, the EITC provides about a thirty-cent supplement for every dollar earned (Blank, 1997). Income increases faster than earnings as workers at very low wages increase their hours of work. For workers who earn more, generally between $11,000 and $29,000, there is some concern that the EITC may not be as helpful, since the amount of the benefit declines as earnings increase. The actual amount received depends on the number of children the family has and its earnings. To receive the EITC supplement, families must file a tax return, even if their incomes are so low that they do not owe income taxes. Thus a

family whose EITC is greater than its tax obligation will receive a check from the government after their tax return has been filed. EITC is a cost-effective way for the government to support poor families.

In a recent study, the National Center for Children in Poverty found that the EITC has had a significant impact on driving down young-child poverty rates. Without the EITC, the 1996 young-child poverty rate would have been 23 percent higher. In contrast, the report found no substantial evidence that state welfare reform efforts contributed to lowering the young child poverty rate from 1993 to 1996, a period during which forty-three states made significant welfare changes. While over one-third of the children living in mother-only families experienced poverty if their mothers worked only part-time, those with single mothers working full time still had poverty rates nearly three times as high as those in "traditional" two-parent families—those with the father working full time and the mother not working (17 percent to 6 percent) (National Center for Children in Poverty, 1998). EITC is likely to become even more important as an antipoverty measure as larger numbers of single mothers enter the labor market.

Child Support Enforcement

In the past, governmental efforts to enforce child support payments have been applied mostly to welfare families headed by women, although the problem of adequate child support from absent fathers is pervasive throughout the country. Many women are not awarded child support payments at all, and others do not receive the amount to which they are legally entitled (Mulroy, 1995). In 1975 the federal government began to make systematic efforts to address child support enforcement. In that year, Congress passed the Child Support Enforcement Act, Title IV-D of the Social Security Act, which offered financial incentives to states to establish a standard means for establishing paternity, locating parents, and obtaining child support. In 1982, the federal government issued regulations on deducting delinquent support payments from federal income taxes owed to custodial parents of children receiving AFDC payments. In 1984, Congress required states to develop guidelines to determine child support awards. However, the law still left local courts free to set the amount of awards.

The Family Support Act of 1988 further increased the federal role in establishing paternity, setting child support awards, and enforcing payment from absent parents. It was intended to apply to all single-parent families, whether or not they received welfare. The Act required states to disregard the first $50 of monthly child support payments when determining a family's benefit or eligibility status. AFDC recipients were required to cooperate with the state in establishing paternity and obtaining child support payments unless recipients were found to have good cause for refusing to cooperate. The cooperation requirement, good cause exemption, and penalties for noncooperation were determined by the federal government. Finally, the Family Support Act authorized demonstration projects to provide JOBS services to noncustodial parents of AFDC children who were unemployed and unable to meet their child support obligations. However, the law left the states considerable discretion in implementation, and many important details were left unresolved.

As we have seen in other areas, the 1996 welfare reform legislation took away most federal restrictions in the area of child support and left the states with much greater discretion in how they would enforce child support. Each state had to weigh for itself how the funds for child support affected a recipient's chances of moving off the welfare rolls. The $50 pass-through was eliminated. Each state was given the discretion to decide how much earnings from child support that it collected would be passed-through to the welfare recipient. Each state now decided what the cooperation requirements would be in determining paternity and locating the father, what the penalties would be for the custodial parent's failure to cooperate, and what constituted causes for exemption. All states now had the authority to suspend professional and recreational licenses of individuals owing past due child support. Finally, states now had the authority to establish procedures for imposing work activity requirements on noncustodial parents who were past due in child support payments (A Comparison of Selected Key Provisions, 1996).

Why do many noncustodial parents fail to meet their child-support obligations? Several reasons have been identified. First, the lower the noncustodial parent's income, the less likely it is that the noncustodial parent will pay. Second, noncustodial parents whose support orders represent a higher proportion of their income than that prescribed by federal guidelines are less likely to pay. Third, those who have visitation rights or joint custody are more likely to pay. Finally, we know that noncustodial parents are more likely to pay if the support orders are diligently enforced by the courts.

Medicaid and CHIP

According to a recent report issued by the Census Bureau, the number of people in this country without health insurance rose sharply in 1997, to 43.4 million, and the proportion of Americans lacking coverage reached the highest level in a decade, 16.1 percent. The number of poor people without insurance stayed about the same at 11.2 million. Still, nearly one-third of all poor people—31.6 percent—were uninsured in 1997. There were 10.7 million children uninsured in 1997, about the same as 1996. Because of Medicare, nearly all people over 65 and older have insurance coverage. It was people aged 18 to 64 who accounted for the increase in the uninsured (Pear, 1998).

Ironically, this increase occurred as the country was experiencing an economic boom. The reasons for such a large increase in the number of Americans without medical insurance were several: Medicaid rolls went down as more poor people were forced to move from welfare to work and find low-paying jobs that did not offer health benefits; some employers cut back health benefits, especially for dependents of employees, because of rising medical costs; and even among higher income families, there was less health coverage due to self-employment or work in small businesses (Pear, 1998).

The federal program designed to address the health needs of the poor is Medicaid. The 1988 Family Support Act required that states provide Medicaid to all AFDC recipients, and that they extend Medicaid for twelve months after a family left AFDC, although the benefit could be limited during the second six months. Under the 1996 Welfare Reform Act, states must provide Medicaid to persons who would have been eligible for AFDC under the prior law. Medicaid transition benefits also remain in force but can be terminated if adults refuse to work. In most states, the children of sanctioned parents are still eligible for Medicaid. Because states now have to maintain dual eligibility systems (one for TANF and one for Medicaid), the federal government established a fund to reimburse states for increased administrative costs.

After much clamoring by advocates and policy specialists that the 1996 Welfare Reform Act did not provide enough protection to children who were without medical coverage, Congress made some corrections in its 1997 Reconciliation Act. That legislation allocated $47 billion over the next five years to allow states to expand health insurance coverage to a larger group of uninsured children. States can provide this added protection either through the Medicaid program or through separate state initiatives, called the Children Health Insurance Program (CHIP) (Currie, 1996). States must contribute 70 percent of what they would have contributed under the matching provisions of the Medicaid program. The result is that states can get federal money to expand health insurance coverage at very favorable match rate.

What is the effect on children likely to be? It is too early to tell, but from earlier studies, we may expect the following. A longitudinal study found that when children are covered by Medicaid they are more likely to have visited a doctor in the past six months and that the effect of being covered by Medicaid is larger than the effect of being covered by private health insurance (Currie, 1996). The study surmised that this is probably due to the fact that Medicaid has no copayments or deductibles, as many private health insurance plans do. Another study found that the expansion of Medicaid led to improved quality of care for children, as measured by the fraction of health care visits that took place in doctor's offices rather than in hospital outpatient clinics or emergency rooms (Currie, 1996).

The 1996 Welfare Reform Act barred new immigrants from receiving Medicaid during their first five years in the United States and gave states new options to determine legal immigrants' eligibility for Medicaid. Some states, such as Michigan, have opted to continue Medicaid coverage of legal immigrants where federal matching funds are available. Federal funds are available for legal immigrants who were in the United States as of August 22, 1996, and to legal immigrants entering after that date following the five-year bar. Michigan will not provide state-funded Medicaid to legal immigrants during the five-year bar (Seefeldt, Pavetti, Maguire, & Kirby, 1998). Illegal immigrants are eligible for emergency services only under the Welfare Reform Act.

Child Care Assistance

The 1996 Welfare Reform Act fundamentally changed federal child care assistance programs (see Chapter 5) by eliminating federal child care entitlements and consolidating the four major child care assistance programs for low-income children into a single block grant to states, called the Child Care and Development Fund (Long & Clark, 1997). Under the Child Care and Development Fund (CCDF), the amount of federal funds provided to a state is tied to the state's level of spending on child care. Under this new arrangement, total funds available for child care is dependent to a large extent on a state's level of investment of its own funds. While states have gained increased flexibility for designing and targeting their child care assistance programs, they also face an increased need for child care among families, as more parents are required to go to work. It is now up to states to determine how to meet this increased demand.

Given the greater flexibility in the design of child care assistance programs, states now face a number of decisions in terms of providing child care assistance to poor families. Some decisions center around funding: a state might choose to maintain its present spending on child care; or it could choose to limit child care funding to federal funds only, and thus put no additional state funds into child care; or a state might choose to maximize the federal dollars available for child care by increasing its own related child care spending above its historic level (Long & Clark, 1997).

Beyond choices about funding levels, states must also make decisions about eligibility. The new law is likely to intensify the trade-offs states face between serving low-income working families who need child care assistance and are not on welfare and poor families that are on welfare. States must make decisions on how to reimburse providers: the new law abolishes the percent of costs per child that must be paid, as well as the need to take into account variations in the costs of providing child care in different settings and to children of different ages. For instance, it is more costly to provide care for infants and very young children, for sick children, and for night-time care. In order to serve more children, states may reduce child care subsidies to providers, thereby increasing the share of cost paid by parents (Long & Clark, 1997).

States must also decide how much families will pay for the cost of child care (i.e., the amount of co-payments). States could limit parent access to higher-priced (and possibly higher-quality) child care. The issue of quality is a major one, since the 1996 Act eliminated the provision that unlicensed providers be registered, the provision that states establish health and safety standards (states need only "certify" that health and safety requirements are in effect), and the requirement that 25 percent of federal child care monies be reserved for activities to improve the quality of child care and increase the availability of early child development and before- and after-school care.

In 1997 the Progressive Policy Institute surveyed the decisions on child care assistance made in the ten states with the largest welfare caseloads: California, Florida, Georgia, Illinois, Michigan, New York, Ohio, Pennsylvania, Texas, and Washington. These states include almost two-thirds (65 percent) of the national caseload. The PPI found that states so far have not taken advantage of the flexibility built into the new law and that they are focusing resources on welfare recipients transitioning to work to the disadvantage of other low-wage workers. Only three states have moved to create a seamless system of child care support for all low-wage workers (that is, they have developed a child care system with eligibility based on income and not on status): Illinois, Michigan, and

Washington. There is no time limit on child care assistance in any of these states (Waller, 1997).

WELFARE-TO-WORK PROGRAMS

State Programs

One of the hallmarks of the 1996 Welfare Reform Act was the flexibility it gave to states to create their own cash assistance programs for families with children, in effect creating fifty different programs, with the states required to follow only very broad federal guidelines. Initially through waivers from the federal government, Wisconsin and Michigan have been involved with reforming their welfare systems for a relatively long period of time. After PRWORA was enacted in 1996, other states looked to Wisconsin and Michigan for recommendations on how to change their programs.

Wisconsin.   In December 1993, Wisconsin Governor Tommy Thompson signed into law a redesigned state welfare program. Calling for a replacement of welfare with work, the state created a program centered around the belief that work fulfills a basic need by connecting individuals to society. The program, called Wisconsin Works (W-2), provides cash assistance and supportive services only to those individuals engaged in one of four work options. The preferred option is unsubsidized employment, followed by trial jobs or subsidized employment, community service jobs, and W-2 transitions. The last category is reserved for those individuals who are unable to perform effectively even in a community service job (Miranne & Young, 1998).

Supportive services such as child care, medical insurance, and transportation reimbursements are in place, but recipients are held responsible for some portion of the cost of such services. Child support payments will now go directly to the working custodial parent. The welfare office has been transferred from the Department of Health and Human Services to the Department of Industry, Labor, and Human Relations. The intent is to replace "the automatic welfare check with a comprehensive package of work options, job training, health-care and child-care services, and even financial planning" (Thompson, as cited in Miranne & Young, 1998, p. 164). Wisconsin has developed a strategy to link welfare reform with children's programs through its Children's Services Network. The network links families participating in TANF with a comprehensive array of community resources and services. Local networks must identify a group of community organizations and service providers that communicate on a regular basis, create a single point of information and access to services for families, and establish a means of assessing community needs (Knitzer & Page, 1998).

Michigan.   As early as 1992, Michigan began to implement changes in its welfare program that emphasized personal responsibility. This initiative, called To Strengthen Michigan Families, continues to provide the state's framework for welfare reform. Since 1992, Michigan has required welfare recipients to engage in activities, for a minimum of twenty hours per week, that would lead to their personal growth or the community's enhancement. Since 1994, the state has created two programs that focus more directly on fostering recipients' transitions to unsubsidized employment: Work First, a statewide mandatory job readiness/job search program for all AFDC/TANF recipients unless they are working twenty hours a week or more, and Project Zero, a demonstration project under which sites are given increased resources for child care and transportation with the goal of zero unemployment among welfare recipients. In 1996, to reflect implementation of the state's block grant plan, the name of the AFDC program was changed to the Family Independence Program (FIP). Families receiving cash assistance from this program receive more assistance than families in most states (Seefeldt et. al., 1998).

Michigan and Vermont are the only two states that have established no time limits for receipt of cash assistance. In Michigan, the only exemptions from the work requirement are age of child and being a victim of domestic violence. Parents with infants under three months are exempt from work requirements. While exempted, parents with infants are subject to other requirements like volunteering in their communities (Gallagher, Jerome, Gallagher, Schreiber, & Watson, 1998). Currently, child care assistance is available to all welfare recipients who are looking for work and

for all working families whose income falls below 85 percent of the state median income. The state does not have a waiting list for subsidized child care. While it hopes to continue to offer child care to all eligible groups, the state has set target priorities for assistance in expectation that child care caseloads are likely to increase and it may not be able to help all groups who are now eligible (Seefeldt et al., 1998). Michigan has maintained the $50 pass-through for child support payments on a temporary basis. Michigan has no strategies to link welfare reform with comprehensive initiatives for young children (Knitzer & Page, 1998).

Other Strategies.   There is considerable variation in how states address the needs of young children. The National Center for Children in Poverty (NCCP) sought information from the states about their explicit efforts to link children's programs with the implementation of welfare reform. It found that only ten states report specific statewide efforts to link welfare strategies with statewide comprehensive program initiatives, excluding child care strategies, on behalf of young children and families (see Figure 4.7). These states are Connecticut, Georgia, Delaware, Indiana, New Hampshire, Ohio, Oklahoma, Vermont, West Virginia, and Wisconsin (Knitzer & Page, 1998).

These states are using TANF dollars to expand or target services specifically to families receiving or at risk of receiving welfare; requiring or encouraging parents of young children to engage in parent education programs or other strategies to enhance their parenting skills in lieu of, or in tandem with, work requirements; giving priority for program enrollment to young children in families receiving, or at risk of receiving, public assistance; and using existing services as "hubs" for multiple services to families receiving assistance, diverted from assistance, or transitioning off assistance. Although state implementation of welfare reform is still in its early stages, the NCCP data suggest that few states see the linking of comprehensive programs for young children and families with welfare reform as part of their agenda. Yet the networks of programs that states are establishing on behalf of young children and families could be "important tools in the effort to promote family self-sufficiency and young child well-being" (Knitzer & Page, 1998, pp. 43–44).

FIGURE 4.7 State Strategies to Link Comprehensive Services for Children and Families with Welfare Reform

---

GIVING PRIORITY TO YOUNG CHILDREN IN FAMILIES RECEIVING TANF FOR EARLY CHILDHOOD PROGRAMS

Connecticut
- The state has targeted families with young children receiving or at risk of receiving public benefits as priority enrollees in its new School Readiness and Child Care Act.

Georgia
- The state is making efforts to link its universal prekindergarten program with efforts to provide full-day child care. It reports encouraging local prekindergarten sites to work with county welfare offices to arrange extended-day child care using child care subsidy funds for families receiving welfare.

REQUIRING PARENTS OF YOUNG CHILDREN TO PARTICIPATE IN SPECIAL PROGRAMS

Delaware
- The state requires that parents of young children participate in a parenting education program in order to receive their full welfare checks (otherwise the checks are reduced).

USING TANF DOLLARS FOR PROGRAMS FOR FAMILIES WITH YOUNG CHILDREN RECEIVING ASSISTANCE

Indiana and New Hampshire
- These states are using TANF dollars for home-visiting programs for TANF recipients, in New Hampshire on a pilot basis, in Indiana linked with Step Ahead community mobilization councils.

Ohio
- The state has targeted $12 million in state money, supplemented by $6 million in TANF funds, to expand Early Start, which links families with infants and toddlers at risk of abuse, neglect, or developmental delay to health, education, and support services, based on individualized plans. Participation helps to meet work requirements. Families being diverted from assistance may also access Early Start.

Oklahoma
- The state reports using TANF dollars for Early Head Start.

USING SYSTEMS DEVELOPMENT AND COMMUNITY MOBILIZATION INITIATIVES FOR YOUNG CHILDREN AND FAMILIES RECEIVING TANF

Vermont
- Vermont's welfare-to-work plan includes incentives for participating in parent education programs, as well as expanded child care and Medicaid coverage. Parent-Child Center staff, state employees, state college staff, and other service providers offer service coordination and assistance to teen parents and other participating families.

West Virginia
- The state is deliberately using the local Family Resource Networks (FRN) to inform families and the community about the new welfare reform provisions; conducting focus groups to get ideas from families about how to implement and improve the new system; and using the FRN's annual consumer and provider interviews to get feedback about the program. It is also using FRN and/or its member agencies to serve as sponsors for Community Work Experience. JOIN, or community service placements. The state is coordinating cross-agency training on the new welfare program and on family-centered practices.
- The state also has explicit plans to use the Starting Points Early Childhood Centers as access sites for welfare through FAIR (Family Assessment, Intake, and Referral). Further, the Personal Responsibility Contract identifies each parent's employment plan, as well as strategies to enhance the well-being of her children (e.g., requiring immunizations and health exams); cash grants and/or support services are provided to those who meet the terms of their Contracts. Efforts are underway to coordinate services for Head Start families enrolled in TANF.

Wisconsin
- Children's Services Networks are required components of the state's welfare reform plan. Local networks must identify and work with providers of children's services.

Source: J. Knitzer & S. Page. *Map and track: State initiatives for young children and families, 1998 edition.* New York: National Center for Children in Poverty, Columbia School of Public Health, 1998.

Nonprofit Programs
and Public-Private Partnerships

Project Match.   Project Match, an innovative program in Chicago that helps women on welfare transition to work, has found that preparing for work involves a long period of personal growth (see Chapter 3). According to the founder of Project Match, Toby Herr, the long process to independence involves "forging or renewing connections with mainstream norms and institutions; reworking basic dispositions toward self and world; becoming ready to struggle to acquire basic skills that should have been acquired in childhood; [and] developing the capacity to construct a future for oneself" (Herr & Halpern, 1991, p. 22). Project Match has found that these tasks may take longer than a few months, and the first steps need to be accessible to parents in their current situation so that they can get early recognition and feedback that they are on track. These first steps may include participating with their children and volunteering on a scheduled basis in community activities.

Project Match has developed the concept of a "ladder that shows how people can move in a series of small steps toward economic independence" (Herr & Halperin, 1991, p. 76). (See Figure 4.8.) To progress up the ladder, people are expected to make gradually increasing time commitments to identified activities, and they progress from family- or community-oriented activities to those that are more directly related to finding and keeping employment. People may move along the ladder in many different sequences, including temporary setbacks, after which they reenter at a lower level.

According to Project Match, many people who live in disadvantaged neighborhoods do not receive the kind of positive feedback from family, friends, teachers, and others that would help them stay motivated to achieve their goals and feel good about themselves. Project Match attempts to recreate this "social scaffolding," as they call it, through public recognition of people's progress on the ladder. Community awards ceremonies, newsletters, and display boards announce that an individual has successfully completed a rung on the ladder and has moved to a new status, such as a change from volunteering within Project Match agencies to volunteering in an outside agency. Public recognition helps establish and reinforce community norms about the expectations for adult behavior.

Federal and state regulations are often too rigid to accommodate the needs of people who are not ready to sustain consistent employment. Participants at risk of long-term welfare dependency may need to start with organized activities that are less demanding than school or work, and build up to more stringent activities. Also, most jobs programs allow only a very limited period of follow-up by case workers after the participant is working. Project Match has found, however, that backsliding is common and should be expected. Therefore, case management services need to be available to help people over the long haul.

Public-Private Partnerships.   On the first anniversary of the 1996 Welfare Reform Act, President Clinton announced that 135,000 former welfare recipients had been hired by about 5,000 businesses participating in the Welfare to Work Partnership (Harris, 1998.) An initiative of the White House, the Partnership is a nonprofit corporation whose purpose is to encourage members of the business community to hire those who are transitioning from welfare to work. One of the early successes of the program is United Airlines, which has hired nearly 800 former welfare recipients. Given the tight labor market and growth in entry-level positions, there is anticipation that more companies will be willing to hire welfare recipients. The Partnership is designed to help ease qualms that employers may have about hiring welfare recipients.

A recent survey of employers' requirements for entry-level workers and their views on hiring people who have recently been on welfare found that most of these employers appear willing to fill their entry-level positions with people who are or have been on welfare, if the applicant exhibits a positive attitude and can be a reliable worker (Regenstein & Meyer, 1998). Most of the employers surveyed had fewer than 50 workers and employed one or more entry-level workers. The survey found that employers generally have positive views of welfare recipients and

FIGURE 4.8 Incremental Ladder to Economic Independence

Source: Reprinted with permission of the Families in Transition Association. © 1995 by Project Match.

The five columns of the ladder (left to right): **Activities with Children — Volunteer Work — Employment — Education/Training — Membership in Organizations**, rising from *–WELFARE DEPENDENCY–* toward *Economic Independence*.

Activities with Children (bottom to top)
- Acts on referrals in a timely manner / Takes child to extracurricular activities regularly / Gets child to school on time
- 1–2 hours/week
- Family literacy programs / Family support programs (e.g., parenting education class, drop-in center)
- 3–4 hours/week
- Other activities (e.g., sports) / Community activities (e.g., Scout leader, coach) / School-based activities (e.g., homeroom mother)
- 5 hours/week or more

Volunteer Work (bottom to top)
- Community center / Community health center / Child's school / Head Start
- Unscheduled hours
- Community center / Community health center / Child's school / Head Start
- Scheduled hours 1–10 hours/week
- Scheduled hours 11–19 hours/week / Outside community (e.g., national organizations) / In community (e.g., church)
- Scheduled hours 20 hours/week or more / Outside community (e.g., hospitals) / In community (e.g., child's school)

Employment (bottom to top)
- Structures activities with stipends (e.g., WIC clerk, Head Start aide) / 7–12 months / 4–6 months / 0–3 months
- Community internships
- On-the-job training / Supported work
- Subsidized work
- Unsubsidized jobs Under 20 hours/week / 7–12 months / 4–6 months / 0–3 months
- Unsubsidized jobs 20 hours/week or more / 7–12 months / 4–6 months / 0–3 months
- Unsubsidized jobs 40 hours/week ($6.00/hour or less) Over 1 year / 7–12 months / 4–6 months / 0–3 months
- Unsubsidized jobs 40 hours/week ($6.00/hour, benefits) Over 5 years / 4–5 years / 1–3 years

Education/Training (bottom to top)
- ABE/GED / Literacy
- 1–4 hours/week
- ABE/GED / Literacy
- 5–10 hours/week
- College / Vocational training / ABE/GED / Literacy
- 11–19 hours/week
- College / Vocational training / High school / ABE/GED
- 20 hours/week or more

Membership in Organizations (bottom to top)
- Head Start parent councils / Support groups (e.g., MYM) / PTA
- 1–2 hours/week
- Church activities / Concerned parent groups / Neighborhood Watch activities
- 3–4 hours/week
- Advocacy groups / Tenant management boards / Local school councils
- 5 hours/week or more

their performance in the workplace. About 70 percent of the employers who held positive views felt that the two most important qualities in an employee—a positive attitude and reliability—described welfare recipients in the workplace.

Another group, led by Vice President Al Gore, seeks to create linkages among state and local governments and nonprofit, community-based groups in an attempt to ensure that the social service needs of welfare recipients transitioning to work will be met. This Welfare-to-Work Coalition attempts to provide a range of resources, including child-care assistance, mentoring opportunities, worker training, and emergency food and housing. Groups involved in the Coalition are quite diverse, including Boys and Girls Clubs of America, Goodwill Industries, National Urban Coalition, and United Way.

Involvement of Unions. At first, labor unions campaigned against the decision by some states to require welfare recipients to work in publicly-created jobs, known as workfare, for fear that currently-employed, low-skilled, public-sector workers would be fired and replaced with the cheaper welfare workers. More recently, labor unions have begun to target some of their organizational efforts among low-skilled workers, including those in workfare jobs. As part of that initiative, labor unions have also begun to work with city and state governments to train welfare recipients in the kinds of skills that are currently needed.

An example of this is the New York City Consortium for Worker Education Satellite Day Care Project. This program trains welfare recipients to become child care providers in their own homes. Unlike licensed family day care centers, where the provider is typically an independent contractor, the satellite provider is an employee of a sponsoring child care center. The current goal is to create 1,000 jobs for welfare recipients while providing 4,000 badly needed child care slots for preschool-aged children in New York City. Up-front costs to the provider are expected to be minimal since the average provider will be caring for children in his or her own home, minimizing the need for new facilities. The project is targeting TANF recipients in public housing and in surround-

ing neighborhoods. These new employees will be covered by a union contract, which provides for entry-level annual salaries of $18,200 and fringe benefits. These jobs will offer supervision and are meant to provide opportunities for career advancement in the child care profession (American Federation of State, County and Municipal Employees, 1998).

EFFECTS OF WELFARE ON CHILDREN

Poverty is a condition that affects about a fifth of all American families with children under age 18. Over half of these children are in single-mother homes. A white child being raised by a single mother has about a 45 percent chance of being poor. African-American and Hispanic children in single-mother homes have about a 65 percent chance of being poor (Blank, 1997). Children in the United States have a far greater chance of living in poverty than children in other industrialized countries. In part this may be because of the higher rates of single motherhood in this country, but another significant reason is the limited public assistance that we give to single-parent families—much less than other industrialized countries provide (Weir, Orloff, & Skocpol, 1988). See Chapter 1 for a discussion of the detrimental effects of poverty on children.

Because of the effects of poverty on children's development and their future life chances, it is important to look at the impacts of public policy on children. Welfare policy in this country has always had significant implications for the well-being of children, and the new Personal Responsibility and Work Opportunity Reconciliation Act (PRWORA) is no exception. Zaslow, Tout, Botsko, and Moore (1998) have completed an analysis of the provisions of this legislation and, based on the findings of earlier research on welfare-to-work programs, identified key provisions that are likely to have significant implications for children. The key provisions that they highlight and their rationales for concern are as follows:

1. *Time limits.* The new law places a sixty-month lifetime limit on welfare receipt, although some states have even stricter time limits (see Table 4.2). States exempt some families from the sixty-month

limit because of specific hardships. The new legislation may result in a sizable number of recipients going to work so they won't reach the sixty-month time limit, but for those who are long-term recipients (and their children), the outlook is problematic. From previous studies we know that, compared to short-term recipients, long-term recipients display more depressive symptoms, have less of a sense of personal control over their lives, and have fewer social supports. They also provide their children with less cognitive stimulation and emotional support, and their children score lower on measures of receptive vocabulary and social maturity.

2. *Employment requirements.* New legislation requires participation in work-related activities, as defined by each state, within twenty-four months of receiving assistance. Findings from earlier studies suggest that children fare slightly better or about the same on measures of development when their mothers are employed than when they are not. This may be due to the better mental health of employed mothers, or it may be due to the infusion of needed economic resources. However, some studies suggest negative outcomes for children when employment is initiated during the first year of a child's life. This is significant, given that under PRWORA, some states are requiring mothers whose infants are as young as zero to three months to go to work (see Table 4.3). Studies also show that outcomes for children vary according to maternal wage level and the quality of the home environment (which may decline when the mother goes out to work).

3. *Paternity and child support.* New legislation strengthened child support and paternity establishment provisions. States are now mandated to have a process in place for voluntary paternity acknowledgment and to establish paternity for 90 percent of all births to unmarried women. Based on earlier studies, we know that various forms of paternal involvement and the provision of child support have been linked to positive developmental outcomes. However, it is not known whether or how child support in a mandatory context influences father-child contact or children's developmental outcomes. In addition, benefits to children may not occur if increased paternal involvement leads to interparental conflict.

4. *Eligibility and entitlement changes.* Under PWRORA, an estimated quarter-million children with behavioral disorders and learning disabilities who received Supplemental Security Income (SSI) are no longer eligible for benefits. In addition, adult welfare recipients in the families of many of these children are subject to work requirements. Likewise, children of legal immigrants who are no longer eligible for food stamps under PWRORA may experience diminished family resources. Some states provide supplemental funds or emergency benefits for such families, but others do not, and these families will have to provide for themselves.

5. *Child care.* Under the new welfare law, states have flexibility regarding child care funding and child care assistance eligibility guidelines. PWRORA combined child care monies into the Child Care and Development Fund, which is a capped grant based on prior state child care expenditures. States vary in the degree to which they use this money to provide subsidies, increase the supply of child care, assist parents in finding child care, and strengthen regulation and monitoring of licensed child care.

   Important to children's well-being is whether states, when providing a child care subsidy to families, require them to use a licensed caregiver or encourage them to use different types of care such as a center or family child care (see Chapter 5). Indications are that a substantial proportion of families turn to unlicensed, informal forms of child care when seeking to fulfill the new work requirements because these offer more flexible hours and are less expensive, but research shows that unlicensed, informal child care is often of lower quality than regulated settings.

6. *Nonmarital and teenage childbearing.* The Welfare Reform Act requires teenage welfare recipients to attend school and live with their parents or other responsible adults. The Act also allows

TABLE 4.3   Time Period Exemptions for Mothers of Infants, by State

States with no exemptions from work requirements for mothers with infants (3 states)
Idaho
Iowa
Utah

States with exemptions lasting three months or less (10 states)

Arkansas	New Jersey
Colorado	Oklahoma
Florida	Oregon*
Michigan	South Dakota
Nebraska*	Wisconsin*

States with exemptions lasting four to six months (6 states)

California	North Dakota
Delaware	Tennessee*
Hawaii*	Wyoming

States with exemptions lasting up to one year (26 states)

Alabama	Minnesota
Alaska	Mississippi
Arizona	Missouri
Connecticut	Montana
District of Columbia	Nevada
Georgia	New Mexico
Illinois	New York
Indiana*	Ohio
Kansas	Pennsylvania
Kentucky	Rhode Island
Louisiana	South Carolina
Maine	Washington
Maryland	West Virginia

*States with exemptions lasting more than one year (6 states)***

Massachusetts	Texas*
New Hampshire	Vermont*
North Carolina	Virginia*

*These states have indicated that the work exemptions for parents with infants *do not* count against lifetime limits.
Source: J. Knitzer & S. Page. *Map and track: State initiatives for young children and families, 1998 edition.* New York: National Center for Children in Poverty, Columbia School of Public Health, 1998.

states to institute a "family cap" that denies additional benefits to families in which more children were born while the families are receiving assistance. States that succeed in reducing nonmarital births receive monetary bonuses. Some recent findings, such as Delaware's A Better Chance program, suggest that family cap policies may not be effective.

Other research findings provide limited guidance on how effective these new requirements on nonmarital and teenage childbearing are likely to be. Staying in school has been shown to be associated with lower first-birth rates to teens, and both staying in school and living with parents have been shown to be associated with lower second-birth rates to teens. However, research has not yet established whether either of these things *causes* the rate of first or repeat teen births to be lower (Wertheimer & Moore, 1998).

TRENDS AND ISSUES

Jobs: Minimum Wages, Unions, and Community Service/Workfare

The current success of welfare reform, as reflected in the dramatic drop in welfare caseloads, is due in large part to the country's robust economy. There are fears among some advocates that, should the economy experience a recession, fewer jobs will be created, especially for entry-level workers with limited skills. Wages have not kept pace with the current growth in jobs. For low-skilled workers, even full-time employment does not provide a living wage, and many of them are trapped in poverty. Poverty is likely to continue to be prevalent among single mothers, who often cannot work full-time and who often have limited education and skills. Getting more education and skills would enhance their life chances, but with the new welfare reform regulations these women are expected to find jobs, not go back to school.

As states attempt to move hard-to-place welfare recipients off the rolls, they may find that these recipients cannot find jobs in the private sector. States may need to create more public service jobs, such as maintaining public parks, painting public buildings, and repairing schools, for these recipients if they want to keep work and personal responsibility as their major goals. However, these kinds of workfare jobs would compete with other entry-level or low-skill jobs held by regular city and state employees. One of the ways to lessen the competition between workfare employees and regular public employees is to ensure that all welfare recipients be paid at least minimum wage for their work. Unions are likely to continue their efforts to organize among workfare workers, as well as partner with public employers and others to develop the skills training and work opportunities that welfare recipients and others who are poor need to get jobs in this changing economy. Creating links among the poor, rather than exacerbating divisions among the welfare poor and the working poor, is an aim of a number of advocates working on behalf of children and their families.

The present emphasis in federal and state welfare programs on work rather than education or skills training is likely to prove more problematic in the coming years. If nothing else, it will ensure that the polarization between the well-to-do and the poor grows wider, since those with limited education are finding fewer employment opportunities with salaries and benefits that support healthy families. The children in these families will continue to be disadvantaged and their life chances narrowed. While employers may like paying lower wages to former welfare recipients, at some point the country's productivity levels will be negatively impacted. A smarter response may be to encourage prospective employees to study and develop skills so that they can become more productive workers.

Race to the Bottom

When the welfare reform legislation was being debated in Congress, some welfare advocates feared that states would attempt to keep their benefits as low as possible for a number of reasons. First, the money that comes to states from the federal government is a block grant, which means that states have a great deal of discretion in how they use the monies to respond to their economic, political, and social needs. Second, the amount of money that comes to states is capped, meaning that states get the same amount of federal money whether their caseloads are rising or falling. In that case, states definitely do not want to create a situation in which increasing numbers of recipients live within their borders. Third, states differ on what approach they take to work and personal responsibility, and the resources that they make available to welfare recipients as they transition from welfare to work. Some states are clearly more punitive in their approach, believing that if a recipient is left with very few options, that person will go to work. Other states have been more generous in their provision of services, and have a longer view of what it takes to move from welfare to work. Child care assistance is a good example: Some states have increased their spending to make more subsidized slots available; others have maintained their historic level of spending. Some states have relaxed the regulations on what is a suitable child-care placement, thus perhaps increasing the affordability of child care but not the quality of care (see Chapter 5).

Welfare Reform's Impact on Families and Children

A mother's going to work need not be traumatic for children. However, if she is stressed by money, transportation, and child care problems, her stress may be felt by the child in a number of ways (Edin & Lein, 1997). She may inflict emotional or physical abuse on the child, or the child may suffer the terror of stress-related domestic violence. Or the child may experience more want as the family's income is lessened by the decrease in welfare benefits, or from periods of unemployment or underemployment.

We also need to be concerned about the children of kinship providers. For instance, what happens when a grandmother's welfare benefits are capped, even if she takes in more of her grandchildren? What happens when a grandmother on welfare, despite the physical and emotional challenges of age, has to go to work and finds herself juggling responsibilities at both home and work? When the mother of a disabled child has to go to work, who will take care of the child? Will subsidized child care be sufficient or will specialized child care be prohibitively expensive? The safety net that used to be available to women when they cycled off work because of these kinds of difficulties is no longer available. Who will take up the slack for these families—nonprofit organizations or other family members?

These are questions that policy makers need to be pondering. The case study at the beginning of this chapter illustrates some of these issues. Denise Jordan was clearly conflicted in having to decide whether she should quit her job and take care of her grandchildren or continue to work in hopes of providing more economic resources to her own children.

CHAPTER SUMMARY

According to federal government calculations, about 13 percent of the U.S. population is poor. The poor are a heterogeneous group, but poverty is especially prevalent among children under 18 and among households headed by African-American and Hispanic females. Poverty figures are highest for children under 6 years old who live in female-headed households. Poverty is caused in large measure by a number of changes in the U.S. economy which make it difficult for families to maintain a decent standard of living, including wage stagnation and a declining need for male workers with few skills and limited education.

Before the Great Depression, providing for the poor was mainly the responsibility of local and state governments. From 1935 until recently, the federal government, in partnership with the states, provided a safety net to eligible poor families with children through the Aid to Families with Dependent Children (AFDC) program. AFDC was a means-tested program which required applicants, mainly single mothers and their children, to meet federal and state criteria of eligibility in order to receive benefits. The AFDC program was increasingly viewed with suspicion, and concern grew that the existing program discouraged work by enabling recipients to subsist on welfare payments.

By the mid-1980s, a number of states began demonstration programs among targeted groups of welfare recipients. In 1988 Congress passed the Family Support Act, which required AFDC recipients to participate in education, job-training, and work programs. The professed intent was to help poor persons leave welfare and become self-sufficient.

Welfare benefits were further linked to approved parental behaviors when, in 1996, Congress passed the Personal Responsibility and Work Opportunity Act (PRWORA). PRWORA eliminated the AFDC program and replaced it with block grants to states to establish Temporary Assistance for Needy Families (TANF) programs. PRWORA places emphasis on work and leaves states responsible for designing and implementing their welfare programs.

TANF, like AFDC before it, provides cash income to poor families. The federal government also provides other kinds of assistance to families in need. These noncash resources include tax credits, food stamps, medical benefits, and child care subsidies. PRWORA affects the way some of these noncash resources are dispensed. For example, Medicaid can be terminated if adults refuse to work, although in most states the children of parents who have been terminated are still eligible for Medicaid.

Because of the flexibility which PRWORA gives to states, today we have fifty different cash assistance programs. Given their relatively long involvement with reforming their welfare systems, Wisconsin and Michigan have become models to which other states look for recommendations on how to change their programs. Wisconsin Works (W-2) provides cash assistance and supportive services only to those individuals engaged in some work activity. Also helping welfare recipients transition to work are nonprofit programs like Project Match and organizations such as unions.

Children in the United States have a much greater chance of living in poverty than children in other industrialized countries, in part because of the limited public assistance that we give to single-parent families. This is unfortunate because poor children face greater risks of premature death, stunted physical and intellectual growth, and neglect and abuse. The Welfare Reform Act has several provisions that may directly impact children, such as a requirement that mothers of very young children go to work and relaxed guidelines on the kinds of child care centers that may be subsidized.

The changing welfare policy environment suggests several trends and issues which may prove problematic. Some of these include the likelihood of increased competition for jobs between the welfare poor and the working poor; the political calculations that states make in deciding whether to be more punitive or more generous in allocating benefits to those transitioning from welfare to work; and understanding the conditions under which a mother's return to work may be beneficial or traumatic for her children. The country must decide whether it wants to punish families that are poor or provide them with the security that they need to thrive.

FOR STUDY AND DISCUSSION

1. Identify five nonprofit organizations in your community that provide resources to the poor. What kinds of resources do they provide? Where do their funds come from?

2. Ask a representative of a welfare rights organization in your community how women and their families are faring under the 1996 Welfare Reform Act.

3. Review the history of public assistance in this country. Identify the premises of major programs, from mothers' pensions through the Personal Responsibility and Work Opportunity Act of 1996. What are the similarities? What are the differences?

4. Talk with a welfare worker (generally called a case worker) and a current or former welfare recipient about why women go on welfare. Identify any similarities and differences in the reasons they give you.

5. Identify two major employers in your community. Ask the employers about the kinds of entry-level jobs their companies provide. What skills and attitudes do they expect of entry-level employees? How much do they pay entry-level employees?

FOR ADDITIONAL STUDY

Blank, R. M. (1997). *It takes a nation: A new agenda for fighting poverty.* New York: Russell Sage Foundation and Princeton, NJ: Princeton University Press.

Edin, K. & Lein, L. (1997). *Making ends meet: How single mothers survive welfare and low-wage work.* New York: Russell Sage Foundation.

Katz, M. B. (1986). *In the shadow of the poorhouse: A social history of welfare in America.* New York: Basic Books.

Mink, G. (1998). *Welfare's end.* Ithaca, NY: Cornell University Press.

Sidel, R. (1986). *Women and children last: The plight of poor women in affluent America.* New York: Viking.

Zaslow, M., Tout, K., Botsko, C., & Moore, K. (1998). *Welfare reform and children: Potential implications.* Washington, DC: The Urban Institute.

INTERNET SITES

Administration for Families and Children. The Administration for Families and Children is a division of the U.S. Department of Health and Human Services. The Web site provides technical information and statistical data in regards to welfare reform. http://www.acf.dhhs.gov

Children's Defense Fund. The Children's Defense Fund is committed to the well-being of children. The Web site provides helpful information about children and welfare reform but focuses mainly on statistics related to the state of children in the United States. http://www.childrensdefense.org

Child Trends, Inc.* Child Trends, Inc. is a nonprofit organization dedicated to research focused on children, youth, and families. The Web site offers comprehensive data on how welfare reform affects children. http://www.childtrends

The Urban Institute: Assessing the New Federalism* The Urban Institute provides extensive information on social and economic issues. "Assessing the New Federalism" is the Urban Institute's project examining welfare reform. In addition to information about all aspects of welfare reform, the site offers thorough and extensive research related specifically to families and children. The Web site also has a database with information about the efforts of each state in addressing welfare reform. http://newfederalism.urban.org

Institute for Women Policy Research* The Institute for Women Policy Research was established to research policies that impact women. A portion of the Web site covers welfare reform and contains information on domestic violence, reproduction, education, and issues that impact women in relation to welfare reform. The site also provides an on-line forum for interested individuals to discuss welfare reform. http://www.iwpr.org

The National Center for Children in Poverty* The NCCP promotes policies and programs that work to reduce child poverty. The Web site provides statistics about children, along with information on how welfare reform affects children. http://www.cpmcnet.columbia.edu/dept/nccp/

The Welfare Information Network* The Welfare Information Network is a foundation-sponsored Web site with extensive information on all aspects of welfare reform, including policies regarding immigrants, child support, teenage parenting, welfare-to-work programs, TANF, domestic violence, and child welfare. http://www.welfareinfo.org

REFERENCES

Abramovitz, M. (1988). *Regulating the lives of women: Social welfare policy from colonial times to the present.* Boston: South End Press.

American Federation of State, County and Municipal Employees. (1998, July). *Thinking creatively about welfare-to-work job creation.* Unpublished manuscript.

Background: Vice President Gore's welfare-to-work coalition: Keeping jobs and sustaining success. (May 19, 1998.). http://www.whitehouse.gov/wh/eop/ovp/work/history.html

Blank, R. M. (1997). *It takes a nation: A new agenda for fighting poverty.* New York: Russell Sage Foundation and Princeton, NJ: Princeton University Press.

Boo, K. (1997, October 19). Painful choices: Denise Jordan is off welfare and loves her job, but what about her daughter? *Washington Post,* p. A1.

*Denotes a Web site with extensive information on welfare reform.

A comparison of selected key provisions of the welfare re-form reconciliation act of 1996 with current law. (1996). Washington, DC: The Urban Institute. Available on-line at http://www.urban.org/welfare/WRCA96.htm

Currie, J. (1996, May). The effects of welfare on child outcomes: What we know and what we need to know. Paper prepared for National Academy of Sciences meeting.

DeParle, J. (1998, July 27). Shrinking welfare rolls leave record high share of minorities. *New York Times,* p. A1+.

DeParle, J. (1997, December 30). Tougher welfare limits bring surprising results. *Washington Post,* p. A1.

Edin, K., & Lein, L. (1997). *Making ends meet: How single mothers survive welfare and low-wage work.* New York: Russell Sage Foundation.

Fix, M. E., & Tumlin, K. (1997). *Welfare reform and the devolution of immigrant policy.* Washington, DC: The Urban Institute.

Gallagher, L., Jerome, M., Gallagher, K. P., Schreiber, S., & Watson, K. (1998). *One year after federal welfare reform: A description of state temporary assistance for needy families (TANF) decisions as of October 1997.* Occasional paper number 6. Washington, DC: The Urban Institute.

Harris, J. F. (1998, May 28). Clinton extols his welfare policies. *Washington Post,* p. A15.

Herr, T., & Halpern, R. (1991). *Changing what counts: Rethinking the journey out of welfare.* Evanston, Ill: Northwestern University. Project Match, Center for Urban Affairs and Policy Research.

Katz, M. B. (1986). *In the shadow of the poorhouse: A social history of welfare in America.* New York: Basic Books.

Kingfisher, C. P. (1996). *Women in the American welfare trap.* Philadelphia: University of Pennsylvania Press.

Knitzer, J., & Page, S. (1998). *Map and track: State initiatives for young children and families.* New York: National Center for Children in Poverty.

Long, S. K., & Clark, S. J. (1997). *The new child care block grant: State funding choices and their implications.* Washington, DC: The Urban Institute. Available on-line at http://www.newfederalism.urban.org/html/anf_a12.htm

Mathews, J. (1990, May 18). Working off welfare: Study sees treasuries in major beneficiaries. *Washington Post,* p. A4.

Mink, G. (1998). *Welfare's end.* Ithaca, NY: Cornell University Press.

Miranne, K. B., & Young, A. H. (1998). Women 'reading the world': Challenging welfare reform in Wisconsin. *Journal of Sociology & Social Welfare, 25,* 155–176.

Mulroy, E. A. (1995). *The new uprooted: Single mothers in urban life.* New York: Auburn House.

Murray, C. (1984). *Losing ground: American social policy, 1950–1980.* New York: Basic Books.

National Center for Children in Poverty. (1998, Spring). Poverty Rates Remain High Despite the Booming Economy, *News and Issues, 3.*

Pavetti, L. (1997, July). *How much more can they work? Setting realistic expectations for welfare mothers.* Washington, DC: The Urban Institute. [Annie E. Casey Foundation] Available on-line at http://www.urban.org/welfare/howmuch.htm

Pavetti, L, Olson, K., Nightingale, D., & Duke, A. (1997). *Welfare-to-work options for families facing personal and family challenges: Rationale and program strategies.* Washington, DC: The Urban Institute. Available on-line at http://www.urban.org/welfare/pave1197.html

Pear, R. (1998, September 26). Americans lacking health insurance put at 16 percent. *New York Times,* A1+.

Regenstein, M., & Meyer, J. A. (1998, July). *Job prospects for welfare recipients: Employers speak out.* Washington, DC: The Urban Institute. Available on-line at http://www.newfederalism.urban.org/html/occ10.htm

Seefeldt, K. S., Pavetti, L., Maguire, K., & Kirby, G. (1998). Income support and social services for low-income people in Michigan. *State Reports.* Washington, DC: The Urban Institute.

Shalala, D. (1993). Welfare reform: A priority for the Clinton administration. *Children Today, 27,* 4–6.

Stout, H. (1996, August 21). Clinton signs measure raising minimum wage. *The Wall Street Journal,* p. 3.

Tweedle, J. (1998, January). Building a foundation for change in welfare. *State Legislatures,* 26–35.

U.S. Bureau of the Census. (1998). *Poverty and health statistics.* Washington, DC: Branch/HHES Division. March Current Population Survey.

U.S. Department of Health and Human Services (1998). *Temporary assistance for needy families, 1936–1998.* Washington, DC: HHS Administration for Children and Families. Available on-line at http://www.acf.dhhs.gov/news/stats/369/htm

Vobejda, B., & Haveman, J. (1998, August 12). States' welfare shift: Stop it before it starts. *The Washington Post,* p. A1+.

Vobejda, B., & Jeter, J. (1997, September 1). And now comes the hard part. *Washington Post National Weekly,* p. 22.

Waller, M. (1997). *Welfare-to-work and child care: A survey of the ten big states.* Washington, DC: Democratic Legislative Committee. Available on-line at http://www.dlcppi.org/texts/social/ccare.htm

Weir, M., Orloff, A. S., & Skocpol, T. (Eds.). (1988). *The politics of social policy in the United States.* Princeton: Princeton University Press.

Wilson, W. J. (1987). *The truly disadvantaged: The inner city, the underclass, and public policy.* Chicago: University of Chicago Press.

Wertheimer, R. & Moore, K. (1998). *Childbearing by teens: Links to welfare reform.* Washington, DC: The Urban Institute.

Zaslow, M., Tout, K., Botsko, C., & Moore, K. (1998). *Welfare reform and children: Potential implications.* Washington, DC: The Urban Institute.

CHAPTER 5

Supporting Families with Day Care and Child Development Programs

There was a child went forth every day,
And the first object he look'd on, that object he became,
And that object became part of him for the day or a certain part of the day,
Or for many years or stretching cycles of years.
—Walt Whitman

CHAPTER OUTLINE

CASE EXAMPLE: A NEIGHBORHOOD DAY CARE NETWORK

The following case example shows a community-based approach to day care that helps family day care providers offer good quality day care in their homes. This fictional case is a composite of similar family day care networks being developed across the country. It illustrates the importance of community organization in the development of good day care options in low-income neighborhoods.

Elisa Hernandez is a day care coordinator at the Casa del Barrio, a community agency for economic and social development, located in a low-income Puerto Rican neighborhood in a large city. A community organizer, she became concerned about the lack of day care in her neighborhood about six years ago. Many of her neighbors are young families, often headed by the mother, who work at low-paying jobs in other areas of town. As welfare became stricter about requiring mothers to work, even if they had infants and toddlers to care for, the shortage of day care slots in the local neighborhood became severe. The only day care center in the area that would accept the low welfare reimbursement rates was always full. Besides, it only took children who were toilet trained and it did not offer evening or weekend services, when many of the mothers worked.

Ms. Hernandez called together a committee consisting of current family day care providers, working parents, and representatives of Head Start, the schools, the public health department, and the public day care licensing department. The group decided to focus on increasing family day care in the area, which would provide scheduling flexibility to parents, be reasonable in cost, and offer parents, many of whom had limited English language skills, caregivers who spoke Spanish and were part of the Puerto Rican culture. An initial grant from a foundation gave the group resources to begin recruiting and training family day care providers, and to offer ongoing support to them. In order to find women who would be capable day care providers, Ms. Hernandez asked people in the area for names of women whom the neighbors trusted to do babysitting and who were considered to know a lot about children. She visited each of these women to get better acquainted and to invite them to an informational meeting.

The Family Day Care Program now has thirty family day care providers serving from seventy to eighty children. The program accepts infants and preschoolers, and older siblings who may come before and after school. Some providers offer care in the evenings and on weekends. Most speak Spanish as well as English.

Training is a major aspect of the program's success. Before caring for any children, providers receive training in how licensing works in the state and get help completing the licensing forms, which are not available in Spanish. They also receive information on the food program available from the state and learn other basics about running a small day care business from their homes. The program learned that many women who were interested in providing day care had been discouraged because they didn't know how to cope with the red tape involved; the program guides them through this process. The program also talks with the potential providers realistically about the rates welfare will pay for day care and how much the provider can expect to earn.

Within the first three months of taking children, providers also receive training in early childhood development, nutrition, health, and child abuse and neglect. Further training is also available in early childhood education. In addition to training, the program offers providers the free use of baby furniture and toys for six months, and can help providers install smoke detectors and make other minor improvements to meet licensing requirements.

During the last year, due in part to welfare reform, more money has been available from the state to improve day care quality. The program was able to access these funds to hire a full-time, bilingual early childhood education teacher, who has been successful in increasing the skills of the providers. She visits each home at least once a month, bringing books and other learning materials. She shows the providers how to use them and consults on any special issues with the children. She helps the parents and providers keep track of the children's immunizations, and she refers children as needed to early screening programs for possible developmental problems.

The providers have developed a support group that meets monthly in members' homes. They share ideas and concerns, and often have guest speakers. Ms. Hernandez believes that these monthly meetings and the training help the providers to develop a sense of professionalism, as they begin to think of themselves less as "babysitters" and more as child care specialists with knowledge of how children grow and develop and of the community service system for children. Providers have learned to identify potential problems in child development and to refer parents to Head Start, the food stamp program, and adult education classes. As one provider observed, "People have always come to me to talk about their kids. The difference is now I know many different ideas to tell them, and not just based on my own experience."

The services offered to providers have also created program stability; few providers quit, so children experience long-term continuity of care. Parents are comfortable with the program; they know that their children are cared for in homes that are connected to the social service system, and that the providers have been screened and trained. Overall, the program has been able to improve the early childhood experiences of numerous children with working parents in the neighborhood, at relatively modest cost, through developing a cadre of dedicated, skilled family day care providers. Unfortunately, neither this day care program nor most others is able to offer day care providers with a decent income. However, for some women, it is a reasonable alternative to outside employment.

INTRODUCTION

With most mothers at work some part of each day, the question of what happens to the children has become an issue of intense national interest. Highly publicized stories of children left in dangerous situations while their parents, oblivious to the problem, were at work, have received widespread coverage in the press. This concern reflects the anxiety parents feel about having to juggle home and work, and their worries about whether, by working outside the home, they are short-changing their children of the care they need, or even jeopardizing their safety (Vobejda & Davis, 1997). The fact that day care is in the national spotlight indicates that, after decades of ignoring the reality that many children were being cared for by people other than their parents, the country is ready to address the issue of what happens to children in a society organized around parental employment outside the home.

The term *child care* encompasses a wide variety of arrangements that parents make for their children's daytime care and development. Unlike most industrialized countries, the United States has lagged in establishing government-assisted arrangements for the daytime care of children of working parents. Reasons for this long delay come from a host of conflicting values in American society about the appropriate role of women as workers and mothers, and about the responsibility of government to participate in what many consider to be the "private sphere" of family life. The high cost of quality child care, the cultural diversity of U.S. families, and the controversy over the effects of day care on children's growth and development have also inhibited the establishment of comprehensive federal policy on children's daytime care and development. Hesitation about encouraging "other-than-mother" care derailed the first major effort to develop a national consensus on federal government support for daycare. In 1971, Congress passed a major piece of legislation that would have vastly expanded the availability of quality child care, but President Nixon vetoed it on the grounds that, "For the Federal Government to plunge headlong financially into supporting child development would commit the vast moral authority of the National Government to the side of communal approaches to child rearing over against the family-centered approach" (Nixon, 1971).

By the 1990s, however, a variety of advocacy groups had continued to press for an effective national child care policy and had achieved a congruence of interests. Today, child care is no longer perceived as a service mainly for poor mothers, for disorganized families, or for children with special needs. Parents from all regions and levels of income have expressed concern about child care and are demanding not only programs that offer nurturance, safety, and affordability but also experiences that advance early childhood education. Politicians' awareness of the gender gap has made them more responsive to issues of concern to women voters. Reflecting on the increased acceptance of child care as a political issue, Mary Frances Berry, former U.S. commissioner on civil rights, observed that, "Continuing concern about poor children and welfare women underscored the issue, yet it was the increasing number of divorces, female-headed households, and middle-class wage-earning white women that ignited the child care movement" (Berry, 1993).

In the last decade, funding for child care has increased substantially. Head Start, a program started in 1965 to provide early child education to poor children, received its largest increase in funding in 1992 and became available as an all-day, full-year program to accommodate working mothers. The Child Care and Development Block Grants, established in 1990, provide states with funds to subsidize child care for low-income families and to improve quality through enforcing higher standards at the state level and through child care worker training. Another child care program established in 1990 was Title IVA At-Risk Child Care, targeted at the child care needs of poor, working families. The welfare reform legislation of 1996 included increased funding for day care for welfare families to ease the transition from welfare to work. In addition to these government-funded programs, the federal government also supports child care through its tax policy. Through tax credits, working families can reduce their tax burden by a percentage of their child care expenses.

These changes in federal policy reflect a consensus that child care is no longer a matter of private concern to individual families, but a legitimate issue for national policy. At the 1997 White House Conference on Child Care, President Clinton's remarks reflected this increased recognition of the importance of child care to the nation: "[P]eople in this country have to be able to succeed at work and at home in raising their children. And if we put people in the position of essentially having to choose one over the other, our country is going to be profoundly weakened. Obviously, if people are worried sick about their children, and they fail at work, it's not just individual firms, it's the economic fabric and strength of the country that is weakened. Far more important, if people fail at home, they have failed in our most important job, and our most solemn responsibility" (W. Clinton, 1997).

In spite of these achievements, advocates for children and working families believe that many gaps exist in providing suitable daytime care for the nation's children. Availability and affordability are still major problems for many families, in spite of increased government help. The quality of care that children receive is also becoming a question of national concern. One recent study concluded that most centers in the country offer care that is poor to mediocre, particularly for infants and toddlers (Helburn, et al., 1995). This problem becomes even more urgent when considered in light of other recent scientific findings that the experiences of young children in their earliest years affect how well they will learn for their entire lifetime. First Lady Hillary Rodham Clinton has pointed out that, "With 45% of our children under the age of one in day care regularly, the issue of quality has tremendous bearing not just on individual lives, but on the future of our nation" (H. Clinton, 1997). Another issue affecting many families is choice. Families have different child care needs depending on their work schedules, the characteristics of their children, and individual preferences. Yet too many families have choices severely limited by what is available and affordable in their community. National attention is also focusing on making it easier and more affordable for parents who want to do so to stay home with their children for some period of time.

The lives of working parents are complicated and demanding. In a society that requires women to work and recruits them into the labor force but has only begun to establish a national policy of child care, maintaining an adequate arrangement for children's care can become a constant source of family tension. Because of the fragmented and uncoordinated patterns of day care provision, working parents usually must rely on multiple arrangements, even within the same day. This is often a package of some in-family care, some out-of-home care, and some group center care, all of which require multiple coping strategies for both children and parents. A major gap in child care services is the lack of coordinated, community-based programs that help families organize work and family life in a comprehensive way.

Whatever the setting or focus, all programs of child care should contain these elements:

- An understanding of a child's individual needs and stages of growth
- Consistent nurture and supportive emotional response
- Attention to the child's needs for healthy physical, emotional, cognitive, and social development
- A team approach to working with the family to minimize stress and discontinuity for the child
- Coordination within the community to minimize fragmentation of services for the family.

In other words, child care should deal with the whole child and her or his family. Children are not well cared for and protected if their need and capacity to learn and acquire competence are not given careful attention. Similarly, their success in learning, even in carefully devised educational programs, is hampered if there is not appropriate response to their feelings and emotions. Neither their education nor their welfare can be well looked after if they have unmet health needs, untended handicaps, or insufficient food and rest. Finally, child care that links its program to the families of the children, and also coordinates with other services in the community, helps create a network of caring adults in which the child is embedded.

FAMILIES NEEDING CHILD CARE

Families with Working Parents

Families at the beginning of the twenty-first century are dynamic and changing. Their needs for child care are evolving, and they are demanding change in the child care system. Parents are not only working in greater numbers but are also attending school, volunteering, and seeking leisure activities to enhance their lives. For all these activities, they may require child care. Welfare recipients are required to work, go to school, or participate in job training, and they need child care to meet these demands. Also fueling the demand for child care is the desire of many parents to provide some form of early educational experience to prepare their children for school.

In 1995, 60 percent of all preschoolers, or about 13 million children, were in some form of day care or early childhood educational program (Casper, 1996).

Overall, about 31 million children under the age of 15 live with working mothers (Casper, Hawkins, & O'Connell, 1994). These figures clearly show that "other-than-mother" care is now normative, rather than the exception, for children in the United States.

Child Care as a Child Welfare Service

Child care is usually considered only in the context of maternal employment. However, child care also has potential as a child welfare service, to strengthen vulnerable families and to prevent abuse, neglect, and the necessity for foster care placement for children. This potential has not been fully developed, partly because child care services are often administered by organizations outside the traditional child welfare service spectrum, and necessary linkages between service systems have not been made (Roditti, 1995; Hershfield, 1995).

Families Needing Specialized Assistance. Families who have characteristics that put them at risk for child maltreatment may need many types of specialized assistance, including access to child care. For example, children whose parents are in a substance abuse treatment program can benefit from child care that offers them a safe environment and developmentally appropriate experiences while their parents are working at overcoming their addiction. Similarly, children of teen parents who are in good quality day care settings may receive the developmental stimulation and oversight on their healthy growth and development that their young mothers are not ready to provide.

Respite care and crisis nurseries are also a valuable supplemental resource for families needing specialized assistance. Respite care is provided in some communities to families who have a child with disabilities or to families at risk of child abuse and neglect (ARCH, 1994). *Physically handicapped* children frequently need more than the usual opportunity for stimulation, training, and socialization as part of their treatment and rehabilitation. Similarly, *mentally retarded* children often need child care—preschool programs, after-school recreational services, and occupational day centers for older youth.

Many children with *serious emotional problems* have parents who can continue to care for them in their homes if proper therapy is provided and if the parents have periods of respite from demanding caretaking duties. Day treatment centers for emotionally disturbed children are a useful alternative to outpatient therapy or full-time residential treatment.

Children of migrant farm workers are vulnerable to serious physical, social, and emotional deprivation. Because their parents have no way of caring for them while the parents are working in the fields, these children may spend their days in hazardous conditions of care. Sometimes they stay in parked cars or buses near the fields with only very occasional attention from adults, or they may be left in the camps under the supervision of an elderly, incapacitated member of the family or with the oldest child—perhaps only 6 or 7 years of age. Community child care centers are needed for infants and preschoolers to get the nutrition and intellectual stimulation they need to achieve success at school.

Families in Crisis. For families who have abused or neglected their children and are at risk of losing them to foster care, child care services can help the family remain together while ensuring the child's safety. Such services allow a child to live at home while spending the day under the care of a trained child care provider, who can supplement the parent's minimally adequate care with developmentally enriching experiences and also can be a "first line of defense" in monitoring risky home situations. At the same time, child care services can provide needed respite to overburdened parents; the children receive appropriate daytime care while the parent attempts to resolve the serious problems which precipitated the child abuse and neglect. Homelessness, mental or physical illness, and mental retardation are among the family situations in which specialized day care services would be an appropriate middle-ground intervention between leaving children in a poorly functioning family with agency supervision and removing the child from the home entirely.

CHANGING PATTERNS OF WORK AND FAMILY

Working mothers are not new in America. Well before the Industrial Revolution of the nineteenth century, mothers worked many hours a day in their homes and on farms to produce goods and services that supplemented the family's income. This essential work often resulted in as much divided attention to children as occurs now among many mothers employed more formally outside their homes. Viewed against this background, the high rate of maternal employment today is not a radically new phenomenon, but an old one modified by new occupations and changed work locale, relationships, and rewards.

We decided to come back here because there were supposed to be jobs, but he couldn't find anything. So we decided I better go back to work—I haven't worked since we were married, but I'm a telephone operator and I knew I could get a job—but first we had to find a babysitter for Shelley. We didn't like the idea—she's two—but then . . . (Family day care user—Collins & Watson, 1976, p. 4)

The most urgent reason that women have entered the labor force in the past and continue to do so today is that like men, they feel a strong pressure to earn money. Women who enter the labor force almost universally do so out of necessity of one kind or another. Historic advances in science and technology have brought about an unprecedented growth and change in the national economy. The shift from an agricultural to an industrial society and the resulting expansion of the urban population has brought changes in the nature of jobs (for example, lessened requirements for physical labor) and greatly expanded job opportunities for women. At the same time, the goods and services mothers once produced in their homes now are produced by industry, and require money income to obtain. As industry has made more and more goods and services available, families have become increasingly desirous of a higher standard of living, improving the likelihood that mothers will take advantage of job opportunities to help achieve it.

For growing numbers of women, an equally compelling reason for working is that, just as in the case of men, work is central to their identities. More women than ever before subscribe to and take for granted the aims and principles of the organized women's movement—women as individual human beings, rather than persons treated collectively without recognition of their interests and capabilities (Chavez, 1987). Even though women receive approximately 70 percent of the average wage earned by men (Women's Bureau, 1990), women are entering and deriving satisfaction from a wide range of jobs at all levels of occupations previously viewed as suitable only for men.

Changed patterns of marriage and childbearing and increased life expectancy in the twentieth century have influenced mothers to work, and in turn have been influenced by women's opportunities and desire for employment. Women complete their families in a shorter time, and they have fewer children. As family ideology has become more egalitarian, there is less support for the idea that the husband, as the dominant family member, must earn all the income and the mother perform all the daily child-rearing responsibilities. The increased likelihood of divorce or widowhood impels women to develop their own economic security through work, rather than rely solely on their husbands for economic support.

At the center of the ambivalence in many quarters about the accelerated rate of mothers in the workforce is the tenacity, despite sweeping change, with which many citizens hold to an emotional and nostalgic view of what the structure of the family should be and the roles that men and women should play in it. Yet the economy has never supported the somewhat romantic, traditional concept of the family except for a select group of upper- and middle-class women during a brief time in the nineteenth century. Opponents of maternal employment have tended to ignore or minimize the family's need for the mother's earnings and to perceive the accelerated entry of women into the labor force as a dangerous consequence of "feminist thinking." The 1996 welfare reform law, which requires parents to work as a condition of eligibility for welfare, recognizes that maternal work outside the home is now normative. It remains to be seen whether this requirement will be fully supported by adequate provision of child care resources for the children of welfare recipients.

When over fifty percent of all married women with young children are in the labor force, it's time to stop blaming the feminists for destroying the family. Whatever personal satisfactions these women may find at work, the cold hard fact of American family life today is that it takes two incomes to live decently and still pay the bills (Rubin, 1987, p. 90)

Although the pattern is changing, women still bear most of the responsibility for housework and child care. Since women first entered industrial work more than a century ago, the way in which work is organized has been a stress factor in family life. Recognition that the "second shift" that is a constant in the lives of many American women, and concerns about the quality of care children receive while parents are working, have led to increased interest in better coordinating work and family life. The Family and Medical Leave Act of 1993 gives parents time off from work to care for a new baby or ill child. Some advocates are also urging shorter work weeks for both men and women and other policies that would allow a parent to stay home for a period of time.

SHARING THE COSTS OF CARE

The Child Care Crunch

Child care is a costly expense for many American families. The Children's Defense Fund (1998) describes the problem: "Full-day care easily costs $4,000 to $10,000 a year—at least as much as college tuition at a university. Yet, half of America's families with young children earn less than $35,000 a year. A family with both parents working full-time at the minimum wage earns only $21,400 a year." Families with preschoolers who required day care in 1993 paid an average of $74 a week (Casper, 1995).

For poor families, child care costs are especially burdensome. Poor families who pay for care spend about 18 percent of their income on child care for preschoolers, compared to 7 percent for the nation's wealthier families (Casper, 1995). Figure 5.1 shows the percentage of income spent by women of different income categories on child care.

In spite of the large percentage they spend on day care, poor families spend less in actual dollars than do wealthier families. The poorest working families spend less than $50 on average a week for child care, whereas the wealthiest families spend $92 a week. See Figure 5.2. Quality of care is related to cost. Recent

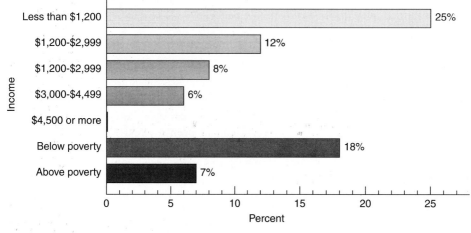

*Limited to families with a preschooler.

FIGURE 5.1   Percent of Monthly Family Income Spent on Child Care by Family Income and Poverty Status*

Source: L. M. Casper. (1995). *What does it cost to mind our preschoolers?* Washington, DC: U.S. Bureau of the Census.

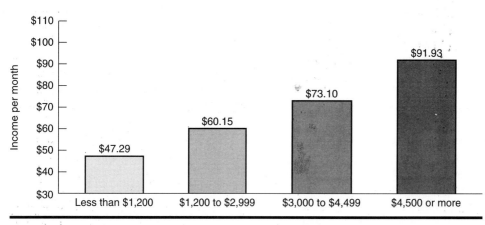

FIGURE 5.2   Weekly Payment for Child Care by Monthly Family Income.

Source: L. M. Casper. (1996). *Who's minding our preschoolers?* Washington, DC: U.S. Bureau of the Census.

research showing that the later learning ability of children depends on the quality of care they receive as infants and preschoolers underscores the importance of ensuring high-quality child care for all children (Barnett, 1995). Women with low earning capacity cannot support their families and pay for child care on their earnings alone. Advocates for children are concerned that without governmental assistance, poor children will be relegated to substandard day care facilities that will not provide the needed emotional, social, physical, and cognitive experiences to help them do well in school and become productive adults.

Recent Federal Legislation

Parents, businesses, and federal, state, and local governments all contribute to the total cost of child care in the United States. The federal role in funding child care changed drastically in the early 1990s as a result of legislation increasing the federal contribution. In 1997, the federal government spent about $10 billion on the three largest federal child care programs: the Child Care Development Block Grant; Head Start; and the Dependent Care Tax Credit (Shalala, 1997).

- *Child Care Development Block Grant* provides funds to states for child care for low-income families, including those in welfare-to-work programs, and for improving the quality and supply of child care. In 1997, the government spent $3 billion on grants and passed legislation authorizing funding for $22 billion over the next seven years. This program has expanded in recent years to address the additional child care costs brought about by welfare reform, which requires welfare recipients to work (Children's Defense Fund, 1997).
- *Head Start* is a federally and locally financed early childhood development program for low-income children. In 1997, the federal share of this program's costs was $4 billion. This program is described in another section of this chapter.
- *Dependent Care Tax Credit* helps families reduce their child care costs by allowing them to deduct a portion of these costs from their federal tax obligation. An important limitation of this program is that it helps only families who earn enough to pay federal taxes. Those earning too little to pay taxes do not get any help from this program on their child care expenses. In 1997, the federal cost of this program was $2.5 billion.

In addition to these programs, numerous smaller funding streams funnel resources to specific populations, such as children with disabilities and Native American children.

Families bear the brunt of expenditures for child care. Researchers have estimated that families pay about 70 percent of the total child care cost in the nation. In 1991, parental expenditures for child care were $23.6 billion (Stoney & Greenberg, 1996).

The Family and Medical Leave Act

The Family and Medical Leave Act was signed into law by President Clinton in 1993, the culmination of seven years of lobbying by child advocacy groups. It addresses the needs of families for both job security and caregiving, and, according to National Association of Social Workers (NASW) president Sheldon Goldstein, was "symbolic of a different day for the families of America" (Landers, 1993, p. 1). The law requires employers of 50 or more workers to grant employees who work 25 or more hours per week, up to 12 weeks of unpaid leave a year, for the birth or adoption of a child, for the care of a seriously ill child or other family member, or for a serious illness of their own. Although the leave is unpaid, employers do have to provide health benefits during the leave. Because part-time workers and workers in small businesses are exempt, only about half the nation's workers are covered by the law. In spite of this limitation, the law is a milestone toward the goal of making work more compatible with family life for American workers and their children, and puts the United States in the company of other industrialized countries, most of which have provisions for leave following childbirth and for child care emergencies.

Child Care and Welfare Reform

Changes in the welfare law are affecting many families with young children. See Chapter 4. Before the 1996 changes in welfare, families with children under age 3 were exempt from work requirements. Now, families with children under the age of one year may be required to work; Michigan, for example, requires parents of children three months old or older to work (United States General Accounting Office, 1997). Under the new law, more mothers are likely to need child care, particularly for very young children. These low-income parents often experience the "day care crunch" described earlier, in which their low incomes cannot cover the costs of day care. Innovative programs are needed to ensure not only an adequate supply of day care slots for the children of parents moving off welfare, but also good quality care which will help these youngsters prepare for success when they enter school.

DAY CARE REGULATION

Although varying in form, today all states have statutory provisions for the regulation of day care for children. The intent of these regulations is to safeguard children from harm and prevent ills that might befall them from poor care and supervision. Regulation is an action of the government to bring an activity in the private sector (in this case the places where and means by which children are cared for outside their own homes) under the control of constituted authority and to require compliance with agreed-on expectations.

Licensing is one of the activities affecting the standard of care that children receive. . . . Its mission is to require services in which the safety and well-being of children are givens. (Terpstra, 1989, p. 442)

Appropriate and well-enforced licensing and regulatory standards are important strategies in assuring quality in day care. Remember, however, that licensing rules represent minimum baseline requirements below which no program may operate. They do not provide a guarantee that day care will be of high quality. States, not the federal government, make and enforce regulations for day care. The states vary considerably in their day care licensing provisions; as the findings of two studies by the Children's Foundation (1991), which surveyed the states on their licensing provisions for day care centers and family day care homes, have verified.

All states do require that day care centers be licensed. Despite many differences, state day care regulations are fairly uniform in the areas they address. Most specify the amount of space that must be available to each child and also define fire and other building safety requirements. Providers may be required to pass health examinations; more and more states are also requiring criminal background checks. Most states require that the providers have certain levels of education and specify required child/adult ratios.

Special Issues in Day Care Regulation

In recent years a number of states have begun to consider and evaluate different ways of regulating family day care. Licensing, the traditional form of regulation, requires that a state agency reviews applications, inspects the day care centers and homes, approves the license, and regularly monitors the centers and homes. This arrangement has proved very costly, and states have not traditionally allocated sufficient resources to provide sound, ongoing assessments of day care homes. Concern has grown about the high costs of licensing day care homes in view of the limited safeguards achieved for children.

Most private day care homes are not regulated at all. One study estimated that 80 to 90 percent of caregivers are not regulated (Willer, Hoffereth, Kisker, Divine-Hawkins, Farquhar, & Glandtz, 1991). Most states exempt various categories of day care providers from regulation; for example, some states exempt homes caring for three or fewer children, or those caring for the children of relatives. States may require only homes that are receiving public funds, such as those caring for the children of welfare recipients, to be regulated. (Galinsky, Howes, Kontos, & Shinn, 1994). Many day care providers simply do not comply with the law, if they find the process of licensing burdensome and intrusive. Some providers do not become licensed because they want to avoid paying taxes on their income.

For all these reasons, only a small proportion of day care homes actually caring for children are brought to the attention of licensing agencies. In fact, if licensing authorities actively undertook to study and evaluate all the homes now giving care to unrelated children, the endeavor would be beyond the capacities of administrative departments as now constituted. This is in contrast to day care centers that by their nature are more easily identified in a community and brought under the jurisdiction of a licensing statute.

Registration: An Alternative to Licensing

Many states are now considering "registration" as an alternative to traditional licensing. The idea of registration is based on the assumption that most family day care providers want to comply with the law and that most of them are in substantial if not complete compliance with the family day care mandatory requirements. This approach to regulation operates as follows: Persons giving family day care to one or a small number of children are required to make this fact known to the state's regulatory agency—that is, to register the day care operation and report the names of children being cared for. The regulatory agency is then responsible for supplying the child care provider with a statement of the mandatory forms to be completed for registration, and other literature deemed to be helpful to anyone caring for young children. Day care providers are instructed to review the requirements carefully, assess their own degree of compliance, and report the degree of conformity to the regulatory agency. In addition, they must supply the parents of the children they care for with a copy of the mandatory requirements and the means by which complaints can be made to the regulatory agency. After registration, day care providers are given access to consultative resources for improving their child care endeavors. The regulatory agency also makes inspection visits to randomly selected registered day care homes to determine whether substantial conformity to standards does in fact exist and, when necessary, to help day care providers overcome obstacles to meeting standards.

To be successful, the regulatory agency must promulgate family day care standards widely. It must also carry out a continuing program of interpretation to the public of required standards of care, the role of the regulatory agency, and ways in which parents can select appropriate day care, monitor it, and report complaints.

Advantages to family day care of registration over licensing include these: (1) regulatory staff members are free to concentrate on problem homes rather than on routine inspections, (2) parents have a greater role in evaluating day care homes, and (3) family day care becomes more socially visible, increasing the feasibility of measuring its extent and evaluating and strengthening its characteristics.

WORKING PARENTS' CHILD CARE ARRANGEMENTS

There are over 19 million employed women with 31 million children under the age of 15 in the United States These children are in a variety of child care arrangements. Child care for children of employed parents is most often an informal arrangement be-

tween private individuals with no organized community involvement or sanction. Licensed family day care homes, day care centers, nursery schools, and organized after-school programs under any auspices play a lesser role in providing care for children of working parents. How then are the nation's children of working parents distributed among the different child care arrangements?

Child Care Arrangements for Preschoolers

Day care often is categorized as falling either (1) inside the family or (2) outside the family, when families use centers or family day care providers in the child care market. Care inside the family may be offered by the parents themselves, if, for example, they work different shifts. Nearly a quarter of all children under 5 whose mothers work are cared for by their parents. Another quarter of children under age 5 are cared for by relatives, especially grandparents. Overall, about half of all families with working mothers and children under age 5 use care within the family, either by the parents themselves or by relatives. This proportion has remained stable over the years (Casper, 1996).

Care outside the family may occur in the child's home, in the provider's home, or in a center. Nonrelatives who come into the child's home, called sitters or nannies, account for only a small proportion of child care arrangements. It would be a preferred option for many parents, especially parents of infants, but is too expensive for most families.

Nonrelative day care providers who offer care in their own homes, an arrangement known as "family day care," are used by about a fifth of working mothers with children under age 5. Day care centers include nursery schools and preschools, particularly used by mothers working part-time, as well as all-day centers. About 30 percent of preschoolers with employed mothers are cared for in centers (Casper, 1996). In addition, many children whose mothers don't work attend preschool or day care centers; currently about half of all 3- and 4-year-olds in the United States attend some form of preschool program. Figure 5.3 shows the child care arrangements for preschoolers in 1993.

Child care arrangements tend to change as the child gets older. Infants and toddlers (ages zero to 2

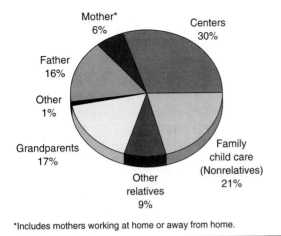

*Includes mothers working at home or away from home.

FIGURE 5.3 Primary Child Care Arrangements Used by Families with Employed Mothers for Preschoolers: 1993

Source: L. M. Casper. (1995). *What does it cost to mind our preschoolers?* Washington, DC: U.S. Bureau of the Census.

years) are more likely than older children to be cared for within the family. A common shift at age 3 is from care inside the family to care in a center (Casper, 1996).

Family Day Care

Made up of many different arrangements between parents and the caretakers of their children, family day care is the most complex system of child care in the country. For over 2 million children, most under age 5, going to someone else's home to be cared for is an integral part of their daily lives. Family day care defies simple description because it is so varied. In general, it can be divided into three major categories, differing in regulatory and administrative structure. The largest category is unregulated family day care, constituting about 90 percent of all family day care (Clarke-Stewart, 1993). These caregivers operate informally and independently of any regulatory agency, even though they may be subject to licensing or registration under the child care statute of the state in which they live. The second category consists of caregivers who are in compliance with state and/or federal regulatory requirements and who are subject to regulatory supervision if complaints about the care they give come from parents or the community, but who otherwise also operate quite independently. The smallest group of caregivers, though one growing in importance, is made up of regulated homes functioning as part of a child care system or network under the auspices of an umbrella sponsoring organization. Day care homes may care for one to six children; licensed group day care homes may care for up to twelve children. Most providers work alone, though about 40 percent have helpers. The cost, in 1990 dollars, of family day care ranges from about $2,000 to $6,000 per year per child, for full-time care (Clarke-Stewart, 1993; Kisker, Hofferth, Phillips, & Farquahar, 1991).

Family day care offers several advantages to parents and children. It is relatively easy to locate, since day care homes are dispersed widely in neighborhoods across the country. Parents can often find day care close to home, which minimizes transportation problems. The arrangements parents make with the providers often can accommodate special situations, such as a parent's unusual work schedule or special needs of the children. It is less expensive than other forms of care. Parents are likely to form a close, personal relationship with the provider, which may continue even after the child leaves care. For children, day care offers the stimulation of playing with other children and relating to nonfamily adults within the comfort and safety of a home setting.

The major disadvantage of family day care is the lack of accountability. Day care homes are private; after dropping off the child, the parent does not know what goes on in the home. The vast majority of providers are not licensed or regulated, and are not part of a network of providers. They operate independently and are unsupervised. They are unlikely to offer educational activities and usually do not have the training to provide ongoing, planned experiences for the children to promote their cognitive development. Another disadvantage is that the day care homes are inherently unstable and are often short-lived. An illness in the family or other event can cause the provider to quit offering care. The quality of care in day care homes varies a great deal. "They offer experiences for the child ranging from concerned and competent care by an involved and happy care provider to neglectful or even abusive care by a depressed and isolated woman who believes she has no marketable skills but needs the money and so takes in babies" (Clarke-Stewart, 1993, p. 45).

Day Care Centers

As with day care homes, there is tremendous variety among day care centers, making general descriptions inadequate. A center may offer care for a few as 15 children or as many as 300, though on average there are about 60 children per center. Children are usually divided into classes based on age; the average size of these groups is seven for infants, ten for toddlers, and fourteen for preschoolers. Most children in day care centers are 3 or 4 years old. The teachers are usually young women who have attended college (Clarke-Stewart, 1993).

Compared with day care homes, day care centers have several advantages. They are more stable and are publicly accountable through licensing and other regulations. They stay open even if staff are sick or go on vacation. Usually, staff have some training in child development and are likely to offer educational activities to children. Children have opportunities to play with other children in a safe environment that may be rich in stimulating games and activities. Their major disadvantages are that they may be farther from home than day care homes located in the immediate neighborhood, and they are often less flexible in hours or in taking sick children than are day care homes. Day care centers may seem large and impersonal to children; poor or mediocre centers often are not sufficiently attentive to the needs and abilities of individual children. Children may not have a close connection with a caring adult who knows them well.

Two major categories of day care centers are (1) nonprofit centers and (2) proprietary or for-profit centers. About 40 percent of all centers are for-profit operations. They differ among themselves in significant ways (Kagan & Glennon, 1982). Some (about 86 percent) of these for-profit centers are independently owned and operated, most often by a husband–wife

team. Not only are these small enterprises more numerous; they also are the most varied. Some of them provide a rich and diversified experience for children; some others provide at best only custodial care.

The other 14 percent of proprietary centers are either chains or franchised operations. Kinder-Care is an example of a chain of centers. This corporation serves more than 700 centers in 36 states and Canada with a clientele of children from infants to 12-year-olds, although mostly the children are 3 to 5 years old. Kinder-Care advertises care from 7:00 A.M. to 6:00 P.M., including before and after-school care. In the printed matter distributed to applicants, parents are assured of a staff–child ratio of 1 to 10 as well as "colorful toys instead of junk food and TV."

About 60 percent of centers are nonprofit. Of these, the majority are run by private community or charitable organizations, faith communities, or parent cooperatives. A small number are sponsored by corporations as a benefit for their employees, and another tiny fraction are run by universities as part of their educational and research missions. About 10 percent of nonprofit centers receive government funding and tend to offer a wide range of services, including health care, meals, transportation, and activities to promote children's educational readiness. Government-funded programs are available mainly to low-income families.

Although both for-profit and nonprofit centers exist in great variety, some characteristics important to quality tend to vary according to whether the center is nonprofit or proprietary. Clarke-Stewart (1993), reviewing recent research, reports that

it is clear that for all counts on which there is a difference, and there is a difference on most, nonprofit daycare centers, especially those supported by public funds, come out ahead. They are more likely to have a trained and experienced staff, to offer a comprehensive program with a child-development component, and to adhere to a higher set of standards. The teachers are more likely to offer the children developmentally appropriate activities. The centers offer more services: screening, testing, immunization, transportation, social work, referral to other agencies or professionals. They pay their teachers higher wages. Although these average differences are not guarantees, they can be of some help in starting a search for the best available daycare. (pp. 52–53)

Day Care Networks in Low-Income Communities

The organization of family day care homes into "day care systems" is a relatively recent development that has significant implications for child care planning and programming (Kisker et al., 1990; Out-of-School Time, 1997). Although these homes are only a small proportion of all day care homes, they are representative of a growing trend more important than their numbers suggest. The U.S. Congress, in enacting the Child Care and Development Block Grant of 1990, called on governors to designate a state lead agency to act as a convener and coordinator for organizing various day care constituencies into an overarching day care system.

As the case example at the beginning of the chapter shows, day care networks are systems that link family day care providers in a geographical area with each other and with professional support and consultation. They are usually organized by established agencies, such as schools, health departments, departments of social services, community-based organizations, or early childhood development and child care services. They improve the quality and supply of family day care in an area by recruiting, screening, training, and offering ongoing support and technical assistance to family day care providers and by linking the providers and the children they care for to other needed services in the community.

Providers participating in a day care system usually have access to ongoing training and support, and are required to adhere to certain health and safety standards. They are likely to receive regular consultation with child development professionals. Studies have shown that day care providers who are part of a network are more likely than other providers to consider themselves child care professionals. They tend to read child care books, go to meetings with colleagues, take classes in child development, keep records on each child in their care, and are more likely than other providers to provide educational activities, nutritious food, and a stimulating home environment (Divine-Hawkins, 1981).

The [network] provided the opportunity for bringing small groups of family day care mothers together for the purpose of discussing strengths and weaknesses of this type of child care. They wanted to compare notes, find more friends, assist each other and learn ways of coping with common problem situations. The staff quickly recognized that the women themselves could and would often provide assistance most needed to improve the quality of life for themselves and those in their care. (June Solnit Sale, Project Director—Collins & Watson, 1976, p. 64)

Providers in day care systems are also more likely to remain stable than other providers, because the system can provide supports that help the provider function better. The system can offer referrals of new families and consultation on fee schedules, taxes, and other business issues. It provides training and opportunities for providers to interact with one another. Expert consultation can help providers manage situations relating to children or their families. Back-up care is available if the provider is temporarily unable to care for children. Day care systems can alleviate such problems with family day care as lack of accountability, instability of provider homes, lack of training, and insufficient attention to children's developmental needs. At the same time, day care systems maintain all the advantages of family day care, such as flexibility, home atmosphere, and the close personal connections that can occur between provider and parent (Sugarman, 1991; Larner & Chaudry, 1993).

Day care networks have potential to improve family day care in all communities, but are particularly valuable in low-income neighborhoods. Families in poor neighborhoods want safe, high-quality day care that is convenient for the family's work schedule just as other families do; however, poor families have more severe financial constraints and there may be fewer options for care in the areas where they live. Their jobs often start early in the morning or last into the night, and many work on weekends. They may need day care only on a part-time basis, and because they have little job security, they may cycle in and out of the labor force. They may lack transportation to day care, and there may be very few providers or centers close to where they live. They or their children may not speak English, further complicating their search for day care.

As Larner (1994) points out, family day care may be especially well-suited to low-income families because it is close to home, flexible, small in scale, relatively affordable, and gives the parents the choice of who will care for their child, particularly regarding cultural and language compatibility. It also provides low-income women with the opportunity to earn a living at home while providing day care, although subsidies are required to supplement what the parents can pay for care.

Larner's research has led her to conclude that there are certain keys to success in creating a viable family day care network in low-income neighborhoods. She describes these as follows:

- It takes resources—financial and material—to enable low-income providers to offer safe and high quality care in their homes.
- It takes local people who are friendly, familiar, and trustworthy to reach low-income providers and draw them into the program's circle of support.
- It takes novel cooperative efforts involving child care experts and representatives of low-income communities to develop and implement effective programs that improve child care in poor neighborhoods.
- It takes time for change to occur in public policies, organizational relationships, and human behavior. Building the family day care supply depends on changes in all of these realms (Larner, 1994, p. 41).

The Child Welfare League of America (Sugarman, 1991) published a handbook on how to establish a day care network. It describes how a day care network organized at the local level might look. The local area could be defined as a county, a city, a school district, a health district, or another geographical area. Aided by an advisory committee from the community, an early childhood coordinator, operating out of a designated lead agency, would handle various operating functions, such as managing grants and contracts. This person would also arrange for working agreements with other agencies and providers for the referral services to health and other agencies. The network would include a wide range of day care providers, including family day care homes, centers, Head Start, school-based programs, faith-community programs, and day care for children with special needs.

Child Care Arrangements for School-Age Children

School-age children are likely to spend time in many different kinds of child care arrangements. Figure 5.4 shows where children aged 5 to 12 who have employed mothers are during after-school hours.

As the table shows, the majority of school-age children are in some form of after-school care: with relatives, in centers, with day care providers, or with babysitters. About two-fifths of school-age children with working mothers do not use any supplemental care. Not all of these children are home alone, as many children are in school during most of the hours their mothers work and don't need supplemental care. However, nearly 5 million school-age children spend time as "latchkey kids" without adult supervision during a typical week. Children are more likely to be "latchkey kids" as they get older and if their mother works full time instead of part time (Casper, Hawkins & O'Connell, 1994; Out-of-School Time, 1997).

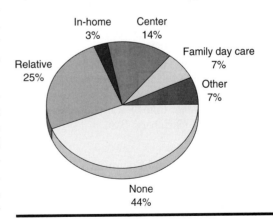

FIGURE 5.4   Use of Supplemental Care for Children Aged 5 to 12 with Employed Mothers, 1997

Source: U.S. Bureau of the Census. (1997). In Out-of-School Time, *Child Care Bulletin,* Issue 17. Available on-line: http://nccic.org/ccb/ccb-so97/outtime.html.

The subject of children in self-care generates controversy and tends to polarize people, perhaps because it reflects the difficult choice that so many parents have to make—working to support the family versus providing conventional supervision of their children after school. Early research on the effects of child self-care showed mixed results, leaving uncertainty as to whether latchkey children are subject to positive or negative consequences (Gray & Coolsen, 1987; Long & Long, 1983). Later findings, within limits, were generally reassuring, in that they found no negative impact from self-care on children's self-esteem, locus of control, or academic achievement (Rodman, Pratto, & Nelson, 1985; Vandell & Corasaniti, 1988).

Steinberg (1986) was interested in whether young adolescents in self-care were more susceptible than other adolescents to negative influences of peer pressure. He examined suburban children who were in adult care and several types of self-care, including self-care children who stay home after school, those who go to a friend's house with no adult supervision present, and those who "hang out" at the mall or elsewhere. He found that children who stayed home alone did not differ from those who were home in adult care. Those who stayed at a friend's house with no adult supervision were more susceptible to peer pressure than were those who stayed home in self-care, and those who were at malls or other public places were the most susceptible. He concluded that self-care per se did not make adolescents more susceptible to peer pressure, but that where the children in self-care spent time after school and the distance they were from home did make a difference; "adolescents who are more removed from adult supervision (either proximal or distal) are more susceptible to pressure from their friends to engage in antisocial activity" (Steinberg, 1986, p. 438).

Parental Monitoring and Community Programs

Steinberg (1986) and other researchers (Galambos & Maggs, 1991) have found that a significant variable in diluting potential ill effects for children in self-care is the extent to which a parent is readily available by telephone and is monitoring the child's after-school activity. Whether someone is there when a child arrives home may be less important than the psycho-

logical connection with the parent that gives the child a sense of parental supervision until the parents arrive home and can further bolster a sense of involvement and genuine parental interest and concern. A number of handbooks are now available for parents with practical suggestions for making self-care fun and safe for children. Some handbooks emphasize particularly the importance of working out with the child a "self-care plan" on how the child will spend time after school (Swan & Houston, 1985).

Many communities are developing programs to address the need for supervision and developmentally appropriate activities for young adolescents in self-care. Schools are frequently used, since transportation to the day care facility is unnecessary and the facilities (gym, library, playground) are available. The challenge in school-based programs is to make the after-school program different enough that it does not seem like an extension of the school day. Recreational facilities such as community centers and YM/YWCAs can provide recreational programs for children on a planned or drop-in basis.

An innovative, community-based program particularly suitable for rural areas has been developed by the Center for Improving Mountain Living at Western Carolina University. This intergenerational program, called *Agelink,* brings together children in self-care with older volunteers.

The seniors spend time with the children alone and in small groups, often teaching traditional skills that are no longer being passed on from generation to generation. This approach to after-school care typically occurs in a group setting (e.g., in a school or community center), but Agelink has also developed three other models: older volunteers may (a) care for up to five children in licensed private homes, (b) provide transportation to sports or scouts programs, or (c) staff telephone call-in services. The program is now being expanded with different activities and emphases to include adolescents up to age fifteen. (Galambos & Maggs, 1991, p. 148)

Child Care Choices and Consumer Education

With "parent empowerment" becoming a watchword for services to families, it is not surprising that parents are increasingly taking responsibility for making informed choices about what kinds of child care their children receive. Recent federal legislation on day care reinforces this trend toward empowerment, requiring that parents have choices regarding the care their children receive under federal programs. This is in contrast to earlier legislation, which required that low-income parents use care in specific centers or day care homes. Current legislation is based on consumer-driven subsidies, in which parents have vouchers that can be applied to various child care possibilities. Some programs require that the state help parents become informed consumers of child care by providing information about licensing regulations and about the child care options available in their area.

In their review of research on parental choice, Mitchell, Cooperstein, and Larner (1992) found that a decision about child care is a complex process in which parents balance out many competing factors: "financial cost; family resources, both human and financial; child rearing values such as love, education, security, discipline, and safety; logistical considerations such as convenient hours and location; and attitudes toward maternal employment" (p. 21). In evaluating child care options, parents are concerned primarily with the quality of care their children will receive, as determined mainly by health and safety issues and the "personality of the provider," "how children get along with each other and the adults," "the provider's childrearing philosophy," and "coordination between home and the provider" (p. 24). Cost and convenience are rated important, but to a lesser degree. Parents of infants overwhelmingly express a preference for not working at all, and do so only if the family needs the money. Most parents of young children prefer that they be cared for by relatives (usually the other parent or a grandparent) and turn to care outside the home only if care by a relative is not available. The authors estimate that overall about two-thirds of parents are content with their child care arrangements, and another third would prefer a type of care other than the one they are using.

In searching for child care, parents generally use informal sources of information, such as immediate family and close friends. The next circle of sources includes neighbors, co-workers, and other relatives and friends. About two-thirds of families locate child care from one of these sources of information. If these sources don't work, parents may check the newspapers and community bulletin boards, and drive around looking for signs of day care centers. About 10 percent of families use a formal source of information, such as a local public service agency offering resource and referral services. This usually consists of a list of local child care providers. Parents may also consult various guides on how to select child care, available in popular magazines and in paperbacks. In general, parents use the same strategies to locate child care that they would to locate other necessities such as a job or housing; they rely primarily on word of mouth from those close to them before consulting more formal sources (Mitchell et al., 1992).

Guidelines for Finding Good Day Care

A number of guides are available to parents to help them assess the suitability of various day care environments for their children. Parents who have consulted published guides, who have developed criteria and expectations about the kind of care they want, and who have plenty of time to search for care increase their chances of finding appropriate day care for their children. It is just as important to stay involved after the child is placed. Forming alliances with the day care staff, visiting on a drop-in basis, talking with the child about her or his day, and asking questions about confusing situations are important ways for parents to continually monitor their children's progress in day care. The following guidelines for parents seeking care are based on the latest research on day care quality and its effects on children.

- *In general, center-based programs are more likely than home-based care to provide educational opportunities for children and to increase their social competence, maturity, and intellectual development.*
- *In general, home-based care is more likely than center-based to offer children frequent one-to-one interaction with the caregiver and discipline and training close to what the mother herself would provide.*
- *Daycare centers that receive some public funds are most likely to offer care of high quality. For-profit*

centers, especially chains, are likely to have higher staff turnover and worse staff-child ratios. . . .

- *Daycare in states with the least stringent childcare regulations is generally of lower quality.*
- *An environment that offers a wide variety of materials and accessible things to do is ideal. . . .*
- *Children do better in daycare groups or classes with a moderate number of children (more than 2, fewer than 10).*
- *The caregiver is the key to daycare quality. Children do best when caregivers are actively involved in talking, teaching and playing. . . . Daycare providers who think of themselves as professionals, have been trained in child development, have had five to ten years of experience, and are part of a training and support network or an educationally oriented center are more likely to provide good care.* (Clarke-Stewart, 1993, pp. 132–134)

RECENT RESEARCH ON CHILD CARE

The Effect of Child Care on Infants

Economic and social changes in the past several decades have influenced "a phenomenon that can only be termed a new social form"—the placement of infants as young as three weeks into out-of-home care (Gamble & Zigler, 1986, p. 26). In percentage increase, child care for infants is currently the fastest growing type of out-of-home care. In testimony before a U.S. Senate hearing on child care, Edward Zigler characterized the issue of the developmental effects on children who experience out-of-home care during infancy as "the hottest debate going on among child development experts in the United States" (Hearings before the Sub-committee on Children, 1987, p. 79). The current debate reflects the public's awareness of the vulnerability of infants and their utter dependence on others for their care. Further, infants are thought to be particularly susceptible to environmental influences, which may have long-term effects on the child's development. This view of the importance of infancy in shaping the future is reflected in the popular adage, "As the twig is bent, so grows the tree."

Recently, the debate about the effect of day care on young children has moved beyond global ques-

tions about whether child care is good or bad, and now focuses on how the different aspects of child care affect children's development in the early years. With so many infants in care because their parents have to work, it may not be possible to ensure that each child is with a parent throughout the day. Therefore, it is important to know about the qualities of day care that tend to help or hinder healthy development.

Results of a major research project conducted by the National Institute of Child Health and Human Development (NICHD), released in 1997, offer important new insights into the relationship of day care to children's well-being (National Institutes of Health, 1997). The Study for Early Child Care found that the quality of child care for very young children is key to their cognitive development. In other words, day care itself is neither harmful nor beneficial for young children, rather it is the quality of care that makes a difference. The longitudinal study began in 1991 by enrolling more than 1,300 families and their children from ten locales across the country. The children were one month old or less at the time of enrollment and were followed by researchers for seven years. The families were diverse in ethnicity, income, family structure, maternal employment status, type and quality of child care, and length of time children spent in care. Child care arrangements included care by fathers and relatives, by nonrelatives in the child's home, child care homes, and centers. The level of positive caregiving and language stimulation measured quality of care. Child outcomes were measured by the child's language abilities at 15, 24, and 36 months, the Bayley Scales of Infant Development, and other measures of school readiness at age 3. The study took into account the effects of other influences on children's development such as family economic status, mother's psychological well-being and intelligence, and infant sex and temperament. The design makes it likely that findings reflect the effects of day care on children, rather than the effects of these other influences.

The main conclusion of this study, important to parents and to policy makers, is that child care need not be harmful to very young children if it is high quality. "The most striking aspect of these results from the early child care study is that children are not being placed at a disadvantage in terms of cognitive development if they have high-quality day care in their first three years," said NICHD Director Duane Alexander (National Institutes of Health, 1997, p. 1).

The study researchers found that children whose caregivers spoke frequently with them, asked them questions, and responded to their vocalizations were likely to have greater language abilities as they grew older than did children whose caregivers did not give them this type of attention. "In this study, we found that the amount of language that is directed at the child in child care is an important component of quality provider-child interaction," said Dr. Sarah Friedman, NICHD coordinator of the study and one of its investigators. "This language input is predictive of children's acquisition of cognitive and language skills, which are the bedrock of school readiness" (National Institutes of Health, 1997, p. 2).

Another important finding of the study was that, although the quality of the care made a difference in the child's language development, home influences were still much more important. The researchers reported that, "While the quality of child care had a small but statistically significant relation to children's cognitive and linguistic outcomes, the combination of family income, maternal vocabulary, home environment, and maternal cognitive stimulation were stronger predicators of children's cognitive development" (National Institutes of Health, 1997, p. 2).

In summary, this study suggests that social workers, parents, and advocates for public policies favorable to children should pay particular attention to the quality of care that young children and infants are receiving in day care. In addition to having nurturing warmth and skill in caring for young children, caregivers need to be aware of the importance of language stimulation to the future school readiness of children. Reading stories, asking questions, listening, and trying to understand the child's vocalizations, all help stimulate the child's cognitive growth. It is also important to remember that the care the child receives in the home, including verbal stimulation, is more influential on the child's future development than the experiences the child has in day care.

The Importance of Quality

The study described above points out the importance of quality of care in assessing the effect of day care on infants. It is discouraging, then, to learn from another recent study that overall the care provided in the nation's child care centers is mediocre, and not of the high quality needed to optimize children's development. The Cost, Quality, and Child Outcomes study collected data in 1993 through visits to fifty nonprofit and fifty for-profit randomly chosen centers in four states: California, Colorado, Connecticut, and North Carolina. Only centers, and not family day care homes, were included in the study. Data collectors conducted interviews and distributed questionnaires to center directors, teachers, and parents and observed classrooms in each center. Data was also collected on the 826 children from the visited classrooms (Helburn et al., 1995). This study designed a scale of quality as follows:

> *1—Inadequate: Children's needs for health and safety not met; no warmth or support from adults observed, no learning encouraged.*
> *3—Minimal: Children's basic health and safety needs met; a little warmth and support provided by adults; few learning experiences.*
> *5—Good: Health and safety needs fully met; warmth and support for all children; learning in many ways through interesting, fun activities.*
> *7—Excellent: Everything in "good" plus children encouraged to become independent; teacher plans for children's individual learning needs; adults have close, personal relationships with each child.* (Helburn et al., 1995, p. 2)

The main finding of the study was that the level of quality at most child care centers in the United States does not meet children's needs for safety, warm relationships, and learning. Fifty-eight percent of the centers fell in the area of the scale from 3 to under 5, which the researchers labeled "mediocre." Another 28 percent of the centers fell below even this mediocre level. Thus, only 14 percent of the centers were rated as "good" or "excellent" and were considered developmentally appropriate by the researchers.

Of particular concern was the quality of center care for infants and toddlers. Of the classrooms serving these age groups, only 8 percent offered "good" or "excellent" quality, while 40 percent rated less than "minimal." The data collectors point out that "[b]abies in poor-quality rooms are vulnerable to more illness because basic sanitary conditions are not met for diapering and feeding; are endangered because of safety problems that exist in the room; miss warm, supportive relationships with adults; and lose out on learning because they lack books and toys required for physical and intellectual growth" (Helburn et al., 1995, p. 3).

The researchers found that good-quality child care was related to such factors as higher staff-to-child ratios and teacher education, specialized training, and wages. States with higher licensing standards had fewer poor-quality centers. The auspices of the center also was related to quality; those operated by public schools, universities, or public agencies, by employers at the work site, or by organizations using public funding which required them to adhere to higher standards were likely to provide higher quality care than other centers. These centers were likely to have more donated resources and subsidies which helped increase the funding available for child care. Centers dependent mainly on parent fees, on the other hand, had fewer resources and, overall, lower quality of care.

This important study confirms that the care children receive in many centers in the United States is not helping them develop cognitively and emotionally, and is not preparing them to enter school fully ready to learn. It also confirms that the costs of child care are high, and that parent fees alone cannot provide sufficient resources to ensure high-quality care. The study's findings strongly suggest that subsidies, from foundations, employers, and the government, are needed in addition to parent fees to ensure that an adequate level of care is offered to all children needing child care in the United States.

SEXUAL ABUSE IN DAY CARE

During the 1980s, the public became aware of a new threat to children's safety—the possibility that they would be sexually abused while in day care. Although sexual abuse in day care has probably been going on for a long time, the McMartin Preschool case in Manhattan Beach, California galvanized the issue for the general public. This case had characteristics that fed public fears: the preschool was located in a prosperous suburb, dispelling notions that "it can't happen here"; the facility was well-established and trusted; and the teachers, who seemed to be typical day care providers, were accused of abusing hundreds of 3- and 4-year-olds with terrifying and bizarre rituals. After six and a half years of legal activity, the jury finally acquitted the defendants on most of the charges and deadlocked on others because of questions about the credibility of the child witnesses (see Chapter 7). The McMartin case undermined confidence that children could be safely left with day care providers. Unfortunately, the McMartin case appeared not to be an isolated incident; hundreds of other cases were also uncovered around the country, many in the wake of the McMartin case publicity (Mason, 1991).

In an effort to understand more about this confusing and frightening phenomenon, the National Center on Child Abuse and Neglect funded a nationwide investigation of sexual abuse in day care, including not only the sensational cases but also "ordinary" ones, which were handled in a more routine fashion. The investigators, Finkelhor, Williams, and Burns (1988), attempted to gather information on all cases of sexual abuse of young children (age 7 or under) in day care centers and group day care homes (licensed for six to twelve children) for the years 1983, 1984, and 1985. Finkelhor and colleagues estimate that about 500 to 550 cases of sexual abuse were substantiated, involving 2,500 victims, over the three-year period. Translated into rates, these figures mean that for day care centers, the risk to children is about 5.5 children sexually abused for every 10,000 children enrolled. While disturbingly high, this risk is lower than the risk of children being sexually abused in their own homes, which is estimated to be about 8.9 per 10,000 children.

In more than 80 percent of the cases the abuser acted alone; half the cases involved a single victim, more often a girl than a boy. The most common forms of abuse were touching and fondling the children's genitals, but "penetration (including oral, digital, and object) . . . is remarkably frequent, considering the young age of the victims; it occurred to at least one child in 93 percent of all cases" (p. 251). Allegations of ritualistic abuse occurred in 13 percent of the cases. The authors were also under the impression that in comparison to other sexual abuse, children in day care cases were more "threatened, coerced, and terrorized" (p. 252). Overall, these findings put sexual abuse in day care in perspective, suggesting that this phenomenon is not an "epidemic" but rather is a reflection of the risk to children in our society of sexual abuse and of the large numbers of children in day care.

The study findings give guidance to parents, day care centers, licensing agencies, and the child welfare and criminal justice systems investigating and prosecuting these cases on how to increase the protection of children in day care. About two-thirds of the abuse took place around toileting, in the bathroom, suggesting that day care centers become more alert to who is taking children to the bathroom and also decrease the amount of private or enclosed spaces in the bathroom. Many children were threatened or coerced into not disclosing the abuse. In half the cases, children did not disclose for a month or more. Finkelhor and colleagues strongly recommend that parents make sure their preschool children understand there are no secrets in day care, and that anything that happens there can be told safely to parents. Day care staff need to be more alert to the possibility that abuse can occur and to be informed frequently of the necessity of reporting suspected abuse to child protective services. Over half the perpetrators were neither owners nor part of the professional staff; they were aides, volunteers, family members of the staff, bus drivers, janitors, or others who had access to the children. This finding suggests more diligence in monitoring who has unsupervised access to the children. Although most of the abusers were men, women made up a surprising 40 percent of the perpetrators; allegations against female staff should not be dismissed without investigation. Parents should be free to drop in to the center at any time, and to have access to all parts of the facility. Law enforcement and child protective services should form collaborative relationships that allow for a coordinated, comprehensive investigation, and should make special efforts to keep parents informed about the progress of the case.

In considering policy implications of their research, Finkelhor and colleagues urge that the risks to children in sexual abuse be kept in perspective, considering the risks to children in their own homes:

While taking the problem of abuse in day care very seriously, policymakers should not give it attention and resources disproportionate to other kinds of abuse. The problem of abuse in day care needs more research, training, and public and professional awareness. But this attention should not come at the expense of attention to other kinds of child maltreatment, which are also neglected and in need of additional attention. In the area of sexual abuse, the problem of intrafamily sexual abuse, particularly by fathers, stepfathers, and older brothers, is clearly the most pressing priority, both because of its prevalence and its devastating impact. . . . Day-care abuse has frightened many parents, baffled investigators, led to a host of misconceptions on the part of the public, and cast a long shadow over the lives of many children. It deserves a high priority on the public agenda. Yet, unfortunately, it is only one entry on a far too lengthy list of unpleasant realities that affect the world of our children today. (p. 260)

DEVELOPMENTAL PROGRAMS FOR FAMILIES WITH YOUNG CHILDREN

Throughout the United States, a large and growing number of programs exist to enhance the development of young children; the intent is for these children to be ready developmentally to start school and move forward on the path to becoming productive, self-sufficient adults. Federal and state governments have greatly increased their investment in early childhood programs over recent decades, and advocates for children are calling for even greater investments in the future. The assumption behind these investments is that early intervention can increase the chance the children will be ready to enter school and to achieve school success. Middle-class families now routinely enroll their preschoolers in developmental programs, convinced that the experiences the children receive there will help them prepare for school. Publicly funded programs attempt to offer some of these same opportunities to lower-income children, who may have even greater need. Since the 1960s, with the founding of Head Start, legislators, policy makers, parents, and professionals in child development and child welfare have focused attention on making pre-school programs available for children of poor fami-lies, who frequently lack access to high-quality early education programs.

The need for these programs is widely recog-nized. Too often children who are reared without stimulating home environments and who have not re-ceived supplemental preschool education find when they start school that they are already behind their peers in mastering skills necessary to succeed in school. Children may become discouraged and fall further and further behind, a pattern that encourages feelings of failure and dropping out early. Children who are not successful in school are at high risk for adjustment difficulties in adolescence, including ju-venile delinquency, early teenage pregnancy, and abuse of drugs and alcohol.

Developmental programs for young children may be offered under a variety of auspices, including vari-ous levels of government, school districts, health and social service agencies, universities, grassroots com-munity organizations, or a combination of sponsors. The programs may resemble those described in the chapter on Family Support and have many of the same features. However, programs that are designed primar-ily to enhance early childhood development have a focus primarily on the child. Thus they are referred to as *child-focused programs,* in contrast to the *family-focused programs* described in the chapter on family support. The difference between family-focused and child-focused programs is one of degree rather than of kind, however, and most child-focused programs in-volve the parents to some extent. The involvement tends to be in relation to the child's learning, as for ex-ample helping the parent learn to read and play games with the child, whereas in family-focused programs the emphasis may be on the parent's own personal devel-opment rather than on the child. Usually, child-focused programs offer a preschool experience for the child with some parental involvement in the classroom, and help in obtaining health screenings and immunizations, access to food programs, and other referrals that di-rectly affect the child's development. The following de-scriptions of three programs—Head Start, Avancé, and Missouri's Parents as Teachers program—illustrate the range and variety of these programs.

Head Start: A Federal-Community Partnership

A major assumption of public responsibility for chil-dren's daytime programs came about through Project Head Start (U.S. Office of Education and Office of Economic Opportunity, 1966). This program was an outgrowth of scientific knowledge about how a child's intelligence develops; it also drew from a government study that had revealed the magnitude of the problems brought on by inadequate early childhood experiences and which had recommended preventive steps. A crit-ical factor in the founding of Head Start was the "war on poverty" in the administration of President Lyndon Johnson. This initiative favored a comprehensive pro-gram with the potential for wide acceptance and quick results. A shared interest in early childhood develop-ment from members of President John Kennedy's family made preschool development an item on the political agenda.

Head Start is intended to give preschool children from economically disadvantaged backgrounds a comprehensive, multidisciplinary program of educa-tion, medical care, social services, and nutritional help. Emphasis is placed on working constructively with all aspects of a child's environment, including the family and the community. Head Start is centered on such goals as improving children's physical health and abilities through medical assessment and reme-dial health programs; helping with their emotional and social development by encouraging qualities such as self-confidence, expectation of success, spontane-ity, curiosity, and self-discipline; improving their mental processes with particular attention to concep-tual and verbal skills; and strengthening the child-parent relationship.

Parents are encouraged to participate in every phase of developing and administering the program. Many work as teachers' aides and in other nonpro-fessional capacities. Parenting education courses have taught parents how to improve the home environment and help young children "learn to learn" at home.

With federal funds covering up to 80 percent of the cost, programs have been organized and administered by local communities. Sponsors have been community-based agencies, institutions of higher education, schools, voluntary agencies, local governmental bodies, and other nonprofit, nonpolitical organizations. In 1990, the federal government took a major step forward in its commitment to Head Start by passing the Head Start Expansion and Improvement Act. This landmark legislation authorized sufficient funding to serve all eligible children by 1994 and contained numerous provisions to strengthen program quality. Among these provisions are funds for additional staff, training, facility renovation, transportation, and equipment.

Does Head Start Have Lasting Effects?

Head Start has been a source of pride for the country for many years. It has maintained consistent bipartisan support in Congress; it has held its popularity even as other programs from the 1960s have failed to reach their early promise and have lost funding. Head Start has been considered a sound investment in the nation's children, and a cost-effective way of reducing school dropout and social failure of poor children. However, with the 1990 legislation promising expansion of Head Start to all eligible children, a controversy arose on whether Head Start actually helps children overcome disadvantaged home environments and increases their chances for success. Part of the reason for the disillusionment with Head Start is that expectations for it have been too high. From the beginning, Head Start has been plagued with over-optimism about what it could accomplish.

Early evaluations of Head Start focused on IQ scores. Results showed that children's IQ scores could be increased by as much as 10 points after just a few weeks of Head Start. However, follow-up evaluations of the program have consistently shown that these early gains fade during the primary grades (Westinghouse Learning Corporation, 1969). These findings have led some observers to conclude that Head Start is ineffective in helping children succeed at school. Defenders of the program point out, however, that chil-

dren do improve in intelligence and achievement while in the program and do start school more ready to learn. If the gains in IQ fade, this may reflect problems at home and in the grade school environment, and should not be blamed on Head Start (Haskins, 1989).

If Head Start cannot permanently increase a child's IQ, can it help children become more socially competent and able to function successfully as teenagers and adults? The Perry Preschool Project, a program similar in some ways to Head Start, has conducted a longitudinal investigation of the children it served in the 1960s to see how they have fared later in life. The results of this follow-up study have shown that the Perry graduates derived many benefits, including reduced grade retention, welfare usage, and crime, and increased school completion and employment rates. A cost-benefit analysis reported that for every dollar spent on the program, taxpayers saved $7 on reduced need for social programs by the time the children reached age 27 (Berreuta-Clement et al., 1984; Schweinhart, Barnes, & Weikart, 1993).

Although Head Start has not received such an extensive longitudinal investigation, a number of follow-up studies have shown benefits that extend into grade school and high school. In their review of the effects of Head Start, Zigler and Styfco (1994) point out that Head Start graduates have been shown less likely to be retained in grade and to be assigned to special education than their counterparts who did not have an early preschool experience. They are likely to have better health, immunization rates, and nutrition. They have better school adjustment than their peers and may perform better academically (Barnett, 1995).

Early development programs cannot guarantee success in life. The Perry Preschool Project graduates, though they were likely to be more successful than their peers who did not attend preschool, nonetheless were less successful than children from middle- and upper-income families. By adulthood, about 30 percent of the Perry graduates had been arrested, and one-third had dropped out of high school. Many Head Start graduates are not able to overcome their disadvantages, and they later may experience social failure. A reasonable conclusion of the effects of early childhood programs is that "they cannot overpower the effects of poor living conditions, inadequate nutrition and health care, negative role models, and substandard schools. But good programs can prepare children for school and possibly help them develop better coping and adaptation skills that will enable better life outcomes, albeit not perfect ones" (Zigler & Styfco, 1994, p. 129). In addition to benefits to children, Head Start has helped numerous parents and had a positive effect on their communities. Thousands of parents obtain training and jobs through Head Start each year, and many go on to further their education and become employed.

Avancé: A Community-Based Program for Mexican-American Families

Many communities across the United States have developed early childhood programs designed to meet the unique needs of their families. One such program is Avancé, a community-based family support and intervention program started in 1973 in the Mirasol Federal Housing Project in San Antonio, Texas. It now has four other sites in other low-income neighborhoods in San Antonio and Houston, serving 2,000 families annually. Like many other community-based programs, Avancé receives funding from a variety of public and private sources, including the City of San Antonio, the United Way, the Texas Department of Human Resources, the federal government, private foundations, and private donations (Johnson, Walker, & Rodriguez, 1991).

I grew up in one of these poor communities, and I saw well-intentioned policies and ineffective and insufficient programs. . . . I have seen proud Hispanic people who at one time came to this country with hope, motivation, and a desire to partake of the American dream, of having a job, owning a house, and being able to raise a family adequately lose that hope, that motivation, and those dreams. As a school teacher, I, too, saw children at the age of six already labeled, tracked and categorized as failures by the school system. I began the Avancé program . . . because I knew old approaches were not effective. They provided too little too late. . . . Supporting the family and helping them in their role as parents is the core of our intervention. Through this approach and through the love and compassion that these people receive, Avancé has been able to rekindle the

spirit of Hispanic people living in poverty, has been able to strengthen families and has been rebuilding communities. (Gloria Rodriguez, Executive Director, Avancé Family Support and Education Program—Hearing before the Select Committee on Children, Youth, and Families, House of Representatives, 101st Congress, First Session, 1989)

The goals of Avancé are to help family members learn to develop their fullest potential, to strengthen families, to alleviate problems of child maltreatment and school failure, and to stabilize the economic condition of the family. The participants are mainly young, single, Mexican-American mothers who live in poverty and who dropped out of school before completing high school. They have a high rate of depression, are socially isolated, are under stress, lack knowledge of child development and child management methods, have a high potential for child abuse and neglect, and lack job skills.

Avancé offers these families the Parent-Child Education Program, a nine-month, three-hour weekly program located in the community in which the family lives. Parents learn to make educational toys, attend class discussions on child development and behavior management, receive home visits, go on field trips to libraries and various community events with their children, and learn about community resources. To help them develop parent-child interaction skills, they are videotaped interacting with their children. Parent-to-parent interaction is encouraged to help families build a strong support network in the community. While the parents are in session, the children receive a developmentally appropriate preschool experience.

I read to my kids now every night. We get a book and curl up in bed and read. (A mother in an early childhood program—Ounce of Prevention Fund, 1993)

The Education and Economic Development Program is available for families successfully completing the Parent-Child Education Program. It was developed in response to the parents' wishes to undertake structured activities to develop their own skills and confidence. Avancé helps parents set realistic, attainable economic goals, including owning a car and a home, and offers classes, in conjunction with the local community college, in English, basic skills, high school equivalency (General Education Development, or GED), and college classes. Transportation and child care are provided by Avancé.

The staff are Avancé graduates, including the directors and parent educators of the various centers, the secretaries, accounting and research assistants, and the direct service staff. They act as role models for new parents and encourage them to "advance" in their own development.

A recent evaluation of the program, comparing program mothers to a control group of mothers living in the same area but not participating in the program, found that it had a substantial effect on the ability of mothers to provide an educationally sound and emotionally nurturing environment for their children. It also had strong effects on child-rearing attitudes and knowledge and on awareness of community resources. The program also helped participants to strengthen their support networks. Mothers participating in the second-year adult-development program were more likely to be enrolled in courses to upgrade their employment prospects than were control mothers. The evaluation concludes that parents "have the necessary skills to provide an educationally stimulating environment and provide emotional support, they value education for themselves and their children, and they have a knowledge base for effective rearing of children" (Johnson & Walker, 1991, p. 4).

Missouri's School-Based Parents as Teachers Program

During the 1980s, state governments took the lead in financing early childhood programs. Most of these state initiatives started as demonstration projects, usually at the instigation of key program advocates and supporters in the legislative and executive branches, and expanded as they demonstrated success and gained political support. These initiatives have developed out of different state agencies, including public health, welfare, and education. State-sponsored programs are unique to each state; however, they share the common elements of having statewide coverage and of a program focus on family and child development.

Missouri's Parents as Teachers (PAT) program started as a pilot project in 1981 to demonstrate the benefits of a high-quality parent education and family-support program to strengthen parents' skills and enhance their children's development from birth to age 3. The Missouri Department of Education, in cooperation with the Danforth Foundation, started the PAT program in four school districts representing metropolitan and rural communities. Evaluation results of this early pilot project were promising, and in 1984, the PAT program became a mandatory service for all Missouri school districts.

Home visits are the primary means of service delivery; families are scheduled to receive them monthly, and most families actually receive seven or eight a year for the first three years of their child's life. Additional services include group meetings for parents and comprehensive health screening for children. In some districts, playtime and/or resource centers are also available, and provide parents and children an opportunity to meet and interact informally. The resource centers lend children's books, toys, and educational materials to participants.

Thirty-seven school districts were chosen for special study because they contained many families at risk for school failure and other problems. The program families in these districts were likely to be poor and headed by a single mother who had not completed high school. About a quarter of the parents were African American or Latino. The families also were more likely to have poor coping skills, family stress, poor parent-child communication and child development delay, child illness, failure to thrive, and homes where English was not spoken. The evaluation found that both children and parents received benefits from program participation. The children at age 3 scored significantly above national norms on measures of school-related achievement. Parents expressed a high level of satisfaction with the program; they liked particularly the home visits focused on the family's needs. The program was particularly successful for families with children identified with developmental delays (Pfannestiel, Lambson, & Yarnell, 1991).

The philosophy behind all these early childhood programs is that the child's home is the most powerful environment affecting her or his development, and therefore interventions to improve the child's ability to succeed in school and at other developmental tasks of growing up depend to a large extent on the ability of parents to provide a nurturing home setting. This concept of parental primacy in their children's development has been captured in the phrase, "the parent is the child's first and most important teacher."

HISTORICAL DEVELOPMENT OF DAY CARE

A review of the development of *day nurseries* and *nursery schools* casts light on some of the problems in evolving a comprehensive approach to programs for children's daytime care and development. Formally organized daytime programs have existed in two parts—child care as a philanthropic undertaking, chiefly under social work auspices, and nursery schools as a form of preschool education. Despite their common elements, these two institutional approaches generally developed quite separately and have served different groups and classes of children.

Child Welfare Day Care

The Early Day Nurseries.   The first program for the daytime care of young children in this country began in Philadelphia in 1798. This first "charitable nursery" was sponsored by a group of Quaker women, and its initial goal was to increase productivity of working mothers in the "spinning room" (Michel, 1988). Another goal soon emerged—to attend to the education and welfare of the children. Early day nurseries were modeled on the French crèche, a form of care for children of working mothers founded in Paris in 1844. The crèche was a response to the rapidly expanding employment of women in factories. In addition, in France, it was used as a weapon against the problem of infant mortality. Mothers of infants nursed their babies in the factory crèches and were taught methods of hygienic child care. French crèches were

considered important enough to receive official recognition by an imperial decree in 1862. Regulations were issued to specify the conditions under which they could open and the standards that had to be met to receive a government subsidy.

The early day nurseries in America lacked this kind of official attention. They were usually sponsored by a church, a settlement house, or sometimes a voluntary social agency. Their purposes were to prevent child neglect during a mother's working hours and to eliminate the need to place children of destitute parents in institutions. They served an underprivileged group, handicapped by family problems. The emphasis was on physical care.

Even well into the twentieth century, many of the nurseries were poorly financed and substandard. Children were fed, often inadequately, and guarded from only the most obvious dangers. Provision for cleanliness and medical care was a common lack. The public generally was unconcerned about the nurseries. For information on the history of early day nurseries, see Forest (1927), Beer (1938), Lundberg (1947), and Fleiss (1962).

Day Care Services.   By the 1930s the social work profession seemed somewhat more agreed that day care, although still very insufficiently provided, was an essential part of a child welfare program. Emphasis was placed on social casework as a means of strengthening family life for the child in day care. Some persons cautioned that the conception of child welfare day care was limited by its definition as a philanthropic activity and as such served only the economically unfortunate. To become a valuable agency for the care and development of the preschool child, day care sponsors and staff would have to solve problems of integration with the health and education fields.

Efforts were made to differentiate day care, as a child welfare service, from nursery schools, as a form of preschool education. Day care was regarded as a sharing of child-rearing responsibilities with parents, a way of keeping families together or helping them to maintain an adequate level of child care. Consequently, day care agencies usually applied some test of economic or social need before making the service available to parents.

Preschool Education

The Nursery School Movement. The American nursery school is a product of the twentieth century, although its roots can be traced to the early infant schools in England and continental Europe. In the eighteenth century, Jean Frederic Oberlin, a Lutheran minister, established an infant school in France. It was a philanthropic venture, designed to give religious and moral training to young children as a means of substituting for their poor home care. At about the same time a contemporary of Oberlin, Johann Heinrich Pestalozzi, was working in Switzerland to improve conditions of the poor through education. His belief that children learn best by using their own senses and discovering things for themselves was discernible in preschools of later years. In the nineteenth century Friedrich Froebel founded the kindergarten and developed a philosophy and procedures in relation to preschool education.

Nursery schools in the United States were an outgrowth of early twentieth-century progress in such fields as biology, medicine, psychology, and psychiatry, which led to scientific interest in early childhood and a new awareness of the importance of the preschool years. The early American nursery schools were developed for such purposes as these: (1) to conduct research in educational curricula and methods—for example, a nursery school at Columbia University Teachers College in 1921; (2) to conduct research in child development—for example, a nursery school organized at the University of Iowa's Child Welfare Research Station in 1921; (3) to serve as a laboratory for the education of students in child care—for example, the Merrill-Palmer School of Homemaking in Detroit in 1922 and, following this, similar laboratories for child study as part of a child development curriculum in many home economics departments of land-grant colleges; (4) to serve as centers for the training of nursery school teachers; (5) to offer the opportunity for parents to provide wholesome play for their children, further understanding of them, and released time from

personal child care—for example, the Chicago Cooperative Nursery School, initiated in 1915 by a small group of wives of faculty members of the University of Chicago; and (6) to provide a supplement to psychiatric clinics—for example, the Play School for Habit Training, established in Boston in 1922.

As a consequence of the nature of these early experiments in preschool education, the nursery school developed as a "normal" service to be used without stigma even though, like day care, it was conceived as an educational and social supplement to the home. Undoubtedly the origin of nursery schools in America, developed from the beginning as a resource for middle- and upper-class families, has contributed to their acceptance and perceived desirability.

[My involvement with young children] was like a whole new world. I will always feel that people in our field feel the same magic. It's like you've discovered childhood all by yourself and nobody else even knew it was there. (Early childhood education specialist— Langlois, 1989, p. i)

The Modern Nursery School. Some persons interested in the care and development of the young child saw very early that there were advantages to be obtained through cooperation between the day nursery and the nursery school, and suggested that the nursery school concept was highly compatible with an "ideal" day nursery. However, preschool educators historically were willing to leave formulations of the nature of "day care" to social work. They were not professionally concerned with the components of "care and supervision" in all-day centers. They were influenced by the view that the day care center was for a dependent or troubled population, and was appropriate, therefore, as a social work service. Also, considerations of status played a part.

Hunt has suggested a further explanation for the failure of those in nursery school education to involve themselves more directly in the educational needs of young children from very poor families. Because of a traditional belief that class differences in ability were the inevitable consequence of heredity, Americans generally were little inclined to provide nursery schools for children of the poor. As a result, nursery schools were adapted to the needs of middle-class children. Consequently, when projects were launched in the 1960s to improve the future academic success of children of the poor, there was no tested technology of compensatory early childhood education at hand that could be counted on to foster in children of the poor those abilities that underlie competence in the dominant society (Hunt, 1969).

Assumption of Public Responsibility

The WPA Program.   There was a major expansion in day care during the Depression of the 1930s, when the federal government made funds available to the states for the establishment of nursery schools for the children of low-income parents. This action was part of the Works Progress Administration (WPA) program, and its immediate purpose was to provide employment for unemployed teachers, nurses, nutritionists, clerical workers, cooks, and janitors.

Federal funds were made available to state departments of education, and the nursery schools were administered by local boards and usually located in public school buildings. For the most part, however, nutritional and health services were stressed rather than educational activities.

The Lanham Act.   As economic conditions improved and fewer teachers were unemployed, it appeared that the public day care program would be ended. But as the United States became involved in World War II, defense industries mushroomed. Many children were exposed to instability in family and community life as their parents moved to overcrowded or new communities to which they were attracted by wartime employment. The Children's Bureau began to receive reports of less-than-adequate child care situations in various communities with a concentration of defense industries. These reports told of children who were left alone, locked in parked cars, or expected to shift for themselves or adjust to other unsatisfactory child care arrangements while their mothers worked.

Pressure mounted for a continuation of public financing for day care, this time for children whose mothers were being drawn into the national defense

effort. Under the Lanham Act of 1941, federal funds were made available to the states on a matching basis for the conversion of WPA facilities or the establishment of new day care centers and nursery schools to serve children of working mothers in war-impacted communities. The United States Office of Education was given responsibility for developing the nursery school program in cooperation with local schools, and the Children's Bureau was given similar responsibility for day care centers sponsored by agencies that were not part of a school system.

> *The attitude of the Children's Bureau . . . was that mothers of preschool children should not be encouraged to work; but if they did indeed work, the community had an obligation to provide services to help parents care for their children, with state and local governments assuming the responsibility for supervising and maintaining adequate standards. Thus, the approach of the Children's Bureau towards the Lanham Act day care program was at best ambivalent. Some within the Bureau looked with misgiving on what they feared would be interpreted as a public sanction of the employment of women. They were joined by some social work leaders who were concerned that the federal stimulus to day care would in the long run be destructive of the family and contrary to basic American values. However, as it became clear that the emergency situation had first priority, the Bureau undertook the stimulation of counseling services in support of day care and developed a comprehensive set of standards for the guidance of communities. (Mayer, 1965, p. 27)*

> *During the war years, you were more concerned with trying to compensate for the lack of a family with the father gone and the mother working, these children were in there from sometimes—when the mother lifted them over the fence to me and I lifted them back at 6 o'clock at night and they hadn't seen their parents or home and went to bed very soon after that. (WPA day care center director—Langlois, 1989, p. 30)*

At the peak of the program in 1944, from 105,000 to 129,000 children were enrolled in nursery schools and day care centers receiving federal funds, most of them sponsored by schools and school people (Pedgeon, 1953; Farmer, 1969).

Federal funds were withdrawn in 1946, after the end of the war, with resulting difficulties for many families. Most programs disappeared. Some people believed that maternal employment would cease to exist on any substantial scale with the end of the war. In some communities the expanding school population required all the available classroom space and other educational resources. And there was undermining disagreement or confusion as to whether daytime programs were a continuing responsibility of welfare or education.

The loss in public day care facilities following the end of World War II was serious. For example, although Chicago had had twenty-three centers operating during the war, there were no programs of public day care early in 1965. The same was true of Detroit, although during World War II there had been eighty centers in that city supported by Lanham Act funds (Fleiss, 1962).

Heightened Interest and Support for Child Care in the 1960s.

Various social, economic, and political forces in the 1960s removed day care from the periphery of social services for children. For example, scientific interest in how a child's intelligence develops and in the social and psychological factors in the intellectual functioning of poor children led to research into preschool curriculum development and evaluation. As a result, enriched experimental nursery school programs were developed as university researchers investigated the area of early childhood education in search of reliable methods of compensatory training.

In addition, the 1960s generally were prosperous, and high levels of employment made industry's recruitment of women into the labor force more visible. Many of these new employees had difficulties on the job because they lacked reliable child care arrangements during their working hours. Also, there was interest in providing parents receiving Aid to Families with Dependent Children (AFDC) with an opportunity to receive job training and a work role in society. If welfare mothers were to take advantage of training and employment opportunities or any other major social, educational, and health services designed to improve their family life, child care programs would have to be considerably expanded.

The heightened support for and interest in child care led many states to reconsider and improve their mandatory licensing standards for day care facilities. Federal agencies—the Department of Health, Education, and Welfare, the Office of Economic Opportunity, and the Department of Labor—joined together to issue a common set of standards and regulations that day care programs under their jurisdiction must meet if they were to receive federal funds (U.S. Department of Health, Education, and Welfare et al., 1968).

Provisions of the Social Security Act.

By a series of amendments to Title V of the Social Security Act in 1962, day care was defined for the first time as a public child welfare service. Funds had to be administered by a public child welfare agency, even though the target population was not limited to abused and neglected children, but also included the children of parents who were working.

With the intent to restore family self-sufficiency and reduce the size of the public assistance caseloads, the 1967 amendments to the Social Security Act introduced a coercive tone and, for the first time, defined day care as an essential element of public assistance. Most federal funding for day care was transferred from public child welfare agencies to public assistance programs. This trend has continued into the present, as funding for day care is a prominent feature of the welfare reform legislation of 1996.

The history of day care in the United States contains two major themes: (1) the separation of day care into two streams—day care as a service to the poor while their mothers were at work, and early childhood education, in the form of nursery schools primarily for children of the middle class; and (2) the reluctance of the federal government and American society to subsidize day care for working mothers, largely due to ambivalence about the role of women and concerns about government involvement in family life. These tensions and contradictions are still apparent in the way day care services are conceptualized, funded, and implemented in this country.

TRENDS AND ISSUES

The Role of Day Care in Welfare Reform

With recent federal changes in welfare, child advocates are concerned about the effects of increasing the work requirement of parents on children. Research described earlier in this chapter on the effects of day care on children underlines the importance of high quality day care to avoid harming children while their parents are working. Yet much day care currently provided in the United States is mediocre at best, particularly for children at the very vulnerable stages of infancy and toddlerhood. Quality is related to the resources day care programs have available to them, leaving poor parents unable to purchase good quality care for their children (Helburn et al., 1995). Therefore, there is cause for very serious concern that welfare reform will force additional numbers of young children into inadequate day care arrangements, unless government at both the state and federal level is willing to increase investments to improve the quality of these programs. At the 1997 White House Conference on Child Care, President Clinton pledged the help of the federal government in improving day care. As this book goes to press, an effort to increase day care funding has failed in the U.S. Congress, but the Children's Defense Fund and other advocacy organizations are certain to renew their efforts to achieve greater public support for day care.

The availability of day care will ultimately affect the success of recent welfare reform efforts. For women on welfare, help with child care is essential if they are to pursue job training, education, or work that will lead to self-sufficiency. A study by the Children's Defense Fund showed that women who are having difficulty finding child care they trust are less likely to remain in programs leading to economic independence. For example, a survey of Illinois welfare recipients found that most parents surveyed said they preferred working and using child care they trusted over staying home with the children and remaining on welfare. However, they encountered major barriers in finding child care: Child care problems were cited by 42 percent of the parents as the reason that they could not work full time, and by 39 percent as the reason they could not go to school (Ebb, 1994).

A further issue is the quality of care. Lawmakers, faced with large federal deficits and demands for tax cuts and less federal spending, may be tempted to shortchange funding for child care. This will be a serious mistake because it will exacerbate the difficulties many children from poor families already face in preparing for school. Short-term budget savings from under-funding day care for welfare and other low-income mothers, which may force children into substandard care, could result in increased federal expenses for remedial programs for children later on, to compensate for the lack of developmental enrichment in earlier day care experiences (Blum, 1994).

The Status of Women in the Provision of Day Care

The issue of quality versus cost is encompassing, and it cloaks other matters of importance. One of the most significant of these has to do with the status and roles of women in the provision of day care. Women constitute virtually all the caregiving personnel in the day care industry in this country. As a class of essential workers, they are underpaid and have access to few government work benefits taken for granted by other wage earners.

Thus we find a large labor force of women who are essential to the economy as well as to the families of working parents. Yet these caregivers are grossly underpaid and denied benefits common to other workers. Child care workers earned an average of $6.12 an hour in 1996. The pay for preschool teachers, many of whom have bachelor's or master's degrees, averaged $7.80. These figures compare to $10.35 for all workers. People taking care of zoo animals earn $2,500 more on average than child care workers (Kids Count, 1998; Rally 'Round the Kids, 1993). Furthermore, the fact that additional training in child-related fields and experience in child care brings no rewards in earnings suggests that the government and the public still subscribe to the sexist notion that "since child care is women's work it is not worth paying for" (Children at the Center, 1979, pp. 21–22).

The devalued perception of child care staff with its low pay and demanding working conditions has led to high rates of turnover in child care. Research has shown that staff are a key component of good child care. A study based on classroom observations and testing of children at over 200 child care centers in five geographically dispersed metropolitan areas established that link. Children in centers with persistently high rates of turnover among caregivers, when compared with children at centers with low rates of staff turnover, were found to be less competent in language and social development. The high rates of turnover were found to be directly related to pay and working conditions (Lewin, 1989).

What must not be overlooked is that the lack of government subsidies for child care maintains the existence of an exploited underclass of women performing child care work that is essential to the economy and to the well-being of the nation's families. The lack of public attention to this injustice unfairly places two groups of women with opposing needs in confrontation with each other. Working mothers who must pay for day care usually feel financial pressures, as do their caretaking substitutes. If problems of the women purchasing care are lessened by lowering prices, the caregiving women suffer. On the other hand, if the caregivers are paid at higher levels, mothers in the labor force may find it no longer feasible to continue to work outside their homes. Responsibility for this dilemma does not belong to either set of working women. Instead it reflects a vacuum of leadership at the national level in efforts to develop a more effective and fair resolution of the issue of day care cost.

Schools of the 21st Century Program

Day care today can be characterized as a patchwork arrangement of multiple funding sources, multiple auspices, and a wide range of child care programs and settings. These various components are not well organized or coordinated, however, leaving many families and communities without adequate day care resources. Parents are left trying to piece together arrangements suitable for their children of different ages, which fit the family budget and don't require too much transportation. Although more children are using day care services now than at any time in our nation's history, the overall system is subject to little oversight, and we have very little information on how the majority of children in care are faring. As Zigler and Lang (1991) have described the situation:

Concerned observers have noted that our society has embarked on a broad social experiment in child rearing, one in which parents continue to raise their children, as they always have, but with a significant difference—mothers and fathers have turned over the supervision of a large part of their children's waking hours to a vast mixed system of child care. The system is subject to few controls, has lacked sustained national commitment, and varies significantly in quality from excellent to harmful. (p. 2)

As noted earlier in this chapter, locally organized, state and federally funded, day care systems can help standardize quality, improve access to day care for parents, and coordinate the myriad federal and other governmental programs for children. As one of several proposals for organizing coordinated systems of child care, Edward Zigler (1989) has proposed the Schools of the 21st Century Program. This program is a vision for a stable, organized system of child care in all communities, which would provide for the needs of children of all ages and offer greater support for families than now exists. Zigler's plan calls for using the current educational system and, where possible, available school buildings, to build a community-based child care system that would offer a variety of child care and family support services. Many of these services may already be available in the community but delivered in piecemeal fashion. The Schools of the 21st Century Program would ensure that these elements would be coordinated into a single system that would operate under the auspices of the school system but separately from the regular school program.

This envisioned program would have five components: two on-site child care components and three other outreach components. The on-site programs would include an all-day, year-round preschool program at the school for children aged 3 to 5, and a before- and after-school and vacation care program for children from kindergarten through grade six. In addition, the program would create a network of family day care providers with the school as the hub. This network would be especially helpful for the care of children under age 3. The program would offer training and general support to family day care providers, and work to improve the quality of such arrangements.

Another outreach service would be an information and referral system that would provide area families with information about child care facilities and programs for children or families with special needs. The third outreach service would be a family support and education program, such as those described earlier in this chapter—Avancé or Missouri's Parents as Teachers program. Family support programs that begin during pregnancy and continue for the first year or two of the infant's life can offer many benefits to families, including early screening and identification of developmental problems, information on child development and child rearing, support through contact with other parents, and referrals to other community services.

As the United States approaches the twenty-first century, it faces an urgent need to better support working families. The trend toward women working outside the home is irreversible, as it is based on large social and economic changes in society. As a society, we have not responded quickly or adequately to the need for day care services for the many children whose parents work. This inattention must be corrected so that today's families, supported by the community, can fulfill their function of rearing children to become caring, productive adults for tomorrow.

CHAPTER SUMMARY

Care for children during the hours that their parents work, long a concern within the private realm of the family, has emerged in the 1990s as a major public policy issue as well. Welfare reform has given impetus to the movement to increase government involvement in funding and planning children's daytime care. Sensational stories from the news and entertainment media, showing children left with abusive or careless babysitters, have reflected the anxieties of parents about leaving their children while they work. Recent research documenting the mediocre quality of many day care centers, combined with research showing the importance of high-quality day care for children's development, have given strong empirical support to efforts to improve conditions under which children are cared for during the day. High-quality care may be expensive and beyond the reach of many working families. Although federal and state support for day care has increased, greater government involvement is needed to reduce the number of children in mediocre or poor care. In addition to cost, other barriers to finding good care include lack of day care resources in the area, and lack of day care for children of parents working nights and weekends.

Families in which parents work and children are in day care have become prevalent in American society. Today, about 60 percent of all preschoolers, or 13 million children, are in some form of day care or early childhood development program. About 31 million children under the age of 15 live with a working mother. In addition to day care for children of working mothers, day care may also be provided as a child welfare service, offering specialized and respite care to abusive and neglectful families as an alternative to placement of children in foster care. Day care arrangements include care by relatives, family day care, offered in the caregiver's home, in-home caregivers, and day care centers. Much day care is unregulated, particularly family day care, and little is known about what kind of experiences children have during the time they are with the day care provider. Most school-age children are in school during the hours that their parents work, but about 5 million children spend time alone, without adult supervision, during the week.

A promising approach to improving quality and accessibility at relative low cost are day care networks. These programs, located in schools, other child development centers, or social or community agencies, offer information and referral services to parents, and recruit and train day care providers. By offering ongoing support to providers, they increase the number of day care homes in an area and help improve the skills of providers in promoting children's intellectual, social and physical development. Another approach to improving care is to offer consumer education to parents on how to find good care and on the importance of staying involved in the day care program. The importance of parental involvement is highlighted by the cases of child abuse in day care; these deplorable situations have illustrated that parents need to encourage children to talk about their day care experiences and to visit the day care facilities as often as possible.

Child development programs, such as Head Start, have as their primary goal the enhancement of pre-school age children's development so that they will enter school ready to learn. These programs focus on the family, as well as the children, and work to help parents become more effective at promoting their children's cognitive, social and physical development. They are based on a large body of research showing the importance of parents as the child's first and most important teacher.

FOR STUDY AND DISCUSSION

1. Discuss why child care personnel remain so poorly paid although they are essential to the economy and to family life. What values within the economy and the status of women come together to maintain this inequity?

2. Look further into the concept of neighborhood day care networks. Are there any in your community? Identify the benefits and barriers to implementation to be derived from this form of organization.

3. What have been some of the effects or influences of the historical separation between day nurseries and nursery schools? What were the positive accomplishments of public nursery school and day care programs under WPA and the Lanham Act? What explanation can you advance for the failure of these two large public programs to lead to a comprehensive provision of programs for the daytime care and development of children?

4. Propose a variety of arrangements that could be made to serve school-age "self-care" children who need outside-of-school supervision and guidance. Is there such a service in your community? Could you bring one about?

5. Visit a child care center in your community to learn its purpose, the population of children that it serves, its means of financing its operations, its staffing pattern, and the focus of its programs. What evidence is there that the program plays a responsible role in a community network of quality daytime programs?

FOR ADDITIONAL STUDY

Clarke-Stewart, A. (1993). *Daycare* (rev. ed.). Cambridge: Harvard University Press.

Helburn, S., Culkin, M. L., Howes, C., Bryant, D., Clifford, R., Cryer, D., Peisner-Feinberg, E., & Kagan, S. L. (1995). *Cost, quality, and child outcomes in child care centers: public report.* Denver: University of Colorado at Denver, Department of Economics.

Larner, M. (1994). *In the neighborhood: Programs that strengthen family daycare for low-income families.* New York: Columbia University School of Public Health, National Center for Children in Poverty.

Larner, M., Halpern, R., & Harkavy, O. (1992). *Fair start for children: Lessons learned from seven demonstration projects.* New Haven, CT: Yale University Press.

National Institute of Child Health and Human Development. (no date). *The NICHD Study of Early Child Care.* Available online at http://www.nih.gov/nichd/html/lpublications.html.

Seitz, V. (1990). Intervention programs for impoverished children: A comparison of educational and family support models. *Annals of Child Development, 7,* 73–103.

Zigler, E., & Styfco, S. J. (1994). Head Start: Criticisms in a constructive context. *American Psychologist, 49*(2), 127–132.

INTERNET SITES

Families and Work Institute.   The Families and Work Institute is a nonprofit organization that addresses the changing nature of work and family life. It is committed to finding research-based strategies that foster mutually supportive connections among workplaces, families, and communities. The Web site describes the institute's research on a broad range of issues on the connections between work and family life, with extensive links to other sites. http://www. familiesandwork.org

National Child Care Information Center. The Center is part of the Children's Bureau, U.S. Department of Health and Human Services. It disseminates child care information in response to requests from states, territories and tribes, policymakers, parents, programs, organizations, providers and the public. The Center also publishes the *Child Care Bulletin* six times a year. http://www.nccic.org

National Institute of Child Health and Human Development. The NICHD administers a multidisciplinary program of research, research training, and public information, nationally and within its own facilities, on prenatal development as well as maternal, child, and family health. The Web site offers access to NICHD publications. http://www.nih.gov/nichd

National Network for Child Care. This nonprofit, educational organization affiliated with the Cooperative Extension programs of state universities attempts to increase and strengthen the quality of nonparental care environments using the expertise of Cooperative Extension's nationwide dissemination system. It offers an e-mail listserv for communication on day care, support and assistance to day care providers and users, and a newsletter. The Web site is an Internet source of over 1,000 publications and resources related to child care. Publications are research-based and reviewed. http://www.exnet.iastate.edu/Pages/ families/nncc/homepage.html

Working Mother Lifenet. This Web site provides information on day care for working parents, with results of state surveys on licensing laws and other consumer information. http://www.womweb.com

REFERENCES

ARCH. (1994). *Respite: Prevention, preservation and family support.* Chapel Hill, NC: Access to Respite Care and Help, ARCH National Resource Center for Crisis Nurseries and Respite Services.

Barnett, W. S. (1995). Long-term effects of early childhood programs on cognitive and school outcomes. *The Future of Children: Long Term Outcomes of Early Childhood Programs, 5*(3), 25–50.

Beer, E. S. (1938). *The day nursery.* New York: Dutton.

Berreuta-Clement, J. R., Schweinhart, L. J., Barnett, W. S., Epstein, A. S., & Weikart, D. P. (1984). *Changed lives: The effects of the Perry Preschool Program on youths through age 19.* Ypsilanti, MI: High/Scope Press.

Berry, M. F. (1993). *The politics of parenthood: Child care, women's rights and the myth of the good mother.* New York: Viking/Penguin.

Blum, B. (1994). Children and welfare reform. *National Center for Children in Poverty: News and Issues, 4*(3), 4–6.

Casper, L. M. (1995). *What does it cost to mind our preschoolers?* (Current Population Reports, P-70, no. 52). U.S. Department of Commerce, Bureau of the Census. Washington, DC: U.S. Government Printing Office.

Casper, L. M. (1996). *Who's minding our preschoolers?* (Current Population Reports, P-70, no. 53). U.S. Department of Commerce, Bureau of the Census. Washington, DC: U.S. Government Printing Office.

Casper, L. M., Hawkins, M., & O'Connell, M. (1994). *Who's minding the kids?* (Current Population Reports, Series P70-36). U.S. Department of Commerce, Bureau of the Census. Washington, DC: U.S. Government Printing Office.

Chavez, L. (1987, July). Women's movement, its ideals accepted, faces subtler issues. *New York Times,* p. 8.

Children at the center: Final report of the national day care study, executive summary. (1979). Cambridge, MA: Abt Associates.

Children's Defense Fund. (1997, November). *Summary of current welfare legislation.* [Online], 6 pages. Available on-line at www.childrensdefense.org [May, 1998].

Children's Defense Fund. (1998, March). *Facts about child care in America.* [Online], 4 pages. Available: www. childrensdefense.org [May, 1998].

The Children's Foundation. (1991). *Daycare center licensing study.* Washington, DC: Author.

Clarke-Stewart, A. (1993). *Daycare.* Cambridge: Harvard University Press.

Clinton, H. (1997). Remarks by First Lady Hillary Rodham Clinton. *Child Care Bulletin, Issue 17, September/ October,* 3 pages. Available on-line at http://Ericps.ed. uiuc.edu/nccic [1997, November].

Clinton, W. (1997). Remarks by President Bill Clinton. *Child Care Bulletin, Issue 17, September/October,* 3 pages. Available on-line at http://Ericps.ed.uiuc.edu/nccic [1997, November].

Collins, A. H., & Watson, E. L. (1976). *Family day care.* Boston: Beacon Press.

Ebb, N. (1994). *Child care tradeoffs: States make painful choices.* Washington, DC: Children's Defense Fund.

Farmer, J. (1969). *Senate hearings on Head Start Child Development Act* (Pt. 1, 91st Cong., 1st Sess.).

Finkelhor, D., Williams, L. M., & Burns, N. (1988). *Nursery crimes: Sexual abuse in day care.* Newbury Park, CA: Sage.

Fleiss, B. H. (1962). *The relationship of the Mayor's Committee on Wartime Care of Children to day care in New York City.* Unpublished doctoral dissertation, New York University.

Forest, I. (1927). *Pre-school education: A historical and critical study.* New York: Macmillan.

Galambos, N. L., & Maggs, J. L. (1991). Children in self-care: Figures, facts, and fiction. In J. V. Lerner & N. L. Galambos (Eds.), *Employed mothers and their children.* New York: Garland.

Galinsky, E., Howes, C., Kontos, S., & Shinn, M. (1994). *The study of children in family child care and relative care: Highlights of findings.* New York: Families and Work Institute.

Gamble, T. J., & Zigler, E. (1986). Effects of infant day care: Another look at the evidence. *American Journal of Orthopsychiatry, 56*(1), 26–42.

Gray, E., & Coolsen, P. (1987). How do kids really feel about being home alone? *Children Today, 16*(4), 30–32.

Haskins, R. (1989). Beyond metaphor: The efficacy of early childhood education. *American Psychologist, 44,* 274–282.

Hearings before the Subcommittee on Children, Family, Drugs and Alcoholism of the Committee on Labor and Human Resources. (1987, June 11). *First session on examining initiatives needed to meet the demand for quality and affordable childcare in the United States.* 100th Cong. Washington, DC: U.S. Government Printing Office.

Helburn, S., Culkin, M. L., Howes, C., Bryant, C., Clifford, R., Cryer, D., Peisner-Feinberg, E., & Kagan, S. L. (1995). *Cost, quality, and child outcomes in child care centers: Public report.* Denver: University of Colorado at Denver, Department of Economics.

Hershfield, B. (1995, Fall). The role of child care in strengthening and supporting vulnerable families. *The Prevention Report.* Iowa City: National Resource Center for Family Centered Practice, University of Iowa, 2–4.

Hunt, J. M. (1969). Black genes—white environment. *Transaction, 6*(7), 20–21.

Johnson, D. L., & Walker, T. (1991). *Final report of an evaluation of the Avance Parent Educaton and Family Support Program.* San Antonio: Avance.

Johnson, D. L., Walker, T., & Rodriguez, G. (1991). *Enhancing the vocational prospects of low-income Hispanic mothers: Results of a family support program.* Paper presented at the biennial meeting of the Society for Research in Child Development, April 18–20, Seattle.

Kagan, S. L., & Glennon, T. (1982). Considering proprietary child care. In E. F. Zigler & E. W. Gordon (Eds.), *Day care: Scientific and social policy issues.* Boston: Auburn House.

Kids Count 1998 Data Online. (1998). *Profile for the United States: Child care indicators.* Available on-line at http://www.aecf.org. [October, 1998].

Kisker, E. E., Hofferth, S. L., Phillips, D. A., & Farquahar, E. (1991). *A profile of child care settings: Early education and care in 1990.* Washington, DC: U.S. Government Printing Office.

Landers, S. (1993). Family leave ushers in new era. *NASW News, 38*(3), 1.

Langlois, J. (1989). *Serving children then and now: An oral history of early childhood education and day care in metropolitan Detroit.* Detroit: Wayne State University.

Larner, M. (1994). *In the neighborhood: Programs that strengthen family daycare for low-income families.* New York: National Center for Children in Poverty, Columbia University.

Larner, M., & Chaudry, N. (1993). *Promoting professionalism through family day care networks.* New York: Columbia University School of Public Health, National Center for Children in Poverty.

Lewin, T. (1989, October 18). Study finds high turnover in child care workers. *New York Times,* p. 9.

Long, T. J., & Long, L. (1983). *Handbook for latchkey children and their parents.* New York: Arbor House.

Lundberg, E. O. (1947). *Unto the least of these: Social services for children.* New York: Appleton-Century-Crofts.

Mason, M. A. (1991). The McMartin case revisited: The conflict between social work and criminal justice. *Social Work, 36*(5), 39–43.

Mayer, A. B. (1965). *Day care as a social instrument: A policy paper.* New York: Columbia University School of Social Work.

Michel, S. (1988, January). *The nineteenth-century origins of the American child care policy.* Unpublished paper, Women's Studies, History and Literature, Howard University, Washington, DC.

Mitchell, A., Cooperstein, E., & Larner, M. (1992). *Child care choices, consumer education, and low-income families.* New York: National Center for Children in Poverty, School of Public Health, Columbia University.

National Institutes of Health. (1997, April 3). *Results of NICHD study of early child care reported at Society for Research in Child Development meeting.* Available on-line at http://www.nih.gov/news/pr/apr97/nichd-03.htm. [March, 1998].

Nixon, R. M. (1971). Veto message of the Child Development Act of 1971. *Congressional Record, December 10, 1971,* 46057–59.

Ounce of Prevention Fund. (1993). *Beethoven's Fifth: The first five years of the Center for Successful Child Development.* Chicago: Author.

Out-of-school time. (1997, September/October). *Child Care Bulletin, 17,* 2 pages. Available on-line at http://Ericps.ed.uiuc.edu/nccic [1997, November].

Pedgeon, M. (1953). *Employed mothers and child care.* Bulletin 246. Washington, DC: Women's Bureau.

Pfannestiel, J., Lambson, T., & Yarnell, V. (1991). *Second wave study of the Parents as Teachers program.* St. Louis: Parents as Teachers National Center, Inc.

Rally 'Round the Kids. (1993, April 21). *Detroit Free Press,* Section E, p. 1.

Roditti, M. G. (1995). Child day care: A key building block of family support and family preservation programs. *Child Welfare, 74*(6), 1043–1068.

Rodman, H., Pratto, D. J., & Nelson, R. S. (1985). Child care arrangements and children's functioning: A comparison of self-care and adult care of children. *Developmental Psychology, 21*(3), 413–418.

Rodriguez, G. (1989). *Avance family support and education programs.* Hearing before the House Select Committee on Children, Youth, and Families. 101st Cong., 1st Sess. Washington, DC: U.S. Government Printing Office.

Rubin, L. (1987). A feminist response to Lasch. *Tikkun, 1*(2), 89–91.

Schweinhart, L. J., Barnes, H. V., & Weikart, D. P. (1993). *Significant benefits: The High/Scope Perry Preschool Study through age 27.* (Monographs of the High/Scope Educational Research Foundation, No. 10). Ypsilanti, MI: High/Scope Press.

Shalala, D. (1997, October). Remarks by Secretary Donna E. Shalala, DHHS. *Child Care Bulletin, Issue 17,* 3 pages. Available on-line at http://Ericps.ed.uiuc.edu/nccic [1997, November].

Steinberg, L. (1986). Latchkey children and susceptibility to peer pressure: An ecological analysis. *Developmental Psychology, 22*(4), 433–439.

Stoney, L., & Greenberg, M. H. (1996). The financing of child care: Current and emerging trends. *The Future of Children, 6*(2), 83–102.

Sugarman, J. (1991). *Building early childhood systems: A resource handbook.* Washington, DC: Child Welfare League of America.

Swan, H. L., & Houston, V. (1985). *Alone after school: A self-care guide for latchkey children and their parents.* Englewood Cliffs, NJ: Prentice-Hall.

Terpstra, J. (1989). Day care standards and licensing. *Child Welfare, 68*(4), 437–442.

U.S. Department of Health, Education and Welfare, Office of Economic Opportunity, and U.S. Department of Labor. (1968). *Federal interagency day care requirements* (DHEW Publication NO. 938-038). Washington, DC: U.S. Government Printing Office.

U.S. General Accounting Office (1997, May). *Welfare reform: Implications of increased work participation for child care.* Washington, DC: Author.

U.S. Office of Education and the Office of Economic Opportunity. (1966). *Education: An answer to poverty.* Washington, DC: U.S. Government Printing Office.

Vandell, D. L., & Corasaniti, M. A. (1988). The relation between third graders' after-school care and social, academic, and emotional functioning. *Child Development, 59*(4), 868–875.

Vobejda, B., & Davis, P. (1997, November). Keeping an eye on the hand that rocks the cradle. *The Washington Post National Weekly Edition,* p. 30.

Westinghouse Learning Corporation. (1969, April). *The impact of Head Start: An evaluation of the effects of Head Start experience on children's cognitive and affective development.* Athens: Ohio University.

Willer, B., Hoffereth, S. L., Kisker, E. E., Divine-Hawkins, P., Farquahar, E., & Glandtz, F. B. (1991). *The demand and supply of child care in 1990: Joint findings from the "National child care survey 1990" and "A profile of child care settings."* Washington, DC: National Association for the Education of Young Children.

Women's Bureau. (1990). *Facts on working women.* (No. 90-2). Washington, DC: Department of Labor.

Zigler, E. (1989). Addressing the nation's child care crisis: The school of the twenty-first century. *American Journal of Orthpsychiatry, 59,* 484–491.

Zigler, E., & Lang, M. E. (1991). *Child care choices: Balancing the needs of children, families, and society.* New York: Free Press.

Zigler, E., & Styfco, S. J. (1994). *Head Start and beyond: A national plan for extended childhood intervention.* New Haven: Yale University Press.

CHAPTER 6

Law and Procedure

Court Intervention with Children, Youth, and Families

Juvenile court history has again demonstrated that unbridled discretion, however benevolently motivated, is frequently a poor substitute for principle and procedure.
—Justice Abe Fortas, *In re Gault* 1967, p. 18

CHAPTER OUTLINE

INTRODUCTION

Perhaps no social institution was founded with higher hopes for its contribution to justice for children than the juvenile court. In the last four decades, however, it has been a center of controversy. Its philosophy, procedures, and achievements have undergone scrutiny, challenge, and demands for radical change. At the heart of the controversy are differences over the proper purpose, focus, and procedures of the juvenile court.

The division of authority between courts and social agencies, particularly state child welfare agencies and the private child welfare agencies providing services under purchase-of-services arrangements with the public agencies, is a constant source of tension for the social worker. In the period of the juvenile court's history when its rules and procedures were informal, social workers were consulted for their expertise in "what's best for the child." Their opinions were given, generally with little questioning of the evidentiary bases for them, and the court acted with significant deference to those recommendations. As the juvenile court system became more structured to conform to legal requirements for admissibility of evidence, standards of proof, rights to attorney representation, and other procedural protections for children and their parents, the social worker's approach has had to adapt.

A constant source of conflict for social workers is that they are required to gather and act on both social evidence and legal evidence. Some situations of children and families do not yield clear legal evidence. Because the questions at issue in such cases are often not simple, social workers may rely on many sources of information, some of which is nonadmissible hearsay evidence or other information acquired informally. In such cases they look for repeated patterns of parent and child behavior and environmental influences. They may offer "voluntary" services to the family with the hope of resolving the concern. Frequently these offers of "voluntary" services are rooted in their knowledge that they have insufficient evidence to proceed to court intervention. This practice is receiving greater scrutiny and commentary within the social work and legal communities. Many argue that when the state intrusion and the treatment plan do not rest on

a documented basis that could pass judicial scrutiny, social workers must carefully evaluate the reliability of any social evidence that in a way affects the rights of children and families and their ability to direct their own lives.

The challenge to social workers is to understand the nature of evidence and the court process, to become skillful in finding and organizing facts, and to integrate this knowledge and skill into their social work values and approaches to helping. In Chapter 2 we highlighted the major Supreme Court case decisions and their impact on the juvenile courts. In Chapters 3, 7, 8, 9, 10, and 11 we focus on the social work issues. In this chapter, we focus on the basics of the juvenile, and increasingly, the family courts in the handling of abuse, neglect, and delinquency matters. Our intent is to orient the student to the structure and processes of the legal systems and their roles in them.

THE JUVENILE COURT MOVEMENT

Juvenile courts were created by a legal and social work cooperative venture. In a spirit of mission, late nineteenth- and early twentieth-century social reformers enjoined the "child welfare" purpose to that of "youth correction." Historical factors in large measure account for the highly complex commingling of the child welfare system and the juvenile justice system that exists today: "The most significant fact about the history of juvenile justice is that it evolved simultaneously with the child welfare system. Most of its defects and its virtues derive from that fact" (Flicker, 1977, p. 27).

Philosophy and Purpose

From its inception, the juvenile court had high aims, combined with heavy responsibilities. Its purpose was conceived of as protection and rehabilitation of the child in place of indictment and punishment. It was based on a philosophy of "individualized justice," which directs the application of law to social ends by individualization, that is, by "dealing with each case as in great measure unique and yet . . . on a basis of principle derived from experience . . . developed by reason" (Pound, 1950, p. 36). The intent was a humanitarian one, based on the conviction that the individual child and his or her needs rather than an offense and its legal penalty should be the focus of consideration.

The concern of the juvenile court founders was directed toward the youthful lawbreaker and children whose circumstances were likely to lead them into delinquency, rather than those who were grossly neglected or in need of other protections.

Judge Julian Mack, one of the early leaders in the juvenile court movement, described procedures prior to the passage of juvenile court legislation:

> *Our common criminal law did not differentiate between the adult and the minor who had reached the age of criminal responsibility, seven at common law and in some of our states, ten in others, with a chance of escape up to twelve, if lacking in mental and moral maturity. The majesty and dignity of the state demanded vindication for infractions from both alike. . . . The child was arrested, put into prison, indicted by the grand jury, tried by a petit jury, under all the forms and technicalities of our criminal law, with the aim of ascertaining whether it had done the specific act—nothing else—and if it had, then of visiting the punishment of the state upon it. (Mack, 1909–1910, p. 106)*

An early description of the aims and the humanitarian concerns of the new court will serve to draw the contrast between the old and the new philosophy:

> *Emphasis is laid, not on the act done by the child, but on the social fact and circumstances that are really the inducing causes of the child's appearance in court. The particular offense that was the immediate and proximate cause of the proceedings is considered only as one of the many other factors surrounding the child. The purpose of the proceeding here is not punishment but correction of conditions, care and protection of the child and prevention of a recurrence through the constructive work of the court. Conservation of the child, as a valuable asset of the community, is the dominant note. (Flexner & Baldwin, 1914, pp. 6–7)*

To implement such a philosophy, the juvenile court was of necessity a court of equity, one intended to temper the strict application of the law to the individual needs of the child. Its justice represented a departure from the concept of justice personified by the traditional symbol: a statue of a woman holding a balanced scale. In one scale, the crime is measured, and in the other, the punishment. When the two sides of the scale balance evenly, it was held, justice prevails. This symbol of justice wears a blindfold so that the wealth or poverty of the accused or other individual characteristics or station in life cannot influence her. She is blind to individual differences, all objective and evenhanded. There were historical reasons for this symbol. It marked a revolt against the tyranny and the inequities of earlier centuries when law was made and interpreted differently for nobles and peasants, rich and poor. It marked a claim of the ordinary person for equal treatment before the law.

But in the philosophy of the juvenile court, the blindfold was, in effect, stripped from the symbol of justice. The characteristics of the child became crucial to the judge, who was under obligation to examine the child and a particular situation with all its differences and to turn away from a scrutiny of the offense and its legal penalty. Julia Lathrop, one of the juvenile court's early founders, said that the outstanding contribution of the juvenile court was that "it made the child visible" (Lundberg, 1947, p. 119).

Founding

The first juvenile court in the United States was created in Illinois on April 2, 1899. The attainment of this significant and far-reaching piece of legislation came through cooperation among a group of discerning and energetic social workers in Chicago, lawyers for the Chicago Bar Association, and civic leaders from various organizations, particularly the Chicago Woman's Club.

The leading female reformer among those who assumed responsibility for securing the juvenile court was a social worker, Julia Lathrop. An early resident of Hull House, she had been challenged by the spirit and potentiality of youths and distressed at the careless and neglectful treatment of many of them.

In 1898, at the annual meeting of the Illinois State Conference of Charities, Julia Lathrop showed leadership in planning an entire conference program on the topic "The Children of the State." Different organizations were found to be considering legislative proposals for benefits to children. The various groups merged their efforts and appointed a committee to secure the cooperation of the Chicago Bar

Association to bring about a draft of a juvenile court act. While there were many revisions, the bill that emerged was approved as a Bar Association bill and introduced into the state legislature (Lathrop, 1925, pp. 290–297). The task of proposing and testifying in behalf of the juvenile court bill was assigned to the lawyers, while the woman's club took responsibility for securing support for the bill (Rosenheim, 1962, pp. 18–19).

This initial piece of legislation, which served as a model for legislation in other states, was broadly entitled "An Act to Regulate the Treatment and Control of Dependent, Neglected, and Delinquent Children." Thereafter, children who violated laws or ordinances were classified as delinquents instead of criminals. The new act was considered a magnificent accomplishment, attained against the weight and opposition of tradition. Jane Addams believed that the new court brought such change that

> there was almost a change in mores when the Juvenile Court was established. The child was brought before the judge with no one to prosecute him and no one to defend him—the judge and all concerned were merely trying to find out what could be done on his behalf. (Addams, 1935, p. 137)

Roscoe Pound said that the juvenile court represented "the greatest advance in judicial history since the Magna Carta" (National Probation and Parole Association, 1957, p. 127). The movement had strong appeal to individual citizens and to groups working in behalf of children. This exciting concept of justice for children and the new legal machinery for helping them was achieved during a period of support for social reforms generally and special interest in the needs of children, a factor that helped to speed the creation of juvenile courts in other states.

By 1945, all states plus the District of Columbia, Hawaii, Alaska, and Puerto Rico had enacted juvenile court legislation, and Congress had authorized similar procedures for use in the federal courts (Nutt, 1949, p. 270).

The Early Question of Constitutionality

Some opposition to the initial passage of the acts came from members of the bar who believed that the court procedures, although intended to protect children, actually took away their constitutional rights. Nevertheless, by finding that juvenile proceedings were not adversarial, the courts firmly established the constitutionality of the juvenile court statutes, substantially reinforcing and extending the doctrine of parens patriae to include juvenile delinquents. In all the leading test cases, the parens patriae tenet was called up and used to justify the state's authority in the new acts, even though this old doctrine had not been a direct antecedent of the juvenile court (Flexner & Oppenheimer, 1922; Lou, 1927). The first major test of the constitutionality of juvenile court procedures was that of the Pennsylvania Act of 1903. An excerpt from the decision is illustrative of the philosophy that prevailed.

> To save a child from becoming a criminal, or from continuing in a career of crime, to end in maturer years in public punishment and disgrace, the legislature surely may provide for the salvation of such a child, if its parents or guardian be unable or unwilling to do so, by bringing it into one of the courts of the state without any process at all, for the purpose of subjecting it to the state's guardianship and protection. . . . There is no probability, in the proper administration of the law, of the child's liberty being unduly invaded. Every statute which is designed to give protection, care, and training to children, as a needed substitute for parental authority and performance of parental duty, is but a recognition of the duty of the state, as the legitimate guardian and protector of children where other guardianship fails. No constitutional right is violated. (Commonwealth v. Fisher, 1905)

When the new juvenile court statutes were challenged on constitutional grounds, the state supreme courts successively upheld them on the basis that the juvenile court was not a criminal court and no child was brought before the juvenile court under arrest and on trial for a crime; hence, constitutional guarantees accorded defendants in criminal cases did not apply to juvenile procedures. The weight of decision was an overwhelming endorsement of the new laws.

Practically, this meant that the child or youth was brought under the power of the juvenile court without the legal safeguards claimed as a constitutional right by an adult accused of law violations. These safeguards are embodied in such procedures as open hearings, right to counsel, proof beyond a reasonable doubt, limitations on the use of hearsay evidence, protection against self-incrimination, and right to bail. This practice of failing to provide the minor with these constitutionally guaranteed protections eventually led to extensive criticism of the juvenile court, on the basis that the rights of the child should be no less highly regarded and no less strictly observed than those of an adult in any court.

Supreme Court Decisions: New Procedural Directions

The *Kent* and *Gault* decisions of the United States Supreme Court began the constitutional review of the juvenile court processes that had been the subject of heavy criticisms. Youth and their parents frequently were not informed of their right to counsel. The absence of suitable facilities had led to the use of jails for children who had been arrested but not adjudicated. The social investigation, designed as a basis for helping the judge make an informed decision, often was sparse or superficial, thus negating its purpose. Clear proof of charges was often lacking even though the result was undesirable labeling of the child, or loss of liberty through commitment to training schools. Frequently there had been no transcripts of court proceedings, or incomplete ones, which made an appeal to a higher court difficult (Beemsterboer, 1960; Ellrod & Melaney, 1950; Elson, 1962; Handler, 1965; Rubin, 1952). Too often there had been failure on the part of the state to provide true rehabilitative facilities following the removal of a child from parental custody, what Ketcham (1962) termed substitution of "governmental for parental neglect."

Supreme Court Justice Abe Fortas cogently pinpointed two of the major problems before the juvenile court, the lack of constitutional guarantees and the lack of rehabilitative treatment resources:

> There is much evidence that some juvenile courts . . . lack the personnel, facilities and techniques to perform adequately as representatives of the state in a parens patriae capacity, at least with respect to children charged with law violation. There is evidence, in fact, that there may be grounds for concern that the child receives the worst of both worlds: that he gets neither the protections accorded to adults nor the solicitous care and regenerative treatment postulated for children. (Kent v. United States, 1966)

The specific facts of the following cases are stated in Chapter 2 and will not be repeated here. The issue in the *Kent* case was the juvenile's constitutional rights during a transfer, or waiver, from the juvenile court to the adult criminal court. The decision specified that the juvenile court must hold a hearing on the matter of a waiver, provide the young person with counsel at this hearing, and make the juvenile court records available to his or her counsel. The second major United States Supreme Court decision in relation to procedural protections for juveniles was *In re Gault*. The issue in this case was the due process and equal protection requirements in juvenile court proceedings. While the Court made it clear that juvenile court proceedings on an adjudication of delinquency need not conform to all the requirements of a criminal trial, it held that such action must measure up to the essentials of due process and fair treatment guaranteed by the Fourteenth Amendment to the Constitution. Specifically, (1) the child and his or her parents must be given written notice of a scheduled hearing sufficiently in advance to provide opportunity to prepare for the hearing, and this notice must set forth the alleged misconduct "with particularity"; (2) the child and his or her parents must be notified of the child's right to be represented by counsel retained by them, or if they are unable to afford this, counsel will be appointed to represent the child; (3) the constitutional privilege against self-incrimination (the right to remain silent instead of admitting or confessing) is applicable in the case of juveniles as well as adults; and (4) the child or young person has a right to confront and cross-examine witnesses who appear against him or her (*In re Gault*, 1967).

Three other U.S. Supreme Court decisions are important in shaping the adjudication phase of a delinquency procedure. *In re Winship* (1970) established the principle of proof beyond a reasonable doubt as a requirement for a finding of delinquency (although not necessarily for finding a child "in need of supervision"). While *Winship* affirmed a required level of proof for minors, two other decisions, *McKeiver v. Pennsylvania* (1971) and *Schall v. Martin* (1984), were in the direction of limiting the legal rights of a minor.

McKeiver held that the due process clause of the Fourteenth Amendment does not require jury trials for youths charged with delinquent acts that could result in incarceration, leading to the criticism that *McKeiver* "continues the tradition of conceptual oscillation when juvenile court procedure is at issue," resulting in "the extension of some rights and the denial of others" (Schultz & Cohen, 1976, p. 28). The *Schall* court decided that pretrial detention to protect an accused juvenile and society from the "serious risk" of pretrial crime is compatible with the "fundamental fairness" demanded by the due process clause. The interest of the state in promoting juvenile welfare is *a parens patriae* interest, and is what "makes a juvenile proceeding fundamentally different from an adult criminal trial" (*Schall,* 1984, pp. 253, 263). Liberty can therefore be circumscribed by the power of *parens patriae.*

The doctrine of *parens patriae* found further expression in the first Supreme Court decision establishing a standard in the dispositional stage of juvenile proceedings. *Thompson v. Oklahoma* (1988) over-turned the death penalty for a boy who was 15 at the time he participated in the brutal murder of his former brother-in-law. The Court's majority held that to execute a person who was under 16 at the time of committing a crime was cruel and unusual punishment and therefore unconstitutional. The court distinguished juveniles from adults in terms of a basic assumption of society about children as a class: "We assume that they do not yet act as adults do, and thus we act in their interest. . . . It would be ironic if these assumptions that we so readily make about children as a class—about their inherent difference from adults in their capacity as agents, as choosers, as shapers of their own lives—were suddenly unavailable in determining whether it is cruel and unusual to treat children the same as adults for purposes of inflicting capital punishment" (*Thompson,* 1988, p. 2693, n. 23).

These precedent-setting cases affirm that in instances of alleged delinquency, juveniles are granted legal rights differentiated from those of adults, and at the same time are afforded due process protections (see Box 6.1).

BOX 6.1 ───

Due Process in Juvenile Courts

These are the due process rights for parties in juvenile court matters:

- *Right to notice and opportunity to be heard.* This means they have a right to know in advance what the charges are; who is making them; what evidence they have to support the charges; the date and time for the court hearing; and the right to bring evidence in support of their side of the story.
- *Right to representation.* This means that parents charged with abuse or neglect and youth charged with delinquent offenses have a right to an attorney. If they cannot afford one, then they have a right to have one appointed at public expense. Children in neglect and abuse matters may or may not have a right to attorney representation, depending on the state statute. They do have the right to have someone speak on their behalf—often a guardian ad litem.
- *Right to remain silent or privilege against self-incrimination.* This means that parents and youth charged with delinquent offenses can choose to not speak on their own behalf and the court cannot interpret that as an admission of or presumption of guilt.
- *Right to confront and cross-examine witnesses.* This means that parents charged with abuse or neglect and youth charged with delinquent offenses have a right to challenge verbally and with documents the testimony and statements of any witness.

THE FAMILY COURT MOVEMENT

The first family court was established in Cincinnati, Ohio in 1914, just fifteen years after the founding of the juvenile court. Family courts, in general, have jurisdiction over a broad range of legal issues involving children and families. Specific jurisdictional issues include divorce; child support, custody, and visitation; paternity establishment; child abuse and neglect, including termination of parental rights; juvenile delinquency; guardianship; emancipation; and emergency medical and mental health treatment authorization. The underlying rationale is that family legal issues are not isolated. A family experiencing child abuse and neglect may already have custody and visitation orders that could conflict with orders arising out of the child abuse and neglect matter. Divorcing parents frequently charge each other with abuse or neglect. The family courts, having the comprehensive jurisdiction to adjudicate all matters arising out of the same situation, spare the parties the multiplicity of court appearances with their potential for conflicting results. One jurist knows all the facts and is responsible for the resolution of all the legal issues (Szymanski, 1993).

As of 1998, eleven states had statewide family courts; fourteen states had family courts in selected areas of the state; nine states had family courts planned or being piloted; and seventeen states had no plans for family courts. The subject matter jurisdictions of the courts vary, with only eleven states' family courts having jurisdiction over all family matters (Babb 1998). Ross attributes these variations to the need to adapt the courts to the particular communities. She identifies four components necessary to classify a court as a "family court":

- *comprehensive jurisdiction, that is, the ability to adjudicate a range of legal issues so that there is an integrated approach to the resolution of problems within the same family;*
- *efficient administration designed to support the concept of "one family, one team," that is, the provision of continuity in decision-makers so that individual solutions are crafted based in knowledge of the family and its total situation;*
- *broad training for all court personnel, that is, establishing mechanisms so that judges, lawyers, so-*

cial workers, and other support personnel are trained in the social, medical, psychological issues that arise in connection with the legal issues;
- *comprehensive services, that is, having a broad array of services available to the family that can be accessed as soon as the family assessment is completed. (Ross, 1998, pp. 15–28)*

As the family court movement progresses, there is a need for critical evaluation of outcomes. In theory the decisions should be more timely with little, if any, conflicts in orders, and services should be available when needed and in the "dosage" required for the individual family situation. Mark Hardin comments

> *If, in the end, it appears doubtful that the resources and organization needed to achieve excellence in child protection cases will be in place when a unified family court is established, then advocates will have to ask themselves whether the proposed unified family court will be an improvement for abused and neglected children or, if not, an improvement for children overall. Where the resources are not in place, advocates in some locations may ultimately choose to work for improvement through specialized juvenile courts. . . . In either event, child protection advocates should be aware of the significance of court reform to achieving change beneficial to abused children. (Hardin, 1998, p. 199)*

THE STRUCTURE OF THE LEGAL SYSTEM

The legal system is complex. Law is the body of rules set and enforced by the government. Its function is to provide order and stability to society. Laws are changed when the society, as a whole, determines that the changes are required to advance the goal of order and stability in an ever-changing society. Laws are established in federal and state constitutions, by statutes or ordinances passed by the legislative branch of federal, state, and local governments, by regulatory agencies in administrative rules and regulations, and by federal and state court case decisions.

The ultimate law of the land is the U.S. Constitution. No federal or state statute and no administrative rule or regulation that violates a provision of the U.S. Constitution will prevail when challenged on constitutional grounds and the federal courts find that the statute, rule, or regulation is in violation of the U.S. Constitution.

Assuming that a specific statute, ordinance, administrative rule or case decision is constitutional, where there is a conflict, the general rule is that

- federal law supercedes state law and administrative rules if the federal law provides a greater benefit;
- state law supercedes administrative rules and local ordinances; and
- administrative rules supercede agency policies.

Case decisions, that is, case law or decisional law, serve to clarify the intent and meaning of federal and state constitutions, statutes, and administrative rules as applied in a specific fact situation or to clarify legal principles if there is no existing statute. Once a higher court of appropriate jurisdiction has ruled on the matter, that ruling serves as the interpretation of the law that all lower courts within the jurisdiction covered by the deciding court must follow.

Trial and Appellate Courts

The court system is comprised of the federal and state courts. Different courts have different jurisdictions, that is, types of legal matters over which it has authority to hear and decide. A trial court is a court where decisions are based on receipt, examination, and evaluation of witness testimony and evidence. Either a jury or judge makes decisions. An appellate court is a court where decisions are based on receipt and review of the written record of the trial court. Parties can submit written and oral arguments identifying the alleged errors made at the trial court level. Appellate courts can overturn (*reverse*) or support (*uphold*) the decision of the lower court based on the record as submitted or can return the case to the trial court with specific instructions or orders (*remand*).

Different states have different statutes and court rules governing appeals. In general there are appeals of right and appeals by application and leave granted. An appeal of right is taken when a specific statute provides that the decision of a lower court can be appealed to and must be heard by the appellate court. If a specific statutory provision granting an appeal of right is not present, the appeal is taken "by leave granted," that is, petition to court with the court having discretion as to whether or not to hear the case. Very few abuse, neglect and juvenile delinquency matters ever proceed beyond the trial court stage.

Jurisdiction

The **jurisdiction** of a court (that is, its legal authority to hear and decide a particular matter) is determined by state statutes. The judge's authority in decision-making is limited to those situations authorized by the statute. In juvenile matters, the primary factors enumerated in the statutes are the subject matter, the maximum age of the children for original jurisdiction, the geographic boundaries of the court, and the matters in which the court has exclusive and/or shared or concurrent jurisdictions.

The **age** of the young person in question is a primary factor that enters into a decision as to whether a juvenile court has jurisdiction. For delinquency matters, in most states the maximum age for original jurisdiction is 17 years; in some states the maximum age is as young as 15. Most states allow the juvenile court to continue jurisdiction over juvenile offenders, once they are adjudicated, beyond the maximum age of original jurisdiction. For abuse and neglect matters, in most states the juvenile court now has original jurisdiction up to 18 years of age, and, if jurisdiction was assumed prior to 18 years of age, it could continue jurisdiction beyond 18 years of age when provided by statute. For status offenses and adoption matters, in most states the jurisdictional age limit is 18 years.

The **subject matter** jurisdiction of the juvenile courts, in general, includes four general areas: abuse, neglect, abandonment, and dependency; delinquency; wayward minor, status offender, and minor in need of supervision; and adoption. With the family court movement, the decisional capacities in many states have been expanded to include paternity establishment; child custody, support, and visitation; guardianship; and emancipation. The specific facts of the case determine the appropriate jurisdictional basis. It is not atypical for dependency, neglect, abuse, and delinquency to overlap in the same case: "Parental neglect can precipitate delinquent conduct and the delinquent child may have been subjected to hostility and child abuse in the home. The neglected child may also be a delinquent who has not yet been caught" (Brieland & Lemmon, 1985, p. 139).

Jurisdictional elements are state-specific. Refer to the specific statutes and court rules for the state in which you are practicing.

Evidence

Evidence includes the full range of information, written and verbal, provided to the court in support of the allegations or statements made. Rules of evidence direct the type of information and the method for presenting that information to the court. These rules are promulgated to ensure the fair administration of justice. You should review the rules for the state in which you will be practicing, specifically the rules related to hearsay, business records, and expert witness testimony. You should document cases and prepare for hearings or trials with these evidentiary rules in mind.

Standards of Proof

A **standard of proof** is the degree of evidence required for the party who has the burden of proof to present to the court in order to sustain its burden, that is, to prove what the party asserts. The standard of proof varies depending on the stage of the hearing process—adjudicatory or dispositional—and the type of case being heard.

The three standards of proof are preponderance of the evidence, clear and convincing evidence, and beyond a reasonable doubt.

Preponderance of the Evidence. This refers to the greater weight of the evidence or evidence that is more credible and convincing. In delinquency matters, this is the standard used in most states for dispositional phase. In neglect or status offense matters, which are not treated as delinquency cases, this is the standard used by most states for adjudicatory phase.

Clear and Convincing Evidence. This proof is beyond preponderance but less than beyond a reason-

able doubt. Some say that this means proof beyond a well-founded doubt. This is the standard used in the adjudicatory phase for cases involving Indian Child Welfare Act cases and in termination of parental rights for all children except Indian children. In some states, this standard is used in delinquency matters where the recommended disposition is placement in a secure facility.

Beyond a Reasonable Doubt. This proof must satisfy a moral certainty, be entirely convincing; the facts proven must establish guilt. In delinquency matters, this is the standard used in adjudicatory hearings. It is also the standard used in termination of parental rights of children covered by the Indian Child Welfare Act.

Indian Child Welfare Act: An Example of Federal Law Superceding State Law

The Indian Child Welfare Act, PL 95-608, was passed in 1978. Its intent was to curb an excessive rate of placement of Indian children in non-Indian foster and adoptive homes. The legislation came about after years of agitation by Indian groups and other advocates of civil liberties who maintained that out-of-home placements contributed to disruption of tribal culture and identity confusion on the part of Indian children and encroached upon the sovereignty of tribes.

The federal legislation was a significant social policy development, unique in acknowledging and protecting cultural values and self-determination of a minority group within the larger American society. In passing the legislation, Congress stated that the policy of the nation was to promote the stability and security of Indian tribes and families by establishing minimum federal standards for the removal of Indian children from their families. The placement of such children in foster homes hereafter would reflect Indian preferences for placement in priority order: extended family; homes licensed by a nontribal entity; or institutions approved by an Indian tribe.

Tribal courts have exclusive jurisdiction over child custody proceedings involving most Indian children whether residing on the reservation or not. This means that the state court has the responsibility to notify the tribal court that it has a custody matter involving an Indian child before it and, if the tribal court elects to take the case, the state court must transfer the case to the tribal court. Custody proceedings include all foster care or adoptive placements of Indian children resulting from abuse or neglect, termination of parental rights, or status offenses of running away, truancy, and curfew violation. The legislation provided for federal funding to assist tribes in developing and operating child and family service programs.

The United States Supreme Court has heard one case involving interpretation of the Indian Child Welfare Act, *Mississippi Band of Choctaw Indians v. Holyfield.* That case involved twins born to an Indian mother who was a member of the Choctaw tribe and who lived on the reservation. The children were born off the reservation, and the mother and father released their parental rights to allow the Holyfields to adopt them. The Holyfields proceeded with the adoption, and the tribe brought a motion to vacate the adoption on the basis that the children were Indian children and the parents did not have the right to release them for adoption by non-Indian persons without tribal permission. The Court stated

> We agree with the Supreme Court of Utah that the law of domicile Congress used in the ICWA cannot be one that permits individual reservation-domiciled tribal member to defeat the tribe's exclusive jurisdiction by the simple expedient of giving birth and placing the child for adoption off the reservation. Since, for the purposes of ICWA, the twin babies were domiciled on the reservation when adoption proceedings were begun, the Choctaw tribal court possessed exclusive jurisdiction pursuant to 25 U.S.C. Section 1911(a). (Id, 490 U.S. 51 (1989), pp. 1610–1611)

The Court expressed its concern about the fact that the children had lived with the Holyfields for three years while the case proceeded through the appellate process:

> We have been asked to make the decision as to who should make the custody determination concerning these children—not what the outcome of that determination should be. The law places that decision in the hands of the Choctaw tribal court. Had the mandate of the ICWA been followed in 1986, of course, such potential anguish might have been avoided, and in any case the law cannot be applied so as to automat-

> ically to reward those who obtained custody, whether lawfully or otherwise, and maintain it during any ensuing (and protracted) litigation. . . . It is not ours to say whether the trauma that might result from removing these children from their adoptive family should outweigh the interest of the Tribe—and perhaps the children themselves—in having them raised as part of the Choctaw community. Rather, we must defer to the experience, wisdom, and compassion of the Choctaw tribal courts to fashion an appropriate remedy. (p. 1611)

The legislation and this decision should leave no doubt that matters involving Native American children that come to the attention of the state child welfare system should be immediately referred to the appropriate tribal authority. State systems have authority to act to protect these children from immediate harm while awaiting response from the tribal authority.

LEGAL MATTERS FOR THE CHILD WELFARE SYSTEM

There are many legal matters involving children, including child abuse, neglect, abandonment, or dependency; juvenile delinquency; status offenses; adoption; guardianship; paternity establishment; support and visitation; child custody, support, and visitation; and emancipation. It is not atypical for a social worker in child welfare or juvenile delinquency to have a single case with a multitude of legal complexities involving the various issues identified.

Abuse, Neglect, Abandonment, or Dependency

The state's reporting law describes procedures for professionals and other citizens to use in reporting suspected instances of child abuse and neglect to the local child welfare agency and/or the local police department. After the report is received and investigated, the agency or police department decides whether to file a petition with the juvenile court. The factors that go into this decision vary. (See Chapter 7.) Important to note is that the child protection agency can find evidence of abuse, neglect, abandonment, or dependency and not bring the matter to the attention of the court.

The juvenile codes of the states typically provide for jurisdiction when it is alleged that the child

- lacks proper guardianship because his or her parents are minors, the parents' whereabouts are unknown, the parents are dead, or the parents are unable to provide acceptable care because of some established mental or physical incapacity; or
- has been physically, mentally, or emotionally abused by a parent or guardian; or
- whose basic needs for food, shelter, clothing, medical care, and education have not been met by the parent or guardian. (See Chapter 7.)

Once the court takes jurisdiction (adjudicates) due to abuse, neglect, or dependency, it has a number of dispositional alternatives, including leaving the child in the home; referring the child to a child welfare agency for placement in foster care, including foster homes (relative and nonrelative), group homes, or residential treatment facilities; and, in extreme situations, immediate termination of parental rights.

Social workers have a particularly important role in juvenile court cases involving abuse and neglect because their agencies are usually charged with the following key responsibilities:

- determining when and whether to file a petition alleging abuse or neglect
- recommending that the child remain at home or be placed out of the home
- in the case of a recommendation for out-of-home placement, showing that the agency made "reasonable efforts" to keep the family together
- recommending a specific out-of-home placement, including placement with relatives, after investigating all possibilities
- establishing a treatment plan with the parent and monitoring progress
- reporting to the court on the parent's progress and recommending reunification or termination of parental rights
- monitoring and supporting reunification, if that is the plan
- preparing evidence to support a judicial decision for termination of parental rights, if it seems unlikely that the child can ever go home and can be adopted
- testifying in court

It is not an exaggeration to say that the extent to which the juvenile court successfully protects children while supporting continuity of family relationships for children depends to a large extent on the persistence of the social worker and his or her knowledge of the case and of court personnel and procedures (Downs & Taylor, 1980). Continuous, meticulous documentation of all contacts with family members is essential if the social worker wishes to influence the decisions that courts make concerning children.

A primary, essential, unavoidable rule is document, document, document. Admittedly, the tedium of the practice is at times overwhelming, and if the parent improves and the children return home, it may not have been necessary. However, proper recording of the worker's activities is directly related to success in court. Depending on legal practices in your state, your case record may be submitted as an evidentiary exhibit. Any issue with possible controversy is secured by case recording and supporting correspondence. (A child welfare supervisor—Downs & Taylor, 1980)

In abuse and neglect situations where the child has been removed from the home, planning is crucial to maintaining momentum for positive change on the part of the parents and to avoiding "foster care drift," in which the child remains in foster care indefinitely because no one takes responsibility for permanency planning. (See Chapter 9).

Juvenile Delinquency

Delinquency jurisdiction arises when a juvenile, as defined by the state or federal statute, is alleged to have violated any federal or state law, or municipal ordinance. States vary somewhat by excluding certain minor offenses such as vagrancy or loitering, by treating traffic offenses differently depending on whether they are heard in traffic court or juvenile court, and in how they define and handle status offenses, that is, those acts that are illegal because of the youth's age or status. However, the primary criterion in defining delinquency is whether the act would be a crime if committed by an adult.

Although delinquency matters account for only 2 percent of the juvenile court dockets nationwide, they receive the headlines and are perceived to be of significantly higher volume (OJJDP, 1996).

Nearly all states have some provision to permit a juvenile or, where appropriate, a family court to waive jurisdiction in the case of major offenses. This means that the juvenile or family court has the right to transfer a case to the criminal court for adjudication, following procedures delineated in the statutes or court rules that are consistent with those required by *Kent v. United States, 1966.* In some states, the case may start in adult court, and it is up to the juvenile to prove that he or she is amenable to treatment in the juvenile system; in still others, the prosecutors have absolute discretion to file cases in adult court, without any hearing at all in juvenile court. (See Box 6.2 for the types of offenses covered by the waiver processes.)

Once the court adjudicates, the dispositional alternatives are similar to those it has in abuse and neglect matters. The youth can remain in the home, be placed in foster care—including foster homes, group homes, and residential treatment facilities—or be placed in a secure facility. The dispositional choice is based on the type of offense committed as well as social factors. Chapter 11 provides a detailed discussion of the juvenile delinquency services system.

The social worker or probation officer is charged with monitoring the treatment and rehabilitation process and making periodic reports to the court.

Status Offenses

Many states provide separate jurisdictional sections for status offenders, wayward minors, or minors in need of supervision within their juvenile codes. For most, jurisdiction arises when it is alleged that the youth is beyond the control of his or her parents or other guardians and displays patterns of conduct deemed incorrigible, uncontrollable, or likely to develop into more serious and dangerous behavior. These situations are often referred to as "status offenses" because the conduct that brings the youth before the court is held to be illegal only because of the youth's age and would not be regarded as illegal if he or she were not a minor. Examples of status offenses include truancy, running away, curfew violations, sexual promiscuity, undesirable companions, and disobedience to parents. Youth

---

BOX 6.2 _____

Offenses for Which a Juvenile May Be Tried as an Adult

Although states vary, in general youths from age 14 to 17 may be tried as adults for the following types of offenses:

- burning a dwelling
- assault with intent to commit murder
- assault with intent to commit great bodily harm less than murder
- assault with intent to rob—unarmed
- assault with intent to rob—armed
- attempted murder
- first-degree murder
- second-degree murder
- kidnapping
- criminal sexual conduct
- assault with intent to commit criminal sexual conduct
- armed robbery
- unarmed robbery
- possession, manufacture, or delivery of a controlled substance

who commit status offenses may be referred to as persons (or minors, or children) in need of supervision, with the corresponding acronyms PINS, MINS, or CHINS. Maintaining status offenses within the jurisdiction of the juvenile court remains highly controversial. Some authorities challenge the wisdom and justice of authorizing the juvenile court to assume jurisdiction over youth who behave in ways encompassed under such general terms as *incorrigibility* or *in need of supervision.* Given the scope, vagueness, and equivocal language of the statutes in many states, almost any child could be brought within the jurisdiction of the juvenile court (Simonsen, 1991).

Concern is expressed that a too-ready transfer of responsibility to bureaucratic discretion is seriously weakening the traditional responsibility of the family for control of children's misbehavior. Within an increasingly adversarial context, some believe the juvenile justice system is being forced to deal with delinquents and status offenders in the same way, that is, to treat status offenses like delinquent acts (Simonsen, 1991). (See Chapter 11.)

Once the court adjudicates it has a number of dispositional alternatives, including leaving the youth in the home or placement in foster care, including foster homes (relative and nonrelative), group homes, or residential treatment facilities. (See Chapter 11.)

Adoption

Adoption is the full transfer of parental rights and responsibilities to persons other than the biological parents, after termination of parental rights or voluntary relinquishment of parental rights. The legal process of adoption, relatively speaking, is simple. A petition is filed, along with the appropriate verifications—original birth certificates, child-specific information as required by statute, an adoptive family home study—and the court may or may not hold a hearing. The court orders the placement with or without supervision, depending on the state's statutory requirements. (See Chapter 10.)

Guardianship

Guardianship, custody, and in loco parentis are frequently confused. *Custody* generally relates to physical/legal placement with a parent; *guardianship* generally refers to physical/legal placement with someone other than the parent, since parents are by law the natural guardians of their children; and *in loco parentis* generally refers to a designated individual having authority to engage in certain parental acts on behalf of a child through statutory authority or a specific court order.

There are important differences between the rights and responsibilities of parents and those of a court-appointed guardian. Guardianship through court appointment is subject to the continuing supervision of the court. Guardianship, unlike parenthood, does not involve the duty to support and educate the ward except from his or her own estate. It does not carry the right to the ward's earnings and services. The parent of a child has the right to control incidental assets of the child such as income from gifts and typical childhood employment. Control over other assets of the child such as insurance settlements, lawsuit awards, distributions from wills and trusts of grandparents and others, or income from professional employment during minority generally requires a specific appointment of the parent or someone else as guardian of the estate. This triggers court oversight of the management of the estate. Children under court-appointed guardianship have statutory rights to inherit from their parents should the parents die without a will (intestate succession); they do not have any statutory rights to inherit from their guardians. If the guardians want the ward to inherit from them, they must specifically identify them and what they wish them to have in the guardians' wills. Parents have the right to choose where their child shall live as long as the care given does not fall below the minimal standards demanded by the community. In contrast, a guardian of the person may or may not have the authority to independently change the ward's residence. Parents cannot independently transfer their rights of legal guardianship. Whether or not the transfer of guardianship is voluntarily or involuntarily, the state court having jurisdiction over guardianship matters must be involved, and that court remains involved, so long as the guardianship is in effect.

There are two basic types of guardianship: guardian of the person and guardian of the estate. The **guardian of the person** becomes responsible for the care and control of the child. Depending on the state law, the guardian can decide the kind of medical care, including permission for major medical, psychiatric, and surgical treatment; or decisions about education, employment, permission for marriage, and permission for entry into the armed forces; and the right to represent the child in legal actions. In certain instances, the guardian of person may have been invested by court action with the power to consent to the adoption of the minor when the parent-child relationship has been fully terminated by judicial decree. Guardians of the person do not have the right to receive and manage property that their wards may acquire unless specifically authorized to do so through a separate appointment as the guardian of the estate.

Guardian of the estate creates a means by which a minor can deal in the business world. Guardians of the estate are in a sense trustees or administrators. Specifically, they have power to govern the estate and act for their wards in matters involving property. The guardian of the estate can mortgage, sell, or otherwise transfer property and make the resources available for the ward's needs during his or her minority. Guardians of estate are persons of presumed integrity and are subject to the continuing supervision of the court. In general, they must submit periodic accountings of the ward's assets and their transactions to the court. Unless the guardian of estate is also named guardian of person, the guardian does not have the right to interfere in personal affairs of the minor but must confine his or her activities to the management of the estate.

While state laws vary, parents in most states can provide for **standby guardians** and **testamentary guardian.** A standby guardian is a person named by the parent to assume guardianship of the child should the parent become disabled and/or unable to care for the child. A testamentary guardian is a person named by the parent in their last will and testament to assume guardianship of the person of the child upon their death. Both are voluntary, independent acts of parents. Both require court approval before the guardians assume their responsibilities. Only a legal parent can name a testamentary guardian, and the testamentary guardian does not automatically assume guardianship responsibilities if another legal parent survives the one designating the testamentary guardian.

Guardianship often has been insufficiently understood as a resource for children who are abused, neglected, or abandoned. Guardianship is a concept, a practice, and a policy issue in child welfare practice. The use of guardianship arrangements instead of foster care for the substitute care of children has been acknowledged as a viable resource for children in the child welfare system by national standard-setting agencies. The Children's Bureau position, stated in 1966, remains unchallenged in principle to this date:

> *All children are entitled to an individual guardian "by birth or adoption or a judicially appointed guardian." This guardian is responsible for safeguarding the child's interests, making important decisions in her or his life, and maintaining a personal relationship with the child. (Children's Bureau, 1961, p. 3)*

The practice of guardianship placement in lieu of foster care or adoptive placement can, depending on the specifics of the state's guardianship statutes, raise significant due process issues for the children, the legal parents, and the guardians. It is not uncommon to see legal guardians charged with neglect or abuse of their wards. Nor is it uncommon to have legal guardians rescind their guardianships when the child becomes "unruly". In voluntary guardianship arrangements, the parent usually retains authority to return and demand physical custody of the child at any time. In involuntary guardianships, the parent's rights may be terminated if she or he fails to complete the agreed-upon plan in the specified time. Often courts do not provide supportive services to parents whose children are under guardianship arrangements, whereas those services are provided to parents whose children are under abuse or neglect jurisdictional arrangements. All of these concerns raise the fundamental issue of protection and permanency for the child. To minimize these concerns and ensure the best use of legal guardianship in child welfare cases, social workers should assess each case situation with these principles as guides:

- Children are individuals with the right to develop their fullest capacities in a stable, supportive adult-child relationship.
- Parents have the first right and responsibility to give care, protection, stability, and support to their children.

- When parental efforts fall short of society's minimum standards, the state has the authority and responsibility to provide substitute care and protection utilizing the jurisdictional basis that will provide the best due process, equal protections, and permanency for child and parent.
- The judicial review and oversight responsibility for legal guardianship should be no less than that imposed for abuse or neglect or dependency, that is, children under legal guardianship arrangements should be entitled to frequent judicial review of their status as wards and the quality of care provided by substitute caregivers.
- The choice of legal guardianship should not be made because the process is easier for the child welfare worker, but because it is in the best interests of the child.

Irrespective of whether or not the transfer of guardianship is voluntarily or involuntarily sought, the state court having jurisdiction over guardianship matters must be involved. Further, that court remains involved so long as the guardianship is in effect.

Paternity Establishment, Support, and Visitation

If a child is born to unmarried parents, the paternity of the child must be established in order for the father to legally assume the privileges, benefits, and responsibilities of parenthood. State statutes govern the process for paternity establishment. In general, there are two procedures:

- acknowledgement voluntarily signed by the mother and father
- adjudication of parentage through a court process should either the mother or father object to a voluntary acknowledgement

Once paternity has been established, by whichever method, the parents' individual and collective abilities to support the child and the visitation rights, if the parents live apart, may be voluntarily agreed to or determined by the court.

The social worker should proceed with paternity establishment early in the processing of a child welfare case, since it is critical to case planning. From a legal

perspective, the legal father and his family become potential care providers if identified early in the case processing or proceeding to permanency through termination of parental rights requires identification of the father and termination of his rights. (See Chapter 9.)

Child Custody, Support, and Visitation

Most controversy over custody, support, and visitation arises with a divorce action. Divorce statutes in all states make provision for awards of custody of children of the marriage. When there are issues of child abuse and neglect or delinquency in the family, child custody, support, and visitation presents additional considerations. Specifically, unless the case is in a "family court" jurisdiction, at least two judges and two different courts will likely handle it. These judges and courts may or may not coordinate decision-making, which may or may not result in conflicting orders with respect to the children's custody, support, and parental visitation.

Some jurisdictions no longer use the adversarial term *custody,* and favor instead "allocating parental responsibilities" or "parenting plans following divorce." Many different options are available with respect to custody, support, and visitation. While custody with the mother had been the norm until the early 1980s, joint custody has become the preference of many courts during the 1990s. This generally results from a court order or a court-approved agreement between parents that provides for joint decision making concerning a child's education, medical treatment, religious training, and care. In some joint arrangements, physical custody is also shared. Rarely does a court, in deciding child custody in a divorce matter, order custody of a child to a third party when the parent(s) are alive. When a child's best interests require it, most states provide for custody to be granted to someone other than one of the parents. Generally in such situations relatives or friends are given preference over social agencies.

The most frequent social work roles in custody actions arising from divorce are mediation with parents to arrive at the best plan for the child or, failing that, carrying out a family evaluation and recommending a particular custody or shared parenting time plan to the judge. Social workers handling child welfare matters may, from time to time, be confronted with conflicting court orders. The divorce order may grant custody to the father, whereas the child abuse/neglect order grants custody to the mother. In general, each state handles these conflicts by court rule. The social worker should know the rules and advise the juvenile court that a prior custody order exists.

Emancipation

Emancipation is the legal process by which a person younger than the age of majority, which is usually 18 years of age, is given the status and privileges afforded someone who is over the age of majority. State statutes specify the condition under which emancipation can occur. Typically they provide that persons who marry or join the military are emancipated by operation of law,

that is, automatically upon execution of the marriage or joining the military. Otherwise a petition is required which must state the reasons for the emancipation and the young person's means of support.

COURT PROCEDURES

An orderly process involving four steps (Figure 6.1) is generally followed when a child comes to the attention of the court: intake, investigation, adjudication, and disposition.

Initiating the Case

Courts do not act as casefinders. Generally, a court concerns itself with children only when a complaint or petition is filed by law enforcement (delinquency matters), the designated child protection agency

---

FIGURE 6.1   Processing a Case Through the Juvenile Court

Complaint/Petition Filed

The agency, police, or other appropriate person claims, in writing, that the child's parent has committed an offense against the child or the youth has committed a delinquent act or status offense.

Preliminary Inquiry/Hearing

The court determines that the case facts, if true, are within its jurisdiction.

Adjudication

The court takes testimony to determine whether the allegations are true. If there is sufficient evidence to support the allegations, then the court takes jurisdiction, that is, it adjudicates.

Initial Disposition

The court determines what to do to remedy the situation. The usual dispositions are

- warn and dismiss
- place delinquent youth on probation
- place child or youth in foster care
- leave child in own home as court ward under supervision of the court or other agency
- terminate parental rights
- terminate court wardship when the reasons for adjudication are eliminated

Review Hearings (Further Dispostions)

The court is required to review the case at regular intervals. These reviews are dispositional in nature, and the court may change the initial and current disposition. Except for cases of termination of parental rights or movement of a delinquent ward into a more secure facility, these reviews may occur without actual hearings.

(neglect, abuse, and dependency matters), the parent or person acting in loco parentis (status offenses, and minors in need of supervision), or in some states the child through an adult acting for him or her (adoption, guardianship, emancipation, and termination of parental rights).

Depending on the state statute and court procedures, the police or child protective services agency files either a complaint or a petition. In filing the complaint or petition, the complainant or petitioner must allege sufficient facts to show that the case comes within the jurisdiction of the court. For example,

> John Brown, born October 1, 1990, was treated at the Children's Hospital for a broken arm. The parent's statement as to how the arm was broken was inconsistent with medical evidence. The hospital filed a complaint with the child protection agency. In addition to the hospital's report, the investigating worker interviewed the parent's mother, who stated that she saw the parent "yank the child by the arm." The worker submits that this is evidence of abuse within the juvenile code. Further, the child and his mother reside in Little Town within the jurisdiction of this Court.

or, if a delinquency matter,

> Susan Sharp is a 14-year-old residing in Midville. On July 3, 1998, she took a sweater from the Big Department Store located in Midville without paying. This act was recorded on security cameras. This act constitutes a violation of the Criminal Code Section 101.

The court clerk or another designated official determines if the complaint or petition meets the requirements for filing. If it does, a date is set for a hearing. The timing of the hearing date is provided in statute or court rules. The child's parents or guardians must be notified of the petition, the time of the hearing, and their right to be represented by counsel.

Preliminary Inquiry or Hearing

Before the court can adjudicate the matter, it must first ensure that it has jurisdiction—that is, make clear the basis for the court's authority to hear and decide the case. The court does so by ascertaining certain facts, such as the age of the child, where he or she lives, where the alleged acts took place, and who committed the acts. If these established facts fit the kinds of situations over which the court has been given authority by statute, then it may proceed with the case. The court also makes a preliminary assessment of the evidence supporting the allegations and, consistent with state law or court rules, determines whether the child should remain with the parent or be removed pending the adjudication or whether the case should be diverted, dismissed, or authorized for adjudication.

Adjudication

The adjudication is the fact-finding or trial phase of the processing of the case. Here the court weighs the facts, properly presented under the rules of evidence by both sides, and decides whether the child, under the law, is delinquent, neglected, or dependent; or is in need of supervision; or requires an award of custody or guardianship. In reaching a decision in a neglect, abuse, or dependency allegation, the judge is expected to determine whether a preponderance of the evidence presented supported the allegations. If it did, then there is basis for taking wardship. If it did not, then the case should be dismissed. In reaching a decision in a delinquency allegation, the judge is expected to determine whether the evidence presented proved beyond a reasonable doubt that this juvenile committed the alleged offense.

Disposition

All court orders entered after the adjudication are dispositional. The disposition is, in essence, the decision as to how the child shall be treated—that is, what is to be ordered or arranged for him or her following the adjudication or case reviews. Judges have a great deal of discretion in the dispositional phase, in contrast to the adjudicatory phase where they are bound by statutes and court rules. After a finding or plea that an act occurred within the statutory definition of abuse, neglect, delinquency, or status offense (adjudication), the judge must decide what to do to alleviate or remedy the condition(s).

If, at the conclusion of the adjudicatory hearing, the judge decides that there is sufficient evidence for the court to take wardship of the child, he or she may order a family and child assessment or social investigation to assist in the establishment of an appropriate disposition and treatment plan. The Adoption and Safe Families Act of 1997 requires courts to assume greater oversight in monitoring the case plan and services to the child and family to ensure permanency as soon as possible. Thus the social investigation and case plan become more important to the legal process as well as the social work intervention (Adoption and Safe Families Act of 1997).

The social investigation may be carried out by the probation staff or by a social agency as a service to the court. Typically probation staff handle delinquency matters and social agencies handle all other matters. In some states, where the social agency also supervises delinquency wards, those agencies are expected to present the social investigation on youth already under their supervision who commit new offenses. In any case, it is important that the court have all the facts necessary to act properly in the best interests of the child and, if a delinquency matter, the promotion of public safety as well. The investigation presents facts and evaluations that help the judge determine what treatment plan is appropriate and what orders, if any, the court needs to make to ensure that the treatment plan is carried out in a timely manner.

Prior to the mid-1990s, judges had almost total discretion in dispositional alternatives. With increasing attacks on family preservation, children in foster care limbo, and community placement for juvenile delinquents, many states through statutory changes have limited the discretion of the judge. If a juvenile commits a certain offense, the disposition is prescribed in statute. If the abuse is so severe or is continuing and chronic, the disposition is prescribed in statute. The most common dispositions remain as follows:

- *Warn and dismiss.* No further action is needed and therefore the case is closed, as in instances of a single, minor delinquent act or status offense when it is believed that the family is able to prevent further misconduct on the part of the child.
- *Probation.* The child is found to be delinquent or guilty of a status offense and is placed on probation and permitted to remain in the community under the official supervision of the court.

- *Temporary wardship with in-home supervision.* The child is found to be neglected or abused and is allowed to remain at home under the protective supervision of a probation officer or a social agency.
- *Temporary wardship with out-of-home placement.* The child, whether delinquent, guilty of a status offense, neglected, abandoned, or abused, may be placed out of the home for protection, care, and treatment. Placements may be in foster homes, group homes, relatives' homes, an independent living situation if the youth is of appropriate age and maturity, institutions, or state training schools.
- *Permanent wardship.* Increasingly, state statutes are providing for immediate termination of parental rights in serious abuse cases or where prior children have been removed and parental rights terminated. Further, all statutes provide specific conditions under which parental rights to a child who has been a temporary ward may be terminated.
- *Termination of court wardship.* This disposition is used when the child has exceeded the age limit for jurisdiction; the conditions that lead to neglect or abuse wardship no longer exist, or the juvenile has been rehabilitated and no longer poses a threat to public safety.

Review Hearings

Dispositional decisions are reviewed by the court at specific intervals established by statute or court rule or at any time upon motion by the supervising agency, the prosecutor, the youth, or other person acting in his or her behalf. At review hearings, the situation is reassessed and a determination is made on whether to order a new disposition. For example, the judge might decide to send a child home from foster care if the conditions that lead to the child's removal had been alleviated to a degree that the child could be safe at home. In a delinquency matter, the judge could decide to move the youth from a secure to a nonsecure facility based on reports of the youth's progress in rehabilitation and the risk to public safety.

The review hearing is a monitoring mechanism to ensure that there is progress toward a permanent solution for the child. The review hearing can be used as a device to resolve controversies between the agency and parent when the agency has custody, such as a dispute over visitation or case planning. It can be used to clarify expectations of all parties and set a time certain for final disposition.

Termination of Parental Rights

Termination of parental rights is the second most extreme action the legal system can take in abuse and neglect cases. The first, of course, is the initial intrusion into the family's autonomy with the removal of the child from the parent. In general, termination of parental rights is based on the following:

- children need permanency and stability in their lives; and
- the child before the court has been in out-of-home care for a statutorily specified time period; and
- the conditions which lead to the removal have not been corrected; and
- there is no reason to believe that they will be corrected in the foreseeable future.

Specific grounds for termination of parental rights are described in the statutes of each state. Pike, Downs, Emlen, Downs, and Case (1977) identified four overarching reasons for termination of parental rights which are present in some form in every state statute to this date: abandonment, desertion, parental condition, and parental conduct.

- Abandonment and Desertion. *State statutes enumerate the failure of parents to identify the child, visit, establish paternity, contribute to the child's support, or maintain contact with the child's custodian for a prescribed period of time as grounds for termination of parental rights.*
- Parental Condition. *State statutes enumerate conditions such as mental illness, emotional illness, mental deficiency, narcotic or dangerous drug addiction, and alcohol addiction which have lasted or are expected to last for a certain period of time as grounds for termination of parental rights.*
- Parental Conduct. *State statutes enumerate conduct such as the chronic and continuing physical neglect of the child, serious physical abuse of the child or a*

sibling of the child, sexual abuse of the child or a sibling of the child and failure of parent to correct the conditions or conduct which lead to the child's removal as grounds for termination of parental rights. (Pike et al., 1977, pp. 5.1–5.8)

The social work issues related to a decision to seek termination of parental rights are discussed in greater detail in Chapter 9. The legal requirements are established in each state's statutes. A hearing to terminate parental rights is usually a formal proceeding like the adjudicatory hearing, even though it is a dispositional action. When contested, it can be lengthy and involve many elaborate, technical, legal procedures.

The burden of proof is clear and convincing evidence, a higher standard than preponderance of evidence but somewhat less stringent than the beyond a reasonable doubt standard. Another indicator of the seriousness of this state action is the attention to ensuring that any adult with possible parental rights to the child is notified and has the opportunity to present evidence in court. This is particularly salient in the case of unmarried fathers, whose rights were at one time disregarded. (See Chapter 2 for a discussion of U.S. Supreme Court decisions on the standard of proof and on the rights of unmarried fathers.)

THE ROLE OF VARIOUS PERSONS IN THE COURT PROCESS

Court proceedings rely on many persons to effectively achieve justice in each case. The most frequently encountered persons include jurists, attorneys, guardians ad litem, probation officers, social workers, court-appointed independent evaluators or fact-finders, and witnesses.

Jurists

Jurists, including judges and referees or hearing officers, carry out their responsibilities within the statutory definitions of their jurisdiction. Statutes are necessarily couched in such general language as to encompass a wide range of situations. Therefore jurists must interpret the meaning and intent of the law. Jurists are responsible for conducting the hearings and, where there is no jury, for determining the facts established by evidence and rendering a decision consistent with the state law.

Attorneys

Attorneys are responsible for presenting the evidence, examining and cross-examining witnesses, and advocating the desires of their client within the boundaries permitted by law. Consistent with Supreme Court decisions, all juveniles charged with delinquent acts must have attorney representation unless they have waived the right and the court determines that the juvenile has the capacity to give an informed waiver and that such waiver is in the juvenile's best interests.

In neglect and abuse matters, state statutes and court rules determine the conditions under which the child and parent must have attorney representation. These requirements vary significantly from state to state.

In most states, the prosecutor represents the interests of the state in delinquency matters. In some states, the prosecutor or the attorney general represents the interests of the state in neglect and abuse matters. He or she influences the handling of the case through charges made, pleas accepted, and general examination and cross-examination of victims, witnesses, and the child.

Guardians *ad Litem*

Some states, by statute or court rule, provide for the appointment of a guardian *ad litem* to protect the child's interests. Commonly, the state statutes offer little guidance as to that person's duties, often containing only the vague phrase that responsibilities include "protection of the child's interests." A guardian *ad litem* may in fact be required to function in at least four separate roles: (1) as an investigator of background information for the judge, (2) as an advocate of the child's rights and interests, (3) as a counsel who helps the child in the expression of his or her wishes in court, and (4) as a court watchdog who submits a written report at disposition, assures that the child's best interests are protected in dispute resolutions, and sees that court orders are followed (Davidson & Gerlach, 1984).

Guardians *ad litem* have a duty to promote the child's best interests and in carrying out that duty could conceivably go against the child's wishes. Some states assign a child an attorney rather than a guardian *ad litem*. An attorney, in contrast to guardian *ad litem,* is bound by the child's own determination of best interests if the child is capable of considered judgment. A dilemma may confront the child's representative when courts combine the roles of child's attorney and guardian *ad litem* or when the child is too young or otherwise impaired in decision making and self-determination (Green & Dohrn, 1996).

The concept of volunteers as guardians *ad litem* developed in juvenile courts as a response to children needing representation. An early program in the juvenile court in Seattle developed a system of trained community volunteers who investigate child abuse cases, monitor the child's progress, and, when necessary, speak up for the child in court. These volunteers, known as court-appointed special advocates (CASAs), usually handle one or two cases at a time and devote about sixty hours to each case. Many courts now use CASAs as well as other volunteers to assist in the dispositional phase of the process. (National Council of Family Law Judges, 1998).

Probation Officers

Probation officers provide social investigations, dispositional recommendations, and supervision of juveniles charged with delinquent offenses.

Social Workers

Social workers, like probation officers, provide social investigations, dispositional recommendations and casework services for both the parents and the child until the court dismisses the case. Depending on the state, social workers provide these services to children who are within the abuse, neglect and delinquency jurisdictions. In the court process itself, they are frequently called on to give testimony in addition to written progress reports, either as a fact witness or as an expert witness. A fact witness is one who gives information as to what they saw, heard, said, or did, in relation to a specific issue before the court. An expert witness is one who is asked to give opinions or provide specialized knowledge on facts presented by others or themselves because they have specialized education, training, and experience. A social worker, depending on the circumstances, can function in both capacities (Dickson, 1995).

Although the thought of testifying may be terrifying to the beginning child welfare worker and a source of ongoing anxiety for the experienced child welfare worker, testifying becomes easier with advance preparation and documentation of evidence. Preparation requires knowing the law involved, knowing the facts of the case, and understanding how those facts and the law relate to one another. Documentation requires distinguishing fact from opinion. Fact, as supported by documents or witnesses, is evidence. Opinions that are based on the application of theoretical knowledge to the facts of the case are important, but opinions that are not based in fact or knowledge provide attorneys with the opportunity to totally discredit the social worker's testimony. If you approach testifying prepared with factual documentation and applicable theoretical knowledge coupled with a clear head, then the techniques used by attorneys in the examination and cross-examination processes should be immaterial.

The basic principles for giving testimony are as follows.

- Keep your temper. If you lose your temper, you discredit yourself and your testimony.
- Answer a question in the shortest possible way. The more you talk, the more likely you will provide the attorney an opportunity to find a small discrepancy in your testimony and use it to discredit you. Don't withhold information; but once you have responded to the question, be quiet.
- Always be willing to admit ignorance, or that your memory has failed you or that you are not sure. If you don't know the answer, say "I don't know." To respond when you don't know opens you up to giving conflicting testimony.
- Never show partiality, or vindictiveness, to either party to the litigation. You have no personal interest in this matter. You represent the state. You are charged with providing facts and opinions based on those facts. If you waiver from the charge, you are subject to rigorous examination designed to show that you are not presenting facts but biased statements.
- Never show reluctance to concede a point in the opposition's favor. If they are right, it is better for you to recognize it and move on. To do otherwise exposes you to challenge as biased.

- Use short, simple language so that your point is immediately comprehensible. Avoid social work jargon. If you must use a specific social work term, explain what it means in plain English.
- Ask for a question to be repeated or rephrased if you do not understand it.
- Prepare ahead of time; but do not memorize your testimony. If you memorize testimony you may forget some parts of it under the pressure of testifying or could lose all memory of the facts. Your preparation should include knowing the pertinent facts and the applicable law so that you can correlate the two while testifying.
- Expect to feel nervous. You never know how you will be examined or cross-examined. Thus you will always feel tense until the process is completed.
- State the facts as you know them based on an unbiased, well-documented inquiry. Do not start with conclusions. The more you rely on facts that you have documented, the less likely you will be to get confused by an attorney's questions. Further, if the attorney engages you in a hypothetical ("what if . . .") discussion, you are able to differentiatie the facts in the hypothetical from the facts in your actual case.
- If you are asked for an opinion or recommendation, first give the facts on which you base your opinion, then state your opinion or recommendation.
- Remain cool, calm, and collected. If you have prepared your case well and available evidence is not brought out by the attorneys or jurists, it is their fault not yours. (Dickson, 1995; Stern, 1997; Stein, 1991; Saltzman & Proch, 1990)

Court-Appointed Independent Evaluators or Fact-finders

The court may appoint independent evaluators or fact-finders, other than CASAs and guardian ad litems when, in its judgment, it needs additional information to make an informed and just decision. These appointees generally receive a specific statement of responsibilities. Their findings are reported directly to the court as written reports and/or as verbal testimony.

Witnesses

Witnesses are persons who have some direct knowledge of the facts and circumstances of the matter before the court. They may be witnesses in support of the petition or complaint or witnesses against it. Both sides have a right to call witnesses and to examine and cross-examine witnesses called by the other side. The social worker, in investigating and preparing the case for court, should interview and follow-up with all persons and source documents that might have information which leads to a more informed decision in the case.

TRENDS AND ISSUES

There are three specific trends to watch over the next five years: establishment of family courts; increase in delinquency adjudications of children and youth who are already adjudicated abused or neglected; and the transfer of jurisdiction over juveniles who commit serious offenses to the adult court system. These trends have begun already but are in the infancy stage and should be carefully watched as they mature in the future. Family courts, that is, courts with broad jurisdiction to hear and decide all matters involving children, will continue to grow. It is hypothesized that this court structure will provide more efficient decisions. While preliminary data suggests that there are some benefits, it is not conclusive that this structure will be beneficial to children.

For years studies have documented the negative impact of childhood maltreatment on youth development and correlated it with increased delinquent acts in adolescence. This trend requires a reexamination of the prevention and treatment interventions provided in the abuse and neglect system. Further, courts that previously have been reticent to hold abused and neglected children accountable for their delinquent behaviors

until the behavior becomes more serious are beginning to reexamine that practice. Everyone agrees that it is necessary to look at the status of children and youth more holistically. (Kelley, Thornberry, & Smith, 1997)

During the 1990s, the adult courts have assumed greater responsibility for handling matters involving juveniles who commit serious offenses. It is anticipated that this trend will continue. (Office of Juvenile Justice and Delinquency Prevention, 1998) (See Chapter 11.)

CHAPTER SUMMARY

This chapter focused on the historical development of the juvenile court system, its transition from a benevolent system with full discretion given to the jurists to a system subject to rules providing for the protection of the parties in abuse, neglect, and delinquency matters. The movement toward family courts is growing throughout the United States. These courts have broader jurisdictions over the multiplicity of matters that arise when children are abused, neglected, or commit delinquent acts. It is hypothesized that family courts will provide administrative efficiency and ensure a consistent treatment of the various independent legal issues.

The standard processing of a case through the juvenile court system has been reviewed. The role of the child welfare worker in the court system has changed as the juvenile court has become more "procedural". The social worker remains responsible for marshalling factual information to assist the court in determining the best plan for the child and his or her parents; however, that information is now subject to more stringent examination by attorneys for the child and the parent. Child welfare workers must understand the roles and responsibilities of their position and those of all the persons involved. This chapter provided a brief summary of these roles and responsibilities.

FOR STUDY AND DISCUSSION

1. Explain and evaluate the aims and guiding philosophy of the early founders of the juvenile court. Discuss ways in which the implementation of the juvenile court deviates from those aims and guiding philosophy.

2. Give arguments to support either the traditional rehabilitative model of the juvenile court or a

model based on constitutional guarantees of due process and legal justice.

3. Obtain a copy of the juvenile court act in your state. Review it in these terms:

   a. What is the expressed intent of the act? How well does this intent reflect a modern juvenile court philosophy?

b. Compare the act's definitions of classes of children who come under the jurisdiction with those discussed in this chapter.

c. What does the statute provide with respect to the child's and parent's constitutional rights? Are there different provisions based on the class of children?

d. How adequate are the act's provisions in regard to the personnel and services of the court?

4. Read your state's statute and interview agency and court personnel to find out what the provisions are in your state for termination of parental rights. How well does the statute protect the parent's rights and also provide for the child's need for permanency?

5. What is your assessment of the potential for family courts to provide for better administration of justice as compared with the juvenile court?

6. Discuss how the court process in your state differs from the standard process discussed in this chapter.

7. Why is paternity establishment so important in child welfare practice? How would you proceed to determine whether paternity had been established in one of your cases?

8. Identify a specific case that you will be testifying on in the next month. State the type of hearing for which testimony will be given. What information does the court need to accomplish the purposes of the hearing as stated in the statute? What information do you have? What are your sources for the information? What information are you lacking? How can you obtain the information?

9. Should juveniles be prosecuted as adults for serious offenses? What factors should be considered in determining whether to treat them as adults or juveniles?

10. If you were designing the ideal court system for handling matters involving children and youth, what would it look like?

FOR ADDITIONAL STUDY

Ayers, W. (1997). *A kind and just parent: The children of juvenile court.* Boston: Beacon Press.

Besharov, D. J. (1990). *Combating child abuse: Guidelines for cooperation between law enforcement and child protective services.* Washington, DC: The AEI Press.

Davis, S. M. (1998). *Rights of juveniles: The juvenile justice system* (2nd ed.). St. Paul, MN: West Group.

Haralambie, A. M. (1993). *The child's attorney: A guide to representing children in custody, adoption, and protection cases.* Chicago: American Bar Association.

Kramer, D. T. (1994). *Legal rights of children* (2nd ed.). Colorado Springs: Shepard's/McGraw-Hill.

Jacobs, T. A. (1995, supp. 1997). *Children and the law: Rights and obligations.* St. Paul, MN: West Publishing.

Pollack, D. (1997). *Social work and the courts: A casebook.* New York: Garland Publishing Co.

The David and Lucile Packard Foundation. (1996, Winter). *The future of children: The juvenile court.* (Vol. 6, No 3). Los Altos, CA: Author.

INTERNET SITES

The following sites provide copies of statutes, case decisions, analyses, and commentary on legal issues affecting children in the juvenile and family court systems.

The American Bar Association Center on Children and the Law—http://www.abanet.org/child/home.html

Center for Law and Social Policy—http://www.epn.org/clasp.html

National Archives and Records Administration, Code of Federal Regulations—http://www.access.gpo.gov/nara/cfr/cfr-table-search.html

National Clearinghouse on Child Abuse and Neglect Information—http://www.calib.com/nccanch/

National Council of Juvenile and Family Court Judges—http://www.ncjfcj.unr.edu/

Juvenile Justice Clearinghouse—http://www.fsu.edu/~crimdo/jjclearinghouse/

THOMAS, Library of Congress—http://thomas.loc.gov/

REFERENCES

Addams, J. (1935). *My friend, Julia Lathrop.* New York: Macmillian.

Babb, B. A. (1998, Summer). Where we stand: An analysis of America's family law adjudicatory systems and the mandate to establish unified family courts. *Family Law Quarterly, 32,* 31–57.

Beemsterboer, M. J. (1960). Benevolence in the star chamber. *Journal of Criminal Law, Criminology, and Political Science, 50,* 464–475.

Brieland, D., & Lemmon, J. A. (1985). *Social work and the law* (4th ed.). St. Paul, MN: West.

Children's Bureau (1961) Legislative guide for the termination of parental responsibilities and the adoption of children. (Publication No. 136). Washington, DC: U.S. Government Printing Office.

Commonwealth v. Fischer, 213 Pa. 48 (1905).

Davidson, H. A., & Gerlach, K. (1984). Child custody disputes: The child's perspective. In R, M. Horowitz, & H. A. Davidson (Eds.), *Legal rights of children.* Colorado Springs: Shepard's/McGraw-Hill.

Dickson, D. T. (1995). *Law in the health and human services: A guide for social workers, psychologists, psychiatrists, and related professionals.* New York: Free Press.

Downs, S. W., & Taylor, C. (1980). *Permanent planning in foster care: Resources for training.* (DHHS Publication No. [OHDS] 81-30290). Washington, DC: U.S. Government Printing Office.

Ellrod, F. E., Jr., & Melaney, D. H. (1950, Winter). Juvenile justice: Treatment or travesty. *University of Pittsburgh Law Review, 11,* 277–287.

Elson, A. (1962). Juvenile courts and due process. In M. K. Rosenheim (Ed.), *Justice for the child* (pp. 95–117). New York: Free Press.

Flexner, B., & Baldwin, R. N. (1914). *Juvenile courts and probation.* New York: Century.

Flexner, B., & Oppenheimer, R. (1922). *The legal aspect of the juvenile court* (Children's Bureau Publication No. 99). Washington, DC: Children's Bureau.

Flicker, B. D. (1977). *Standards for juvenile justice: A summary and analysis* (Institute of Judicial Administration and American Bar Association, Juvenile Justice Standards Project). Cambridge, MA: Ballinger.

Green B. A., & Dohrn, B. (1996). Forward: Children and the ethical practice of law. (Proceedings of the Conference on Ethical Issues in the Legal Representation of Children.) *Fordham Law Review, (64)* 4, 1281–1323.

Handler, J. F. (1965). The juvenile court and the adversary system: Problems of function and form. *Wisconsin Law Review, 7,* 7–51.

Hardin, M. (1998, Summer). Child protection cases in a unified family court. *Family Law Quarterly, 32,* 147–203. Chicago: American Bar Association.

In re Gault, 387 U.S. 1 (1967).

In re Winship, 397 U.S. 358 (1970).

Indian Child Welfare Act, PL 95-608.

Kelley, B. T., Thornberry, T. P., & Smith, C. A. (1997). *In the wake of childhood maltreatment.* Washington, DC: Office of Juvenile Justice and Delinquency Prevention.

Kent v. United States, 383 U.S. 541 (1966).

Ketcham, O. W. (1962). The unfilled promise of the American juvenile court. In M. K. Rosenheim (Ed.), *Justice for the child* (pp. 95–117). New York: Free Press.

Lathrop, J. C. (1925). The background of the juvenile court in Illinois. *The child, the clinic, and the court.* New York: New Republic.

Lou, H. H. (1927). *Juvenile courts in the United States.* Chapel Hill: University of North Carolina Press.

Lundberg, E. O. (1947). *Unto the least of these: Social services for children.* New York: Appelton-Century-Crofts.

Mack, J. W. (1909–1910). The juvenile court. *Harvard Law Review, 23.*

McKeiver v. Pennsylvania, 403 U.S. 538 (1971).

Mississippi Band of Choctaw Indians v. Holyfield, 490 U.S. 51 (1989).

National Council of Family Law Judges (1998) *Court Appointed Special Advocates.* Reno, NV: National Council of Family Law Judges.

National Probation and Parole Association. (1957). *Guide for juvenile court judges.* New York: National Probation & Parole Association.

Nutt, A. S. (1949). Juvenile and domestic relations court. In *1949 social work yearbook* (pp.270–276). New York: Russell Sage Foundation.

OJJDP (1998) Juveniles in adult courts. Washington, DC: Office of Juvenile Justice and Delinquency Prevention.

Pike, V., Downs, S. W., Emlen, A., Downs, G., & Case, D. (1977). *Permanent planning for children in foster care.* (No. OHDS 77-30124). Washington, DC: U.S. Department of Health, Education and Welfare.

Pound, R. (1950) The juvenile in the service state. In *1949 yearbook.* New York: National Probation and Parole Association.

Rosenheim, J. K. (Ed.) (1962). *Justice for the child.* New York: Free Press.

Ross, C. J. (1998, Summer). The failure of fragmentation: The promise of a system of unified family courts. *Family Law Quarterly, 32,* 3–30. Chicago: American Bar Association.

Rubin, S. (1952, November–December). Protecting the child in the juvenile court. *Journal of Criminal Law, Criminology and Political Science, 43,* 425–440.

Saltzman, A., & Proch, K. (1990). *Law in social work practice.* Chicago: Nelson-Hall.

Schall v. Martin, 467 S.Ct. 253 (1984).

Schultz, L. L., & Cohen, F. (1976). Isolation in juvenile court jurisprudence. In M. K. Rosenheim (Ed.), *Pursuing justice for the child.* Chicago: Univeristy of Chicago Press.

Simonsen, C. (1991). Status offenders: An attempt to clarify the system. *Juvenile Justice in America.* New York: Macmillan.

Stein, T. J. (1991). *Child welfare and the law.* White Plains, NY: Longman.

Stern, P. (1997). *Preparing and presenting expert testimony in child abuse litigation: A guide for expert witnesses and attorneys.* Thousand Oaks, CA: Sage Publications.

Szymanski, L. A. (1995). *Family courts in the United States.* Washington, D.C.: Office of Juvenile Justice and Delinquency Prevention.

Thompson v. Oklahoma, 487 U.S. 815 (1988).

CHAPTER 7

Protecting Children from Neglect and Abuse

The little world in which children have their existence, whosoever brings them up, there is nothing so finely perceived and so finely felt, as injustice.
—Charles Dickens

To raise up and to restore that which is in ruin
To repair that which is damaged
To rejoin that which is severed
To replenish that which is lacking
To strengthen that which is weakened
To set right that which is wrong
To make flourish that which is insecure and undeveloped.
—Huisa M. Karenga, *Selections from the Huisa: Sacred Wisdom of Ancient Egypt*

CHAPTER OUTLINE

CASE EXAMPLE: A PROTECTIVE SERVICES INVESTIGATION

No case can stand as a typical example of a protective services investigation because of the great range of family situations that are reported. The alleged maltreatment may be categorized as neglect, physical abuse, sexual abuse, emotional maltreatment, other concerns about poor child care, or a combination of problems. The case presented here shows the protective services investigator "in action" as she attempts to learn the truth about child care patterns in the home.

Theresa McDaniel, a protective services worker in a large, midwestern city, received a call one Monday from a Head Start director concerning a 4-year-old named Danny, who is usually dirty and smelly when he arrives at the center. He also has head lice. On this day, he has a bruise on his cheek and stripe marks on the backs of his legs and buttocks. As a mandated reporter, the director, Ms. Berg, is making a formal report of suspected child abuse and neglect. In further conversation, Ms. Berg tells Ms. McDaniel that Danny's mother, Ella Robinson, has recently started to work due to welfare reform, and that her partner, Charles Hudson, usually brings Danny to school. Sometimes a 10-year-old sister picks him up. She says that Danny has been acting aggressively to other children lately and gets frustrated easily. Mrs. Robinson missed the last parent-teacher conference because of her work schedule. When Ms. Berg asked Danny this morning how he got the bruise and marks, he hung his head and got busy with a toy truck, refusing to talk about it.

Ms. McDaniel made an unannounced home visit to the Robinson home that afternoon. She found Mr. Hudson at home, who told her that he had lived there for the past two years as a partner to Mrs. Robinson. A six-month-old infant, Bobby, was their joint child, while Danny and his older sister, Sandra, were Mrs. Robinson's children by a former partner. Mr. Hudson said that since Mrs. Robinson had started back to work, he stayed home during the day to look after the children. He continued to make deliveries for a scrap-metal business on an occasional basis. He readily acknowledged having spanked Danny over the weekend; he said that Danny needed to learn the hard way not to hit the baby and to quit "messing his pants."

Ms. McDaniel noted that the house was messy and poorly furnished, but saw no immediate health hazards to the children; the refrigerator contained adequate food. She observed that Bobby was appropriately dressed in a shirt and diaper and had a bottle of milk. He seemed comfortable being carried by Mr. Hudson. Danny and Sandra were not at home; Mr. Hudson said that they were "out playing." Ms. McDaniel told Mr. Hudson that she would need to come back to see Mrs. Robinson and Danny because the marks on Danny might be indicators of child abuse, as defined by state law. She explained that as a protective services investigator, she needed to have a complete understanding of the events surrounding the incident of Danny's spanking. Ms. McDaniel thought she smelled alcohol on Mr. Hudson's breath. His apparent lack of concern about the older children caused her to wonder about Sandra as well as Danny. She put in a quick call to the school and learned from the teacher that Sandra had frequently been absent during the past two months; she was becoming increasingly withdrawn and her grades were falling.

That evening, Ms. McDaniel returned to the Robinson home and was met at the door by Mrs. Robinson. Mr. Hudson was out. Mrs. Robinson expressed confusion and fear about why Ms. McDaniel was investigating her family. She said that she had taken a job at a fast food restaurant because the welfare department had threatened to cut off her check. She was worried that welfare would take away her children because she wasn't working enough. She said that Mr. Hudson was good to the children; he bought Pampers for Bobby and took care of the kids. She said that the children behave better now that he is in charge of them, and that she doesn't feel so lonely. She also indicated that she met Mr. Hudson after he had been released from jail for armed robbery, and he had moved in with her soon after they met. Mrs. Robinson assured Ms. McDaniel that she would get the kids cleaned up and make sure that Sandra went regularly to school.

Concerned about Sandra, the next day Ms. McDaniel arranged to interview her at school. Sandra was reluctant to talk, but said she missed school because "Charles wants me at home to look after the baby." In response to questions, she said that she had trouble sleeping and that the thought of eating made her feel sick; she avoided the other kids at school and would rather be alone. She was worried about her mother, who was under pressure from going to work. Ms. McDaniel suspected that there was a possibility that Sandra was being sexually abused. She asked her if anyone at home touched her private areas or expected her to touch theirs. Sandra remained silent and seemed unable to talk. Ms. McDaniel brought out anatomically correct dolls, and Sandra showed the female doll performing oral sex on the male doll. She was able to state that when Charles drank and smoked dope, he insisted that she "take care of him." She also said that he had threatened to hurt both her and Danny if she told anyone.

Ms. McDaniel next examined Danny at the Head Start center, and verified the bruises and stripe marks. Danny said that Charles had hit him and then "whupped" him with a coffee pot cord, because Danny had "pooped" his pants. In a call to the public health nurse, Ms. McDaniel learned that Danny was behind on his immunizations but was in the normal range for height and weight for his age.

That evening Ms. McDaniel talked again with Mrs. Robinson. She told her that she had found substantial evidence of sexual abuse of Sandra and physical abuse of Danny. Mrs. Robinson said she had no idea of the sexual abuse because she and Charles had an active sex life, and denied the physical abuse, saying that the children got out of hand sometimes and needed firm discipline. Ms. McDaniel explained that Danny and Sandra could not be left unsupervised with Mr. Hudson and that together they needed to make a plan on how these children would be protected. Mrs. Robinson refused to consider asking Mr. Hudson to leave. She didn't believe that he had abused Sandra. She needed him to help with the kids, and said she could not afford other day care and didn't know where to find it. She was not interested in working out an alternative day care plan for Bobby and Danny. When confronted again with the fact that the children could not be left unsupervised with Mr. Hudson, Mrs. Robinson indicated that perhaps they could stay temporarily with her mother, who lived about ten blocks away.

Mrs. McDaniel contacted the grandmother, and learned that she was extremely worried about her daughter and grandchildren. She was concerned that her daughter might be smoking dope and drinking with Mr. Hudson ever since they had told her to stay away from the house. She agreed to take Danny and Sandra on a temporary basis, and to participate in a family meeting to decide on a long-range plan for them.

This case shows how a protective services investigation can grow as the investigator learns more about the family. Starting with a situation of possible abuse and neglect of a 4-year-old boy, the case now involves possible sexual abuse as well as neglect of all three children. Over the next several months, Ms. McDaniel will ensure the children's safety by removing them from the home, continue her investigation, and engage the family, including extended family members, in developing a long-range plan for the children.

In child welfare and perhaps in all social services, there is no situation that instigates such concern or outrage as the neglect, abuse, or exploitation of children by parents or others responsible for their care. Fueled by media coverage of sensational instances of abuse and by considerable research and other scholarly attention, the last 30 years have witnessed a dramatic new concern for these child victims.

INCIDENCE

No fully accurate figures are available to judge the incidence of child neglect and abuse. Data come from three sources: the National Child Abuse and Neglect Data System; the National Incidence Study of Child Abuse and Neglect; and various surveys.

Reported Child Abuse and Neglect

The National Child Abuse and Neglect Data System (NCANDS), managed by the National Center on Child Abuse and Neglect, has the responsibility to collect information on official reports of abuse and neglect made to child protective services agencies in each state and the District of Columbia. It is important to remember that the data are based on existing state child abuse and neglect reports. A count of reported cases is a serious underestimate of actual incidence of child abuse, particularly of "hidden" abuse, such as undetected child sexual abuse or other abuse. Estimates are that fewer than half of all child maltreatment is reported to child protective services agencies (Besharov & Laumann, 1996.)

In 1996, states received over three million reports of child abuse and neglect, an 18 percent increase over 1990. Although three million reports were received, only about one in three cases were confirmed, after investigation, as victims of maltreatment, for a total of just under one million children. The NCANDS data break down child maltreatment into the following categories: neglect, physical abuse, sexual abuse, medical neglect, and emotional or psychological maltreatment. Neglect was the most common type of maltreatment, suffered by 52 percent of victims, while about a quarter (24 percent) suffered physical abuse. About 12 percent of victims were sexually abused. Children suffering medical neglect and emotional maltreatment accounted for 3 percent and 6 percent of victims, respectively. Approximately 16 percent of victims suffered other types of maltreatment, such as abandonment, congenital drug addiction, and "threats to harm the child." Many states count victims in more than one category when more than one type of abuse or neglect has occurred, so the total of the percentages is more than 100 percent (U.S. Department of Health and Human Services, 1998).

The Child Victims. The NCANDS data for 1996 provide information on the age, sex, and race or ethnicity of victims, and on service action taken. Over half (56 percent) of the victims were under age 8, with 28 percent under age 4. Neglect and medical neglect were more common among young children, while the percent of physical and sexual abuse increased with age. Slightly over half (52 percent) of the victims were female. About 53 percent of all victims were white, and 27 percent were African-American children. Hispanic children made up about 11 percent of victims, Native American and Alaska Native children about 2 percent, and Asian/Pacific Islander about 1 percent. "Other" and "unknown" categories accounted for 2 percent and 4 percent, respectively. Most of the perpetrators of maltreatment to these children were parents (77 percent), and an additional 11 percent were relatives. About 10 percent of the perpetrators were classified as noncaretakers or "unknown," and about 2 percent of perpetrators were foster parents, facility staff, and child care providers. Women were the perpetrators in about three-quarters of the neglect and medical neglect cases, while male perpetrators accounted for about three-quarters of the cases of sexual abuse (U.S. Department of Health and Human Services, 1998).

National Incidence Studies

By Congressional mandate, the U.S. Department of Health and Human Services has conducted three national incidence studies of child abuse and neglect, in 1979–1980, 1986–1987, and most recently in 1993–1994 (Sedlak & Broadhurst, 1996). The information from these studies comes from a nationally representative sample of community and public agency professionals, who are asked to provide comprehensive information about maltreated children whom they have observed. It also includes all cases reported to child protective services in the area. The study differs from the NCANDS data in that cases include all those observed by professionals, whether or not they were reported to a child protective services agency. Thus the national incidence studies provide the most comprehensive information on the extent of child abuse and neglect available.

The studies collect data using two different definitional standards of abuse and neglect:

1. The " harm" standard is relatively stringent and requires that the child suffer observable harm as a result of the abuse or neglect. Data using this definition has been collected in all three National Incidence studies.
2. The "endangerment" standard includes all children who meet the "harm" standard as well as children who have been abused and neglected but have not suffered observable harm from the maltreatment, according to the community profes-

sionals who submitted the information to the study researchers. Data using this standard has been collected only on the last two studies, in 1986 and 1993.

The 1993 study found that 1,553,800 children had suffered observable harm from maltreatment. When the definition is expanded to include all those who were endangered as well as those suffering observable harm, the number of abused or neglected children rose to 2,815,600 children, or about 42 abused or neglected for every 1,000 children in the United States. (Sedlak & Broadhurst, 1996).

A comparison between the 1986 and 1993 studies shows that the number of abused and neglected children increased substantially, in both the "harm" and the "endangerment" categories. Figure 7.1 shows the increases for four categories of maltreatment: neglect, physical abuse, emotional abuse, and sexual abuse, using both the " harm" and the "endangerment" definitional standards.

Self-Report Surveys

A number of surveys have been conducted of parents or victims of maltreatment, asking them questions concerning their participation in child abuse or neglect. These surveys show higher rates of maltreatment than those reported to public agencies. Researchers of the National Family Violence Survey of 1985 interviewed a nationally representative sample of over 3,000 families. Parents were asked to report abusive behavior toward their children; abusive actions were those considered to have a high probability of injuring a child, such as kicking, biting, punching, hitting or trying to hit a child with an object, beating up a child, burning or scalding, and shooting or threatening a child with a gun. Results of this survey indicated that 1.5 million children in 1985 experienced acts of violence, and 450,000 were injured by their parents or caretakers (Straus & Gelles, 1986).

A 1995 Gallup poll of 1,000 parents found even higher rates of self-reported abusive behavior. According to that study, about 3 million children suffered physical abuse from their parents, a rate that is 16 times higher than that reported to public agencies (Gallup, Moor, & Schussel, 1997).

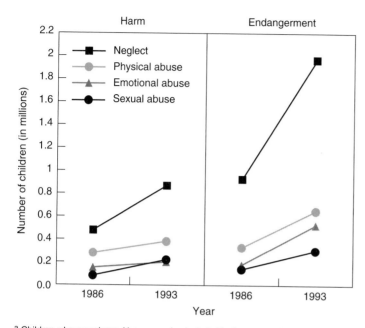

a Children who experienced harm are also included in the counts of children who were endangered.

FIGURE 7.1   Child Abuse and Neglect Observed by Professionals: Number of Children Identified as Experiencing Harm from or Being Endangered by Abuse or Neglect in 1986 and 1993*

Source: D. J. English. (1998, Spring). The extent and consequences of child maltreatment. *The Future of Children, 8*(1), p. 45. Reprinted with permission. Based on data from: A. J. Sedlak & D. D. Broadhurst, *The third national incidence study of child abused and neglect.* Washington, DC: U.S. Department of Health and Human Services.

As with physical abuse, self-report surveys of sexual abuse also show higher rates than do official reports. A 1985 survey found that 27 percent of women and 16 percent of men disclosed a history of having been sexually abused. In this study, noncontact abuse was counted as well as sexual contact (Finkelhor, Hotaling, Lewis, & Smith, 1990). The 1995 Gallup poll found that 23 percent of adults reported having been sexually abused by an adult or an older child (Gallup, Moor, & Schussel, 1997).

In summary, although it is not possible to get fully accurate figures of the numbers of children affected by maltreatment each year, reporting methods have improved over the years. Official studies show that reports of child abuse and neglect have gone up each year since reporting began in the 1970s. These large numbers of families affected by maltreatment have strained the public child welfare system in its efforts to respond appropriately to each situation.

Behind each statistic is a child, a child whose immediate safety, comfort, welfare, and future development are jeopardized or whose very life may be at stake. Parents also exist behind these numbers, parents who may have their child removed from their care or at least have their autonomy as parents eroded. For society, the costs are similarly high. Balancing society's desire to maintain and support the integrity of the family while protecting the welfare of its children is a complicated proposition demanding clarification of our national values. The care and protection of children consumes large amounts of money. Research suggesting that child maltreatment is linked to future delinquency, substance abuse, and crime indicates that the indirect costs to society may be much higher than the direct costs (Sandberg, 1989).

AIMS AND SPECIAL ATTRIBUTES OF CHILD PROTECTIVE SERVICES

Child protective services are intended to guard children from further detrimental experiences or conditions in their immediate situations, bring under control and reduce the risks to their safety or well-being, prevent further neglect or abuse, and restore adequate parental functioning whenever possible or, if necessary, take steps to remove children from their own homes and establish them in foster situations in which they will receive more adequate care.

Protective services today reflect the conviction that among parents whose level of child care is unacceptably poor, many can be reached on behalf of their children and can be helped to improve their parental functioning. The focus of child protective services is on both the investigation of reported maltreatment that initiates agency responsibility and on stabilizing and improving the children's own homes by helping parents to perform more responsibly in relation to their children's care. Protective services also are concerned with social planning to organize and coordinate collaborative efforts among community agencies involved in the child protection system (Carroll & Haase, 1987; Melton & Barry, 1994).

Child protective services are characterized by certain distinctive features: (1) the way in which service is initiated; (2) the increased agency responsibility that accompanies work with parents of children at risk; (3) the kind of agency sanction, or community authorization; and (4) the balance required in the use of authority in relation to the rights of parent, child, and society.

1. *Child protective services are authoritative.* The protective agency initiates the service by approaching the parents about a complaint from some element of the community, such as police, schools, public health nurses, neighbors, or relatives. Because the protective service is involuntary, the situation that justifies an agency's "intruding" into family life must strongly suggest that parents are not providing the love or basic care a child needs for healthy growth and development.

2. *Child protective services carry increased social agency responsibility, since they are directed toward families where there are children at risk.* Children are highly vulnerable when their homes lack normal levels of care or protection. Children cannot make effective claims by themselves for the enforcement of their rights. If just and quick initiation of services does not follow a complaint from the community, lasting harm may result for a child who is experiencing physical abuse or neglect.

Social workers in the protective agency must act promptly; their decisions about the nature or seriousness of the complaint and the action to be taken must be based on accurate fact-finding. Moreover, the social agency cannot withdraw from the situation if it finds the parents uncooperative or resistant to taking help, as it may in situations where individuals have voluntarily sought help. Once protective service has been initiated, the agency can responsibly withdraw only when the level of child care in the home has improved to acceptable levels or when satisfactory care has been arranged elsewhere, as in a relative's home or in foster care.

The protective agency, then, has a high degree of responsibility to the child at risk; to the child's parents, who are usually found to be experiencing great stress; and to the community, which charges the agency to act for it in the provision of child protection.

3. *Child protective services involve agency sanction from the community.* A child protective agency has been delegated responsibility by statute or by charter to receive reports about instances of unacceptable child care, to investigate them, and if necessary to initiate service to the family even though the parents have not requested help. Other social agencies expect and look to the child protection agency to act.

The provision of child protective services is regarded as a fundamental public agency responsibility. By the 1970s, protective services under public welfare auspices were present in all states, the District of Columbia, Puerto Rico, the Virgin Islands, and Guam (Hildenbrand et al., 1979). Concern about child neglect and abuse has spread throughout the country, and public agencies in all the states have attempted to strengthen and extend their services more effectively.

4. *Child protective services require a crucial balance in the use of the agency's authority.* Child neglect or abuse is both a social and a legal problem. The fact that the agency approaches a family about its problems without a request from the family itself denotes some invasion of privacy, however well motivated the services may be. Furthermore, an integral part of the protective agency's methods is to reserve the right to invoke the authority of the court by filing a petition alleging parental neglect or abuse if the parents do not improve their level of care. This "threat," implied or acknowledged, is recognized by the family and may be perceived as either subtle or overt coercion—pressure to cooperate or conform to other ways of child care. The protective agency has the difficult task of maintaining a just and effective balance in its use of authority in relation to the child at risk, whose rights and protection depend on other persons; to parents, whose right to rear their children without outside intervention is being questioned; and to society, which has delegated a responsibility for the protection of children from neglect or abuse.

These four attributes of child protective services will assume fuller meaning as we consider the specific social services that are extended and the issues involved in doing so. But first it is important to look at the origins and subsequent growth of the protective service idea.

HISTORICAL DEVELOPMENT OF PROTECTIVE SERVICES

Early Attitudes Toward the Treatment of Children

Accepted ideas on ways to rear children have undergone many changes through the centuries. We tend to lose sight of how recently the general public has strongly objected to indifferent parental care or to aggressive actions toward children by other members of society.

For many hundreds of years, history has recorded mistreatment of children. The Bible contains examples of cruelty to children, including Herod's order to slay "all the children that were in Bethlehem, and in all the coasts thereof, from two years old and under" (Matthew 2:16). Infanticide by different means was carried out in a number of societies to assure the survival of only strong, healthy infants who could become able to serve the state in combat, and to rid the society of "undesirable" offspring—females, out-of-wedlock children, or any infant who did not seem to be a promising child. Parents who were poor sometimes abandoned children, exposing them to weather and hunger, to escape the burdens of rearing them; richer parents often did the same to avoid dividing property into too many small parts. Even in the Roman family, children were the father's property, and he had absolute power over them, including the privilege of ordering their death, selling them, or offering them in sacrifice. Speculators mutilated or maimed children before setting them up as beggars so that their injuries would arouse pity and increase their rewards from begging.

> Violence toward children and youth has been expressed in endless ways in the history of this country. Deeply rooted in many places, it has been resistant to control. Indifference and inaction in the face of violence to children was hardest to identify when it occurred within the family. It was also difficult to uncover or to challenge when practiced by social institutions. (Polier, 1989, p. 27)

During colonial times and even later, parents often enforced absolute obedience to the demands of adults or emphasized breaking the children's will to free them from the evil disposition with which they supposedly had been born. Drugs, particularly laudanum (a form of opium), were given by parents or servants "almost indiscriminately" to infants to stop their crying (Sunley, 1963). Flogging and caning were used extensively and brutally by schoolmasters.

Beginnings of Care for Neglected Children

After the Revolutionary War, various states passed legislation that recognized the needs of neglected children to the extent of authorizing the binding out, or commitment to almshouses, of children who were found begging on the street or whose parents were beggars. Homer Folks cited the year 1825 as the beginning of more general recognition and application of the principle that public authorities have a right and duty to intervene in cases of parental cruelty or gross neglect of children and "to remove the children by force if necessary, and place them under surroundings more favorable for their development" (Folks, 1911, pp. 168–169). Before the end of the nineteenth century, special laws were passed in nearly all states to provide for the protection of children from neglect or ill-treatment by authorizing the courts to remove them from parents or guardians and commit them to some proper place of care.

Societies for the Prevention of Cruelty to Children

The new laws provided a legal basis for acting in behalf of neglected or abused children if they became objects of attention by a child-saving agency or a children's institution, or if the police chose to bring the situation to the attention of the court. However, there were no clear lines of responsibility among agencies or officials for *finding* neglected and abused children unless families were already requiring support from public or voluntary relief funds. Organizations were needed to bring about the enforcement of existing laws for the "rescue" of neglected children. As a consequence, voluntary societies for the prevention of cruelty to children (SPCCs) were established, the first in New York City in 1875.

Examining the circumstances under which the first SPCC came into existence provides an aid to understanding the purposes and focus of the early societies and the means by which some late-nineteenth-century reformers attempted to act as child advocates. Late in the year 1873, Etta Wheeler, a church worker visiting tenement homes in New York City to try to relieve the suffering of sick and lonely people, heard the story of a 9-year-old girl who for two years had been cruelly whipped and frequently left alone, locked in an inner room during a long day. The thin partitions between the tenement apartments let other occupants hear the child's cries and other evidence of the cruel treatment inflicted on her by the man and woman with whom she lived. They had obtained the child from an institution at two years of age, but no inquiry about her well-being had been made by institution personnel during the intervening seven years. Concerned occupants of the house had not known to whom to complain or how to get help for the child. The tenement visitor went to great lengths to investigate the report and establish evidence of the abuse and neglect. Then, when she sought advice as to how to obtain protection for the child, no one seemed to know of any legal means to "rescue" the child. Up to that time the legal removal of children from cruel or neglectful parents was rare if not impossible. Finally, the tenement visitor took her report to Henry Bergh, who had founded the New York Society for the Prevention of Cruelty to Animals. He arranged to file a petition to have the child removed from her present custodians and placed with persons who would treat her more kindly. The abusing foster mother was sentenced to prison and Mary Ellen eventually gained loving parents. In 1875 the New York Society for the Prevention of Cruelty to Children was established.

The Mary Ellen case was not the sole cause of the emerging child protection movement. Large social movements rarely, if ever, are traceable to accidental causal beginnings. The Mary Ellen instance of private violence becoming "public property" is best explained by a fortuitous coming together and fusing of varying and sometimes competing factors. Among such factors were these: (1) Wide and often lurid publicity was given to the Mary Ellen case; (2) Mary Ellen was an "illegitimate" child and beaten by someone other than her natural parents, a circumstance that muted the old precept of a parent's right to determine the nature and severity of a child's punishment; (3) public awareness had been awakened to the plight of children in a system of child-saving where public authority added to the neglect of children by failing to set standards and supervise child placement activities; (4) gaining in influence was the women's rights movement of the 1870s and its overarching influence on various thrusts toward social justice, one of which was the ideal of "protected childhood" and cultural rejection of child abuse and punitive corporal punishment (Costin, no date).

The formation of the New York Society for the Prevention of Cruelty to Children (SPCC) triggered a rapid growth of other child cruelty societies. By 1898 more than 200 SPCCs had come into existence in the United States. The primary function of the new societies was to investigate cases of alleged cruelty or neglect, present the facts to the courts, and assist the police and public prosecutors in bringing to justice the adults who were responsible for crimes against children. Although these societies were largely private bodies, agents were sometimes given police powers.

These new societies sponsored the passage of child protective or "wrongs-to-children" laws. In New York the SPCC drafted an act to prevent the establishment or spread of the scandalous "baby farms." In addition, action was directed against the *padrone* system of importing children who had been sold by their parents in Italy, against abuses in the employment of children in theatrical and acrobatic performances, and against other similar practices that endangered child life.

Who Should Do Protective Work and What Should Be Its Functions?

After the "discovery" of child abuse in 1874 and the formation of the Societies for the Prevention of Cruelty to Children, child abuse seemed to disappear from public consciousness as well as from the practice of child welfare, only to be "rediscovered" in the early 1960s. After the turn of the century, child welfare practice was marked by confusion and uncertainty as to which agencies should undertake protective work and how this work should be conducted. As some early leaders recommended, with the basic principles and practices of child protection work established, the government now should assume the responsibility for this protection. However, appropriate governmental agencies did not exist and there was little public interest in creating a public agency with a mandate to intrude into the privacy of family life to protect children (Costin, 1992).

The private agencies, for their part, continued to move away from child protection work. The use of

authority, necessary in protective work, made social workers uncomfortable. Within the profession as a whole, the lack of clarity about the nature of authority and its potential for constructive help fostered a weak endorsement of protective work and played a large part in the dormancy of child protective services (Costin, 1992).

The long dormancy of child abuse as a major professional and public issue might have continued had it not been interrupted by new knowledge and the skills of radiologists in identifying suspicious injuries in some children. Sadly, "the rediscovery of child abuse in the 1960s revealed the same tenacious problem, evoked a similar naive public alarm, and posed parallel obstacles to solutions, as it did in the 1870s" (Gordon, 1988, p. 171).

The Rediscovery of Child Abuse: The Battered Child Syndrome

The "rediscovery" of child abuse began in the early 1960s, when Kempe and colleagues identified the "battered child syndrome" (Kempe, Silverman, Steele, Droegemueller, & Silver, 1962). Advances in the technology of radiology made it possible for physicians to identify patterns of injuries, observable by X-rays, that were likely to have been inflicted rather than accidental. In the deluge of interest and publicity that followed this discovery, public interest in addressing child maltreatment was renewed. The interest quickly took the form of establishing official procedures whereby those who knew of instances of child abuse could report them to the authorities.

With new knowledge and diagnostic skill in pediatric medicine, physicians became able to detect with far greater certainty that particular children had been deliberately injured by another person. Even so, they frequently were unwilling to report such cases because of fear of litigation against them by angry parents, or reluctance to divulge what they considered to be confidential information between themselves and their patients, or lack of knowledge or confidence about whom to report the situation to so that prompt and constructive help would be given. If physicians were to be required to report abuse cases uniformly, they would have to be given immunity from resultant legal action.

The American Academy of Pediatrics supported mandatory reporting legislation. The Children's Bureau and the American Humane Association each published guidelines for model legislation in 1963 as a way of assisting states to draft effective reporting laws. In the following several years, child abuse legislation was passed by the individual states with almost unprecedented speed (American Humane Association, 1963; Children's Bureau, 1963).

The Child Abuse Prevention and Treatment Act

In 1974, under the sponsorship of Senator Walter Mondale, the Child Abuse Prevention and Treatment Act (CAPTA) was passed. This act required the Department of Health and Human Services to establish a National Center on Child Abuse and Neglect, which would be a clearinghouse for the development and transmittal of information on research and demonstration programs in child protection. The center was authorized also to make small grants to states for innovative programs.

In order to receive funds, states had to have enacted a law which (1) gave immunity from prosecution to those reporting instances of child abuse and neglect and (2) required certain categories of professionals to report suspected abuse and neglect, and encouraged nonprofessionals to do so. States also had to have provisions for dissemination of information to the general public on prevention and treatment of child maltreatment (Besharov, 1996). Although funding of this act has been meager, it has greatly affected child protective services in the states through its requirement that states pass reporting laws (*Abused Children*, 1987; Schene, 1998).

The history of society's response to children's need of protection in the United States shows a progression from early efforts of local governments and communities, through the development of private charitable organizations in the nineteenth century, to the increasing involvement of state and federal government today. However, as in the past, the focus of attention continues to be mainly on the poor, and involves an often harsh, intrusive investigation and possible removal of children from the home. Although the connection between the needs of children and the conditions in which their families live is obvious, there are still too few supportive services to families to help them offer a higher level of care and ameliorate the sometimes deplorable environmental conditions in which they live. Services continue to be offered on a residual basis, available to families only after a stigmatizing label of abuse or neglect has been given. Although the family support movement described in Chapter 3 shows promise, it is still the case that too many families do not receive preventive services at all and do not come to the attention of the service system until they are reported for child abuse or neglect.

Child abuse is wrong. Not only is child abuse wrong, but the nation's lack of an effective response to it is also wrong. Neither can be tolerated. Together they constitute a moral disaster. (U.S. Advisory Board on Child Abuse and Neglect, 1990, p. 3)

THE DEFINITIONAL DILEMMA

There is no consensual definition of either child abuse or neglect. The type of extreme cases most frequently reported by the media offer few problems, but such cases are relatively rare. The great majority of cases fall into more ambiguous categories in which complex sets of factors must be taken into account. The difficulty and the importance of developing clear definitions can be understood if viewed as a society's attempt to establish minimum standards for the care of children. The development of research-based knowledge, treatment, prevention, and legislative and judicial decision-making depend on a foundation of agreement on what constitutes child maltreatment.

The Child Abuse Prevention and Treatment Act of 1974 (CAPTA) gave a national definition of child maltreatment: "The physical and mental injury, sexual abuse, neglected treatment or maltreatment of child under age 18 by a person who is responsible for the child's welfare under circumstances which indicate the child's health and welfare is harmed and threatened thereby. . . ." (Child Abuse Prevention and Treatment Act, 1974). This definition clarifies that only parents or other caregivers can be charged with abuse or neglect. Harmful behavior to children committed by other adults is considered assault and is handled by the criminal justice system. The definition is a broad one, in that it includes mental injury and neglect as well as physical and sexual abuse.

The CAPTA legislation left many specific details of defining abuse and neglect to the states, and states vary considerably in their definitions. For example, some states include educational neglect (failing consistently to get the child to attend school) while others do not. States also vary in how they screen and process reports of abuse and neglect. In 1996, reports of child maltreatment per 1,000 children nationally was 43.5, but the number ranged from 8.2 per thousand in Pennsylvania to 107.7 in Washington, D.C. (U.S. Department of Health and Human Services, 1998). Only about one-third of all reports were substantiated upon investigation. These large differences indicate a lack of consistency in how child maltreatment is defined.

Broad and Narrow Definitions

One definitional problem is distinguishing between acts of maltreatment that are deliberate or intentional and those that are not. It is not always easy to differentiate between accidental and intentional behavior. "For example, did the mother's placement of her baby's foot in scalding water result from an intentional act to harm the baby, an accident when she slipped while testing the water, or an accident with some unconsciously intended elements?" (Hutchison, 1990, p. 71). Many times child abuse reflects a mixture of intentional and chance elements, as for example, when harm to the child results from parental discipline. Some unintentional accidents may be the result of neglecting the supervision or physical care of a child. Specifying intentions or motivations is hazardous at best.

Another definitional controversy is whether or not to include "endangerment" in the definition of maltreatment. Some situations of potential harm seem clearly dangerous—for example, a parent wielding a knife, chasing a child through the yard threatening to stab him. But many instances of potential harm are dependent on the perception and opinion of the observer. The national incidence studies include both definitions —observable harm as well as endangerment—in recognition of the lack of consensus on this question.

Related to the question of actual or potential harm is the issue of "cumulative harm." As English (1998) points out, "Maltreatment behaviors that are associated with ongoing neglect and with repeated emotional maltreatment typically result not in a discrete injury, but in cumulative harm—the child's well-being or developmental trajectory is impaired" (p. 41). Examples of "cumulative harm" might include persistent verbal abuse, such as calling a child stupid and ugly, over a long period of time, or ongoing neglect in providing medical care. These parental behaviors may not have an immediate effect on the child's development, but are damaging in the long run.

Another problem is distinguishing less than optimal care from care that is actually harmful. Hutchison (1990) pointed out that maltreatment falls somewhere along a continuum of child care. For example, "Can a school-age child be left alone for 30 minutes? 2 hours? overnight? Can a parent hit a child with a hand? with a belt? with a baseball bat?" (p. 71).

Whether a broad or a narrow definition of child maltreatment is selected has implications for the policy and practice of child protective services. Proponents of a narrow definition would prefer to see only cases of observable harm, such as broken bones or burns, handled by child protective services. This policy would simplify the operation of protective services and provide clarity for all concerned—parents, those reporting maltreatment, and other professionals—on the scope and role of protective services in the community. Proponents of a broad definition, on the other hand, are concerned that many children suffering endangerment or cumulative harm would be left entirely unprotected and unnoticed if a narrow definition were adopted. They argue that the definition should include situations in which the child is at serious risk of suffering harm or negative developmental outcomes in the future.

Cultural Attitudes

In the large, culturally diverse society of the United States, differences among cultures in child-rearing practices and perceptions of acceptable parental behavior complicate the problem of providing clear definitions of child abuse and neglect (Giovannoni & Becerra, 1979; Garbarino & Ebata, 1983; Ahn & Gilbert, 1992). Korbin (1994) points out the dilemma posed by cultural factors in determining whether a situation constitutes abuse or neglect: An extreme ethnocentric position, which disregards all cultural differences and imposes a single standard for child care on everyone, risks including situations which appear to constitute maltreatment but are not. On the other hand, an extreme position of cultural relativity runs the risk of ignoring situations that may in fact be harmful for children, even if accepted by the children's culture.

Korbin (1994) offers the example of "coin rubbing" among southeast Asians to illustrate this dilemma. The practice of *cao gao,* believed to cure illness, involves pressing metal coins "forcefully on the child's body, leaving a symmetrical pattern of bruises" (p. 187). These bruises are, indeed, nonaccidentally inflicted and may leave a pattern of bruises that appear more serious than the bruises resulting from being hit with a belt. An ethnocentric position would require that the case be reported for child abuse, even though the bruises were inflicted in a medical context. In fact, these cases are rarely reported because it is recognized as a cultural practice with good intentions.

However, the relativistic view also has pitfalls. Sometimes children subjected to this treatment become seriously ill or die, not from the coin rubbing but because they did not receive standard medical treatment. A relativistic position would seem to endorse different standards of medical care (with risk of harm) for different cultural groups. Because this position seems unacceptable, the American Academy of Pediatrics (1988) has recommended against allowing exemptions from medical treatment on religious grounds. Unfortunately, this position seems to place western medicine at a higher level than other medical practices. Korbin (1994) speculates that in a reverse situation, American parents in Asia might become extremely upset if told that they could not have antibiotics for their child's ear infection and must rely instead on local healing methods.

Korbin suggests that in resolving this dilemma, the first principle must be that, in general, cultural differences must be respected and understood within their cultural context. However, she also distinguishes among "different kinds of cultural differences" (p. 190). Some cultural practices become harmful if the environment changes. For example, the Maoris in New Zealand frequently expect children from about age 8 or 10 to care for their infant and toddler siblings. This practice becomes a problem if the family moves to an urban area with more dangers and without the supportive network of the home setting. Other cultural practices may be quite harmful to children and should be changed, even though the intent is benign. Korbin offers the example of a medical practice in the southwest part of the United States, in which children with stomach problems are given an indigenous medicine which is almost pure lead. Educational efforts in the community have been successful in eliminating this harmful practice, which puts children at risk for lead poisoning (Korbin, 1994, p. 191).

Sometimes, a cultural practice acceptable within the community is taken to an extreme and then becomes a form of maltreatment. For example, a frequent cause for a child neglect report among the Navaho Indians is that children have been left alone or unattended. Parents justify this behavior by pointing out that Navaho culture endorses sibling care-taking of younger children and entrusts children with a high level of responsibility. However, a survey of Navaho parents found that most mothers disapproved of leaving young children alone or with siblings who were not much older for overnight or other long periods of time. Many of the neglect cases were for children as young as five. These situations could not be justified as culturally acceptable, but were in fact a departure from cultural norms exacerbated by problems of poverty and alcohol (Korbin, 1994, p. 193). Sibling care-taking as it was meant to be practiced within this culture should not be condemned, Korbin points out, but should be kept within acceptable limits.

Similarly, Korbin suggests that culturally acceptable forms of physical discipline cannot always be considered as abuse. Within the culture, physical discipline may be considered appropriate and necessary if it does not harm the child. Child protective services workers tend to see only the cases in which children are left with bruises, welts, and other wounds, yet most physical discipline within the culture leaves the children without such marks.

A final, important consideration is that abuse and neglect can occur at a societal level as well as within individual families or cultures in that society. The United States tolerates a high level of poverty, homelessness, deprivation, and failed educational institutions for children. These conditions affect parents' ability to provide for their children, and it seems unfair to define their effects on children as evidence of parental mistreatment. Both societal and parental abuse and neglect may overlap in exposing some children disproportionately to deprivation and exploitation.

Other Legal Provisions

Besides state reporting laws, two other sources of legal provisions help to define child abuse and neglect. These sources are provisions in criminal law and laws regarding the juvenile court.

In the criminal code of every state there are punishable crimes, including murder, assault, and sexual exploitation, that can be applied to parents who inflict injury on their children. Some people believe that criminal prosecution is an undesirable response to abuse and neglect. Imprisonment divides the family, and the hostility engendered by the adversarial proceedings can make it impossible to establish a therapeutic casework relationship. On the other hand, sometimes arrest and criminal prosecution are appropriate. Jailing the perpetrator can solve the immediate problem of protecting the child by getting the adult out of the house. If the adult is not detained, the child may have to go through the additional trauma of being removed from home and placed in foster care. Some policy makers believe that criminal prosecution in some cases reaffirms community standards on what constitutes unacceptable domestic behavior. The National Council of Juvenile and Family Court Judges (1992) has stressed "the importance of treating family violence as serious criminal conduct," and the need for a coordinated community response, including arrest, in domestic violence cases (p. 2).

Violence in the home strikes at the heart of our society. Children who are abused or who live in homes where parents are battered carry the terrible lessons of violence with them into adulthood. . . . To tolerate family violence is to allow the seeds of violence to be sown into the next generation. (U.S. Department of Justice, 1984)

Juvenile court statutes in all the states, with their varying definitions of neglect and abuse, also serve as a determinant of the conditions under which intervention into family life is justified in behalf of children. The differences in statutory language indicate what evidence is necessary to sustain a charge of neglect. In some there must be evidence of direct parental involvement in a child's neglected or abused condition, while in others an inference of parental responsibility may be sufficient, as in the case of an infant severely malnourished or repeatedly injured, who is in the custody of his or her parents and cared for most of the time by them.

REPORTING CHILD MALTREATMENT

As described above, during the 1960s, every state and the District of Columbia passed a child abuse reporting law, and all states now require reporting by physicians and other medical personnel, mental health professionals, social workers, teachers and other school officials, day care or child care workers, and law enforcement personnel. About twenty states require all citizens to report, and all states permit any citizen to report (Besharov, 1996).

The last twenty years have witnessed radically improved performance in the reporting of suspected child maltreatment. The reporting process is strengthened by publicity campaigns, 24-hour hot lines, and administrative linkages between agencies likely to report, such as schools, welfare, and visiting nurses, and the legally mandated child protection agency in the community. Recognition of abuse and neglect is improving among those mandated to report, and this results in increased reporting. The rate of reported child maltreatment was 10 cases per thousand children in 1976, while by 1996 the rate ranged from 8 to 110 children per thousand, depending on the state (U.S. Department of Health and Human Services, 1998). As a result of improvements in reporting, many children have been saved from serious injury or death. Besharov (1996) estimates that in the past twenty years, deaths from child abuse and neglect have fallen from about 3,000 a year to about than 1,000 a year. New York State experienced a 50 percent reduction in child fatalities within five years of passage of a comprehensive reporting law.

In 1996 data on child abuse and neglect reports showed that the majority of these reports came from professionals such as teachers, welfare workers, and health care workers; others came from family members of the victims, including the victims themselves, and from neighbors and friends. Another 20 percent of reports were from anonymous or other sources (U.S. Department of Health and Human Services, 1998). Figure 7.2 shows the sources of reports for 1996.

Problems with the Reporting Laws

In spite of improvements in reporting, two major problems remain: the large number of cases that go unreported, and the large number of unfounded reports. The plight of many vulnerable children continues to go unreported. Although legally mandated to do so, many professionals do not report cases in which they suspect child maltreatment. According to the national incidence study in 1993, child protective

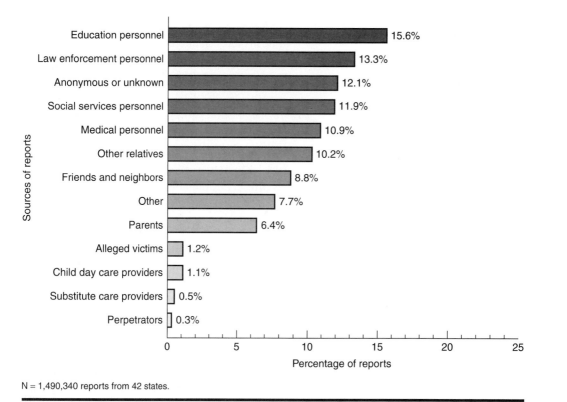

N = 1,490,340 reports from 42 states.

FIGURE 7.2   Sources of Reports, 1996

Source: U.S. Department of Health and Human Services. (1998). *Child maltreatment 1996: Reports from the states to the national child abuse and neglect data system.* Washington, DC: Author.

services investigated fewer than one-third of the cases identified by professionals in the study, either because the professionals did not report the case to child protective services or because child protective services screened out the referral without investigation (Sedlak & Broadhurst, 1996). Reasons for this reluctance to report include lack of clarity on which situations require reporting, concern about confidentiality and the effect of reporting on the therapeutic relationship, concern about lawsuits or reprisals from clients, reluctance to become involved, and a belief that reporting will not help the situation (Diesz, Doueck, George, & Levine, 1996; Warner-Rogers, Hansen & Spieth, 1996).

A second problem is the large number of reports that, on investigation, are found to be without enough basis to warrant further action. These "unfounded" or "unsubstantiated" reports currently constitute about two-thirds of all reports made to child protection agencies (U.S. Department of Health and Human Services, 1998). Figure 7.3 shows the disposition of child maltreatment reports for 1996. Very few of these unfounded reports are made by malicious people trying to cause trouble. Many are made by "nonmandated" reporters, such as neighbors and relatives (U.S. Department of Health and Human

Services, 1998), who may not know the definitions of child maltreatment used by the local child protection agency. Another reason for the large number of unfounded reports concerns agency policy regarding which kinds of situations to substantiate. As indicated above, states vary in the inclusiveness of their definitions of abuse and neglect, and local and county agencies also vary in what kinds of situations they believe warrant a thorough investigation or a decision to substantiate.

Unfounded reports are of concern because of the possible conflict between a family's right to privacy and the state's interest in protecting children who may be abused or maltreated. A protective service investigation is intrusive. Workers must inquire into intimate details of family life. The children usually must be questioned, and also friends, school personnel, day care workers, clergy, and others who know the family. The fact of the investigation is stigmatizing, even if the report is later unfounded. Justice Hugo Black pointed out that the parent "is charged with conduct—failure to care properly for her children—which may be viewed as reprehensible and morally wrong by a majority of society" (*Carter v. Kaufman,* 1971, p. 959). Critics question a system that infringes on the family's right to privacy without giving much assurance that the lives of children will be improved as a result of this infringement (Besharov, 1996; Lindsay, 1994).

Another troublesome aspect of the large number of unfounded reports is that agency resources are necessarily deployed to investigate reports while children already identified as abused are insufficiently served by the agency. The large increase in reports of child maltreatment has not been accompanied by an increase in appropriations for child protection agencies, so staff must spend time investigating new cases rather than treating families already known to them.

The large number of unfounded reports also affects the credibility of the agency. If those reporting begin to perceive that their reports are likely to be unfounded, or the family is not helped as a result of the report, they may lose confidence in the system and be less likely to report suspected cases (Levine, 1996).

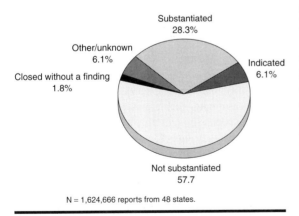

N = 1,624,666 reports from 48 states.

FIGURE 7.3   Investigated Reports by Disposition, 1996
Source: U.S. Department of Health and Human Services. (1998). *Child maltreatment 1996: Reports from the states to the national child abuse and neglect data system.* Washington, DC: Author.

Filing a Report

States include nearly every category of professionals serving children, such as teachers, social workers, day care workers, probation officers, and health care professionals, as mandated reporters who are required to report suspected abuse or neglect. Mandated reporters may face civil and criminal penalties if they fail to report, and have immunity from legal action by parents for reporting. They are also protected by confidentiality provisions in the reporting laws; the identity of the reporter is supposed to remain unknown to the parents.

Those reporting child abuse and neglect are not expected to have conducted an investigation to ascertain whether or not child maltreatment occurred. They are asked to report instances in which they have "reasonable cause to suspect" child maltreatment. Then child protective services will conduct the investigation. As indicated above, many professionals are confused about what types of situations are considered "abuse" or "neglect" by their local child protective agency. However, the general rule for mandated reporters is to report all cases in which they have "reasonable cause to suspect" child abuse or neglect, whether or not they believe that the child protective agency will act on the referral. By doing so, they are protecting themselves from any possible legal penalties as well as working to protect children.

The procedures for filing a report are quite simple in most states and are described in the state's reporting law. Generally, the reporter may make an oral report, such as a telephone call, to be followed by a written report within twenty-four hours. Reporters are encouraged to give as much information as possible, such as relevant names, addresses, and phone numbers, and specific information regarding the maltreatment, such as physical evidence and the statements of children or perpetrators. In some states, child protective services is required or encouraged to let the reporter know the results of the investigation.

AN ECOLOGICAL VIEW OF CHILD MALTREATMENT

Conditions leading to the neglect or abuse of children cannot be defined in simple, discrete terms. Multiple causes and conditions interact, reinforce each other, and generate new influences that lead to family malfunctioning. In general, child maltreatment results from the interaction of environmental stress, personality traits of the parent, and child characteristics (English, 1998; Belsky, 1993). Environmental conditions that increase risk of child maltreatment include poverty, unemployment, hostile or demeaning work settings, unsupportive or dangerous neighborhoods, and unresponsive service systems. Characteristics of parents also, of course, affect the type and quality of care they offer their children. Parents who were maltreated as children or who grew up in abusive households are more at risk than other parents of mistreating their children. Other parental conditions considered risky include mental or severe, chronic physical illness, mental retardation, unemployment, domestic violence, and drug and alcohol abuse. Children also may have characteristics that put them at special risk for maltreatment or that may exacerbate the consequences.

No one factor causes child maltreatment; rather the interaction among environmental and parental and child characteristics creates situations in which child maltreatment is likely to occur. For example, a young, isolated mother may be particularly at risk if she is suffering from severe postpartum depression and if her infant is colicky and difficult to care for.

Community Deficits

Environmental conditions that contribute to child neglect and abuse often can be identified within a community's system of social services. There can be lack of early casefinding techniques, resulting in a pattern of providing social services only after a child is observed to be in an already dangerous situation, or when the care he or she is receiving finally reaches such a low level that it defies what a neighborhood or community can tolerate. A deficiency in "case accountability" is another factor, reflected in such practices as (1) giving inadequate or incomplete services, (2) failing to follow through on referrals for another service, (3) setting up barriers of communication or bureaucratic procedures that cut off some people from asking for or receiving help, (4) showing concern only about fragments of family life that present symptoms troublesome to the community, and (5) failing to develop an agency function that is an active part of a community-wide program of services. Preventive services may be unavailable to avert the onset of family problems that sometimes occur at normal transitional points of family life—for example, marriage, pregnancy and childbirth, early infancy, and school entrance—and at other times of peak demand on family functioning (see Chapter 3).

Serious social problems abound in our communities today, and all of these, directly or indirectly, tend to increase the incidence of child neglect and abuse. Some of the most pressing social problems are a large-scale incidence of mental ill health and substance abuse; escalating health costs and unequal medical services; poverty in the midst of affluence; lack of jobs for youth and heads of families; deplorable housing for large numbers of the population; high rates of delinquency; inadequate and irrelevant education for much of the nation's youth, with a lack of preparation for jobs, higher education, parenthood, and other aspects of adult responsibility; and a pervading sense that individuals lack the power of self-direction and are subject to the restrictive rules of bureaucracies or intangible outside forces that limit daily experiences for them and their children.

Societal Attitudes

We live in a culture saturated with images of violence. The media glamorizes violence in movies, books, television, and music, and reinforces the widely held view that violence is a culturally-approved way of resolving disputes. Child abuse must be viewed within the context of a society which accepts, if not condones, violence in the domestic sphere and in the community. A survey by Gil revealed that physical force in child rearing is accepted by various segments of American society, leading to the conclusion that child abuse is founded on a "culturally determined permissive attitude toward the use of a measure of physical force in caretaker-child interaction" (Gil, 1970, p. 135).

Demographic Characteristics

Poverty. The relation of poverty to child maltreatment has been recognized at least since the nineteenth

century, when the Societies for the Prevention of Cruelty to Children were founded to work almost exclusively among the poor. Research consistently shows a correlation between socioeconomic status and child maltreatment rate. The 1993 National Incidence Study, like the two previous NIS reports, found "significant and pervasive differences in the incidence of maltreatment . . . in relation to family income" (Sedlak & Broadhurst, 1996, p. 5–2). The poorest children were three times more likely to suffer maltreatment than children in families with incomes between $15,000 and $29,000 and more than twenty-five times more likely to be maltreated than children in the most affluent categories. Figures 7.4 and 7.5 show the differences in maltreatment rates for children in families of different incomes. Some studies have found that sexual abuse and emotional maltreatment are not closely related to family income, but the 1993 National Incidence Study found that income is correlated to all types of maltreatment except child fatalities.

Child abuse and neglect occur at all income levels. To some extent, the differences in rates between income groups may reflect differences in recognition

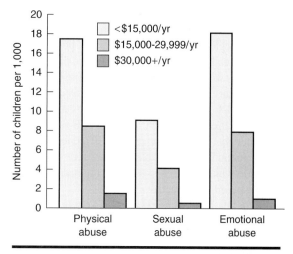

FIGURE 7.4 Incidence of Types of Abuse Under the Endangerment Standard for Different Levels of Family Income

Source: A. J. Sedlak & D. D. Broadhurst. (1996). *Third national incidence study of child abuse and neglect.* Washington, DC: U.S. Department of Health and Human Services.

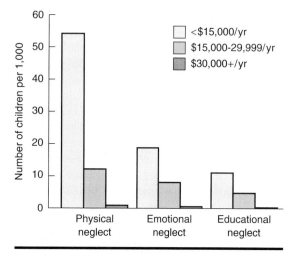

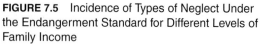

FIGURE 7.5 Incidence of Types of Neglect Under the Endangerment Standard for Different Levels of Family Income

Source: A. J. Sedlak & D. D. Broadhurst. (1996). *Third national incidence study of child abuse and neglect.* Washington, DC: U.S. Department of Health and Human Services.

of maltreatment rather than differences in occurrence. Deviant forms of child treatment are more easily concealed in families of higher social status. It is also important to remember that most poor families do not abuse or neglect their children, and many poor parents raise their children successfully in the face of great obstacles. However, the magnitude and consistency of the difference in rates among the three income groups in the NIS suggest that family income is a powerful predictor of child maltreatment. The NIS researchers conclude that "the income-related differences in incidence found in the NIS reflect real differences in the extent to which children in different income levels are being abused or neglected" (pp. 8–12).

The reasons for the correlation between poverty and maltreatment are not fully understood. Class differences in child rearing may explain some of the difference in maltreatment rates. Poorly educated people at the bottom of the social and economic ladder may express their abuse more readily in direct, aggressive actions, whereas those in higher income groups may resort to other means, such as verbal attacks or withdrawals of affection. The stress of living in chronically

poor conditions is also a factor. Researchers have found that unemployment is related to family stress and child abuse (National Research Council, 1993).

Race/Ethnicity. African-American children are more likely to be reported for child maltreatment than are children of other ethnic groups (Berrick, Needell, Barth & Jonson-Reid, 1998). In 1996, African-American children accounted for about 15 percent of the total child population but comprised nearly 29 percent of children reported to child protective services (U.S. Department of Health and Human Services, 1998). There are also differences among the races in the type of maltreatment for which they are reported. For example, white children make up a disproportionate number of those reported for sexual abuse and emotional maltreatment. African-American children are less likely to be reported for sexual abuse and emotional maltreatment, but are more likely to be reported for medical neglect (U.S. Department of Health and Human Services, 1998). Figure 7.6 shows the proportions of victims, as reported to child protective service agencies, in comparison to the proportion of children of each race.

There is much debate on whether the differences in reporting reflect real differences in the rate of maltreatment among the races, are a result of biases in reporting, or simply reflect the higher poverty rate of African Americans. The national incidence studies have found no differences among the races in the rate of maltreatment as observed by professionals, although there were large differences in reporting patterns (Sedlak & Broadhurst, 1996; Ards, Chung, & Myers, 1998). This finding has remained consistent over the fourteen years in which these three studies have been conducted.

The impact of race is linked closely to the impacts of poverty, substance abuse, and living in inner-city communities. Families in these communities are more likely than others to come into contact with social workers, police, and medical personnel who are mandated reporters, and therefore they may be somewhat more likely to be reported to the authorities. It is difficult to separate out the effects of race from those of poverty and substance abuse, two factors which are strongly linked to child maltreatment.

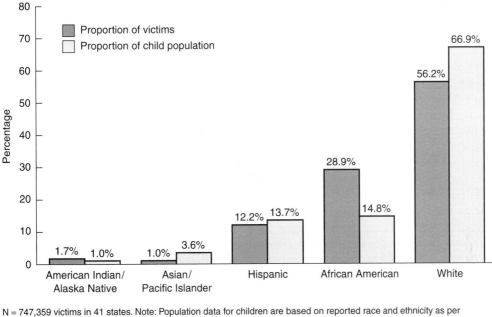

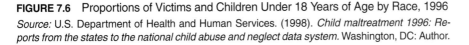

N = 747,359 victims in 41 states. Note: Population data for children are based on reported race and ethnicity as per 1994 Census estimates in the 41 states. The percentages are based on the number of victims excluding children of "other" or "unknown" race.

FIGURE 7.6   Proportions of Victims and Children Under 18 Years of Age by Race, 1996

Source: U.S. Department of Health and Human Services. (1998). *Child maltreatment 1996: Reports from the states to the national child abuse and neglect data system.* Washington, DC: Author.

Berrick and colleagues (1998) conclude, based on a review of the literature, that ethnicity alone is not closely linked to child maltreatment rates, and that when large differences in reporting rates for different races are found, the explanation lies in other family and community characteristics.

Characteristics of Parents and Families

Family Structure.   Abuse and neglect are more likely to occur in single-parent households, with father-only families at somewhat higher risk than mother-only families (Sedlak & Broadhurst, 1996). Single parenthood is related to poverty and the additional risks that the difficulties of living in poverty entail. Single parents, trying to fulfill both parental roles, may be more susceptible to stress, which can result in lashing out at children. They also have to try to handle the child care and other parenting tasks on their own, without a par-

enting partner. Another family characteristic related to abuse and neglect is the number of children at home; those with more children are at higher risk than are small families, probably due to increased demands on parents (Sedlak & Broadhurst, 1996).

Substance Abuse.   Drug abuse has increased tremendously in recent years, with devastating effects on the lives of adults and children. Substances such as alcohol, marijuana, cocaine, crack, PCP, and heroin are widely available. The Child Welfare League of America estimates that substance abuse is a factor in as many as 80 percent of all cases substantiated for abuse and neglect (Child Welfare League of America, 1990).

Substance abuse affects children in many ways. Parents who abuse substances, especially if they are addicted, are often unable to provide consistent, nurturing care that promotes their child's development. Those who are addicted have lost control over their use of the desired substance; they are preoccupied with their addiction, despite the consequences. Parents in this situation place their substance use above the welfare of their children, resulting in the increased likelihood of both abuse and neglect. Feeding the addiction takes needed resources from the family, so that children may lack sufficient food and clothing and decent housing. Parents involved with substances are likely to be inattentive to the physical and developmental needs of their children; they may not see that the children attend school or receive needed medical care, or give the children the time and attention that they need to become socialized adults. Use of psychoactive drugs also increases the risk of abuse. Chemical substances lower inhibitions; an angry parent, when drunk, may become a physically abusive parent. Some parents recruit their children into selling drugs, prostitution, or other extremely damaging activities in order to obtain money to buy drugs or alcohol (Zuckerman, 1994).

Often addiction is related to a constellation of other problems that also affect the parent's ability to provide an adequate level of care for their children. Many women who are addicted experienced sexual or physical abuse as children. For them, use of drugs and alcohol may be an effort to dull the painful memories associated with these events. Those suffering from clinical depression may also be susceptible to substance use in order to alleviate their symptoms. Substance-abusing women are more likely to be the victims of domestic and other violence. These interrelated conditions, of which substance usage is a part, compound the risks to children's healthy development (Zuckerman, 1994).

Although child welfare professionals have been aware for many years of a link between child maltreatment and drug and alcohol abuse, only recently has this connection been seriously studied and addressed in the service delivery system. The gap between knowledge and action may be explained in part by the failure of two service systems—child welfare and substance abuse treatment programs—to coordinate services. Thus child welfare agencies, although aware of a substance abuse problem in a family, focused only on the child maltreatment issues. With the

great increase of family problems related to the crack cocaine epidemic, which began in the mid-1980s, child welfare agencies became overwhelmed with families who seemed unreachable because of the pervasive effects of addiction on family functioning. In the past decade, professionals in both service systems have become more aware of the importance of an integrated approach, incorporating substance abuse treatment and help with parenting (Azzi-Lessing & Olsen, 1996).

Domestic Violence. Studies indicate that domestic violence and child maltreatment are linked (Herskowitz & Seck, 1990; Walker, 1984). A national survey of 6,000 families found that half of the men who frequently assaulted their wives also frequently abused their children, and that mothers who are beaten by their partners are more likely to abuse their children than are mothers who are not victims of violence (Straus & Gelles, 1990).

Social Isolation. Social isolation from other families and from relatives can be related to child maltreatment (Tracy & Whitaker, 1987). Polansky et al. (1981) observed that "among neglectful parents are many who make their circumstances worse by self-imposed aloneness, and who must thus live with dreadful loneliness" (p. 210). Social interaction with trusted neighbors or friends helps parents relieve everyday stress and can also help them learn new ways of managing their children and of locating needed resources. Friends and relatives are also a resource for child care and household help in times of family crisis or just to help parents get away and have time to themselves. Socially isolated families not only lack needed social support but also may be overly insulated from social control. Child maltreatment tends to take place in secrecy and isolation, and most parents do not want others to know that they are mistreating their children. Interaction with neighbors, members of one's faith community, extended family members, and others can help parents keep a check on their impulsivity, which might lead them to commit acts of abuse.

Psychological Factors. Personality and health problems of parents are associated in varying degrees with child abuse and neglect. Research has revealed an array of psychological problems experienced by neglectful mothers, suggesting that they are "hostile, impulsive, poorly socialized, lonely, depressed, have deficient problem-solving skills, and may be substance abusers" (Nelson, Saunders, & Landsman, 1990, p. 6). Some mothers are borderline psychotic. For many maltreating mothers of young children, life is a chronic experience of depression, serious enough that they have been hospitalized or have seen a mental health professional for "nerve problems" (Zuravin, 1988). They may feel that nothing is worth doing and experience emotional numbness, loneliness, and lack of competence. They may display anger expressed through passive aggression and hostile compliance, reluctance to talk about feelings, poor problem-solving skills, and an ability to bring forth the same feelings of futility in others, primarily as a defense against change (Polansky, Chalmers, Buttenwieser, & Williams, 1981).

Interactional Factors. Abusive and neglectful caretakers often have inappropriate expectations of their children. They may lack parenting skills and knowledge of child development and are likely to have unreasonably high expectations of young children's ability for self-care and for care of younger siblings. They may also have unreasonable expectations for compliant behavior. When these expectations are not met, the parent assumes the child is being willful or defiant and lashes out physically. For example, a parent believes that a three-month old infant who keeps on crying after being told to stop, just "won't mind" and needs a spanking.

Some parents have a very limited repertoire of techniques for guiding their children's behavior. They know how to spank a child but not how to use time-outs, explanations, negotiation, diversion, and positive reinforcement. Lack of knowledge of parenting skill, combined with lack of empathy and belief in authoritarian control can precipitate child maltreatment.

Maltreating parents may express more negative and neglectful feelings about their children than do other parents. Their interactions with their children are often limited, negative, controlling, and lacking in emotional nurturance. They may make many requests of their children but at the same time are unlikely to respond to requests from them.

Having been mistreated as a child puts a parent at greater risk of abusing and neglecting a child. Widom (1989), after reviewing research, estimates that about one-third of those who were abused as children will neglect or abuse their own offspring, and that two-thirds will not. Thus, the "cycle of violence" from one generation to the next does exist, but it is not inevitable.

The ability to form attachments is thought to depend on the quality of care the parent received as a small child, so failure to bond tends to get transmitted intergenerationally. Steele (1987) observed that parents who suffered massive emotional deprivations and physical abuse in early life often manifest a marked lack of empathy for their children. They seem unaware of and insensitive to their children's affective needs and moods, and are unable to respond appropriately. This deficit is observable in hospital maternity wards in the first interactions of the parent and child. The parent may seem cold, uninterested, and unwilling to attend to the newborn infant's needs. He or she may avoid eye or body contact with the child. Particularly when under stress, unempathic parents find the satisfaction of their own needs to be so compelling that they disregard those of the child (Erickson & Egeland, 1996).

Child Characteristics

Younger children, premature infants, and children with irritable temperaments are at higher risk for abuse and neglect. Girls are at higher risk for sexual abuse, but other types of maltreatment affect boys and girls equally. Infants, with fragile bodies, are more likely than other children to die of maltreatment (English, 1998; Berrick, Needell, Barth, & Jonson-Reid, 1998).

CONSEQUENCES OF CHILD MALTREATMENT

Children experience disruptions to normal development as a result of maltreatment, leading to physical, psychological, cognitive, and social impairments. The extent of these effects vary depending on the age of the child when maltreatment occurred, the severity and duration of the maltreatment, and the type of maltreatment suffered.

Child Fatalities

The death of a child from maltreatment is a great tragedy. Each day three children in the United States die from abuse or neglect. In 1993, 1,299 children were known to die from mistreatment. This is probably a low estimate since some percentage of child deaths officially listed as accidental death, homicide, or sudden infant death syndrome (SIDS) would be attributed more accurately to mistreatment (McCurdy & Daro, 1994). Somewhat more children die from abuse (55 percent) than from neglect (40 percent), while about 5 percent of child deaths are attributable to both types of mistreatment. Most maltreatment fatalities occur to children under age 5, a fact which highlights the extreme vulnerability of young children.

Fewer than half the families in which fatal mistreatment occurs are known to child protection agencies before the child's death. To develop better community systems that can find and monitor potentially lethal family situations, many states have established death review committees, with representatives from health services, law enforcement, child protective services, the medical examiner's office, and the prosecutor's office. These multidisciplinary groups review the circumstances leading to the death, including the extent to which social and health agencies were involved with the family. They also develop and implement policies to improve the response of the community to endangered children (Daro & Mitchel, 1989; McCurdy & Daro, 1994).

Effects on Children's Development

Children suffering from very poor care in infancy (see Failure to Thrive, below) may suffer lasting growth retardation. Sexual abuse victims may become infected from sexually-transmitted diseases. Severe physical abuse can lead to long-lasting and irreversible physical disabilities and mental impairment, if the brain has been injured.

Psychological and social problems are prevalent, including lack of empathy, inability to trust, and difficulty with peer relations. Abused children are often more aggressive toward peers, unable to handle stress or frustration, and may have difficult temperaments. Neglected children are more likely to be passive and withdrawn and to exhibit helplessness under stress. Both groups may suffer language disorders and moderate or severe developmental delays. When children cannot master developmental tasks at the appropriate life stage (such as learning to trust) they face compounded difficulties in mastering the tasks of subsequent life stages.

Older children who have been abused or neglected are likely to do poorly at school. Delinquency, suicidal thoughts, depression, emotional problems, substance abuse, eating disorders, sleeping difficulties, and sexual problems are more common in adolescence among abused and neglected children. As adults, these developmental problems are likely to continue (Dodge, Bates, & Petit, 1990; Kurtz, Gaudin, Wodarski, & Hoving, 1993; Erickson & Egeland, 1996; English, 1998).

The Resilient Child

Recently, interest has turned to children who seem to transcend seriously neglectful or abusive childhoods to become successful adults. It seems likely that both environmental and personal factors account for resiliency. Personal qualities of resilient children include good intellectual ability, a positive attitude toward others, physical attractiveness, enthusiasm, and an internal locus of control. External protective factors that may make a difference are the presence of caring adults outside the abusive family who take a strong interest in the child, and parents who, in spite of being abusive, are able to offer some family stability, expectations of academic performance, and a home atmosphere in which the abuse is sporadic rather than a constant, pervasive element (Starr & Wolfe, 1991; Smith & Carlson, 1997).

Case Example. The following case study shows how both individual qualities and external supports worked to allow one child to escape the life patterns set by her parents, while her sibling could not.

> Marisha, age 19, was a college freshman. Her 18-year-old brother, Marcus, had dropped out of school and

was living at home. He had a history of delinquency and suicidal threats. Their parents had abused the children physically and sexually over a long period of time. The children had required hospitalization for burns inflicted by the parents and had also suffered broken bones. The parents were alcoholics and drug abusers, with no regular employment, who used all family resources to obtain addictive substances. Fortunately, the children had a supportive aunt and uncle, Mr. and Mrs. Collins. Childless themselves, they cared deeply for the children, who lived with them intermittently for years. While in high school, Marisha chose to leave her family and moved in permanently with the Collinses. Fortunate in having a good singing voice and a conscientious attitude toward school, she received personal attention and encouragement from her choir director at church and from teachers. She developed a realistic plan to become a music teacher, and determined not to remain passive and dependent as her mother had done.

Marcus remained at home, unwilling to meet the Collins's demands that he return to school, participate regularly in counseling, and attend supervised after-school activities. He engaged in acts of violence in the community and was abusive to his girlfriend.

For Marisha, a critical factor appears to have been her early decision to be different from her parents. She seemed to be able to let go of her parents and find love and approval from other adults. Her brother, in contrast, remained mired in an abusive home situation and acted out aggressively. He did not attract the sustained attention of other caring adults who might have helped him develop a positive self-image.

IDENTIFYING CHILD NEGLECT

Incidence

Physical neglect is the predominant form of child maltreatment in the United States; the 1993 National Incidence Study found that 1,961,300 children were physically neglected, for a rate of 20 children per thousand (Sedlak & Broadhurst, 1996). Not only is child neglect more prevalent than physical abuse, it is nearly as dangerous. About 45 percent of all child fatalities involve neglect (McCurdy & Daro, 1994). In spite of its seriousness, child neglect has not received the media and scholarly attention accorded to child abuse. Furthermore, the attention given to neglect often fo-

cuses only on observable physical harm. Neglect does often leave physical indications, but much of the damage from neglect accrues over time. It is the cumulative effects of malnutrition, medical neglect, inattention to education, and emotional deprivation that are likely to have the most serious long-term consequences to the developing child. "Whether or not the child sustains physical injury, at the core of maltreatment is lasting damage to the child's sense of self and the resultant impairment of social, emotional, and cognitive functioning" (Erickson & Egeland, 1996, p. 5).

Definition of Physical Neglect

Zuravin (cited in Nelson, Saunders, & Landsman, 1990), after analyzing definitional issues of neglect, concluded that most definitions agree it is an act of omission "judged by a mixture of community values and professional expertise to be inappropriate and damaging" and is "failure to perform parental duties related to supervision and physical needs of the child" (p. 9). Rose and Meezan (1997), after reviewing definitions of neglect over time, conclude similarly that:

> *The greatest degree of consensus and consistency in the definition of neglect over time appears to be the categories of inadequate food, clothing, shelter, and supervision (including abandonment). This consensus may be due to the almost universal agreement that the basic requirement of physical care of a child is the responsibility of parents, and that the absence of such care has clear consequences for the child. (p. 18)*

The National Incidence Study includes the following categories of physical neglect: inattention to remedial health care needs; custody issues such as abandonment, expulsion, and repeated shuttling of children among multiple caretakers; inadequate supervision; conspicuous inattention to avoidable hazards in the home; inadequate nutrition, clothing, or hygiene; and other forms of reckless disregard of the child's safety and welfare, such as driving with the child while intoxicated, leaving a young child unattended in a motor vehicle, and so forth. Excluded from these definitions are cases where the parent was financially unable to provide reasonably safe, hygienic living conditions (Sedlak & Broadhurst, 1996).

Examples of physical neglect, noted by professionals participating in the 1996 National Incidence Study, include the following:

> *A teen whose mother refused to provide needed medication for his seizures; an infant whose parents delayed 24 hours before seeking medical attention for his serious head injury and loss of consciousness; a 12-year-old whose mother abandoned him; a preteen whose mother threw him out of their home and told him not to return; a 2-year-old, reported as endangered, who was found wandering in the street late at night, naked and alone; an infant who had to be hospitalized for near-drowning after being left alone in a bath; a 3-year-old who had roaches in her leg cast; children endangered when their mother left a 6-year-old in charge of an infant and toddler so long that the older child feared her mother would not return and called 911 for help; and children endangered by living in a home contaminated with animal feces and rotting food. (Sedlak & Broadhurst, 1996, pp. 2–17, 2–18)*

Children of Neglectful Families

The label *neglect* is commonly attached to those symptoms denoting parental failure to adequately perform essential child care tasks, or parental failure to perform certain duties at all. Some of these symptoms are observable in children's personal appearance or behavior. For example, common signs of child neglect include chronic hunger, possibly manifested by a distended stomach; inappropriate dress, such as a lack of warm clothing in cold weather; poor hygiene, as shown by unclean clothing, hair, and possibly lice or other skin conditions; abandonment or lack of supervision; and unattended medical needs. Neglected children may display such behaviors as stealing and hoarding food; falling asleep or listlessness; frequent unexplained absences from school; self-destructive activity; and frequent reports that no caretaker is at home (American Humane Association, 1997; Besharov, 1990a, cited in Berrick, 1997).

Home Conditions

Children's neglect may be directly observable in home conditions that affect them adversely, including dilapidated housing without the essential material equipment for normal family life, overcrowding, and lack of

privacy. Children may experience eviction and homelessness. A mother may maintain such low housekeeping standards that her family lives in squalor. Children may not have an adequate place to sleep. Young children may be left alone in the house or be very poorly attended when their parents are away. The home may contain physical hazards, such as poisons within reach of a young child, or unsafe heating equipment, or unprotected stairways. Children may experience unwholesome or demoralizing circumstances at home—violence, excessive quarreling, parental dishonesty, defiance of proper authority in society, or lack of love or concern for each other's welfare among family members (Helfer, 1987). In assessing neglect, it is important to be aware that poor home conditions may reflect lack of resources and poverty. In these situations, caseworkers attempt to help parents get the resources they need to maintain decency rather than focus on changing parental behavior. Often neglect reflects a combination of poverty and parental inattention, requiring a multifaceted approach to treatment.

Family Characteristics

Neglectful families, like maltreating families in general, are likely to be poor, to be headed by a single parent, and to have a large number of children (see An Ecological View of Child Maltreatment, above). They are often socially isolated, perhaps because they tend to be shunned by others rather than because they, themselves, avoid social contact. The parents lack empathy, have difficulty relating to others, may be impulsive, and do not communicate effectively. They tend not to demonstrate nurturing behaviors to their children, and their interactions with their children lack warmth. Their lives often seem chaotic, with many conflictual relationships (Berrick, 1997). Neglectful parents tend to have a low opinion of their own competency and abilities, and lack a sense of well-being (Gaudin & Dubowitz, 1997).

Lack of Supervision

Lack of supervision (LOS) refers to situations in which children are without a caretaker or the caretaker is inattentive or unsuitable, and therefore the children are in danger of harming themselves or possibly others (American Humane Association, 1984). Also included are situations in which children are allowed to remain away from home overnight without the parents' knowing or attempting to find out the child's whereabouts, expulsion from home or refusal to allow the child to return home, and abandonment.

In a study of 375 LOS cases in New York State, Jones (1987) found that in many cases, the child was left unsupervised because the parent was engaged some essential activity, such as school, work, or errands. In other cases, parents were socializing, engaged in illegal or irresponsible activity, or were hospitalized or incarcerated. About half of the parents believed that there was nothing wrong with what had happened. For example, a parent who left a child with a slightly older sibling may be convinced that the caretaker was competent. In most other cases, the parent did acknowledge a supervision problem but blamed someone else or said it was unavoidable.

Jones concluded that about half the families could have been helped with regular day care or as-needed baby-sitting. The other half of the cases were thought to need "supplementary child care . . . to shore up, stabilize, or enhance the caretaker's child care functioning," such as homemaker service, respite care, or foster care (Jones, 1987, p. 29). Day care alone would not have been enough to ensure the child's safety.

An obstacle to developing a consensus on minimum standards of supervision is the relationship of lack of supervision to poverty, inadequate housing, and dangerous neighborhoods. Families with better houses in safer neighborhoods may need to provide less supervision to keep their children safe than do those residing in poor areas. A solution is to increase the day care and baby-sitting services available to poor families so that children are supervised while parents need to be away. A more modest but useful goal would be to increase public awareness and educational activities so parents understand minimally acceptable levels of supervision. See Chapters 3 and 5.

Expelled and Runaway Youth

Adolescents told to leave home by a parent who has made no adequate arrangement for their care by others and who refuses to accept the youth's return may be labeled as expelled or "throwaway" youth. "Runaways" are adolescents who have left home with or without permission for an extended period of time. Although the circumstances of their departures vary, these teenagers may make up one homogeneous group who are characterized primarily by having extensive problems at home. Many have been chronically abused and neglected. A recent national survey estimated that there are about 500,000 expelled and runaway youth yearly under age 18 and that 150,000 youth are homeless during a year, with "homeless" defined as "without a safe place to sleep" (Barden, 1990).

"Failure to Thrive" as Neglect

Failure to thrive (FTT) refers to chronic, severe undernutrition of an infant. Medical staff may diagnose FTT if the infant's weight is 20 percent below the ideal weight for the infant's height. Poor weight gain over time is another indicator of FTT. Thirty percent of FTT cases have an organic cause, 50 percent are due to extreme neglect and dysfunctional parenting, and the rest are caused by errors in formula preparation or breast-feeding problems. Infants are thin with prominent ribs and wasted buttocks. If their condition is due to neglect, they may also show poor hygienic care, such as diaper rash, untreated impetigo, uncut nails, and dirty clothes. These babies may also show signs of abuse and of dehydration. When offered food, underfed babies will often eat voraciously. FTT infants have stunted development and show delays in social interaction and speech. They may avoid eye contact and resist cuddling. Mothers are observed to interact very little with their infants during feeding and may act angry at the child (Schmitt, 1988). FTT appears to be the result of insufficient attachment between the mother and the baby. Explanations for the lack of bonding include early deprivation of the mother during her own childhood, difficulties during the pregnancy or childbirth resulting in prematurity or congenital defects, acute illness of mother or baby, and stressful current life events. Mothers of FTT infants are more likely than other mothers to have experienced abuse, neglect, and sexual abuse as children (Halsey, Covington, Gilbert, Sorentino-Kelly, & Renoud, 1993).

Results of FTT can be serious. <u>If untreated, it can result in permanent retardation and ongoing psycho-logical problems</u>. In extreme cases, the infant must be hospitalized and possibly later placed in foster care until the medical condition is alleviated. In most cases, however, the infant can be treated at home if the parents are engaged in therapy. Skill and effort are required to establish the exact nature of the failure to thrive and its causes. A team of professional workers may be needed not only to diagnose but also to treat the ailment and manage the case at physiological, social, and psychological levels.

Case Example.   The following case example shows how a health clinic social worker, in collaboration with a medical team, provided services to a family with a failure-to-thrive infant.

Mr. and Mrs. R brought their eight-month-old daughter, Miranda, to the hospital clinic on a referral from the pediatrician. Miranda weighed six pounds at birth and had barely doubled her weight. She did not roll over or sit alone and appeared listless. She was slow to respond to social stimulation and did not seek out attention. The medical social worker, Ms. G, reviewed the medical records and began exploring whether there was an environmental cause for Miranda's failure to grow and develop properly. While the social worker gathered family history and observed the family's interactions, physicians administered tests in search for organic causes.

Mr. and Mrs. R were in their early twenties and had not planned this pregnancy. They had been married eighteen months. Mr. R did not come home from work until late every evening although he worked an average number of hours. He did not account for his after-work activities and denied any alcohol or substance abuse. Mrs. R stayed home with the baby and was isolated from friends and family. She spoke quietly, without emotion, and avoided eye contact. Her appearance was unkempt although she was an attractive woman.

In the waiting room the couple did not converse or face each other. Neither attempted to engage Miranda or take her out of the car seat. When she cried, they gave her a bottle without interacting with her or removing her from her seat. During the initial interview, the parents were cooperative, but Mr. R made it clear that child care was his wife's domain and he did not feel he needed to be involved. He felt that Miranda's poor health was Mrs. R's fault.

Ms. G worked to establish a relationship with the family and engage them in the treatment process. She respected the stated family roles of the mother as being in charge of child care and reinforced her abilities to parent Miranda. She also emphasized the important role of the father in keeping his family healthy and functioning well, the importance of a male role model, and the special relationship fathers have with their daughters. Ms. G modeled how to hold Miranda closely and how to face her and make her smile. Then she gave Miranda to Mr. R and encouraged him to try to make her smile. As the parents interacted with Miranda, Ms. G praised their efforts, introduced new activities, and explained what Miranda was learning. At the end of the first session, Ms. G and the parents agreed that they would spend half an hour each day playing with Miranda.

In subsequent sessions, Ms. G continued to encourage the parents to stimulate Miranda socially. Mrs. R joined a community support group for full-time mothers and enrolled Miranda in a parent-tot swim class. A cycle began to develop in which Mr. and Mrs. R engaged Miranda, she would react, and the parents would be encouraged to interact again. Mr. R spent less time away from home and expressed pride in his relationship with his daughter.

As the family gained trust in Ms. G and self-confidence based on Miranda's progress, they were willing to discuss marital problems and other parenting issues. The family continued to strengthen as these core issues were addressed and the family developed a support system. The medical team continued to monitor Miranda's muscle tone and weight, which steadily increased. The parents were instructed in proper nutrition and exercise as well as child development. After several months of intervention, Miranda was approaching normal weight and had made developmental gains. Ms. G's intensive involvement with the family ended, but Mrs. R continues to attend her support group. (Gleason, 1994)

Medically Fragile Children

Disregard for Fetal Development.   Although it has been known for many years that pregnant women sometimes behave in ways that may harm a growing fetus, only recently have some of these behaviors been categorized as fetal abuse or neglect and come to the attention of child welfare agencies. Neglecting to get prenatal care and not acting on sound medical advice are ways that pregnant women might show insufficient care for the developing fetus. Reasons for maternal medical neglect include mental illness, particularly depression, mental retardation, and addiction to chemicals (Kent, Laidlaw, & Brockington, 1997).

Psychoactive substances used by pregnant women can affect the fetus's developing brain and cause learning disabilities and behavior problems. For example, pregnant women who use alcohol excessively may give birth to children who have fetal alchohol syndrome, a constellation of physical, psychological, and cognitive developmental disabilities. Estimates range from 100,00 to 300,00 infants born exposed to illegal substances nationwide (McCurdy & Daro, 1994). The long-term effects of in-utero exposure to psychoactive drugs is not yet known. However, use of drugs and alcohol in pregnancy is often a precursor of other substandard parenting practices to which the child is exposed over the ensuing years, and the cumulative effects on children are very damaging (Zuckerman, 1994).

Scientific advances have made it possible to diagnose problems in the fetus and to treat the fetus directly, raising policy questions concerning the competing rights of the fetus and of the mother. Possible areas of conflict include

> *forced cesarean sections and drug therapies for the benefit of the fetus; required prenatal screenings to detect fetal abnormalities; control over nutrition, alcohol, drug use, smoking, and vitamins; and the prohibition of behaviors considered situationally dangerous to the fetus, such as exercise, intercourse, and some work-related activities. These behaviors that occur within the 'geography of pregnancy' pose varying degrees of risk to the fetus and restrictions on the mother's liberty rights. (Madden, 1993, p. 130)*

Judges, politicians, and other policy makers are tempted to create laws that use restrictions or punishment to force pregnant women to adhere to medical advice as a way of protecting the fetus and ensuring its healthy development. Some women's advocates oppose such restrictions on the grounds that they constitute an impermissible infringement on the rights of women.

State courts are now hearing and deciding child protection cases relating to fetal protection and appear to be "willing to find maternal behaviors such as drug or alcohol ingestion to be abuse given the overwhelming research on the risk of birth defects and developmental delays in children" (Madden, 1993, p. 134). Child welfare workers can expect to become increasingly involved in these cases as petitioners, advocates, and treatment planners.

Some state reporting laws require that newborns who test positive for drugs be referred to child protection agencies. However, evidence of prenatal drug use by the mother may not, by itself, provide sufficient evidence for the child protection investigator to find the mother neglectful or for the child to be subsequently removed from the home. Judges may require additional evidence of ongoing drug use by the mother and demonstrated inability to care for the child (Stein, 1998).

It is necessary to look at the reporting of fetal abuse in relation to the help such action will make available to the parents. If the purpose of such a report is to lay the groundwork for removing the child from the mother's custody immediately after the child's birth, mothers may become wary of using medical services for fear of this outcome. However, if the purpose of the report is to help the mother access services that would otherwise be unavailable, the report will further the effort to have a caring and capable parent for the arriving baby. "In examining the legal and social policy implications of fetal abuse, the question that must be asked is whether society's goal is control of the woman or protection of the baby. Ultimately, the child's interests will best be served by supporting the mother and providing the resources to meet her diverse needs" (Madden, 1993, p. 139).

Children with AIDS. According to the Centers for Disease Control and Prevention (CDC), by early 1995 a total of 8,000 children had been diagnosed with AIDS since the beginning of the epidemic. About 5,000 of these children were under the age of 5. AIDS is transmitted to children in several ways. Infected mothers transmit the disease to their children in utero, during labor and delivery, or postnatally through breastfeeding. Most of those who become infected prenatally have mothers who are intravenous drug users or are sexual partners of intravenous drug users. In addition to prenatal transmission of AIDS, children may become infected from blood transfusions, a particular risk if they have hemophilia. Adolescents are at risk for infection through sexual contact and intravenous drug use.

In 1994, the results of research were announced indicating that the drug AZT could reduce perinatal HIV transmission by as much as two-thirds in some infected women and their babies. For HIV-infected women and their infants to benefit optimally from AZT and other medical treatment, it is best for women to know if they are HIV infected early in pregnancy. They will then be able to seek out and receive the care they need for themselves and for reducing the chances of transmitting HIV to their infants. To help women plan appropriate care, the CDC has published guidelines that call upon medical professionals to provide HIV counseling and voluntary testing for all pregnant women. If women do not receive prenatal care, or if for any reason their HIV status is unknown, the guidelines recommend that HIV testing be offered to the mothers or their babies at or shortly after labor and delivery (Public Health Service, 1995).

Many of the parents of children with AIDS or who are HIV positive are poor, of minority ethnicity, lack medical insurance and health care, and are in ill health themselves. They are very likely to need the services of local child welfare agencies for help in caring for their children. Child welfare agencies are concerned, therefore, not only with the children's current well-being, but also in testamentary planning for them after a parent's death (Stein, 1998). See Chapter 8 for practice approaches to families affected by HIV.

IDENTIFYING CHILD ABUSE

Incidence

Each year in this country substantial numbers of children are beaten, cut, or burned by their caretakers in circumstances that cannot be explained as accidents.

Moreover, their injuries usually result from recurring acts of violence rather than from a single expression of anger or loss of control by the adults who care for them. The severity of such injuries ranges from a mild form of abuse, which may not come to the attention of a doctor or other persons outside the home, to an extreme deviancy in child care resulting in extensive physical damage to the child or even death.

The National Incidence Study found that 614,000 children had been physically abused in the United States in 1993, for a rate of about nine children out of every 1000. After physical neglect, physical abuse is the most common type of child maltreatment. Teenagers aged 12 to 14 are more likely to be abused than any other age group; boys and girls are about equally likely to be physically abused (Sedlak & Broadhurst, 1996).

Definition of Child Abuse

Physical abuse includes such parental actions as hitting with a hand, stick, strap, or other object; punching; kicking; shaking; throwing; burning; stabbing; or choking a child. In the National Incidence Study, examples of physical abuse as observed by professionals included

A 1-year-old child who died of a cerebral hemorrhage after being shaken by her father; a teen whose mother punched her and pulled out her hair; a child who sustained second- and third-degree "stocking" burns to the feet after being held in hot water; a preteen whose grandfather gave her a black eye; a teen who sustained bruises after being beaten with an extension cord; and a 3-year-old who had welts and bruises from being beaten with a belt by his father. (Sedlak & Broadhurst, 1996, pp. 2–10)

Symptoms of Child Abuse

The primary symptom of child abuse is the evidence on the child of suspicious injuries that the parents cannot explain satisfactorily. Children often get bumped or bruised in the course of play and their daily activities, so not all injuries lead to a suspicion of child abuse. Physical indicators of physical abuse include unexplained bruises, welts, bite marks, bald spots, burns (especially cigarette-shaped burns or immersion burns in the shape of a glove or stocking), fractures, and lacerations. Some marks leave the shape of the object that was used to hit the child, such as belt buckles or hot irons (American Humane Association, 1997).

Abused children may also display behaviors that are suggestive of physical abuse. For example, they may be very aggressive or very withdrawn; they may complain of soreness, move uncomfortably, or wear inappropriate clothing to cover their body; they may be afraid to go home or continually run away.

Besharov (1990a) has identified a number of factors that lead to the suspicion that an injury was caused by abuse rather than by an accident. The location of the injury is important: Accidents cause injury to chins, foreheads, hands, shins, and knees, but injuries to other parts of the body, such as thighs, genitals, buttocks, and torso are often caused by physical assault. Corner or joint fractures are usually not caused by accidents but by violent shaking or twisting. Another indicator is the presence of old as well as new injuries. Although physical abuse can occur in a single episode, it is often a pattern of behavior that goes on over time. Children with injuries such as those described here should be reported to the child protection authorities. An accurate determination of the exact cause of the injury can then be made through medical diagnosis and social investigation.

Physical Abuse and Reasonable Discipline

Society sanctions corporal punishment of children. Even though many people believe that any physical punishment of children is wrong and contributes to their emotional maladjustment, all states recognize the rights of parents to use physical force to discipline their children. The difficulty, for those concerned with reporting child abuse, is to differentiate between reasonable discipline and child abuse. Besharov (1990a) has provided guidelines for making this distinction. Discipline would be considered unreasonable if its *"reasonably foreseeable consequence was or could have been the child's serious injury.* This includes any punishment that results in a broken bone, eye dam-

age, severe welts, bleeding, or any other injury that requires medical treatment" (p. 67). He points out that physical punishment of infants is always of concern because infants are not developmentally able to understand the reason for the physical assault on them and because their soft tissues make any physical violence dangerous. A forceful attack on the head of a child of any age is also dangerous and unreasonable punishment. In assessing cases of physical punishment, a number of factors should be considered, including "the child's age and physical and mental condition, the child's misconduct on the particular occasion and in the past, the parents' purpose, the kind and frequency of punishment inflicted, the degree of harm done to the child, and the type and location of the injuries" (p. 68).

Parent and Family Characteristics

Families of abused children tend to be larger than average. The caretakers tend to be young, with higher rates of abuse reported for parents under 27 years than for other age groups (Connelly & Straus, 1992; Wolfner & Gelles, 1993). Poverty is strongly linked to child abuse, as families with low income and parents who are unemployed or lack a high school diploma are at greater risk of child abuse (Wolfner & Gelles, 1993).

Family structure also plays a part in child abuse. Single parents are more likely to abuse their children than are parents who live together. Abuse in single-parent families appears to be linked to poverty and may be explained by the stresses of living with very low income (Gelles, 1989). Single fathers are more prone to abusing their children than are single mothers. Particularly at risk are children in poor, single-father households. Gelles (1989) found that these fathers have a rate of severe violence toward their children—406 per 1,000, a rate higher than for any other group of parents.

Families with nongenetic caretakers have received attention from researchers and those working with abusive families. Most reports show that stepparents are more likely than genetic parents to abuse the children in their home (Gelles & Harrop, 1991). Daly and Wilson (cited in Gelles & Harrop, 1991) have explained this difference by biosocial theory, which holds that people behave in ways to enhance the likelihood of reproductive success. According to this view, people are more likely to care about their own children and avoid squandering effort on the offspring of others. Thus "when people are called upon to fill parental roles toward unrelated children, we may anticipate an elevated risk of lapses of parental solicitude" (p. 197). However, some research shows no evidence that stepparents are more likely than biological parents to abuse children, so more information is needed to clarify this issue (Gelles & Harrop, 1991).

Mothers' boyfriends are often thought to have a high risk of abuse, and although little research has been conducted, Margolin's recent study (1992) supports this view. She points out that boyfriends have characteristics often associated with higher risk of abuse: being nongenetic caretakers, being male, and being located in a single-parent family. She suggests that the lack of an accepted, legitimate social role may put boyfriends on the defensive and make them more likely to react to perceived threats to their authority. Particularly if they are not supporting the family or fulfilling a parental role in other ways, they may be challenged by the children when they try to exercise authority and may then react with violence. Further, a mother's boyfriend may be in conflict with the children because both are competing for the mother's time, and the children may feel that the boyfriend is displacing their own father's role in the family.

Abusive parents are more likely than other parents to have suffered abuse themselves as children. They have learned negative behavioral models of parenting that they duplicate when they themselves become parents. Substance abuse or a psychiatric diagnosis of hostile or explosive personality are linked to higher rates of physical child abuse. Abusive parents tend to see their children in a more negative light than do nonabusive parents. They are apt to have inconsistent child-rearing practices, characterized by sporadic harsh coercion. Family members tend to communicate through arguments and other negative, hostile interactions (Kolko, 1996). See An Ecological View of Child Maltreatment, above, for a more complete discussion of characteristics of maltreating parents.

IDENTIFYING PSYCHOLOGICAL MALTREATMENT

Definition of Psychological Maltreatment

The study and identification of psychological maltreatment, also referred to as emotional abuse and neglect or mental injury, has been hampered by the lack of a sound definition of the problem. In general, psychological maltreatment refers to a repeated pattern of behavior that conveys to a child that he or she is unwanted, worthless, valued only to the extent that he or she can meet others' needs, or is threatened with physical or psychological attack. Recently, Hart, Brassard, and Karlson (1996) developed an operational definition comprising six categories of behavior:

- *Spurning,* including belittling, degrading, shaming, ridiculing; singling out one child to do most of the household chores or to criticize and punish; and publicly humiliating
- *Terrorizing,* including threatening to hurt, kill, or abandon a child; placing a child in recognizably dangerous situations; and threatening or perpetuating violence against a child's loved ones or objects
- *Isolating,* including confining the child or placing unreasonable limitations on the child's freedom of movement or on social interactions with peers and adults in the community
- *Exploiting/corrupting,* including modeling, permitting, or encouraging such antisocial behavior as prostitution, performance in pornography, criminal activity, or substance abuse; encouraging developmentally inappropriate behavior such as parentification or infantilization of the child; extreme overinvolvement or intrusiveness; and restricting cognitive development
- *Denying emotional responsiveness,* such as being detached and uninvolved, interacting only when absolutely necessary, and failing to express love and affection to the child
- *Mental health, medical, and educational neglect,* such as ignoring or refusing to provide for the child's needs in these areas (p. 74)

Psychological maltreatment is related to other forms of maltreatment; it is the psychological dimension of abuse, neglect, and sexual abuse. Terrorizing may be embedded in physical abuse; denying emotional responsiveness may be the psychological aspect of physical neglect. However, psychological maltreatment may also exist by itself, without other forms of maltreatment (Burnett, 1993; Hart, Brassard, & Karlson, 1996).

Incidence

The 1993 National Incidence Study identified 532,000 cases of emotional abuse, 584,100 cases of emotional neglect, and 397,300 cases of educational neglect (Sedlak & Broadhurst, 1996). Boys were more likely to be emotionally neglected than girls, and older children were more likely to be emotionally abused and neglected than were infants and toddlers. Emotional abuse and educational and emotional neglect were more common in low-income families. No ethnic or racial differences were reported

Psychological maltreatment is underreported to child protection agencies, partly because there is confusion as to what constitutes psychological maltreatment and partly because the parental behavior often takes place in the privacy of the home and is unobserved. A view of the actual prevalence of psychological maltreatment may be found in a study by Vissing, Straus, Gelles, and Harrop (1991). In a telephone survey of a nationally representative sample of 3,346 families with children, the researchers reported that two-thirds of U.S. children are abused verbally each year.

Impact on Children

The damage that psychological maltreatment does to children may be more serious than physical abuse, but the damage may not surface for years. "While physical injuries hurt immediately and may be long in healing, some research shows that humiliation, rejections, and verbal assaults devastate the integrity and self-image of the child, with damage lasting well into adulthood" (Baily, 1988, p. 47). Children vary in how

they respond to psychological maltreatment. Some children will direct their anger outward and become physically or verbally aggressive. Other children will turn their pain inward, becoming at risk for suicide, drug and alcohol abuse, and depression.

Children evidencing these behaviors have not necessarily been psychologically maltreated, so by themselves these signs of dysfunction are insufficient evidence that a child is suffering maltreatment. As a general guide for identifying a situation as psychological maltreatment, Besharov (1990) suggests a two-tiered approach. For extreme acts of mistreatment, such as close confinement or torture, the parental behavior is sufficient evidence to ascertain that mistreatment has occurred. For less extreme forms, such as not allowing the child social and emotional growth or failure to provide a loving home, some relationship should be established between the parental behavior and the child's problems. Particularly important in a finding of psychological maltreatment would be the parent's refusal to accept help for the child's emotional problems.

SEXUAL ABUSE OF CHILDREN

Definition of Sexual Abuse

Sexual abuse has been defined as "any act occurring between people who are at different developmental stages which is for the sexual gratification of the person at the more advanced developmental stage" (Faller, 1988a, p. 11). This definition includes situations where both the perpetrator and the victim are children as long as they are at different developmental stages. For example, an adolescent may abuse a latency or preschool-aged child, or a child may abuse another child of the same age who is retarded. This definition assumes that sexual gratification plays a role in sexually abusive interaction. Even though other motivations may be involved, it is the sexual element that distinguishes this form of abuse from others (Faller, 1988a).

Sexual abuse of children includes various types of sexual behaviors. The National Incidence Study counted situations in which oral, anal, or genital penetration had occurred, other forms of genital contact, the touching of other intimate body parts, and inadequate or inappropriate supervision of children's voluntary sexual activities (Sedlak & Broadhurst, 1996). Other definitions may also include noncontact behavior such as "sexy talk," perpetrator's exposure of intimate body parts to the victim, and voyeurism and sexual exploitation in the form of child pornography or child prostitution. Often more than one type of behavior is involved (Faller, 1988a).

Incidence

Every year, many children are sexually abused. The 1993 National Incidence Study found that an estimated 4.5 children per thousand, for a total of 300,200 were sexually abused, according to the study's definition (see above) (Sedlak & Broadhurst, 1996). Many other children are abused but their situation remains unknown. A recent national survey of adults in the United States found that 27 percent of the women and 16 percent of the men disclosed a history of having been sexually abused (Finkelhor, Hotaling, Lewis, & Smith, 1990). In this study, noncontact abuse was counted as well as sexual contact.

In the last twenty-five years, a number of studies have increased public awareness that child sexual abuse is much more prevalent than most people had thought. Reports of sexual abuse have increased greatly since 1976, the first year that national statistics were collected (American Association for Protecting Children, 1986). This trend probably reflects increased willingness of the public to identify and report sexual abuse, not an increase in incidence (Berliner & Elliot, 1996). Unlike other more obvious forms of maltreatment, child sexual abuse can remain hidden unless the victim chooses to disclose the abuse. In the past, victims very often chose to remain silent because they feared retribution from their attacker, because they were ashamed and blamed themselves for the abuse, and because they felt, often correctly, that they would not be believed. With increased public understanding of the dynamics of sexual abuse, victims are more likely than in previous years to tell someone about the abuse, though it is still underreported.

Females are more likely to suffer sexual abuse than males, though the discrepancy is less than was once thought (Cermak & Molidor, 1996). Finkelhor (1993) estimates that about 29 percent of victims are male, though boys are less likely to be reported to child protective services than girls. Children of any age may experience abuse, but studies indicate that vulnerability increases at about age 10. Members of all races appear equally likely to suffer from sexual abuse (Sedlak & Broadhurst, 1996; Finkelhor, 1993). Sexual abuse does appear to be more common among those with very low incomes; the National Incidence Study found that poor children were eighteen times more likely to be sexually abused than children in higher-income families (Sedlak & Broadhurst, 1996).

Family and Parent Characteristics

Some family characteristics place children at greater risk for abuse. Although most stepfathers do not abuse their stepchildren, the presence of stepfathers in the home does increase somewhat the risk of sexual abuse for girls. Children in single-parent families and those in which the mother is disabled, dead, mentally ill, or out of the home for extensive periods are at somewhat higher risk than other children, particularly if there are no other caring female adults for the child to confide in. Other parental characteristics associated with increased risk for children include reliance on punitive discipline, extreme marital conflict, social isolation, disorganized family life, substance abuse, and depression. Children from such families may be emotionally deprived and more susceptible to the ploys of child molesters who offer attention and affection (Finkelhor, 1993; Fleming, Mullen, & Bammer, 1997). Children with disabilities are more likely to be sexually abused than other children (National Center on Child Abuse and Neglect, 1993). These characteristics are too general to be useful in identifying specific cases of sexual abuse. They are perhaps most helpful to social workers in selecting groups of children for prevention programs.

Sexual abuse that comes to the attention of child protective services is usually perpetrated by a family member, neighbor, or friend. The police handle cases of stranger rape and abuse. (See Chapter 5 for a discussion of sexual abuse in day care.) Patterns of sexual abuse vary widely. Multiple abuse episodes are common (Berliner & Eliott, 1996). In Faller's (1988a) clinical sample of 148 Michigan cases, on the average a given perpetrator victimized a child twenty-three times. Sexual contact was the most prevalent type of abuse, with noncontact abuse accounting for only 15 percent of the sexual acts. In more than half the cases, some form of force was used by the perpetrator to gain compliance. In cases where force was not used or threatened, the children had a history of deprivation and abuse, and viewed sexual abuse as a way of receiving nurturance. Victims reported the abuse about three months after it began, on average. About half the perpetrators made some kind of admission or confession to the abuse (Faller, 1988a).

The vast majority of perpetrators are male, though women also commit sexual abuse. Perpetrators are characterized by a failure to control their sexual impulses toward children. They are likely to have suffered sexual abuse themselves as children (Sebold, 1987). As adults they often have ambivalent or hostile relationships with members of the opposite sex and have limited ability to develop intimate relationships or show affection. They also demonstrate excessive self-centeredness, strong dependency needs, and poor judgment (Bresee, Stearns, Bess, & Packer, 1986). Alcohol and drugs, which act as disinhibitors and also weaken guilt pangs, are frequently used by perpetrators.

Mothers of sexual abuse victims frequently have been abused themselves as children, or they were nonvictimized members of incestuous families (Faller, 1988a)

Case Example

The following protective services investigation concerns incestuous attacks by a father on his two young teenage daughters. It illustrates some of the dynamics of incest.

The Smith family was referred to the agency by the police department. When Jill Smith was picked up for shoplifting earlier in the day, she informed the police that she shoplifted in order to get someone's attention. Her father had been making sexual advances toward her, and she was frightened. Jill indicated that the same

thing had happened to her older sister, Nicki. [Nicki, Mr. Smith's daughter by a previous marriage, lives with her mother but saw Mr. Smith on visits.]

When Mr. Smith was questioned by the police, he admitted that he made sexual advances toward both Nicki and Jill. The incident with Nicki occurred about two years ago when she was visiting the family for the summer. She was 13. Mr. Smith had removed her panties, touched her breasts and genital area, and penetrated her vagina with his finger. The incident with Jill occurred about a year later. Mr. Smith kissed her, putting his tongue in her mouth, and he attempted to reach inside her blouse and touch her breasts. He did not try to undress her or convince her to do so.

Nicki returned to her mother's home immediately after her father made sexual advances toward her. She has not visited at her father's home since then.

According to Jill, her father had not made any other sexual advances toward her since that incident. However, he had begun to ask her to sit near him and to put his hands on her thighs even though she asked him not to do it. She described it as "creepy" and was afraid that he would try to become more intimate with her.

After questioning Jill and Mr. Smith, the police referred the case to the state attorney's office. The police also informed Mrs. Smith that she should not leave Jill alone with Mr. Smith under any circumstances.

[The CPS worker interviewed the family and learned that] the family consisted of Mr. Smith (age 39), a sales representative, Mrs. Smith (age 34), director of a day care center, and their daughter, Jill. Jill, age 13, is an eighth grader who is making satisfactory academic progress. The Smiths have been married for 14 years. This is Mrs. Smith's first marriage and Mr. Smith's second.

Mr. Smith moved out of the home immediately after the police filed the report with the agency. He stated that he would continue to live away from home until the agency allowed him to return. He has scheduled an appointment with a psychiatrist at the local mental health center. He denies being sexually attracted to either Nicki or Jill, and he cannot offer any explanation for his sexual advances toward them. "It was just something that happened." He would like to resolve his problems and return to his wife and daughter.

Mrs. Smith cannot understand why her husband made sexual advances toward Nicki and Jill, and why neither girl had told her what had happened. She thought that she had a close relationship with them and that they trusted her. She is ambivalent about her husband; she did not feel that she could accept him as her husband again, but she hated the thought of living without him. She believes perhaps he did it when he was drunk and unable to control himself. Mrs. Smith expressed anger and concern over Jill's shoplifting. She thinks Jill told the police about her father not because she was afraid he would assault her but in order to elicit sympathy and get out of a sticky situation.

Jill reiterated the sequence and details of her father's sexual advances toward her to the child protection worker. She denies she told the police about his advances as a way of distracting attention from the shoplifting. She is adamant that she shoplifted purposely in order to have the opportunity to talk with someone. When asked why she did not simply call the police to report her concerns, she stated that she did not know that a report could be made by telephone. She hopes her mother will divorce her father. She said she hates him for what he did to her, for forcing Nicki to leave the family and therefore depriving her of a sister, and for the embarrassment his frequent intoxication caused her. (Proch, 1982, pp. 49–51)

Identifying Child Sexual Abuse

Child protective service workers may have great difficulty substantiating allegations of sexual abuse, unless the child or a witness discloses the abuse. Physical indicators include torn or stained underclothing, pain or injury in the genital area, difficulty walking or sitting, venereal disease, and frequent urinary or yeast infections (American Humane Association, 1997). Physical evidence exists in only a small percentage of cases, and, if present, may not identify the abuser (Rosenberg & Gary, 1988).

Sexually abused children may exhibit such behaviors as depression, excessive seductiveness, sudden massive weight loss or gain, substance abuse, suicide attempts, hysteria, sudden school difficulties, avoidance of physical contact, devaluation of self, and inappropriate sex play or premature understanding of sex (Browne & Finkelhor, 1986; Hibbard & Hartman, 1992; Chandy, Blum & Resnick, 1996; Harrison, Fulkerson, & Beebe, 1997). By themselves, without physical evidence, these behaviors may not be enough for child protective agencies to substantiate sexual abuse (Oberlander, 1995).

Corroborating witnesses are a good source of evidence, but they rarely exist since sexual abuse usually takes place in secrecy. Perpetrators are likely to deny that they have engaged in sexual abuse, fearing rejection, shame, and criminal prosecution.

Children do not often make false allegations or misunderstand innocent behavior. Interviewing sexual abuse victims requires specialized knowledge and techniques. Children making true allegations can usually give detailed information about the context in which the incidents occurred, and describe the sexual victimization and their own emotional state (see below) (Faller, 1988b; Oberlander, 1995).

Legal Intervention

Legal entities that may intervene in sexual abuse cases include child protective services, law enforcement, the juvenile court, prosecuting attorneys, and the criminal courts. These agencies often are not well coordinated. Children who are sexual abuse victims may suffer additional trauma by having to describe the circumstances of their abuse to many investigators. If the case is criminally prosecuted, children face public court appearances, confrontation with their abuser, and cross-examination. The process may be even more painful if the accused is a family member rather than a stranger, since the child and others in the family may have mixed feelings about criminally prosecuting a close relative of the child. The child wants the abuse to stop but may not understand the need for legal interventions to stop it (Berliner & Barbieri, 1984).

The Child Witness. Decisions on whether to prosecute a sex abuse case through the criminal justice system depend on the plan that is developed to protect the child. When the plan requires that the legal system become involved, several innovative techniques and procedures have gained acceptance as ways to reduce trauma to the child during the investigative phase. These are identified by Duquette (1988) as follows:

1. Adopt the federal rule of evidence establishing the presumption that the child witness is competent. This would eliminate the need to have the child's

trustworthiness as a witness established through interviews with judges and court personnel.

2. Reduce the number of interviews and interviewers the child must endure by coordinating the procedures of different agencies. Videotape the initial interview, so that those who need to know the child's story can watch the videotape. Employ "vertical prosecution," in which a single prosecutor is assigned to the case through all stages of juvenile and criminal court proceedings. Videotapes can often substitute for the child's live testimony at preliminary and grand jury hearings.

3. Allow an emotionally supportive adult, such as a relative or a victim/advocate, to accompany the child through all stages of the legal process. This escort can make the child much more comfortable as he or she encounters unfamiliar people and situations.

4. Allow children with limited vocabularies to use anatomically correct dolls and drawings with which they can show interviewers and judges what happened to them.

5. Expedite the legal process.

Two recent U.S. Supreme Court decisions have clarified procedures courts may use to protect child witnesses during a trial of the accused abuser. The use of closed-circuit television and the admission of statements made to third parties raise constitutional issues. The Bill of Rights grants the accused the right "in all criminal prosecutions . . . to be confronted with the witnesses against him." This confrontation does not directly occur if the witness is on closed-circuit television or if her or his statements are reported by a third party.

In Maryland v. Craig, by a five-to-four majority, the Supreme Court found that because the state has a compelling interest in protecting child victims of sex crimes from further trauma and embarrassment, testimony on closed-circuit television was admissible if the trial judge first determined that this procedure was necessary to protect the welfare of the particular child being called to testify. The Court noted that the Maryland law ensured that all other elements of the confrontation were in place—the oath of the witness, cross-examination, and the opportunity for the court to observe the demeanor of the witness—even though the child was appearing on closed-circuit television.

However, in a related case, the Court limited the ability of prosecutors to present as evidence statements the child made to third parties. In Idaho v. Wright, an Idaho court had admitted as evidence a pediatrician's testimony about his interview with a 3-year-old girl whose mother and a male acquaintance were accused of sexually abusing her. In another five-to-four decision, the Supreme Court ruled that the pediatrician's testimony was not admissible because no evidence had been offered to show that the circumstances of the interview were such as to ensure the reliability of the child's statements to the pediatrician (Greenhouse, 1990). See Interviewing in Child Protective Services, below, for information on forensic interviewing.

Social Work Intervention

The first goal of intervention is to stop the sexual abuse. Victims need protection not only from further abuse but from retribution from family members for disclosing the sexual abuse. Intervention possibilities include permanently removing the child from the home, criminal prosecution of the perpetrator, permanent exclusion of the perpetrator from the family unit, and reunification. Careful assessment of each parent is needed to guide case planning decisions. Mothers who are financially independent, or are able to become so, and who are loving and protective to their children can fruitfully be involved in a family rehabilitation plan. For perpetrators, key factors are their general level of functioning as providers and family members, the extent to which they acknowledge and feel guilty about the abuse they have inflicted on a child, and the duration, intensity, and frequency of the abuse (Faller, 1988c).

Individual and group treatment of sexual abuse victims can be effective in ameliorating the effects of abuse. Therapy is usually supportive and psychoeducational; topics include feelings about the abuse and the offender, education on sex abuse prevention, preparation for court appearances, and development of a support system. Treatment for victims with sexual behavior problems usually follows standard interventions for other types of child behavior problems, with a close focus on changing specific behaviors. Family therapy is often needed because the families function poorly; issues specific to the sexual abuse include helping parents work through their initial negative reactions to the disclosure and to the court procedures, and addressing the psychological distress of siblings, if incest was involved (Berliner & Elliott, 1996).

Cases of child sexual abuse raise particularly difficult issues for professionals in the human services. Many people are bewildered or repelled to learn that adults could have sexual feelings toward children. Discounting or disbelieving the child or rage at the perpetrator are understandable but unhelpful reactions, as are blaming the victim or the mother (Faller, 1988a). Another reason that sexual abuse cases are difficult to manage is that they require the specialized knowledge of several disciplines. The medical, legal, mental health, and child welfare fields each contribute needed knowledge to the resolution of sexual abuse cases. Multidisciplinary teams are an effective way for the community to respond to sexual abuse cases. Through a team approach the resources of the community can be effectively coordinated to arrange a case plan that is most likely to assist the victim's recovery (Faller, 1988a).

Survivors of Sexual Abuse

Children suffer in many ways from sexual abuse. The behaviors listed in the section Identifying Child Sexual Abuse show the powerful effects that these traumatic events can have on children's emotional and social functioning. Sexual behavior is common, manifested by excessive masturbation, sexual play with dolls, sexual statements, or behavior interpreted by others as seductive. These behaviors are the result, not the cause, of the abuse, and they do not imply acceptance of the sexual role by the victim (Faller, 1988a; Ryan, 1996). Many victims, particularly boys, become sexually aggressive, thus perpetuating the abusive cycle by victimizing other children (Burton, Nesmith & Badten, 1997).

The effects of child sexual abuse can last into adulthood. Adults who were abused as children, in comparison to adults with no history of child sexual abuse, are more likely to have sexual disturbance or dysfunction, to report homosexual experiences, to have a diagnosable anxiety disorder, to show evidence of depression, to have difficulty expressing anger, and to have suicidal ideas and behavior. They are also susceptible to revictimization; they may be victims of battering, sexual assault, or rape. Women who have multiple personality disorder or borderline personality disorder often have child sexual abuse or physical abuse in their background. Male victims of sexual abuse are at risk for sexual dysfunction, gender-identity conflict, homosexuality, and an increased risk of becoming sex abuse perpetrators (Beitchman, Zucker, Hood, DaCosta, Akman, & Cassavia, 1992).

Persons who have suffered overwhelming trauma may develop post-traumatic stress disorder (PTSD), which is manifested by recurring memories of the traumatic events through flashbacks, nightmares, and intrusive thoughts. Studies show that between one-third and two-thirds of sexual abuse survivors suffer PTSD, particularly if the abuse was severe and of long duration (Berliner & Elliott, 1996).

Some survivors cope with the overwhelming pain of memories of sexual abuse through dissociation, including disengagement, depersonalization, psychic numbing, and amnesia. Clinicians and survivors report the phenomenon of an adult recalling traumatic abuse that occurred in childhood, after a period of not remembering these events. A controversy has arisen over whether these events did in fact ever happen, or if the adult is fantasizing (Loftus, 1993). Research in this area is still preliminary, but one recent study has found that many adult survivors of abuse report that they had periods in their lives when they could not remember their abuse, suggesting that it is possible for people to repress memories of traumatic events (Melchert & Parker, 1997). More research is needed to understand the relationship between memory and childhood trauma.

The effects of child sexual abuse on adult behavior vary; some survivors report very few symptoms, while others experience overwhelming difficulties. The severity of the adult survivor's problems are related to characteristics of the abuse she or he experienced. Serious, long-term adjustment problems are more likely to be reported by adult survivors who suffered abuse that was of long duration; was accompanied by violence, force, or threat of force; involved penetration; or was committed by a father or stepfather rather than another member of the family or a nonrelative. Abuse perpetrated by a father is more traumatic than other abuse because it involves betrayal and loss of trust. Further, it is usually accompanied by other symptoms of severe family disturbance and may indicate a lack of support and care of the child. Disclosure may increase the trauma to the child if it leads to the breakup of the family or to blaming the victim. The family's response to the abuse may affect the adjustment made by the survivor. Families that are supportive and have higher general functioning can help the victim's recovery. The ability of the mother to be warm, supportive, and caring makes a big difference in the long-term adjustment of her child to the abuse (Beitchman et al., 1992; Berliner & Elliott, 1996).

Ritualism and Child Sexual Abuse

Social workers helping families and children involved in sexual abuse may encounter, at some time in their practice, stories of bizarre, perverse, and sadistic sexual events. Descriptions of these events come from children and from adults recalling past abuse. These descriptions share some commonalities, including sadistic elements such as poking objects into body orifices; costuming, such as robes, masks, and animal paraphernalia; pornography; satanic rituals and belief systems, torture and sacrifice of animals and humans, including infants; and threats of extreme physical violence to ensure silence of the children. Events including these kinds of elements have been termed "ritualistic abuse," defined as "abuse that occurs in the context linked to some symbols or group activities that have a religious, magical, or supernatural connotation, and where the invocation of these symbols or activities, repeated over time, is used to frighten and intimidate the children" (Finkelhor, Williams, & Burns, 1988).

Reliable estimates of the prevalence of ritualistic abuse do not exist, but the National Center for Child Abuse and Neglect recently surveyed professionals regarding their contact with such cases. In this survey, cases of religion-related abuse, such as abuse by clergy, corporal punishment to "beat the devil" out of children, and withholding medical care were included along with cases of ritualistic abuse. The study found that 31 percent of mental health professionals and 23 percent of prosecutors, law enforcement agencies, and child protection agencies who responded to the survey had encountered at least one case of ritualistic or religion-based abuse. The respondents overwhelmingly believed both the ritualistic abuse and the religion-related allegations (Goodman, Bottoms, & Shaver, 1994).

Reports of ritualistic sexual abuse usually involve multiple perpetrators and multiple victims, with males and females about equally likely to be victims (Kelley, 1996).

Therapists are aware of the extremely serious effects ritualistic abuse has on children. Affected children experience greater psychopathology than do other sexually abused children, with increased symptomatology and persistent fears related to their victimization (Jones, 1991; Kelley, 1996).

A central issue for therapists and law enforcement officials is the credibility of those who allege to have been abused. To date, most of the evidence for ritualistic practices comes from children and adults who claim they were abused as children. Very little evidence has come from police to corroborate these stories. Investigations of crime scenes have not found corpses or other physical evidence of violent murders (Lanning, 1991).

In reviewing the evidence to date, Jones (1991) urges a cautious approach. In his view, "some allegations are possibly true despite lack of evidence, others largely or entirely fictitious, and a third group true but with a large overlap of confused and muddled added memories" (p. 167). Kelley (1996) points out that children's memories may be distorted because they were given drugs or because of the overwhelming nature of the events. Perpetrators may purposely use satanic rituals, bizarre paraphernalia, and simulated torture and murder of animals and humans in order to scare children into not disclosing the abuse. More information is needed on ritualistic abuse before questions on the extent and effects of this phenomenon are understood.

Preventive Programs for Children

Widespread attention to sexual abuse of children has led to a variety of books, films, and group interventions aimed at teaching children protective behaviors. The intent is to empower children to an extent that will enable them to exercise more control over what happens to them in an often unfriendly world.

However, these programs have been criticized for inadvertently giving children the understanding that they bear most of the responsibility for protecting themselves from adult behaviors that adults themselves do not understand sufficiently and find abhorrent. Furthermore, teaching "good touches," "bad touches," "private zones," and skepticism of strangers is a simplistic approach. Most sexual abuse of children goes on in the child's own home and involves someone she or he has been led to trust. "Do we not overstate the degree of empowerment that a young child can maintain in such situations and ignore the complexity of the judgments as to when 'good touches' that were first introduced gradually within an atmosphere of affection and trust become 'bad touches?' (Costin, 1985, pp. 210–211).

In a study of the effectiveness of preventive sexual abuse programs, Reppucci and Haugaard (1989) evaluated selected programs for effectiveness and the untested assumptions that guide them. They found that few, if any, of the prevention programs were comprehensive enough to have a meaningful impact in the complex process a child goes through in an attempt to repel an abusive approach or to report the act of abuse. A recent evaluation of prevention programs for middle school–aged children found that children did increase their sense of control over a potentially abusive situation, but this effect was not long-lasting. Older children developed more negative feelings about physical touches of any kind while younger children appeared to be overwhelmed by the subject matter (Taal & Edelaar, 1997).

For a thorough discussion of recent evaluations of child sexual abuse prevention programs, including an analysis of prevention lessons at different ages and discussions of the role of parents, teachers, and public policy in child sexual abuse prevention, see *With the Best of Intentions: The Child Sexual Abuse Prevention Movement,* by Jill Duerr Berrick.

THE PRACTICE OF CHILD PROTECTION

Public child welfare agencies have a number of functions related to the protection of children. They are best known for their work in investigating allegations of abuse and neglect within families. However, public agencies also have other programs that provide protection for children. In every state but Alaska, the protective services agency conducts investigations of abuse and neglect in licensed child care facilities, such as day care, group care, foster family care, and residential care. In this book, discussions of child protection in these settings is provided in the chapters on foster care and day care. In many states, the public agency is also responsible for investigating maltreatment allegations against nonfamily members such as strangers, school employees, coaches, and baby-sitters in nonlicensed facilities. However, many states have assigned responsibility for investigating nonfamilial maltreatment to law enforcement agencies (National Commission, 1990).

Core Services of Child Protective Services

Child protective services in a democracy must provide safeguards for the rights of the child, the parents, and society; the development of clear standards and rules, as a basis for agency intervention, and the proper observance of legal provisions which will help to ensure that decision making is reasonable and based on relevant criteria.

Child protective service (CPS) agencies provide full geographic coverage throughout each state. These agencies vary in size and complexity, but they all should offer a basic set of services to protect children. Guidelines created by the National Association of Public Child Welfare Administrators (1988) emphasize that the purpose of CPS agencies is to assure the child's safety, but that "all decisions and activities should be directed toward enhancing the family's functioning and potential for growth. The agency's policies, procedures, and practices should reflect its focus on 'family based' child welfare" (p. 27).

All CPS agencies provide a basic set of core services, as follows.

Intake.   The intake service receives reports of abuse and neglect. When a member of the community makes a report to CPS, it is the function of intake to take the report and screen it for suitability for investigation (Wells, Stein, Fluke, & Downing, 1989). Agencies may screen out reports if the situation is not within the legally mandated mission of the agency, such as reports of delinquency, family eviction, or mental health problems.

Investigation.   The investigation involves the timely gathering of information, through contact with the child, the parents, and individuals who can provide collaborating information. CPS staff should be trained to conduct an investigation in an objective, thorough, but unobtrusive manner which is sensitive to the difficulties an investigation imposes on the family. The investigation should be done within specified time limits.

Disposition Determination.   The disposition determination involves timely decisions about the status of the abuse or neglect report and the need for further CPS action. In making the disposition, the agency should put the case in one of three categories:

1. Unsubstantiated (not confirmed): No credible evidence of abuse or neglect has been identified.
2. Substantiated (confirmed): Credible evidence has been identified that abuse or neglect has occurred.
3. Family moved—unable to locate: This category records the fact that the agency was unable to take action on the report.

The terms *unsubstantiated* or *not confirmed* are often misunderstood. They mean that the agency was unable to find credible evidence of maltreatment according to its definitions. However, it is quite possible that the family has some deficits in child-rearing that are not serious enough to be labeled abuse or neglect but need attention. In this case, the families should be referred to agencies where they can receive help on a voluntary basis.

Crisis Intervention.   Crisis intervention services should be available from CPS as needed during the time that CPS is engaged with the family, including the intake phase. These services should provide for immediate protection of the child and help families remain together during short-term emergencies. Crisis nurseries, domestic violence shelters, emergency housing, short-term placement with relatives, removal of the perpetrator, and 24-hour emergency homemakers should be available to help stabilize families during a crisis (Gentry, 1994).

Case Planning and Coordination.   Case planning and coordination services are also the responsibility of CPS. For substantiated cases, the agency workers should design an individualized, goal-oriented case plan that clearly sets out what the agency expects parents to do in order to keep their children in the home. The CPS agency may provide the services listed on the case plan, or it may refer families to other service providers through purchase agreements. In either case, the CPS worker stays involved to monitor the parents' progress and coordinate the work of other agencies providing services to the family (Horejsi, 1996). See Chapter 8.

Discharge.   Discharge services are appropriate when the CPS agency determines that one of the following conditions exist: (1) The child is no longer at sufficient risk to warrant CPS involvement; (2) the family is voluntarily receiving services from another agency to strengthen family functioning, and CPS involvement is not needed because the child is no longer at risk; or (3) the agency places the child in substitute care (National Association, 1988).

Central Registries.   A central registry is a centralized data system of child abuse and neglect reports maintained by states in compliance with their child maltreatment reporting laws. These registries are used to aid CPS agencies in their investigations and to maintain statistical information. In addition to CPS agencies, other individuals and organizations such as police officers, court personnel, and physicians may have access. Increasingly, registries are being used as screening devices for child care workers and foster parents. Central registries have come under criticism because the information is not always accurate or updated, and because of concerns about confidentiality for both the reported families and the reporter.

Although this is the model for most CPS agencies, it must be acknowledged that CPS is not always able to carry out these functions well. CPS suffers from high community expectations combined with insufficient resources. Staffing problems exist, including rapid turnover and low morale. Working with resistant, problem parents, with unsatisfactory care of children the pressing concern, is a heavy responsibility, requiring a range of knowledge and acquired competencies. Increased staff-development programs, lower workloads, improved relationships with the juvenile court, and skilled, available supervision are needed if CPS workers are to meet society's expectations of them.

Other considerations also interfere with the ability of CPS to meet the sometimes unrealistic expectations of society. It must be remembered that the job is complex, and most of the decisions are not clear-cut. Very few of the family situations are of the sort that make headlines; most are in the gray area of marginally adequate child care. Also, there is tremendous variation across jurisdictions in the staffing and organization of CPS. This makes it difficult to gain a consensus on what reforms are needed and what the appropriate focus of CPS should be. A further problem is that there are limits on the knowledge we have about how to intervene effectively in some families. Finally, a major difficulty for CPS is that it operates with conflicting values: On the one hand we are protecting children, but we also believe in the integrity and autonomy of the family. This conflict sometimes leaves CPS workers caught in a double bind and at best requires a careful weighing of factors before a decision is reached (Forsythe, 1987).

Nature and Use of Authority

To make effective use of the authority essential to protective services, all those who provide these services must understand its nature and source, and convey it clearly and objectively; the parents, in turn, must be able to some degree to accept the authority if their child care and family functioning are to improve.

Sociolegal and Psychological Authority.   Authority is a complex phenomenon. It is the power to influence or command thought, opinion, or behavior. The key concepts—*power, influence,* and *behavior*—appear in definitions of authority, sometimes used in such a way as to result in a sociolegal emphasis, and in other instances, to focus more on the psychological aspects of authority.

Sociolegal authority stems from the authority of an office, or designated position, and the possession of this formal power is a legitimate one, a matter of right attached to the person who occupies a specified and socially endorsed position in the institutional structure of a society. Psychological authority, the power to bring about change through influencing behavior, is subject to another person's perception of authority and readiness to be influenced, directed, or controlled.

To be effective in protecting children from neglect and abuse, the worker must rely on and use both the sociolegal and the psychological aspects of authority. The worker who extends child protective services is given sociolegal authority by the law authorizing the agency to act in ways that will protect children from neglect and abuse. A caseworker's position and role in a publicly mandated child protective agency, then, embodies a legitimate and formal assignment of authority. This legal aspect of authority in child protection is expressed most centrally in the agency representative's duty to investigate complaints about the care of children, and if substandard care or maltreatment is found, to continue to visit the home until the level of care is improved or until the children are cared for adequately in another setting. Legal authority, then, brings what De Schweinitz and De Schweinitz refer to as the power "to be there" (1964, p. 288).

While legal authority is a necessary element in protective services, it is not sufficient by itself. The power of someone else "to be there" can lead to an oppressive sense of restriction on parents that may only exacerbate their feelings of inadequacy and resistance to change. Whether the agency representative who exercises the authority "to be there" can then motivate neglecting or abusing parents to face their need to change—the first step toward improved child care—will depend in large measure on the extent to which the psychological aspect of her or his authority—that is, knowledge and skill in ways of helping people—is developed and used.

Psychological authority does not imply some intangible quality that a child protective worker may or may not happen to possess; it can be learned through study and experience. It encompasses an understanding of the law and administrative policies that relate to child protection, and of a community's standards in such areas as family life, health, and housing; the capacity to ascertain and evaluate relevant facts; a grasp of the nature of the protective worker's authority and an ability to use it constructively; sound judgment about the capacities of a particular parent; and an ability to develop, interpret, and implement a variety of treatment plans (De Schweinitz & De Schweinitz, 1964).

Use of Authority in Practice. Authority need not be a necessary but negative part of protective services; it can be utilized as a factor to enable inadequate parents to fulfill their responsibility to their children more satisfactorily. The social worker who presents authority skillfully can use it to create a climate of communication that may motivate resistant parents toward change.

Certain difficulties commonly occur, however, and the social worker cannot expect parents to be motivated simply because he or she comes to them representing an agency with authority. This very action may tap a variety of negative feelings on the part of parents, who probably already have had harsh and demeaning experiences with persons in an authoritative relationship. Parents who become clients involuntarily respond to the agency's offer to help in varying ways, such as superficial compliance, hostility, passive resistance, and belligerent defiance. Some parents are deeply distrustful of authority, while others may welcome it as a means of escaping their burdens and responsibilities.

Whatever the parents' initial response, the social worker attempts to accept with empathy the basis for their feelings, but proceeds to identify objectively the areas of child care that are of concern to the community and tells the parents the first concrete tasks they can perform in using the service, for example, taking a child to a medical clinic, getting him or her off to school each day, serving food regularly, following through on a search for employment, or applying for assistance.

One of the principal tasks of the social worker is to develop alternatives, or choices of action, for the parents to consider, and to create opportunities for them to use their own initiative to improve their situation. The social worker must convey that their freedom is restricted in only one direction—they are not free to neglect or abuse their children. Furthermore, the community endorses the right of the parents to receive help in improving their level of child care before declaring them neglectful, and the social worker stands ready to try to help them without resorting to legal action; but the community will not cease to be concerned until the level of child care is improved, and the social worker "will not disappear or be denied" (Moss, 1963, p. 388).

The social worker in protective services cannot expect marked improvement immediately. The parents' problems are very great and their capacities are limited, so expectations, although presented consistently, must be reasonable. Encouragement and endorsement of even very minimal achievements toward improved family functioning are necessary.

In extending protective services, especially to very low-income or "problem" families, one of the most difficult matters facing the agency and its staff is the maintenance of proper balance in the use of authority. The families are difficult, often exasperating and defeating. The children are vulnerable and dependent on others for improvement in their care. Citizens in the neighborhood and community are affronted by the family and expect the social agency to act and effect improvement in the situation promptly. Under such pressure, administrative actions that dangerously erode the right to direct one's own life may come to be regarded as inevitable. It is important that administrative and legal procedures be in place to safeguard the rights of the families, or these rights may be ignored in an effort to respond to the problems they present to their children and to the community.

Informed Consent. Recently, the issue of informed consent has arisen in relation to child protective services. *Informed consent* means that "clients have a right to information about the type of social work treatment they are about to receive and the efficacy of that treatment in addressing their particular problem"

(Regehr & Antle, 1997). However, when social workers are in a position to consider not only the interest of the client but also the needs and interests of the community, an ethical dilemma can arise. Social workers need to be aware of the limits of confidentiality in child protective services practice and to inform their clients that information shared during the course of social service intervention may be used in court. See Chapter 12 for a further discussion of ethical issues in child welfare practice.

Decision-Making in Child Protective Services

A number of factors influence the protective service worker's decision to substantiate a report of abuse and neglect (Jones, 1993).

Direct Evidence. Direct evidence of maltreatment includes physical evidence on the child and in the home; parental admission of maltreatment; the child's statements about the maltreatment; and the reports of witnesses. This evidence is valuable but is not always available. Sexual abuse in particular is often hidden; witnesses are not present, and parents have a powerful motivation to deny that the abuse occurred. Children may not be believed or may not be able to tell the story clearly. The nature and severity of the injury is often used as an indicator of abuse by investigators (American Humane Association, 1996). Medical research has provided useful information on differentiating between intentional injuries and accidents. However, workers may rely too heavily on the severity of the injury in substantiating abuse, and overlook more subtle evidence of chronic maltreatment (Jones, 1993).

Parental Response. The parent's response is often a key factor in the worker's decision to substantiate, particularly when direct evidence is not available. Workers assess the appropriateness of the parent's response to the situation and whether they can provide consistent and credible explanations of the child's injury. Workers are more likely to substantiate abuse if parents are uncooperative with the investigation. Assessing cooperation can be quite subjective; some families are uncooperative because of the way they

perceive they are being treated by the agency; other families may be deemed uncooperative because of their appearance, their ability to verbalize feelings, or because of the worker's class or cultural biases. On the other hand, some parental responses are "red flags" of serious problems. In cases of obvious maltreatment, workers assess the extent to which the parents take responsibility for the maltreatment, express remorse, and acknowledge that the treatment the child received is harmful.

Family and Parent Characteristics. Family and parent characteristics include parental mental or physical illness, substance abuse, prior history of abuse or violence, social isolation, and physical conditions in the home that threaten the child's health and safety.

Child's Vulnerability. Workers are more likely to substantiate if the child is very young, has a serious mental or physical illness, exhibits unusual behavior problems, or is developmentally delayed. Other considerations are the interactions between the parent and child and the child's reaction to the parent, such as flinching or avoiding contact.

Assessing Risk

Risk assessment can be defined as "the systematic collection of information to determine the degree to which a child is likely to be abused or neglected at some future point in time" (Doueck, English, DePanfilis, & Moote, 1993, p. 442). Risk assessment, like an investigation of a report of abused or neglect, involves collecting information on the family. However, risk assessment is oriented toward the future; it attempts to establish the likelihood, or an educated prediction based on a careful examination of the data, that the child will be maltreated at another time. Risk assessment should be a process that continues throughout the course of CPS involvement, from time of initial screening of a report to discharge (National Association, 1988). CPS agencies use risk assessment to prioritize cases for investigation and services, and to help determine the level of service that a family will receive. For example, a family rated as "high risk" would receive immediate and intense interventions, compared with a family rated as "low risk."

Items on risk assessment instruments are those that research and practice experience have shown to predict later maltreatment of a child, whether or not maltreatment has already occurred. The following is a list of risk factors compiled by the National Association of Public Child Welfare Administrators (1988).

- Impact of parental behavior: CPS intervenes if behavior is serious and harmful even if harm to the child is not easily observed, such as, psychological maltreatment or sexual abuse
- Severity of abuse or neglect
- Age and physical and mental ability of the child
- Frequency and recency of alleged abuse or neglect
- Credibility of the reporter
- Location and access of child to perpetrator
- Parental willingness to protect child and cooperate
- Parental ability to protect

Risk assessment instruments hold promise of standardizing data collection and helping to make decisions more consistent within an agency, because all workers will collect the same areas of information on families and share, to some extent, a common understanding on how to assess the information collected (Schene, 1996). Risk assessment instruments are still under development and have received little validation so far when used under field conditions (Doueck, Bronson, & Levine, 1992). Proponents of risk assessment emphasize that they are intended as an aid to worker judgment. They are not yet accurate enough to replace the experienced judgment of seasoned caseworkers and should not be relied on as the sole basis for case decisions (Doueck et al., 1993; Schene, 1996).

Protecting Children in Their Own Homes

A crucial phase of child protective work is the determination that children can be properly protected within their own home, or that they should be in foster care. In the past, practice in relation to neglected and abused children was heavily weighted toward removing them from their homes and placing them in foster care. In

1980, the Adoption Assistance and Child Welfare Act required that states make "reasonable efforts" to preserve families before placing children in foster care. (See Chapter 8.) Social workers today generally hold that it is better to serve children in their own homes, whenever possible, and to extend social work effort to the strengthening of their family situations. Nevertheless, not all children can remain at home, and some must be removed for their own safety and well-being.

Investigators of child abuse agree that parents who inflict serious and extreme assaultive abuse on their children either are not amenable to treatment or require extensive therapy before they can care for their children safely. Consequently, the protective agency must try to remove these severely abused children from their homes in order to prevent further damage (Jones & Alexander, 1987).

Families that show only moderate child neglect are more hopeful in terms of preserving and strengthening the home as a place for the care of children. Parents in these families often have greater adequacy in their social functioning. They can be expected to respond in greater numbers to a constructive use of agency authority and social work services. Also, if a greater investment of the nation's resources is made to alleviate some of the serious social problems that impinge on these families, the outlook should be improved very considerably for strengthening not only these homes but also the level of child care so that foster placements need not occur. (See Chapter 8.) For a discussion of legal issues in maintaining children in their own homes under protective supervision, see Chapter 2.

INTERVIEWING IN CHILD PROTECTIVE SERVICES

Much of the evidence in a child maltreatment investigation comes from the statements of children and the families being investigated. Interviews for the purpose of gathering information are often termed "forensic interviews," in contrast to therapeutic interviews, whose purpose is to alleviate difficulties of the client. Forensic interviews have an approach and practice methodology that are specific to their information-gathering function.

Particularly if the case goes to court, the information from interviews and the way that the interviews were conducted are essential considerations in the admissibility of evidence and the weight given to it. The quality of the interviews that investigators are able to conduct with concerned parties determines, to a great extent, whether or not the investigation will arrive at the truth concerning an allegation of abuse. The circumstances surrounding the interviews are often very difficult; the topics are ones usually considered taboo; children, particularly young ones, may not be able to explain events in a credible way; children of any age may not want to disclose the truth for many reasons or may recant earlier disclosures; parents may be hostile, fearful, defensive, and may be motivated to hide the truth rather than disclose it. For these reasons, social workers involved in interviewing families concerning neglect and abuse need to have expert interviewing skills and be able to use them in adverse circumstances.

Interviewing in child abuse and neglect requires the same basic skills that apply to all social work interviews. Suggestions for special techniques and considerations specific to forensic interviewing in child maltreatment are presented below, based on material from Wiehe (1996), Stattler (1997), and the American Humane Association (1992).

Planning the Interview

The interviewer should prepare for the interview by deciding its purpose, location, and who is to be interviewed, and making special arrangements for children.

Purpose.   It is important to have reviewed all available information prior to the interview and to have a clear idea of what issues are to be discussed. Usually the purpose of the interview is to obtain information on the allegations of maltreatment, and to assess the condition of the child and the possible need for immediate protective intervention.

Interviewing Separately or Together.   In cases of sexual abuse, it is necessary to interview the parents separately. In neglect cases, it may be more advantageous to interview the parents together, to obtain a more dynamic understanding of the family. Children should never be interviewed in the presence of the al-

leged perpetrator. Siblings should be interviewed separately. If the interview is in the client's home, neighbors or relatives may be present when the interviewer arrives. The parents should be consulted on the presence of others at the interview.

Age of Child.   Children under the age of 3 may not have sufficient language skills to be interviewed. Between the ages of 4 and 6 or 7, children can reliably recount events that they have witnessed, but the questioner must be careful not to influence the child's answers. The interview needs to be conducted at the child's developmental level, with consideration for attention span, special words for body parts, and sexual terms (e.g., pee-pee for vagina or penis). Child-sized furniture and a home-like atmosphere will help to make the child comfortable.

Location.   The client's home may provide a convenient and comfortable setting for the family. Safety considerations, however, may indicate an office setting or a neutral meeting place, such as a neighborhood center, for the interview.

Multidisciplinary Interview Centers.   If there are allegations of sexual abuse or severe physical abuse that may involve criminal charges of a perpetrator, it is recommended that children be interviewed in multidisciplinary interview centers. These settings provide a comfortable atmosphere for children, support staff who can answer parents' and children's questions about the investigative and legal processes, and the opportunity for prosecutors and police to observe the interview behind one-way glass or by TV monitor. This procedure will eliminate the need for children to undergo multiple interviews on the painful circumstances of their abuse.

Establishing Rapport

The interviewer attempts to create an atmosphere of calmness and mutual respect as a background for the exploration of the interview topics.

Respect.   Respect of those being interviewed is communicated through using titles, such as "Mr." and "Mrs." and explaining clearly the reason for the interview. "Hello, Mrs. Taylor, my name is Edna Macken-zie and I am from the county children's services agency. I am here because of a report the agency received concerning some burns on Robert. The agency has to look into the report."

Cultural Considerations.   Interviewers of the same ethnic/racial background as the person being interviewed may encounter fewer barriers to effective communication. Understanding the meaning of nonverbal communication, such as lack of eye contact, within the context of the interviewee's culture will reduce the likelihood of misinterpreting behavior. Non-English speakers should have an interviewer who can conduct the session in the interviewee's own language. Using a translator is a less desirable option.

Handling Resistance.   Acknowledging the interviewee's feelings may defuse the situation to some extent. If the client is angry, an approach might be, "I realize that my asking you these questions must make you angry." Passive, mute clients may be encouraged to talk if the interviewer acknowledges their difficulty: "I understand that it may be difficult to talk about such personal, private family matters." If possible, give the client an opportunity to vent anger, fear, and frustration before proceeding with the investigative questions. Ignoring hostility or fear will rarely make them disappear.

Some workers, in an attempt to overcome resistance, give the impression that they are on the client's side against the person who reported the abuse. This misguided strategy will have unfortunate consequences if it develops that the allegations are true and the worker proceeds to substantiate the report. The client will feel betrayed and tricked into disclosing information, and be less likely to cooperate with the agency in a treatment plan. The interviewer must attempt to maintain a neutral position, with a focus on gathering information, while communicating understanding of the difficulties faced by the client.

When interviewing a child, it is important to communicate respect for the parents, even if they have harmed the child. Children may depend on and be strongly attached to the parents, and become resistant if the interviewer appears to be trying to recruit the child into a conspiracy against them or to

rescue the child from them. Children also need reassurance that they are not in trouble, and that the abuse is not their fault. If the child disclosed the abuse, they should be reassured that it was the right thing to do.

Types of Questions

The style of questions can shape the client's response. Certain kinds of questions are more likely than others to elicit fuller responses from clients. With children, there is concern that the interviewer may lead the child to make up events or embellish them. Particularly if the content of the interview may become evidence in a court proceeding, it is important to ask questions that are unlikely to be challenged as having influenced the child's answers. The following categories of questions are adapted from Wiehe (1996) and American Humane Association (1992).

- *Open-ended questions* encourage the client to talk. Examples are, "Why do you think that you were asked to come and see me today?" and "How do you get along with your dad?" The questions may become more focussed, if necessary: "Tell me about how Bobby got those marks on his buttocks" and "What happened on the day your daddy baby-sat?"
- *Probing questions,* also in an open-ended format, encourage the client to explore the information at deeper levels; for example, "Mr. Jones, you mentioned that you sometimes get pretty upset with Elizabeth. What do you do when that happens?" "Mrs. Baker, you said that you got upset when Andrew told you that he had shoveled the snow off the sidewalk, but he had not. What did you say to him?" "What did Andrew do then?"
- *Close-ended questions* encourage the client to give only yes or no answers and do not tend to elicit information. In general, they are to be avoided. "Did you hit him at that time?"
- *Refocusing the interview.* If the client talks incessantly, the interviewer may need to interrupt and restate the purpose of the interview. "Mrs. Allen, we need to get back to the main point here. Please tell me what you have tried to do about making sure that Stuart has clean school clothes."

- *A continuum of types of questions for children.*
  This continuum, developed by Kathleen Faller, a
  nationally recognized therapist and expert witness in the area of sex abuse, shows the types of
  questions that elicit more or less confidence in
  the accuracy of the child's answers. Open-ended
  questions and focused questions are preferable in
  forensic interviewing, because the children's answers are less likely to be influenced by the interviewer. In contrast, in multiple-choice and
  yes/no questions, the interviewer is providing information to the child which could influence his
  or her answers. Further, a child might select an
  answer in order to get the interview over with or
  for other reasons, but the answer may not reflect
  the reality of the child's experience. Sometimes,
  multiple-choice and yes/no questions are necessary, because more general questions may not
  elicit a response. They are particularly appropriate as a follow-up to a child's earlier disclosure,
  in response to an open-ended question, as the example in Figure 7.7 illustrates.
- *Use of interview aids with children.* Particularly
  with younger children, interviewers use drawings, dolls, puppets, and other props as a means
  of communication. The use of anatomically correct dolls has been criticized as leading children
  into making statements, or implying sexual activity through their play, about sexual events that
  may not, in fact, have happened. In general,
  anatomically correct dolls should not be used in
  an interview until *after* the child gives indication
  of sexual abuse and is able to verbalize some specific details of the victimization (American Humane Association, 1992).

ASPECTS OF COMMUNITY SUPPORT
AND INFLUENCE

The way in which a protective agency discharges its
responsibilities is influenced not only by the quality
of its staff and its organization and structure, but also
by factors within a community. Public attitudes and
level of community support affect the responses of
government, the professions, and voluntary associations to protect children from abuse and neglect.

Multidisciplinary Teams

An increasingly prevalent model for organizing community professionals in protective services is the multidisciplinary team. A 1983–1984 survey found that
every state had at least one multidisciplinary team,
with over 900 teams identified nationwide (Kaminer,
Crowe, & Budde-Giltner, 1988). The development of
this approach continues to be characterized by a diversity of forms and purposes with little empirical
data attesting to their efficacy. In the 1983–1984 survey, all teams included a social worker; other disciplines identified by at least half the teams were
psychologists, nurses, physicians, lawyers, educators,
and law enforcement and public health representatives. Most teams were involved in assessment and
case planning, but others were involved in providing
crisis service, case management, direct services to the
family and child, public education, community organization and program planning, and advocacy. The
team can work out of a hospital or be affiliated with
a private or public child welfare agency (Bross, Krugman, Lenherr, Rosenberg, & Schmitt, 1988).

The use of a multidisciplinary team in relation to
a particular case provides flexibility in the kinds of
arrangements that can be made when a family crisis
occurs. It helps to prevent a service from becoming
wholly committed to traditional methods or narrow
professional identifications because the variations in
background, training, and special interests of the team
members can be used to foster a climate that will stimulate innovation and response to newly perceived
needs of families. It provides an opportunity for mutual support among staff members, which can lessen
their need to receive some appreciation from a family
or see some sign of progress prematurely. It can spread
responsibility for crucial decision making—for example, for deciding when an infant can safely be left in
the care of a parent who has injured him or her.

Advocacy Organizations

Tremendous public and media attention has been given
to the plight of abused and neglected children since the
reporting laws were passed in the early 1970s. Public
concern for these children has found expression in a
number of national advocacy groups. The Children's

FIGURE 7.7   Questioning Typology by Kathleen Faller

OPEN-ENDED		**MORE CONFIDENCE**

Type of Question	Definition	Example

———————— MOST PREFERRED QUESTIONS ————————

Type of Question	Definition	Example
General question	Open-ended inquiry about the child's well-being or salient issues; it does not assume an event or experience.	How can I help you? How are you feeling today? Is there something I can help you with?
Invitational question	Open-ended inquiry that assumes there may be an event or experience.	Can you tell me everything you can remember about going to the doctor? (Saywitz et al.) I heard something may have happened to you. Tell me about it as best you can. (Boychuk)

———————— PREFERRED QUESTIONS ————————

Focused question	One that focuses the child on a particular topic, place, or person, but refrains from providing information about the subject. (Myers, Goodman, & Saywitz)	Can you tell me about daycare? Tell me about your dad? (Are there things you like about him? Are there things you don't like about him?) Can you tell me about penises? (Who has one? What are they for? Did you ever see one? Whose did you see?)
Follow-up strategies	Strategies that encourage continued narrative.	
1. Facilitative cue	Interviewer gesture or utterance aimed at encouraging more narration.	Un Huh (affirmative) Anything else? And then what happened?
2. Specific question	Follow-up inquiry to gather details about the child's experience.	Do you remember where it happened? What were you wearing? Were any clothes taken off? Did anything come out of the penis?

———————— LESS PREFERRED QUESTIONS ————————

Multiple choice question	A question that presents the child with a number of alternative responses from which to choose.	Did he do it one time, two times, or lots of times? Did it happen in the daytime or night or both?
Externally derived question	A question that relies on information not disclosed in the child interview.	Do you remember anything about a camera? Did John say anything about telling or not telling?
Direct question	A direct inquiry into whether a person committed a specific act.	Did John hurt your peepee? Was your father the one who poked your butt?
Repeated questioning	Asking the same question two or more times.	Did anything happen to your pecker? Do you remember if anything happened to your pecker?

———————— LEAST PREFERRED QUESTIONS ————————

Presumptive question	A question that takes for granted facts.	
1. Leading question	A statement the child is asked to affirm.	Isn't it true that your brother put his penis in your mouth?
2. Misleading question	A question that assumes a fact that is not true, which the child is explicitly or implicitly asked to confirm.	What color scarf was the nurse wearing? (When she wasn't wearing one) Show me where the doctor touched you. (When he didn't touch)
Coercion	Use of inappropriate inducements to get cooperation or information.	If you tell me what your father did, we can go for ice cream. Don't tell my boss that I was playing. (And gives child a piece of candy)

CLOSE ENDED		**LESS CONFIDENCE**

Source: Kathleen Faller, Ph.D. (1990). Reprinted with permission.

Trust Fund provides state revenue to fund programs to prevent child abuse and neglect, bypassing the traditional legislative appropriation process. Kansas was the first state to establish such a trust in 1980; currently, most states have established trusts. Revenues for the trust program are raised in various ways in the different states, including surcharges placed on marriage licenses, birth certificates, or divorce decrees, or voluntary check-off plans using state tax refunds. The common feature of these methods is that they are separate from the ordinary state tax and revenue-collecting processes, and the money is earmarked especially for child abuse and neglect prevention.

Responsibility for administering the trusts rests with community boards made up of public representatives and, in some states, heads of relevant governmental departments. These boards provide small grants to community groups to fund child abuse prevention programs. Among the projects are resource centers for preschoolers and their parents in high-risk neighborhoods, parent education programs from pregnancy through the infant's first year, training of volunteers to act as advisers to new parents, and play programs for children of violent homes (Cohn & Birch, 1988). These programs, proponents believe, have given the public a way to respond meaningfully to the child abuse problems in their own communities. So far, the trust programs have not appeared to deflect state legislatures from continuing more substantive funding appropriations for ongoing state programs.

The American Humane Association: Children's Division is a private, nonprofit organization located in Denver, Colorado. Founded in 1877 to protect children from abuse and neglect, its mission continues to be the protection of children and the prevention of child maltreatment. Its chief functions are to provide information on child maltreatment and to be an advocate for children and families in relation to effective service delivery systems in all communities.

The National Committee to Prevent Child Abuse is a volunteer-based organization dedicated to involving all concerned citizens in actions to prevent child abuse. Donna J. Stone, a Chicago philanthropist, founded the Committee in 1972 out of concern for the number of infant deaths that appeared to be caused by inflicted injury. The Committee's mission is to prevent child abuse through prevention programs, public awareness, education and training, research, and advocacy.

A backlash to child maltreatment investigations has developed in the formation of a citizen's organization called Victims of Child Abuse Laws (VOCAL), founded by people who stated that they were wrongly accused of abuse. It has lobbied state legislatures to drastically decrease the scope of child protective service investigations. The public also became aware of the possibilities of false accusations and false denials from caretakers, perpetrators, and sometimes children, particularly in the context of child custody disputes. However, these counter-trends do not appear to have lessened public interest in reducing child abuse.

The National Center on Child Abuse and Neglect, though not an advocacy group, is included here because of the national leadership it provides in the area of child maltreatment. Established by the Child Abuse Prevention and Treatment Act of 1974, it is the primary federal agency with responsibility for assisting states and communities in developing capacity for child abuse prevention, identification, and treatment. The National Center allocates child abuse and neglect funds appropriated by Congress and coordinates federal child abuse and neglect activities. The National Center is located within the Department of Health and Human Services, Administration for Children, Youth, and Families.

TRENDS AND ISSUES

Due Process for Parents and Children

What is the appropriate scope of state intervention into parental child rearing practices? Some contend that neglect and abuse jurisdiction should be narrowed, giving a high degree of recognition to parental autonomy. They believe that, in the wake of large-scale public awareness campaigns, child protective service agencies have become overwhelmed with reports on relatively minor situations involving poor parenting practices. Besharov (1990b, p. 37) takes this view: "Many unfounded reports involve situations in which the person reporting, in a well-intentioned effort to protect a child, overreacts to a vague and often misleading possibility that the child may be maltreated. Others involve situations of poor child care that, though of legitimate concern, simply do not amount to child abuse or neglect." Current concern about the use of computerized central registries also relates to the issues of fairness, due process, and confidentiality for accused parents.

Others advocate extending the reach of child neglect and abuse laws. For example, Finkelhor (1990) disputes Besharov's view that the system is casting too wide a net. Rather, he says, "the picture is of large numbers of seriously abused children, whose families and abusers have managed in past years to successfully evade detection, now finally being discovered by professionals and community members who have been sensitized to the problem. Many of these serious cases are still, for one reason or another, not getting into or are being rejected by the CPS system. The big overload of new cases does indeed make it difficult for CPS to work efficiently. But to deal with these problems, the system may need to be expanded rather than cut back" (p. 26).

Many social workers and juvenile court judges take a position somewhere between the views of Besharov and Finkelhor, often with considerable ambivalence. Clearly, some level of unsubstantiated reports is appropriate and necessary. The system depends on persons in the community calling in to report situations about which they have reasonable suspicions that child maltreatment has occurred. Only an investigation can reveal the truth of the situation, so it is reasonable to expect that some reports will turn out to be unfounded. There is agreement that the system could be improved in order to better protect children and become more proficient at targeting cases for intervention. Various reforms have been suggested that would help agencies and those reporting to become more expert at assessing situations and screening those cases that appear to need services. More education would help professionals identify cases appropriate for a report to child protective services. Clarification is needed on what kinds of evidence would justify a report, and on what kinds of situations

can be considered abusive or neglectful, particularly in the area of psychological maltreatment. Agencies need to continue to develop procedures for prioritizing cases for investigation and for screening reports at intake, to ensure that potentially serious situations are responded to in a timely way.

Child Protective Services in a Comprehensive System

A problem related to the issue of assuring due process for parents is the one of configuring child protective services as a part of a comprehensive system of child welfare. Many are concerned that child protective services has absorbed a large proportion of resources available to child welfare, leaving gaps in services. Kamerman and Kahn (1990), in a survey of state child welfare agencies, found that the activities of public child welfare agencies focus on investigating allegations of abuse and neglect and on treating those families for whom maltreatment is substantiated. Families with less severe problems are not able to find help. Resources may also have become more limited for needed foster care and adoption services for children whose families cannot maintain a minimally sufficient level of care.

Many forces have combined to create the current situation. The passage of the reporting laws in the 1970s caused a huge increase in child abuse and neglect reports. Public awareness campaigns contributed to the realization that many children lived in perilous or unnurturing environments in their own homes. At the same time, cutbacks in federal funding during the Reagan years caused services to families outside the child protection system to wither. During this same time period, social problems became exacerbated, with the drug epidemic, AIDS, and a declining standard of living for young families increasing the vulnerability of children to harm.

There have been a number of proposals for reconfiguring the child welfare system so that child protective services becomes part of a larger whole rather than the force driving the entire system. The National Association of Public Child Welfare Administrators (1988) has recommended that child protective services limit intake to a core of family situations, including physical and sexual abuse, serious psychological maltreatment, and physical neglect if the parent has the means to provide and refuses to do so. Under this plan, other service systems would be responsible for other family and child problems, in which help is clearly needed but not necessarily the authoritative approach of protective services. Situations that would be referred to other agencies include neglect cases in which the parent wants to provide for the child but has inadequate resources, and various child-centered problems, including status offenses and school truancy. The U.S. Advisory Board on Child Abuse and Neglect has called for a national child protection strategy that integrates the contributions of social service, mental health, and educational and legal professionals into a service delivery system offered at the neighborhood level (U.S. Advisory Board, 1993).

As the child welfare system attempts to adapt to the increased intake of cases generated by reports to child protective services, children and their families remain under-served by a system that is strained beyond capacity. Simply reorganizing existing services will not be enough to respond to the needs of abused and neglected children; a more comprehensive approach is needed that offers more and higher-quality services to these children and their families.

Staffing Child Protective Services

The quality of the staff in CPS is a critical factor in the quality and effectiveness of services provided to people whose lives are in turmoil, pain, and danger (Terpstra, 1992). Child protective service workers have an exceedingly difficult job. They deal daily with the misery and exploitation of some of society's most vulnerable members, children, and their families, who failed to protect them or who harmed them. They must confront the mistrust, hostility, and sometimes aggression of family members who may feel threatened by an investigative process that implicates them as having failed as parents. Workers function in a service system that is overstrained; hospital emergency rooms, the juvenile court, mental health agencies, and the public schools all may be overwhelmed with the seemingly insurmountable problems of those who need help.

The child protection agencies themselves usually have too few resources to help families or to provide the kinds of support the workers need to maintain a professional level of performance in their difficult work. The large increase in child protection cases has not been matched by increases in staffing. Many agencies report difficulty in recruiting staff because of low salaries and high caseloads. Lack of resources has forced some agencies to hire staff with no experience and, in some cases, without a college degree, even though the work they perform requires them to make accurate assessments about confusing and highly charged family situations (National Commission, 1990). Workers complain that they do not get the support they need, yet are blamed by the public and their own administrators if a child on their caseload is harmed in a situation which, in retrospect, seemed preventable.

A major challenge for the coming decade is to improve the quality of staff and the conditions in which they work. Some have called for a return of the close alliance between the social work profession, including social work education, and child welfare services. Social work is the conceptual parent of child welfare services, but "in recent decades that connection has largely been lost, as has much of the conceptual social work base" to child protective services (Terpstra, 1992). To remedy this situation, schools of social work are renewing their commitment to make social work education relevant to the needs of public child welfare services, and agencies are becoming increasingly committed to hiring staff with a social work education and to involving schools of social work in ongoing staff training (Briar, Hansen, & Harris, 1992). These efforts, even when fully implemented, will not be enough to ensure a high quality of child protective services. Increased resources for agencies are needed as well, so they can hire qualified staff, assign them manageable caseloads, and offer competent supervision in well-managed agencies.

CHAPTER SUMMARY

Media reports of abused and neglected children disturb us and make us aware of the appalling conditions in which many children live. Child protective services represents the organized response of each community to the circumstances of mistreated children and their families.

The actual number of children abused or neglected is not known, but it is thought that the number is increasing. About three million children are reported for some form of child abuse or neglect each year, of whom one million are found, after investigation, to have suffered maltreatment. Another source of data, the national incidence studies, has found that about three million children are abused and neglected, many of whom are never reported to child protective services. All surveys point to the conclusion that large numbers of children in the United States are harmed or endangered by their parent's mistreatment of them.

Types of maltreatment are neglect (including physical neglect, abandonment, lack of supervision, and medical neglect), which comprise more than half of all cases of mistreatment; abuse, comprising about a quarter of all cases of mistreatment; sexual abuse; psychological maltreatment; and educational neglect. Many times, more than one type of maltreatment is involved.

Violence toward children has been pervasive in American history. During the nineteenth century, concerned citizens formed Societies for the Protection of Cruelty to Children, to investigate instances of child abuse and report them to the police. These Societies (SPCCs) are the precursors of today's child protective services agencies. In the 1960s, the "discovery" of the "battered child syndrome" led to the passage of the Child Abuse Prevention and Treatment Act in 1974 and ushered in a new era of child protection.

Today all states have reporting laws, which require professionals to report all cases of suspected child abuse or neglect to CPS. However, the implementation of these laws is hampered by the lack of clear definitions of types of child abuse and neglect. Factors to be considered in definitions are the severity of the harm, the cumulative harm to the child over time, endangerment of the child even if the child has not yet suffered observable harm, intentional harm versus accidental harm, and cultural issues.

There are problems with over-reporting and under-reporting child maltreatment. Only about a third of all reports are substantiated, which leaves many parents feeling that they have suffered an invasion of privacy and the stigma of having been the focus of a child abuse investigation. On the other hand, many cases of maltreatment are not reported because the potential reporters believe that reporting will not help the family and may make matters worse.

The causes of child maltreatment are complex and overlapping, and are best understood from an ecological perspective. No one factor causes abuse or neglect, but rather a combination of circumstances. Risk factors include social conditions, such as deprived, dangerous neighborhoods with few supports or social services and widespread societal tolerance for interpersonal violence. Poverty is highly associated with all forms of maltreatment and is the single most important risk factor for children. Race and ethnicity do not appear to be related to maltreatment, though people of color are more likely to be reported to CPS. Many family and parent characteristics and conditions are associated with abuse and neglect, including single parenthood, mental illness, substance abuse, domestic violence, social isolation, and a history of having been mistreated as children (though many children who are maltreated do not grow up to mistreat other children). Maltreating parents tend to lack empathy, express negative attitudes and hostility to their children, lack the ability to form attachments, and use the children to meet their own needs.

Children suffer in many ways from maltreatment, including death, permanent injury, and impaired physical, cognitive, social, and emotional development.

All child protective service agencies offer a set of core services, including intake, investigation, and case planning. While investigating families, the workers must also assess the current and future risk to the child, and take steps to remove the offender or child from the home when necessary. The preference is to maintain the child in his or her own home, if possible, by providing services to help the family. CPS workers have the legal authority to intervene in the lives of families and must develop strategies for using that authority to help parents achieve a minimally sufficient level of care.

A major issue today is the appropriate scope and authority of child protective services. One view is that CPS should only be involved for serious cases of child maltreatment and that less serious situations should be referred to other social service agencies. It is thought that this would protect families from needless, intrusive investigations and free up resources for the most serious situations. Others believe that CPS should be expanded, since many abused and neglected children are not receiving any services and may, in fact, be unknown to any social service agency. Many policy makers believe that CPS must become more connected to the community, through partnerships with schools, police, and neighborhood groups, to form a comprehensive system for protecting and serving children.

FOR STUDY AND DISCUSSION

1. Discuss the factors contributing to the underreporting of sexual abuse. What steps could be taken to improve the reporting?

2. Explain what you see as the principal causes of child neglect or physical abuse, and what in your opinion is a major direction for treatment.

3. Differentiate between sociolegal and psychological authority. Enumerate guidelines or ways of presenting and using authority constructively.

4. Discuss the feasibility of having two levels of definitions of child abuse and neglect: narrow definitions of the various categories of maltreatment for legal purposes and broad definitions for the purpose of determining the need for services. Give examples of narrow and broad definitions for one of the categories of child maltreatment.

5. In view of the characteristics of neglected and abused children as you have come to see them, make suggestions for new treatment approaches in direct work with such children.

6. Draw together what you regard as significant aspects of agency organization and community support if effective protective services are to be provided. Then study the protective service agency in your community in relation to these aspects.

7. Read transcripts or watch videotapes of interviews with children or adults in protective service investigations. Observe and comment on the techniques used by the interviewer.

8. Obtain a risk-assessment guide or a protocol for a child maltreatment investigation from your local child protective services agency. Comment on its usefulness as a decision-making guide.

FOR ADDITIONAL STUDY

American Humane Association. (1996). *Guidebook for the visual assessment of physical child abuse.* Englewood, CO: Author.

Berrick, J. D. (1997). Child neglect: Definition, incidence, outcomes. In J. D. Berrick, R. Barth, & N. Gilbert, (Eds.). *Child welfare research review, vol. 2* (pp. 1–84). New York: Columbia University Press.

Briere, J., Berliner, L., Bulkley, J. A., Jenny, C., & Reid, T. (Eds.). (1996). *The APSAC handbook on child maltreatment.* Thousand Oaks: Sage.

Center for the Future of Children. (1998, Spring). *The future of children: Protecting children from abuse and neglect.* Vol. 8, No. 1. Los Altos, CA: The David and Lucille Packard Foundation.

Faller, K. C. (1988). *Child sexual abuse: An interdisciplinary manual for diagnosis, case management, and treatment.* New York: Columbia University Press.

Helfer, R. E., & Kempe, R. S. (1987). *The battered child* (4th ed.). Chicago: University of Chicago Press.

Melton, G. B. & Barry, F. D. (Eds.). (1994). *Protecting children from abuse and neglect.* New York: Guildford Press.

National Association of Public Child Welfare Administrators. (1988). *Guidelines for a model system of protective services for abused and neglected children and their families.* Washington, DC: American Public Welfare Association.

Sedlak, A. J. & Broadhurst, D. D. (1996). *Third national incidence study of child abuse and neglect.* Washington, DC: U.S. Department of Health and Human Services.

Wiehe, V. R. (1996). *Working with child abuse and neglect: A primer.* Thousand Oaks, CA: Sage.

INTERNET SITES

American Humane Association   This national advocacy organization for abused and neglected children has numerous resources on policy and practice in child protective services. http://www.americanhumane.org

National Clearinghouse on Child Abuse and Neglect Information   This is a national resource for professionals seeking information on the prevention, identification, and treatment of child abuse and neglect, and related child-welfare issues. The National Center for Child Abuse and Neglect may be accessed at this Web site. The site contains numerous resources and links to other sites. http://www.calib.com/nccanch

National Committee to Prevent Child Abuse.   This is the Web site of a national advocacy organization whose purpose is to prevent and reduce child maltreatment. The site has numerous resources for advocates, including information packets, publications of statistics and trends, and lists of local chapters. http://www.childabuse.org

Children's Bureau, Administration for Children, Youth, and Families, U.S. Department of Health and Human Services.   Contains information on federal initiatives in foster care and adoption and statistics, child abuse and neglect, and other programs. http://www.acf.dhhs.gov/programs/cb/

REFERENCES

Abused children in America: Victims of official neglect. A report of the Select Committee on Children, Youth, and Families, U.S. House of Representatives. (1987). Washington, DC: U.S. Government Printing Office.

Ahn, H. N., & Gilbert, N. (1992, September). Cultural diversity and sexual abuse prevention. *Social Service Review, 66,* 410–427.

American Academy of Pediatrics. (1988). Religious exemptions from child abuse statutes. *Pediatrics, 81* (1) 169–171. Cited in Korbin, J. E. (1994). Sociocultural factors in child maltreatment. In G. B. Melton & F. D. Barry (Eds.), *Protecting children from abuse and neglect: Foundations for a new national strategy.* New York: Guilford Press.

American Association for Protecting Children, Inc. (1986). *Highlights of official child neglect and abuse reporting 1984.* Denver: American Humane Association.

American Humane Association. (1963). *Guidelines for legislation to protect the battered child.* Denver: American Humane Association, Children's Division.

American Humane Association. (1984). *Trends in officially reported child neglect and abuse.* Denver: American Humane Association, Child Protection Division.

American Humane Association. (1992). *Helping in child protective services.* Englewood, CO: Author.

American Humane Association. (1996). *Guidebook for the visual assessment of physical child abuse.* Englewood, CO: Author.

American Humane Association. (1997). *Guidelines to help protect abused and neglected children.* Englewood, CO: Author.

Ards, S., Chung, C., & Myers, S. (1998). The effects of sample selection bias on racial differences in child abuse reporting. *Child Abuse & Neglect, 22*(2), 103–115.

Azzi-Lessing, L., & Olsen, L. J. (1996). Substance abuse–affected families in the child welfare system: New challenges, new alliances. *Social Work, 41*(1), 15–23.

Baily, W. (1988). Defining emotional maltreatment in child protective services. In National Association of Public Child Welfare Administrators, *Guidelines for a model system of protective services for abused and neglected children and their families.* Washington, DC: American Public Welfare Association.

Barden, J. C. (1990, February 5). Toll of troubled families: Flood of homeless youth. *New York Times,* A1, B7.

Beitchman, J. H., Zucker, K. J., Hood, J. E., DaCosta, G. R., Akman, D., & Cassavia, E. (1992). A review of the long-term effects of child sexual abuse. *Child Abuse & Neglect, 16,* 101–118.

Belsky, J. (1993). Etiology of child maltreatment: A developmental-ecological analysis *Psychological Bulletin, 114,* 413–434.

Berliner, L., & Barbieri, M. K. (1984). The testimony of the child victim of sexual assault. *Journal of Social Issues, 40*(2), 125–137.

Berliner, L., & Elliott, D. M. (1996). Sexual abuse of children. In J. Briere, L. Berliner, J. A. Bulkley, C. Jenny,

& T. Reid (Eds.). *The APSAC handbook on child maltreatment* (pp. 51–71). Thousand Oaks, CA: Sage Publications.

Berrick, J. D. (1991) *With the best of intentions: The child sexual abuse prevention movement.* New York: Guilford.

Berrick, J. D. (1997). Child neglect: Definition, incidence, outcomes. In J. D. Berrick, R. P. Barth, & N. Gilbert (Eds.). *Child welfare research review, vol. 2,* pp. 1–12. New York: Columbia University Press.

Berrick, J. D., Needell, B., Barth, R. P., & Jonson-Reid, M. (1998). *The tender years: Toward developmentally sensitive child welfare services for very young children.* New York: Oxford University Press.

Besharov, D. (1990a). *Recognizing child abuse: A guide for the concerned.* New York: Free Press.

Besharov, D. (1990b). Gaining control over child abuse reports. *Public Welfare, 48,* 34–41.

Besharov, D. J., & Laumann, L. A. (1996). Child abuse reporting. *Society, 33*(4), 40–46.

Bresee, P., Stearns, G. B., Bess, B. H., & Packer, L. S. (1986). Allegations of child sexual abuse in child custody disputes: A therapeutic assessment model. *American Journal of Orthopsychiatry, 56*(4), 560–569.

Briar, K. H., Hansen, V. H., & Harris, N. (Eds.). (1992). *New partnerships: Proceedings from the National Public Child Welfare Training Symposium, 1991.* Miami: Florida International University.

Bross, D., Krugman, R., Lenherr, M., Rosenberg, D., & Schmitt, B. (Eds.). (1988). *The new child protection team handbook.* New York: Garland.

Browne, A., & Finkelhor, D. (1986). Impact of child sexual abuse: A review of the research. *Psychological Bulletin, 99,* 66–77.

Burnett, B. (1993). The psychological abuse of latency age children: A survey. *Child Abuse and Neglect, 17,* 441–454.

Burton, D. L., Nesmith, A. A., & Badten, L. (1997). Clinician's views on sexually aggressive children and their families: A theoretical exploration. *Child Abuse & Neglect, 21*(2), 157–170.

Carroll, C. A., & Haase, C. C. (1987). The function of protection services in child abuse and neglect. In R. E. Helfer & R. S. Kempe (Eds.), *The battered child* (4th ed., pp. 137–151). Chicago: University of Chicago Press.

Carter v. Kaufman, 8 Ca.App.3d 783, 87 Ca. Rptr. 678 (1970), *cert. denied,* 402 U.S. 964 (1971). (J. Black dissenting in separate opinion at 402 U.S. 954, 959).

Cermak, P., & Molidor, C. (1996). Male victims of child sexual abuse. *Child and Adolescent Social Work Journal, 13,* 385–400.

Chandy, J. M., Blum, R. W., & Resnick, M. (1996). History of sexual abuse and parental alcohol misuse: Risk, outcomes and protective factors in adolescents. *Child and Adolescent Social Work Journal, 13* (5), 411–432.

Child Abuse Prevention and Treatment Act, Public Law 93–247, 42 U.S. C. 5101 (1974), sec. 3.

Child Welfare League of America. (1990). *Crack and other addictions: Old realities and new challenges.* Washington, DC: Author.

Children's Bureau. (1963). *The abused child—Principles and suggested language for legislation on reporting of the physically abused child.* Washington, DC: U.S. Government Printing Office.

Cohn, A. H., & Birch, T. L. (1988). Building resources for prevention programs. In D. C. Bross et al. (Eds.), *The new child protection team handbook* (pp. 598–615). New York: Garland.

Connelly, C. D., & Straus, M. (1992). Mother's age and risk for physical abuse. *Child Abuse & Neglect, 16*(5), 709–718.

Costin, L. B. (n. d.) *"The Cruelty." Rescuing the victims of child abuse, 1874–1960.* Unpublished manuscript.

Costin, L. B. (1985). Protective behaviors. *Social Work in Education, 7* (4), 210–211.

Costin, L. B. (1992). Cruelty to children: A dormant issue and its rediscovery, 1920–1960. *Social Service Review, 66*(2), 177–198.

Daro, D., & Mitchel, L. (1989). *Child abuse fatalities continue to rise: The results of the 1988 annual fifty-state survey* (Working paper number 808). Chicago: National Committee for the Prevention of Child Abuse, National Center on Child Abuse Prevention Research.

Deisz, R., Doueck, J. J., George, N., & Levine, M. (1996). Reasonable cause: A qualitative study of mandated reporting. *Child Abuse & Neglect, 20*(4), 275–287.

De Schweinitz, E., & De Schweinitz, K. (1964). The place of authority in the protective function of the public welfare agency. *Child Welfare, 43*(6), 286–291.

Dodge, K. A., Bates, J. E., & Petit, G. S. (1990, December). Mechanisms in the cycle of violence. *Science, 250,* 1678–1683.

Doueck, H. J., Bronson, D. E., & Levine, M. (1992). Evaluating risk assessment implementation in child protection: Issues for consideration. *Child Abuse & Neglect, 16*(5), 637–646.

Doueck, H. J., English, D. J., DePanfilis, D., & Moote, G. T. (1993). Decision-making in child protective services: A comparison of selected risk-assessment systems. *Child Welfare, 72*(5), 441–452.

Duqette, D. N. (1988). Legal interventions. In K. C. Faller, *Child sexual abuse: An interdisciplinary manual for diagnosis, case management, and treatment.* New York: Columbia University Press.

English, D. (1998). The extent and consequences of child maltreatment. *The Future of Children: Protecting Children from Abuse and Neglect, 8*(1), 39–53.

Erickson, M. F., & Egeland, B. (1996). Child neglect. In J. Briere, L. Berliner, J. A. Bulkley, C. Jenny, & T. Reid (Eds.), *The APSAC handbook on child maltreatment* (pp. 4–20). Thousand Oaks, CA: Sage Publications.

Faller, K. C. (1988a). *Child sexual abuse: An interdisciplinary manual for diagnosis, case management, and treatment.* New York: Columbia University Press.

Faller, K. C. (1988b). Criteria for judging the credibility of children's statements about their sexual abuse. *Child Welfare, 67*(5), 389–401.

Faller, K. C. (1988c). Decision-making in cases of intrafamilial child sexual abuse. *American Journal of Orthopsychiatry, 58*(1), 121–128.

Faller, K. C. (1990). An approach to questioning children alleged to have been sexually abused. *The Advisor, 2*(2).

Finkelhor, D. (1990, Winter). Is child abuse overreported? *Public Welfare, 48,* 22–29, 46–47.

Finkelhor, D. (1993). Epidemiological factors in the clinical identification of child sexual abuse. *Child Abuse & Neglect, 17,* 67–70.

Finkelhor, D., Hotaling, G., Lewis, I. A., & Smith, C. (1990). Sexual abuse in a national survey of adult men and women: Prevalence, characteristics, and risk factors. *Child Abuse & Neglect, 14*(1), 19–28.

Finkelhor, D., Williams, L. M., & Burns, N. (1988). *Nursery crimes: Sexual abuse in day care.* Newbury Park, CA: Sage.

Fleming, J., Mullen, P., & Bammer, G. (1997). A study of potential risk factors for sexual abuse in childhood. *Child Abuse & Neglect, 21,* 49–58.

Folks, H. (1911). *The care of destitute, neglected, and delinquent children.* New York: Macmillan.

Forsythe, P. (1987). Redefining child protective services. *Protecting Children, 4*(3), 12–16.

Gallup, G. H., Moor, D. W., & Schussel, R. (1997). *Disciplining children in America.* Princeton, NJ: The Gallup Organization.

Garbarino, J., & Ebata, A. (1983). The significance of ethnic and cultural differences in child maltreatment. *Journal of Marriage and the Family, 45,* 773–783.

Gaudin, J. M., & Dubowitz, H. (1997). Family functioning in neglectful families. In J. D. Berrick, R. P. Barth, & N. Gilbert (Eds.). *Child welfare research review, vol 2,* pp. 28–62. New York: Columbia University Press.

Gelles, R. J. (1989). Child abuse and violence in single-parent families: Parent absence and economic deprivation. *American Journal of Orthopsychiatry, 59*(4), 492–501.

Gelles, R. J., & Harrop, J. W. (1991). The risk of abusive violence among children with nongenetic caretakers. *Family Relations, 40*(1), 78–83.

Gentry, C. E. (1994). *Crisis intervention in child abuse and neglect.* Washington, DC: U.S. Department of Health and Human Services, National Center on Child Abuse and Neglect.

Gil, D. G. (1970). *Violence against children: Physical child abuse in the United States.* Cambridge, MA: Harvard University Press.

Giovannoni, J. M., & Becerra, R. M. (1979). *Defining child abuse.* New York: Free Press.

Gleason, B. (1994). Unpublished manuscript. Detroit, MI: Wayne State University, School of Social Work.

Goodman, G. S., Bottoms, B. L., & Shaver, P. R. (1994). *Characteristics and sources of allegations of ritualistic child abuse* (Executive summary of the final report to the National Center on Child Abuse and Neglect [Grant No. 90CA1405]). Washington, DC: National Center for Child Abuse and Neglect.

Gordon, L. (1988). *Heroes of their own lives: The politics and history of family violence.* New York: Viking.

Greenhouse, L. (1990, June 28). Child abuse trials can use television. *New York Times,* AI, A12, A13.

Halsey, S., Covington, S., Gilbert, J., Sorentino-Kelly, L., & Renoud, S. S. (1993). A legacy of violence in nonorganic failure to thrive. *Child Abuse & Neglect, 17*(6), 709–714.

Harrison, P. A., Fulkerson, J. A., & Beebe, T. J. (1997). Multiple substance use among adolescent physical and sexual abuse victims. *Child Abuse & Neglect, 21*(6), 529–539.

Hart, S. N., Brassard, M. R., & Karlson, H. C. (1996). Psychological maltreatment. In J. Briere, L. Berliner, J. A. Bulkley, C. Jenny, & T. Reid (Eds.), *The APSAC handbook on child maltreatment.* (pp. 72–89). Thousand Oaks, CA: Sage Publications.

Helfer, R. E. (1987). Litany of the smoldering neglect of children. In R. E. Helfer, & R. S. Kempe (Eds.), *The battered child* (4th ed.). Chicago: University of Chicago Press.

Herskowitz, J., & Seck, M. (1990). *Substance abuse and family violence, part 2: Identification of drug and alcohol usage in child abuse cases in Massachusetts.* Boston: Massachusetts Department of Social Services.

Hibbard, R. A., & Hartman, G. L. (1992). Behavioral problems in alleged sexual abuse victims. *Child Abuse & Neglect, 16,* 755–762.

Hildenbrand, W. S., et al. (1979). *Child protective services entering the 1980s: A nationwide survey.* Englewood, CO: American Humane Association.

Horejsi, C. (1996). *Assessment and case planning in child protection and foster care services.* Englewood, CO: American Humane Association.

Hutchinson, E. D. (1990). Child maltreatment: Can it be defined? *Social Service Review, 64* (1), 60–78.

Jones, D., & Alexander, H. (1987). Treating the abusive family within the family care system. In R. E. Helfer, & R. S. Kempe (Eds.), *The battered child* (4th ed., pp. 339–359). Chicago: University of Chicago Press.

Jones, L. (1993). Decision making in child welfare: A critical review of the literature. *Child and Adolescent Social Work Journal, 10*(3), 241–262.

Jones, M. A. (1987). *Parental lack of supervision: Nature and consequence of a major child neglect problem.* Washington, DC: Child Welfare League of America.

Jones, P. H. (1991). Ritualism and child sexual abuse. *Child Abuse & Neglect 15*(3), 163–170.

Kamerman, S. B., & Kahn, A. J. (1990, Winter). If CPS is driving child welfare—where do we go from here? *Public Welfare, 48,* 9–13.

Kaminer, B., Crowe, A., & Budde-Giltner, L. (1988). The prevalence and characteristics of multidisciplinary teams for child abuse and neglect: A national survey. In D. Bross et al. (Eds.), *The new child protection team handbook* (pp. 548–567). New York: Garland.

Karenga, M. H. (1989). *Selections from the Huisa: Sacred wisdom of ancient Egypt.* Los Angeles: Sankore Press. Quoted in: Sullivan, M. (1996, Spring). An Afro-centric perspective on developing cultural identity. *The Prevention Report, 6.*

Kelley, S. J. (1996). Ritualistic abuse of children. In J. Briere, L. Berliner, J. A. Bulkley, C. Jenny, & T. Reid (Eds.), *The APSAC handbook on child maltreatment.* (pp. 90–99). Thousand Oaks, CA: Sage Publications.

Kempe, C. H., Silverman, F. N., Steele, B. T., Droegemueller, W., & Silver, H. K. (1962, July). The battered child syndrome. *Journal of the American Medical Association, 181.*

Kent, L., Laidlaw, J. D., & Brockington, I. F. (1997). Fetal abuse. *Child Abuse & Neglect, 21*(2), 181–186.

Kolko, D. J. (1996). Child physical abuse. In J. Briere, L. Berliner, J. A. Bulkley, C. Jenny, & T. Reid (Eds.), *The APSAC handbook on child maltreatment.* (pp. 21–50). Thousand Oaks, CA: Sage Publications.

Korbin, J. E. (1994). Sociocultural factors in child maltreatment. In G. B. Melton, & F. D. Barry (Eds.), *Protecting children from abuse and neglect: Foundations for a new national strategy* (pp. 182–223). New York: Guilford Press.

Kurtz, P. D., Gaudin, J. M., Wodarski, J. S., & Hoving, P. T. (1993). Maltreatment and the school-aged child: School performance consequences. *Child Abuse & Neglect, 17*(5), 581–589.

Lanning, K. V. (1991). Ritual abuse: A law enforcement view or perspective. *Child Abuse & Neglect, 15*(3), 171–173.

Levine, M. (1996). Reasonable cause: A qualitative study of mandated reporting. *Child Abuse & Neglect, 20*(4), 275–287.

Lindsay, D. (1994). *The welfare of children.* New York: Oxford University Press.

Loftus, E. F. (1993). The reality of repressed memories. *American Psychologist, 48,* 518–537.

Madden, R. G. (1993). State actions to control fetal abuse: Ramifications for child welfare practice. *Child Welfare, 72*(2), 129–140.

Margolin, L. (1992). Child abuse by mothers' boyfriends: Why the overrepresentation? *Child Abuse & Neglect 16,* 541–551.

McCurdy, K., & Daro, D. (1994). *Current trends in child abuse reporting and fatalities: The results of the 1993 annual fifty-state survey.* Chicago: National Committee to Prevent Child Abuse.

Melchert, T. P., & Parker, L. (1997). Different forms of childhood abuse and memory. *Child Abuse & Neglect, 21*(2). 125–135.

Melton, G. B., & Barry, F. D. (Eds.). (1994). *Protecting children from abuse and neglect: Foundations for a national strategy.* New York: Guilford Press.

Mencher, S. (1960). The concept of authority and social casework. In *Casework papers, 1960.* New York: Family Service Association of America.

Moss, S. Z. (1963). Authority—An enabling factor in casework with neglectful parents. *Child Welfare, 43*(8), 385–391.

National Association of Public Child Welfare Administrators. (1988). *Guidelines for a model system of protective services for abused and neglected children and their families.* Washington, DC: American Public Welfare Association.

National Center on Child Abuse and Neglect. (1993). *A report on the maltreatment of children with disabilities.* Washington, DC: Department of Health and Human Services.

National Commission on Child Welfare and Family Preservation. (1990). *Factbook on public child welfare services and staff.* Washington, DC: American Public Welfare Association.

National Council of Juvenile and Family Court Judges (1992). *Family violence: State-of-the-art court programs.* Reno, NV: Author.

National Research Council. (1993). *Understanding child abuse and neglect.* Washington, DC: National Academy Press.

Nelson, K., Saunders, E., & Landsman, M. J. (1990). *Chronic neglect in perspective: A study of chronically neglecting families in a large metropolitan county, final report.* Oakdale: National Resource Center of Family Based Services, University of Iowa.

Oberlander, L. B. (1995). Psycholegal issues in child sexual abuse evaluations: A survey of forensic mental health professionals. *Child Abuse & Neglect, 19*(4), 475–490.

Parsons, T. (1954). *Essays in sociological theory* (rev. ed.). Chicago: Free Press of Glencoe.

Polansky, N. A., Chalmers, M. A., Buttenwieser, E., & Williams, D. P. (1981). *Damaged parents: An anatomy of child neglect.* Chicago: University of Chicago Press.

Polier, J. W. (1989). *Juvenile justice in double jeopardy. The distanced community and vengeful retribution.* Hillsdale, NJ: Lawrence Erlbaum Associates.

Proch, K. (1982). *Child welfare case notebook.* Urbana: University of Illinois at Urbana Champaign, School of Social Work.

Public Health Service. (1995). *Questions and answers on PHS guidelines for HIV counseling and voluntary testing for pregnant women.* Atlanta: Centers for Disease Control and Prevention.

Regehr, C., & Antle, B. (1997). Coercive influences: Informed consent in court-mandated social work practice. *Social Work, 42*(3), 300–306.

Reppucci, N. D., & Haugaard, J. J. (1989). Prevention of child sexual abuse: Myth and reality. *American Psychologist, 44*(10), 1266–1275.

Rose, S., & Meezan, W. (1997). Defining child neglect: Evolution, influences, and issues. In J. D. Berrick, R. P. Barth, & N. Gilbert. (Eds), *Child Welfare Research Review, vol. 2* (pp. 13–27). New York: Columbia University Press.

Rosenberg, D. A., & Gary, N. (1988). Sexual abuse of children. In D. C. Bross et al. (Eds.), *The new child protection team handbook.* New York: Garland.

Ryan, K. (1996). The chronically traumatized child. *Child and Adolescent Social Work Journal, 13,* 287–310.

Sandberg, D. N. (1989). *The child abuse–delinquency connection.* Lexington, MA: Lexington Books.

Schene, P. (1996). The risk assessment roundtables: A ten-year perspective. *Protecting Children, 12*(2), 4–8.

Schene, P. (1998). Past, present, and future roles of child protective services. *The Future of Children, 8*(1), 23–38.

Schmitt, B. D. (1988). Failure to thrive: The medical evaluation. In D.C. Bross et al. (Eds.), *The new child protection team handbook.* New York: Garland.

Sebold, J. (1987). Indicators of child sexual abuse in males. *Social Casework, 68*(2), 75–80.

Sedlak, A. J., & Broadhurst, D. D. (1996). *Third national incidence study of child abuse and neglect: Final report.* Washington, DC: U.S. Department of Health and Human Services, National Center for Child Abuse and Neglect.

Smith, C., & Carlson, B. E. (1997, June). Stress, coping, and reslience in children and youth. *Social Service Review,* 231–256.

Starr, R. H., Jr., & Wolfe, D. A. (Eds.) (1991). *The effects of child abuse and neglect: Issues and research.* New York: Guilford Press.

Stattler, J. N. (1997). *Clinical and forensic interviewing of children and families.* Jerome N. Stattler, Publisher, Inc.

Steele, B. (1987). Psychodynamic factors in child abuse. In R. E. Helfer, & R. S. Kempe, (Eds.), *The battered child* (4th ed., pp. 81–114). Chicago: University of Chicago Press.

Stein, T. (1998). *The social welfare of women and children with HIV and AIDS.* New York: Oxford University Press.

Straus, M., & Gelles, R. (1986, August). Societal change and change in family violence from 1975–1985 as revealed by two national surveys. *Journal of Marriage and the Family, 48,* 465–79.

Straus, M., & Gelles, R. (Eds.). (1990). *Physical violence in American families.* New Brunswick, NJ: Transaction Publishers.

Sunley, R. (1963). Early nineteenth-century American literature on child rearing. In M. Mead & M. Wolfenstein (Eds.), *Childhood in contemporary cultures.* Chicago: University of Chicago Press.

Taal, M., & Edelaar, M. (1997). Positive and negative effects of a child sexual abuse prevention program. *Child Abuse & Neglect, 21*(4), 399–410.

Terpstra, J. (1992). Foreword. In K. H. Briar, V. H. Hansen, & N. Harris (Eds.), *New partnerships: Proceedings from the National Public Child Welfare Training Symposium, 1991.* Miami: Florida International University.

Tracy, E. M., & Whitaker, J. K. (1987). The evidence base for social support interventions in child and family practice: Emerging issues for research and practice. *Children and Youth Services Review, 9,* 249–270.

U.S. Advisory Board on Child Abuse and Neglect. (1990). *Child abuse and neglect: Critical first steps in response to a national emergency.* Washington, DC: U.S. Government Printing Office.

U.S. Advisory Board on Child Abuse and Neglect. (1993). *The continuing child protection emergency: A challenge to the nation.* Washington, DC: U.S. Government Printing Office.

U.S. Department of Health and Human Services. Children's Bureau. (1998). *Child maltreatment 1996: Reports from the states to the national Child Abuse and Neglect Data System.* Washington, DC: U.S. Government Printing Office.

U.S. Department of Justice. (1984). *Attorney General's Task Force on Family Violence (Final Report).* Washington, DC: Author.

Vissing, Y. M., Straus, M. A., Gelles, R. J., & Harrop, J. W. (1991). Verbal aggression by parents and psychosocial problems of children. *Child Abuse & Neglect, 15,* 223–248. Cited in Hart, S. N., Brassard, M. R., & Karlson, H. C. (1996), Psychological maltreatment. In J. Briere, L. Berliner, J. A. Bulkley, C. Jenny, & T. Reid (Eds.) *The APSAC handbook on child maltreatment,* 72–89. Thousand Oaks, CA: Sage Publications.

Walker, L. E. (1984). *The battered woman syndrome.* New York: Springer.

Warner-Rogers, J. E., Hansen, D. J., & Spieth, L. E. (1996). The influence of case and professional variables on identification and reporting of physical abuse: A study with medical students. *Child Abuse & Neglect, 20*(9), 851–866.

Wells, S. J., Stein, T. J., Fluke, J., & Downing, J. (1989). Screening in child protective services. *Social Work, 34*(1), 45–48.

Widom, C. S. (1989). Child abuse, neglect, and adult behavior: Research design and findings on criminality, violence, and child abuse. *American Journal of Orthopsychiatry, 59*(3), 355–367.

Wiehe, V. R. (1996). *Working with child abuse and neglect.* Thousand Oaks, CA: Sage.

Wolfner, G. D., & Gelles, R. J. (1993). A profile of violence toward children: A national study. *Child Abuse & Neglect, 17,* 197–212.

Zuckerman, B. (1994). Effects on parents and children. In D.J. Besharov (Ed.), *When drug addicts have children,* (pp. 49–63). Washington, DC: Child Welfare League of America and the American Enterprise Institute.

Zuravin, S. (1988). Child maltreatment and teenage first births: A relationship mediated by chronic sociodemographic stress. *American Journal of Orthopsychiatry, 58*(1), 91–103.

CHAPTER 8

Family Preservation

Intervention with Family-Based Services to Protect Children and Strengthen Families

Each family is so complex as to be known and understood only in part even by its own members. Families struggle with contradictions as massive as Everest, as fluid and changing as the Mississippi . . . Yet when practical the preference should be for family.

—Maya Angelou

CHAPTER OUTLINE

CASE EXAMPLE: USING INTENSIVE FAMILY-BASED SERVICES TO PREVENT PLACEMENT

The following case example is one of countless family preservation efforts—each complex and unique—which successfully holds a family together when the events of that family's existence threaten dismemberment or a profound dislocation.

Amy is a 23-year-old mother of three young children. Jimmy, who is the father of Jeremy, age 6, and Tiffany, age 4, drifts in and out of their lives. When he is sober he visits and sometimes brings toys or food. When he has been drinking he becomes sullen and verbally abusive. Amy has learned to keep him from bothering them. Amy's youngest child, Ashley, is medically fragile—Amy was using crack heavily during her pregnancy.

Amy doesn't remember who Ashley's father might be. Amy's life has been a blur of misfortune in the last few years. She has been evicted from apartments twice for nonpayment of rent. They spent weeks going from homeless shelter to homeless shelter until her cousin took them in. Both Amy's stepmother and Jimmy have threatened to have the children taken from her. She struggles to stay free of crack. As a result of substance abuse treatment after Ashley's birth, Amy has had periods of nonuse and a brief relapse. Her nerves are frayed from the children's constant fighting and whining and Ashley's irritable, fretful crying. Amy tries to keep the children quiet because they annoy her cousin, who threatens to kick her out. She needs a drink or a joint to tolerate the children when they get out of control. Amy is frightened because she has been hitting the children in futile discipline attempts. She left bruises on Jeremy's buttocks and left arm after hitting him with a belt to show him that he couldn't hit his sister. When she took Ashley to the emergency room because the infant seemed very congested, a nurse noticed Jeremy's bruises and was concerned about Ashley's nutrition, as she was below the twentieth percentile. The hospital called child protective services.

Ten years ago, the children might have been placed in foster care. After a careful assessment of risk, the CPS worker referred Amy to a program that offers intensive, comprehensive, family-based services designed to preserve the family unit, protect the children, and keep the children out of care.

Carolyn, the family-based services worker, carries a beeper so that she is available to Amy and the children around the clock, if needed. Because her caseload is limited to two or three families at a time, she is available, during the next six weeks, to work with the family. She will work to keep the family together by identifying and supporting their strengths, bringing in resources, teaching them problem-solving skills, and providing hope. She will engage Amy by helping her to locate housing and furniture, working with her at household tasks, and being an understanding, caring, and constant figure in her life. Carolyn will use a wide range of techniques and strategies, drawn from family therapy and social learning sources, to enable Amy to face and solve the problems that have led to the threat of child placement. She will also begin to put into place a safety net of ongoing community resources that will meet the children's developmental needs and Amy's needs during a long recovery process.

CONTROVERSY CONCERNING FAMILY PRESERVATION PHILOSOPHY AND SERVICES

The controversy concerning family preservation exists on several levels and is articulated in many different ways. First is the issue of family preservation as a *philosophy* in child welfare. According to Warsh, Pine, and Maluccio (1995), "Family preservation is a philosophy that supports policies, programs and practices which recognize the central importance of the biological family to human beings" (p. 625). When viewed as a philosophy, family preservation concepts can relate to kinship care, reunification from foster care, and child protective services decision-making. In some domains, the philosophy has become a catch-phrase applied to many of the failures and tragedies of the entire child protection/child welfare system, with child death and child safety being a primary concern.

The term *family preservation* is also used to describe a specific type of service involving intensive, family-based services as discussed in this chapter. Controversy regarding family preservation *programs* focuses more specifically on issues such as evaluation, targeting of services, effectiveness of service delivery, impact on family functioning, and cost effectiveness. These issues are discussed in this chapter's section on evaluation.

The field is currently experiencing a pendulum swing. Initially there was wide acceptance of family preservation philosophy and programs. An air of optimism stimulated the family and children's services system in the early 1990s.

> That family preservation can be the catalyst for rehabilitating the entire service delivery system is the hope, already glimpsed and beginning to be realized, of its advocates. Family preservation supporters believe that the service—its values and its characteristics—can be understood not as an isolated kind of "magic bullet" to fix something that's wrong with a state's placement decisions, but as a means of examining a host of related issues, including the responsibility of the community to families and why there should be a very strong bias toward relying on families as the primary way to take responsibility for children. (Barthel, 1992, p. 75)

More recently, the concept of family preservation has been called into question by professionals and media alike. Some of the questions raised by critics include the following: Does family preservation harm children? Does it try to maintain families in which the parents are incapable of parenting? Has the concept of reasonable effort gone too far? Is family preservation being substituted for prevention services that are lacking for lower-risk families?

Mixed Reactions to Family Preservation

In *McCall's*, a popular women's magazine, an article titled "The Little Boy Who Didn't Have to Die" told of the death of a child returned to his parents from the foster care system:

> Gregory appears to have been doomed by a decade-old national policy determined to patch up troubled parents and preserve families. Despite mounting evidence that family preservation programs aren't working, child-welfare policy remains so focused on reuniting families that its original aim—keeping children safe—has become almost secondary. (Spake, 1994, p. 146)

The result of some recent failures to protect children from harm has been a growing backlash against family preservation (Hartman, 1993). Lindsey, writing for a professional audience, observes:

> Obviously children should not be taken from their family if it is possible to keep them safe at home. The problem is that the child welfare field has not developed a proven technology, which can assure the adequate safety of endangered children. The risk with inappropriate removal of a child is that it may tear apart a family unnecessarily. However, the risk of leaving a child in an endangered home is a child fatality. Neither is acceptable, but protecting the child's life must always be paramount. (Lindsey, 1994, p. 279)

It is difficult to maintain a balance between the goals of preserving families and protecting children. This tension has been exacerbated by inflammatory media coverage, which generally focuses on the systemic failure rather than the success of social work intervention. Family preservation proponents cannot afford to dismiss media coverage as ill-informed, because popular attention influences policy formation and political controversy. They do note that many complaints should more appropriately be targeted specifically to mistakes in child protection units, community failure to report abuse, and legal decisions to leave children in the home or to return children home from foster care. Family-based services to prevent placement are hardly responsible for problems in other parts of the child welfare system, which members of the public are unable to distinguish or differentiate from the general philosophy of family preservation.

There also exists considerable divergence of opinion among researchers and practitioners. Gelles (1993) pointed out that it is unpopular to argue against family preservation, because it draws support from conservatives for limiting state intervention in the private sphere and from liberals for supporting needy and disadvantaged individuals, families, and children. Yet he asserted that "We are not sure under what circumstances family preservation is a penicillin and under what conditions it is a poison. My most important argument is that family preservation and family reunification should not be the sole or even main means of treating and preventing child maltreatment" (Gelles, 1993, pp. 558–559).

In *The Book of David: How Preserving Families Can Cost Children's Lives*, Gelles (1996) calls for the abandonment of the family reunification/family preservation model as an official and unofficial child welfare policy, and cites the "overselling" of the concept by several influential foundations, which "marketed family preservation with a near-religious zeal" (p. 134). His rationale for changing the prevailing family preservation philosophy is complex. Some of the factors cited are the issues of child safety and child deaths; changing political winds; the rigidity of the "reasonable efforts" legal standard; the lack of sufficient evaluation data to prove program effectiveness; and the tendency of child welfare workers to preserve families at all costs.

From a feminist perspective, Bernard (1992) examines "the dark side" of family preservation, reminding readers that the American family is one of this country's most violent institutions and a cornerstone of women's oppression. She cautions us to "consider carefully the full implications of the family-preservation policy without buying into the nostalgia for and mythology of families that are presented by an administration that has consistently undercut the goals of equality and social justice" (p. 159).

Maluccio, Pine, and Warsh (1994) acknowledge that family preservation is viewed as competing with child protection and in particular cases may be incompatible. However, they state, "At the philosophical and policy levels family preservation and child protection are complementary rather than competing values. In essence, the best way to protect children is to preserve as much of their families as possible" (p. 295).

Wells and Tracy (1996) recommend that the current rationale for family preservation—the prevention of placement—should be abandoned and a new rationale developed. They argue that family preservation services should be integrated closely with child development services, with drug treatment programs, and with family development services such as employment and literacy programs. Such programs should be aimed at families with young, physically neglected, and abused children who do not require placement. Further, these services should be linked with longer-term plans, including up to two years of home visiting, and should be evaluated in terms of developmental outcomes for children.

In a printed debate on family preservation, Seader (1994) asserts that both policy and actual services place children at unnecessary risk, with services limited by phenomena such as agency biases, worker competencies, and community resources. She argues that social workers report pressure to maintain families that they know cannot be rehabilitated. Nelson's (1994) rejoinder clarifies that family preservation is not universally applied; that safety is a central concern; that family preservation workers typically recommend placement of the child in from 5 percent to 50 percent of their cases; and that there is empirical evidence that family preservation cases show significant improvement in functioning.

Dore (1993) reminds social workers that family preservation intervention is less effective with maltreating families characterized by extreme poverty, single-parent status, low educational attainment, and mental health problems. She concludes that "Family preservation will truly occur when many families with children no longer struggle to exist at less than subsistence level, when poor parents are freed from anxiety and depression generated by raising children in hostile environments, and when it is widely acknowledged that the real cause of family breakdown is the failure of our society to value and support the parenting role" (p. 553). A careful examination of the historical development of family-based services to preserve families sheds further light on the current controversy.

Historical Development of Family Preservation Concepts

The child welfare system's way of thinking about family has evolved in the twentieth century, as indicated by a series of reforms. At the 1909 White House Conference on Children, emphasis was placed on the importance of moving children from institutions to a family setting in a foster home. Consequently the foster family became the focal family of child welfare practice, with emphasis on helping the child adjust to the foster home and helping the foster family create an environment that promoted the child's development. In the 1970s, with the advent of permanency planning reforms, the primary focus shifted to freeing children for placement in adoptive families. In the 1980s the Adoption Assistance and Child Welfare Act focused on the biological family, as family preservation began to emerge conceptually. In the 1990s it appears that the focus on the biological family has expanded to the child's extended or augmented family, with kinship caregivers becoming a new focal family setting in a family-continuity paradigm.

Although social work has long been concerned with the family—the first direct practice journal was named *The Family*—historically the focus in child welfare has been largely on the well-being of the child, rather than on the family. Hartman and Laird (1983) played a pivotal role by refocusing an emergent national interest in family therapy back onto practice with the vulnerable and the poor. Another return to the historic roots of social work is viewing the family in the context of the neighborhood and community. Settlement houses, which flourished in the late-nineteenth and early-twentieth century, were the earliest ancestors of family preservation and left a number of important legacies, including recognition of the interrelationship between family and community (Kaplan & Girard, 1994).

The social work profession and the family have traveled a long distance together, sometimes in close companionship and sometimes on divergent paths, only to meet once again on the same road. (Hartman & Laird, 1983, p. vii)

In the 1980s, family-systems thinking and the dissemination of evaluations of the successful Homebuilders model of family preservation intersected with a strong government response to the problems of child welfare. The field had been prepared by forces leading to the passage of several critical pieces of federal legislation. The Child Abuse Treatment and Prevention Act of 1974 had called public attention to the severity of child maltreatment as a social issue, but the nation was unprepared for the dramatic increases in reporting.

A review by Sudia in 1981 noted that existing child abuse treatment programs lacked effectiveness; the families were poor and on welfare; services need to be easily available and in a form that was acceptable to the families; and that new directions were needed. It became clear to all involved with child welfare that foster care was not the solution to compli-

cated, multifaceted family problems that adversely affected children. The 1980 Adoption Assistance and Child Welfare Act established—among other key provisions—mandates that "reasonable efforts" be made to keep families together. It gave federal support to state efforts to preserve the family before placing a child in foster care. With the intent to protect children from unnecessary separation from their parents, the act required that reasonable efforts be made to preserve and strengthen families by preventing placement and reuniting children in foster care with their families in a timely way. The legislative purpose was to encourage agencies to work with families in more than a cursory way.

There have been numerous projects to operationalize the concept of "reasonable effort," including an implementation guide developed by the American Bar Association (Ratterman, Dodson, & Hardin, 1987) and a protocol for reasonable efforts in drug-related cases developed by the National Council of Juvenile and Family Court Judges (1992). There was consensus that intensive family preservation programs are a key component of family and children's services programs and practice.

In 1981 the National Resource Center on Family Based Services (now known as the National Resource Center for Family Centered Practice) was established by government funding at the University of Iowa, building on earlier efforts there by Marvin Bryce to make information on in-home services available. A major accomplishment of the National Resource Center was that, in cooperation with Minnesota and several state associations, the National Association for Family-Based Services was formed, with over 1,000 professionals attending national conferences (Sudia, 1993). Between 1981 and 1993 there were statewide initiatives for family based programs in thirty states, with twenty-seven recognized state associations for family-based services developed (Allen & Zalenski, 1993).

The Family Preservation and Support Services established by the Omnibus Budget Reconciliation Act of 1993 was the first piece of major child welfare reform legislation since 1980. It bolstered services that enhance parental functioning and protect children in vulnerable families. This act was seen as an opportunity to establish a continuum of coordinated, culturally relevant, and family-focused services.

Adoption and Safe Families Act

The passage of the Adoption and Safe Families Act, Public Law 105-89, in 1997 was the culmination of a philosophical and political shift away from some of the original tenets of family preservation presented earlier. While the preponderance of the act concerns foster care and adoption, discussed in later chapters, some sections contain oblique references to family preservation through their emphasis on safety in the home, which reflects a public concern with child protection, family-preservation philosophy, and the use of family preservation services. The act continues funding services for the prevention of abuse and for supporting families when children can be safely maintained at home. Additionally it increases treatment options for families, particularly when a caretaker parent is in need of substance-abuse treatment, when the family is homeless, or in domestic-violence cases.

Practitioners' Response to Controversial Issues

The initial issue is that family preservation was sold to state legislatures as a cost-effective approach. It is a cost-effective approach, but they cut the line far, far too close. So that even some of the family preservation programs that started at three to six weeks have expanded to three months, and now they have announced six-month programs, then nine-month programs, and there are some programs with enough wisdom to give people what they want and need. Karl Dennis, executive director of Kaleidoscope (Dennis, in Golden, 1997, p. 172)

To realize the full potential of family preservation as both a philosophy and a practice approach, committed professionals enter the professional and political discourse reiterating that child safety is their first concern, while advocating for social and economic justice for families. Practitioners in family preservation programs remain committed to their program and philosophy. They understand that poverty is indeed related to many family problems and that we cannot adequately preserve families who are ground into despair by want, need, and hostile surroundings. These practitioners assist with—and are intelligent consumers of—program evaluation and research efforts aimed at revealing in which cases family preservation is most effective, and in which cases it may be dangerous for the child. They serve families compassionately, but must be vigilant and quick to summon protective intervention when needed. When terminating with cases, family preservation workers should ensure that an ongoing combination of kinship networks and community services are in place as supportive and protective structures.

CHARACTERISTICS OF FAMILY PRESERVATION SERVICES

Principles of Family Preservation Services

Family-based services for the prevention of placement are often known by names such as family preservation, intensive family services, families first, Homebuilders, in-home services, or prevention services. These services represent a rapid proliferation of a philosophy that families are important, that they should be kept together, and that intensive focused efforts will mobilize family strengths. As articulated by the National Resource Center on Family-Based Services, now known as the National Resource Center for Family Centered Practice, this philosophy is rooted in the belief that

- children need permanency in their family relationships in order to develop into healthy, productive individuals;
- families should be the primary caretakers of their own children; and
- social service programs should make every effort to support families in this function (National Resource Center, 1994).

Nelson, Landsman, and Deutelbaum (1990) have identified three distinct models of family-centered placement prevention: crisis intervention, home-based treatment, and family treatment. Each model has its own underlying assumptions, theoretical base, and organizational or structural features, yet there are many similarities in the models. Common elements of intensive, family-based placement prevention programs include the following aspects:

- commitment to maintaining children in their own homes
- focusing on the entire family system rather than on individuals
- accepting for service only those families at actual risk of having children placed
- beginning service as soon as the referral has been made—no waiting lists
- seeing and working with families in their own homes
- maintaining flexible hours seven days a week, with round-the-clock response to family needs
- providing intensive service over a limited period of time (from one to five months)
- keeping caseload size small—often two to three cases at a time—enabling the worker to deliver intensive services
- providing comprehensive services meeting a variety of therapeutic, concrete, and supportive needs
- teaching family members skills
- offering counseling or therapy within the home
- basing services on client need rather than agency categories
- having access to flexible funding to support the case plan
- offering ongoing, in-service training and support to staff
- following up and evaluating family progress and program success

(Nelson, Landsman, & Deutelbaum, 1990; Edna McConnell Clark Foundation, 1985; Whittaker, Kinney, Tracy, & Booth, 1990).

Theoretical Base

The conceptual frameworks for family based prevention services draw from and integrate a number of theoretical sources. The ecological systems metaphor examines the transactions and exchange of energy and resources between the family and its environment, and views the family holistically in terms of interrelationships of systems. When children experience problems, for example, those difficulties need to be viewed in the context of the child's family, the family's community, and the community's involvement in the larger society.

Theories of coping and adaptation in both maturational and situational life transitions (Germain & Gitterman, 1980) are also applied, with the understanding that coping with ongoing conditions is part of family functioning. According to Bain (1978), the family capacity to cope is a function of the magnitude of the stress and the richness, relevance, and coherence of the "social container" within which the stress is experienced. The concept of the social container includes both the family's social networks and its formal institutional relationships. Such a view of family dysfunction suggests several options for intervening to enhance family coping, reduction of stress, facilitating the response of formal institutions, strengthening the social network, or enhancing the effectiveness of family members.

Another theoretical source for many family-based prevention programs is crisis intervention theory (Caplan, 1974; Parad, 1965). Families seen in family preservation programs are usually experiencing one of two crises: (1) child protective services has said that the family is not providing adequate child care and is planning to remove one or more children, or (2) problems between parents and children have grown so severe that a parent is refusing to allow the child to continue to live at home, or the child is running away (Kinney, Haapala, & Booth, 1991). Crisis intervention theory postulates that people's familiar coping mechanisms break down during periods of high stress, so that they become more open to change. With competent intervention at the time of crisis, the opportunity is created for healthier adaptation following resolution of the crisis.

Many family-based service programs, especially Homebuilders, integrate social learning theory into their approach. A key to understanding behavior is recognizing the rewards or penalties, which follow the behavior, and the antecedents that stimulate or trigger the behavior (Patterson, 1975). The expectations and cognitions about behavior also provide reciprocal influence with the behavior itself (Bandura, 1977). The clarity and specificity of cognitive-behavioral approaches fit with the focused intervention of most programs.

Family-systems theory, which takes note of family structure, family roles, family life cycle, multigenerational family issues, and the nature of family transactions, also undergirds a family-based services approach. It helps the social worker to understand the circular nature of interactions and behaviors that may jeopardize the safety of the child in his or her own home. The use of family-systems theory enhances the assessment of how the family "works." Many therapeutic techniques—such as eco-maps and genograms, increasing the clarity of communication, understanding the structure of the family, working with boundary issues, helping families change maladaptive roles, and establishing positive family rituals—come directly from family therapy sources. Other theoretical approaches to family work focus on identifying and treating family pathology. In intensive, family-based prevention services, the focus is nearly universally on identification of family strengths, reframing family perceptions to maximize strengths, and mobilizing families to use their strengths.

Some see the family-systems theory base and the cognitive-behavioral theory base as dichotomous, or the divergent approaches as potentially competitive or conflictual. Friedman (1993) cautions against reductionism or reification as threats to humane, creative, and effective practice. He encourages bridge-building between the two perspectives to integrate theory so that clinical work will reflect the complexity of clients' lives.

Thus family preservation or intensive family-based services for prevention of placement is more than a collection of program elements or a single theoretical perspective. It is an attitude toward families that focuses on the positive aspects of any family with a commitment to avoid the pain of dismemberment whenever possible. In the words of Maya Angelou,

Too often our system, in focusing on the individual, endangers the group. When a child is protected, but its family is shattered, we are forced to question if indeed our process has succeeded. Or, are we, in fact, living the cliche that the operation was a success but the patient died? (Angelou, 1985, p. iv)

PROGRAMS THAT PREVENT PLACEMENT AND PRESERVE FAMILIES

The Intensive Family Preservation Services National Network Directory identified 223 programs in 1994, a dramatic increase from the 20 programs listed in the 1982 directory of the National Resource Center on Family-Based Services. A recent study conducted for Congress by the General Accounting Office (1997) found implementation of family preservation programs utilizing federal funds in all fifty states (U.S. GAO, 1997). While there is tremendous variety and diversity within the existing programs, they have in common a commitment to intensive, family-based services.

The Homebuilders Model

Homebuilders, an intensive in-home crisis intervention and education program for families, has pioneered concepts of family preservation since 1974. The families are referred by state workers when there is a child at imminent risk of placement. Workers serve only two families at a time, providing a wide range of services, including help with basic needs and counseling regarding family relationships. The Homebuilders philosophy includes several important assumptions: It is our job to instill hope; clients are our colleagues; people are doing the best they can (Kinney, Haapala, & Booth, 1991).

When a family is accepted into the program a face-to-face meeting takes place within twenty-four hours. Homebuilders therapists are on call to the client families and have flexible schedules so that they can meet with clients as needed, even on weekends, nights, or holidays. While much of the work takes place in the home, therapists also go where the problems are, whether that is a school or a teen hangout. The goal of all services is to enable families to resolve their own problems. Program goals are limited: to prevent out-of-home placement, and to teach families the skills necessary to remain living together.

The therapist is involved in doing concrete tasks such as cleaning the apartment or driving to the grocery store with the family members. The therapist also uses a variety of educational and therapeutic techniques as the situation warrants, including teaching behavior-management skills, assertive skills, problem-solving skills, cognitive skills, and communication skills.

The brevity of the Homebuilders model, four to eight weeks, fits with a crisis-intervention theoretical foundation. The services are intense during the time-limited period, serving to keep therapist and family focused on the specific goals established by the family.

In addition to initiating the family preservation approach in 1974, Homebuilders has made several significant related contributions to the field. From its inception, an evaluation component was built into the model. This focus on accountability provided impetus for widespread adoption of Homebuilder concepts. It also demonstrated to state legislatures that the program was cost effective and would save money if placement was avoided. The architects of Homebuilders published numerous books and articles describing varied aspects of the approach, disseminating it broadly to the field and to professional education programs. Thirty states, including Missouri, have family preservation programs based on the Homebuilders model.

In Missouri, a statewide family preservation services program has been operating since 1992. The program has succeeded in diverting about one-third of the children who otherwise would have entered foster care. One such case, described by Vanessa, an FPS worker, involved Heidi, a former foster child who was homeless and pregnant at age 18, and in danger of losing her son a year later. With the help of FPS she began working toward her goal of becoming a nurse. During the period of services Heidi was helped to locate housing, shop for furniture at garage sales, improve nutritional habits, feed the baby regularly, and obtain medical care. When Heidi left the FPS program at the end of six weeks, she was assigned an aftercare worker to continue the case plan (Kolb, 1993).

Other Models

A multisystems approach to family preservation has been implemented in Illinois through a training curriculum developed for the Illinois Department of Children and Family services. While the Homebuilders

training manual reflects a cognitive-behavioral approach, the Illinois curriculum is based on the multisystems approach, which works with larger systems outside the family. The need for a multisystems approach in working with African-American families had been pointed out by Boyd-Franklin (1989).

A multisystems approach offers definite strategies for balancing the seemingly conflicting goals of child protection and family empowerment. It also requires coordinating the demands of systems affecting the family, such as juvenile court, school, other social services, and the extended family (Cimmarusti, 1992). Cimmarusti delineates four levels in each family preservation case: the family, the extended family, the community, and the family preservation intervention group, which includes the agency, the family preservation worker, the legal system, and other service providers. He cites a case in which a young mother began to use drugs again as services were coming to an end. The worker discussed the relapse with the mother, who voluntarily placed the child with a relative and resumed drug treatment. The example illustrates how the seemingly conflicting demands of family empowerment and child protection were managed, and how the worker coordinated the systems levels (Cimmarusti, 1992).

A model of family preservation services with two workers has been used in a number of places, from Maryland to Adelaide, South Australia. Advantages of having a staff pair to work with a family include the ability of the team to keep each other on target, to provide extra energy for difficult or complex tasks, and to keep a positive focus on family progress. The following case illustrates the need for teamwork:

A family preservation team intervened in a situation where the parent had allowed garbage and trash to pile up to the ceiling in the home. The media had photographed the housing inspector staring at the huge mounds of refuse and ran the photograph on the front page of the local newspaper with the headline "The Dirtiest House in the State". The mother was so shamed that it took three days before the family preservation team could go into the house. They met with the mother on the front porch and made clean-up plans. It took a contractor with three dumpsters to empty the house of rubbish, and a large group of relatives and volunteers to scrub, clean, and paint. When the house had been restored to order and the mother engaged with mental health services in the community, the team reflected on their success. They realized that it would have been much harder to counter the media criticism, ameliorate the depression and shame of the mother, and handle the overwhelming nature of the mess if they had been working singly, not as a team.

Typically such an arrangement consists of a professional social worker and a paraprofessional or case aide. The pair is usually part of a larger team which meets regularly to provide support and celebrate success.

A variation on the use of brief, intensive, family preservation services was found in an experimental program in which IFPS workers were assigned to families at the front end of a child protective services investigation, before rather than after a CPS determination has been made. The family preservation workers assessed families in terms of strengths, and the CPS workers assessed risks in a collaborative decision-making process. The IFPS workers helped families establish a network of services for a strengthened environment, including informal support such as extended family members, friends, neighbors, and clergy. Families in the experimental group had fewer cases opened than did those in the control group and were more satisfied with the agency's services. By front-loading services to the time of CPS intake, child safety may be enhanced (Walton, 1997).

Another form of services targeted at the prevention of placement addresses the needs of children and youth at risk of being sent from the community into costly residential care, or young people returning to family and community from a more structured setting. The "wraparound" approach was developed in Alaska by the former coordinator of Children's Mental Health Services and has been continued by the Community Resources Cooperative. The model has been replicated in over 100 sites nationwide (Vandenberg, Grealish, & Schick, 1993). A wraparound service is developed by a community-based child and family team, which may include parents ("customers"), child welfare, mental health, juvenile justice, education, law enforcement, health, vocational rehabilitation, clergy, developmental disabilities, family advocates, and other concerned staff and community representatives. An individualized resource coordinator identifies those people already in the child's life and configures a wraparound team. This team, operating on the premise "never give up" develops culturally competent individualized services in the life domain of the child and family. Life domains include the basic human needs such as a place to live, family, social, friends, psychological/emotional, safety, and so forth. Family strengths—"the good news about families"—are assessed, and problems are reframed. A family resistant to assistance might be commended for being a wise shopper for services, or an assaultive child might be reframed as someone who tries to stick up for himself. Creative approaches to meeting life domain needs might include hiring a college student who models acceptable behavior while keeping a youth from running away or doing destructive behaviors. Parent involvement is key to the wraparound approach. Wraparound services are funded through integration of funding streams for children's services and are cost effective in the prevention of expensive residential care or hospitalization.

Family preservation approaches are also used by some mental health agencies to meet the needs of children who might otherwise need psychiatric hospitalization or residential care. These programs provide a variety of family-based mental health services, including assertive community treatment teams for intensive and flexible crisis intervention; family intervention specialists who work as a team in providing home-based clinical services; and early intervention teams who handle intake, provide on-call crisis services, and carry cases up to three months. Some also work with wraparound services for young people involved with the Department of Social Services and the juvenile court. Like other family preservation programs, they incorporate the use of other community resources at time of closure to maintain the family's progress. Similarly, in some states intensive, family-based service programs are providing service to women in domestic violence shelters as they make the transition from the shelter to a new life in the community.

New models to coordinate substance abuse treatment with child welfare and maternal child health services are being conceptualized and implemented in response to the epidemic of crack cocaine addiction.

The number of infants in New York City reported with positive drug toxicology increased 268 percent between 1986 and 1988. During the peak twelve-month period of the crack crisis, between July 1988, and June 1989, there were 20,900 new admissions into foster care in New York (Sabol, 1994).

Parental addiction is seen as "a chronic relapsing disorder" (Besharov, 1994, p. ix) which requires that current child welfare programs must be radically re-oriented. Recognition of the severity of substance abuse and addiction—especially to crack cocaine—has led to a number of collaborative or cooperative approaches which often involve health, substance abuse treatment, child development, and child care and child welfare services. Many of these initiatives involve longer-term case management than the typical family preservation, short-term, crisis-intervention program. Family preservation teams serve substance-affected families in a short-term intervention. While working with the family they may help to substantiate that there is a problem, help parents consider the need for treatment, help parents access treatment, and help develop structures for the child's safety. The vast majority of children from drug-involved families are probably under the court's supervision (Barth, 1994), although many other such children are being monitored by the extended family kinship networks, under the watchful eye of the grandmothers or aunts providing informal kinship care.

Time-limited, intensive, family preservation services are not adequate for substance-affected families. Such cases need ongoing services for children who are not placed in foster care but who continue to need supervision and help in the form of services to the family, including transitional housing for recovering parents, family-focused rather than individually focused treatment, family planning services, and child care options. Recovering addicts should be trained to anticipate their own drug-using episodes and seek protection for their children before the crisis hits (Jones, 1994). Kinship care can be viewed as a form of family preservation that provides safe and supportive environments for children of addicts (Johnson, 1994). Barth (1994) proposes that intensive family preservation programs for drug users should be augmented by ongoing case management, shared family care, early childhood services, developmentally focused services, and child care to improve developmental outcomes while protecting children. The National Council of Juvenile and Family Court Judges developed a "reasonable efforts" protocol for substance-abuse cases. In examining the social service agency response to a substance abusing parent, some of the questions to be asked are as follows:

Has there been adequate intra-agency coordination to ensure that concrete services have been made available in a timely manner?

Have all relatives been contacted and their ability to care for the child been assessed?

How has the social service agency helped the substance-abusing parent obtain treatment?

Have referrals to treatment programs been appropriate . . . to programs experienced in treating women with the mother's particular addiction and problems with small children?

Has the availability of the following service programs been examined:
    family-centered drug treatment services
    intensive family preservation services
    emergency housing
    in-home caretaker
    out-of-home respite care
    teaching and demonstrating homemakers
    parenting-skills training
    transportation, etc.

(National Council of Juvenile and Family Court Judges, 1992, p. 19)

I was so scared that I'd lose my kids. I guess I might have deserved it because I'd been messing up and staying high for days at a time. If my worker hadn't gotten me into treatment I could be dead today. She gave us all a second chance, and we want to make it work. (a parent)

THE PRACTICE OF FAMILY-BASED SERVICES

The family-based services practitioner operates on values that form the bedrock of the family work. These values and beliefs enable the practitioner to enter a troubled family system effectively, engage family members, build hope, and begin the change process. One of the most important beliefs is in that workers and clients are partners in change. Another belief is that a crisis is an opportunity for change. However, the most important belief is that safety is the first concern.

While individual family preservation programs may follow fairly specific service delivery models, they generally focus on such practice components as engaging and building trust carefully; working in the clients' home whenever possible; providing concrete services; being available nights and weekends, with 24-hour-on-call backup; de-emphasizing diagnostic labeling; building on family strengths; setting specific client generated goals; and using client priorities (Kinney, Haapala, & Booth, 1991; Pecora, Whittaker, Maluccio, Barth, & Plotnick, 1992). The following case examples illustrate the unique aspects of family-based services practice.

Case 1: Protecting Children from Sexual Abuse and Domestic Violence

Reason for Referral.   Tammie had fled with her children, Kelly, age 3, and Bethany, age 1, to a domestic violence shelter in another county after being beaten by Pete, the father of her children. At the shelter she and the staff discovered that Kelly's statements seemed to indicate sexual abuse by Pete. Fearing a referral to child protective services, Tammie left the shelter precipitously, moved in with a new boyfriend, Tom, (who lived with several other men), and hid the children at her great-aunt's house so their father couldn't find them. She told her relative that she would get the children as soon as she found housing, but at the present time there was no room for them at Tom's place.

The great-aunt knew about the possibility of sexual abuse and was concerned about getting help for the children, so she called the local child protective services. The CPS worker was aware that Tammie had a previous referral in the county where the domestic violence shelter was located, and that her earlier living conditions had exposed the children to sexual and physical abuse. Other concerns were that Tammie's ability to protect the children was uncertain and that there appeared to be substance abuse in

the mother's current living situation. Tammie needed to learn how to protect her children and to fulfill her parenting responsibilities, and she needed assistance in establishing a home. The case was referred to the local family-preservation program.

Family Members.   Tammie, age 20, had run away from home at age 16, and lived on the streets of the nearest small city using drugs and occasionally trading sex for food or shelter. She was taken in by Pete, who fathered at least one of her two children. Tammie had left high school before her sixteenth birthday. As a young teen she had been sexually abused by her father when her mother was in a mental hospital. She left home before her mother returned from the hospital. Before the birth of her first child she tried to reach out to her parents, only to find that they had moved away and left word that they didn't want her to try to follow them. She is ambivalent about her parents, alternately missing them and hating them. Tammie is petite, attractive, and looks much younger than her years.

Kelly is 3½ years old. She appears healthy and strong for her small size although she eats mostly junk food. She resists going to sleep, but generally sleeps well with only occasional nightmares. She has had recurring bladder infections and is behind on her immunizations.

Bethany is 1 year old. She is quite small in size, which may be related to her mother's petite stature. She appears slightly developmentally delayed in motor skills in that she attempts to crawl but has not tried to stand yet. She appears attached to her mother.

Engagement and Developing Trust.   Elise, the family-preservation services worker, met Tammie at the child welfare office. Tammie was angry with her great-aunt for calling child protective services, dismayed that she was "in trouble," and angry that she couldn't just pick up her children and move on. Elise drove Tammie to see the children and listened on the way to her tearful explanation of why she had left the children. Their father, Pete, had taken Tammie in when she was on the streets at age 16. When Tammie became pregnant by Pete she realized that she was terribly dependent on him because her parents had moved away without her and she had nowhere to go. Before Tammie gave birth to Kelly, Pete became increasingly physically abusive to her. She tried working at a fast food restaurant to earn enough money to be able to leave Pete, but she was afraid to leave Kelly at home with him. She became increasingly depressed, quit her job, and was completely isolated. When she came home from the hospital after having their second child, Bethany, Kelly complained to her of a "sore bottom." Tammie wondered if Kelly had been sexually abused, but was too afraid and depressed to confront Pete and too ashamed to ask for help. When she was ready to leave Pete she took the children with her to the shelter, planning to leave the children with her great-aunt as soon as possible.

She felt lucky that Tom was taking care of her, but knew that it wasn't a good place to bring the children. She didn't know whether Tom or his friends could be trusted and Tom didn't want kids around anyway. Besides, she was just too upset to take care of them at the moment.

Elise listened quietly to the outpouring of despair as they drove to the great-aunt's home. She noted that Tammie was shaking and offered her a jacket to help keep her warm. She waited while Tammie visited with the children and observed that the little ones ran to their mother, clinging to her and kissing her. After the visit she dealt with Tammie's tears by asking how she could help and by reminding Tammie that the purpose of family-preservation services was to keep families together. Tammie identified her first goal—finding housing—and her greatest fear—that Pete would find her or the children.

Assessment of Strengths.   Although Tammie had had a traumatic adolescence and appeared very young because she was physically petite, she showed maturity in her wish to be a good parent to her daughters and to locate housing. Tammie and the children appeared bonded to each other and showed appropriate emotion at their visit. Tammie is attractive, personable, and shows normal intelligence. She has made efforts to remove herself from a difficult situation, the first time when she tried to work so that she could leave Pete, and the second time when she actually left and found

a safe place for the children. Tammie was excited that family-preservation services would work with her to locate housing and establish a home for the children.

Goal Setting.   Tammie, with Elise's help, established four goals for the time they would be working together:

1. Secure affordable housing and furnishings for the family that could be maintained over time
2. Protect the children from further physical or sexual abuse and herself from Pete's violence
3. Improve parenting and child management skills
4. Improve her self-esteem regarding relationships with men and her ability to select men who would not be a danger to her and the children

Action Steps to Reach Goals.   Elise and Tammie worked together to locate a mobile home that could be rented reasonably. FPS flexible funding paid the security deposit and the first month's rent. Tammie applied for Temporary Assistance to Needy Families (TANF), foodstamps, and WIC. Elise took Tammie to the distribution point for free commodities. They went grocery shopping together, and Tammie learned that nutritious snack foods such as apples and bananas are actually cheaper than potato chips and cheese curls. Elise referred Tammie to the county extension family nutrition program. They purchased a copy of "The Cheapskate's Gazette," a local bargain-hunter's newsletter, and scoured thrift shops in order to furnish the trailer and locate equipment such as a toddler car seat for Bethany. Tammie was also referred to the public assistance employment program with the goal of finding work that would fit her long-range goal of obtaining a GED or completing high school. Tammie and Elise talked about how to network with her new neighbors and barter goods or services such as child care or a ride to town. These action steps related to the goal of being able to live on assistance and maintain housing until she found adequate employment.

Legal action was begun for a restraining order to protect Tammie from Pete. According to the prosecuting attorney there was insufficient evidence to initiate criminal charges of sexual abuse against him.

However medical exams, and the great-aunt's report that Kelly was displaying the sexual behavior of "humping" with her toys, indicated that sexual abuse had in all likelihood occurred. Elise provided Tammie with several books and a videotape about protecting children from sexual abuse and discussed protection plans with her. They discussed sleeping arrangements for the children, who could be trusted with the children, and how to manage sexual acting-out behaviors. They also worked on other safety issues, such as a fire escape plan, putting all cleaning substances and other poisonous or hazardous supplies in high or locked cupboards, and generally child-proofing the inside and the yard of the mobile home.

In preparation for the return of the children from the great-aunt's house, Elise began teaching Tammie child-management skills, including environmental controls, time-out, active listening, positive reinforcement, and natural and logical consequences. The children were returned to their mother several days after the mobile home was ready. Tammie and the worker spent many hours together as Tammie tried her new parenting techniques. One resource available in the rural community was a Head Start program that provided transportation and had a parent support group. Kelly was enrolled in Head Start after having been reunited with her mother for two weeks. Elise took Tammie to the first parent support group at the Head Start Center. The county nutritional aide began visiting. Tammie went to the county health department for the well-baby clinic and family planning services.

Tammie thought carefully about her dependency on men and the reasons she had gravitated to a relationship that would turn abusive to her and the children. Elise gently helped her see that she had characteristics, such as intelligence and sensitivity, that were as important as the "sexiness" that Tammie thought was her prime attribute. As her capacity to parent increased, Tammie realized that she had strengths of her own which meant she was not dependent on a male for survival. Tammie's relationship with her boyfriend Tom continued, but she began to look at how she might survive if the relationship should end. She began to examine this relationship for clues that Tom, too, might be abusive to her or the children. She listened to

tapes on how to overcome past dysfunctional family rules in order to have healthier adult relationships. Elise coached Tammie on assertiveness-training skills.

Termination. After five weeks the goals had been attained and the safety net of ongoing services was in place. The child protective services case would remain open. A public health nurse would make home visits, watch Bethany's development, and ensure that the children's immunizations continued. The nutrition aide would assist Tammie in meal planning and accessing commodities. Head Start and the parent support group would help her meet Kelly's developmental needs. The great-aunt would provide child care for brief periods if Tammie needed a break. Tammie could get transportation to town with a neighbor or her landlady. A restraining order against Pete would remain in effect, and Tammie's location remained a secret.

Elise had spent sixty-eight hours providing services to Tammie, including many hours of driving to services in the rural area. She had also spent slightly over $800 in flexible funds to cover initial costs of housing and furnishings plus some lunches and reading materials. Elise reflected in retrospect, "All that time I spent driving paid off. When Tammie and the kids were in the car with me we talked and interacted productively. When they weren't with me I used my recorder for dictation. Working in a rural area has its problems, like isolation and poverty, but you know all the key players in the helping system so you can get things done quickly. Besides, I appreciate the fresh air and wide open spaces."

Case Commentary. Family-preservation services lends itself well to rural social work. The worker creates clinical interventions and brings them to the home, counterbalancing the reality concern that many services do not exist or are inaccessible to a young mother isolated in a trailer in the hills with two small children and no transportation. If Tammie had lived nearer to the battered women's shelter or had known earlier how to access that service system in the nearest city, she might have left an abusive relationship before her child was ever molested and would not have come to the attention of child protective services.

One might wish that a local sexual abuse survivors group or support group for women who had experienced battering had been available, so Tammie could continue to look at her dependent relationships with men. It is also clear that she has many unresolved family of origin issues. Perhaps she will be able or willing to address them as she matures; perhaps she won't. But Tammie is young and resilient. She has one family member in her support network who can help provide some stability. It is unfortunate that in this somewhat isolated county there is no children's play therapist available to work with Kelly regarding the trauma of sexual abuse, witnessing violence, and experiencing temporary separation from her mother. For the time being the family is together and has survived a crisis. Protective services involvement could be helpful in negotiating future developments with Pete, or in financing other needed services. The short-term goals have been accomplished, and the family is stabilized. There are supportive services in place, as a step down from the intensive family-based services, which should help the family to stabilize further and begin working toward long-range goals. In the future as Tammie grows and pursues her goals there will be time for more changes.

This case illustrates the importance of providing concrete services to keep a family together and the use of multiple techniques to strengthen a parent's competence. The worker's reflections capture much of the essence and challenge of rural social work.

Case 2: The Importance of Cultural Competence

Patricia Sandau-Beckler, Riccardo Salcido, and John Ronnau (1993) present a case study of cultural competence with a Hispanic family in an international border community. Understanding the nuances of culture is a critical skill for family preservation workers engaging families across ethnic and cultural boundaries.

Reason for Referral. The 10-year-old daughter of the N. family was referred to child protective services by the school because she had black-and-blue marks on her left arm and a circular bruise on her right arm. The girl indicated that her mother had hit her with a belt. When the father was contacted he stated that there had been disagreements and that he felt remorseful because he had been present but had not intervened when the girl was beaten by her mother. In a home visit (conducted in Spanish by the CPS worker) Mrs. N. stated that she had verbally and physically abused her children in the past and that she was willing to work with a family preservation counselor.

Family Members. Mr. N. spoke both Spanish and English, and had traditional values that made him uncomfortable with asking for help from outsiders. He felt that family matters were nobody's business. Mrs. N. lacked experience and knowledge of the norms in the United States and often relied on extended family members' perceptions of situations. She felt a great deal of shame about what she had done, but denied physical abuse. She was attempting to use the same forms of discipline with her 10-year-old that she had experienced as a child. She was also very concerned that her 17-year-old daughter had abused her privileges by having sexual relations with her boyfriend. The 17-year-old daughter thought she might be pregnant. When she had tried to run away earlier, her mother ripped off her blouse, pushed her out of the home, and locked the door. There was also a 7-year-old son.

Engagement and Building Trust. The family preservation counselor was bilingual with a third-generation Mexican-American parent deeply rooted in traditional values. Her heritage helped her to be sensitive to the values and cultural practices of first-generation Mexican-American families. For example, she was careful to wait at the door until invited into the home. She attempted to learn about the family's values and culture by asking about their families of origin in Mexico and the traditions that the family followed, encouraging the family to give her information about their experiences. Ideas about candy-making, a recipe for homemade tortillas, and stories about their Mexican lineage were exchanged. The counselor showed respect for the father's traditional values and explored with the mother the changes she would like to see in the family. These conversations were part of the counselor's attempt to acknowledge both their shared values and their differences.

Assessment of Strengths.   Together the counselor and the mother identified strengths, such as the concern the mother had for her children and the mother's attempt to provide support for the children as they adjusted to the new culture. The counselor complimented the mother on the way that she took pride in the home, her concern for her children and husband, her ability to express herself even though she was shy, and her recognition that there was a problem. The children in the family were all above-average students and this was highlighted. The father's concern about the children's discipline was also a strength.

Goal Setting.   Together the family preservation counselor and the mother explored and decided on the following goals:

1. Better communication between family members
2. Anger management
3. A more involved role in discipline by the father
4. Improved relationships with her daughter
5. More ease in displaying affection with her children
6. Marital counseling for conflicts she was experiencing with her husband

Culturally Competent Intervention.   Among many interventions aimed at reaching Mrs. N.'s goals, a number of them illustrate the cultural competence of the family preservation counselor. She explored cultural issues and recognized the importance of being aware of her own culture and the differences between her values and the more traditional values of the client family. She modified her approach when Mr. N. told his wife privately that he felt uncomfortable talking to outsiders, especially one who was a woman. Instead of providing marital therapy, she met privately with Mrs N. to help her mourn the loss of the ideas she had about her children's adherence to traditional cultural values. The mother was concerned that her husband did not want her to work outside the home, wear makeup, take dance lessons, or do things outside the home. Many of these issues related to strong cultural

traditions about the role of women in Mexican society. The counselor showed restraint in not moving the family toward adapting American cultural traditions unless the family made that choice.

Termination.   At the time of case closing, after eight months, the changes in this family included the mother's full realization that physical abuse of the children was unhealthy. She was able to successfully put an end to the abuse. The 17-year-old's feelings about her abuse as a child were acknowledged and validated by the mother. The daughter's acting-out behavior subsided and she began to exhibit more open communication with her family. The mother's affection for the children was apparent, and the mother's parenting of the younger children changed considerably as she recognized the long-term effects of her abusive behavior on her older daughter. Although Mr. N. was an active participant in only two family sessions, he accepted the changes in all family members (Abridged and adapted from Sandau-Beckler, et al., 1993, with permission from the American Counseling Association).

Case Commentary.   Although this case example is an illustration of work with one family from a particular cultural background, it aptly demonstrates generalizable strategies for the culturally competent provision of services. The flexibility of the family-preservation model and the family-oriented values are an important part of this worker's ability to sort out her own cultural values and respond appropriately to the family's more traditional stance. Family-based services for family preservation are relevant to the social work emphasis on diversity. Family preservation thinking has also been applied to African-American families (Gray & Nybell, 1990); Native American families (Cross, 1987; Mannes, 1993); poor families (Ronnau & Marlow, 1993); and lesbian families (Faria, 1994). Respecting clients' cultures and beliefs, learning about the family's cultural context, sorting out differences in one's own values, advocating for one's clients, and dispelling stereotypes and myths are all ways in which family preservation workers can operationalize social work knowledge, values, and skills about diversity.

Other Approaches That Help High-Risk Families

Child protective services case workers make determinations about whether a child can be protected within his or her family or whether placement of the child in out-of-home care is necessary, based on a thorough investigation and assessment of risk (see Chapter 7).

Although the newer family-based services are seen as a potent force and the prevailing model for the prevention of placement, many other services continue to form a first line of defense against child abuse and family dismemberment, to prevent child abuse, and to support or treat families before placement or after family reunification. Children can be maintained in homes, and family life can be sustained, through a variety of programs, including family counseling, parent education, recreational groups, day treatment, drop-in or respite child care, homemaker services, parent aides, foster grandparents, and Head Start. These programs are used in a variety of combinations to work with families' diverse situations and family members' unique needs for nurture, stimulation, comfort, competence, contact, well-being, and protection. (See Chapters 4 and 5.)

Many of the treatment approaches discussed here can be used with families and children whether or not the child has been removed from the home. In some cases they are also part of a family reunification plan. (See Chapter 9.) These services are reasonable efforts to keep families together and are often offered as long-term follow-up after the intensive service phase of family preservation (four to eight weeks) has been completed. Such interventions include parent education, groups, and various forms of ongoing treatment using family systems, behavioral-cognitive, psychosocial, Transactional Analysis, play therapy, and other modalities.

Treating Loneliness. This phrase grew out of the observation that "among neglectful parents are many who make their circumstances worse by self-imposed aloneness, and who must thus deal with dreadful loneliness" (Polansky et al, 1981, p. 210). Although the roots of isolation may lie in circumstances of the parent's childhood, it can to some extent be remedied by providing parents the opportunity to be with people.

Group treatment of parents being served by CPS has been used as a medium for dealing with individual problems, marital problems, and child-management techniques. An often-overlooked function of these groups, apart from other benefits, is that they give parents an opportunity to interact with other adults.

An example of groupwork with abusive parents is a twelve-week program designed to build social support networks for low-income abusive mothers who received training in conversational skills, self-protection, and assertion. In the first session women examined various types of friendships and were encouraged to identify features or patterns in their social networks. The term *friend* carried negative connotations—members reported being hurt and taken advantage of by persons they had considered friends. In the second session they identified danger signs of relationship problems, such as drug problems or lying. In the fourth session the right to feel safe was emphasized, with discussion of protective techniques. During the next few sessions participants focused on basic social skills such as initiating, maintaining, and ending conversations. In sessions eight through eleven, the women learned how to assert themselves and handle criticism. In the final session a shopping outing provided an opportunity for members to practice new social skills (Lovell, Reid, & Richey, 1992).

Treatment with individual parents can also incorporate the concept of strengthening social networks. Tracy, Whittaker, Pugh, Kapp, and Overstreet (1994) report that social network mapping used with family preservation clients yielded rich data about the importance of social support in helping families avert placement. One result of the mapping was that gathering social network data was often a critical step for workers in engaging the families in treatment, as well as enhancing social empowerment.

C is a 26-year-old African-American single mother with a 20-year-old male partner and a 2-year-old son. The mother was reported for neglect, leaving her son unsupervised for two to three hours at a time, and also for spanking the child excessively with a belt. Review of the social network map showed that she received insufficient support from the extended family . . .

The goals for this family were to teach basic child-care skills and to capitalize on the support system that was in place. Family meetings were held to strengthen family relationships. The parents were encouraged to contact family or friends when they needed help (Tracy et al., 1994, p. 487).

In some incestuous sexual abuse situations, children are left in the home contingent on the removal or departure of the perpetrator. The decision to remove the perpetrator rather than the child is largely related to the assessment of the mother's understanding of the situation and her strength in establishing boundaries to protect the child (Ryan, Warren, & Weincek, 1992). Intensive sexual abuse treatment programs (Giarretto, 1982) work with each member of the family system individually, in groups, and later in family treatment. Self-help and support groups such as Parents United and Sons and Daughters United also strengthen the treatment process and contribute to the possibility that a child can be maintained in his or her own home.

Help with Reality Problems.   For neglecting and abusing parents, actions usually speak louder than words. The disorganized daily living pattern of neglecting families means that family workers must relate directly to everyday problems and behaviors, and give direct help with pressing reality problems. These parents are not ready to deal with introspective questions.

Reality-oriented services are typically used when problems have been detected that are not quite serious enough to warrant removal of the children without an attempt to rectify the problem and meet the needs of the family and children. Each type of service can have multiple functions. In a "dirty house" case, a homemaker can mobilize the family to clean up the litter of dirty laundry, decaying food, animal feces, and dirt piles. The homemaker may also demonstrate housekeeping skills, teach basic techniques, model positive attitudes toward housecleaning, help the mother develop a cleaning routine, and break through the atmosphere of discouragement and depression surrounding the neglected home environment.

A parent aide can bring new input to an entropic situation of a young parent marooned with small children. She may provide transportation for shopping, set up recreational activities to stimulate and cheer a depressed mother, and counteract the isolation that heightened the risk of child maltreatment. Yet the success of a parent aide may depend more on intangible qualities of the relationship that develops between parent and aide than on activities. Kind and supportive comments by the aide may nurture the parent and provide role modeling of effective interaction, which can carry over into discipline of the children.

Head Start, which stimulates social and cognitive development to prepare preschoolers to succeed in school also has additional benefits for other family members, even as it is nurturing the child. Aside from the obvious respite it provides to stressed parents, it also offers adult socialization and learning opportunities, as parents engage in parent groups and programs.

Housing is an extremely important element of family preservation. In the past many children were at risk of placement due in part to homelessness or inadequate housing. The Family Unification Project falls under the general category of family preservation services and supports, and is unique in that its central element is housing assistance. This program brings together child welfare agencies and housing agencies in collaborative efforts to make the needs of child welfare families and persons in domestic violence shelters a top priority. In 1993, in participating cities, some 1,275 foster care placements of children were avoided through this collaboration (Doerre & Mihaly, 1996).

Coordinated Service Delivery.   Cases of abuse and neglect are complex, often involving families with multiple problems that create a state of disorganization. Coordination of efforts is critical. This may done by a child protective services worker or an ongoing case manager. Shapiro's study (1979) found that families who received several services did better than families who received only one or two. Other studies of comprehensive services indicated the following:

1. An appropriate array of services must be available—not counseling alone or concrete services alone, but a combination.
2. Outreach services are critical; merely having services available is not enough. Clients must be

enabled to use these services through such mechanisms as physically bringing clients to the service by providing transportation; advocacy efforts to access needed services; and skill in case management (Jones et al, 1981, p. 73).

The impetus of practice is toward family-based, in-home services, with ongoing case management of wraparound or "step-down" services once the immediate crisis period is over.

Few programs combine family support and family preservation, so developing an integrated approach hinges on the integration of disparate organizational cultures and paradigms. Family-support programs work primarily with communities, schools, and hospitals, while family-preservation programs are tied to public or private child welfare agencies (Kaplan & Girard, 1994). A significant shift toward integration of these services can be seen in the recent collaboration of the National Resource Center on Family Centered Practice and the National Resource Center for Family Support Programs. The Family Partnership Project, another collaborative effort, involves the two National Resource Centers (above) with the Child Welfare League of America and the National Association for Family-Based Services in exploring further connections between family support and family preservation (Prevention Report, 1994).

EVALUATION OF FAMILY PRESERVATION PROGRAMS

Family-based services, which is a generic term, and intensive family preservation services (IFPS, which refers to Homebuilders-based models) share a common difficulty in evaluation—they are prevention programs. It is difficult to demonstrate that an event was prevented and that, if it was, a certain intervention is causally linked with the nonoccurrence of the event. Moreover, the program evaluation criteria and research design of many projects have come into question. A comprehensive review of family-preservation literature questioned whether target families in many studies were actually at risk of imminent placement (Blythe, Salley, & Jayaratne, 1994). Hess, Folaron,

and Jefferson (1992) remind us that using nonplacement or family reunification as the singular definition of success (rather than a successful placement outcome) reflects a potentially dangerous implementation of family preservation.

Other issues in the evaluation discourse include the importance of evaluating family functioning and differentiating characteristics or types of families with whom the approach is successful. In a review of family preservation program evaluations, Rossi (1992) identified a number of shortcomings: (1) the numbers of subjects were too small to detect effects reliably; (2) the programs evaluated were not given enough time to be fully operational before being evaluted; (3) the major criterion of success—placement avoidance—is arguably insufficient; and (4) the analysis strategies used were overly simple. Thus he concluded that the evaluations neither support nor contradict the effectiveness of family preservation strategies (Rossi, 1992).

As the prototypical family preservation program, Homebuilders set an expectation for program evaluation. They defined success in terms of cost-effectiveness and the prevention of placement. Working with a population considered to be "at imminent risk of placement," Homebuilders defined success as the prevention of placement at twelve months from the initiation of service. Using these criteria, Homebuilder's success rate varied from 73 percent to 91 percent of families served. The per-child cost of Homebuilders, $2,700, compared favorably with the average costs of placement—$5,113 for foster care, $19,673 for group care, $25,078 for residential care, or $100,200 for psychiatric hospitalization (Kinney, Haapala, & Booth, 1991). Forsythe (1992) said of Homebuilders, "Its superiority for reform purposes lay particularly in its strong documentation of methodology, proven replicability, and a decade of data that supported its claims of cost effectiveness and reduced unnecessary placement" (p. 40).

A similar framework for program evaluation has been used in a number of programs derived from the Homebuilders model. Michigan's Families First evaluated services to 225 children, of which 96 percent were at risk of placement according to referring workers. These cases were compared to a matched group of 225 children previously placed in foster care, and

Homebuilders had a consistently lower out-of-home placement rate at three, six, and twelve months after intervention. If foster care placement for 85 percent of the children was averted by Families First, savings to the state amounted to $46,651,000 the first year after intervention (Bergquist, Szwejda, & Pope, 1993).

However, a damper on these optimistic estimates of cost savings and placement prevention came in 1992 with an extensive evaluation of Illinois' Family First program. The study, done by Chapin Hall with the Illinois Department of Children and Family Services, found that the risk of placement for cases served by the Family First program was actually quite low. Therefore the program could not be said to prevent placement. In addition, the evaluation found that the program had no effect on rates of subsequent reports of maltreatment after program intervention (Scheurman, Rzepnicki, & Littell, 1992a). This information was used by media to reach the simplistic conclusion that family preservation didn't work.

It should be noted that the media used these suggestions that Family First was less than had been promised in accounts that were somewhat distorted and over-simplified, causing some private agency and CFS staff to be unhappy about what they considered to be an attack on the program precipitated by the evaluation (Scheurman, Rzepnicki, & Littell, 1992). The social and political ramifications of program evaluation are evident in this example.

A critical issue raised in Scheurman's research is a common problem in the implementation of social programs—that the programs may not be provided to those for whom they are intended. Family preservation services are targeted at families in which a child is at "imminent risk of placement." However, many, if not most, of the children in both the comparison and treatment groups (to which they had been randomly assigned) were not at imminent risk of placement. The researchers suggest that family preservation services should take their place in a larger agenda of reform in the child welfare system, including attention to improving the communities in which children live, because the families receiving services have great needs and the services are not necessarily being wasted (Scheurman, Rzepnicki, Littell, & Budde, 1992b).

The impact of this research continues, with Littell (1997) providing an additional analysis of Chapin Hall data and concluding that "it appears that the duration, intensity, and breadth of family preservation services have little impact on subsequent child maltreatment, out-of-home placement or the closing of cases in child welfare" (p. 34). Responding to the Chapin Hall research, Courtney (1997) concludes that two issues are clear: "Service and support approaches should be developed for clearly defined subpopulations of families and children. . . . one size simply doesn't fit all" (p. 73) and "A retreat from the unrealistic early objectives of the family preservation movement is reasonable" (p. 74).

Recently researchers have directed attention away from the global question of whether family preservation works and toward specific issues, such as what kinds of family characteristics are associated with success in a family preservation program and what influences family preservation programs have on family functioning.

Thieman and Dail (1997) examined predictors of out-of home-placement in a family preservation program to ascertain if welfare recipients are particularly vulnerable. They concluded that neither low income nor receiving public assistance was predictive of having a child removed from the home. The predictors were child-centered and parent-centered risk factors. Further research is needed to determine to what extent family dysfunction is a result of poverty and to identify effective programs for different family issues. However, Bath, Richey, and Haapala (1992) found family income (and parental mental health problems) to be the only predictive variables for child placement.

Scannapieco (1993) acknowledged the effectiveness of family preservation services in preventing placement, but raised the critical issue of family functioning. Until recently there has been little research on the relationship between family functioning and placement. Scannapieco found improved family functioning for 75 percent of families who had participated in a family preservation program. She also found that 78 percent of the families did not experience placement during the program period, and that there is a relationship between family functioning improvement and placement prevention (Scannapieco, 1993).

Wells and Whittington (1993) studied family functioning in a population of families served by a mental health agency. Data show that many of the problems that families had at admission were either eliminated or improved by follow-up. However, these families were functioning lower than the nonclinical samples, suggesting that they were still vulnerable. They point out that intensive family preservation services are intended to help families achieve some basic skills considered necessary to keep children at home; they are not designed to effect major changes in ways in which families function. They add, "It is unclear whether it is a positive outcome for an emotionally disturbed child designated as at imminent risk of residential placement to remain at home with the help of intensive family preservation services if residential treatment could resocialize that child and alter highly dysfunctional patterns of family functioning. . . .We argue, as a result, that intensive family preservation services should be evaluated case by case with an eye towards the goals of the placement services that they are intended to replace" (Wells & Whittington, 1993, p. 77).

Another key issue in the evaluation of family preservation programs is the examination of group differences between neglectful and abusive families. Bath and Haapala (1993) found that the outcome picture for neglect cases was less positive than for other treatment categories. Using the referring worker's reason for referral as the basis of the maltreatment categories (sexual abuse, physical abuse, neglect, and combination), they examined outcomes for each group. While the majority of children in all treatment groups avoided out-of-home placement, significantly fewer physical abuse group children were placed than those in the neglect and combined groups. Neglectful families are affected by a greater range of environmental, social, and personal difficulties, and suffer the effects of poverty more than their abusive counterparts. The authors suggest that further research is needed to determine whether a longer time intervention may be useful with neglect families (Bath & Haapala, 1993).

Berry's (1992) evaluation of family preservation services focused on fitting agency services to family

needs also indicated that the services were not as effective with neglectful families. She found that while neglect cases were open longer, they received somewhat less service time overall. The neglect families were assessed by DSS workers as having significantly poorer family functioning than others. Mentally incapacitated families were somewhat more likely to experience adjudicated child neglect and to have a higher placement rate. The proportion of worker time spent in the home is highly related to success. Families that received larger proportions of their service time in the home were more likely to stay together. The type of service provided also made a difference in outcome. Families were best served and more likely to stay intact when services were concrete, such as medical care, help in the securing of food, and financial services (Berry, 1992).

A key dimension of program evaluation in family preservation services is client satisfaction. Consistent with a family empowerment value orientation, most programs ascertain client perceptions of services given. An evaluation of the Michigan Families First program showed that client families were highly satisfied with the services:

- 92 percent gave the top rating of "very satisfied" to their overall interaction with their worker, and an additional 6 percent were "somewhat satisfied."
- 98 percent would recommend Families First to another family in a similar situation.
- 98 percent of families agreed that the Families First worker listened to and understood their situation, and 94 percent said that they felt neither hurried or pressured.
- 82 percent reported behavioral changes in family interactions as a result of Families First intervention, while examples focused on improved communication, appropriate discipline, and better care of children (Bergquist, Szwejda, & Pope, 1993).

There are many challenges for program evaluation and research in family preservation services. Some of the issues that will continue to be addressed are the targeting of imminent risk (determining whether the children are really at risk); further development of experimental design utilizing control groups; whether prevention of placement should be the only or main criterion of success; whether implementation of family-based services actually reduces entry into foster care, thus saving money and essentially paying for itself; with which types of families and children is a particular model most effective; and how family functioning is improved by particular types of services. Pediatric researchers call for more attention to be directed to the *child's* functioning, particularly in the domains of cognitive and social development (Heneghan, Horwitz, & Levanthal, 1996).

In examining what has been learned from the family-preservation initiative, Maluccio and Whittaker (1997) conclude that there are three tasks of knowledge-building through more relevant, sophisticated, and practice-oriented research: (1) identify areas of consensus about what has been learned; (2) pinpoint areas of disagreement to be framed as empirical questions for the next generation of research; and (3) develop protocols and guidelines to guide future research and program demonstration.

KINSHIP CARE AS FAMILY PRESERVATION

An historic tradition of mutual assistance within kinship networks is part of many diverse cultural groups. From the villages of Africa and the clans of Scotland, our ancestors brought to the New World an understanding that the extended family cared for children when parents were unable to or unavailable. Kinship care is increasingly viewed as both the context and an integral part of culturally competent family-preservation practice. According to the North American Kinship Care Policy and Practice Committee of the Child Welfare League of America,

> Care of children by kin is strongly tied to family preservation. Family strengths often include a kinship network that functions as a support system. The kinship support system may be composed of nuclear family, extended family, blended family, foster family or adoptive family members, or members of tribes and clans. The involvement of kin may stabilize family situations, ensure the protection of children, and prevent the need to separate children from their families and place them in the formal child welfare system. (Child Welfare League, 1994, p. 1)

It was through efforts of the original people of the United States that concepts of kinship were first enacted into child welfare law. Beginning in the nineteenth century, official U.S. policy emphasized forced assimilation of Native American people. Indian boarding schools were established, which disciplined children harshly for speaking their own language, made them cut their hair and wear uniforms rather than uniquely decorated native clothes, and eradicated vestiges of culture (Horesji, Heavy Runner, & Pablo, 1992). In these schools several social problems, abusive physical discipline, and sexual abuse were inflicted on the children and thus introduced to the native cultures. These problems distorted the intergenerational transmission of parenting and led to further involvement by the child welfare system. Countless Native American children had been removed from their families in the decades prior to passage of the Indian Child Welfare Act.

Native American Kinship Care

The Indian Child Welfare Act of 1978 affirmed the extended family structures that are part of the culture. Children were no longer to be removed to white foster or adoptive homes. Rather they were to be placed in their own extended family, in their tribe, or with another Native American family if they couldn't remain with their own family. Jurisdiction over children was returned to tribal courts. Similarly, in Canada Native people demanded more control over child welfare programs affecting their communities (McKenzie, 1989).

Before the era of dominance by non-Indian influences, Indian communities had a cohesive communal life, which protected children, based on the values and teachings of the society. Within the extended family network, child rearing was shared. Children were safeguarded because they were under the watchful eye of an aunt, grandmother, or tribal elders. Children belonged not to an individual or couple but rather to the entire community. The interdependence of extended family members provided a strong substitute care system (Cross, 1986). With the passage of the Indian Child Welfare Act of 1978, P.L. 95-608, which restored jurisdiction over their children to a sovereign people, the importance of kinship ties was thrust into the consciousness of child welfare. This federal legislation provided the opportunity for tribes to serve Native American children and their families in a culturally sensitive way and to undo the shameful legacy of colonialism, which had separated countless children from their tribal families.

The Indian Child Welfare Act of 1978 was also a precursor of the family preservation movement. Although the act addressed the issue of Native American tribal sovereignty and was designed to stop the alarmingly high percentages of Native American children placed in non-Indian foster homes, adoptive homes, and institutions, it brought into clear focus the issues of culture and extended family kinship networks. Kessel and Robbins (1984) called for the infusion into social work practice literature of knowledge of Indian culture, traditions, family, and child rearing, knowledge of the extended family system and community network for reservation and nonreservation Indians, and skills in a variety of social work methods from micro to macro.

Since implementation of the Indian Child Welfare Act, Indian child welfare programs have had to develop placement standards that are culturally sensitive to unique tribal traditions. Tribal and nontribal Indian children and youth have been placed with aunts, uncles, grandparents, and others. These kinship-care placements are often mistakenly viewed by the non-Indian child welfare system as temporary or long-term foster care settings. Native American organizations and tribal governments have struggled to get states to accept extended family placements as legitimate (Mannes, 1993). To many, extended family placement *is* a form of family preservation. Additionally, a number of intensive family preservation programs have been developed by tribes to work with parents, in the context of community, tribe, and cultural tradition.

African-American Kinship Care

In the United States during the 1980s, kinship care, long a strength of the African American community, was increasing as more and more children affected by parental addiction and substance abuse were being raised by grandparents and other relatives. Kinship care in the foster care system had earlier been called "relative placement" and was used infrequently. By the 1990s, kinship care had been reconceptualized as a form of family preservation (Gray & Nybell, 1990; Child Welfare League of America, 1994) and was used extensively. In 1990, half of New York City's foster care population was in kinship care (Meyers & Link, 1990), as was typical of other major urban areas. Additionally, many other children across the country were being raised in "informal" kinship care outside of the foster care system.

In the African-American community, kinship care or informal adoption has long been a positive survival mechanism (Boyd-Franklin, 1989; Gray & Nybell, 1990). Autobiographical works by Langston Hughes, Frederick Douglass, and Maya Angelou show their grandmothers as strong caregivers who instilled in them a sense of worth and humanity. Despite the upheaval and damage created as a result of slavery, African Americans have preserved many of the characteristics associated with the strong family and community life of their African ancestors. The function, role, and revered status of the grandmother can be traced to the position and responsibilities grandparents held in West African society (Hill-Lubin, 1991).

Although the increase in grandparent caregiving in the 1980s and 1990s resulting from the epidemic of crack cocaine cuts across all ethnic lines, it has been particularly pronounced in the African-American community, where 12 percent of children live with their grandparents, compared with 5.8 percent of Hispanic and 3.6 percent of white children (U.S. Bureau of the Census, 1991). Many of these arrangements are *informal as* differentiated from formal placements made by the child welfare system. In informal situations, grandparents, aunts, and other relatives provide care for children of substance-affected mothers. In some instances, the mother and the extended family caregivers may share a common household.

Minkler, Roe, and Price, studying a sample of African-American kinship caregivers, found that grandmothers de-emphasized their health problems and reported good emotional health, which suggests an overly optimistic picture when contrasted with their qualitative responses about the stress of caregiving and the pain of watching the children's parents deteriorate with crack usage. The authors suggest that a contributing factor to the discrepancy may be fear that the grandchildren might be placed in foster care if they were unable to take care of them (Minkler, Roe, & Price, 1992). Grandmothers caring for their grandchildren need a variety of supports to meet the needs of young children, some of whom may have been affected by their mother's prenatal substance abuse. In informal care, the only financial support available is Temporary Assistance to Needy Families (TANF), whereas in formal kinship care, when the child has come under the jurisdiction of the court, the kinship caregiver may be licensed as a foster parent and receive a much higher rate of payment (Johnson, 1994). Family members often care for children at great sacrifice of their own needs. Grandmothers may have to quit their employment in order to provide care for young children. They discover that there aren't enough hours in the day to pursue their own age-appropriate interests and still be available for children. Some of the primary needs of kinship caregivers are respite care and support groups. When asked in a focus group what would help her the most, one grandmother replied, "I pray night and day for my daughter to recover from crack. I'll do anything I have to do to take care of these babies, but I want to know that you social workers are trying everything you can do to help my daughter recover."

Family Group Decision-Making

Indigenous people in many countries became aware of the Indian Child Welfare Act and its implications. In New Zealand, the Maori people who were taking the first steps toward the child welfare reform which would lead to the family group decision-making model of child protection work with extended family systems, were influenced by the U.S. Indian Child Welfare Act.

The family decision-making model in New Zealand has evoked wide interest in those working in family-based services in the United States. This model, emanating from the report Te Puao-Te-Ata-Tu, challenged the domination of the Maori people by the New Zealand descendents of English colonists.

Provisions from the treaty of Waitangi in the early nineteenth century granted Maoridom authority over its people, thus leading to the Children, Young Persons, and their Families Act of 1989, which acknowledged the rights of the Maori to make decisions for their own families. Although the family decision-making model was initially intended to honor the Maori culture through culturally appropriate methods, it has also been used with other Pacific Island peoples, and with members of the dominant Anglo-European culture. The family decision-making model has also recently been implemented in Australia with the Children's Protection Act of 1993.

The family decision-making model involves implementation of a conference of extended family members following an investigation of child abuse by a child protection worker or the police. The parents of the affected children agree to involve their extended kinship network in planning. The kinship network, or *Whanau*, is invited to participate and may converge from all parts of the two islands that comprise *Ao Tearoa* (New Zealand). The family decision-making conference is facilitated by a care and protection coordinator, with a Department of Social Welfare worker. It takes place in a comfortable setting and may last for several days. During the conference, information is shared by professionals about factors that place the child at risk. Then the professionals leave the conference, although the conference facilitator may remain available in a nearby room for consultation. The extended family develops a plan for protecting the child and providing a home within the kinship network if needed. The conference coordinator records the decisions and accesses resources needed for implementing the plan (Smith & Featherstone, 1991).

Adapting the family decision-making model to an American setting raises many issues (Zalenski, 1994; Merkel-Holguin, 1998). Child welfare practice in the United States has until recently had a strong focus on control by the social worker. Legal constraints around confidentiality, court processes, and liability may make it difficult to involve the extended family in planning (Hardin, 1994). Yet the model is being transplanted to a number of states and communities in the United States. Over 250 individuals from thirty-five states participated in a recent series of family group decision-making (FGDM) roundtables sponsored by the American Humane Association. Twenty-five states are planning or have implemented family group decision-making programs (American Humane Association, 1998). An estimated fifty communities in the country are involved with family group decision making (Merkel-Holguin, 1998.) As used in the United States, family group decision-making has a philosophy similar to the New Zealand model from which it was adapted. If families, communities, and the government partner to protect children, then extended families must be involved to make decisions in a nonadversarial process.

In practice in the United States, the child protection worker investigating a case determines that the case will be referred to a family group conference coordinator. In most states families are referred voluntarily, although in a few locations such meetings may be court-ordered. Merkel-Holguin (1998) identifies four distinct phases in the process:

Phase 1: Referral to hold an FGDM meeting
Phase 2: Preparation and planning
Phase 3: The family conference or meeting
Phase 4: Follow-up

The coordinator prepares and plans for the meeting, a process which may take weeks. This involves working with the family; identifying concerned parties and members of the extended kinship network; clarifying their roles and inviting them to a family group meeting; establishing the location, time, and other logistics; and managing other unresolved issues. At the meeting the coordinator welcomes and introduces participants in a culturally appropriate manner, establishes the purpose of the meeting, and helps participants reach agreement about roles, goals, and ground rules. Next, information is shared with the family, which may involve the child protection workers and other relevant professionals such as a doctor or teacher involved with the child. If the program strictly adheres to the New Zealand model, the coordinator and other professionals withdraw from the meeting in the next stage, in order to allow the family privacy for their deliberations. (Some programs have adjusted the model

to their local norms and allow the coordinator to remain in the meeting.) As a result of this process, the kinship network responds to several issues, including the safety of the child and the care of the child if they consider that protection is needed (American Humane Association, 1996). There is generally some type of follow-up involved to provide support to the designated caregivers and to plan for permanence when needed. It should be noted that the coordinator and/or child protection worker retain the right to veto a family plan if they believe the child will not be protected. In reality, this veto is rarely used.

Working with family group decision making requires a new approach to family-centered practice. The social worker must expand his or her ideas about the family to recognize the strength and centrality of the extended kinship network, particularly in communities of color. Use of the strengths perspective is critical. The worker must understand the greater investment of kin in the well-being of the child and should also understand that, even when parts of the kinship system may seem to be compromised or dysfunctional, the healthier kinfolk can assess and deal with the problem. One of the greatest challenges for the social worker is incorporating the sharing of power or returning of power to the kinship network. Many social workers trained as family therapists or child welfare workers have assumed a power role and may find it difficult to relinquish a sense of control. This may be manifested in worker concerns about the meeting being disrupted or concerns about the family's ability to make appropriate decisions to protect the child.

In the New Zealand model, the family meeting is conducted in private, without the presence of the coordinator or other professionals. In the United States, some communities do not use the concept of private family time. This central feature of FGDM seems to be a sticking point for some child welfare professionals who believe that "this family is too dysfunctional to make a rational decision" or "they need me to guide them" (Merkel-Holguin, 1998, p. 12). Such responses are identified by Turnell (1998) as paternalism, the process whereby the child welfare professional approaches the service recipient with the attitude that his or her opinions are most important in the interaction. Generally speaking, most FGDM workers welcome the opportunity to work in partnership with kin families and find it to be congruent with their values.

The following case illustrates the adaptation of this model in the United States and implementation within the American child protection system.

Case Study of Mental Health Consumers

Judy and Ronnie R. are parents of a 7-year-old son, Chad. Judy and Ronnie had met in a community drop-in center for consumers of mental health services. Judy, the adopted daughter of Tom and Sandy J., had complex special needs, including developmental and learning disabilities, occasional seizures, and motor difficulties. Ronnie, the son of Mary Ellen R., was diagnosed with a mental illness. Both received SSI for their disabilities. When Judy's pregnancy became evident, both families supported the marriage of the young couple and became actively involved as grandparents for Chad. From time to time Judy and Ronnie would leave their child with paternal or maternal grandparents when they felt unable to cope. Several times Tom and Sandy had gone to the R.'s apartment to pick up Chad and actively intervene in his behalf. Gradually Judy and Ronnie began to isolate themselves from the extended family and refuse to allow Chad to have his regular visits with the relatives.

A referral was made to child protective services by Chad's teacher and the school social worker. Chad had missed twenty days of school in the first semester and appeared dirty and hungry when he was in school. He had difficulty focusing on his work, slept in class, and cried frequently. The school social worker had attempted to engage the parents but was not allowed into their apartment. Ronnie was threatening and belligerent to the school social worker and refused to let Judy speak.

When the protective service worker visited the home, he found it to be dirty to the point of being a health hazard. He noted that Ronnie appeared to spend much of his time locked in the bedroom, and Judy was absorbed in the TV. In a visual assessment

of Chad he noted several bruises. The medical evaluation of Chad's condition was that he was suffering from malnutrition, was neglected, and that bruises on his back and buttocks were in the shape of handprints. In discussions with Judy, the protective service worker discovered that grandparents had been involved with Chad before Judy and Ronnie had shut them out. Both parents indicated that they would rather have the grandparents reinvolved with Chad than risk the possibility of placement outside the family. Ronnie and Judy agreed to have a family group decision-making conference. Chad was allowed to stay temporarily with the paternal grandmother, Mary Ellen, while the case was referred to a family group conference coordinator.

The coordinator received the names and telephone numbers of both paternal and maternal grandparents. She met with Tom and Sandy, and also with Mary Ellen, doing genograms with each family to identify members of the kinship network. Both sets of grandparents helped contact other family members. The conference coordinator talked with each potential participant to explain the FGDM process and purpose.

The conference was held within two weeks of the initial referral, at the small grass-roots agency where the coordinator worked. A number of persons attended the conference, including both sets of grandparents, Judy's two sisters and their husbands, her godparents, and her cousin. Ronnie's father, stepmother, and brother also attended. Ronnie and Judy chose not to attend the meeting. The coordinator explained the purpose of the meeting: to plan for the care and protection of Chad. After people became comfortable, with introductions and light refreshments, the coordinator invited the protective service worker to speak. He discussed the medical report, the teacher's concerns, and the condition of the apartment when he had called. The coordinator then asked the family to decide whether they thought Chad needed care and protection by his extended family. The professionals left the room, explaining that the family could have their discussion in private, but that the coordinator would be available as a consultant if they needed her. Within fifteen minutes, she was called back into the room by Tom, the maternal grandfather.

The grandparents took turns speaking. First Tom stated that their family was aware of Judy's limitations and that they had tried hard to support her, until they found themselves shut out by Ronnie. They believed that Chad needed to live away from his parents in order to receive proper care. Mary Ellen, the paternal grandmother, stated that their family had been increasingly concerned about Chad over the past several years and that she knew from having Chad with her the past several weeks that he had not been properly cared for by his parents. Ronnie's father stated that everyone realized that Chad had been neglected and abused and that it was time for the family to step in decisively.

The coordinator then outlined several options and asked the family to develop a plan for caring for Chad. Again, the coordinator let the family plan privately. After an interval of about three hours, during which the coordinator worked in her office on other matters and lunch was brought in to the family, she was summoned back to the family meeting. This time, Judy's sister and brother-in-law, Marjorie and Ed, served as spokespersons for the family. They stated that the families had looked at many complicated issues, including Judy and Ronnie's disabilities, and had decided that in all likelihood Chad might need a home within the extended family for all of his growing-up years. Thus they reasoned that, while the grandparents wanted to remain strongly involved, it might be best for Chad to live with younger family members. Marjorie and Ed, who lived near both sets of grandparents, felt that they could raise Chad to adulthood, if needed, and could keep him in contact with both maternal and paternal relatives. Ronnie's father and brother stated that they would make sure Ronnie would not further abuse Chad or make trouble for Marjorie and Ed. Mary Ellen would provide day care for Chad on school holidays, and Tom and Sandy would provide respite care as needed. Marjorie and Ed would apply for guardianship of Chad. All grandparents would contribute to Chad's support through the purchase of clothing, furniture, and provision of money for allowance and incidentals. The family would try to work with Judy and Ronnie on cleaning up their apartment and using mental health services. Until the situation stabilized, the parents would have to visit Chad at the grandparents' homes. The family would make sure they continued to have a part in Chad's life.

This understanding was written down in a "family compact," which was approved by the coordinator and the protective service worker.

Case Commentary. Not all family group decision-making cases are as easily resolved as this one. Both maternal and paternal relatives were able to reach a position of agreement and trust with each other. Both sets of kin had attempted to support the family and protect the child earlier. However, until empowered by protective service intervention, they were unable to overcome the barriers posed by the parents' isolation. Thus empowered, they promised to take specific roles in supporting the placement of the child and assisting the parents. This case illustrates the strengths and potential of a kinship network to develop a realistic plan based on the needs and situation of the child and family. It appears that both of the parents have conditions that will continue to affect their parenting. It should be noted that this family system had tried diligently to support the child prior to protective service intervention, but they were shut out by the parents. The protective service worker and family group conference coordinator empowered the extended family, enabling them to continue and intensify their efforts with the child.

Several key elements which contributed to the success of this family group conference were the consent of the parents, the strengths of the extended family members, the ability of the coordinator to enlist the cooperation of all members through careful planning, and the family's focus on the long-term needs of Chad. The signed family compact clarified the roles of all, the financial arrangements, the legal arrangement to be made, and the conditions under which protective services might have to be reinvolved.

Policy and Program Issues in Kinship Care

A final glance at the New Zealand child welfare system can help to frame policy issues for the United States. In New Zealand, the financial assistance most extended family caregivers receive is considerably less than that received by unrelated foster caregivers. Additionally, because many of the children show disturbed behaviors similar to those of children in foster care, the caregivers need supports to stabilize the children within the extended family. In a small qualitative study of kin caregivers, Worrall (1996) found that five out of six kin placements broke down over a six-year period. The families cited a lack of supportive services and believed that with better services they could have maintained the placement. Children move within the extended family itself, and when placements are in difficulty, the families are reluctant to re-engage the formal child welfare system (Worrall, 1996). While such findings must be viewed within methodological limitations, the study suggests that for placements to maintain over time supportive services must be available. Thus the issue of long-term supports to kinship caregivers may be as important in the United States as it appears to be in New Zealand.

In the United States, the debate continues as to whether kinship caregivers should be treated as family members or should be licensed, trained, and reimbursed as foster parents. To view kinship care simply as another form of foster care ignores the unique dynamics and varied definitions of family within a multicultural context and places the kinship caregiver in a conflictual role (Johnson, 1994). Yet there are currently few mechanisms to adequately support kinship caregivers under existing funding streams and federal programs. For example, if a kinship caregiver has been licensed as a foster parent and wishes to obtain guardianship of the child and exit the system, he or she will lose the higher foster care rate. There is little clarity about how best to support the extended families. Some feel that relatives should not receive extra funding for "taking care of their own." However kinship caregivers are generally less affluent than foster parents and have access to fewer services. The extended family may be subject to the same sort of economic conditions which affected the child's parents. They may need assistance with housing, respite care, support groups, transportation, and special health and educational services to meet the needs of the children. Organizations such as the American Association for Retired Persons are funding small demonstration pro-

jects such as telephone "warm lines," grandparenting classes, and support groups, but these efforts do not compensate for the lack of government attention to the needs of the children and their caregivers.

Those informal kinship caregivers, whose involvement prevents children from entering the foster care system, have no options for financial help other than their own resources or TANF payments. Children in protective cases who are placed informally may face all the risks that PL 96-272 and other federal and state legislation were designed to avoid: lack of permanency planning, lack of services to the parent and other family members, and lack of preplacement screening or post-placement supervision (Takas, 1993).

One promising development is that the El Paso County, Colorado public welfare agency has developed a specialized unit of kinship workers to assist kin families who are receiving public assistance for their relatives. These intensively trained workers do a wide range of supportive services with kinship families, including accessing resources for the children, providing supports for the caregivers, and working with the extended families to plan for protection and permanence for the children. Offering kinship support services on the "front end" and promoting community support of kinship care promises to enhance family preservation by maintaining kinship placements outside the child welfare system (Berns, 1998).

To further clarify policy issues, the federal government has convened an advisory committee on kinship care, which will work with the Children's Bureau and provide input to Congress on needed policy and legislation regarding kinship care. While kinship caregivers continue to divert HIV orphans, children affected by maltreatment, and the children of substance-abusing parents from the formal foster care system, the policy discourse will undoubtedly transpire in an atmosphere of increasingly conservative fiscal and political sentiment.

Family Preservation and Kinship Support for HIV Families

One of the serious challenges continuing to face family and children's services as well as the health care system is the AIDS crisis. In the early 1990s it was estimated that 80,000 healthy children would be orphaned by AIDS before the twenty-first century, with approximately one-third that number expected to enter the child welfare system (Taylor-Brown & Wiener, 1993) At the end of the decade, in New York State, HIV/AIDS now surpasses any other single cause of death for women 25 to 44 years of age, and consequently 58,000 children in the state have been or will be orphaned (Taylor-Brown, Teeter, Blackburn, Olnen, & Wedderburn, 1998). These children will struggle with complex burdens of loss and stigma.

Family preservation approaches that will support these children, their ill parents, and their kinship network through the disease and bereavement processes are being developed. Taylor-Brown and others (1993) are working with HIV mothers to videotape a legacy for their children. The videotape is presented to the mother as a means for her to share her love with her child. The messages in the tape about who will be taking care of the child, cultural and spiritual beliefs, and the importance of relationships will support the children as they adjust to bereavement and their changed living situations.

Support for HIV-infected children and their families is available now through national telephone support groups. Teleconferencing for groups including grandparents, foster parents, infected and noninfected parents, HIV-infected children, and noninfected siblings enable those affected by AIDS to live with life-threatening illness and share their strength, compassion, courage, and hope (Wiener, Spencer, Davidson, & Fair, 1993).

In order to address the complex health care and support needs of such families, the Michigan Department of Social Services established the Medically Fragile Unit in Detroit, which collaborates with the hospital, the health department, and other community agencies. Workers within the unit assume a variety of roles to meet the needs of families. They may work to access concrete resources such as beds or housing; provide transportation to health care services, arrange enrichment activities for children, counsel mothers, work with kinship networks to mobilize support, help bereaved family members with loss, arrange guardianship for relatives who will assume full care of the children, and locate foster or adoptive homes when requested. The staff activities transcend the job and unit boundaries found elsewhere in the DSS to provide comprehensive and holistic services for these vulnerable families. Their work is aimed at family preservation both with the ill parents and with the vulnerable children, in the context of kinship supports.

Kinship Care and Social Work Practice

In 1979, Joan Laird foreshadowed the current conceptual return of practice and values to kinship care:

> *Human beings are profoundly affected by the family system of which they are a part. Kin ties are powerful and compelling, and the individual's sense of identity and continuity is formed not only by the significant attachments in his intimate environment but also is deeply rooted in the biological family—in the genetic link that reaches back into the past and ahead into the future. . . . Ecologically oriented child welfare practice attends to, nurtures and supports the biological family. Furthermore, when it is necessary to substitute for the biological family, good practice dictates that every effort is made to preserve and protect important kinship ties. (Laird, 1979, p. 175)*

Reexamination of extended family traditions and values in diverse cultures supports kinship caregiving as a vital and central part of the family preservation movement. Development and implementation of family preservation practice models, which empower kinship networks in decision making and support deeply rooted cultural forms of shared parenting and family interdependence, will further enhance all of family-based practice. Kin caregivers and the children they serve have unique needs and complex family dynamics (Crumbley & Little, 1998; McFadden, 1995) which should be addressed in culturally responsive programs, supports and practice which take into account the special issues of kinship care.

TRENDS AND ISSUES

Assessment of Family Functioning

Outcome research conducted in Los Angeles County with two voluntary agencies examined changes in family functioning during home-based family preservation services, as well as changes in child behavior, home environment, traits of parents, and placement outcomes for children (McCroskey & Meezan, 1997). The experimental program differed from the typical family preservation program in that the services provided were for a three-month period (as opposed to the four- to six-week crisis intervention model); the program provided less intensive service to a broader range of families than those with imminent risk of placement; and the program had different standards of program success than the avoidance of placement or cost-savings. In many respects, the program appears to address significant issues raised by earlier evaluation (see Evaluation of Family Preservation Programs), especially with its approach to assessing family functioning.

The two agencies involved used a specially developed family assessment form (Children's Bureau of Southern California, 1997) which addressed family functioning in the following areas: (1) environment (physical environment, family finances, and social supports); (2) caregiver (caregiver's history, personal characteristics, and child-rearing ability); (3) family interactions (caregiver to children, children to caregiver, and caregiver to caregiver); and (4) children (developmental status, behavioral concerns, and child summary). Other studies of family preservation have used tools to assess family functioning. For example, the Child Well-Being Scales (Magura and Moses, 1986) has been used in studies of family preservation with drug-exposed infants (Potocky & McDonald, 1996), while the Family Risk Scale (Magura, Moses, & Jones, 1987) was used in research (Thieman & Dail, 1997) on predictors of out-of-home placement.

The Family Assessment Form used in Los Angeles is a practice-oriented assessment protocol developed to collect standardized data with which to evaluate the effectiveness of the program, as well as to allow the worker to monitor the progress of families. Since then it has been used with families in many different program settings in agencies all over the world (Children's Bureau of Southern California, 1997). The instrument was developed by the agency practitioners (with the help of researchers) to meet their needs. Additionally, the Family Assessment

Form measures family functioning from an ecological perspective and identifies family strengths. In doing so, it integrates family assessment and case planning with program documentation.

While studies of family preservation have always been dependent on case data, this approach appears to involve the practitioner more thoroughly in the process of family preservation program evaluation and research, while addressing the crucial issue of improved family functioning. In a parallel development in social work education, students are learning to assess family level of functioning in order to select the appropriate model of intervention (Kilpatrick & Holland, 1995).

A second significant trend is toward utilization of family preservation services to improve developmental outcomes for children. Wells and Tracy (1996) recommend that the current rational for family preservation—the prevention of placement—should be abandoned. The new rationale could be in terms of developmental outcomes for young physically neglected and abused children who do not require placement. Instead of family preservation services being brought to bear at the time of imminent risk of placement, they should be integrated closely with the child development services and/or with drug treatment programs that serve the parents of young children. In other words, the preventive aspects of family preservation should be utilized far earlier and with a more specific focus on the needs of children. Another critical part of this approach would be to develop strong linkages with community programs such as infant mental health, Head Start, and family support programs.

The future direction of family preservation, in response to earlier critiques, appears to be in the direction of broadened services targeted beyond families at "imminent risk" of placement, earlier intervention, differential strategies based on assessment of family level of functioning and types of family problems, and heightened evaluation based on outcomes targeted at change in family level of functioning.

CHAPTER SUMMARY

Intensive family-based services, typically known as family preservation, have been demonstrated to be helpful to families struggling with multiple problems. These services are time-limited and are provided primarily in the home and other environments within the family's ecosystem. Within an overall family-systems framework, a variety of approaches and techniques may be used, including but not limited to the following: cognitive-behavioral, crisis intervention, provision of concrete resources, parent education, mobilization of community supports, and operating from a strengths-based perspective. Flexible funds and the availability of the worker on a round-the-clock basis if necessary help to stabilize families in crisis and provide a wide range of resources for change. Workers understand the importance of engaging family members and instilling hope of positive change. The approach is congruent with social work's historic concern and values about families.

While proponents of the services believe that they often prevent out-of-home placement of children and ensure the safety of children who remain in the home, recent program evaluations call into question the targeting of services to families at risk of placement and the concept of placement prevention. There is some agreement on the usefulness of the services to families, but researchers and practitioners alike call for further research on developmental outcomes for children, the effect of services on levels of family functioning, and the types of families for whom the family preservation approach is most effective. The trend appears to be toward a wider application of family-based services and greater flexibility in the area of time limitation.

Despite media criticism of the philosophy of family preservation as a risk to the safety of children, such programs continue to proliferate. Certainly some of the criticisms are unjustified, as media attacks often address failures of the legal system or child protective decision making, rather than family preservation

programs *per se*. However, the issue of child safety continues to generate a significant amount of heat among child advocates. It is critical to note that family preservation workers do call in CPS staff and recommend removal of children if the situation is not safe. All those who are committed to family-based services to protect children, improve the functioning of families with multiple problems, and prevent unnecessary separations need to be knowledgeable and informed spokespersons in behalf of their programs.

Another important form of family preservation is the use of kinship care. Particularly among communities of color, involvement by extended families in child rearing is normal and has been an adaptive survival mechanism. Program approaches borrowed from New Zealand to involve the extended kinship network in the protection of children from abuse and neglect are proliferating and appear thus far to be successful. The field awaits focused evaluation of these efforts.

A significant concern for proponents of kinship care is the lack of congruent policy and supports for informal kinship caregivers. There have been projects and programs developed such as "warm lines," caregiver support groups, and children's support groups. However, federal support and policy development for kinship care has been at best inconsistent. The new, federal-level Kinship Advisory Board is a promising step.

Intensive family based services require knowledgeability of systems, and a high level of teamwork and collaboration. Many communities are developing multipurpose collaborative bodies that work toward improved communication between services, flexibility in funding to provide better services for families, articulation of services between family preservation and "step down" family support programs, and community partnership in the challenge of preserving families at risk of placement.

FOR STUDY AND DISCUSSION

1. In your community, is there an intensive, family-based services program which works for family preservation with families of children at imminent risk of placement? Visit the agency or invite a staff

member to class to discuss assessment and safety issues. How does the agency operationalize the value, "safety is our first concern"? How do they respond to attacks in the media? How are they evaluating the effectiveness of their program? What is the practitioner's role in evaluation?

2. Identify those agencies in your community providing support to relatives who are involved in kinship care. Are there support groups and/or advocacy groups? They may be framed as "grandparents raising grandchildren groups," forums for kinship caregivers, or parent-education classes for relative caregivers. Is there a "warm line" or information and referral service available to them? Talk to kinship caregivers and find out what they need.

3. Does your community have any community collaboratives for family support and family preservation? How do service delivery systems (mental health, child protective services, schools, and family preservation agencies) work together to identify needs, allocate resources, provide interdisciplinary team planning for "wrap around" services, and coordinate the "step-down" services when a family moves from family preservation to community-based family support?

4. Talk with your child protection agency. Has your state or community piloted a project on family group decision-making? Why or why not? If so, what involvement do the courts and child protection play in the process? What follow-up is available for assuring the children's safety and permanence?

5. Examine current media (newspapers, magazines, television, and talk shows) to identify issues being raised in your state and community about family preservation and safety of children. Do a simple content analysis to identify recurrent themes. Then research the evaluation of family preservation and write a letter to the editor or similar rejoinder to correct any media distortions.

6. Contact your local domestic violence, children's mental health, or HIV support agency. Inquire how they see family preservation and what intensive, family-based services are being offered to their clientele.

7. Invite a family preservation social worker to speak to your class on the *specifics* of her or his job. How does he or she engage families? How does he or she provide hope? How do families respond to the worker's identifying strengths? What are the greatest challenges? What are the rewards?

FOR ADDITIONAL STUDY

Besharov, D. (Ed.). (1994). *When drug addicts have children: Reorienting child welfare's response.* Washington, DC: Child Welfare League of America, American Enterprise Institute.

Crumbley, J., & Little, R. (Eds.). (1997). *Relatives raising children: An overview of kinship care.* Washington, DC: Child Welfare League of America.

Kaplan, L., & Girard, J. (1994). *Strengthening high-risk families.* New York: Lexington Books.

Kilpatrick, A., & Holland, T. (1995). *Working with families: An integrative model by level of functioning.* Boston: Allyn & Bacon.

McCroskey, J., & Meezan, W. (1997). *Family preservation & family functioning.* Washington, DC: Child Welfare League of America Press.

Children's Bureau of Southern California. (1997). *Family assessment form: A practice-based approach to assessing family functioning.* Washington, DC: Child Welfare League of America Press.

INTERNET SITES

American Humane Association. This nationally recognized organization, known primarily for work in the area of child protection, provides references to publications specific to family group decision-making. http://www.americanhumane.org

Child Welfare League of America. This organization has a general child welfare site, with specific pages related to developments in family preservation and lists of topically related publications provided by CWLA. http://www.cwla.org

National Family Preservation Network. The central coordinating point for a network of family-preservation staff and programs. http://www.nfpn.org

National Resource for Family Centered Practice. This federally funded resource center, which provides technical assistance and training to states and programs, has a comprehensive Web site which includes lists of materials available, bibliographies, and *The Prevention Report.* http://www.uiowa.edu/~nrcfcp

REFERENCES

Allen, M. (1992). *Working with families with substance abuse concerns. (Curriculum)* Iowa City, IA: National Resource Center on Family Based Services.

Allen, M., & Zalenski, J. (1993, Spring). Making a difference for families: Family-based services in the nineties. *The Prevention Report, 1*–3.

American Humane Association. (1998). *1997 National roundtable series on family group decision-making: Summary of proceedings, assessing the promise and implementing the practice.* Englewood, CO: American Humane Association.

American Humane Association. (1996). The practice and promise of family group decision-making. *Protecting Children, 12* (3).

Angelou, M. (1985). Introduction. In *Keeping families together: The case for family preservation.* Edna McConnell Clark Foundation.

Bain, A. (1978). The capacity of families to cope with transitions: A theoretical essay. *Human Relations, 31*(8), 675–688.

Bandura, A. (1977). *Social learning theory.* Englewood Cliffs, NJ: Prentice-Hall.

Barth, R. P. (1994). Long-term in-home services. In D. Besharov (Ed.), *When drug addicts have children* (pp. 175–194). Washington, DC: Child Welfare League of America, American Enterprise Institute.

Barthel, J. (1992). *For children's sake: The promise of family preservation.* Philadelphia: Winchell Company.

Bath, H., & Haapala, D. (1993). Intensive family preservation services with abused and neglected children: An examination of group differences. *Child Abuse & Neglect, 17,* 213–225.

Bath, H., Richey, C., & Haapala, D. (1992). Child age and outcome correlates in intensive family preservation services. *Children and Youth Services Review, 14,* 389–406.

Bergquist, C., Szwejda, D., & Pope, G. (1993, March). *Evaluation of Michigan's Family First program summary report.* Lansing, MI: University Associates.

Bernard, L. D. (1992). The dark side of family preservation. *Affilia, 7*(2), 156–159.

Berns, D. (1998). Personal communication to author.

Berry, M. (1992). An evaluation of family preservation services: Fitting agency services to family needs. *Social Work, 37*(4), 314–321.

Besharov, D. (Ed.). (1994). *When drug addicts have children: Reorienting child welfare's response.* Washington, DC: Child Welfare League of America, American Enterprise Institute.

Blythe, B., Salley, M., & Jayaratne, S. (1994). A review of intensive family preservation services research. *Social Work Research, 18*(4), 213–224.

Boyd-Franklin, N. (1989). *Black families in therapy: A multi-systems approach.* New York: Guilford Press.

Caplan, G. (1974). *Principles of preventive psychiatry.* New York: Basic Books.

Children's Bureau of Southern California. (1997). *Family assessment form: A practice-based approach to assessing family functioning.* Washington, DC: Child Welfare League of America Press.

Child Welfare League of America. (1994). *Kinship care: A natural bridge.* Washington, DC: Child Welfare League of America.

Cimmarusti, R. (1992). Family preservation practice based upon a multisystems approach. *Child Welfare, 71*(3), 241–255.

Courtney, M. (1997). Reconsidering family preservation: A review of *Putting Families First. Children and Youth Services Review, 19*(1/2), 61–76.

Cross, T. (1987). *Cross-culture skills in Indian child welfare: A guide for the non-Indian.* Portland, OR: Northwest Indian Child Welfare Association.

Cross, T. (1986). Drawing on cultural tradition in Indian child welfare practice. *Social Casework,* May, 283–289.

Crumbley, J., & Little, R. (Eds.). (1997). *Relatives raising children: An overview of kinship care.* Washington, DC: Child Welfare League of America Press.

Dennis, K. (1997). Advocate's narrative. In R. Golden, (Ed.), *Disposable children,* (pp. 169–172). Belmont, CA: Wadsworth.

Doerre, Y., & Mihaly, L. (1996). *Home sweet home: Building collaborations to keep families together.* Washington, DC: Child Welfare League of America Press.

Dore, M. M. (1993). Family preservation and poor families: When "homebuilding" is not enough. *Families in Society, 74*(8), 545–554.

Edna McConnell Clark Foundation (1985). *Keeping families together: The case for family preservation.* New York.

Faria, G. (1994). Training for family preservation practice with lesbian families. *Families and Society, 75*(7), 416–422.

Forsythe, P. (1992). Homebuilders and family preservation. *Children and Youth Services Review, 14,* 37–47.

Friedman, R. (1993, Spring). Homebuilders, family systems and false dichotomies: Reflections on cross-currents in family preservation thinking and steps toward integration. *The Prevention Report.* Iowa City, IA: National Resource Center on Family Based Services, 7–9.

Gelles, R. (1993). Family reunification/family preservation: Are children really being protected? *Journal of Interpersonal Violence, 8*(4), 557–562.

Gelles, R. (1996). *The Book of David: How preserving families can cost children's lives.* New York: Basic Books/Harper Collins.

Germain, C., & Gitterman, A. (1980). *The life model of social work practice.* New York: Columbia University Press.

Giarretto, H. A. (1982). *Integrated treatment of child sexual abuse.* Palo Alto, CA: Science and Behavior Books.

Golden, R. (Ed.), (1997). *Disposable children: America's welfare system.* Belmont, CA: Wadsworth.

Gray, S. S., & Nybell, L. (1990). Issues in African-American family preservation. *Child Welfare, 69*(6), 513–523.

Hardin, M. (1994, May). Family group conferences in New Zealand. *ABA Journal and Child Welfare Law Reporter.*

Hartman, A., & Laird, J. (1983). *Family centered social work practice.* New York: Free Press.

Hartman, A. (1993). Family preservation under attack. *Social Work, 38,* 509–512.

Heneghan, A., Horwitz, S., & Leventhal, J. (1996). Evaluating family preservation programs: A methodological review. *Pediatrics, 97*(4), 535–542.

Hess, P., Folaron, G., & Jefferson, A. (1992). Effectiveness of family reunification services: An innovative evaluative model. *Social Work, 37,* 304–311.

Hill-Lubin, M. (1991). The African-American grandmother in autobiographical works by Frederick Douglass, Langston Hughes, and Maya Angelou. *International Journal of Aging and Human Development, 33*(3), 173–185.

Horesji, C., Heavy Runner, B., & Pablo, J. (1992). Reactions by Native American parents to child protection agencies: Cultural and community factors. *Child Welfare, 71*(4), 329–342.

Johnson, I. (1994). Kinship care. In D. Besharov (Ed.), *When drug addicts have children,* (pp. 221–228). Washington, DC: Child Welfare League of America, American Enterprise Institute.

Jones, B. (1994). The clients and their problems. In D. Besharov (Ed.), *When drug addicts have children,* (pp. 115–124). Washington, DC: Child Welfare League of America, American Enterprise Institute.

Jones, M. A., Magura, S., & Shyne, A. W. (1981). Effective practice with families in protective and preventive services: What works? *Child Welfare, 60*(2).

Kaplan, L., & Girard, J. (1994). *Strengthening high-risk families.* Lexington, MA: Lexington Books.

Kessel, J., & Robbins, S. (1984). The Indian Child Welfare Act: Dilemmas and needs. *Child Welfare, 63*(3), 225–232.

Kilpatrick, A., & Holland, T. (1995). *Working with families: An integrative model by level of functioning.* Boston: Allyn & Bacon.

Kinney, J., Haapala, D., & Booth, C. (1991). *Keeping families together: The homebuilders model.* New York: Aldine de Gruyter.

Kolb, L. (1993, Spring). Family preservation in Missouri. *Public Welfare,* 8–19.

Laird, J. (1979). An ecological approach to child welfare: Issues of family identity and continuity. In C. Germain (Ed.), *Social work practice: People and environments,* (pp. 174–209). New York: Columbia University Press.

Lindsey, D. (1994). Family preservation and child protection: Striking a balance. *Children and Youth Services Review, 16*(5/6), 279–294.

Littell, J. (1997). Effects of the duration, intensity, and breadth of family preservation services: A new analysis of data from the Illinois Family First experiment. *Children and Youth Services Review, 19*(1&2), 17–39.

Lovell, M., Reid, K., & Richey, C. (1992). Social support training for abusive mothers. *Social Work with Groups, 15*(2/3), 95–107.

Magura S., & Moses, B. (1986). *Outcome Measure for Child Welfare Services: Theory and Applications.* Washington, DC: Child Welfare League of America Press.

Magura S., Moses, B., & Jones, M. (1987). *Assessing risk and measuring change in families.* Washington DC: Child Welfare League of America Press.

Maluccio, A., & Whittaker, J. (1997). Learning from the "family preservation" initiative. *Children and Youth Services Review, 19*(1/2), 5–16.

Maluccio, A., Pine, B., & Warsh, R. (1994). Protecting children by preserving their families. *Children and Youth Services Review, 16*(5/6), 295–307.

Mannes, M. (1993). Seeking the balance between child protection and family preservation in Indian child welfare. *Child Welfare, 72*(2), 141–152.

McCroskey, J., & Meezan, W. (1997). *Family preservation & family functioning.* Washington, DC: Child Welfare League of America Press.

Merkel-Holguin, L. (1998). Transferring the family group conferencing technology from New Zealand to the United States. Paper presented at the twelfth International Congress on Child Abuse and Neglect, Auckland, New Zealand.

Meyers, B., & Link, M. J. (1990). *Kinship foster care: The double edged dilemma,* study for the New York Task Force on Permanency Planning for Children. Rochester, New York.

Minkler, M., Roe, K., & Price, M.(1992). The physical and emotional health of grandmothers raising grandchildren in the crack cocaine epidemic. *The Gerontologist, 32*(6), 752–761.

National Council of Juvenile and Family Court Judges. (1992). *Protocol for making reasonable efforts to preserve families in drug-related dependency cases.* Reno, NV: National Council of Juvenile and Family Court Judges.

National Council of Juvenile and Family Court Judges, Child Welfare League of America, Youth Law Center and National Center for Youth Law (no date) *Making reasonable efforts: Steps for keeping families together.* San Francisco, CA: National Center for Youth Law.

National Resource Center on Family Based Services. (1994). Project proposal. Iowa City, IA.

Nelson, K. (1994). Do services to preserve the family place children at unnecessary risk? Yes. In E. Gambrill & T. Stein (Eds.), *Controversial issues in child welfare,* (pp. 59–72). Boston: Allyn & Bacon.

Nelson, K., Landsman, M., & Deutelbaum, W. (1990). Three models of family-centered placement prevention services. *Child Welfare, 69*(1), 3–21.

Parad, H. J. (Ed.). (1965). *Crisis intervention: Selected readings.* New York: Family Service Association of America.

Patterson, G. (1975). *Families.* Champaign, IL: Research Press.

Pecora, P., Whittaker, J., Maluccio, A., Barth, R., & Plotnick, R. (1992). *The child welfare challenge.* Hawthorne, New York: de Gruyter.

Polansky, N., Chalmers, M., Battenmeier, E., & Williams, D. (1981). *Damaged parents: An anatomy of child neglect.* Chicago: University of Chicago Press.

Ratterman, D., Dodson, G. D., & Hardin, M. (1987). *Reasonable efforts to prevent foster placement: A guide to implementation.* Washington, DC: American Bar Association.

Ronnau, J., & Marlow, C. (1993). Family preservation, poverty, and the value of diversity. *Families in Society, 74*(8), 538–544.

Rossi, P. (1992). Assessing family preservation programs. *Children and Youth Services Review, 14,* 77–97.

Ryan, P., Warren, B., & Weincek, P. (1992). Removal of the perpetrator versus removal of the victim in cases of intra-familial child sexual abuse. Final report. Ypsilanti, MI: Institute for the Study of Children and Families, Eastern Michigan University.

Sabol, B. (1994). The call on agency resources. *When drug addicts have children* (pp. 125–144). Washington, DC: Child Welfare League of America, American Enterprise Institute.

Sandau-Beckler, P., Salcido, R., & Ronnau, J. (1993). Culturally competent family preservation services: An approach for first generation Hispanic families in an international border community. *The Family Journal, Counseling and Therapy for Couples and Families, 1*(4), 313–323.

Scannapieco, M. (1993). The importance of family functioning to prevention of placement: A study of family preservation services. *Child and Adolescent Social Work Journal, 10* (6), 509–520.

Scheurman, J., Rzepnicki, T., & Littell, J. (1992a). *Evaluation of the Illinois Family First placement prevention program: Progress report.* Chicago, IL: Chapin Hall.

Schuerman, J., Rzepnicki, T., Littell, J., & Budde, S. (1992b). Implementation issues. *Children and Youth Services Review, 14,* 193–206.

Seader, M. B. (1994). Do services to preserve the family place children at unnecessary risk? Yes. In E. Gambrill & T. Stein (Eds.), *Controversial issues in child welfare,* (pp. 59–72). Boston: Allyn & Bacon.

Shapiro, D. (1979). *Parents and protectors: A study in child abuse and neglect.* New York: Child Welfare League of America.

Smith, D., & Featherstone, T. (1991). Family group conferences—the process. In *Family Decision Making.* Lower Hutt, New Zealand: Practitioners Publishing.

Spake, A. (1994, November). The little boy who didn't have to die. *McCall's,* 142–151.

Sudia, C. (1981). What services do abusive and neglecting families need? In L. H. Pelton (Ed.), *The Social Context of Child Abuse and Neglect,* (pp. 268–290). New York: Human Services Press.

Sudia, C. (1993). The origins and development of family-based services—from a government servant's perspective. *Prevention Report,* a publication of the National Resource Center on Family-based Services. Iowa City: pp. 4–6.

Takas, M. (1993). Kinship care: Developing a safe and effective framework for protective placement of children with relatives. *Zero to Three,* December/January, 12–17.

Taylor-Brown, S., & Wiener, L.(1993). Making videotapes of HIV-infected women for their children. *Families in Society, 74*(8), 468–480.

Taylor-Brown, S., Teeter, J., Blackburn, E., Olnen, L., & Wedderburn, L. (1998). Parental loss due to HIV: Caring for children as a community issue—the Rochester, New York experience. *Child Welfare, 77*(2), 137–160.

Thieman, A., & Dail, P. (1997). Predictors of out-of-home placement in a family preservation program: Are welfare recipients particularly vulnerable? *Policy Studies Journal, 25*(1), 124–139.

Tracy, E., Bean, N., Gwatkin, S., & Hill, B. (1992). Family preservation workers: Sources of job satisfaction and job stress. *Research on Social Work Practice, 2*(4), 465–478.

Tracy, E., Whittaker, J., Pugh, A., Kapp, S., & Overstreet, E. (1994). Support networks of primary caregivers receiving family preservation services: An exploratory study. *Families in Society, 75*(8), 481–489.

Turnell, A. (1998, September). Aspiring to partnership: The signs of safety approach to child protection. Paper presented at International Society of Professionals in Child Abuse and Neglect Conference, Auckland, New Zealand.

U.S. Bureau of the Census. (1991). *Current population reports. Marital status and living arrangements: March 1990.* Series P-20, No. 450.

U.S. General Accounting Office. (1997). States' Progress in Implementing Family Preservation and Support Services. Washington, DC: General Accounting Office, Health Education and Human Services Division.

Vandenberg, J., Grealish, M., & Schick, C. (1993). *Wraparound guidelines.* Lansing, MI: Michigan Department of Social Services.

Wald, M. (1988). Family preservation: Are we moving Too fast? *Public Welfare, 46*(3), 32–38, 46.

Walton, E. (1997). Enhancing investigative decisions in child welfare: An exploratory use of intensive family preservation services. *Child Welfare, 76*(3), 447–461.

Warsh, R., Pine, B., & Maluccio, A. (1995). Essay, the meaning of family preservation: Shared mission, diverse methods. *Families in Society: The Journal of Contemporary Human Services,* 625–626.

Wells, K., & Whittington, D. (1993, March). Child and family functioning after intensive family preservation services. *Social Service Review,* 55–83.

Wells, K., & Tracy, E. (1996). Reorienting intensive family preservation services in relation to public child welfare practice. *Child Welfare, 75*(6), 667–692.

Whittaker, J., Kinney, J., Tracy, E., & Booth, C. (1990). *Reaching high-risk families.* New York: Aldine de Gruyter.

Wiener, L., Spencer, E., Davidson, R., & Fair, C. (1993). National telephone support groups: A new avenue toward psychosocial support for HIV-infected children and their families. *Social Work with Groups, 16*(3), 55–71.

Worrall, J. (1996). *Because we're family: A study of kinship care of children in New Zealand.* Thesis. Massey University, Albany, New Zealand.

Zalenski, J. (1994). A new/old practice to care for children: New Zealand's family decision making model. *The Prevention Report* (pp. 11–14). Iowa City, IA: National Resource Center on Family Based Services.

CHAPTER 9

Foster Care
A Service for Children and their Families

Children begin by loving their parents; as they grow older they judge them; sometimes they forgive them.
—Oscar Wilde

I never really got that badly hit. I never really got hit when I was younger, that much. Just for doing bad things. But I was seeing my father beat up my mom and my brother too. My dad used to be an alcoholic so that's why he hit her. My mom hit me one day, and I just hauled off and hit her back and ever since that day she never talked to me . . . I came into care because my mother tried to kill herself, she almost died. She had a lot of problems.
—(Youth in care—Raychaba, 1993, p. 18)

CHAPTER OUTLINE

CASE EXAMPLE: TEAMWORK IN FOSTER CARE

In foster care practice, as in all social work practice, each case situation is unique. Each family member has many strengths and compelling needs. Each family in need of out-of-home care for children suffers its own pain from dismemberment. Placement of a child in care is like major surgery for a family system—necessary, perhaps, in serious situations, but not to be undertaken lightly. The following case material illustrates a family-centered approach used when placing children in foster care was necessary.

Elena and Ricky came into care when she was 5 years old and he was 3. They had been found by neighbors wandering in the street at 11 p.m. They were looking for their mother, who had left them at home alone a day earlier when she went off with her boyfriend. An elderly woman took them in for the night. When their mother still hadn't returned the next morning, child protective services was contacted. There were no known relatives who could care for the children. The woman who had watched over them temporarily was unable, for health reasons, to keep them on a long-term basis. The child protection worker contacted the court for permission to place the children in a foster home and brought them to the Williams foster home.

Laurella Williams met Elena and Ricky at the door and knelt down to their level while she explained that they could stay with her while Mr. Harrison tried to locate their mother. She said that she understood they might be feeling worried and scared, and that she, her husband, and the other children would try to help them feel at home. She asked them if they had a favorite kind of food and if they were hungry. Then she showed them to a room where they could put their things.

While the foster parents were helping Elena and Ricky look over their new home, the CPS worker filed a petition with the juvenile court, alleging that the children had been without proper care and supervision and that the parents had not been located.

When Mrs. Williams bathed the children at bedtime she noted a number of bruises on Ricky's back and the back of his legs. She also noted that both children had head lice and Elena appeared frail and unduly thin. The following morning she took both children to the pediatrician for a complete physical exam. The physician reported that Ricky's bruises suggested abuse and that Elena appeared seriously malnourished.

Four days later, their mother, Juanita H., contacted child protective services wanting the children. She told the worker that she had gone with her boyfriend for a few drinks. They lost track of time because they had a fight and were driving home when they had an auto accident. She spent the day in the emergency room. She thought a girlfriend had gone to check on the kids. When she got home the children were gone and she found the CPS worker's card. She had been so upset that she couldn't make the call for several days.

The worker explained that a petition had been filed, and that there would be a court hearing to determine whether the children should stay in care or return home. He asked Juanita if the foster parent could call to tell her how the children were doing and to get some information. Soon Laurella Williams called Juanita H., providing reassurance that the children missed their mother and were otherwise doing okay. Juanita told the foster parent that Ricky's birthday was coming up, and that he was due for another shot at the health department. She also mentioned that Elena had an allergy to wheat products and she was afraid of dogs. The foster parent thanked her for the valuable information and thus laid the groundwork for a working relationship with the parent based on their common concern for the children.

Following the court hearing, in which it was decided that the children would remain in care temporarily, the case was transferred to a foster care worker, who met with Juanita. After a careful assessment of the family

situation, the worker drew up a service agreement. The goal was to return the children home. There would be visits with the children twice a week. Juanita acknowledged that substance abuse had led to her neglecting the children, and that she and her boyfriend had hit Ricky with a belt when he had problems with toileting. She agreed to attend parenting classes and counseling to improve her parenting skills, and to attend outpatient treatment and a twelve-step group to deal with her substance abuse problem. She would have weekly tests to determine whether she was substance-free. She understood that there would be a review in three months and a review hearing at six months as part of the permanency planning process.

Juanita met with Mr. and Mrs. Williams and the foster care worker at the agency to discuss ways to have meaningful visits with the children. Following an initial visit with the children in the agency playroom, she would visit with the children in the Williams home and work on parenting skills, especially around Ricky's toilet training. Mrs. Williams and Juanita would work together on nutrition planning for Elena to address her allergies. At the first visit in the Williams home, they would celebrate Ricky's birthday.

The foster parents developed a supportive relationship with Juanita. The foster care worker monitored the progress in Juanita's plan. She enrolled in substance abuse treatment, attended AA, and had regular urine screens. Within three months the children were returned to their mother's care, with the support of family reunification services and the foster parents who had acted as extended family to the children and their mother. The family reunification worker stayed involved for four weeks after the children were returned, and the family remained under foster care supervision for another six months. The foster parents continued to see the family occasionally, providing brief respite care when needed.

PERMANENCY, SAFETY, AND FAMILY CONTINUITY: CRITICAL CONTEMPORARY ISSUES

Adoption and Safe Families Act of 1997

With the passage of Public Law 105-89, the Adoption and Safe Families Act, in 1997, the American people, through their legislators, moved the issues of child safety and permanency into the forefront of foster care policy, programs, and practice. Long intended as a "temporary" service for children and families, foster care—and the child welfare system—had become increasingly problematic. Many children did not find timely permanency outcomes (that is, return to their parents, placement with kin or adoption) while waiting in foster homes. At least one-third of the estimated 500,000 children currently in foster care will never return to their birth parents. Minority children, who made up over 60 percent of children in care in 1994, waited twice as long for permanent homes as did other foster children (U.S. General Accounting Office, 1998).

The issue of child safety was of equal concern to American policy makers and legislators. Nearly 3.2 million children were abused or neglected in 1997—up 41 percent since 1988. In 1996, 41 percent of the estimated 1,046 children who died of abuse or neglect were known to child protective services (Pizzigati, 1998). Despite significant advances in family preservation policy, practice, and programs, there was a rising chorus of criticism of the services that help keep children with their families and prevent entry into care, and of foster care practices that return children to their families when the family is unable to provide adequate care. Additional criticism focused on programs that allow children to remain too long in foster homes or group settings rather than being placed for adoption transracially. A sustained campaign of media attention was promulgated by child advocates, adoption advocates, and critics of family preservation philosophy. (See Chapter 8). Public concern mounted as citizens read in their daily newspapers about children at risk in their families or in the systems designed to protect them.

The new law made specific provisions related to the safety of children. It clarified that the health and safety of the child are paramount concerns in deciding about removal from—or reunification with—the child's family. It also specified certain situations in which *reasonable efforts* to keep children with their families, as previously required by PL 96-272, are no longer required. In fact, it required mandatory filing of termination of parental rights petitions when there had been the murder of another child by the parent, abandonment of an infant, or felony assault resulting

in serious bodily harm to a child. In order to promote safe homes for children in the foster care system or in adoptive homes, the law required states to check prospective foster and adoptive parents for criminal backgrounds. The legislation also emphasized accountability of state systems for safety. It required the Secretary of Health and Human Services to issue an annual report on state performance in protecting children. (See Chapter 10.)

As the United States prepared to enter the new millennium there was brief renewed interest in using orphanages as a means of solving social problems and an acknowledgment that foster care is in a state of unparalleled crisis. Class action suits challenged foster care in a number of states, in an effort to protect the rights and safety of children in the system, bringing to light certain flaws in the system, while politicians and other critics of the social service system again called for a return to orphanages as a preferred way of caring. However, as a result of incentives in the Adoption and Safe Families Act, it appears that states will attempt to move toward increased use of adoption rather than orphanages for those children who wait in foster homes and group care. (See Chapter 10).

Child welfare services operate in a social and political atmosphere characterized by powerful feelings and deep values. These values affect political support, including financial resources and other legislation that affect child welfare. Seeing all these forces or the interplay among them is not possible. (Terpstra, 1997, p. 1)

Specific provisions of the Adoption and Safe Families Act relate directly to foster care, in an effort to emphasize permanency. While the federal law does not establish grounds for termination of parental rights, it does expedite procedures and requires states to file a petition to initiate termination of parental rights for any child in foster care for fifteen of the most recent twenty-two months, unless the child is in the care of a relative, or unless a compelling reason is documented why such a filing would not be in the best interest of the child, or unless the state has not provided the family of the child such services as would be necessary for the safe return of the child.

The law authorizes state and local child welfare agencies to use the Federal Parent Locator Service to locate absent parents in proceedings dealing with termination of parental rights.

An interest in kinship care or services that promote family continuity is also evident in the Adoption and Safe Families legislation. As noted, placement with a relative is an exception to the mandatory initiation of termination of parental rights. The legislation requires the Secretary of Health and Human Services to prepare a report for Congress on the placement of children with relatives. The Act also authorizes a U.S. Advisory Board on Kinship Care, which will be convened to review the report on kinship care. Additionally, the act underscored a concern for parental rights, stating that nothing in the act is intended to disrupt the family unnecessarily or to intrude inappropriately into family life, to prohibit the use of reasonable methods of parental discipline, or to prescribe a particular method of parenting.

Cultural Issues and Family Continuity: Multiethnic Placement Act and the Indian Child Welfare Act

A controversial child welfare issue is whether children should be placed transracially in foster or adoptive homes. As many adoptions of children in the system are by foster parents, a foster home placement can become potentially a de facto adoptive placement. The Multiethnic Placement Act of 1994 sought to decrease the length of time that children wait in foster care to be adopted by eliminating race-related barriers to adoption. Minority children, who made up over 60 percent of the children in foster care in 1994, waited twice as long for permanent homes as did other foster children (U.S. General Accounting Office, 1998). The original act explicitly allowed race to be considered as one of a number of placement-related factors. However, a 1996 amendment to the Multiethnic Placement Act created a firm prohibition on using race as a placement factor. In effect, child welfare agencies have been put on notice that they are subject to civil rights principles banning racial discrimination when making decisions related to adoption or foster care placements.

An examination of the social work positions on transracial placement over the past two decades shows that this has been an ongoing and controversial issue. In 1972, the National Association of Black Social Workers affirmed "the inviolable position of Black children in Black families where they belong physically, psychologically and culturally in order that they receive the total sense of themselves" (National Association of Black Social Workers, 1972). The Child Welfare League standards reflect changing practice. The 1958 standards discouraged transracial placement, while the 1968 standards gave it tacit acceptance. Standards published in 1978 stated that it is preferable to place children within their own racial background. Revised standards (1995) call for cultural competency, stating in part "Culture and ethnicity are vital components of the assessment and service-planning process. . . . Culturally competent assessments and service plans recognize relationships with family members, siblings and kin" (Child Welfare League, 1995, p. 31). Concerning adoption of foster children, the revised foster care standards state: "Children in need of adoption have a right to be placed into a family that reflects their culture or race. . . . Agencies have a responsibility to aggressively recruit families of the same cultural and racial background of the children who are placed for adoption. . . . The best interests of the child should be paramount. If aggressive ongoing recruitment efforts are unsuccessful in finding families of the same culture or race as the child, other families should be considered" (Child Welfare League, 1995, pp. 79–80). (See Chapter 10.)

A contributing factor to the use of transracial placement is the shortage of foster homes. Many agencies have intensified their recruitment of people of color and increased the use of kinship care as a way of maintaining children within their own culture. Changing long-standing social work principles in order to conform with federal law is a challenge to state child welfare administrations.

Currently children are being placed in foster homes and adoptive homes of different ethnic groups and cultures, but not to the extent of making the child welfare system color-blind. Implementation of the Multiethnic Placement Act has been affected by a number of factors, including the need to change existing state laws, regulations, and policies; the personal and professional values and beliefs of caseworkers; and the challenge to the federal Department of Health and Human Services to provide policy guidance, technical assistance, training, and monitoring of compliance (U.S. General Accounting Office, 1998).

Many social workers are personally reluctant to make transracial placements, although they are aware that the law requires that race not be considered a factor. When making such a placement, workers might explore the following issues:

- Racial attitudes of the foster family and their surrounding community
- Community resources (churches, schools, friends) that affirm the child's identity
- Availability of materials such as books, toys, food, and music of the child's culture in the foster home
- The foster parents' ability to handle grooming for skin and hair
- The foster parents' ability to teach "survival skills" to a child confronted by racism
- The training and experience of the foster home

While matching a child with the culture and ethnicity of a foster home is still considered important by many social workers, there are other important dimensions of matching, such as the age or sex of child desired by the foster family; the types of behaviors that the family can or can't handle; and the "chemistry" between the child and the foster family. Much of the placement process relates to the worker's professional judgment of what is in the best interest of the child. However, agencies can no longer routinely assume that placing children with parents of the same race is in the best interest of a child or that same-race parents are more capable of passing on a cultural heritage than parents of a different race (U.S. General Accounting Office, 1998).

The Indian Child Welfare Act of 1978 does still affirm the rights of Native American children to be placed (in order of priority) with members of their extended family, within their tribe, or with a Native American family from another tribe. The Multiethnic

Placement Act specifically affirmed that it should not be construed to affect the application of the Indian Child Welfare Act of 1978 (PL 104-188, 1996). Foster care workers thus face several dichotomies of principles. Native American children are protected from transracial placement by federal law, yet children of other minority groups must be treated in a legally color-blind way. While standards, practice history, and professional ethics support cultural competence and acknowledge the critical impact of culture on identity, the federal law would consider as discriminatory many of the time-honored practices of cultural assessment and matching.

Although current child welfare reform movements and federal legislation stress accountability, safety, and permanency, it is important to recognize that the foster care system is extremely complex, reflects larger societal issues, and is closely interrelated with child protection, family preservation, adoption, and other services. The African American Child Welfare Summit, convened by the Black Administrators in Child Welfare (BACW), developed goals reflecting systemic complexity, which included the following:

To reach consensus on action steps to be taken by the African American leadership in creating new structures and providing policy directions to the African American community and the larger child welfare system, to substantially alter or ameliorate current trends and practices." (Brisett-Chapman & Issacs-Shockley, 1997, p. 7) Regardless of where the systemic child welfare reforms begin, they must ultimately encompass all systems that serve vulnerable families and children (Usher, Gibbs, & Wildfire, 1995).

HISTORICAL DEVELOPMENT: EARLY BEGINNINGS

The history of foster care is in many respects the history of family and children's services (or child welfare, as it is still known to many people). When examined within its historical, social, and political context, foster care can be viewed as a dialectic, synthesizing opposing perspectives, or as an evolutionary response to the needs of families and children over time. In examining the twentieth century journey from orphanages to family preservation, we can apply lessons learned in the past to contemporary concerns.

Indenture, Almshouses, and Institutions

In ancient historic times orphaned children were usually cared for by their kinfolk through mechanisms embedded in clan or tribe and culture. Both Jewish and Christian religions made the care of dependent children a duty under law. Slingerland (1919) found that orphanages and homes for infant children began at the close of the second century. For a thousand years or more these forms of child care continued.

Child placement for profit began under a system of indenture in England in 1562 and was imported into the American colonies. By statute in many towns and counties, trustees of the poor were authorized to "bind out" to a master artisan poor, orphaned, or illegitimate children old enough to work. Such children became members of their master's household and were taught a craft or trade. In return the children owed obedience and labor until they reached maturity. Indenture had two main purposes: (1) to fix responsibility for the support and care of a dependent child and (2) to provide training for work. The system of indenture passed into disuse and disrepute by 1875.

During the early years of this country some destitute parents were provided with "outdoor relief"—material aid—which kept children in their own homes. Punitive attitudes toward the poor made this alternative less favored than almshouses, where needy children and their families were often sent. In 1842, J. V. N. Yates, then Secretary of State in New York, surveyed the condition of paupers in that state and strongly recommended that every county in New York maintain a poorhouse. Thirty years later, an investigation of poorhouses found them to be "the worst possible nurseries" for the young (Report of Select Senate Committee, 1857). After a time orphanages and institutions were developed as a more humane way of caring for children.

In the nineteenth century public and private agencies set up institutions for children who were blind, delinquent, or mentally retarded. They also established orphanages for dependent children to protect them from neglect and abuse. The trend grew not only because of dissatisfaction with almshouses, but also because of the practice of awarding subsidies from the public treasury to voluntary agencies. Some of the orphan asylums were established under the auspices of religious groups, which combined religious zeal with lack of individualization of children. However, as other churches developed child care institutions, many began to place children in family homes and planted the seeds of community-based services for children as early as the 1830s, through missions—ministries—located in the slums (Garland, 1994).

The vast majority of orphanages were representative of the dominant culture, operated by white people for white children. By and large children of color were served by informal kinship placements, but in 1888 several African-American women community leaders founded the St. Louis Colored Orphans Home in Missouri. This agency evolved into the Annie Malone Children and Family Service Center, which still provides leadership in the African-American service community today (Brissett-Chapman & Issacs-Shockley, 1997).

Orphan Trains and Free Foster Homes

The Rev. Charles Loring Brace (1872) worked with the Five Points Mission in New York and became deeply disturbed about the hundreds of youngsters fending for themselves on the streets without supervision or protection. With several of the city's clergymen, he founded the New York Children's Aid Society, which initiated a program for relocating neglected and abandoned urban children to rural homes. The child "placing-out" movement spearheaded by Brace took children from the cities, by train, to farm communities in the Midwest. Brace described his method as follows:

> We formed little companies of emigrants, and, after thoroughly cleaning and clothing them, put them under a competent agent, and, first selecting a village where there was a call . . . for such a party, we dispatched them to the place. The farming community having been duly notified, there was usually a dense crowd of people at the station, awaiting the arrival of

the youthful travelers. The sight of the little company of the children of misfortune always touched the hearts of a population naturally generous . . . The agent then addressed the assembly, stating the benevolent objects of the Society and something of the history of the children. The sight of their worn faces was a most pathetic enforcement of his arguments. People who were childless came forward. . . . Others, who had not intended to take any into their families, were induced to apply for them; and many who really wanted the children's labor, pressed forward to obtain it. (pp. 231–232)

Between 1853 and 1929, 31,081 children were placed in family homes by way of the orphan trains (Thurston, 1930). Even though this program may have left much to be desired, it demonstrated that family foster care and adoption were realistic options. Some child welfare leaders had little enthusiasm for the program, as most of the homes in which children were placed were Protestant. In contrast, most of the children came from immigrant families, largely Catholic. Objections that children had been removed from the religion of their parents added a stimulus to the growth of sectarian agencies and to legislating religious matching as one determinant in the choice of foster or adoptive homes.

The White House Conference on Children

By the last quarter of the nineteenth century, foster homes and institutions prevailed as fairly well-developed forms of care for dependent children. States grappled with the task of getting children out of almshouses. A philosophy of child care centered on the question "What does the child really need?" began to emerge. A consensus developed, articulated at the White House Conference on Children in 1909, that all children need families and that family care was the preferred environment to meet the needs of developing children.

TWENTIETH-CENTURY CHILD WELFARE REFORMS

Phase One: Family Foster Care, a Response to Institutional Care

From the White House Conference in 1909 through the 1960s, the main goal of the foster care program was to provide a safe, nurturing environment for children who

could not live at home because of parental maltreatment or inadequacy. Child welfare practice focused on helping the child adjust to the foster home and helping the foster family with the child's development. The serious limitations of this phase were the lack of incentives within the system to work toward family reunification and the lack of recognition that the family of origin was important to the child in care. Since the main emphasis was on the child's well-being, it usually appeared safer to leave the child in care indefinitely. The focus on children essentially excluded their families from consideration. The focal family of this period was the foster family, not the biological family.

Phase Two: The Permanency Planning Movement and Adoptive Families

A major impetus for reform was the growing recognition that although foster care had been intended as a temporary substitute for the child's own home, many children remained in foster care for years, sometimes moving through many different foster homes (Maas & Engler, 1959). The work of Bowlby (1969) and others (Geiser, 1973; Littner, 1975) lent theoretical weight to the notion that separations and disruption of emotional attachments would lead to difficulties in forming healthy attachments and would be damaging to children.

In response to these concerns, and because the critical mass of children in care had risen to over 520,000 by 1977, the 1970s saw the advent of permanency planning. *Permanency planning* is the "systematic process of carrying out, within a limited period, a set of goal direct activities designed to help children and youths live in families that offer continuity of relationships with nurturing parents or caretakers, and the opportunity to offer lifetime relationships" (Maluccio & Fein, 1983, p. 197). Moving children out of care into adoption became a desired goal, articulated by adoption activists who saw the children's rights philosophy as an extension of the earlier Civil Rights movement. Throughout the 1970s the legal, attitudinal, and procedural barriers to moving children into adoptive families were systematically addressed through a variety of demonstration programs and national dissemination efforts (Pike, Downs, Emlen, Downs, & Case, 1977; Emlen, 1978; Fanshel & Shinn,

1978; Jones, 1978,). In many states statutes were revised to make clearer the grounds for termination of parental rights, and to mandate case review and case planning. Underlying this phase was the belief that "no child is unadoptable" (Churchill, Carlson, & Nybell, 1979) and the concept that placement of children in permanent families is a primary goal of the child welfare system (Downs, 1981).

Phase Three: Family Preservation and Biological Parents

As professionals demonstrated that the backlog of children in indeterminate foster care could be reduced, they promoted the understanding that some children would not have needed care in the first place if services had been available to their families. In the early 1980's, this awareness sparked practice strategies and legal reform to prevent family breakup (Nelson, Landsman, & Deutelbaum, 1990). Two major pieces of federal legislation, the Indian Child Welfare Act of 1978 and the Adoption Assistance and Child Welfare Act of 1980, gave federal support to state efforts to make diligent and focused efforts to preserve the family before deciding to place a child in foster care (Ratterman, 1987). By 1984 the number of children in foster care (both foster family and group care) declined to 275,000 as result of vigorous permanence planning and family preservation services.

Phase Four: Family Continuity and Kinship Care

By 1991 the number of children in care had risen to 429,000 (Tatara 1992) and continued to rise despite family preservation and permanency planning. The onset of the crack cocaine epidemic, combined with economic stressors on families caused by structural unemployment, recession, and downsizing, were contributing factors to the fragmentation of families. Other salient issues were homelessness and AIDS, as well as the usual constellation of factors leading to neglect and abuse. As the number of children entering care increased, the number of foster families declined from 137,000 in 1984 to 100,000 in 1989 (U.S. General Accounting Office, 1989). In 1995 the number of children in out-of-home care was estimated by Terpstra (1995) to be 500,000, with 80 percent in family

foster homes and the remaining 20 percent in group and residential care.

The National Commission on Family Foster Care was convened by the Child Welfare League of America to develop *A Blueprint for Fostering Infants, Children and Youths in the 1990s,* which focused national attention on strengthening family foster care as an essential service option. The National Commission made recommendations for legislative action, initiated areas of agency action, focused on foster parent and worker teamwork responsibilities, and supported the significance of kinship care (National Commission of Family Foster Care, 1991).

The focus in the 1990s has turned increasingly to kinship care, in part because of the pressures of the amended Multiethnic Placement Act. Members of the child's extended family network, primarily grandparents, aunts, and uncles, are being licensed as foster families to provide care for their young relatives. The focus on kinship acknowledges the family forms of diverse cultural groups and honors the importance of family connection and culture for the developing child. Increased knowledge about family systems and the development of identity, plus feedback from former foster children who have searched for their origins, points to the importance of maintaining significant emotional ties with kinfolk. Considering the legal ramifications and restrictions of the amended Multiethnic Placement Act, many social workers view kinship care as a compelling option for keeping children's family and cultural ties intact. Current practice supports continuity of relationships over time and integration of earlier experience with family into a child's current or future family situation. Thus staff at group and residential settings now work with the child's family as part of treatment; foster parents are encouraged to adopt children and help them maintain earlier ties when family reunification is not possible; adoptive parents assist their children in "searching"; and relatives continue the tradition of "taking care of your own" by providing respite, temporary care, or permanent care through guardianship or adoption.

Figure 9.1 outlines the four phases of child welfare reform in the twentieth century and shows how the focus has expanded from foster care to adoption, and from biological to extended family, so that the family is now viewed with a wide-angle lens. It also

FIGURE 9.1   Child Welfare Reforms in the Twentieth Century

PHASE	TIME	REFORM	FOCUS	CUMULATIVE CONTRIBUTION TO FIELD
One	1909–1970 White House Conference	Family Foster Care	Foster Family	Children belong in a family rather than an institution
Two	1970s	Permanancy Planning	Adoptive Family	Children belong in a permanent family; no child is unadoptable
Three	1980s Adoption Assistance and Child Welfare Act	Family Preservation	Biological Parents	Children belong with their biological parents; reasonable efforts must be demonstrated to maintain family
Four	1990s	Family Continuity	Extended/ Augmented Family	Children belong in a family network that continues relations over time

Source: E. J. McFadden & S. W. Downs, (1995, April). Family continuity: The new paradigm in permanence planning. *Community Alternatives.*

illustrates how each phase has made a significant and cumulative contribution to the field. Each new contribution adds to and enhances earlier practice but does not detract from the ongoing importance of earlier concepts.

The paradigm shift to a unifying framework for all family and children's services in the 1990s is known as *family continuity* (Allen, Lakin, McFadden, & Wasserman, 1992; McFadden & Downs, 1995). The concept of family continuity integrates principles of family preservation into all aspects of child welfare by underscoring the necessity for continuing important relationships throughout life and acknowledging that children need to be embedded in family and community networks of caring. The evolution of services for children and families in the twentieth century has culminated in a wide-angle family focus that increases for children the possibility of family connection throughout life and has increased the engagement of all formal child welfare services with families and communities.

Dickens's summation of the French Revolution— "It was the best of times, it was the worst of times"— can apply to contemporary foster care. Innumerable advances have been made in knowledge and understanding about foster care. There have been many programmatic advances such as applying family preservation approaches to the family reunification process and training foster parents to work supportively with the child's family, while providing specialized services to children with multiple needs. A wide array of placement options are now considered, including shared family care (families fostering entire families), kinship care, open adoption, long-term family foster care, treatment foster care, small group home care, programs that prepare youths for independent living, and a host of residential and treatment settings. Yet the number of children needing protection strains the system to its utmost limits, foster parents and child care staff continue to leave in distress, and worker turnover is high. With the country spending over $6 billion annually on child welfare services, foster care funding has become vulnerable to fiscal cuts. Ironically, orphanages— congregate care settings for children—are far more costly than family foster care, which is in turn more costly than family preservation. Child welfare professionals find themselves looking backward to the lessons of history, in order to be able to look forward to a creative new era that builds on and integrates a century of reform (Terpstra & McFadden, 1993).

BASIC CHARACTERISTICS OF FOSTER CARE

As a service to children and their families, foster care has certain distinguishing characteristics:

1. Foster care is arranged by a public or voluntary social agency.
2. Responsibility for children's daily care usually is transferred from the biological parents because of a serious situation—a complex set of interacting conditions or parental characteristics that makes the parents unable to care for their children properly and necessitates community assumption of responsibility.
3. Foster care is full-time care, twenty-four hours a day, outside the child's own home.
4. Foster care or out-of-home care may be given within a family foster home, a treatment foster home, a small group home, a cottage setting or a larger congregate care facility.
5. In contrast with adoption, foster care is supposed to be a temporary arrangement, with the expectation that the child will return to the parents or extended family, be placed for adoption, or be discharged from care on reaching legal maturity.

Using social work methods, the social agency plays a major role in planning and carrying out the child's care. Typically the parents retain many of their rights even if the court has assumed temporary wardship of the child. Thus the agency shares the broad responsibility for the child with the court, the parents, and the community, even while the foster parents, house parents, or child care staff provide the day-to-day services for the child.

Children and youths who enter care have usually had difficult experiences, including the maltreatment and/or parental problems which necessitate care, and this is compounded by the painful separation from parents, siblings, kinfolk, and familiar environments. They may have unresolved conflicts in relation to their parents, or divided loyalties between original family and substitute caregivers. Because of their life experiences—physical neglect, abuse, emotional neglect, sexual abuse, abandonment, or exploitation— young persons in care often have many unmet developmental needs. Consequently, for the foster care experience to be nurturing and successful, it must involve far more than a change of setting: The services must be child-focused and family-centered so that attention can be given to continuity of important emotional ties.

Underlying Principles

Certain generalizations or principles underlie contemporary foster care practice. Some have remained relatively stable during this century, while others have evolved:

1. The parent-child relationship and adequate parenting are of utmost importance to the child. Society's first responsibility is to try to preserve the child's own home. If that is not possible, the kinship network or extended family should be supported to provide the child continuity of relationships.
2. If parental care cannot be restored to a level that will protect children and provide at least minimally adequate care, and the kinship network cannot maintain the child, then family foster care can provide nurture within a family setting until a permanent family situation can be achieved for the child.
3. Different settings within the foster care system— family foster homes, specialized or treatment homes, group homes, and congregate care—are an array of services from which the most appropriate service can be selected, based on the unique needs of the individual child and family.
4. In all settings the family is the identified client, with focus on the needs of the child within the context of the family system. The initial service goal is usually family reunification, with improved family functioning and safety for the child.
5. The foster caregiver (foster parent, houseparent, or child care staff) is an integral part of the service team. The caregiver participates in forming a permanency plan, serves as a role model to the family, and aids in facilitating family reunification.
6. When decisions crucial to the future of the child are made, special consideration must be given to ensure that the legal rights of the child are protected. This must be balanced with attention to

constitutional rights of parents and the presumed rights of children to be part of a family and maintain family connections.

WHY CHILDREN ARE PLACED
IN FOSTER CARE

It is clear that in earlier decades children were placed in care for reasons other than neglect and abuse. These reasons included physical (29 percent) or mental (11 percent) illness of the parents, and personality or emotional problems of the child (17 percent). Only 10 percent of children were placed because of abuse and neglect (Jenkins & Sauber, 1966). This contrasts sharply with current placement data.

One-half (50.2 percent) of the children who entered substitute care in 1990 did so because of protective service reasons (abuse and neglect); another 20.9 percent entered care because of parental conditions or parental absence, such as illness, death, handicap, or financial hardship. Another 11.3 percent of children entered care because of status offenses such as running away, truancy, or delinquent behavior, while 12.5 percent entered care for other reasons such as parent-child relationship problems, a plan for adoption, deinstitutionalization, and unwed motherhood. Only 1.9 percent of the children entered care because of the child's disability or handicap (a physical, mental, or emotional problem) and only 0.8 percent entered care because of the relinquishment of parental rights. (Tatara, 1993).

Bromley and Blacker's study (1991) of children who are placed in care because of severe handicapping conditions indicated that the reasons for placement included parents' perceptions of daily stress, the child's level of functioning, child behavior problems, and the feelings of specific family members such as unaffected siblings or a spouse.

Effects of the Substance Abuse Epidemic

Since crack cocaine hit inner city neighborhoods in 1986, the well-being of hundreds of thousands of children has been affected (Besharov, 1994). From 1982 to 1991 the number of children in the United Sates living in foster care increased by 63.4 percent due to a decline in the rate in which children exited care (Tatara,

1992). This pattern reflected the difficulty child welfare agencies were having in adjusting to changing circumstances of children and families, and suggested that children entering care were from more seriously disturbed families, necessitating longer stays in care. Children in foster care in the 1990s are far more likely to be from families involved in serious and chronic substance abuse—especially crack cocaine (Horn, 1994). Officials in New York state estimate that 75 percent of foster children come from alleged drug-abusing (including alcohol) families (Child Welfare League of America, 1990). Nationally it is estimated that 80 percent of drug-exposed children declared "dependent" in 1989 received out-of-home placement. (Feig, 1990). The recent increase of the number of children in foster care is attributed to the two major epidemics to affect child welfare—HIV and crack cocaine (Groze, Haines-Simeon, & Barth, 1994).

In the 1970s Fanshel (1975) did a major longitudinal study of children who entered foster care in New York City, which drew out evidence of the fate of a subgroup of children in the study population—children with drug-abusing mothers. With minor exceptions, all children in the total study sample reflected family situations of extreme deprivation at the time that foster care became necessary.

These mothers were assessed as among the most damaged in the study population. They tended to become unable to care for their children earlier in their maternal careers than did other mothers in the study. Consequently, their children came into care at young ages. Social workers found the drug-abusing mothers to be extremely difficult to involve in meaningful planning for their children's future. Visiting patterns were erratic, and the children could seldom count on sustained parental contact. Although these mothers were almost totally disabled as maternal figures, they were strongly ambivalent in relation to parenthood, showing negative attitudes toward releasing their children for adoption and toward temporary foster care as a resource for their children. Given their mothers' critical inability to resume maternal responsibilities, these children became locked into the foster care system in disproportionate numbers (Fanshel, 1975).

Although one might argue that the addicted mothers of the 1990s are different than those referenced by

Fanshel, there seem to be similarities. Chasnoff (1990) describes contemporary addicted mothers:

> They are less well educated, more frequently unemployed, with less stable housing than their non-drug–using counterparts. They come from dysfunctional, often chemically dependent families, and have a long history of violent or unhealthy relationships. They are more likely to have been victims of early sexual or physical abuse. They are less likely to receive prenatal care, and are more likely to have multiple health problems. (p. 112)

Substance abuse treatment ideally takes two to four years of therapy and twelve-step group support to move the abuser beyond the likelihood of relapse into a solid recovery. Foster care, on the other hand, mandates that permanence be attained within a six- to eighteen-month time frame. This disjuncture in time frames becomes a critical issue when the child of a substance-abusing parent is placed in care. Premature return of the child may compromise the parent's recovery, yet to allow several years to lapse before starting family reunification can delay permanency.

> I work with infants and young children. . . . The terrible tragedy for the families of these children is that they live in incredible poverty and are up against the worst odds in a time of unbelievable unemployment. They can't get jobs even if they are hard workers. If you dull your senses your kids are taken. (Denise Plunkett in Golden, 1997 p. 173)

Not all infants born to addicted mothers are placed in care. The child's situation should be carefully assessed by examining the mother's functioning, the availability of support systems, particularly the extended family, access to treatment, and adequacy of the living situation (Wightman, 1991). It should be reemphasized that children are *not* placed in care simply because a parent abuses alcohol, crack cocaine, or other drugs. The usual reason children are separated from their parents is that they have been neglected or abused by their parents or others. However, the maltreatment may be related to a parent's substance abuse, and that becomes a factor in placement decisions.

An estimated 80,000 women of child-bearing age may be infected with the HIV virus (Gwinn, Pap-

palioanou, & George, 1991). There is some overlap between HIV and parental drug use as issues affecting child welfare. In a pediatric HIV/AIDS study, 98 percent of the mothers had used drugs while pregnant (Leeds 1992). Thus a number of HIV-infected children in care may also be substance affected, and vice versa. Some HIV-infected children have been placed because their parents have already died. A sizable group of children and youth needing permanency planning are those estimated 80,000 healthy older siblings who have been or will be orphaned by AIDS before the twenty-first century (Taylor-Brown & Garcia, 1995). Only one-third of that number are expected to enter care, with the others being served by informal kinship care with close relatives. Stein (1998) indicates that the percent of children from HIV families who actually enter foster care hovers around 28 percent, with significant state-by-state variation, ranging from a low of 1 percent in Florida to a high of 41 percent in New York. (See Chapter 8). New courses of drug treatment are enhancing the life expectancy of both mothers and children affected by HIV.

Despite difficulties in working with addicted parents or substance-affected children, there are many ways in which these families can be helped. In the mid-1990s, a collegial effort by the American Enterprise Institute, the American Public Welfare Association, The American Bar Association, the U.S. Department of Health and Human Services, the U.S. Department of Justice, and the U.S. Office of National Drug Control Policy brought forth new approaches to and new ways of thinking about child welfare and substance-addicted families (Besharov, 1994). Some of the strategies, including increased use of kinship care and acknowledging the extended period of time required for recovery, are addressed in Chapter 8. Other salient issues are discussed later in this chapter.

Impact of Poverty and Racism

Racism plays a large part in the social context of family situations that bring children into care. In a study of urban families referred for child neglect, the most startling finding was the economic disparity between African-American and Caucasian families. Although almost all of the families in the sample were poor,

African-American families suffered even more from economic inequality than those in the general population. The interrelationship of racism and poverty is evident in de facto segregated housing patterns. Stress is endemic to families experiencing substandard housing, unsafe neighborhoods, and overcrowded conditions (Saunders, Nelson, & Landsman, 1993). While most of the children served by the foster care system are affected by poverty, families of color are more likely to be poor. Racial discrimination and a history of economic marginality have rendered African-American families more vulnerable to large-scale technological and economic changes (Billingsley, 1992).

Racism in the larger society is reflected by the over-representation of minority children in the system (Stehno, 1982; Stehno, 1990; National Black Child Development Institute, 1989; Goerge, Wulczyn, & Harden, 1996). In 1990, children who entered substitute care were 47.2 percent white, 30.8 percent black, 13.7 percent Hispanic, and 4.6 percent other races (Asian, Pacific Islander, Native American, Alaskan Native). A significant decline occurred in the percentage of white children who entered care—from 56.4 percent in 1983 to 47.2 percent in 1990. The percentage of black children who entered care rose somewhat from 26.7 percent (49,100 children) in 1983 to 30.8 percent in 1990. For Hispanic children, the percentage rose from about 10 percent in 1983 to 13.7 percent in 1990 (Tatara, 1993). In 1994, Caucasian children constituted 75 percent of the child population in the United States, African-American children constituted 15 percent and Latino children constituted 10 percent. (Groze, Haines-Simeon, & Barth, 1994). This disparity points to the effects of racism.

Latino families have been marginalized as a result of social and economic disadvantages, including poverty, limited educational resources, and obstacles to accessing social service organizations. Thus Latino children are coming into care at ever-increasing rates and are remaining in care longer than non-Hispanic white children. The term *Latino* does not adequately portray the diversity of the Latino community, which includes Guatemalan or Salvadoran refugees, Mexican-Americans, Puerto Ricans, and many other ethnic groups (Zambrana & Dorrington, 1998). Therefore,

the National Latino Child Welfare Advocacy Group asserts that Latino children in the system are "invisible and unaccounted for" (Ortega, Guillean, & Najera, 1996). Their report also reminds us that Latino parents who are refugees or immigrants encounter difficulties with the system due to the cultural gap in what constitutes acceptable discipline.

The thread of poverty is woven throughout the foster care system . . . in financial deprivation among families, and in communities who have rarely been willing to appropriate adequate funds for supportive services. Child welfare agencies have thus suffered their own kind of "poverty". (Boehm, 1970, pp. 674, 676)

Family Characteristics

Problems relating to parental characteristics and social conditions that precede foster care are in most instances very serious ones, not easily corrected by existing services. Although the child welfare concept of foster care emphasizes its temporary nature, foster care often can become a long-term experience. Contrary to popular belief, children in care are not orphans; at least, they have not lost their parents through death. Children in foster care usually have at least one living parent who may or may not visit and assume responsibility. As a result, these children have been termed "orphans of the living" to emphasize the emotional, social, and legal limbo in which they frequently live. Too often they are tied to their parents by unmet needs and unresolved conflicts, but are unable to live with them and may consequently be trapped in a succession of foster homes or institutions.

For some, this may become a multigenerational cycle of poverty and insecurity. Homeless people, for example, who have a foster care history, are more likely than other homeless people to have their children in care. Research does not indicate that foster care is a cause of homelessness but that it is one element in a complex web of familial, social, and institutional failures that affect children (Roman & Wolfe, 1997).

The incarceration of women also is a reason for foster care placement. The children of incarcerated fathers usually live with their mothers, but when women who are the sole caregiver of their children are arrested, their children are placed in care, often under traumatic conditions as when the children are present at their parent's arrest. Of approximately 42,000 children of incarcerated parents in out-of-home care, most live with nonrelative foster families or group homes, while some are in kinship foster homes (Beatty, 1997).

Although data are incomplete about the children in foster care and their earlier experience with their parents, one fact stands out clearly: The primary reason why children come into foster care is family breakdown or incapacity, exacerbated by severe environmental pressures. This breakdown may reflect one or, more frequently, a cluster of critical and visible individual and environmental problems, such as neglect and abuse of children, physical or mental illness of parents, unmarried parents, parental use of alcohol and other drugs, and continuing poverty or marginally low income.

Children who enter foster care, particularly those who then are in danger of growing up in foster care, usually have parents with a configuration of serious personal and environmental problems that have grown over time and who have insufficient support from other adults. It is difficult to identify a single principal reason for each placement. When problems are categorized, overlapping is evident and social worker's judgments inevitably are subjective and imprecise in varying degrees. For example, children's disturbed behavior may stem from situations of serious marital discord, or a neglecting or abusing parent may also be mentally ill and trying to self-medicate with alcohol or other drugs. A series of studies and reports over the past few decades have provided evidence that the major problems bringing children into foster care are not their emotional or behavioral disorders, but *problems related to parental functioning* (Phillips, Shyne, Sherman, & Haring, 1971; Jenkins & Norman, 1972; Jones, Magura, & Shyne, 1976; Fanshel, 1982; National Commission on Family Foster Care, 1991; Besharov, 1994).

An early, classic study by Jenkins and Sauber (1966) looked at the *onset* of problems that brought about placements. Interviews with 425 families in New York City documented that families had a number of crises, including physical illness of parents (29 percent), mental breakdowns (11 percent), personality or emotional problems of children (17 percent), neglect or abuse (10 percent), and breakdown in family life or relationships (33 percent). The interviews were rich and descriptive. One mother described how she had recognized her own incapacity and managed to initiate placement herself:

> I had a nervous breakdown and I knew I was not myself. I asked my neighbor to call the police because I was so nervous and confused. My vision was blurred. I could not touch anything that was not colored blue. I was not paying attention to the baby. I would feel sad for long periods of time. My sister committed suicide four years ago, so when I began not to feel myself I got help. The police came for the baby. (pp. 103–104)

Fanshel's (1982) review of family conditions of 26,865 children in care in New York City in 1979 found that parental or adult functioning failures accounted for at least 80 percent of the reasons children were in care. Again, in an examination of the national foster care statistics for 1984, in over three-fourths of the cases the primary problem was found to lie in some aspect of parental functioning (Duva & Raley, 1988).

Recent findings on factors affecting foster care placement of children are generally consistent with earlier research efforts. Parent (maternal) characteristics significantly influenced the placement decision. Professional concerns about parental substance-abuse problems had more influence on decision-making than any other characteristic. Families who had a recurrence of abuse were also at increased risk for experiencing placement (Zuravin & DePanfilis, 1997).

A brief retrospective of reasons for placement shows that the precipitating factors leading to placement of a child in care have been complex. Despite the current use of family-based services to prevent placement, children continue to come into care in increased numbers. These children generally have more intense needs, and the families have greater problems and/or conditions, which take longer to resolve. These situations include now, as in the past, poverty and family dysfunction, to which have been added contemporary issues such as crack cocaine, homelessness, and children orphaned by AIDS.

Standards for Decision-Making

Characteristics of the decision-maker—particularly the social worker—are among the nonclient variables that have been given research attention. Important case decisions, including the decision to place, are being made by social workers with less specialized education and child welfare experience than in the past. Difficult tasks are often performed by persons who do not have the necessary skills and training. A majority lack professional graduate social work education. The situation is exacerbated by staff turnover. A past appraisal of the situation had this to say: "Obstacles to recruitment and retention of professional social workers exist in many public agencies. Many states have declassified and reclassified social work positions. In these states, applicants for highly sensitive positions are not required to have a BSW or MSW degree. Salaries are low, and caseloads have tripled on the average in the past decade" (Harris, 1988, pp. 483–484). The new partnership between social work education and public child welfare is beginning to develop more credentialed and better-prepared staff.

The importance of the decision-maker as the processor of information has long been recognized, suggesting that the placement decision may be more a function of the decision-maker than of case characteristics. Professional and personal characteristics have not yet been shown to be highly relevant to placement decisions. Jones (1985) found that the worker variable of child welfare experience resulted in fewer children entering care. The placement decision-maker operates in an environmental context. The processing of information is influenced by contextual elements such as place, time, and persons involved in the decision-making. For example, large caseloads allegedly contribute to less-than-adequate service delivery. Child welfare practitioners are forced to operate on a crisis-to-crisis basis, which limits the information collected and the time allowed for processing it. This can lead to decisions based on expediency. Another dimension of the decision is the range of persons involved in the decision-making process. Although the principal decision-maker is usually the case worker, this decision is rarely made unilaterally. There may be input from family members, other staff in the child welfare agency, and professionals within the community who have been working with the child and family. A preliminary decision to seek removal of a child from the family must be taken to the court and affirmed or denied through a legal process.

The decision about whether to place a child is influenced not only by the characteristics of the case and the decision-making context, but also by the criteria that have been established for such decisions. Standards for public agencies are promulgated through legislation and administrative rules. All states have statutes authorizing intervention to protect children. On a national level, the Adoption Assistance and Child Welfare Act of 1980 set a standard that agencies must make "reasonable efforts" to keep children in their homes rather than foster care placement. Before a child could be removed from the family, a judge had to determine, *for each case,* that the agency had indeed made reasonable efforts.

The legal standards for making "reasonable efforts" were operationalized by organizations such as the American Bar Association (Ratterman et. al., 1987; Hardin, 1989) and the National Council of Juvenile and Family Court Judges (1992). For example, the National Council of Juvenile and Family Court Judges redefines "reasonable efforts" in work with families of drug-exposed infants. Overriding principles involved in the development of the reasonable efforts protocol include the provision of practical help to families; availability and use of drug treatment resources; working with the extended family to support and care for the child; provision of comprehensive medical services; coordination and collaboration of public agencies, including law enforcement; and removal of a child only when there is a substantial risk of harm that cannot be ameliorated through family strengthening services (National Council of Juvenile and Family Court Judges, 1992). Examples of the checklists to be applied during adjudicatory or dispositional hearings with substance-affected families and further discussion of reasonable effort are found in Chapter 8.

The concept of "reasonable effort" was not fully realized in policy and practice, as had earlier been hoped, because of restricted funding, minimal federal leadership, and the tremendously increased demand for services. The "reasonable efforts" mandate was a cornerstone in practice, a much-needed link in balancing parental rights with the protection of children (Kopels & Rycraft, 1993). However, under the Adoption and Safe Families Act, enacted in 1997, the reasonable effort criterion has been placed in the larger context of child safety, and as discussed earlier, the requirement to apply the standard has been waived in certain extreme situations.

CHARACTERISTICS OF CHILDREN IN CARE

Age, Ethnicity, and Other Variables

Current data on foster care are available through the federal government's Adoption and Foster Care Analysis and Reporting System (AFCARS) and can be accessed on the Web at http://www.afc.dhhs.gov/programs/cb/stats/afcars. Prior to implementation of AFCARS, the Voluntary Cooperative Information System (VCIS) of the American Public Welfare Association covered foster care activities from 1982 through 1990. According to the American Public Welfare Association, not all states and jurisdictions were able to respond to every question in the survey, so VCIS data should be considered "rough" national estimates.

In 1986 Congress approved an amendment to Title IV-E of the Social Security Act. This amendment required the establishment of an advisory committee that would make recommendations for establishing a system for collecting data on adoption and foster care in the United States. The committee recommended a mandatory system for collecting data on all children covered by section 427 of Title IV-B of the Social Security Act. In 1993 the Department published final rules regarding the implementation of AFCARS.

AFCARS data were available at the time of this writing only through 1996 and are incomplete. While thirty-eight states submitted foster care data, data from twenty-two states had to be excluded from the tables because of data quality issues or at the specific request of the states. The data are estimated to represent 55 percent of the total number of children served by foster care systems in 1996. Thus the 287,727 children reported in care represent only a fraction of the actual number.

According to AFCARS, in 1996 white non-Hispanic children constituted 38 percent of children in care, with 45 percent black non-Hispanic children, 14 percent Hispanic, 1 percent Asian/Pacific Island, and 2 percent Native American/Alaskan Native. It must cautioned that these figures relate only to the twenty reporting states, many of which failed the Children's Bureau standard for data quality (Adoption and Foster Care Analysis and Reporting System, 1998).

Children in foster care are, as a group, younger than they were during the early years of permanency planning in the 1970s and early 1980s. The percentage of infants in care increased from 9.9 percent in 1983 to 16.1 percent in 1990. The number of adolescents in care decreased from 38.5 percent in 1983 to 31.1 percent in 1990. The median age of children entering care decreased substantially from 10.2 years in 1983 to 7.8 years in 1990 (Tatara, 1993). According to the Adoption and Foster Care Analysis and Reporting System (1998), the age distribution in 1996 of reporting states was as follows: 4 percent under 1 year; 29 percent 1 to 5 years; 27 percent 6 to 10 years; 25 percent 11 to 15 years; 14 percent 16 to 18 years; and 1 percent age 19 or over. These figures do not represent the total population of children in care, only children in those states that reported to AFCARS. Of reporting AFCARS states, 51 percent of children in foster care are male and 49 percent are female.

In an archival study of five states (California, Illinois, Michigan, New York, and Texas) the Chapin Hall research team found disproportionate increases in placement of young children under the age of five. The most notable feature of the age distribution was the large and increased number of infant placements over a ten-year period (Goerge, Wulczyn, & Harden, 1996). Because there are so many infants and young children in care, child welfare services need to become more developmentally sensitive (Berrick, Needell, Barth, & Johnson-Reid, 1998). Children in care are more likely now to be children of color, infants, or young children, and to be affected directly or indirectly by parental substance use. However, only about one-fifth of the current foster care population has one or more disabling conditions (Tatara, 1993).

Each child in care is unique and cannot be adequately described by statistics. Even very young children have likes, dislikes, feelings, memories, and hopes. More research is needed to capture children's perceptions of their situation. A study by Johnson, Yoken, and Voss (1990) examined the child's perspective on foster care placement. They held intensive interviews with fifty-nine youngsters between the ages of 11 and 14, living in public and private agency foster homes in Cook County, Illinois. These children were reasonably clear on the reasons that they were in care, although they were confused about the circumstances of their removal. Almost all the children had been placed in different neighborhoods, were attending different schools, and were making new friends. The children valued their caseworkers because they worked with the biological parents and spent time with the children. Most children felt it was sometimes good to be in a foster home, but a number offered alternatives to placement such as living with a relative or removing the abuser from the family's home, rather than removing them.

WORKING WITH THE PLACEMENT PROCESS

When a child is referred to a social agency because placement outside his or her own home is likely to be necessary, the agency must undertake a series of tasks. Many of the tasks relate to the legal processes of foster care, such as preparing for review hearings, or documenting the work toward a permanency goal. (See Chapter 6.) The use of a systematic placement process helps to assure that the agency meets its responsibilities for

1. trying to maintain or restore the child's home;
2. selecting an appropriate form of care if the decision has been made to place the child;
3. helping the child separate from parents and move into the new child care arrangement;
4. helping foster parents or child care staff carry out their responsibilities successfully; and

5. seeing that a permanent home is provided for the child, either with her or his parents or relatives, or in a new permanent home through adoption, guardianship, or other forms of planned long-term care.

Parental Involvement

Removing children from their homes to place them into the foster care system is a very serious step with far-reaching consequences. It cannot be stated too often that this step should be undertaken only when it becomes clear that, even with outside help, the children's parents cannot continue to care for them.

To make such a crucial decision, the social worker must reach out to the child's parents and try to understand them—their life experiences, the ambivalent feelings they may have about their child, and their strengths and weaknesses in parenting and how these affect the child. Parents should be involved in planning the placement to the greatest degree possible and should continue to be involved in all aspects of the placement process. Parents are to be viewed as partners (Maluccio & Sinanoglu, 1981) and as a valuable resource for the child in care (Blumenthal & Weinberg, 1983).

Parents are often the best source of information about the child's likes, dislikes, habits, and needs (McFadden, 1980; Ryan, McFadden, & Warren, 1981) and should communicate with the foster parents early in the placement process, preferably before the child goes to the foster home. In some situations it is helpful if the foster parent and parent meet before the placement is made, to allay the parent's anxiety and to help the parent give the child a supportive message about the move. The foster parent can answer the parent's questions about care and can benefit from detailed practical information about the child. Even if parents are in crisis, are angry about the removal of the child, or are highly negative about the child, the engagement process should be attempted by the foster care team at the earliest feasible time. Involving the child's parents in the placement processes is termed "inclusive practice." Research on foster care social workers who received focused in-service training on inclusive practice suggests that workers can be influenced to become more inclusive of parents in their placement practice and in the lives of the children in out-of-home care (Palmer, 1997).

When the decision is made to move a child into foster care, the court often orders parental visits and provision of child support. The social worker makes realistic plans with the parents about their contributions to the child's support as well as arrangements to visit the child under circumstances that will reinforce their affection and commitment to the child. It is important that parents be helped to understand their continuing rights and responsibilities. Time is a critical factor in determining whether foster children can return to their own homes or move into a new permanent home through adoption. Therefore it is essential that the social worker strive to help parents establish a realistically attainable plan to restore their home, or, if this is not possible, to maintain a constructive tie to their child in foster care, or to release the child for adoption. Especially because many children who enter foster care do not have adoptive homes available for them even though they could become legally free for adoption, it is important that whatever is of value in the parent-child relationship be supported. It is very useful, when planning the placement, to do a genogram with the parent to identify members of the kinship network who can be a resource for support of the child and parents during placement, and who might conceivably become a resource for permanency.

Helping Parents with Separation

Considerable attention has been given to the effects on children of separation experiences. In contrast, insufficient attention has been given to understanding the experiences of parents when their children enter foster care. Jenkins and Norman (1972) term this reciprocal aspect of the placement transaction "filial deprivation." They recognize the likelihood that in a society where the prevailing expectation is that parents will rear their children themselves, failure to do so will have serious consequences for parents whose children are placed in care. When they interviewed over 400 mothers and fathers, parents reported that they had felt sad, worried, nervous, empty, angry, bitter, thankful, relieved, guilty, ashamed, numb, and paralyzed (Jenkins & Norman, 1972).

The separation of children from parents is a crisis—of dismemberment—that impacts the entire family system. The worker's handling of the actual separation may have an important influence on the parent's ability to remain invested in the children or to be emotionally available. A parent whose children were placed following an episode of serious abuse recollected the impact of the separation on her:

> I had already lost my husband. Now I was losing everything, my self-respect, my children, I was losing myself. I felt like a piece of shit. My father had told me that I'd get no help from the family because I had disgraced them. I knew that I'd lose my financial assistance [AFDC]. Something was dying in me. I wanted to kill myself. Thank God my Parents Anonymous sponsor came down to the hospital emergency room while my children were being examined and taken away. She told me I shouldn't kill myself because if I killed myself I wouldn't get my kids back. I think I probably would have done myself in if she hadn't been there to help me at a time when I lost everything. (McFadden, 1984, p. 596)

Parents should be prepared with anticipatory guidance for the painful feelings surrounding placement. In acknowledging the difficulty of the separation, the worker can help the parent identify the supportive people in their environment who can assist them in the sad and anxious hours following the separation. The worker's skill in restating visiting plans, and the plans made to achieve reunification, may provide a needed element of hope, which can sustain the parent's motivation. For the parent to provide a verbal or written message to the child about the reasons for the separation and the hopes for the placement period, can be helpful to both parent and child.

Selection of Appropriate Care for the Child and Family Needs

Few empirical data exist to support decisions about selection of a care option from the array of foster care services available. Nevertheless, certain guidelines generally prevail in choosing between family care and group care.

Kinship Care. *Kinship placements* are often preferred because they promote continuity of relationships for the child in a familiar environment. They are less likely to disrupt than regular foster care placements (Berrick, Barth, & Needell, 1993). Kinship homes provide a placement within the child's own ethnic or cultural group. They are not appropriate if the relative cannot establish boundaries with the parent, is afraid of the parent, or there is any indication that the relative may have been involved either in abusing the parent or supporting the parent's maltreatment of children.

Family Foster Care. *Family foster homes* continue to be preferred over group care for the majority of children. For infants and preschool-age children a family setting is almost mandatory, except for those with very severe problems requiring specialized service. For children who are able to participate in family life, attend community schools, and live in the community without danger to self or others, family foster care is preferred.

Treatment Foster Care. *Treatment foster homes* are appropriate for children with emotional or behavioral problems that can be handled in a therapeutic family milieu. Specialized, highly trained foster homes that take medically fragile children and work closely with the hospital and medical team are appropriate for children with severe and multiple needs for individualized care who might otherwise be hospitalized (Hochstadt & Yost, 1991).

Group Care. *Group care* is rarely used for young children and is generally considered to be appropriate for adolescents who are unable to tolerate the demands of family living. Many adolescents do well in general or treatment foster homes, and are desirous of having a positive experience with family life. For some adolescents, small or family-type group homes are a good solution. For others, group homes or cottages in which the child care staff are more role models than parent figures may be appropriate. A few group or residential settings accept both child and parents into placement (Gibson & Noble, 1991) or provide intensive work with families (Jenson & Whittaker, 1987).

Children who cannot make use of family living are usually referred to residential care—for example, troubled adolescents who are trying to free themselves of closer family ties and for whom peer influences and group experiences may have greater value than family life. If youths have difficulty in forming relationships with substitute parenting figures because of past family experiences, they may fare better in group settings. Some parents may be more comfortable seeing their children in residential care because they do not have to see other "parents" succeeding where they could not. Some children have experienced successive replacements in poorly selected foster homes and can use the institution as a stable setting that provides continuity and physical if not emotional "roots" and a chance to seek out a few accepting or "safe" adult staff with whom to try to form ties.

Institutional Care. Children and young persons who act out in aggressive ways dangerous to themselves or others or who display other behavior that the family or community will seldom tolerate are often served in an institutional setting. Some children are cared for in institutions because their communities lack appropriate educational, medical, or psychiatric resources that they need. Group care is not often chosen for initial placement in "the system." There is a tendency to use kinship care, family foster care, or treatment foster care rather than group settings, based on the belief that children need to be in families and the legal principle of the "least restrictive environment." Practice has also moved in the direction of moving young people back from institutional settings to the community, using wraparound services. Of the estimated 500,000 children in care in 1995, approximately 80 percent are in family foster care (general or treatment) with only 20 percent in group care (Terpstra, 1995).

Placement Considerations: Sibling Groups, Matching, and Cultural Needs

A critical placement issue involves keeping siblings together. When children have been neglected by their parents they often develop a primary bond with each other (Banks & Kahn, 1982). Research shows that the presence of even one attachment figure can be a protective factor to promote resilience in children who suffer separation or trauma (Garbarino, DuBrow, Knostelny, & Prado, 1992; Rutter, 1985). Staff and Fein (1992), in a study of sibling placements with Casey Family Services, found that siblings who were placed together were more likely to stay in their first placement than siblings who were placed separately. In Grigsby's (1994) study of attachment in foster care, he found that siblings placed together had a shorter duration in care than siblings placed separately, and he recommends that protective services workers receive better training in maintaining attachments. Child Welfare League of America standards state clearly that siblings should be kept together (Child Welfare League of America, 1989, 1995). In the past it was not uncommon for siblings to be separated in order to prevent a "caretaker" older sibling from continuing in the role. There is no support in the literature for that practice (Hegar, 1988). Perhaps the only sound rationale for separating siblings is safety. If one sibling seriously abuses the other sibling, physically or sexually, and the foster parent cannot guarantee intensive supervision, it may be necessary to find separate homes. Still, every effort should be made to keep the siblings in contact in order to help them work through past traumatic events (McFadden, 1985). For large sibling groups, licensing may be a problem in that the number of siblings may exceed the number of children for whom a foster home is licensed. Exceptions should be sought to keep siblings together.

There is agreement in the literature that matching the child to the foster family is important. The use of temporary shelter care can allow sufficient time to develop a home that is a good match. The general concept behind matching is matching the *child's needs* to the *strengths of the foster family,* paying careful attention to how the presence of the child would affect and fit in with the roles, ages, and developmental stages of children already in the home. Foster parents self-assessed preferences as to age, gender, handicapping conditions, and behavior that can be handled should also be considered.

Despite the strictures of the amended Multiethnic Placement Act, there is still a consensus in the practice community that racial or ethnic matching is an important placement variable and should be taken into consideration, although not considered as the only placement determinant. Folaron and Hess (1993), in discussing placement of children of mixed African-American and caucasian parentage, assert that the "burden of misplacement can deprive a child of the timely social and cultural development essential to learning coping skills and to establishing a positive sense of racial identity" (p. 122). They recommend assessment of numerous factors, including the child's preference regarding foster parent race; the comfort of the child's family with the foster family; the opinions and attitudes of the foster family about race; the knowledge the foster parents have about care of skin, hair, and diet; the presence of literature in the home endorsed by members of the child's culture and heritage; the racial makeup of the foster parents' neighborhood; and perceptions of school personnel concerning racial identity.

Child Welfare League standards for family foster care discuss several factors for selection of the most appropriate family for a child. These areas of concern include the age, gender, and culture of the child; competencies training and strengths of the foster family to meet the needs of the child; proximity to the child's parents and kin; the ability of the foster family to help the parents remain connected to the child; and the availability of community resources to meet the needs of the child and family (Child Welfare League of America, 1995). For many children it may be very important to remain in their own school district so that important ties with the educational process, their friends, or a caring teacher are not disrupted. Despite these guidelines, decisions as to the choice of foster care placement settings are often determined by practical factors such as what is available, proximity of the facility or foster home, and existing agency contracts with other child placement agencies (Stein & Rzepnicki, 1984; Briar, 1963; Fanshel, 1963). The matching process has been compared metaphorically to a blindfolded worker tossing darts until a balloon is popped on a dartboard (Chiaro, Marden, Haase, & Guedes, 1982). In fact, failure to match a child with the foster family's abilities or preference is one factor correlated with abuse in foster homes (Miller, 1982).

MEETING THE NEEDS OF CHILDREN
IN FOSTER CARE

Separation, Attachment, and Resilience

Children who leave their own homes and enter foster care have experienced varying kinds and degrees of deviation in parental care. They are highly vulnerable to a stressful separation from their parents, their kin, and their familiar surroundings. Strangely, very limited attention has been directed toward children's loss by separation from siblings (Ward, 1984; Hegar, 1988). Social workers have given considerable attention to assessing the likely long-term effects of poor parental care, particularly poor mothering, and to finding ways to help children with the distress they feel at separating from their parents, even neglectful or rejecting ones.

Child welfare practice was strongly influenced by the publication of Bowlby's *Maternal Care and Mental Health* (1951) and other early reports in the literature that described deviating patterns of maternal care, labeled "maternal deprivation," which were thought to be associated with later disturbances in intellectual and social functioning (Lowrey, 1940; Goldfarb, 1945). One outcome of this influence was that child welfare personnel became more cautious about admitting children into foster care and less optimistic about the gains they expected for them in their new foster care situation.

Later analysis of the early research on maternal deprivation brought a more hopeful outlook (Bowlby, 1961; Yarrow, 1961; Ainsworth, 1962; Rose, 1962). It became apparent that a range of deviations and conditions of infant care had been subsumed under the label "maternal deprivation": institutionalization, separation from the mother, multiple caregivers, and distortions in quality of mothering. While it could be generally concluded that these deviations tended to be associated with later disturbances in the child, the effects were not necessarily irreversible nor as adverse as had been earlier thought. It was recognized that maternal deprivation and separation are not synonymous and that children do not react in uniform ways to separation from parents. Different types of separation have different long-range and short-range

effects. Important variables include the child's age at the time of separation, the impact of early learning experiences, varying constitutional sensitivities; the characteristics of the mother from whom the child had been separated, and the amount, quality, and consistency of mothering provided by the mother substitute.

The current practice focus is on the reverse side of the same coin, assessing the child's *attachment* to parenting figures rather than separation or maternal deprivation (Bowlby, 1969; Goldstein, Freud, & Solnit, 1979; Hegar, 1993; Fahlberg, 1991; Grigsby, 1994). Attachment commonly refers to a close emotional bond that endures over time. By the age of 18 months, children are usually attached to more than one individual, with fathers and siblings sharing the attachment with mothers, who are generally the primary attachment figures. There are a number of indicators for disordered attachments, including the following: lack of warm and affectionate interactions; indiscriminate affection with unfamiliar adults; lack of comfort-seeking when frightened, hurt, or ill; lack of compliance with caregiver request or, conversely, compulsive compliance; failure to check back with caregiver in unfamiliar surroundings; and failure to re-establish interaction after separation (Levy & Orlans, 1998). Attachment problems create great difficulty in foster and adoptive homes, and later in life. Preserving the attachment to parents, siblings, and kinfolk is an important goal of contemporary child welfare practice. Fahlberg (1991) has described the critical role of foster parents in nurturing the child's ability to attach, preserving the child's attachment to parents, and helping to transfer the attachment back to natural parents, or on to adoptive parents.

Attachment appears to be an important protective factor for *resilience*. While concepts of resilience are somewhat controversial, some children from severely maltreating backgrounds do not evidence apparent adverse effects (Knutson, 1995). Gilligan (1997) suggests that attachments to family of origin, kin, and other social networks may be crucial to young persons in care to help them build a more positive view of their own social identity. The social, psychological, and environmental conditions that promote warm and supportive attachments are themselves protective factors.

Such attachments occur first and foremost because of a positive, caring caretaker. Children who have attachments are widely known to function adaptively across settings. (Thomlison, 1997).

Even though the long-term effects of separation from parents need not be as damaging to children as thought in early studies, the social worker should be aware that separation is an extremely stressful and often traumatic experience for children. Although each child's reaction to separation from parents is unique, certain painful feelings are common to the placement process. Children may be torn between conflicting feelings of love and anger toward their parents. Yet no matter how appalling their homes might appear to others, the homes are familiar to children and they have developed ways of coping. In the situation of being separated from the parents for the purpose of placement, children sense that they have no control and almost inevitably feel powerless. They feel abandonment, rejection, helplessness, and worthlessness. They may feel shame or guilt about their "terrible" behavior that caused their parents to give them up or give up on them. These feelings can affect the child's self-concept and sense of reality and distort the child's interpretation of old and new environments (Freud, 1955; Littner, 1975).

Trasler (1960) described some of the traits and attitudes that emerged among foster children as a reaction to separation from their parents. Because they could not understand that their parents were overwhelmed by circumstances, the children tended to interpret separation as the withdrawal of their parents' affection. Children often responded with alarm, unhappiness, or bewilderment. Some others, particularly those who had suffered earlier rejections, showed no initial overt signs of distress. In either instance, the initial reactions usually subsided. With more time, the children tended to develop other traits and attitudes that contributed to the disruption of the foster home placement. For example, sometimes a child displayed hostility toward "rejecting parents" by separating from adults. Children who might have repressed this anger or who feared repeated harm began to display fear and anxiety, reflected in tenseness, restlessness, nervous habits, or somatic reactions. Still other children showed fear of being rejected again by an unwillingness to risk establishing a new trusting relationship, so they withheld themselves from responding to affection. And last, some children reflected their anxiety by alternating between reaching out and withdrawing, which made their behavior appear to foster parents to be unpredictable and inconsistent.

Identity Issues

It appears that children can modify their relationships to parents more effectively if their parents are not denied to them, and if they are not expected to abandon their parents completely. For the significant persons in the foster care system not to talk about a child's parents or earlier experiences is a form of denying the child's reality and increasing the child or youth's confusion about identity.

To understand more about the identity issues of children in foster care, Weinstein (1960) interviewed sixty-one children 5 years old or older who had been in placement for at least one year. The interview consisted of twenty open-ended questions in relation to children's conception of their situations vis-à-vis their family and their foster family, their concepts of the role of the agency, and their patterns of identification with their biological or foster parents. The findings were as follows:

1. *Continuing contact with the biological parents is important for the child's adjustment in placement and tends to have an ameliorative effect on the otherwise detrimental consequences of long-term foster care.*
2. *The child's predominant family identification is an important factor in his or her well-being in placement. On the average, children who identified predominantly with their biological parents had the highest ratings of well-being of any group in the study. Children who identified predominantly with the foster parent or who had mixed identifications were significantly lower. Interestingly, the two most problematic groups were those children with mixed identification and those with foster parent identification whose biological parents did not visit them.*
3. *Adequate conceptions of the meaning of foster status and the role of the agency are important for the child's well being. (Weinstein, 1960, p. 39)*

Identity development in foster care introduces a twist to the trajectory of normative adolescent development, according to Kools (1997). Identity development may be influenced by internalizing the stigmatization of foster care, with diminished status and negative stereotypes. Foster caregivers and clinicians need to develop strategies to confront this stigmatization through anticipatory guidance, problem-solving, role-playing, and focusing on the young person's strengths (Kools, 1997).

Treatment Needs of Children in Care

Many studies suggest that psychological or adjustment problems are common among children in care (McIntyre & Keesler, 1986; Fanshel & Shinn, 1978; Gruber, 1978). Despite the variety of situations children entering care have experienced, most have in common a background of insufficient parental nurturance, exposure to intrafamilial or extrafamilial violence, and a separation from attachment figures. Clearly children coming into the foster care system are at risk for mental health problems. Frank (1979) suggests that the vicissitudes of life in foster care may engender for some children more psychological problems than did the maltreatment that was the reason for placement.

Clinicians who treat children in foster care must continually balance the developmental and therapeutic needs of the foster child with the expectations of a complex network of caretakers and professionals with whom the child interacts (Kates, Johnson, Rader, & Streider, 1991). Frequently the children have been traumatized both by the history of maltreatment that led up to the separation from their families and by the fact of separation, which may thereafter loom large as the marker event of their lives (McFadden, 1991; Oyserman, Benbenishy, & Ben-Rabi, 1992). The younger the children are at the time of placement, the more confusing the separation may seem in retrospect. The lingering grief and uncertainty of loss of parental figures will often color the child's view of the world like a lens, with the child's self-image distorted like the reflection in a carnival funhouse mirror. The therapist must also be aware that children and young people in care have a multidimensional inner life, rarely visible to caregivers, and not easily accessible to social workers, therapists, and other helpers.

Whether the foster care permanency plan is family reunification or a move to adoption, therapeutic work with the child's multiple families (foster and biological) is often centered on helping the families deal with the child's confusion about the separation and divided loyalties; the aggressive behavior that reenacts earlier trauma; the fear of rejection leading the child to test a family's commitment with an escalating barrage of unacceptable behaviors; or the problems in adjustment to family, school, or community expectations. Therapists are often asked for opinions in child custody and permanency planning hearings, based on their assessment of a child's bonding or attachment. Stokes and Strothman (1996) have provided a number of guidelines and a framework for such clinical work. They recommend a semistructured observational session in which the evaluator provides materials and tasks to the adult-child dyad. They caution, however, that interpretations of the bonding interview must be made in the context of all that is known about the individuals and their interactions with the child welfare system (Stokes & Strothman, 1996). Gilligan (1997) cautions that reliance on a legal definition of permanence may have gone too far, and that the concept of resilience has greater potential for assessing and responding to a child's developmental needs in the areas of a secure base, self-efficacy, and self esteem.

Charles and Matheson (1990) apply separation theory in noting the cumulative effect of incomplete resolution of the separation process. "If a child has difficulty separating in one situation, the next attempt at completing the process will likely be impaired. As the ability to separate decreases, so does the ability to attach. The experiences of repeated separations and abandonments, as is often the case with a child in care, will elicit ever-increasing anger and related dysfunctional responses" (pp. 39–40). Attachment disorders underlie many of the clinical diagnoses that have been used traditionally to label extremely troubled foster children, such as conduct disorder, oppositional defiant disorder, autistic disorder, reactive attachment disorder of infancy, and identity disorder (Delaney, 1991).

Fahlberg (1991) identifies the salient factors that influence the child's reaction to separation:

- *the child's age and stage of development*
- *the child's attachment to the parent*
- *the parent's bonding to the child*
- *the child's perceptions of the reasons for separation*
- *the child's preparation for the move*
- *the "parting message" the child receives*
- *the "welcoming message" the child receives*
- *the post-separation environment*
- *the child's temperament*
- *the environment from which he is being moved (p. 14)*

These variables underscore the need for teamwork by worker, foster parents, and biological parents in the placement process and in the clinical treatment of the child.

Therapeutic and socio-educational groups for children and young persons in care can help address the child's perceptions of the separation and assist in the child's adaptation to care (Palmer, 1990). One of the advantages of groupwork with children and youth in care is that they discover the similarity and normalcy of their feelings (Rice & McFadden, 1988). Another is that the faulty attributions and self-blame about the reasons for placement can be opened up and resolved. Groupwork can prepare adolescents for entering care (Murphy & Helm, 1988) or for emancipation from care (McFadden, Rice, Ryan, & Warren, 1989).

A unique approach that is helpful for children in the process of handling separation and adaptation to a foster family is bibliotherapy. There are many books for children and adolescents about foster care and the issues faced by children in care. For bibliotherapy to be effective, an adult—a social worker or foster parent—should explore the child's reactions to books that have been read. While talking about the books may be effective, it may also be helpful to use other methods, such as asking the child to draw a picture about the book, writing a letter to a character in the book, or enacting the story with puppets (Pardeck & Pardeck, 1987). Books written by children and youths in care can be particularly effective in reaching other children. One such book, *Finding Our Place,* was developed by young people after the International Foster Care Organization's youth conference. It is full of useful infor-

mation, such as questions to ask your new foster parents, advice for the first day, and how to connect with other children (Human Service Associates, 1998).

In addition to family treatment, teamwork in the placement process, groupwork, and bibliotherapy, individual treatment such as play therapy or counseling may also be helpful to the child making a transition into care. In working with the individual child to master past traumatic events, techniques such as puppet play, drawing, dollhouse play, or work with clay can help the child express hidden pain and reenact confusing or frightening events until some mastery is gained.

There may be additional treatment concerns related to racism and poverty for minority children in care, including difficulty in developing self-efficacy, denial of their racial or ethnic identity, and adaptive defense mechanisms such as hypervigilance when relating to members of the dominant culture. Black children placed in white foster homes may internalize stereotypes of the dominant culture and feel too uncomfortable to tell their foster parents about experiences with racism (Jackson & Westmoreland, 1992).

Many children in out-of-home care have difficulty with developing age-appropriate peer relationships, often due to their history of rejection, inappropriate touching, lack of nurture, and miseducation in social skills. Clinicians need specific tools and strategies to help the child who doesn't fit in understand the experience of social rejection and learn proactive and appropriate ways of engaging others (Nowicki & Duke, 1992). Both group and individual treatment can help children who have been physically or sexually abused to be more empowered in dealing with adults as well as with other children.

Mental health services are needed for an estimated 50 to 80 percent of children using the services of the foster care system. These services should be integrated with the service delivery system of child welfare agencies, should focus on prevention as well as dysfunction, and should be tailored to the various reasons for placement (Schneiderman, Connors, Fribourg, Gries, & Gonzales, 1998). This might involve clinical consultation for workers; assessment and screening of all children entering care; orientation groups for children; groups dealing with a wide range of issues, including grief; groups for children of substance abusers; socialization groups for children with attention deficit and conduct disorders; parent-infant groups to promote attachment; groups for children and adolescents exposed to violence; and groups for children traumatized by victimization and abuse. Individual treatment, family treatment, and other modalities should be used in conjunction with groupwork.

Meeting Critical Health Care Needs

Currently, children in foster care often do not receive timely, high-quality medical services. Children entering foster care are likely to suffer from both acute and chronic—even severe or disabling—medical problems that have often been neglected prior to placement (Klee, Soman, & Halfon, 1992; Chernoff, Coombs-Orme, Risley-Curtis, & Heisler, 1994). Child Welfare League of America (1988) standards for children in out-of-home care address the need for entry-point health assessment for children coming into care, which would consist of comprehensive health, mental health, and developmental assessments within thirty days of placement in shelter care. Klee et al. recommend the following: collection of information on health history; initial health evaluations within 24 hours of placement; comprehensive health evaluations within fourteen to thirty days of placement; and development of an individual health care plan for each child.

A health care initiative of the Maternal and Child Health Bureau, the Administration on Children and Families, the Child Welfare League of America, and the American Academy of Pediatrics to improve the health of children in out-of-home care surveyed the states and developed recommendations. Twenty-five states have a specific program or strategy for delivering health care services to children in out-of-home care. Recommendations include making children's health care a priority for child welfare agencies; building strong collaborations between child welfare and health care; and providing training on health issues to caseworkers and foster parents, while training health care providers in the workings of the child welfare system (Battistelli, 1998).

The approach to providing health care to children in out-of-home care varies from community to community. One community, in Ononadaga County, New York has successfully used a comprehensive multidisciplinary approach to health care for foster children. The ENHANCE program, located in the University Hospital outpatient pediatric department, has an experienced department of social services caseworker on site as a liaison. When a child enters care, an appointment is made with the program. Clinic staff meet for a "preview session" that reviews the young patient's history. Foster parents are involved in all evaluations. A comprehensive examination follows one month after the initial assessment appointment. Developmental testing, and behavioral and emotional treatment are part of the overall coordinated health plan (Blatt, Saletsky, Meguid, Church, O'Hara, Haller-Peck, & Anderson, 1997).

Because children entering care suffer from a variety of conditions, including the effects of lack of preventive medical care and the sequelae of various forms of maltreatment, it seems imperative to develop comprehensive medical services targeted at their unique needs and situation. The impact of managed care health plans for children in out-of-home care has not yet been adequately evaluated. Those concerned with child advocacy should carefully monitor developments in health care for foster children. The trend for managed health care has potential to address the health needs of children in foster care, yet such plans have limited experience in serving children with complex medical and psychosocial needs. To make managed health care work for foster care, departments of child welfare and Medicaid must partner together (Battistelli, 1996).

Gay and Lesbian Youth in the Foster Care System

Gay and lesbian young people in out-of-home care continue to be underserved. They continue to be ignored and rejected by parents, foster parents, or other caregivers. Not only are they underserved by child welfare agencies, often their very existence is denied. "Because of negative societal portrayals, many gay and lesbian youths live a life of isolation, alienation, depression and fear. As a result, they are beset by recurring crises disproportionate to their numbers in the child welfare system" (Child Welfare League of America, 1991, p. 2).

A significant factor among agencies that retards help to gay and lesbian youths within their care is an inability to identify gay and lesbian youths from other youths. Not all gay or lesbian youths are gender-nonconforming, nor does gender nonconformity assure that an adolescent is gay or lesbian. These young people have been socialized to fear admitting their sexual orientation and often have internalized societal homophobia. They need skilled help and understanding from caregivers who can accept them for who they are, and a safe environment where they can talk openly about their concerns, meet peers and adults who can become role models, and learn skills that will enable them to live as a gay adult in a straight society (NASW News, 1993).

While a few West Coast agencies specifically recruit foster homes from the gay and lesbian community (Ricketts, 1991) in order to meet the diverse needs of gay and lesbian youths, many agencies have difficulty facing the issues implicit in acknowledging the presence of gay and lesbian youths in their care. To do so, they need to provide comprehensive training to staff and foster parents, and be willing to become vulnerable to public backlash in a time when bias appears to be intensifying.

PERMANENCY PLANNING: FAMILY REUNIFICATION

Concurrent Planning

When the U.S. Congress passed the Adoption and Safe Families Act in 1997, several barriers to timely permanence for foster children were addressed. The law states that in certain serious situations the courts do not need to require "reasonable efforts" toward family reunification, but can more forward without delay with termination of parental rights. In such cases, a permanency planning hearing must be held within thirty days. Additionally, in those cases in which "reasonable efforts" for family reunification are being implemented, the law permits the use of concurrent planning. This means that states may plan to place a child for adoption or with a legal guardian at the same time that family reunification is tried. Concurrent planning means that two plans are being implemented simultaneously, so that an alternative plan is already in place in the event that family reunification should fail. (See Chapter 10). Concurrent planning requires that agencies and workers prepare for different outcomes at the same time, instead of sequentially. While at times this may feel like an ethical dilemma to the practitioner, the goal of reunification can be in the foreground of practice efforts, with the goal of adoption in the backround as a fail safe option if the primary goal is not achieved.

Under concurrent planning, children may be placed with a foster family that has indicated an openness to adoption, or with a potential adoptive family that has been licensed for foster care, with the understanding that the children may return home if the family reunification part of the plan works out. This can create pressure for termination of parental rights if the foster parents become attached to the child and hope to be able to adopt. The boundary between foster and adoptive families continues to become increasingly diffuse as many foster parents eventually adopt their foster children, and in many states foster and adoptive parents are recruited and trained together.

Family-Centered Practice for Family Reunification

Family reunification, usually the preferred goal for permanency planning, is defined by Pine, Krieger, and Maluccio (1993) as "the planned process of reconnecting children in out-of-home care with their families by means of a variety of services and supports to the children, their families and their foster parents or other service providers. It aims to help each child and family to achieve and maintain, at any given time, their optimal level of reconnection—from full reentry of the child into the family system to other forms of contact such as visiting—that affirms the child's membership in the family" (p. 6).

In earlier years, family reunification was viewed *only* as physical return of the child to parental care, with full parental rights returned, after a limited period of supervision. It is interesting to note that family reunification is now seen as a continuum of relationship and reconnection, an acknowledgment of the importance of family continuity. A child may remain, for compelling reasons, in planned long-term care but may still be reconnected to parents.

Despite numerous problems within the system, family reunification is the most frequently used option for permanency. In 1990, 66 percent of children who left substitute care were reunited with their families or placed with a parent or relative caretaker (Tatara, 1993). In 1996, 63 percent of foster children, according to the federal Adoption and Foster Analysis and Reporting System report, exited the system by being reunified with their families (Adoption and Foster Analysis and Reporting System, 1996).

> *My kids is my life. There is not much in this world for me but my kids, and I do love them. I do not want my kids taken away from me. I do not like to be separated from them. (a parent, Marcenko & Striepe, 1997, p. 44)*

Ethnographic research of a small sample of mothers of children in care identifies factors contributing to reunification. The mothers were all impoverished and mostly African-American mothers of young children. They had at least one of the following histories: substance abuse, homelessness, domestic violence, psychiatric illness, incarceration, HIV infection, or lack of social support. Despite the many concerns the women faced, they were reunified with their children. Contributing factors to this outcome included the following: strong love for their children; the help of family or partners; drug treatment; a belief in oneself; and spirituality (Marcenko & Striepe, 1997). It would appear that working with a strengths perspective and acknowledging a mother's love for her children are important parts of the reunification process.

Parent Problems After Foster Care Placement

Does foster care help parents resolve some of the serious problems that made it necessary for their children to have care away from them? There is widespread agreement that it is better to provide intensive in-home services to resolve problems in the family without separating children and parents. However, when separa-

tion becomes necessary there is no guarantee that foster care will improve, not exacerbate, the family situation. Parents may become further immobilized by the grief of losing their children, and the parent-child attachment may be compromised, particularly if visits are infrequent or discouraged. Foster care will, however, usually provide protection and nurturing for children at severe risk in their own families.

In the past, foster care has been partially helpful. Jenkins and Norman (1975) concluded in a study assessing the circumstances of reunified families that family problems had not been solved as a result of placement. Parents were still living below the poverty level, more of the mothers were receiving public assistance, and they moved more often than the general population. Foster care has not been able to counteract the effects of chronic poverty or societal racism.

Many agency services for restoration of family life are of insufficient strength and direction to have a sustained impact. The more effective programs emerging include the following elements: (1) a wide variety of helping options; (2) a primary and continuing social work staff team; (3) small caseloads; (4) crisis intervention services around the clock; (5) use of natural helping resources in the neighborhood and community; (6) intensive counseling services; (7) provision of transportation, health services, respite care, and child care payments; and (8) availability and use of substance abuse treatment (Pecora et al., 1992; Berry, 1988; Ten Broeck & Barth, 1986; Besharov, 1994). Intensive family-based services—often the same services used to prevent placement—have been effectively used to reunify families where placement has occurred (Walton et al., 1993, Gillespie, Byrne, & Workman, 1995).

Barriers to Family Reunification

Some parental conditions or situations may make reunification difficult or unlikely. In a risk-assessment matrix Katz and Robinson (1991) present a framework for differential diagnosis and case planning early in service delivery. Parents who have killed or severely injured other children, or who are dangerous or violent, are obviously not likely prospects for reunification.

Chronically severely mentally ill parents and addicted parents who have not responded to treatment are less likely than other parents to resume care of their children. Yet the majority of families are reunified. Under PL 96-272, the Adoption Assistance and Child Welfare Act, the agency had to show that reasonable efforts have been made to correct the problem situation that brought the children into care. With the Adoption and Safe Families Act, the reasonable efforts requirement is suspended in certain serious situations.

A special project at Casey Family Services applied family preservation-type services that demonstrated "reasonable effort" to family reunification. Evaluation of the project showed that families with multiple and serious problems can be reunified if the agency has the resources to offer intensive services (Fein & Staff, 1993).

The child welfare system of services often acts as a barrier to permanency when social workers are indecisive about goals. Child welfare workers who make effective decisions provide services as soon as possible following a child's entry into care; keep frequent contact with parents; encourage parents to visit their children; and clearly define case objectives to counteract the tendency for "drift" (Gambrill & Stein, 1981). Given the importance of the social worker's evaluation of the mother as a predictor of discharge, and worker's difficulties in assessing maternal adequacy, pessimistic attitudes can act as a barrier to planning children's return to their own families (Shapiro, 1976).

Casework behavior that tends to lead to early discharge from foster care includes higher frequency of worker contact with the parents, which in turn increases parental visits. Both factors together increase the probability of discharge (Fanshel, 1975). A high frequency of caseworker contact increases discharges during the first year of placement, but the impact diminishes after that, suggesting that intensity of effort in a short period may be more productive than a diffuse effort over a long period (Shapiro, 1976). One reasonable interpretation is that intense casework effort circumvents parental bereavement. Normal grief lasts between one and two years following a significant loss and culminates in a "letting go." Intensive casework early in the placement process maintains the parent-child bond so that neither parent nor child "disconnects" from their attachment after several years of minimal contact and foster care drift.

Parental ambivalence can be a barrier to reunification. In a study of forty cases of unsuccessful family reunification, Hess and Folaron (1991) found that persistent ambivalence about the parental role and family reunification was a characteristic of twenty-nine of the parents, and that in twenty-three cases the parent's ambivalent attitude was found to contribute directly to placement reentry. Ambivalence can be explored only when the worker caseload is low enough to permit the development of a working relationship between worker and parent. Some parents are able to verbalize their mixed feelings. Others have difficulty expressing their concerns to the worker and appear to sabotage the case plan with their behavior:

Mr. and Mrs. W. had been working for the return of their infant daughter from foster care. Mr. W. was released from jail, where he had been held on burglary charges. He found employment, complied with his parole, and attended parenting classes with his wife. She had been in counseling and had visited her daughter faithfully. Neither parent had ever admitted to breaking the baby's arm, and both still claimed that the abuse must have been a result of their three-year-old son's yanking the baby's arm through the bars of the crib. The worker noticed a pattern developing. Whenever she spoke with the parents about the possibility of the baby returning to them, they missed the next visit at the foster home. When the judge told them, at a review hearing, that they could have their child returned soon, the Ws appeared glad. However, the following day Mr. W. violated his parole and was incarcerated, and Mrs. W. left town. The worker surmised that the parents were showing through their behavior the ambivalence that they could not express. Much later, Mrs. W. told the foster parents, who had adopted the infant, that she had been afraid the baby would return to them, and be abused and perhaps killed this time. The agency never ascertained who in the family had been the perpetrator of the original abuse.

When workers engage the parents and open up honest communication about the permanency plan, parental ambivalence can be addressed more effectively. Some parents can be helped to articulate their need or desire to relinquish parental rights. (Jackson & Dunne, 1981). Others can be supported to move toward reunification.

Parent-Child Visiting

In good foster care practice, every visit between parent and child has a plan and a goal. The overall purpose of visits is to move toward the permanency goal of reunification and to maintain the parent-child bond. The immediate goal of a particular visit might be to work on an aspect of parenting such as behavior management; to reassure the child; to celebrate the child's birthday and show him he is important; to demonstrate a skill such as comforting a tremulous, substance-affected child; or to learn to take pleasure and enjoyment in contact with the child. Teamwork with foster parents is especially critical for visits. Trained foster parents can use visits as times to help teach skills to parents, to involve parents in trips to the doctor or school conference to empower the parents in working with resources for the child, and to develop helping relationships, which enhance the parents' self esteem (Ryan et al., 1981).

Visits can occur at the agency when strict supervision is needed; at the foster home if the parent needs to see how and where the child is living; in a relative's home if the kinfolk are involved; in the parent's home to prepare for reunification; or at a neutral site such as a fast food restaurant or park. Foster parents are often instrumental in bringing children to visits and working with the parents to reach the goals for the visit.

Hess and Proch (1988) describe three phases of visiting. In the first phase, the family, foster parents, and worker are building a relationship, with the focus on assessment and goal planning. Because of the risk of parental pressure for children to recant their statements about maltreatment, visits are often closely supervised. In the middle phase, in which the family is working to meet case goals, visit activities are chosen to provide ways to learn and practice new patterns of behavior. Visits typically occur for long periods with diminishing supervision. In the transitioning phase, the case goals have been reached and preparation is made for the child's return. Emphasis is placed on securing services the family will need to maintain

reunification. Visits (usually at home) provide maximum opportunity for parent-child contact, and remaining stress points are evaluated.

The visiting of children in foster care by their parents is a factor that powerfully affects rates of discharge from care. The issue of unvisited children was first established by Maas and Engler (1959) and confirmed by subsequent studies.

Fanshel and Shinn's five-year longitudinal study (1978) revealed that the frequency of contact between the mother and her child in care showed a strong statistically significant relationship to the child's return to the parental home. Parents who visited the child regularly and took full advantage of all opportunities to do so were able to effect the child's discharge in 73 percent of the cases during the first year, while 64 percent of those children who were not visited during the first year were still in foster care five years later (Fanshel, 1975).

Earlier studies showed that in practice, regular parental visiting occurred in considerably less than half of foster care placements (Gruber, 1973). A more recent study shows a higher proportion of parental visiting, perhaps due to greater emphasis on visiting by the child welfare system (Fanshel, 1982).

Studies of parent-child visiting in out-of-home care situations point out beneficial effects for the emotional well-being of the children as well as the detrimental effects of the absence of visiting. Foster children in a study of child behavior and parental visiting who were visited regularly had fewer behavior problems than children who were visited marginally or not at all (Cantos, Gries, & Slis, 1997). Ongoing contact between children and their biological families is fundamental to a sense of self, personal significance, and identity (Colon, 1978).

A number of conditions discourage visiting by parents. In Jenkins and Norman's classic study (1975), one-quarter of mothers reported "no problem" in visiting. The rest gave the following reasons why visiting was difficult: illness of the mother; distance and lack of travel money; inconvenient visiting times set by the agency; visiting made difficult by foster parents; visit emotionally upsetting to the mother; and visit emotionally upsetting to the child. Visits are particularly difficult to arrange when the parent is incarcerated (Beckerman, 1989). White, Albers, and Bitonti (1996) found that social worker–parent contact appears strongly related to the occurrence of parent-child visits during a child's period of out-of-home placement. They also found that not only did minority children have fewer parental visits, but that workers had fewer contacts with parents and made fewer efforts to solve problems. This differential service to minority children and their families is but one example of the child welfare system's inability to effectively address the needs of the minority population.

Fanshel and Shinn (1978) concluded that, with a few exceptions, parental visiting is linked to discharge from foster care, and that this holds across ethnic and religious groups and is persistent over time. They found visiting patterns of parents—whether they visit and how often they visit their children in foster care—to be the strongest correlate of discharge from foster care. Other studies have also affirmed continuing visits by parents as central to family reunification (Weinstein, 1960; Fanshel, 1975; Mech, 1985; Milner 1987; Proch & Howard, 1986).

It is interesting to note that in Festinger's study (1983) of young adults formerly in foster care, these young people felt that they should have been consulted along the way as to what they wanted or needed, particularly about "the atmosphere surrounding visits, about timing and about whom they saw or did not see" (p. 96).

Using a teamwork approach, children and youths can be prepared by foster parents for the visit (Folaron, 1993) and can be involved in the preparations by making a picture, baking cookies, and assembling their mementos to show their parents at the visit. If parents fail to keep an appointment for the visit, trained foster parents can help the child deal with disappointment not by blaming the parents, but by providing reassurance and support to the children.

Social work practice in foster care focuses strongly on getting parents to visits, with a variety of techniques ranging from transporting the parents; arranging for agency paraprofessional transporters; providing bus tokens; bringing the children to the parents; planning the visit with the parents; observing the visit to determine signs of attachment; working with foster parents about their involvement in visits; and

so forth. Parents often are also encouraged to attend the child's medical appointments, school conferences, sports events, and other important aspects of the child's life, often accompanied by the foster parent. A parent describes such a visit as a turning point toward reunification:

> I had no confidence in myself. I was having lots of heavy treatment, but I was still thinking of myself as stupid and sick. I knew that I wanted my kids but I didn't deserve them. The foster parents of my son gave me tickets to take my son to the circus, so I could do something for him. They could have told him that they were taking him and had invited me to go along, but instead they told Joey that I was taking him. It made a big difference, feeling like I could actually do something for him. It was scary with the lions and tigers and all—I had never been to the circus before. But Joey loved it, and he never forgot. Even after he'd been home from care a long time, he'd say "Remember, Mom, how you took me to the circus, when I was in foster care? I knew how much you loved me, then."

Parent-Agency Service Agreement

In the early days of permanency planning, a project in California experimented in using contracts with parents of children in care. Stein, Gambrill, and Wiltse (1974) reported the successful outcomes of the innovation. Treatment included the use of "hard" services such as housing and financial assistance, along with the "soft" services of counseling. The aim of the project was "to introduce an intensive relationship which will help to rebuild the parent's sense of parenthood and sense of authority to make the decision about his or her children." Possible decisions were to return the child from foster care; to terminate parental rights, with adoptive placement following in most instances; and to continue foster care, usually with a long-term foster care agreement or with a guardianship arrangement. Intensive casework services were offered to the biological parents, and contracts with them were used as a tool to encourage parental participation in planning and decision making, and as a means to prevent or interrupt foster care drift.

Contracts were written documents that specified particular agreements between the project director, the social worker, and the client. They provided a focus for services by explicating long-range goals for children, problems that required remedies, the treatment method to be used, alternative consequences of parental participation, and time limits for accomplishing goals.

The social workers assumed an active role, making clear the range of alternatives for the child's future as well as the consequences if parents did not participate. They also took a firm stand that parents should visit, and they often provided transportation.

Parents almost uniformly were positive about the use of a contract, often indicating that it was the first clear direction they had received as to what must be done in order to move toward the return of their children. Court judges also reacted positively to the contracts because of the specificity and the minimum conditions set forth for the return of the child. At the end of two years, the results were significantly different between the 148 experimental and the 148 control children, with 41 percent of the cases in the experimental group and 25 percent of those in the control group closed after restoration of children to their parents, or after completed adoption or guardianship plans (Stein & Gambrill, 1977).

This successful project still influences contemporary practice. Use of contracts, or agency-parent service agreements as they are sometimes called, creates a sharply focused direction for practice. The contract typically relates to the allegations found on the petition leading to the court assuming jurisdiction over the child. If the court found that the parental home was filthy and unsafe, and that the parents had neglected to feed or provide medical care to the child, then those conditions would become key components of the contract. The contract spells out the permanency planning alternatives; the goal—usually return to the parents—and what must be done to correct the elements of neglect found in the court petition. For example, the contract might specify that the agency would provide homemaker services to assist the parent in cleaning up the filthy home; that the agency would refer the parent to nutrition classes and a nutrition aide; and that the parent would be encouraged to attend medical visits for the child. The parents' responsibilities might include cleaning the home so that it would pass inspection by the health department; at-

tending nutrition classes and demonstrating adequate food preparation skills; demonstrating an understanding of the child's medical needs; and participating in ongoing medical care. As is often the case in contemporary practice, a frequent component of contracts is that the agency provide referral for substance abuse treatment and twelve-step groups, and that the parent use treatment, attend a self-help group, and provide clean drug screens on a weekly basis. It is important to spell out in the contract what is an acceptable level of performance by the parent. Attending a parenting class does not necessarily mean that a parent will improve discipline techniques. The contract should show that using counseling and attending parenting classes are related to the goal of using effective discipline without severe corporal punishment.

Family-Centered Casework Practice: A Case Study

Although frequency and intensity of service are important, contact alone is rarely enough; goal-directed and coordinated services to the biological parents are essential (Stein, 1976). Various tasks are performed by caseworkers with families of foster children. As a catalyst the worker uses community resources, stimulates new ones, and identifies natural networks useful to families (Maluccio & Sinanoglu, 1981). Foster care social workers act as initiators of parent-child contact and other services, and as brokers for the family to reduce isolation and stressors. The worker becomes a mediator "between the parent-child relationship and the external forces that affect the relationship. In the process, duration of foster care is directly affected" (Milner, 1987, p. 121). The social worker is also a *teacher* and *model* of child management skills during parent-child visits (Blumenthal & Weinberg, 1983), although this function is often assumed by trained foster parents (Ryan, McFadden, & Warren, 1981).

Lack of service to biological parents may occur because of limited agency resources and high caseloads, leading to patterns of reacting to crisis, rather than planful intervention. In agency after agency the pattern is often one of handling emergencies rather than providing systematic services and support to children and their parents. Multiple placements of children in the foster care system and the lack of continuity and security that results are exacerbated by the turnover of caseworkers. In a national study of child welfare service, Shyne (1980) reported:

> The number of caseworkers to whom the child had been assigned rose steadily with the length of time in foster care. For example, 48 percent of those in care for two years or longer had had at least four caseworkers, compared with 9 percent of children who had been in foster care for less than two years. The instability of placements and the changing of worker's assignments underscore the importance of concentrated efforts to effect the early return of children to their parents or relatives or the incorporation of the children in a new family by adoption. (p. 80)

Despite these problems, or perhaps in response to them, it appears that many states and the federal government have shifted emphasis to support and preventive services. "There has been a conscious departure from efforts that centered on removing mistreated or neglected children from their natural homes" (Harris, 1988, p. 483) At the same time, while there is little doubt that more services to families can prevent or shorten many placements, it is evident more services are needed, with training of workers to use the additional services.

Intensive family-based services, similar to front-end family preservation services, are being used increasingly to bring about family reunification from care. Typically, the family-based worker is assigned when the reunification process has reached the final transitional phase. The family based services worker works intensively with the family as the children are reintroduced back into the family, preparing the family for child management, restructuring of family life and routines, and working with all aspects of reconnection. This specialized worker also is involved in developing a safety net of community services to support the reunified family. Training has been developed to help the reunification worker develop teamwork with foster parents. An example of the reunification process follows:

> Selena Q. had completed treatment for her addiction, attended a twelve-step support group, and was making steady progress in her recovery. Raymond, her es-

tranged husband, was still using heavily and on the streets. Selena had returned to her earlier employment and located housing. She was responding to clear expectations spelled out in the parent-agency service agreement (contract). At first she had felt angry with the foster care worker for telling her what she had to do to get the children back, but now she appreciated the help she had gotten in working toward her goals. She felt shaky and anxious about maintaining sobriety, but had an NA sponsor and a relapse prevention plan. She knew that she could not reconcile with Raymond unless he stopped using and was in recovery. She wanted the children back but felt that she could not cope with all of them at once.

Her two middle children, girls aged 5 and 7, had been placed with her aunt in a kinship foster care situation, but her son, aged 14, was in group care for treatment, as he had been a sexual abuse perpetrator to his 5-year-old sister. The baby was in a specialized foster home because he had special medical needs. Selena had maintained contact with all four children through visits, although she had spent the most time with the two children placed with her aunt.

The worker and the mother decided together it would be wise to phase the return of the children. First, Selena stayed on the weekends with her aunt to resume care of her two middle children. Then the children returned to her new home, with the aunt providing day care while Selena worked. The family reunification worker was available to her around the clock, seven days a week, and met with her every evening to help her reconnect with the two girls who had been returned. The girls showed some anger and defiance, telling their mother that they only had to listen to Aunt Fay, and they didn't have to listen to her. The worker showed Selena how to set limits and have family meetings.

They then had a meeting with the reunification team, which included the parent, her aunt, the foster care worker, the foster parent, the group care worker, and her son's therapist. They developed a plan in which the baby would be returned next, and her son would start to visit in the home, with close supervision by the mother and the family reunification worker.

Selena and her aunt spent time with the foster parent learning the special techniques involved in baby Jeffrey's care. She and the mother went together to the doctor, the rehab clinic, and the public health department. The plan was that Jeffrey would visit first for long weekends, with the foster parent "on call" for problems. When the baby returned home, Selena reduced her hours of work and used public assistance as her main source of income. She continued to work part time because as she felt it was an important part of her recovery process to also have time away from the children and to keep the feeling of satisfaction she got from her job. The first week that Jeffrey was at home, she called in her family reunification worker frequently, as she was feeling very stressed and found herself having cravings for her drugs. The worker and Selena's sponsor helped her get past the cravings, and the foster parent came in to provide respite so that Selena could get to more meetings of her twelve-step group. The sponsor, the reunification worker, and Selena developed a specific relapse prevention plan.

The worker examined the network of support for the family: Aunt Fay who was providing child care; the foster parent, who supported Selena with little Jeffrey; Selena's sponsor and her twelve-step group. The job helped Selena's self-esteem, and a public health nurse was monitoring Jeffrey's development. The family had stabilized with three children.

A serious concern was whether the return of Tyrone from group care would upset the precarious homeostasis and make Selena once again vulnerable to relapse. Selena was fearful that Tyrone might reoffend with the girls. She was also having flashbacks to her own sexual abuse as a child.

The family reunification worker helped Selena decide to get help for her survivor issues. She took Selena to a survivor's group and gave her some survivor workbooks. She helped Selena educate the girls about good touches and bad touches, the importance of "telling" and saying no. They decided that since Tyrone had completed the treatment program, it might be a good idea to bring him home while the family reunification worker was still involved.

The entire family, including Aunt Fay and the worker, went to a final treatment session at Tyrone's group facility. At this session, Tyrone got down on his knees in front of Jessica and apologized for his actions. He cried when he apologized to his mother for hurting one of the children. Aunt Fay promised to be the outside person who would monitor Tyrone's behavior to Jessica and Roshelle. Selena was helped to set very firm limits for Tyrone. Tyrone was to be enrolled in a new school, and assigned an adult male mentor.

The first week Tyrone was back, Selena again went into crisis because Raymond, her estranged husband, showed up high, wanting money and demanding to take Tyrone with him for "some fun." The family reunification worker stepped in to support Selena in making Raymond leave and handling Tyrone's reactions to his father's visit.

Eight weeks after the first two children were returned home, the family was together, with the exception of Raymond, the father, who had not dealt with his addiction. Each of the older children had a support system, including school, Al-A-Tot or Al-A-Teen, neighborhood activities at a nearby church, and Tyrone's mentor. Their aunt was involved in their lives, and she was introducing them to other relatives who had distanced themselves earlier when Selena had been using.

Selena had good days and bad days. There were times when her cravings were hard to take. She used her twelve-step support group and her sponsor to deal with the urge to relapse. She attended the sexual abuse survivors group from time to time as painful feelings emerged. The family reunification worker got Selena on a waiting list for sexual abuse counseling at a local agency. Selena began to realize that part of her substance use had been to cover childhood pain. She also consulted an attorney about obtaining a divorce from Raymond. She was clear that she did not want to risk losing the children again. The family reunification worker ended her intensive services, although the family remained under supervision by the court and the foster care worker for another six months.

Case Commentary. This case illustrates many of the strong points of contemporary foster care practice. The focus was family centered and involved the kinship network in planning and helping. Teamwork was essential, with active involvement by the foster parent, the group care facility, and community resources in implementation of the plan. The task of parenting was shared by the kinship caregiver, the parent, and the foster parent. All cooperated in working toward the goal of reunifying the family. The foster care worker and the family reunification worker worked from a family empowerment focus, despite the strong element of social control underlying the child protection intervention. Decision-making was by consensus among multiple stakeholders, including the mother, her aunt, the group treatment agency, and the workers. One limitation of the resolution of the case was that neither worker was able to reach Raymond, the children's father. They did, however, support and empower Selena in creating boundaries that would prevent his addiction from intruding into the reformed family in recovery. Special attention was paid to the realities of the recovery process, including development of a relapse prevention plan. The phased return of the children took into consideration the unique needs of the children and the mother's vulnerability to relapse. Although in some states there might be prohibitions against allowing Tyrone back into the home (certain statutes prohibit funding family reunification if there is a perpetrator in the home), he had completed a treatment program, and there was a plan for close supervision and monitoring of the sibling group.

Preparing the Child for Family Reunification

When children have been placed away from their families, they have gaps in their knowledge. They may be confused as to why they are in placement, believing it was because they were "bad" or because they wet the bed, and not realizing it was due to parental incapacity. This may be part of a set of defenses that keeps them from acknowledging the severity of parental maltreatment. It is, after all, important to children to believe they are loved and to long to maintain attachments. The social worker, a therapist, or a treatment foster parent needs to help children assimilate reasons they are in care and the reasons for the plan to return. Folaron (1993) indicates that to ensure the safety of children after return they must be helped to effectively communicate needs, feelings, and problems, and to understand and practice the safety plan that will be in effect. For example, in the Selena Q. case, the plan was that the children would tell Aunt Fay if their brother tried again to molest them, if their mother showed signs of relapse, or if there were other troubles that bothered them.

Figure 9.2 illustrates some differences between an earlier case management model in foster care and the contemporary family continuity focused approach

FIGURE 9.2 Evolution from Permanency Planning to Family Continuity

ASPECTS	PERMANENCY PLANNING	FAMILY CONTINUITY
Definition of family	Nuclear	Extended, augmented
Criterion for permanence	Secure legal status	Perception of belonging
Starting point	Entry into foster care	First contact with system
Decision-making	Legal focus, agency and court	Family empowerment focus: Involving parents and extended families in planning continuity of past with future
Time orientation	Permanence in future	Continuity of past with future
Practice with children	Help adjust to separation and prepare for move to adoptive or biological home	Maintain connections
Practice with families	Case management: Assessment, contracting, documenting reasonable efforts	Family centered, comprehensive services, shared parenting models, empowerment, collaboration between services and cooperation among families—biological, kin, foster, adoptive consensus-building among multiple stakeholders
Scope	Foster care and adoption	All family and child services

Source: E. J. McFadden & S. W. Downs (1995, April). Family continuity: The new paradigm in permanence planning. *Community Alternatives.*

to practice, which integrates principles of family preservation into the process of permanency planning.

Concerns Related to Family Reunification

Unfortunately, not all states and agencies have the necessary resources to provide intensive family reunification services. The Selena Q. case may represent the favorable exception, rather than the rule. Studies are beginning to reveal that children placed because of parental abuse of alcohol and other drugs, as compared with children placed for other reasons, stay in out-of-home placements longer, move from one placement to another more frequently, are less likely to return to their biological parents, and have lower rates of adoption; this is particularly true for minority children (Besharov, 1990; National Black Child Development Institute, 1989; Walker, Zangrillo, & Smith, 1991).

An additional concern related to family reunification is the problem of reentry of children into care. While reentries could be regarded as failures of family reunification, they may also be viewed as part of a safety net for children after return home. In the 1970s and 1980s reentry rates ranged from 3 percent to 33 percent (Fanshel & Shinn, 1978; Block & Leibowitz, 1983; Fein, Maluccio, Hamilton, & Ward, 1983; Jones, 1985). Part of the range in the rates is that some studies included children leaving residential treatment or children returning from disrupted adoption, as well as children returning from family reunification. A report by the U.S. General Accounting Office in 1991 showed data from three sources, indicating that from 3 to 27 percent of children return to care after discharge to their families following a first placement. The report showed additionally that stays in care of less than a year were significantly associated with increased reentry levels (U.S. General Accounting Office, 1991).

Festinger (1994) studied 254 children in New York state, of whom 210 were returned to their parents and 44 went to their relatives. Of those who returned to their parents, 27 children (12.9 percent) reentered care. Of those returned to relatives, only 4 (9.1 percent) reentered care, mainly because the relatives felt unable to handle and abide the children's behaviors. Of those children returning to care from their parents' homes, the

parental problems linked to reentry included limited parenting skills and limited social support networks. Festinger cautions, "Policies that mandate speedy discharge (a needed response to past problems in foster care) run the risk of creating new problems—producing the child welfare equivalent, albeit on a smaller scale, of what occurred in the mental health field, when hospitals were emptied without adequate supports in place. It is likely that because of pressures to discharge, we have generated a revolving door for some, with the attendant dislocation that this entails" (Festinger, 1994, p. 89).

Case Review

In the past, children remained in foster care for extended periods of time for no reason other than that no one in the agency reviewed the case. Decision points in many cases simply passed by without any action being taken. If, for example, a caseload was uncovered after a worker left the agency, it would sit unattended until a new worker was assigned. It might take the new worker months to become acquainted with the particulars of the cases and even longer to be able to formulate plans for permanency.

Systematic and regular case review procedures are essential to clarifying mutual expectations of parents and caseworkers in moving toward the permanence goal for the child. The purpose of subsequent review is to determine whether a specific child should be returned to parents, continue in foster care, or be freed for adoption, and if adoption is chosen to identify an adoptive home and carry out the placement process. All successful early permanency planning projects, according to one researcher, contained as one element, a review system (Jones, 1978).

All states now have review systems, typically judicial review, with some having combinations of judicial review, administrative review, or citizen's review boards. Court review is the most authoritative. It can be a social worker's report, a hearing, or a full evidentiary trial (Dodson, 1983).

Citizen review boards are operated by three to five citizen volunteers, who receive specialized training and often operate under state auspices related to courts. Reviewers examine the following issues:

Is case information adequate?

Is decision-making timely?

Are court hearings complete and detailed?

Do court hearings address reasonable effort?

What are the barriers to timely decision making?
(National Association of Foster Care Reviewers, 1994)

Citizen reviews typically review only a sampling of cases; however, their data collection process can offer a window on the system to monitor permanency services for children in care. Within eighteen months after the establishment of the South Carolina citizen review boards, the number of children in foster care there was reduced from 4,000 to about 3,300, and adoptions increased by 44 percent (Chappell, 1975). A strength of the citizen review approach is that it demonstrates community commitment to foster children.

There is some controversy regarding external review. Jordan (1994) argues that external review systems composed of citizen reviewers have advantages over systems that use judges or attorneys for review. Benefits include protection against conflict of interest, independence from both the courts and the child welfare system, the input of fresh ideas, and representation of community values. Franklin (1994), in a rejoinder to Dr. Jordan, asserts that the foster care system is dysfunctional and needs to be changed, but that citizen review boards can be co-opted, that they can be denied substantive information, and that the system may see external reviewers as a policing agent.

The National Association of Foster Care Reviewers has completed guidelines for foster care review. *Safe Passage to Permanency* (1998) includes a new framework for using review to analyze the effectiveness of systems as a first step toward improving outcomes of safety and permanency for children.

Agency or administrative reviews by the agency that holds custody are often done even when judicial review takes place. Agency reviews may involve supervisory and administrative staff of the public and private child welfare agencies. Hardin reports on a small urban court in Michigan where an effective flow of information between DSS and the court on foster care cases has resulted in reduced average stays in out-of-home care. Average lengths of stay in the county for the 372 children in care are low: 12.3 months for children reunited with their families and 14.5 months for children freed for adoption (Hardin, Rubin, & Baker, 1995).

Within each method there are variations from state to state. Periodic review every six months is a minimum frequency required by the Adoption Assistance and Child Welfare Act of 1980. Thoennes (1996) studied and compared judicial, administrative, and citizen foster care review programs. No single review model is decidedly superior in producing positive care outcomes, and there were few overall differences in case outcomes by type of review. In discussing the strengths and weakness of the three types of review, Thoennes concluded that citizen and administrative boards are advisable in systems that lack judicial resources to ensure regular, thoughtful review hearings (Thoennes, 1996).

Options for Permanence

There are many ways in which a permanent home can be obtained for a child in care. Parents can voluntarily relinquish parental rights (Mylniec, 1983) to make their child free for adoption by a foster parent, a relative, or a new family. The use of guardianship for long-term kinship care is increasingly being considered as a form of permanence, because the child's sense of connection with relatives and the commitment of a family bond are ongoing (Child Welfare League of America, 1994). However, there are many forms of guardianships (Hardin, 1983), and some do not offer the requisite protection for the child and new permanent family caregivers. Proponents of long-term foster care argue that when a child or youth has strong connections to the original family, adoption will not serve the young person's interests, and that being maintained in a foster home where emotional ties have been formed, and in which foster parents will work to maintain connection to the original family, is in the best interest of the child or youth. Bryant (1994) asserts:

We tend to place greater emphasis on achieving the legal outcomes of permanency planning than on building the relationships that support and sustain them. We need to recognize, or allow ourselves to recognize out loud, what we should have known all along—that true permanence is more a function of relation than location. Real permanency cannot be legislated. When we behave as if it can be, we are putting carts before horses and marriage before courtship. . . . When we focus on relationship first . . . we are more likely to recognize and support the value of other types of relationships, such as those in permanent foster care, or in situations where children divide time between birth and foster homes. (pp. 2–3)

The preferred permanence option, once return to the original family has been ruled out, is adoption. Adoption offers a secure, legal arrangement that is the legal equivalent of biological parenthood. Adoptions can be arranged that promote the concept of family continuity, allowing the child or young person to maintain physical or emotional contact with biological parents and the kinship network. This openness may occur when children are adopted by foster parents who have supported the child's family relationships throughout the out-of-home placement process.

Termination of Parental Rights: One Avenue to Permanency

There are some families who will not respond to services provided, or whose difficulties are so pervasive that children should probably not be returned to them. Under the mandates of the Adoption Assistance and Child Welfare Act of 1980, the Adoption and Safe Families Act of 1997, and statutes in each of the states, children in foster care are not allowed to languish in an impermanent and temporary setting if family reunification does not occur. There are checks and balances through judicial review in the courts, plus additional citizen or administrative review processes. Although the states differ in implementation of new legislation, generally speaking, after a child has been in care one—or at the most two—years without family reunification being accomplished, a permanency hearing is held. If the goal at this hearing becomes adoption, it may take several years before the termination of parental rights (TPR) can be completed. In Kentucky, for example, before a special TPR project, the total average time that

children waited from the point when the goal became adoption until the TPR process was complete was two years and two months. After the project, the time had been shortened to just under one year and two months (Farley, 1993). While this may still be too long, the study demonstrates that significant change is possible.

In order for a child to be legally free for adoption, parental rights must be terminated, if they have not been relinquished voluntarily. For many foster care social workers, planning for termination of parental rights is challenging and difficult. Typically, working toward termination of parental rights involves teamwork with attorneys, knowledge of legal procedures, amassing of evidence, contacting witnesses, and handling one's own ambivalence about the procedure. Workers who have a strong commitment to family reunification may have feelings of failure and sadness that they have not been able to help parents fulfill the terms of the parent agency agreement (contract) for permanency planning. They are also sensitive to the pain of both parents and children in having the most elemental tie severed by legal mechanisms:

A termination of parental rights is the ultimate legal infringement on the family. The severance is absolute and permanent; it is as if the parent-child relationship never existed. There are few state-imposed deprivations more unyielding and personal than the permanent and irrevocable loss of one's children. Termination of parental rights is more severe than a criminal sanction. Only the death penalty is a more severe intrusion into personal liberty. (Hewett, 1983)

Regardless of the worker's commitment to permanency for children and hopes for securing the child's future in an adoptive home, the worker is confronted with the dynamics of loss implicit in this legal step. Additionally, some workers dread the adversarial court proceedings when they must testify against parents they worked with and regarded as clients.

In preparation for termination of parental rights, workers review case documentation of all service contacts provided by the agency, in order to demonstrate that reasonable efforts have been made to reunify the family. The records of visits, including documentation kept by foster parents, are reviewed to determine whether the parents failed to show continuing interest in the child. Since termination of parental rights is a legal process, not a casework decision, it is necessary to meet with an attorney to develop the allegations that will be drafted for the termination petition to be filed with the court. There are a number of issues, depending on individual state statute, that may be alleged as grounds for termination of parental rights, including abandonment, nonsupport, repeated or severe abuse, chronic drug abuse, imprisonment, mental illness or retardation, failure of the parent to improve, and harm to the child (Mylniec, 1983). The worker and lawyer decide which allegations can be supported with evidence, and the attorney typically draws up the petition.

Foster care workers need to be familiar with state statutes so they know the acceptable reasons for termination. They should also be aware of the *Santosky v. Kramer* decision by the Supreme Court, which requires a standard of proof of *clear and convincing* evidence needed in termination of parental rights cases (Brieland & Lemmon, 1985). It is the foster care worker's responsibility to document all aspects of the case meticulously, so that evidence can be presented in the TPR hearing (Stein, 1991). Some agencies have specialized workers who handle preparation of TPR materials. In some agencies the TPR is handled in foster care, and in other agencies in the adoption unit as part of adoption planning.

Reaching Timely Permanency Decisions

There are a number of ways to shorten the length of time children stay in out-of-home care, as is now mandated in the Adoption and Safe Families Act of 1997. Obviously, the use of intensive family preservation services to prevent placement, or strengthen family reunification, is paramount. In several states—Michigan, Kentucky, New York, Oregon, Washington, and Idaho—special collaborative projects brought about changes in the system by changing laws and administrative codes, improving practice, building stronger interagency collaboration, and increasing resources dedicated to helping children and their families. Some of the strategies are as follows:

- Build shorter timelines into state laws.

- Change state laws to allow open adoption; parental visiting after TPR papers have been filed; provide legal representation for the agency from the early stages of each case; and reducing the time required to declare an infant abandoned.
- Change court rules for improvements in court docketing and scheduling; give priority assignment to TPR cases.
- Clarify the reasonable efforts standard in TPR cases. Several experts recommend statutory changes that when the best interest of a child would be served by TPR, the state be allowed to terminate parental rights on a standard of the parents' capacity to perform adequately during the rest of the child's childhood, not on how well the agency or the parents did or did not perform in the past.
- Improve legal and social work practice through training to increase technical skill with special problems such as mental illness and parental addiction; to advocate more aggressively for decision making; to develop expertise in court work for caseworkers; to develop judicial and legal expertise in child welfare; and to address cultural variations.
- Improve interagency collaboration through cross training between disciplines; develop interagency task forces; improve the interagency flow of information; and clarify roles, including those of CASA volunteers, citizen review panels, foster parents, and other advocates and caregivers.
- Enhance service resources by increasing staff to reduce caseload size and funding more timely services to parents. (Cahn & Johnson, 1993)

TYPES OF FOSTER CARE

Formal Kinship Care

Kinship care in its many forms is generally viewed as a form of family preservation:

> *Family strengths often include a kinship network that functions as a support system. The kinship support system may be composed of nuclear family, extended family, blended family, foster family, or adoptive family members or members of tribes or clans. The*

involvement of kin may stabilize family situations, ensure the protection of children, and prevent the need to separate children from their families and place them in the formal child welfare system. (Child Welfare League of America, 1994, p. 1)

The ever-increasing phenomenon of *informal kinship care,* which takes place without formal involvement by the foster care system, is discussed in more detail in Chapter 8. *Formal kinship care* is often used as an alternative to family foster care or group care placement. In formal kinship care, the child is placed by the court in the legal custody of the child welfare agency; financial support for the care of children is often made through foster care payments; kinship homes are expected to meet licensing or approval standards for foster parents; and the kinship caregivers are generally expected to comply with foster parenting roles, such as participating in training and cooperating with the agency in implementing a case plan.

The Adoption Assistance and Child Welfare Act of 1980 (PL 96-272), which continues to drive child welfare practice today, did not specifically mention relative placement or kinship care. However, a phrase in the act, "least restrictive environment," has been interpreted by some practitioners as a preference for placement with relatives (Child Welfare League of America, 1994). The use of kinship care as a formal child welfare option has been affected by several legal actions.

In L. J. v. Massinga, a class action suit brought against Maryland by the Baltimore Legal Aid and the Children's Defense Fund, the primary focus was on the failure of the system to protect foster children from neglect and abuse while in the system. A consent decree, approved in 1988, focused on systemic reform in a number of issues. It established the principle that children in kinship care should have access to specialized services formerly only provided to children in licensed foster homes. In Miller v. Yoakim, a case originally filed in federal district court in Illinois, and later appealed to the U.S. Supreme Court, the principle was established that states cannot discriminate against kinship caregivers under the federal foster care program. In essence, foster care payments should be provided to kinship caregivers when the following conditions are met: (1) the child is eligible for federal Title IV-E assistance by being eligible for TANF; (2) there is a judicial determination of abuse and neglect; (3) the kinship home meets state licensing requirements; and (4) the child is under the custody of the agency.

Many unresolved policy issues concerning kinship care may affect case planning. For example, some kinship caregivers do not wish to adopt their young relatives, for a variety of reasons (Thornton, 1991). Often the caregiver is a grandparent who does not wish to relinquish her current role and status as grandmother and become the legal mother. Many grandparents are reluctant to have parental rights terminated so that they can adopt. It feels unnatural, contrary to cultural expectations, and it may mean a final relinquishment of hope that their adult child will recover from the problems that led to the placement of the children. For these caregivers, long-term foster care or guardianship might be a more workable permanency solution. One grandmother stated, "After all, he knows I'm his granny, I always was and I always will be. I'll always love him and I'll always take care of him. He knows we're permanent. We don't need no adoption to feel permanent."

The problem is that under current federal law, the child must have a "permanent" home—that is, must return to his or her biological parents—or an adoptive home as preferred outcomes of a permanency plan. If the grandparent is given guardianship and the case moves out of the system, the caregiver will lose the higher foster care rate. On the other hand, if the grandparents adopt the child, they will probably be eligible for an adoption subsidy. Proponents of kinship care suggest that subsidized guardianships may promote a new kind of permanency in formal kinship care (Child Welfare League of America, 1994). Others advocate for a new form of adoption—kinship adoption (Takas, 1993; Hegar & Scannapieco, 1999).

Assessment of Kinship Homes. Although formal kinship care may be a very appropriate placement option, some child welfare staff are reluctant to use it. Worker concerns about kinship care are often expressed in the phrase "the apple doesn't fall far from the tree," indicating that the problems of the child's parents are related to their family of origin. A competent assessment of the kinship family will address safety and protection issues. The Child Welfare League Kinship Care Policy and Practice Committee recommends consideration of the following factors in assessment:

- the nature and quality of the relationship between the child and the relative
- the ability and desire of the kinship parent to protect the child from further abuse and maltreatment
- the safety of the kinship home and the ability of kin to provide a nurturing environment for the child
- the willingness of the kinship family to accept the child into the home
- the ability of the kinship parent to meet the developmental needs of the child
- the nature and quality of the relationship between the birth parent and the relative, including the birth parent's preference about placement of the child with kin
- any family dynamics in the kinship home related to the abuse or neglect of the child
- the presence of alcohol or other drug involvement in the kinship home. (CWLA, 1994, pp. 44–45)

In assessing such homes, foster care workers must be aware of their own biases. Kinship caregivers are typically grandparents of the children (Thornton, 1991; Dubowitz, 1990), although children are also given care by aunts, older siblings, and other relatives. While many grandparents or even great-grandparents are neither aged nor infirm, workers may feel that a younger home might be better. Kinship homes are predominantly people of color (Dubowitz, 1990; Thornton, 1991; Berrick, Barth, & Needell, 1993), who may be suspicious of "the system," requiring cultural competence on the part of the social worker in engagement and developing trust. Kinship homes are often less educated than unrelated foster homes, and compared to foster homes they tend to have limited incomes (Berrick, Barth, & Needell, 1993). Workers therefore may feel less comfortable working with kinship care or be biased toward established foster parents who are known to the agency, have more financial resources, and are better educated.

In making determinations about the suitability of a relative as a placement option, the worker must be careful to avoid bias against the potential kinship caregiver, and examine the paramount factors of the child's emotional connection and familiarity with the caregiver

and the home. Berrick, Barth, & Needell (1993) found that children in kinship care who had comparable health and educational status with children in foster homes were doing somewhat better in school, had greater placement stability, and were perceived as less problematic by their caregivers. With a few exceptions—as in the case of transracially adopted children who return to care—children placed with relatives have an appropriate match in race, culture, and ethnicity.

A genuine concern in placing children with relatives, particularly older relatives, is whether kinship caregivers have sufficient resources to support them in their efforts with the children. Use of an eco-map can help workers determine what supports are available in the environment and what supports are needed to meet the developmental needs of the children. Meeting with the entire kinship network often provides evidence that while the caregiver's resources are limited, there are others close by who will provide respite care, transportation, help with the child's homework, or other important forms of support. The following case example illustrates many assessment issues discussed above.

> Mrs. G. approached the child welfare agency in great distress. Her four grandchildren had been placed in three different foster homes due to the neglect related to their mother's alcoholism. The baby showed signs of fetal alcohol effect (FAE) and all the children had been dirty, bruised, and underfed when child protective services had investigated. Mrs. G., a quiet, 50-year-old Native American woman, asked to have the children placed with her. The placing worker had not known that a grandmother existed. The new foster care worker wondered how a 50-year-old woman could care for four children, and what Mrs. G. had done to her daughter to contribute to the alcoholism. Thus the worker was opposed to the thought of Mrs. G. assuming care for the children. She did, however, agree to visit the G. home to explore a placement. When she arrived at the home, she found ten people there waiting to see her. Patiently they explained that they were all relatives and that they could all be involved in caring for the children. They reminded the worker that the children should come under the jurisdiction of tribal courts under the Indian Child Welfare Act and be placed with the grandmother in the most culturally appropriate setting. When the worker objected that the grandmother might not have the appropriate training to care for an

infant with FAE, she was assured that the local health service would assist and that each person in the room would help with the nurture of all the children.

The worker needed cultural competence training to understand how Native American families collectively take responsibility for children, and to become aware of the unique role of the grandmother in the culture. As she continued to explore the situation of Mrs. G., she began to identify many strengths and resources for the children that could not be duplicated in their current foster care situation. The Indian Child Welfare worker contacted her and helped her to see the positive aspects of returning the children to their family. As she worked with Mrs. G. to make the placement, the worker realized that the grandmother was strong and healthy and that age should not be a factor. She felt quite comfortable in placing the children with the extended family, because she observed the reciprocal attachment and emotional bonding between the children and their relatives.

Advantages and Disadvantages of Kinship Care.
With kinship care, as with all other placement options, assessments must examine, and decisions must reflect, the unique situation of each child and family, and generalizations may not apply. However, when a kinship home can provide safety for children, there are some advantages other than the critical one of maintaining the child's emotional ties. The child is with people who share a common history and can provide valuable information and help with identity in the context of the family. The child is perceived as one of their own, not an outsider coming into the family circle. Kinship caregivers have more positive perceptions about the children placed with them than do nonrelated family foster caregivers (Gebel, 1996). If the case plan supports it, the child can have easier access to parents to support reunification. With shared parenting a given, transitions are less traumatic. Children placed in kinship care are often better able to address unresolved family issues and traumas (Crumbley & Little, 1997).

The disadvantages in a kinship situation might be that a parent could have too easy access to a child or the caregivers may have difficulties establishing boundaries with the parent. A real concern is that the child might be caught up in existing family dynamics, such as mother-daughter conflict between a grandmother caretaker and the child's parent, or sibling rivalry between a father and his sister, the caregiver aunt. Unless adequate supports are put in place to assist the caregivers, they may feel burdened but unable to complain or ask for help. Several studies indicate that children in kinship care and kinship caregivers lack services and supports (Dubowitz, 1990; Berrick, Barth, & Needell, 1993; Task Force on Permanency Planning, 1990).

The question of safety in kinship homes is critical. While relatives may appear stable, they may also have some denial about the risk the parents represent to the child, or there may be undetected substance abuse or maltreatment patterns in the family system. A recent study of maltreatment in foster care reports that kinship homes are at less risk for maltreatment than nonrelated foster homes (Zuravin & DePanfilis, 1993). To date there have been no other studies comparing the incidence of maltreatment by kinship caregivers with maltreatment in foster homes or group care. Studies do indicate that there is less monitoring of kinship homes than of unrelated foster homes (Berrick, Barth, & Needell 1993; U.S. Department of Health and Human Services, Inspector General, 1992).

In summary, the widespread use of kinship care is fairly new. It is used extensively in New York, Illinois, California, and Maryland (CWLA, 1994). A survey by the Office of the Inspector General, U.S. Department of Health and Human Services, found that state policies vary widely, with twenty-nine states requiring preference for placement with relatives, twenty states routinely or occasionally using relative placements but not mandating a preference, and two states discouraging but not prohibiting placement with kin (1992). There is a growing agreement that when children cannot be reunited with their parents, efforts should be made whenever possible to keep them with their kin (Takas, 1993).

There is currently limited research on the outcomes or characteristics of kinship care. Recommendations on kinship care practice and policy from the Child Welfare League of America (1994) establish a research agenda to fill knowledge gaps. Areas for study regarding kinship care should include but not be limited to demographic information; service needs of children; characteristics of the parents; reasons for placement; reasons for the selection of kinship care; information on kinship parents; outcomes for children in kinship care in terms of their physical, emotional, and developmental well-being; and comparisons of outcomes between informal and formal kinship care, and between kinship care and other forms of out-of-home care. In discussing current research findings, Berrick, Barth, & Needell (1994) summarize:

> A careful comparative assessment of the well-being of children placed in kinship care as compared to other alternatives would be informative, but it is impossible as long as kinship foster parents receive fewer services and less financial support than other providers. Kinship foster parents in this sample suggested that their relationship to the child was warm and close; their expectations that the child would experience a bright and promising future attest to the potential strength of the family in raising children. Kinship foster parents maintain close ties to birth parents and indicate that they consider the child to be family. They love the children they take into their homes. A family's love is certainly not enough, but is there a better place to start? (p. 83)

Shared Family Care

The newest form of out-of-home care is still at the stage of innovation and experimentation. Kufeldt and Allison (1990) state that "the principle of shared care reinforces the notion of support of the family to maintain the child at home. Where a child does have to be taken into care, this principle establishes the basis for an inclusive orientation to foster care" (p. 10). They describe a form of foster care in which foster families foster the children and their parents. Cornish (1992) writes of a program for homeless families, in which they were provided transitional housing with fostering families. Nelson (1992) describes "whole family foster care," which involves the placement of families and their children with experienced foster families known as "host families":

> The foster provider's role is not to be the prime parent, but to share in the parenting tasks by modeling nur-

> turing and discipline, and enabling the parent to claim a rightful parental role in her or his family. The foster family becomes the basis of support for a stressed family by offering an environment in which healing can take place. (pp. 578–579)

The different kinds of families that have made use of the opportunity to stay with foster families include those with developmental delays, recovering parents, homeless parents, and those with unstable physical or mental health. Nelson (1992) describes a client family of the HSA agency:

> Ms. M., a 29-year-old woman with three preschool children, was a victim of ritualistic abuse. Because of safety concerns for the family, as well as M.'s difficulties with parenting when she dissociates or is depressed, a whole-family foster placement was ideal. M. now lives with "Grandpa and Grandma" far away enough from her abusive family of origin for safety, yet close enough to home to continue with her and the children's intensive therapy, to which the foster family offers transportation. (p. 581)

Barth (1994) points out that many forms of shared care already exist, identifying five types of shared family care living arrangements that "have evolved to keep parent and child together: (1) drug and alcohol treatment programs for adults that also offer treatment for children, (2) drug treatment programs for mothers with children, (3) residential programs expressly developed to offer care to pregnant and parenting mothers, (4) foster homes that offer care of parent and child, and (5) child care homes (residential treatment programs for children) that also offer residence and treatment for their parents" (p. 517).

The drug treatment programs mentioned by Barth are not part of the child welfare system, but the other types do exist. A number of agencies offer foster care services for adolescent parents, including the Lula Belle Stewart program in Detroit, the Children's Home and Aid Society of Chicago, and various programs for pregnant teens considering adoption or young mothers who will eventually decide to release their children (Sisto, 1985).

Model licensing requirements for the care of young mothers and their infants include specialized training in both adolescent treatment and infant care, services to the young fathers as well as the young mothers, health requirements, and promoting parenting responsibilities and parenting education (Murray, 1992).

Gibson and Noble (1991) describe a shared family care program in a residential care agency, in which parents stay in a "cottage" with a staff family. Service plans are developed with each resident parent, with such services offered as counseling and day care while the parent looks for employment. Children in placement with their parents are not taken into protective custody, unless circumstances warrant it. Of the first twenty families served, only two later required the separate placement of their children (Gibson & Noble, 1991).

Program Challenges in Shared Family Care. Federal Title IV-E funds, which provide for the majority of children in foster care, apply to children in out-of-home care but not to their parents, as the child must be separated from parents to be eligible. Such care can be funded through state or local child care funds. Block granting of funds may enable states to use funds more creatively, yet there is little evaluation to demonstrate effectiveness of such an approach.

Another program challenge is to prepare and support foster families so that they might be able to foster the families of the children for whom they care. It is one thing to manage the behavior of children in care—it might require an entirely different set of parenting skills to negotiate with parents living in one's home about what is permissible and what is not allowed. It should be noted that Human Services Associates of Minnesota, a pioneer in shared family care and well known as a treatment foster care agency, has a highly trained and professional group of foster parents. This model, used successfully by HSA, might not be effective if attempted with less well-trained and professional foster care providers.

The International Foster Care Organization (IFCO) views family care as an option for children, adults, and the elderly, while in the United States there are rigid demarcations between children's foster care and adult foster care. In many states, foster homes are not allowed to have unrelated adults in their home if they are fostering children. Special licensing considerations may develop if shared family care emerges as a trend in family foster care.

The few programs in the child welfare system serving parents and children in shared family care may represent the first wave of a emergent trend. Conceptually, the idea of shared family care is buttressed by philosophy and values of family preservation. The Out-of-Home Care Task Force of the Child Welfare League of America (1989) called for the reconceptualization of out-of-home care as part of a comprehensive coordinated system of services that support children and their families and posited the concept that foster homes and group care are in fact *supportive* not *substitute* care. Shared family care seems to be the logical next step and a point of convergence between in-home services to preserve families and out-of-home services to support families.

Family Foster Care

Family foster care (Figure 9.3) is a social system with many component parts and complex interrelationships between those parts. The foster child, the parents, the foster parents, the siblings, the foster siblings, the agency social worker, the court-appointed guardian—each party is an integral element of the whole. As an open system, foster home care is in continuous change, and no part of it can be affected without affecting the whole. The foster home system has a set of external influences, which, added to the physical surroundings, makes up the care environment. These influences include such forces as the placing agency's supervisory and administrative structures, the court, the permanency planning laws, the licensing regulations of the state, the treatment resources within the community, the schools, and community norms about child caring.

Social Work with Foster Parents. The social agency responsible for the child in care has a continuing obligation to monitor the placement situation to see that proper care and treatment are given, and to consult with foster parents in a teamwork approach. Ul-

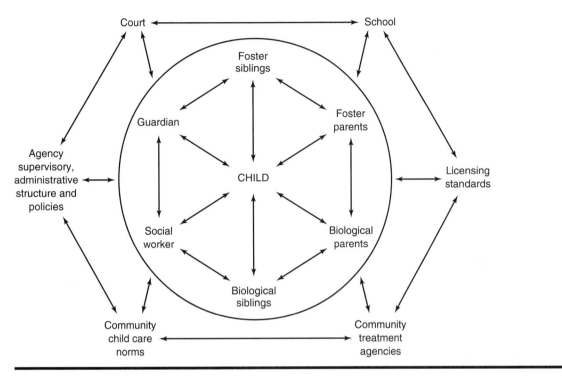

FIGURE 9.3   Foster Care System

timately this collegial relationship is shared by all team members (Fimmen & Mietus, 1988). The social worker has agency-constituted authority, as well as the influence derived from knowledge and competence. Consultation by the social worker about care of the child and work with the family augment the knowledge and skills foster parents have gained through training. Negotiation between social worker and foster parents about specific tasks to be performed, and role clarification, are part of the social work process with foster homes. In working with foster families to support the plan for the child in care, social workers must be aware of the need to communicate with all family members, especially foster fathers who are key decision makers in the family, but who are often ignored by workers who visit the foster home only when the foster father is working.

What kind of problems arise in family foster care to which the foster parent and social worker must give attention? In undertaking the challenges of foster par-

enting, competent adults enter a new situation in which they risk failure. Threats to adequacy cannot be met fully by the social worker's reassurance. Fostering places increased demands to share relationships and possessions on the family, so problems of rivalry and jealousy may come into play. Foster parents' own children may have difficulty coping with the loss implicit in the foster care situation (Twigg, 1997). Foster families are an open family system, sometimes facing acute and chronic crises of accession, dismemberment, and sometimes demoralization as a result of multiple separations and the intrusion of agencies into family boundaries (McFadden, 1996). Foster mothers may see their roles more as "mothering" than providing care in a professional sense (Meidema & Nason-Clark, 1997). Foster parents may find themselves uncertain about actions to control behavior of the children, especially in light of agency discipline policies, which prohibit spanking and other child management techniques, that might be acceptable within a specific community with one's own children, but which would be inappropriate with abused children in a foster home.

A study of 145 new foster parents provides important leads in the ways in which workers can be most helpful (Cautley, 1980):

1. In predicting a successful placement, the extent of preparation by the social worker (length and frequency of contacts) and inclusion of the foster father is critical.
2. The most frequent criticism of the social worker by foster fathers was her or his unavailability when help or information was needed.
3. After six months of placement, foster parents were clearly more satisfied after workers responded to their requests for help.
4. After one year of placement, foster parents reassessed their situation in terms of the rewards for their investment. The social worker needs to help by pointing out progress in the child and by providing encouragement.

Being a foster parent is a demanding and intense experience which carries with it enormous pressure and expectations from the agency and the community. Despite the critical role foster parents play in the child welfare system, they are frequently neglected by agencies and social workers. This neglect contributes significantly to the high turnover rate among foster parents. Payments to foster parents have traditionally been low, especially in view of the demanding service they provide. Most states pay only enough to cover the actual costs of the child's care. Typically the board payment rate for children under 13 years of age is about $12 per day. One compares that to the federal poverty level of $9 per day for a child, or the cost to board a dog in a kennel, which is around $10 per day. This begs the question of Temporary Assistance to Needy Families (TANF) payments of $2 to $3 per day, per child.

In addition to the monthly board payment, agencies provide the additional costs of medical and dental care (although it is hard for foster parents to locate medical care providers who will accept Medicaid), clothing, and some incidental expenses. Most foster parents simply are not compensated for the services

they provide. Prompt reimbursement of costs and fees to foster parents is "an essential part of the agency's plan of care for the child and an investment in both the child and society. The agency should also acknowledge that there are children with special needs of all ages, and establish a cost schedule accordingly" (National Association of Social Workers, 1997, p. 139).

The future of foster care payment may be in providing salaries for those homes providing treatment-oriented foster care. The cost of treatment foster care, ranging usually from $40 to $90 per day, is more than the cost of general foster care but is significantly less than the costs of group care, which runs from $100 to $200 per day, and up.

A second aspect of the neglect of foster parents is their feeling that they do not receive the help they need from agencies or social workers. Rising caseloads and high staff turnover lead to reduced levels of worker contact with foster parents, as does the expectation that workers will commit increased time to the children's parents to facilitate family reunification.

Types of Family Foster Homes

Shelter Homes.   Family foster homes may provide temporary shelter for children during the period of initial assessment and determination by the court of a need for out-of-home care. Although children's agencies must have access to temporary shelter homes, assessment of children's need for placement can be made more reliably when they are still in their own homes, rather than after they are abruptly separated from parents and placed in an unfamiliar temporary situation. Temporary shelter care requires that foster parents have a high degree of skill and training, so that they can assist in the initial assessments through their astute observations. It may be unwise for foster parents whose children are young to provide shelter care. The large numbers of children, about whom little is known, entering and exiting from the home, may present a risk to foster parents' own children. Studies of foster care maltreatment indicate that foster parents' own children have occasionally been abused by older foster children (McFadden & Ryan, 1991). Foster family shelter homes need additional training and support to manage the complexities of their role.

Long-Term Foster Homes.   Long-term foster homes are sought for children who have no chance to return to their parents, who need permanent family living, and who do not wish to be adopted or who have been denied adoption due to a shortage of parents wanting to adopt children of a certain age or with certain developmental problems. Some foster parents may feel unable to assume guardianship for, or to adopt, children in their care but are willing to give a particular child a stable environment and the assurance of lasting relationship. The Casey Family Homes successfully provide well-resourced long-term care to young people with histories of multiple placements and other problems (Walsh & Walsh 1990).

Specialized and Treatment Foster Care

Specialized family foster homes are used by some agencies for children who can profit from family living, although they may have special needs such as emotional problems or developmental disabilities. Some homes specialize in adolescents and take a major role in preparing the youths for independent living. Remuneration is higher in specialized foster homes arrangements than in the usual family foster home arrangement.

Growing use is made of specialized foster homes for infants born with fetal alcohol syndrome or with cocaine addiction. Other medically dependent children in specialized care include youngsters with respirator-assisted breathing. The development of AIDS-specialized family foster homes began in New York. They are now found in at least five states, and many other states are writing policy on the foster care of children affected by HIV or AIDS (Gurdin & Anderson, 1987; Tourse & Gunderson, 1988).

Treatment Foster Care.   Treatment foster care—also called therapeutic foster care—has been established in most states. Hudson, Nutter, & Galaway (1994) identify 321 treatment foster care programs operating in the United States and Canada. The last decade has witnessed a tremendous increase in the use of treatment foster care and the development of new programs.

Treatment foster family care has the following elements:

> 1. *Care is provided within a family setting—a home owned or under the control of the foster care providers.*
> 2. *The program is targeted to children and youth who would otherwise be in more restrictive settings (usually institutions).*
> 3. *Programs have a clearly articulated philosophy with strong community linkages and individual treatment and educational plans.*
> 4. *Foster care providers are selected and trained to provide care to children and youth who have special needs that may result from emotional disturbance, developmental disabilities, behavioral difficulties, special medical needs, or special cultural needs.*
> 5. *Foster providers receive support, consultation, and supervision from human service professionals who carry a limited case load.*
> 6. *Foster care providers receive payment above and beyond the out-of-pocket cost of providing care.*
> 7. *The treatment foster family care program is administered by agencies specializing in treatment foster care or, if part of a host agency, by a unit specifically identified as a treatment foster care program. (Hudson, Nutter, & Galaway, pp. 2–3)*

In-home treatment affords the special needs child a family setting that is less restrictive than group care or institutional treatment. In this type of care, family life offers a normalizing and socialization experience for the child. The foster parents act as the principal source of treatment for the child in care. The intensive service provided in the foster home distinguishes treatment foster care from regular foster care. Treatment foster care is "something of an adaptive hybrid combining elements of residential treatment programming and the foster family environment. . . . This model offers an alternative to both the family foster home and the institution for youngsters who are not appropriately or adequately served in either type of program" (Bryant & Snodgrass, 1990, p. 2). Treatment families have a high degree of training, with an emphasis on behavioral management theory and technique in so that they can act as therapists for the children in their care (Meadowcroft & Grealish, 1990). The treatment family is held accountable for meeting written and measurable treatment goals for the child (Hudson, Nutter, & Galaway, 1994). Outcome studies of the effectiveness of treatment foster with children and adolescents offer conclusions of positive results. Reddy and Pfeiffer (1997) found improvement in children's social skills, with reduced behavior problems and increased psychological adjustment. Increased stability of placement has also been found in treatment foster care (Reddy & Pfeiffer, 1997; Staff & Fein, 1995).

In addition to the sophisticated training they receive, treatment homes are part of a coordinated program of agency staff support, which enables them to maintain a balanced perspective of their stressful work. Fine (1993) describes a developmental network approach to therapeutic foster care, which works with the primary network (foster family, parents, and others), the secondary network (classrooms, clubs, play groups), and tertiary networks (organizations such as the foster care review board, health maintenance organizations, and the child placing agency).

The Foster Family-Based Treatment Association (FFTA) is an agency-led organization of treatment foster care providers established in 1988 with an initial purpose of defining and refining treatment foster care practice. Since the fall of 1989, FFTA member agencies have participated in a series of regional meetings throughout the United States and Canada to develop specific standards for treatment foster care. Program standards that specifically address the nature and requirements of treatment foster care are now available from FFTA. These standards reflect the rigorous approach to quality care that differentiates treatment foster care from general family foster care. Not only shall treatment foster families be subject to licensing criteria of their state or province, they must adhere to a discipline policy that prohibits physical punishment; must be willing to become culturally competent; must complete at least 30 hours of skill-based training before the placement of a child in their home; must also have first aid and CPR training before the placement of a child; must complete 24 hours of in-service training annually; and must submit to a criminal record and child abuse registry check (Foster Family-Based Treatment Association, 1994). These standards prohibit discrimination against foster parents on the basis of sexual orientation.

Predictive Factors in the Selection of Foster Parents

Foster parents are selected by means of a homestudy and licensing/approval process from persons in the community who apply for the purpose of giving care to children. Standards of the agency, as well as general foster home licensing standards, apply, and the decisions made by the agency in matching a particular child with a particular home depend largely on the availability of families most likely to succeed with the types of children for whom the agency must arrange care.

Recruitment that is specifically targeted to finding families for the kinds of children the agency is placing is more productive than is a generalized campaign to interest as many families as possible. Targeted recruitment emphasizes the need for foster families to provide temporary care for children while working as part of a team to serve the children and their families and maximizes agency development of specialized homes (Ryan, 1987).

Agencies recruit new foster parents through newspapers, radio, and television announcements. Media and marketing consultants bring a new approach to foster care recruitment campaigns. Some foster parents are involved as part of recruiting teams that make speeches to community groups. Consultation with community leaders is vital to vigorous recruiting of foster parents from minority racial and ethnic groups, so that children can be placed in families with a background similar to their own.

The agency must be aware of its reputation in the communities it serves; must identify resources needed for the recruitment effort; and must have a commitment to staff training. In serving children of color, the agency must assess the offices and services available to families in targeted communities. It must also determine whether agency policies, procedures, and practices are culturally competent (Lakin, Whitfield, & Anderson, 1997).

Nevertheless, the literature on foster parenting yields evidence of a diminishing supply of foster homes at a time of increased demand (Duva & Raley, 1988; U.S. General Accounting Office, 1989). Various factors have contributed to this imbalance: the "aging out" of existing foster parents; competing occupational opportunities for women; greater financial stresses on families, requiring that both parents work; inadequate compensation for the exacting service required; fear of allegations of maltreatment; and lack of knowledge within the community about foster care programs.

With attrition as high as 60 percent in the first year, retaining foster homes is as important as new recruitment (Ryan, 1987). A good working relationship between foster parent and worker, and foster parent support group attendance are two of the strongest predictors of foster care retention. Among participants in foster parent organizations or other support groups, 82 percent remained active foster parents for two or more years (Anderson, 1988).

There is ongoing debate about the use of gay and lesbian foster parents. Agencies in some areas, particularly on the West Coast, have liaisons to the gay and lesbian community to recruit homes to meet the needs of homeless gay and lesbian adolescents, HIV-affected children, or other children (Ricketts, 1991). Other agencies quietly approve gay or lesbian foster parents without ever officially addressing the controversial issue of sexual orientation. Still other agencies, especially ones with a religious affiliation, are more conservative in their attitudes toward the use of gay and lesbian homes. It is quite probable that in some instances gay or lesbian people who wish to foster children simply conceal their orientation in order to avoid discrimination.

Foster parents often reveal multiple reasons for wanting to give care. The earlier literature on foster care (Stanton 1956; Hutchinson 1943) placed great emphasis on workers' determining the motivation of applicants, but current approaches to foster parent selection focus on prospective foster parents' ability to assess their own strengths and weaknesses (Pasztor & Burgess, 1982). Various motives have been identified: a liking for children, a desire to secure a playmate for their own child, identification with neglected or unhappy children, a wish to provide community service, and so forth. Usually foster parents have multiple reasons for wishing to care for other people's children.

Even though some reasons may appear promising, and some appear suspect, it is more important to focus on parents' skills and strengths in working with children. The social worker involved in foster home development should also realize that preservice training serves an important screening function as prospective foster parents gain adequate information on which to make a sound decision.

Predicting the success of foster families has been a recurring theme in the research literature on foster care. Predictive power continues to be elusive, but a study by Cautley (1980) found eight factors predictive of success:

1. Experience with children as a parent or older sibling.
2. Having grown up with parents who provided good parenting models.
3. Willingness to work with the social worker and the agency (acceptance of visits).
4. Parenting skills in handling specific behavior incidents.
5. Parenting skill in responding to a "difficult" child.
6. Democratic decision making by the couple.
7. Parenting attitudes (degree of differentiation, sensitivity of foster father, and the foster father's extent of child-centeredness).
8. Older mothers up to 45 years old. (Cautley, 1980)

In a study of the maintenance of placements in the Casey Family Homes, Walsh and Walsh (1990) found four factors to be predictive of successful overall functioning of the foster family. These predictors related to the comfort of foster parents in their several roles; to their being motivated to take a foster child by a genuine liking for children; to the foster mother possessing strong emotional coherence; and to the ability of the family to tolerate unassimilated aspects of the child (Walsh & Walsh, 1990).

Fine's study of treatment foster care showed that factors predictive of success as treatment foster parents were "consistent with the personal qualities generally associated with effective psychotherapy, such as outstanding interpersonal skills, a tolerance for different types of children and a positive sense of self" (Fine, 1993, pp. 77–78).

Residential Group Care

The Child Welfare League of America characterizes residential group care as "a child welfare service that provides 24-hour care for a child in a residential facility designed as a therapeutic environment" (Child Welfare League of America, 1982, p. 15). Moreover, out-of-home care is characterized as "part of a comprehensive coordinated system of services that support children and their families . . . with its most important role to support changes necessary to move the family as well as the child, where possible, toward reunification or life in the community" (Stuck, 1992, p. 484). Varying types of residential group care facilities share a common goal—"for every child to return to life in the community with improved ability to cope and succeed, whether with his or her own family or a substitute family, in another type of group care (for example, a group home) or for older youth, through independent living" (Whittaker, 1987, p. 673).

Types of Group Care Facilities and Their Populations.

Although all "institutions" have common characteristics, different types have been established to deal with particular sets of problems and serve distinct categories of children. These facilities may be under public or voluntary auspices and be administered by persons with a primary orientation to social welfare, education, medicine, psychiatry, or juvenile corrections.

Group care facilities include (1) residential group facilities for the care and protection of dependent and neglected children, including temporary shelters; (2) correctional institutions for delinquent and predelinquent young persons, including training schools, detention homes, and diagnostic reception centers; (3) treatment facilities for the emotionally disturbed, including psychiatric inpatient children's units, residential centers, and mental hospitals; (4) residential drug and alcohol programs; (5) facilities for developmentally disabled children and youth; and (6) private boarding schools.

Wherever children are cared for, some degree of restrictiveness in the environment exists. Proch and Taber (1987) offer this ranking of types of placements, with rank 1 being least restrictive and 9 most restrictive:

Home of parent, 1
Home of relative, 2
Foster family home, 3
Specialized foster family home, 4
Group home, 5
Private child welfare institution, 6
Shelter, 7
Mental health facility, 8
Correctional facility, 9

Drawing from a series of systematic surveys of children and youth in group residential care, Whittaker (1987) states that in 1981 there were more than 125,000 children and youth living in 3,900 residential group care facilities, in contrast to the 1965 figures of 155,000 children in 2,300 facilities. As the population declined, the number of facilities increased. In 1966 less than 50 percent of facilities had fewer than 26 children in care; by 1982 the majority of residential care group care facilities were of this size (Whittaker, 1987).

Pecora et al. (1992) trace four phases in the development of group care. First was a period in which dependent, "defective", and delinquent children were extricated from almshouses, jails, and the like, and moved into a separate institutions. In the late nineteenth century the old barracks-style institutions were replaced with smaller, family-style units staffed by house parents, sometimes containing more than twenty-five children. The third phase had a psychological focus and began in the early part of the twentieth century. Concepts from the child guidance movement and psychoanalytically grounded concepts about the therapeutic milieu combined with attention to factors such as group dynamics, with greater focus on child care staff as agents of treatment. The current phase, known as the environmental or ecological phase is based on outcome evaluations that show the importance of postplacement community supports (Pecora et al., 1992).

Most of the children's "institutions" still caring for children today were established before 1920 or after 1945, as institutions were less favored in the 1920s, 1930s, and early 1940s. The early era gave rise to institutions for neglected and dependent children, while the most recent period has produced a growth in facilities for emotionally disturbed and delinquent children and youth.

The U.S. General Accounting Office (1994) has studied residential settings as an approach for dealing with youth at risk for not becoming self-sufficient members of society, engaging in three or more of the following behaviors: poor performance in school, substance abuse, delinquency, and early unprotected sexual activity. In examining a wide range of residential programs ranging from tents in the wilderness to family-like residences, they found the following:

- Although programs report positive outcomes for youths, few programs conduct rigorous evaluations to measure effectiveness.
- Longer-term data are needed to test the endurance of treatment effects.
- The annual cost of serving one youth ranged from about $20,000 to about $132,000, with a median cost of about $44,000.

Special Attributes of Group Care.   Certain characteristics of the group residential care setting can be specifically useful in helping some disturbed children and young persons. These characteristics, which are different from those of the family home, in principle permit a controlled living process and a consciously designed therapeutic environment that can be varied to meet the needs of a particular group of children.

Momma
Every day we grow farther and farther apart
And now I know you didn't love me from the start
Daddy didn't want me and neither did you
It was then you saw there was nothing you could do.
You had to keep me or give me away
And I can see you regret keeping me to this day.
You don't have to lie, it doesn't hurt any more.
I'll just give a last sigh as I close the final door.
    (poem by 16-year-old girl in residential care,
    personal communication to author)

In contrast to a family home setting, young people in residential care can be freed from an obligation to form close personal relationships. The troubled child can keep relationships with others diluted so that there is less need to persist in old ways of reacting. Thus energy can be channeled into new learning processes. The group setting can allow greater variation in behavior than a family unit, and the impact of difficult behavior—"acting out"—may be less because it is diffused among a series of adults who work shifts, rather than being on duty 24 hours a day as parents and foster parents are.

The young person in group care has an opportunity for a variety of interpersonal relationships and patterns of behavior as he or she has access to more adult role models and other supportive relationships. The wider choice can permit the youth to remain relatively detached from relationships that in the past had been undesirably disturbing, but return to those relationships (parents, former foster parents, adoptive parents, mentors) that are rewarding, supportive, and productive. The peer group is an important resource and often a catalyst for constructive change. It offers an opportunity for interaction with others who share the same experience day by day.

A greater range of remedial and therapeutic programs and group activities can be brought together in a residential setting and made available for planning positive daily living experiences. The accessibility of the child to the staff facilitates diagnosis, observation, and treatment. Therapy for emotional problems, remedial programs for learning problems, and controls for behavioral problems can be integrated and related directed to the young person's daily life.

The consistent routine of group care may contribute to a disturbed child or youth's sense of continuity, regularity, and stability. Many young persons requiring group care have come from very disorganized home environments and need structure to facilitate impulse control.

Staff members in group care, by accepting formal employment conditions, assume an obligation for professional functioning and can be readily accessible to regular inservice training and supervision. They work in a context of back-up and support by other professionals, which helps to minimize their reactivity to the problems of young residents in the facility.

These attributes of group care, which can create a therapeutic environment, are not automatically self-fulfilling. If not used with professional skill, each attribute could become a barrier to treatment. Depersonalizing influences can also penalize children and youths who need individual personalized attention. In group living there is always an implicit lack of privacy. Opportunities to make choices may be lost. Some children are overstimulated by the variety of relationships and activities in group care. Without appropriate supervision and controls, acting-out behaviors by young people in care can jeopardize other group members. Although institutional staffs are increasingly aware of the need to involve children and youths in the mainstream of community life, often the campus of the facility is geographically isolated from community influence. In the case of young people in trouble with the community, the isolation may be an advantage during the period in which new controls are being established, but a disadvantage when it becomes time to reintegrate the youth back into the mainstream of community life.

While young people in out-of-home care may have a wide range of issues to be addressed, youths who are gay, lesbian, or bisexual are especially at risk in placement. These young people are often isolated, cut off from families and kin after disclosure of their orientation, and confused about their own emerging sexual orientation (Phillips, McMillen, Sparks, & Ueberle, 1997). They may have internalized societal homophobia or been told that they are sick, deviant, or just going through "a phase." Green Chimneys, a voluntary, nonprofit child welfare agency in New York City, has developed a unique program serving the developmental needs of gay and lesbian youths in out-of-home care. The Triangle Tribe program provides an environment of support in which young persons can understand their identity issues, as well as training and consultation to other child welfare agencies on the issues facing gay and lesbian youths (Mallon 1997).

Family Work in Residential Settings. Within the last few years, greater attention has been paid to the need for working with a child or young person's family if therapeutic change is to be maintained. A variety of creative approaches have been developed to integrate family treatment into the therapeutic modality of the facility. One residential facility in a rela-

tively remote area brings families in to stay on campus for a period of intensive treatment. A similar approach involves family, when possible, in a "ropes" course with their family member in care. The Family Empowerment Program at Wedgwood Acres in Michigan involves family members in every decision made for their young person in care. If the young person needs a consequence for inappropriate behavior, the parents are called, informed of the problem, and asked to decide how to handle the consequence. The Boysville approach involves families in counseling sessions, which may continue for up to six months after discharge, and provides parent support groups. A wilderness camp facility brings families to the camp for family conferences and parent therapy groups. Wraparound services are being used to reintegrate young people back into their families, or into the community in other family settings such as family foster care or kinship care.

Methods and Results. The range of specific approaches to a planned therapeutic residential environment includes individualized psychotherapy, behavior modification, play therapy, milieu therapy, group work, and positive peer culture. Although individual psychotherapy was dominant in earlier times, it has largely been replaced by various forms of group work, and behavior modification as preferred models of treatment. In all such approaches, the attempt is to use the everyday living environment as a therapeutic tool.

Group work approaches have emphasized social and peer supports and sanctions as a means of establishing new patterns of behavior. Youths are given selected responsibilities for the day-to-day operation of the unit and for governing their own and each other's behavior. The youth group assigns, schedules, and monitors the necessary chores, activities, and privileges. The use of recreational challenges, such as wilderness trips, high ropes courses, and camp situations also strengthens young persons' perceptions of responsibility to the peer group goals. Staff act as facilitators or guides with the group interactions, as well as maintaining standards of expected behavior.

Behavior modification remains a dominant treatment approach in many settings. This approach is based on the idea that behavior is learned, and is largely controlled or reinforced by the consequences of a behavior. The staff have the task of making both the desired behavior and consequences explicit to residents and of managing the system of consequence—rewards and punishments—to support and reinforce expectations. Familiar techniques in this approach include token economies, in which young people work for points or tokens to attain varied levels of privilege.

Do institutional care and treatment work well for children and youth? More comprehensive outcome research is needed. From an analysis of follow-up studies of children and youth discharged back to their families or communities from residential care, Whittaker (1987) identified a cluster of common findings with respect to their postdischarge well being:

1. Whatever definition is given to success in residential care, and irrespective of gains the children and youth made while in the residential program, "ecological factors"—supports available in the post-treatment community environment—are critical.

2. Contact between the children and their biological parents, as full partners in the helping process, from the time of a child's entrance into group care is a vital component of treatment.

3. Constructive "linkages between the neighborhood, the peer group, the world of work and other potential sources of support in the environment" are imperative for postplacement well-being. Without these supports, in a stressful family or community situation gains made by youth during residential care are likely to erode.

4. Social work can and should assume a role, not only in the design and implementation of services within the residential unit, but also in post-discharge services—parent education, family support groups, community liaison work, and consultation with informal helping networks.

Without attention to these findings, Whittaker concludes, "it is doubtful that any model of residential treatment . . . can improve on the meager results emerging from outcome studies with respect to ultimate community reintegration" (p. 680).

Agency Group Homes

Many children and young people in the foster care system have needs that may make them unsuited to either family foster homes or residential care. Adolescents—even young adolescents—frequently fall into this group. They may have serious unresolved conflicts in relation to their parents, making it difficult for them to accept the traditional family foster home setting. Yet they will benefit from more casual community experiences and informal living than would be available in an institutional setting. They may have been in a more closed residential setting but are now ready for a transitional experience to test out their readiness to move back into their own homes and communities. In order to benefit from group home care they must be able to function in an open setting.

The Uniqueness of the Group Home. The agency-operated group home is especially useful in serving different kinds of children, although it has been mostly used with adolescents. The group home is typically a large single dwelling or apartment, either owned or rented by an agency or other organization, and located in a residential part of the community. Child care staff members are usually viewed as counselors rather than as foster parents. Some agency group homes have a married couple—group home parents—and child care staff, giving young people the benefit of family-like contact plus the additional opportunity to relate to child care staff as young adult role models. Other professional personnel serve the group home regularly—social workers, a psychiatric consultant, a psychologist, and perhaps at times other resource persons such as recreational therapists, special education consultants, or nutritionists. While the parent agency or institution has administrative and supervisory responsibility, however, the group home reaches out to the community for many activities.

Certain problems are typical of group homes. One is resistance from neighborhood individuals and groups that halts or delays attempts to establish new group homes. The NIMBY (not in my back yard) phenomenon may come into play with neighbors' fearfulness that the presence of young people (or other "different" groups) will threaten the peace, security, or property values of the neighborhood (Pierce & Hauck, 1981). Strategies for overcoming this opposition may be low-profile or high-profile. Low-profile strategies eschew neighborhood education and assume the right to locate a group home in that location. The high-profile strategy involves considerable effort to educate and involve the community in each stage of the planning process. The literature provides successful examples of both approaches (Weber, 1978).

Meeting the expectations of multiple constituencies is another problem for group homes. The constituencies include schools, police, the children or youths' families, and neighbors. Group homes are an open system, so interaction is frequent. Community relations functions are extremely important in the management of a group home. Use of community volunteers and community advisory groups is helpful in promoting positive transactions and community understanding of the needs of the young people in care.

Independent Living Services

Unanticipated increases in the number of adolescents in foster care triggered a new challenge to the child welfare system—the necessity of preparing large numbers of at-risk foster adolescents for independent living or, as is preferred by Maluccio, Krieger, and Pine (1990), *interdependent* living, a phrase that underscores adolescents' need to relate to other people and the community. In the past, young persons who remained in foster care until the age of majority (or the age at which laws of the states allowed agencies to discontinue services) have been discharged into the community with the expectation that they could assume care for themselves. For many young persons exiting care, the lack of planning had disastrous results, with their ending up in homeless shelters with no place to go, no financial resources, and no family connections to fall back on. Many youths leaving foster care ended up on public welfare rolls (Allen, Bonner, & Greenan, 1988).

After a series of hearings, in 1987 Congress authorized the Independent Living Initiative by amendment to Title IV-E of the Social Security Act, P.L. 96-272., which continued into the 1990s. The funds were to be used for a broad range of services for youths in care who were from eligible AFDC families. The legislative intent was to enable such youths to seek a high school diploma, participate in vocational training, enroll in a program for learning life skills, use individual or group counseling, integrate and coordinate all other services available to eligible youth, and provide each participant with an individualized written independent living case plan (Allen, Bonner, & Greenan, 1988).

Despite already heavy demands, the child welfare field responded by developing a variety of programs aimed at enabling foster youth to develop skills to live successfully outside the foster care system. By 1988 several hundred programs existed to provide independent living programs for adolescents preparing for emancipation from the foster care system. The response continued into the 1990s. Currently a wide range of programs exist, including special group homes that teach life skills, supervised apartment living, mentorship programs, groupwork for young people who are receiving in-home training from their foster parents, and specialized foster homes established to teach life skills and assist the emancipation process. A culturally specific African-American rites-of-passage program teaches youths in care life skills for the transition to adulthood using Afrocentric mentoring and ritual (Gavazzi, Alford & McKenry, 1996).

Problems of Youth at Discharge from Foster Care.

In an effort to establish the need for transition programs, the New Jersey Division of Youth and Family Services carried out a study of 357 youths, randomly selected, aged 16 to 21 and serviced by the Division of Youth and Family Services. The sample was drawn from urban, suburban, and rural counties. Data were collected from case records to provide a profile of characteristics of these youth and an assessment of their needs (Wood, Herring, & Hunt, 1989).

The profile showed that many of these foster adolescents had serious behavioral and emotional problems requiring an array of services ranging from intensive mental health care to education and training in survival skills. A relatively small group had developmental disabilities that limited their ability to function independently. Sixty percent belonged to racial minorities. A substantial number had been placed in foster care from four to nine times. For over 70 percent, the record showed incidents of maltreatment that had been confirmed by the foster care agency (Wood, Herring, & Hunt, 1989).

Educational deficits and lack of readiness for employment were present for a large majority of the New Jersey sample, an especially troubling finding. Other researchers have also warned about the unmet educational needs of foster children (Fanshel & Shinn, 1978; Barth, 1986; Gershenson & Kresh, 1986; Westat, Inc., 1986), leading Mech (1988) to conclude that "the interaction between foster placement and educational deficits is of such a magnitude that it cannot be ignored" (p. 489).

They should have demanded more of me . . . I was capable of doing much better in school, but nobody seemed to care much about that. (cited in Festinger, 1983, p. 114)

The need was confirmed as well in Festinger's follow-up study of young adults who had been former foster children (1983). The youths were each asked how much, on the whole, the foster care agency had prepared the to go out on their own. Twenty-five percent said they had been prepared "a lot"; 23 percent replied "some"; and 43 percent said "very little" or "not at all" (p. 64). When the youths were asked what areas of preparation before discharge were most needed, two areas stood out—education and work (p. 290). Learning problems at the time of their discharge from care had affected their employment and work confidence.

Program Elements. In a two-year study of operating independent living programs in the United States and Canada, Stone (1987) identified and ranked elements that staff members and youth from the programs thought were common to successful programs. Among the ten most frequently selected elements thought to be needed, six were selected by all the respondents as essential: financial management; finding housing; accepting responsibilities; medical care/basic health; decision-making; and developing a support system.

Regardless of variation in programs, Stone (1987) identified three basic principles that should be common in all:

1. *The developmental tasks of adolescence are the priorities in the lives of adolescents regardless of their situations or problems. Separating from parents, developing peer and adult relations, discovering their identity, defining a place outside the home in society, and entering the world of work are necessary life tasks at this time and therefore become the basic areas for learning and support in any independent living program;*
2. *The program needs to be integrated into the total agency program, not operated as an extra service that is tacked onto current workloads. . . . Policies and practices that create opportunities for increasing self-reliance—for sharing household tasks, for decision-making or risk-taking—are essential to all phases of agency programming for children in foster care.*
3. *For those youths . . . who have not learned the appropriate developmental tasks of childhood and preadolescence . . . the program must take on a remedial character . . . and do so at an accelerated pace prior to age 18. (pp. 41–42)*

Emotional Readiness for Emancipation. In addition to tangible independent living skills, young people emancipating from care often require assistance with the intangible aspects of emancipation, including reliving the original separation experience and confusion about their identity. Under the best of circumstances, emancipation can be a difficult process requiring a series of complex adaptations. The young person in placement often experiences a double loss. There is the real loss in the here and now of leaving the foster home or group home, saying goodbye to child care staff or foster family members, leaving the neighborhood and school. Additionally the youth re-experiences, consciously or unconsciously, the original loss of his or her biological family. For many youths this is experienced as loss of self. Foster parents, child care staff, and other members of the team must be aware of this potential for *reactivation of earlier losses* (McFadden et al., 1989). In some cases, young persons preparing for emancipation set themselves up to be rejected—as they may believe they earlier had been by their parents—or may sabotage the independent living plan for fear of leaving the only security they may have known. Others may act out in ways that show an identification with their biological parents. These maladaptive responses to separation may be thematic to the young person who has endured multiple placements.

He tells me "You're going to move out on your own" No way man, that's what I'll say. Not ready. Not ready. Not ready. (Male in care, Martin & Palmer, 1997, p. 44)

Another theme workers and caregivers should understand is the phenomenon of the *reunion fantasy.* Young persons may have entertained for years secret thoughts about finding their parents and receiving the love and nurturing that they missed during a childhood in foster care:

Although Jason had not seen his father for years—parental rights had been terminated when Jason was 8—he longed to see his father again. He couldn't remember his mother, who had left when he was 2 years old. During the years that Jason had been adopted, he had a recurring dream about finding both of his parents and telling them he was sorry that they weren't together. When the adoption broke down and Jason came back into care, he had tried to locate his father, but to no avail. He did have a plan. After he left the group home, he would move back to the city where he had lived with his parents. He would go back to the old neighborhood and look in all the bars for his father. He knew his father was an alcoholic and figured that when he found his father he could take care of him, and help his father to quit drinking. Then together, he and his father would look for his mother.

Young people may know or understand—at an intellectual level—the circumstances that brought them into care. They may realize that finding a parent or living with that parent is an unrealistic dream. Yet on an emotional level, it can be a very deep vestige of an old attachment. Effective family continuity practice encourages young people leaving care to reconnect with significant relationships, whether it is the kinship network, or a former foster parent. It is helpful to see the reality of one's family situation, and even if one's parents are incapable of providing support to emancipating youth, there may be other people who are capable of being ongoing "family" during the adult years:

Kevin, like Jason, returned to care from a broken adoption. He knew that his original father was an alcoholic, but wanted to find him to ask some questions about his childhood, which remained a jumble of confusing memories. Kevin's independent living worker helped him find his original family, only to discover that Kevin's father was near death from cancer and that Kevin's mother had disappeared years ago. The worker accompanied Kevin on several trips to the hospital to visit with his father and supported him through his grief. While at the hospital, Kevin rediscovered his grandmother, whom he had last seen at age 4. The grandmother had a family picnic to welcome Kevin back to the family. Kevin took part in the family activities surrounding his father's funeral and decided to attend college in the city where his extended family lives. He lived with an aunt and uncle during his first two years of school. They helped him make contact with his former adoptive family, for some healing of the painfully severed relationship.

Empowerment of Young People Leaving Care. In all probability young persons leaving care have experienced years of disempowerment, in which they were expected to adapt to the rules and lifestyles of several different sets of foster families or other care settings, years in which they had little choice or control over placement decisions that deeply affected their lives, years in which they may have been maltreated or scapegoated in the very system set up to protect them. As an outgrowth of independent living programs, many states and countries now have organized advocacy groups of young people in care or young persons who were formerly in care.

Groups such as the National Youth in Care Network of Canada or the National Association of Young People in Care in the United Kingdom have conducted research projects, set up youth advocacy groups, influenced legislation, and published books and magazines (Raychaba, 1989; Saddington 1988). Young people in care from many countries, including the United States, are part of the International Foster

Care Organization's conferences, and other international efforts for the empowerment of young people in out-of-home care. Organized feedback from young persons exiting the system provides consumer-oriented quality control.

TEAMWORK IN OUT-OF-HOME CARE

Foster care, as a service to children and families, encompasses an array of out-of-family care options. In all the varied types of foster care—family foster care, group care, and residential care—teamwork between staff is critical. The social workers, primarily charged with implementing permanency plans, and the caregivers, who provide the day-to-day nurture that promotes development and healing of earlier trauma, must coordinate their activities with collateral professionals who also provide service to children and their parents, including therapists, health care providers, educators, and others who are part of the overall plan. Thus the team is part of a larger helping system brought into play by the social worker's brokering and coordinating functions. On a different level, there needs to be collaborative teamwork between the management of the child welfare agency, the court, and mental health and substance abuse treatment agencies.

Critical elements of teamwork are necessary to achieve the purposes of out-of-home care in the areas of roles, knowledge, goals, and coordinated effort. In foster care teamwork, clarification of roles is critical. The roles of worker and foster parent (group home parent or child care staff) have changed considerably, with concomitant shifts in ascribed power and duties. Each has clearly differentiated duties toward the child and family in the permanence planning process, and both share certain responsibilities. While team members need similar knowledge about the foster care system and the needs of children and their families, they also need specialized knowledge. Workers' knowledge is more in the area of legal processes and family systems issues, while caregiver's knowledge is more specialized in areas such as creating a nurturing environment, handling separation trauma, and managing a child's behavior effectively. To work effectively in a team all participants must share a com-

mon goal. The goal of teamwork is the goal of the permanency plan. The area of coordinated effort in teamwork involves such skills as sharing information, joint planning, addressing issues of power and control, establishing time frames and specific plans, negotiating specific task performance, managing conflict, decision making, and evaluating team effort.

The National Commission on Family Foster Care, convened by the Child Welfare League of America, proposed, in *A Blueprint for Fostering Infants, Children and Youths in the 1990s,* numerous recommendations to strengthen foster care to meet contemporary challenges and to focus national attention on family foster care as an essential service option. One significant category of recommendations addressed teamwork as a cornerstone of foster care practice:

> *The unique individual needs of infants, children and youths and their families are multidimensional and complex. . . . Successful family foster care must use a teamwork process that begins with the foster parent and social worker and involves the courts and other professionals as well. The family and the child or youth in care should be involved to the fullest possible extent in making and carrying out plans. The team is only as effective as its ability to understand, represent and assist the client. (National Commission on Family Foster Care, 1991)*

While the commitment to teamwork spelled out in the *Blueprint* has not yet been operationalized in all foster care practice, it is part of an international trend toward the professionalization of foster parents, group care houseparents, and child care staff. One of the themes of this shift is the understanding that caregivers are not usually *substitute parents,* rather they are *supplemental* to the child's own parents as caregivers. In the United Kingdom, people who provide foster care are known as "carers" rather than "parents":

> *Present-day foster carers are now very much aware that the foster child's legal parent is the local authority, and their actual parents are people other than themselves. Foster carers have a job of work to do that involves them in carrying out tasks with, for and in behalf of the child and must do so in a way that includes the child's social worker and family. This means that the motivation which may once have attracted many*

to consider becoming foster carers—the opportunity to look after children as if they were one's own—is no longer appropriate. (Lowe, 1991)

Training Foster Parents, Child Care Staff, and Workers

In this respect, foster parents' roles are becoming more professional, like the roles of group home "parents" or "counselors" or residential care staff who may fill roles of milieu therapists. In general, all caregiver roles in out-of-home care have evolved from less specialized to more specialized, from lay to paraprofessional or professionalized, and from strictly child-focused to work with child and family, in order to work within the contemporary context of permanency planning and family continuity. Teamwork is critical in all aspects of foster care.

There are many ways to implement teamwork in foster care settings. In a treatment home, the foster parent (or parent-counselor) may be in partnership with a therapist and a worker. In residential care, child care staff may work with therapist, teacher, and other members of the therapeutic team. The permutations of a team approach are numerous, depending on the setting and its philosophy. The child's parents are also viewed by many child welfare professionals as partners and members of the team. (Maluccio & Sinanoglu, 1981, Jenson & Whittaker, 1987). Training is a key component of teamwork for all those working in foster care.

Foster Parent Training.   The value of systematic training for foster parents is well established. Foster parent training has been shown to have potential for reducing the incidence of failed placements, increasing the probability of desirable placements, and encouraging foster parents to remain licensed (Boyd & Remy, 1978). In a demonstration of joint training of foster parents and caseworkers, attitudes of both groups were significantly strengthened with respect to a teamwork approach to case planning and management. A common definition of the foster parent role was achieved—that of a specialized professional who provides temporary, not long-term, care for children (Fimmen & Mietus, 1988). Use of training materials

about work with children's parents has demonstrated the capacity of foster parents to assume new roles, focused on helping the family not just the children (Ryan et al, 1981; Lee & Nissivoccia, 1989). Foster parent training is now mandated in most if not all states, along with preservice training, inservice training, or both (Ryan, 1995).

There are a number of fully developed foster parent training curricula. The *Fostering Families* series is a curriculum developed at the School of Social Work, Colorado State University to bring foster parents and social workers together for collaborative learning about chemical dependency, religion in foster homes, medically fragile children, and other topics of interest (Schatz, 1991–1992). This endeavor brought together the resources of social work education and the public child welfare agency, with collaboration at management levels enhancing teamwork at the practice level.

The Model Approach to Partnerships in Parenting (MAPP) is a foster home selection and training program used in many states. It includes ten three-hour group meetings and several home visits led by a team of two licensing workers and a seasoned foster parent. The program combines take-home study and meetings to teach the team approach to permanency planning and problem-solving in foster care. Foster parent candidates explore their experiences and perspectives with the training team in a mutual assessment of their readiness and commitment to foster parenting (Anderson, 1988). The MAPP program has been culturally adapted for use in the Netherlands (Van Pagee, Van Miltenberg, & Pasztor, 1991).

A curriculum for training foster parents developed at Eastern Michigan University is comprised of seventeen course outlines and training manuals on a variety of topics (emotional development of children in care, working with natural parents, handling lying, dishonesty and destructive behavior, fostering sexually abused children, team work, etc.) plus a series of manuals on preparing youths in care for independent living and a training program for staff and foster parents on preventing abuse in foster care. These curricula have been distributed nationally and internationally through the Institute for the Study of Children and Families and the National Foster Care Resource Center.

The Child Welfare League of America, in collaboration with a number of participating states, has developed a training curriculum, Foster Pride/Adopt Pride, which covers a wide range of issues for preservice and inservice training. This curriculum has been implemented in European countries as well as in the United States. The Child Welfare League also has available a videotape series for foster parent training, with accompanying study guides, illustrating with case materials topics such as teamwork, work with a sexually abused child, family reunification, and issues of identity affecting youths in care. The audiovisual series was produced by private foundations and the state of Oregon.

National organizations such as the National Foster Parent Association and the Association of Treatment Homes hold yearly training conferences with topics of interest to foster parents, foster care staff, and others. Many states have well-developed service delivery systems. Oregon has regional foster parent training consultants who provide training to isolated rural areas (Whitmore, 1991). The technology of video satellite uplink has been used in the state of Kentucky in a collaborative effort between the state public child welfare agency and state universities to provide statewide interactive training sessions for foster parents at distant sites.

The continuing role shift for foster parents is evident in the literature directed toward their unique tasks of parenting other people's children. Stahl (1990) has written a handbook for foster parents that addresses the difficulties and challenges of fostering. It focuses not only on parenting issues, but also on the value and ethical dilemmas inherent in fostering.

Child Care Staff Training. Training for child care staff existed long before foster parent training was developed. Many agencies and organizations have developed career ladders for child care staff, with comprehensive curricula focused on the emotional social and behavioral needs of children and youths in care. There is a National Organization of Child Care Worker Associations. Some multifunction agencies train child care staff and foster parents together, along with social work and other treatment staff. Other organizations, such as Boys Town, offer training workshops on a wide spectrum of issues. The National Resource Center on Youth Services provides comprehensive training packages to agencies, organizations, and states as well as training conferences. The principles of teamwork in helping the child or youth in group care have been established for years.

The contemporary trend in group care involves a reorientation to the ecological perspective, with a focus on working with the family as well as the child or youth in care. Youth care workers will increasingly perform the following tasks:

1. Teach children and families practical skills to cope effectively with their environments.
2. Work to enhance natural support networks where they exist and help create them where they do not.
3. Operate on the premise that "environmental helping" is not synonymous with aftercare: it begins before placement, continues during placement, and lasts as long after placement as it is needed. (Pecora et al, 1992)

Several initiatives involve training of residential care staff in family work. The Albert E. Trieschman Center has developed training packages on family reunification in group care, which are being used in several states. Boysville of Michigan has used a family-based model for years and has implemented staff training to support family reunification practice.

Training of child care staff and other agency staff in the area of diversity is important. Not only must staff be culturally competent in serving young persons from a variety of racial, cultural, and ethnic groups, but they must also be sensitized to the unique needs of gay, lesbian, and bi-sexual young persons in care. The Triangle Tribe project has offered training and consultation in developing supportive environments for sexual minority young persons (Mallon, 1997). There are a number of training issues to be addressed. For example, general staff training regarding suicide should include information about the elevated suicide rate among gay and lesbian adolescents. Additionally, specific training on gay and lesbian issues is needed to address issues of safety, myths and stereotypes, using gender-neutral language, and intervening when hurtful homophobic language is used (Phillips, McMillen, Sparks, & Ueberle, 1997).

An emerging focus of training, that of positive youth development, is an organizational concept, which applies to all staff members within the child caring agency. It is a proactive commitment to quality of service, expectation of change, and promotion from within that creates an organizational culture focused on the positive development of young persons in care, rather than on "the problem" (Robertson, 1997).

A similar use of parallel process is the staff development and intervention approach, know as *competency development,* which is used with juvenile offenders in out-of-home care as well as in community-based programs. Viewing delinquent youths as resources, rather than as victims or villains, leads to seeing young persons as potentially productive members of society. This perspective can be seen in the proliferation of outdoor adventure, challenge, and "ropes" courses, in which staff are trained to provide role modeling for youth participants (Bazemore & Terry, 1997).

Worker Training. The National Commission on Family Foster Care established recommendations for training foster care workers. One recommendation was for collaboration with schools of social work to develop curricula that adequately prepare BSW and MSW graduates for work in foster care. Curricular topics recommended include the following: working with separation, loss, and grief; chemical dependency; the effects of illness, handicapping conditions, and stigmatization on human functioning; and the interdisciplinary team approach. The Commission recommended that all topics emphasize teamwork and culturally competent practice.

The Project for Practice in Permanency Planning, a collaborative effort between the National Foster Care Resource Center, the National Resource Center for Family-Based Services, and the National Resource Center for Special Needs Adoption, established competencies for family continuity practice. These training competencies were predicated on assumptions of empowering families and working in a teamwork capacity with biological, foster, adoptive, and kinship parents, and in increasing teamwork between branches of children and family services such as foster care, adoption, and family-based services for prevention of

placement (Allen, McFadden, & Wasserman, 1992). Competencies for child welfare inservice staff training have also been developed (Hughes & Rycus, 1989).

Competencies for graduate social work education in child welfare have been developed in several states. The competencies for MSW family and children's services developed in Michigan in a partnership effort involving the Michigan Department of Social Services and six graduate schools of social work can be found in the instructor's manual that accompanies this textbook.

Foster care workers must be able to work across boundaries with many other disciplines. A critical area of training is in legal issues related to permanency planning. In order to function effectively within the legal system, staff need to be grounded in legal terminology, understand legal processes related to permanency planning, know the legal basis of child welfare practice including constitutional rights of parents, be able to document all aspects of casework, be able to present effective testimony and prepare for court hearings, and be able to work collaboratively with attorneys on specific procedures such as preparation for termination of parental rights.

One way foster care workers learn about teamwork is to be cotrained with foster parents, or with other professionals. Wasson and Hess (1989) also cite the use of foster parents as foster care educators. In several states foster parents have taken an active role in training workers and other foster staff about effective teamwork practice for permanency planning.

The skills of casework, while still valuable for foster care workers, must be supplemented with the ability to do groupwork, to develop resources within the community, to be an internal change agent within an organization, and to advocate for families and children at the level of social policy. In order to be effective, family and children's services workers must be able to be generalists in their skills but specialists in their knowledge of issues affecting families and children.

PROTECTING CHILDREN AND YOUTHS IN OUT-OF-HOME CARE

When the community, through courts and agencies, intervenes in the life of a family, they have a moral and legal obligation to provide adequate care if the child is placed away from the family. Besharov (1985) states: "Courts usually hold that by assuming custody of a child—either pursuant to a court order or with the parents' consent—and by making decisions about the child's care, agencies and workers accept a degree of legal responsibility for the child's health, safety, and well-being, and for the child's behavior" (p. 109).

The existence of maltreatment by caregivers and others in out-of-home settings is cause for serious concern and careful vigilance by foster care professionals. The knowledge base of maltreatment in family foster care is still in early stages of development. In the 1980s reports (Ryan et al., 1987; Miller, 1982; Tobias, 1981) and journal articles (Bolton et al., 1981) brought the issue to professional awareness. Prior to that period, maltreatment by foster parents, if recognized at all, was typically viewed as an aberration or an isolated incident. Litigation, including a class action suit, L. J. v. Massinga, and a rash of civil liability suits by outraged parents and others soon brought the issue to the forefront of professional attention.

As agencies monitored homes more closely and began tracking abuse complaints against foster parents, there were unanticipated consequences. Foster parents began to leave fostering as a result of having been investigated or for fear of having allegations made against them. Although some allegations made against foster parents were substantiated on careful investigation, some were unfounded. A number of foster parents denied any maltreatment and perceived themselves as victims of manipulations by the foster child or the child's family. Carbino (1991) examined the impact of allegations on the life of the foster families and found they had many negative experiences, including abrupt removals of children from their homes, being cut off from communication with the agency, feelings of loss and injustice, and damaged reputations. Foster parent organizations have set up response teams to support foster parents during the investigatory process. Kulp (1993) and the Canadian Foster Family Association (1993) have written guidelines to help foster and adoptive parents understand the risks and the investigative processes, and to support them in developing appropriate boundaries and discipline techniques.

Dynamics of Maltreatment in Family Foster Care.
When maltreatment occurs in a family foster home, it may be related to a configuration of factors in three areas: the system, the child, and the foster family. System-related factors include lack of foster parent training, failure to match the child with the family, failure to monitor the child in the home, poor home-study, failure to decertify homes known to be deficient, and overloading of the foster home. Factors related to the child include a number of attributes and behaviors that tend to make children high-risk, including wetting, soiling, and noncompliant behaviors, sexually acting out behaviors, multiple placements, and being an adolescent. In one study, there was no relationship between maltreatment and a number of foster family characteristics, including socioeconomic status, age of parents, and marital status, with the exception that there was a very low incidence of sexual abuse in foster families headed by a single woman (McFadden & Ryan, 1991). Zuravin et al., (1993) found that "foster home characteristics alone may not be important predictors of maltreatment. Occurrences of maltreatment may be dependent on the interactions between the foster home, the foster child and agency practice characteristics" (p. 594).

Maltreatment in Group and Residential Care.
Legal actions in the 1970s—*Wyatt v. Stickney* (1971) and *Morales v Turman* (1973) brought to light the issue of institutional abuse. The devastating effects of abuse on youths in "warehouses" was reported by Wooden (1976), often in their own words and poetry. In a landmark study, Rindfleish and Rabb (1984) estimated that abuse in residential care may occur at twice the rate at which it occurs in families. Durkin (1982) noted that there is strong resistance to reports of institutional abuse and likens the institutional response to those defensive maneuvers found in families when confronted with abuse.

Bloom (1992) identifies a current vacuum in the literature and suggests that it is necessary to believe that maltreatment can happen. His recommendations include the following steps: Take allegations seriously; suspend the employee with pay during the initial investigation; reach out to the child's family; act to cut off retribution by staff members or peers; and flood the child with support. He also details in his protocol steps to maintain the organization during an investigation and ways of supporting the staff, including treating the alleged perpetrator with respect and dignity (Bloom, 1992).

Protecting Children and Youths in Out-of-Home Care. Daley and Dowd (1992) acknowledge a sad reality—that over the last several decades out-of-home care programs have sometimes been places of harm. They propose focusing on the characteristics of a harm-free environment, such as providing support for caregivers, reducing burnout, using a proactive model of care, focusing on positive behavior, using input from the consumers, evaluating programs, and using an internal program audit to investigate events that are questionable but may not be reportable as abuse and neglect. They emphasize the importance of interviewing children and youths confidentially, at least annually, to determine whether any adult has treated them improperly. Raychaba (1993, 1989), a former youth in care, reported on youth forums for Canadian young people in care. When talking to their peers, whom they could trust, Canadian foster children opened up for the first time to disclose their maltreatment by foster parents or child care staff. The description of their pain is eloquent. Some children and youths are reluctant to tell their workers of their problems; others may perceive that the maltreatment in a foster home is 'normal' because it resembles earlier maltreatment they endured in their own homes.

The foster care worker has a vital role in child protection (McFadden, 1986). By assessing children carefully, making careful placements that don't overload the home; giving caregivers full information about the risk characteristics of the children, supporting caregivers, training caregivers in positive behavioral techniques, listening carefully to young people, and monitoring the home or facility for changes, the worker can promote quality and harm-free care.

The worker's responsibility for the safety and well-being of children in placement is very clear. This would include not only child protection issues but also address other critical problems, such as multiple placements or foster care drift—all of which are damaging to children. Professional ethics demand protection for the most vulnerable. (See Chapter 10, Advocacy.) Some social workers have taken great risks as "whistle-blowers" when their best efforts could not rectify a serious situation. There is a related responsibility, with which conscientious professionals must struggle—how to acknowledge limitations of the foster care system without discrediting groups, such as foster parents, or the system itself.

TRENDS AND ISSUES

There is serious interest in applying the concept of managed care, which has been used in health care, to child welfare. Managed care is both a philosophy, related to distributive justice in an era of limited resources, and a new way of providing service. An estimated 105 million people in the U.S. now receive their behavioral health care through one of twelve large managed care organizations (MCOs) (Penkert, 1998). The principles of managed care—having diagnostic categories with related lengths of stay or paying a flat fee for certain types of care, no matter how long it might take to achieve the permanency goal—come from the medical model, which does not seem clearly related to the way the foster care system has operated in the past. Managed care has been applied for some children and youths receiving mental health treatment services under Medicaid funding.

The Child Welfare League of America has established the Managed Care Institute to identify and describe current and potential changes in the way child welfare agencies are delivering services consistent with managed care principles. Some thirty child welfare administrators say they are implementing or planning to implement initiatives that include managed care features (Hutchins, 1997). In some states the public child welfare agency will contract with providers but handle case management functions. Other states may contract with a managed care entity that would contract with service providers (McCollough, 1997).

Managed care is related to the privatization of child welfare services. Kansas was one of the first states to move in this direction, when, in 1996 and 1997, three major child welfare services—family preservation, foster care, and adoption—were transferred to contracted private providers in a modified form of managed care. This involves a capitated case rate for each family or child. This case rate is expected to meet all of the crisis needs of the family and/or children for the duration of each of the services. Kansas officials carefully designed outcome measures to value child safety at all times (Eggars, 1997). Unlike their counterparts in the health care field, the child welfare contractors do not control the intake into their system. While there was considerable agreement that the child welfare system had past problems and was in need of system change, not all reports on the new system has been positive. The Kansas chapter of the National Association of Social Workers enumerated concerns about the implementation of the new systems, and developed a set of recommendations, including:

- Develop community advisory boards.
- Adopt a set of best-practice standards to ensure child safety.
- Provide training for new case managers.
- Institute a grievance process.
- Create an ombudsman/advocate. (Kansas NASW, 1997)

Child welfare organizations are developing networks, partnerships, and mergers in order to successfully navigate the new managed care environment. Four key reasons for doing so are that they can provide more efficient and effective services, can have increased fiscal stability, and can increase their organizational control. Attention to leadership, economics, and qualitative improvements can develop strong organizations that can compete in the changing marketplace (Emenhiser, King, Jaffe, & Penkert, 1998). As funding patterns are affected by managed care or become more flexible in order to move services toward the prevention end, foster care practice may see an increased emphasis on innovation such as shared family care, kinship care, family decision-making for permanency planning, and other prospects that promote family continuity.

While the concept of managed care in foster care service delivery has many converts, and the prestigious Child Welfare League of America has established an Institute to study the phenomenon, it is too early to predict long-range success. There has not yet been adequate evaluation of the concept in its direct application and its effect on children and families, or on service providers such as casework staff or foster parents. Certainly a capitation on service dollars provides a strong incentive to keep children from growing up in foster care and moves the system toward permanency outcomes.

CHAPTER SUMMARY

As indicated throughout this chapter, foster care is moving conceptually toward an ecological model that is community-based, culturally competent, and family-focused. Foster care in its broadest sense refers to a wide array of out-of-home placement options, including kinship foster care, shared family care, family foster care, specialized foster care, treatment foster care, group home care, group care in residential treatment, and institutional care. Although the number of children in out-of-home care decreased after the implementation of permanency planning in the early 1980s, the number of children in care has continued to escalate due to a multicausal mix of poverty, racism, and parental incapacity due to substance abuse, disability, intergenerational family dysfunction, disease, and despair.

While the primary aim of foster care is the safety and protection of children, a steady focus remains on the children's families—parents, siblings, and kinfolk. Family reunification is the permanency outcome attained by most foster care cases. Preserving attachments and family continuity for the children is a guiding principle of foster care social work practice. Greater knowledge of trauma and resilience informs a variety of treatment approaches needed by children and youths in care.

The Adoption and Safe Families Act of 1997 has built on the Adoption Assistance and Child Welfare Act of 1980 to provide time-limited permanency planning for children in care and to expedite the movement of children through the system to permanent outcomes. The placement of children transracially continues to be a matter of some controversy: While the amended Multiethnic Placement Act facilitates such placements, child welfare professionals continue to promote maintaining a child's cultural heritage, especially through the culturally competent recruitment of foster and adoptive homes and in the ever-increasing use of kinship placements.

In a sense, the history of foster care is the history of child welfare. Throughout the twentieth century the philosophical assumptions of child welfare legislation and programs have evolved and will continue to do so, especially as new service delivery structures are promoted under managed care. Foster care review shows promise of helping the foster care system work toward outcomes of child well being, safety, and permanency.

During the past decade there has been concern about the safety of children *within* the system, as reports of maltreatment in foster homes and group care have surfaced. There have been system responses in terms of protocols, consent decrees, and increased monitoring. But throughout the last century and into the next, the immediate responsibility for the safety of children and adolescents rests with the care team: foster parent or child care staff and a disciplined and dedicated foster care social worker. Teamwork must be supported by training and agency expectation. Foster care is a great challenge to all who work with the system.

FOR STUDY AND DISCUSSION

1. Identify both positive and negative vestiges of the historical development of foster care practice that may be seen in current agency practice.

2. Talk with a placement specialist from a child placing agency in your community to determine which options (shared family care, kinship care, family foster care, treatment foster care, group homes, and residential care) are available in your community. What criteria are applied for selecting a particular care option for a child and family?

3. Meet with a protective services supervisor to determine under what circumstances children in your community would be removed from their families and put into care. What are the critical problems or clusters of problems causing foster care placement?

4. Attend a foster parent association meeting and survey foster parents on their perceptions of social worker teamwork. Talk with foster care social workers about what they believe constitute characteristics of good foster parents. Compare points of convergence and discrepancies.

5. Invite a former foster child, or a panel of young adults who have been in care, to discuss their experiences with you in class.

6. Read more extensively on the needs and experiences of parents whose children are in care and talk with one in person.

FOR ADDITIONAL STUDY

Berrick, J. D., Needell, B., Barth, R., & Johnson, M. (1998). *The tender years: Toward developmentally sensitive services for very young children.* New York: Oxford University Press.

Braziel, D. (1996). *Family-focused practice in out-of-home care: A handbook and resource directory.* Washington, DC: Child Welfare League of America Press.

Etter, J. (1997). *Mediating Permanency Outcomes: Practice manual.* Washington, DC: Child Welfare League of America Press.

Fahlberg, V. (1991). *A child's journey through placement.* Indianapolis: Perspectives Press.

Hegar, R., & Scannapieco, M. (1999). *Kinship foster care: Policy, practice, and research.* New York: Oxford University Press.

Kulp, J. (1993). *Families at risk. A guide to understanding and protecting children and care providers involved in out-of-home or adoptive care.* Minneapolis, MN: Better Endings, New Beginnings Press.

Levy, T., & Orlans, M. (1998). *Attachment, trauma, and healing.* Washington, DC: Child Welfare League of America Press.

Warsh, R., Pine, B., & Maluccio, A. (1996). *Reconnnecting families: A guide to strengthening family reunification services.* Washington, DC: Child Welfare League of America Press.

INTERNET SITES: FOSTER CARE

Children's Bureau, Administration for Children and Families, Department of Health and Human Services, Adoption and Foster Care Analysis and Reporting System (AFCARS). This government site provides data on foster care. www.acf.dhhs.gov/programs/cb/stats/afcars

Child Welfare League of America. This organization has a general child welfare site, with specific pages related to developments in foster care and lists of topically related titles by Child Welfare League of America Press. www.cwla.org

Children's Defense Fund, Washington, DC. This site provides information on child care, current news as it relates to children, the black community, publications, and other related links. It also gives data on population and family characteristics, economic security, and federal program participation. www.childrensdefense.org/states/data.html

National Foster Parent Association. Information on becoming a foster parent is available at this site. This site explains the purpose of the National Foster Parent Association and provides membership information. It offers a comprehensive site called KidSource, which addresses information on children, newborn through adolescence, as it relates to fostering. www.kidsource.com/nfpa/index.html

National Resource Center for Permanency Planning. Provides information services, training, and technical assistance to ensure that children have safe families to grow up in. This site focuses on the following issues: Permanency planning, kinship foster care, concurrent planning, family group decision making, and HIV/AIDS. http://www.hunter.cuny.edu/socwork

REFERENCES

Ainsworth, M. D. (1962). The effects of maternal deprivation: A review of findings and controversy in the context of research strategy. In *Deprivation of maternal care: A reassessment of its effects.* Geneva: World Health Organization, Public Health Papers no. 14.

Allen, M., Bonner, K., & Greenan, L. (1988). Federal legislative support for independent living. *Child Welfare, 67*(6), 515–527.

Allen, M., Lakin D., McFadden, E. J., & Wasserman, K. (1992). *Family continuity: Practice competencies.* Ypsilanti, MI: National Foster Care Resource Center.

Anderson, S. (1988). *Foster home retention survey: Findings from foster parents in 10 Bay area counties.* San Francisco, CA: Community Task Force on Homes for Children.

Adoption and Foster Care Analysis and Reporting System (AFCARS) U.S. Department of Health and Human Services, Administration for Children and Families, Children's Bureau. Washington, DC.

Bank, S., & Kahn, M. (1982). *The sibling bond.* New York: Basic Books.

Barth, R. (1986). Emancipation services for adolescents in foster care. *Social Work, 31*(3), 165–171.

Barth, R. (1994). Shared family care: Child protection and family preservation. *Social Work, 39*(5), 515–534.

Bazemore, G., & Terry, W. C. (1997). Developing delinquent youths: A reintegrative model for rehabilitation and a new role for the juvenile justice system. *Child Welfare, 76*(5), 665–718.

Battistelli, E. (1996). *Making managed health care work for kids in foster care.* Washington, DC: Child Welfare League of America Press.

Battistelli, E. (1998). *The health care of children in out-of-home care.* Washington, DC: Child Welfare League of America Press.

Beatty, C. (1997). *Parents in prison: Children in crisis.* Washington, DC: Child Welfare League of America Press.

Beckerman, A. (1989). Incarcerated mothers and their children in foster care: The dilemma of visitation. *Children and Youth Service Review, 11,* 175–183.

Berrick, J., Barth, R., & Needell, B. (1993). A comparison of kinship foster homes and family foster homes. In R. P. Barth, J. D. Berrick, & N. Gilbert (Eds.), *Child welfare research review.* New York: Columbia University Press.

Berrick, J., Barth, R., & Needell, B. (1994). A comparison of kinship foster homes and foster family homes:

Implications for kinship foster care as family preservation. *Children and Youth Services Review, 16*(1–2), 33–63.

Berrick, J., Needell, B., Barth, R., & Johnson-Reid, M. (1998). *The tender years: Toward developmentally sensitive child welfare services for very young children.* New York: Oxford University Press.

Berry, M. (1988). A review of parent training programs in child welfare. *Social Service Review, 62*(2), 302–322.

Besharov, D. (1985). *The vulnerable social worker.* Silver Springs, MD: National Association of Social Workers.

Besharov, D. (1990). Crack children in foster care: Re-examining the balance between children's rights and parents rights." *Children Today,* July–August, 21–25.

Besharov, D. (Ed.). (1994). *When drug addicts have children.* Washington, DC: Child Welfare League of America/American Enterprise Institute.

Billingsley, A. (1992). *Climbing Jacob's ladder: The enduring legacy of African-American families.* New York: Simon & Schuster.

Blatt, S., Saletsky, R., Meguid, V., Church, C., O'Hara, M., Haller-Peck, S., & Anderson, J. (1997). A comprehensive, multidisciplinary approach to providing health care for children in out-of-home care. *Child Welfare, 76*(2), 331–347.

Block, N. & Leibowitz, A. (1983). *Recidivism in foster care.* New York: Child Welfare League of America.

Bloom, R. (1992). When staff members sexually abuse children in residential care. *Child Welfare, 71*(2), 131–145.

Blumenthal, K., & Weinberg, A. (1983). *Establishing parental involvement in foster care agencies.* New York: Child Welfare League of America Press.

Boehm, B. (1970). The child in foster care. In R. H. Bremner (Ed.), (1974), *Children and youth in America: A documentary history,* (Vol. 3, Pts. 5–7, 1933–1973, pp. 673–677). Cambridge, MA: Harvard University Press.

Bolton, F., Lanier, R., & Gai, D. (1981). For better or for worse? Foster parents and children in an officially reported child maltreatment population. *Children and Youth Services Review, 33,* 37–53.

Bowlby, J. (1951). *Maternal care and mental health.* New York: World Health Organization.

Bowlby, J. (1961). Separation anxiety: A critical review of the literature. *Journal of Child Psychology and Psychiatry, 1*(2), 251–269.

Bowlby, J. (1969). *Attachment and loss.* London: Hogarth Press.

Brace, C. L. (1872). *The dangerous classes of New York and twenty years' work among them.* New York: Wynkoop and Hallenbeck.

Briar, S. (1963). Clinical judgments in foster care placement. *Child Welfare, 42*(4), 161–168.

Brieland, D., & Lemmon, W. A. (1985). *Social work and the law (4th ed.).* St. Paul, MN: West Publishing Co.

Brissett-Chapman, S., & Issacs-Shockley, M. (1997). *Children in social peril: A community vision for preserving family care of African American children and youths.* Washington, DC: Child Welfare League of America Press.

Bromley, B., & Blacker, J. (1991). Parental reasons for out-of-home placement of children with severe handicaps. *Mental Retardation, 29*(5), 275–280.

Bryant, B. (1994). Panacea watch: Permanency planning. *The Review, 8*(3), 2–3.

Bryant, B., & Snodgrass, R. (1990). Therapeutic foster care past and present. In P. Meadowcroft and B. Trout (Eds.), *Troubled youth in treatment homes: A handbook of therapeutic foster care.* Washington, DC: Child Welfare League of America.

Cahn, K., & Johnson, P. (Eds.). (1993). *Children can't wait: Reducing delays in out-of-home care.* Washington, DC: Child Welfare League of America.

Canadian Foster Family Association. (1993). *Safeguarding children and foster families: Preventing abuse and false allegations through knowledge and guidelines.* Ottawa, Ontario: Author.

Cantos, A., Gries, L., & Slis, V. (1997). Behavioral correlates of parental visiting during family foster care. *Child Welfare, 76*(2), 309–329.

Carbino, R. (1991). Child abuse and neglect reports in foster care: The issue of foster families and "false" allegations. *Child and Youth Services, 15*(2), 233–247.

Cautley, P. W. (1980). *New foster parents.* New York: Human Sciences.

Chappelle, B. (1975). One agency's periodic review in foster care—the South Carolina story. *Child Welfare, 54*(7), 477–486.

Charles, G., & Matheson, J. (1990). Children in foster care: Issues of separation and attachment. *Community Alternatives, International Journal of Family Care, 2*(2), 37–49.

Chasnoff, I. (1990). Maternal drug use. In *Crack and other addictions: Old realities and new challenges for child welfare* (pp. 110–120). Washington, DC: Child Welfare League of America.

Chernoff, R., Coombs-Orme, T., Risley-Curtis, C., & Heisler, A. (1994). Assessing the health status of children entering foster care. *Pediatrics, 93,* 594–601.

Chiaro, J., Marden, G., Haase, C., & Guedes, B. (1982). *Mismatching of the foster parents and the sexually abused preschool child: Critical factors.* Paper presented at the Fourth International Congress on Child Abuse and Neglect, Paris.

Child Welfare League of America. (1982). *CWLA standards for residential centers for children.* New York: Child Welfare League of America.

Child Welfare League of America. (1988). *Standards for health care services for children in out-of-home care.* Washington, DC: Child Welfare League of America.

Child Welfare League of America. (1989). *Out-of-home care: An agenda for the nineties.* Washington, DC: Child Welfare League of America.

Child Welfare League of America. (1989). *Standards for services for abused and neglected children.* Washington, DC: Child Welfare League of America.

Child Welfare League of America. (1990). *Crack and other addictions: Old realities and new challenges for child welfare.* Washington, DC: Child Welfare League of America.

Child Welfare League of America. (1991). *Serving gay and lesbian youth: The role of child welfare agencies.* Washington, DC: Author.

Child Welfare League of America. (1994). *Kinship care: A natural bridge.* Washington, DC: Child Welfare League of America.

Child Welfare League of America. (1995). *Standards of excellence for family foster care services: Revised edition.* Washington, DC: Child Welfare League of America.

Churchill, S., Carlson, B., & Nybell, L. (Eds.). (1979). *No child is unadoptable.* Beverly Hills, CA: Sage.

Colon, F. (1978). Family ties and child placement. *Family Process, 17,* 289–312.

Cornish, J. (1992). Fostering homeless children and their parents: A unique approach to transitional housing for homeless families. *Community Alternatives, International Journal of Family Care, 4*(2), 43–59.

Crumbley, J., & Little, R. (1997). *Relatives raising children: An overrview of kinship care.* Washington, DC: Child Welfare League of America Press.

Daley, D., & Dowd, T. (1992). Characteristics of effective harm-free environments for children in out-of-home care. *Child Welfare, 71*(6), 487–495.

Delaney, R. (1991). *Fostering changes: Treating attachment-disordered foster children.* Fort Collins, CO: Walter J. Corbett Publishing.

Dodson, D. (1983). Advocating at periodic review proceedings. In M. Hardin (Ed.), *Foster children in the courts* (pp. 86–127). Boston: Butterworth Legal.

Downs, S. W. (1981). *Foster care reform in the 70s: Final report of the permanency planning dissemination project.* Portland, OR: Regional Institute for Human Services.

Dubowitz, H. (1990). *The physical and mental health and educational status of children placed with relatives: Final report.* Baltimore, MD: University of Maryland.

Durkin, R. (1982). No one will thank you: First thoughts on reporting institutional abuse. *Child and Youth Services Review, 4*(1), 109–113.

Duva, J., & Raley, G. (1988). *Transitional difficulties of out-of-home youth.* Washington, DC: Youth and America's Future/William T. Grant Foundation Commission on Work, Family and Citizenship.

Eggars, W. (1997). There's no place like home. *Policy Review,* May–June, 43–47.

Emenhiser, D., King, D. W., Joffes, S., & Penkert, K. (1998). Washington, DC: Child Welfare League of America Press.

Emlen, A. (1978). *Overcoming barriers to planning for children in foster care.* Portland, OR: Regional Research Institute for Human Services.

Fahlberg, V. (1991). *A child's journey through placement.* Indianapolis: Perspectives Press.

Fanshel, D. (1963). Commentary on "clinical judgement in foster care placement." *Child Welfare, 42,* 170.

Fanshel, D. (1975). Parental failure and consequences for children: The drug-abusing mother whose children are in foster care. *American Journal of Public Health, 65*(6), 604–612.

Fanshel, D., & Shinn, E. B. (1978). *Children in foster care: A longitudinal investigation.* New York: Columbia University School Press.

Fanshel, D. (1982). *On the road to permanency: An expanded data base for service to children in foster care.* New York: Child Welfare League of America/Columbia University School of Social Work.

Farley, B. (1993). Effective practices: Changing a system to change a child's life. In K. Cahn & P. Johnson (Eds.), *Children can't wait: Reducing delays in out-of-home care* (pp. 75–104). Washington, DC: Child Welfare League of America.

Feig, L. (1990). *Drug-exposed infants and children: Service needs and policy questions.* Washington, DC: U.S. Department of Health and Human Services.

Fein, E., Maluccio, A., Hamilton, V., & Ward, D. (1983). After foster care: Outcomes of permanency planning for children. *Child Welfare, 62*(6), 485–558.

Fein, E., & Staff, I. (1993). Goal-setting with biological families. In B. Pine, R. Warsh, & A. Maluccio, (Eds.), *Together again: Family reunification in foster care* (pp. 67–92). Washington, DC: Child Welfare League of America.

Festinger, T. B. (1983). *No one ever asked us . . . A postscript to foster care.* New York: Columbia University Press.

Festinger, T. B. (1994). *Returning to care: Discharge and reentry in foster care.* Washington, DC: Child Welfare League of America.

Fimmen, M. D., & Mietus, K. J. (1988). *An empirical analysis of the impact of joint training upon child welfare practitioners.* (DHHS Award No. 05CT1022/01). Macomb, IL: Western Illinois University.

Fine, P. (1993). *A developmental network approach to therapeutic foster care.* Washington, DC: Child Welfare League of America.

Folaron, G. (1993). Preparing children for reunification. In B. Pine, R. Krieger, & A. Maluccio (Eds.), *Together again: Family reunification in foster care* (pp. 41–154). Washington, DC: Child Welfare League of America.

Folaron, G., & Hess, P. (1993). Placement considerations for children of mixed African-American and caucasian parentage. *Child Welfare, 72*(2), 113–125.

Foster Family-Based Treatment Association. (1994). *Program standards for treatment foster care.* New York: Author.

Frank, G. (1979). Treatment needs of children in foster care. *American Journal of Orthopsychiatry,* 256–263.

Franklin, C. (1994). Have external reviews improved the quality of care for children? No. In E. Gambrill, & T. Stein (Eds.), *Controversial issues in child welfare* (pp. 141–147). Boston: Allyn & Bacon.

Freud, C. (1955). Meaning of separation for parents and children as seen in child placement. *Public Welfare, 13*(1), 13–17, 25.

Gambrill, E. D., & Stein, T. J. (1981). Decision-making and case management: Achieving continuity of care for children in out-of-home placement. In A. Maluccio, & P. Sinanoglu (Eds.), *The challenge of partnership: Working with parents of children in foster care* (pp. 109–134). Washington, DC: Child Welfare League of America Press.

Garbarino, J., DuBrow, N., Knostelny, K., & Pardo, C. (1992). *Children in danger: Coping with the consequences of community violence.* San Francisco: Jossey-Bass.

Garland, D. (1994). *Church agencies: Caring for families and children in crisis.* Washington, DC: Child Welfare League of America.

Gavazzi, S., Alford, K., & McKenry, P. (1996). Culturally specific programs for foster care youth. *Family Relations, 45,* 166–174.

Gebel, T. (1996). Kinship care and nonrelative family foster care: A comparison of caregiver attributes and attitudes. *Child Welfare, 75*(1), 5–18.

Geiser, R. (1973). *The illusion of caring.* Boston: Beacon Press.

Gershenson, C., & Kresh, E. (1986). School enrollment status of children receiving child welfare services at home or in foster care. *Child Welfare Research Note #15.* Washington, DC: Office of Human Development Services.

Gibson, D., & Noble, D. (1991). Creative permanency planning: Residential services for families. *Child Welfare, 70*(3), 371–382.

Gillespie, J., Byrne, B., & Workman, L. (1995). An intensive reunification program for children in foster care. *Child and Adolescent Social Work Journal, 12*(3), 213–228.

Gilligan, R. (1997). Beyond permanence? The importance of resilience in child placement practice and planning. *Adoption and Fostering, 21*(1), 12–20.

Goerge, R., Wulczyn, F., & Harden, A. (1996). New comparative insights into states and their foster children. *Public Welfare, 54,* 12–25.

Golden, R. (1997). *Disposable children: America's child welfare system.* Belmont, CA: Wadsworth.

Goldfarb, W. (1945). Effects of psychological deprivation in infancy and subsequent stimulation. *American Journal of Psychiatry, 102,* 18–33.

Goldstein, J., Freud, A., & Solnit, A. (1973). *Beyond the best interests of the child.* New York: Free Press.

Grigsby, K. (1994). Maintaining attachment relationships among children in foster care. *Families in Society, 75*(5), 269–276.

Groze, V., Haines-Simeon, M., & Barth, R. (1994). Barriers in permanency planning for medically fragile children: Drug affected children and HIV infected children. *Child and Adolescent Social Work Journal, 11*(1), 63–85.

Gruber, R. (1973). *Foster home care in Massachusetts.* Boston: Governor's Commission on Adoption and Foster Care.

Gruber, R. (1978). *Children in foster care: Destitute, neglected, betrayed.* New York: Human Sciences Press.

Gurdin, P., & Anderson, G. R. (1987). Quality care for ill children: AIDS-specialized foster family homes. *Child Welfare, 66*(4), 291–302.

Gwinn, M., Pappaioanou, M., & George, J. R. (1991). Prevalence of HIV infection in childbearing women in the United States. *The Journal of the American Medical Association, 265,* 1704–1708.

Hardin, M. (Ed.). (1983). *Foster children in the courts.* Boston: American Bar Association/Butterworth Legal Publishers.

Hardin, M. (1989). The judicial determination of reasonable efforts: How and why. *Protecting Children, 6*(2), 7–11.

Hardin, M., Rubin, H. T., & Baker, D. R. (1995). *A second court that works: Judicial implementation of permanency planning reforms.* Washington, DC: American Bar Association Center on Children and the Law.

Harris, D. V. (1988). Renewing our commitment to child welfare. *Social Work, 33*(6), 483–484.

Hegar, R. (1988). Sibling relationships and separations: Implications for child placement. *Social Service Review, 62*(3), 446–467.

Hegar, R. (1993). Assessing attachment, permanence, and kinship in choosing permanent homes. *Child Welfare, 72*(4), 367–378.

Hegar, R., & Scannapieco, M. (1999). *Kinship foster care: Policy, practice, and research.* New York: Oxford University Press.

Hess, P., & Folaron, G. (1991). Ambivalences: A challenge to permanency for children. *Child Welfare, 70*(4), 403–424.

Hess, P., & Proch, K. (1988). *Family visiting in out-of-home care: A guide to practice.* Washington, DC: Child Welfare League of America.

Hewitt, C. (1983). Defending a termination of parental rights case. In M. Hardin (Ed.), *Foster children in the courts* (pp. 229–264). Boston, MA: Butterworth Legal Publishers.

Hochstadt, N., & Yost, D. (Eds.). (1991). *The medically complex child: The transition to home care.* New York: Harwood Academic Publishers.

Horn, W. (1994). Implications for policy-making. In D. Besharov (Ed.), *When drug addicts have children* (pp. 165–174). Washington, DC: Child Welfare League and American Enterprise Institute.

Hudson, J., Nutter, R., & Galaway, B. (1994). Treatment foster family care: Development and current status. *Community Alternatives, 6*(2), 1–24.

Hughes, R., & Rycus, J. (1989). *Target: Competent staff: Competency based inservice training for child welfare.* Washington, DC: Child Welfare League of America.

Human Services Associates. (1998). *Finding our place: The inside story of foster care.* St. Paul, MN: Rummel Dubs & Hill.

Hutchins, H. (1997). Managing managed care for families. *Children's Voice, 7*(1), 28–29.

Hutchinson, D. (1943). *In quest of foster parents: A point of view on homefinding.* New York: Columbia University Press.

Jackson, H., & Westmoreland, G. (1992). Therapeutic issues for black children in foster care. In L. Vargas, & J. Koss-Chioino, (Eds.), *Working with culture: Psychotherapeutic interventions with ethnic minority children and adolescents* (pp. 43–62). San Francisco: Jossey Bass.

Jenkins, S., & Sauber, M. (1966). *Paths to child placement: Family situations prior to foster care.* New York: Department of Welfare and the Community Council of Greater New York.

Jenkins, S., & Norman, E. (1972). *Filial deprivation in foster care.* New York: Columbia University.

Jenkins, S., & Norman, E. (1975). *Beyond placement: Mothers view foster care.* New York: Columbia University Press.

Jenson, J. M., & Whittaker, J. (1987). Parental involvement in residential treatment: From pre-placement to aftercare. *Children and Youth Services Review, 9,* 81–100.

Johnson, P., Yoken, C., & Voss, R. (1990). *Foster care placement, the child's perspective.* Discussion paper No. 036. Chicago: University of Chicago, Chapin Hall Center.

Jones, M. (1985). *A second chance for families: Five years later.* New York: Child Welfare League of America.

Jones, M. L. (1978). Stopping foster care drift: A review of legislation and special programs. *Child Welfare, 57*(9), 571–580.

Jones, M., Magura, S., & Shyne, A. (1976). *A second chance for families.* New York: Child Welfare League of America.

Jordan, C. (1994). Have external review systems improved the quality of care for children? Yes. In E. Gambrill & T. Stein (Eds.), *Controversial issues in child welfare* (pp. 136–140). Boston: Allyn & Bacon.

Kansas chapter, National Association of social workers. (1997). Kansans talk back: Early responses to the privatization of child welfare services. http://www.naswdc.org/PRAC/Kansans.htm.

Kates, W., Johnson, R., Rader, M., & Strieder, F. (1991). Whose child is this? Assessment and treatment of children in foster care. *American Journal of Orthopsychiatry, 61*(4), 584–591.

Katz, L., & Robinson, C. (1991). Foster care drift: A risk assessment matrix. *Child Welfare, 70*(3), 347–358.

Klee, L., Soman, L., & Halfon, N. (1992 March/April). Implementing critical health services for children in foster care. *Child Welfare, 71*(2), 99–110.

Knutson, J. (1995). Psychological characteristics of maltreated children: Putative risk factors and consequences. *Annual Review of Psychology, 46,* 401–31.

Kools, S. (1997). Adolescent identity development in foster care. *Family Relations, 46,* 263–271.

Kopels, S., & Rycraft, J. (1993). The supreme court rules on reasonable efforts: A blow to child advocacy. *Child Welfare, 72*(4), 397–406.

Kufeldt, K., & Allison, J. (1990). Fostering children—Fostering families. *Community Alternatives: International Journal of Family Care, 2,* 1–18.

Kulp, J. (1993). *Families at risk. A guide to understanding and protecting children and care providers involved in out-of-home care or adoptive care.* Minneapolis, MN: Better Endings, New Beginnings Press.

Lakin, D., Whitfield, L., & Anderson, G. (1997). *Necessary components of effective foster care and adoption recruitment.* (Working paper) Southfield, MI: National Resource Center on Special Needs Adoption.

Lee, D., & Nissivoccia, D. (1989). *Walk a mile in my shoes: A book about biological parents for foster parents and social workers.* Washington, DC: Child Welfare League of America.

Leeds. S. (1992). *Medical and developmental profiles of 148 children born HIV-positive and placed in foster families.* New York: Leake and Watts Services.

Levy, T., & Orlans, M. (1998). *Attachment, trauma and healing.* Washington, DC: Child Welfare League of America Press.

Littner, N. (1975). The importance of the natural parents to the child in placement. *Child Welfare, 54*(3), 175–181.

Lowe, M. (1991). The challenge of partnership: A national foster care charter in the United Kingdom. *Child Welfare, 70*(2), 151–156.

Lowery, L. (1940). Personality distortion and early institutional care. *American Journal of Orthospychiatry, 10,* 576–785.

Maas, S., & Engler, R. E. (1959). *Children in need of parents.* New York: Columbia University.

Mallon, G. (1977). Basic premises, guiding principles and competent practices for a positive youth development approach to working with gay, lesbian and bi-sexual youths in out-of-home care. *Child Welfare, 76*(5) 591–610.

Maluccio, A. & Fein, E. (1983, May–June). Permanency planning: A redefinition. *Child Welfare, 62*(3), 195–201.

Maluccio, A., Krieger, R., & Pine, B., (Eds.). (1990). *Preparing adolescents for life after foster care: The central role of foster parents.* Washington, DC: Child Welfare League of America.

Maluccio, A., & Sinanoglu, P. (Eds.). (1981). *The challenge of partnership: Working with parents of children in foster care.* New York: Child Welfare League of America.

Marcenko, M., & Striepe, M. (1997). A look at family reunification through the eyes of mothers. *Community Alternatives: The International Journal of Family Care, 9*(1) 33–47.

Martin, F., & Palmer, T. (1997). Transitions to adulthood: A child welfare youth perspective. *Community Alternatives, the International Journal of Family Care, 9*(2), 29–58.

McCollough, C. (1997). Managed care and privatization trends in child welfare promoted by states. *The Children's Vanguard,* September, 7–8.

McFadden, E. J. (1980). *Working with natural families.* Ypsilanti, MI: Eastern Michigan University.

McFadden, E. J. (1984). Practice in foster care. In A. Hartman & J. Laird (Eds.), *Handbook of child welfare.* New York: Free Press.

McFadden, E. J. (1985). *Preventing abuse in family foster care.* Ypsilanti, MI: Eastern Michigan University.

McFadden, E. J. (1991). The inner world of children and youth in care. Paper presented at the Seventh International Foster Care Organization Converence, Jonkopping, Sweden.

McFadden, E. J. (1996). Family-centered practice with foster parent families. *Families in Society, 77*(9) 545–557.

McFadden, E. J., & Downs, S. W. (1995). Family continuity: The new paradigm in permanence planning. *Community Alternatives: The International Journal of Family Care, 7*(1), 44.

McFadden, E. J., Rice, D., Ryan, P., & Warren, B. (1989). Leaving home again: Emancipation from foster family care. In J. Hudson and B. Galaway (Eds.), *Specialist foster family care: A normalizing experience.* New York: Haworth.

McFadden, E. J., & Ryan, P. (1991). Maltreatment in family foster homes: Dynamics and dimensions. *Child and Youth Services, 15*(2), 209–231.

McIntyre A., & Keesler, T. (1986). Psychological disorders among foster children. *Journal of Clinical Child Psychology, 15*(4), 297–303.

Meadowcroft, P., & Grealish, E. M. (1990). Training and supporting treatment parents. In P. Meadowcroft & B. Trout (Eds.), *Troubled youth in treatment homes: A handbook of therapeutic foster care.* Washington, DC: Child Welfare League of America.

Mech, E. (1985). Parental visiting and child placement, *Child Welfare, 64*(1), 67–72.

Mech, E. (1988). Preparing foster adolescents for self-support: A new challenge for child welfare serrvices. *Child Welfare, 67*(6), 487–495.

Meidema, B., & Nason-Clark, N. (1977). Foster care redesign: The dilemma contemporary foster parents face. *Community alternatives, the International Journal of Family Care. 9* (2) 15–28.

Miller, F. (1982). *Protection of children in foster family care.* New York: Vera Institute of Justice.

Milner, J. (1987). An ecological perspective on duration of foster care. *Child Welfare, 66*(2), 113–123.

Murphy, S. & Helm, M. (1988). Group preparation of adolescents for family placement. In J. Trisiliotis (Ed.), *Groupwork in adoption and foster care.* London: B. T. Batsford, Ltd.

Murray, L. (1992). Critical issues in residential care for young mothers and infants: An overview of model licensing rules. *Child Welfare, 71*(2), 157–163.

Mylniec, W. (1983). Prosecuting a termination of parental rights case. In M. Hardin (Ed.), *Foster children in the courts* (pp. 193–218). Boston: American Bar Association/Butterworth Legal Publishing.

National Association of Black Social Workers. (1972). Position statement on transracial placement.

National Association of Foster Care Reviewers. (1994). Court improvement project: The citizen review role. *The Review, 8*(3), 1–2.

National Association of Foster Care Reviewers. (1998). *Safe passage to permanency: Using third-party review to improve outcomes for children in foster care.* Atlanta, GA: author.

National Association of Social Workers (1993, April). *NASW News.*

National Association of Social Workers. (1997). Foster care and adoption policy statement. *Social Work Speaks.* Washington, DC: Author.

National Black Child Development Institute. (1989). *Who will care when parents can't: A study of black children in foster care.* Washington, DC: National Black Child Development Institute.

National Commission on Family Foster Care. (1991). *A blueprint for fostering infants, children and youths in the 1990s.* Washington, DC: Child Welfare League of America Press.

National Council of Juvenile and Family Court Judges. (1992). *Protocol for making reasonable efforts to preserve families in drug-related dependency cases.* Reno, NV: National Council of Juvenile and Family Court Judges.

Nelson, K. (1992). Fostering homeless children and their parents too: The emergence of whole family care. *Child Welfare, 71*(6) 575–584.

Nelson, K., Landsman, M., & Deutelbaum, W. (1990). Three models of family-centered placement prevention services. *Child Welfare, 69*(1), 3–21.

Nowicki, S., & Duke, M. (1992). *Helping the child who doesn't fit in.* Atlanta, GA: Peachtree Publishers.

Ortega, R., Guillean, C., & Najera, L. (1996). *Latinos and child welfare/latinos y el bienestar del niño, voces de la comunidad.* Ann Arbor, MI: University of Michigan.

Oyserman, D., Benbenishty, R., & Ben-Rabi, D. (1992). Characteristics of children and their families at entry into foster care. *Child Psychiatry and Human Development, 22*(3). 199–211.

Palmer, S. (1990). Group treatment of foster children to reduce separation conflict associated with placement breakdown. *Child Welfare, 69*(3), 227–238.

Palmer, S. (1997). Training workers to include families in child placement. *Community Alternatives: The International Journal of Family Care, 9*(1), 49–70.

Pardeck, J., & Pardeck, J. (1987, May–June). Bibliotherapy for children in foster care and adoption. *Child Welfare, 66*(3), 269–278.

Pasztor, E., & Burgess, E. (1982). Finding and keeping more foster parents. *Children Today, 36,* 2–6.

Pecora, P., Whittaker, J., Maluccio, A., Barth, R., & Plotnick, R. (1992). *The child welfare challenge.* New York: Walter de Gruyter.

Penkert, K. (1998). *Marketing to managed care organizations,* Washington, DC: Child Welfare League of America Press.

Phillips, S., McMillen, C., Sparks, J., & Ueberle, M. (1997). Concrete strategies for sensitizing youth-serving agencies to the needs of gay, lesbian, and other sexual minority youths. *Child Welfare, 76*(3), 393–409.

Phillips, M., Shyne, A., Sherman, E., & Haring, B. (1971). *Factors associated with placement decisions in child welfare.* New York: Child Welfare League of America.

Pierce, L., & Hauck, V. B (1981). A model establishing a community-based foster group home. *Child Welfare, 60*(7) , 477–482.

Pike, V., Downs, S. W. Emlen, A., Downs, G., & Case, D. (1977) *Permanent planning for children in foster care* (No. OHDS 77–30124). Washington, DC: U.S. Department of Health Education and Welfare.

Pine, B., Krieger, R., Maluccio, A. (Eds.) (1993). *Together again: Family reunification in foster care.* Washington, DC: Child Welfare League of America.

Pizzigati, K. (1998). Safety and permanence: New federal law reemphasizes both. *Children's Voice, 7*(3), 12–13.

Proch, K., & Howard, J. (1986). Parental visiting of children in foster care. *Social Work, 31*(3), 178–181.

Proch, K., & Taber, M. A. (1987). Alienated adolescents in foster care. *Social Work Research and Abstracts, 23*(2), 9–13.

Public Law 105-89, (1997). The Adoption and Safe Families Act. Washington, DC: U.S. Government Printing Office.

Ratterman, D., Dodson, D., & Hardin, M. (1987). *Reasonable efforts to prevent foster care placement: A guide to implementation.* Washington, DC: American Bar Association.

Raychaba, B. (1993). *Pain, lots of pain: Family violence and abuse in the lives of young people in care.* Ottawa, ONT: National Youth in Care Network.

Raychaba, B. (1989). *We got a life sentence: Young people's response to sexual abuse.* Ottawa: National Youth in Care Network.

Reddy, L., & Pfeiffer, S. (1997). Effectivenss of treatment foster care with children and adolescents: A review of outcome studies. *Journal of American Academy of Child and Adolescent Psychiatry, 36*(5), 581–588.

Report of Select Senate Committee to visit charitable and penal institutions. (1857). (New York Senate Document No. 8). Reprinted in S. P. Breckinridge (1927). *Public welfare administration in the United States: Select documents.* Chicago: University of Chicago Press.

Rice, D., & McFadden, E. J. (1988, May–June). A forum for foster children. *Child Welfare, 67*(3), 231–243.

Ricketts, W. (1991). *Lesbians and gay men as foster parents.* Portland, ME: University of Southern Maine, National Child Welfare Resource Center.

Rindfleish, N. & Rabb, J. (1984). How much of a problem is resident mistreatment in child welfare institutions? *Child Abuse and Neglect, 8,* 33–40.

Robertson, R. (1997). Walking the talk: Organizational modeling and commitment to youth and staff development. *Child Welfare, 76*(5), 577–590.

Roman, N., & Wolfe, P. (1997). The relationship between foster care and homelessness. *Public Welfare,* Winter, 4–10.

Rose, J. A. (1962). A re-evaluation of the concept of separation for child welfare. *Child Welfare, 41*(10), 444–458.

Rutter, M. (1985). Resilience in the face of adversity: Protective factors and resistance to psychiatric disorder. *British Journal of Psychiatry, 147,* 598–611.

Ryan, P. (1987, Summer). Recruitment and retention. *Fostering Ideas, 1*–8.

Ryan, P. (1995). Personal communication.

Ryan, P., McFadden, E. J. & Warren, B. (1981). Foster families: A resource for helping parents. In A. Maluccio and P. Sinanoglu (Eds.) *The Challenge of Partnership* (pp. 189–199). New York: Child Welfare League of America.

Saddington, A. (1988). In my experience. *Who cares: The Only National Magazine for Young People in Care.* London, England: National Association of Young People in Care.

Saunders, E., Nelson, K., & Landsman, M. (1993). Racial inequality and child neglect: Findings in a metropolitan area. *Child Welfare, 72*(4) 341–354.

Schatz, M. S., Series Editor, (1991–1992). *Fostering families: A specialized training program for foster care workers, and foster parents; Fetal alcohol syndrome, crack and AIDS babies; The game board of family dynamics; Exploring attachment to primary caregivers.* Fort Collins, CO: Department of Social Work, Colorado State University.

Schneiderman, M., Connors, M., Fribourg, A., Gries, L., & Gonzales, M. (1998). Mental health services for children in out-of-home care. *Child Welfare, 77*(1), 29–40.

Shapiro, D. (1976). *Agencies and foster care.* New York: Columbia University.

Shyne, A. (1980). Who are the children? A national overview of services. *Social Work Research and Abstracts, 16*(1), 26–33.

Sisto, G. (1985). Therapeutic foster homes for teenage mothers and their babies. *Child Welfare, 64*(2), 157–163.

Slingerland, W. (1919). *Child placing in families.* New York: Russell Sage Foundation.

Staff, I., & Fein, E. (1992). Together or separate: A study of siblings in foster care. *Child Welfare, 71*(3), 257–270.

Staff, I., & Fein, E. (1995). Stability and change: Initial findings in a study of treatment foster care placements. *Children and Youth Services Review, 17*(3), 379–389.

Stahl, P. (1990). *Children on consignment: A handbook for parenting foster children and their special needs.* New York: Lexington Books.

Stanton, H. R. (1956). Mother love in foster homes. *Marriage and Family Living, 18*(4), 301–307.

Stehno, S. (1982). Differential treatment of minority children in service systems. *Social Work, 27,* 39–46.

Stehno, S. (1990). The elusive continuum of child welfare services: Implications for minority children and youth. *Child Welfare, 69,* 551–562.

Stein, T. (1976). Early intervention in foster care. *Public Welfare, 34*(2) 38–44.

Stein, T. (1991). *Child welfare and the law.* White Plains, NY: Longman.

Stein, T. (1998). *The social welfare of women and children with HIV and AIDS.* New York: Oxford University Press.

Stein, T., & Gambrill, E. (1977). Facilitating decision-making in foster care: The Alameda project. *Social Service Review, 51*(3), 502–513.

Stein, T., Gambrill, E., & Wiltse, K. (1974). Foster care: The use of contracts. *Public Welfare, 32*(4), 20–25.

Stein, T., & Rzepnicki, T. (1984). *Decision-making in child welfare services: Intake and planning.* Boston: Kluwer-Nijhoff.

Stokes, J., & Strothman, L. (1996). The use of bonding studies in child welfare permanency planning. *Child and Adolescent Social Work Journal, 13*(4), 347–367.

Stone, H. (1987). *Ready, set, go: An agency guide to independent living.* Washington, DC: Child Welfare League of America.

Stuck, E. (1992). Foreword to special practice issue on papers from the 1991 North American Out-of-Home Care Conference. *Child Welfare, 71*(6). 483–485.

Takas, M. (1993). *Kinship care and family preservation: A guide for states in legal and policy development.* Washington, DC: American Bar Association Center on Children and the Law.

Task Force on Permanency Planning for Foster Children. (1990). *Kinship care: The double-edged dilemma.* Rochester, NY: Author.

Tatara, T. (1992). Child substitute care population trends, FY 82 through FY 91—A summary. *VCIS Research Notes, 6*(Sept), 1–5

Tatara, T. (1993). *Characteristics of children in substitute and adoptive care.* Washington, DC: American Public Welfare Association, VCIS.

Taylor-Brown, S., & Garcia, A. (1995). Social workers and HIV-affected families: Is the profession prepared? *Social Work, 40*(1), 14–15.

Ten Broeck, E., & Barth, R. (1986). Learning the hard way: A pilot permanency planning program. *Child Welfare, 65,* 281–294.

Terpstra, J. (1995). Personal communication to author re orphanages.

Terpstra, J. (1997). Child welfare, from there to where. Unpublished paper.

Terpstra, J., & McFadden, E. J. (1993, Spring). Looking backward, looking forward: New directions in foster care. *Community Alternatives, 5*(1), 115–133.

Thoennes, N. (1996). *Foster care review: Reducing delay and expense in the juvenile court.* Alexandria, VA: State Justice Institute.

Thomlison, B. (1997). Risk and protective factors in child maltreatment. In M. Fraser (Ed.), *Risk and resilience in childhood.* Washington, DC: National Association of Social Workers Press.

Thornton, J. (1991). Permanency planning for children in kinship foster homes. *Child Welfare, 70*(5), 593–601.

Thurston, H. S. (1930). *The dependent child.* New York: Columbia University Press.

Tourse, P., & Gunderson, L. (1988). Adopting and fostering children with AIDS: Policies in progress. *Children Today, 17,* 15–19.

Trasler, G. (1960). *In place of parents.* London: Routledge & Kegan Paul.

Twigg, R. (1995). Coping with loss: How foster parents' children cope with foster care. *Community Alternatives: the International Journal of Family Care, 7*(1), 1–14.

U.S. Department of Health and Human Services, Inspector General. (1992) *Using relatives for foster care and state practices in using relatives for foster care.* No. OEI-06–90–02391. Washington, DC: U.S. Government Printing Office.

U.S. General Accounting Office. (1989). *Foster parents: Recruiting and preservice training practices and evaluation.* Washington, D.C.: U.S. General Accounting Office.

U.S. General Accounting Office. (1991). *Foster care: Children's experiences linked to various factors; better data needed.* HRD-91–64. Washington, DC: U.S. General Accounting Office.

U.S. General Accounting Office. (1994). *Residential care. Some high-risk youth benefit, but more study is needed.* Report to the Chairman, Subcommittee on Oversight of Govenment Management, Committee on Governmental Affairs, U.S. Senate. Washington, D.C.: U.S. General Accounting Office, Health and Human Services Division.

U.S. General Accounting Office. (1998). *Foster care: Implementation of the multiethnic placement act poses difficult challenges.* Washington, DC: U.S. General Accounting Office, Health, Education, and Human Services Division.

Usher, C. Gibbs, D., & Wildfire, J (1995). A framework for planning, implementing, and evaluating child welfare reforms. *Child Welfare, 74*(4), 859–876.

Van Pagee, R., Van Miltenberg, W., & Pasztor, E. (1991). The international transfer of foster parent selection and preparation technology: The example of the Netherlands and the United States. *Child Welfare, 70*(2), 219–227.

Walker, C., Zangrillo, P., & Smith J. (1991). *Parental drug abuse and African American children in foster care: Issues and study findings.* Washington, DC: National Black Child Development Institute.

Walsh, J., & Walsh, R. (1990). *Quality care for tough kids.* Washington, DC: Child Welfare League of America.

Walton, E., Fraser, M., Lewis, R., Pecora, P., & Walton, W. (1993). In-home family-focused reunification: An experimental study. *Child Welfare, 72*(5), 473–487.

Ward, M. (1984). Sibling ties in foster care. *Child Welfare, 63,* 321–332.

Wasson, D., & Hess, P. (1989, Spring). Foster parents as child welfare educators. *Public Welfare, 16–22.*

Weber. D. E. (1978). Neighborhood entry in group home development. *Child Welfare, 57*(10) 627–642.

Weinstein, E. A. (1960). *The self-image of the foster child.* New York: Russell Sage Foundation.

Westat, Inc. (1986). *Independent living services for youth in substitute care.* (contract no. 105–84–1814). Washington, DC: Department of Health and Human Services.

White, M., Albers, E., & Bitonti, C. (1996). Factors in length of foster care: Worker activities and parent-child visitation. *Journal of Sociology and Social Welfare, 23*(2) 75–84.

Whittaker, J. K. (1987). Group care for children. In A. Minahan (Ed.), *Encyclopedia of social work,* (18th ed., pp. 672–682). Silver Spring, MD: National Association of Social Workers.

Whitmore, J. K. (1991). Mobilizing training resources for rural foster parents, adoptive parents, and applicants in Oregon, U.S.A. *Child Welfare, 70*(2), 211–218.

Wightman, M. (1991). Criteria for placement decisions with cocaine-exposed infants. *Child Welfare, 70*(6) 653–663.

Wood, L., Herring, A. E., & Hunt, R. (1989). *On their own: The needs of youth in transition.* Elizabeth, NJ: Association for the Advancement of the Mentally Handicapped.

Wooden, K. (1976). *Weeping in the playtime of others.* New York: McGraw-Hill.

Woodley Brown, A. and Bailey-Etta, B. (1997). An out-of-home care system in crisis: Implications for African American children in the child welfare system. *Child Welfare, 76*(1), 65–83.

Yarrow, L. (1961). Maternal deprivation: Toward an empirical and and conceptual reevaluation. *Psychological Bulletin, 58*(6), 459–490.

Zambrana, R., & Dorrington, C. (1998). Economic and social vulnerability of Latino children and families by subgroup: Implications for child welfare. *Child Welfare, 77*(1), 5–27.

Zuravin, S., Benedict, M., & Somerfield, M. (1993). Child maltreatment in family foster care. *American Journal of Orthopsychiatry, 63*(4), 589–596.

Zuravin, S., & DePanfilis, D. (1997). Factors affecting foster care placement of children receiving child protective services. *Social Work Research, 21*(1), 34–42.

CHAPTER 10

Families by Adoption

In every child who is born, under no matter what circumstances, and of no matter what parents, the potentiality of the human race is born again and in him, too, once more, and each of us, our terrific responsibility towards human life.
—James Agee

Bandele. (Follow me home.)
—Swahili saying.

CHAPTER OUTLINE

CASE EXAMPLE: HELPING AN OLDER CHILD USE ADOPTION

This case shows how a social worker, using an approach emphasizing continuity of family relationships, helped a child with a history of traumatic experiences move successfully through the adoption process. She supported him as he worked through his conflicting loyalty toward his birth family and his adoptive family, and his hesitancy to trust a new relationship after experiencing earlier rejection.

Ms. Franklin, an adoption specialist, met Grant when he was 10 years old and living temporarily in a residential center, where he had gone after his adoption of one year had disrupted. Her responsibility was to help Grant, if possible, to move into a new adoptive placement.

The first task was to get to know Grant well. She learned that he had entered the child welfare system at age 7, along with his older brother, Oliver. Their mother had been unable to manage the boys, who were often truant and were causing problems in the community. She had abandoned them at the child welfare agency and later voluntarily relinquished her rights. Their father was a gambler and involved in other illegal activities; during a period of time when the boys were in his care he had exposed them to "nightlife" and had not met their basic needs. He too relinquished his sons voluntarily.

Grant was originally placed in foster care with a single, middle-aged woman who had raised her own family. After a year, she adopted Grant. Initially, things went well, but Oliver, who had not wanted to be adopted and was living elsewhere, began to exert a strong influence on Grant. He let Grant know that "this is not your real family, I'm your real family." The more the adoptive mom put pressure on Grant to distance himself from Oliver, the more Grant felt a conflict of loyalties. His behavior began to reflect the conflict he was feeling and the adoptive mother decided she could not cope. So the adoption disrupted, and Grant was placed in the residential center. He had been there for several months when Ms. Franklin met him.

After assessing Grant's needs, Ms. Franklin felt he needed a home with a strong father figure, since he had had conflicts with two mothers. The family she found consisted of Mr. and Mrs. Robinson and their three children. Grant would be one of the middle children. Because Grant was an average student, Ms. Franklin was interested that the Robinsons did not put undue pressure on the children to excel in school but did expect the children to be conscientious students. Mr. Robinson had a steady job as a laborer, and Mrs. Robinson was a practical nurse. Ms. Franklin thought that this family would provide structure and guidance, and that Grant could meet their expectations.

The mother had a strong spiritual base and was active in church. Strong family networks on both sides, whose members were supportive of the placement, welcomed Grant as a cousin and grandson.

Because of Grant's previous experiences, Ms. Franklin and the Robinsons decided that Grant would feel less pressure if the placement started as foster care, which could develop into an adoption later if both sides wanted it.

Ms. Franklin visited the home twice a month for the next year to provide support and information about resources. During that time, Grant and the Robinsons, parents and children, decided to formalize the arrangement through adoption.

This decision made the adoption very real to Grant and he began to act out his anxiety over the upcoming change in his status. He started to cut classes at school and forged signatures to cover up his truancy. No matter what the parents did to establish consequences, Grant seemed unaffected. They began to question whether Grant wanted the adoption. Oliver reappeared at this time and encouraged Grant to refuse adoption. Also, at this time, Grant learned of his birth mother's whereabouts and visited her.

Ms. Franklin knew that finalizing an adoption can be very stressful for older children as it raises concerns they have over their earlier experiences. She had to help the family and Grant work through this difficult period so they would not rush into a decision during a time of crisis.

She went back over Grant's life history with the Robinsons and discussed how the earlier losses of a family might affect his attitude. She pointed out that both the birth mother and the previous adoptive mother had reneged on a commitment, so Grant was perhaps afraid that that would happen again once the adoption was finalized. She encouraged them to help Grant explore his feelings, and Grant was able to express that he was afraid of what his brother would say about the adoption.

Ms. Franklin helped the family develop several strategies to deal with the confusion everyone was feeling. One strategy was that the adoptive father, who had been from the first an involved and available parent, became more involved with Grant. He told Grant about some incidents from his own school days and how he had tried to resolve them, and took extra time to share activities with him. Another strategy was to keep an open line with the school to avoid an escalation of the crisis by having Grant suspended or expelled. The adoptive parents worked out an arrangement with the counselor and teachers so they all could work on Grant's truancy as a team.

To deal with the influence of Oliver, Mrs. Robinson spoke with him personally and reassured him that he would not lose his brother, and that he would be welcome in her home. She also let him know that the family loved Grant, wanted to take care of him, and would not harm him. She reassured him that they were not denigrating Grant's birth family. Ms. Robinson also met Grant's birth mother and exchanged information with her. The Robinsons let her and Grant know that it was fine for them to stay in touch with each other. Grant himself was able to come to a decision that he wanted to live in the Robinson family. He seemed to understand that the new family would not replace his earlier family but could meet his current needs.

This period of uncertainty also gave the Robinsons a chance to clarify their own feelings about making Grant a permanent member of the family. After weathering this period, they came to believe even more strongly that "this is our kid."

After the adoption was finalized, Ms. Franklin gradually cut back her involvement with the family. She let them know that they were in charge and that the agency trusted them to take full responsibility for Grant's welfare. She continued to be a resource for information on services, and she assured them that she would be available to help them manage a crisis. She also worked to help Grant transfer his trust from the adoption worker to the adoptive parents. Though Grant is now grown, he still stays in touch with Ms. Franklin occasionally. He graduated from high school and is doing well.

CONTROVERSIAL ISSUES

Adoption is a social and a legal process whereby the parent-child relationship is established between persons not so related by birth. By this means a child born to one set of parents becomes, legally and socially, the child of other parents and a member of another family, and assumes the same rights and duties as those that obtain between children and their biological parents. Adoption is a lifelong process of benefits to and adjustments by all members of the adoptive triad—the adopted person, the birth parents, and adoptive parents. The complex legal framework for adoption reflects its importance to the families affected; it is the most drastic state intervention into families, as it creates new families from those not so related by blood.

A recent national survey of attitudes toward adoption has revealed that Americans are deeply ambivalent about an innovative adoption practice known as "cooperative" or "open" adoption (Lewin, 1997). In contrast to the years when contact between biological and adopting parents was discouraged, today many agencies are facilitating varying levels of personal contact or information exchanges between the two sets of parents. The persistence with which many adult adoptees have sought out information or contact with their biological family, in spite of great legal and bureaucratic barriers, has spurred change in both the legal and practice arenas to make possible more information among adoptive parents, children, and biological parents.

The survey also showed that Americans are divided about another controversial issue: whether or not unmarried teenagers should be encouraged to relinquish their children for adoption. About the same percentages believe that adoption is good for the child and the mother as believe that mothers and their infants should remain together (Lewin, 1997). This issue has taken on renewed urgency with the advent of welfare reform, which requires teen mothers to stay in school and to work in order to receive benefits. The results of this survey indicate that although most people support the concept of adoption, they have questions about the experience of children and parents who participate in this profound alteration of biological family relationships.

Adoption is a means of meeting the developmental needs of a child by legally transferring ongoing parental responsibilities for that child from birth parents to adoptive parents, recognizing that in the process we have created a new kinship network that forever links those two families together through the child who is shared by both. The kinship network may also include significant other foster families, both formal and informal, who have been a part of the child's experience. (Adoption agency director—Reitz & Watson, 1992)

Adoption has been at the center of recent federal efforts to reform the child welfare system so that children's need for continuity in family relationships is protected. A well-publicized problem has been the long waits of children in foster care during a too-extensive decision-making process on whether or not to terminate the rights of their parents and thereby free the children for adoption. Another major problem in the child welfare system has been the large backlog of children who are free for adoption and awaiting adop-

tive placement, but for whom no adoptive homes have been found. Both these groups of children are ill-served by the child welfare system, which is supposed to protect them, as they spend years of their childhood without the fundamental security of knowing that they are living with a family who will remain with them permanently. To address these problems in the child welfare system, President Clinton established "Adoption 2002" in 1996, an initiative with the goal of doubling by the year 2002 the number of children adopted or placed in other permanent homes each year (U.S. Department of Health and Human Services, 1997). To meet this goal, states will have to modify their current procedures for moving children through the foster care system and into adoption, so this goal can be reached more expeditiously. (See Adoption of Children with Special Needs.)

Another controversy that has achieved national headlines concerns the placement of children in adoptive homes of a race other than their own. In 1997 the U.S. Congress passed legislation that prohibits "states or private agencies that receive federal funds from delaying or denying adoptions on the basis of race, color, or national origin of the child, biological parent, or adoptive parent" (NASW News, 1997, p. 15). This legislation follows years of debate about what state policy should be regarding the transracial placement of children. Some groups advocating for children of color have traditionally strongly opposed transracial adoption, and consequently many states have permitted only or mainly same-race adoptions in the past three decades. Adoptive and foster parent groups and some child advocacy organizations for children, on the other hand, have vehemently supported transracial adoption as a strategy for moving children out of foster care and into permanent homes, particularly if no same race homes are available. (See Transracial Adoption.) The new legislation clarifies that race cannot be used as a factor in placement planning if it delays or prevents adoption.

HISTORICAL DEVELOPMENT

The adoption of children dates back to antiquity. References to adoption can be found in the Bible and in legal codes of the Chinese, Hindus, Babylonians, Romans, and ancient Egyptians. Its purpose has varied considerably by country and by period of time—for example, to make possible the continuance of family religious traditions, to provide an heir, to overcome difficulties in recognizing an out-of-wedlock child, or, more recently, to provide permanent homes for children in need of them.

Early Adoption Practices in the United States

The nature and social purpose of adoption as it is conceived today in many countries began to emerge in the United States during the latter part of the nineteenth century. Up to that time, inheritance had run through the history of adoptions so much more prominently than any other factor that its importance can hardly be overestimated (Witmer, Herzog, Weinstein, & Sullivan, 1963). Massachusetts in 1851 was the first to enact an adoptive statute in line with present concepts of the purpose of adoption. The Massachusetts law required a "joint petition by the adopting parents to the probate judge and the written consent of the child's parents, if living, or of his guardian or next of kin if the parents were deceased. The judge if satisfied that the adoption was 'fit and proper' was to enter the adoption decree" (Abbott, 1938, pp. 164–165). The state's new adoption statutes put adoptive status on a firmer legal ground by giving a state some control in adoptive situations before a contest arose, and they secured permanent status for the child in a new family as well as a right to an equitable share of the adoptive parent's estate.

Infant Adoptions

During the first half of the twentieth century, statutes reflected interest in secrecy, confidentiality, anonymity, and the sealing of records (Carp, 1995). Originally, these practices "were not designed to preserve anonymity between biological parents and adopters, but to shield the adoption proceedings from public scrutiny. These statutes barred all persons from inspecting the files and records on adoption except for the parties to the adoption and their attorneys" (Hollinger, 1991, p. 13). However, from the 1920s through the 1940s,

states progressively amended their statutes to deny access of the records to everyone except on "a judicial finding of 'good cause' " (Hollinger, 1991, p. 13). The identities of the birth parents were to remain secret; the original birth certificate was sealed and a new one issued at the time the adoption was finalized (Sokoloff, 1993, p. 22).

During the early decades of the twentieth century, adoption became more and more popular, especially for infertile couples wishing to adopt infants. Previously, adoption was relatively rare, due in part to concern about "bad blood" associated with waifs and foundlings. Two developments that began to change the general reluctance to adopt were the wider availability of infant formula, making adoption of newborns more feasible, and the growing view that children were more profoundly influenced by environment than by heredity (Sokoloff, 1993).

After World War I, demand for infants grew rapidly, prompting the growth of black market adoptions by unregulated "baby brokers." In response, many states amended their statutes to require social investigations and a court hearing before a judge to finalize the adoption. During the 1920s, many specialized adoption agencies were founded to offer professional adoption services. Adoption services were used almost entirely by white couples to adopt white babies; adoption for children of other races rarely occurred through formal agency auspices and was more apt to be done informally, within the extended family network.

Social workers, supported by physicians, defined an "adoptable" child as one who was nearly perfect in health and development and, as far as could be determined by extended observation and examination, one who posed minimal risk to the adopting adults. Well into the middle of the twentieth century, infants released for adoption by their biological mothers did not go immediately after birth to adoptive parents. The newborn infant was usually placed first in a foster home for a three- to six-month period of observation. During this time, infants received physical examinations and intelligence testing. Many social workers made fine distinctions from the psychological report as to the intellectual qualities that should be sought in the infant's adoptive family. Eventually it was acknowledged that a careful "matching" of intellectual abilities or physical characteristics between parents and children, even were this possible, was no guarantee of a successful adoption.

By the 1940s, agencies were faced with having many more adoptive parent applicants than children to offer, a condition that influenced them to develop procedures to restrict the number of applicants. "Matching" of socioeconomic and religious background was common. Agencies placed restrictions on the age and financial status of the applicants, even though they acknowledged that many of the applicants they rejected would make good parents (Michaels, 1947).

The mismatch between the numbers of those desirous of adopting healthy, white infants and the supply available for adoption has increased throughout the latter half of the twentieth century. The rate at which women relinquish their infants for adoption has declined dramatically. Between 1982 and 1988, 3 percent of white women relinquished their children for adoption, dropping from 19 percent in the period between 1965 and 1972. The rate of relinquishment among black women has consistently been under 2 percent for unmarried births. The rate of relinquishment among Latina unmarried women has also been consistently at or under 2 percent. (Mosher & Bachrach, 1996.) The decrease of infants available for adoption can be attributed to a number of social developments of the 1960s: increasingly available, effective contraception; the rise in the abortion rate after abortion was legalized in 1973; and the increasing acceptability of single mothers keeping their infants rather than placing them out for adoption (Dukette, 1984). Families interested in adopting infants turned to transracial adoption and now increasingly to international adoption. Also, "as advances in technology have permitted, couples have sought help through alternative means of reproduction including artificial insemination by donor, in vitro fertilization, embryo transfer, and most recently, surrogate parenting" (Sokoloff, 1993, p. 23).

Today, adoption of infants is often handled through private agencies or through "independent adoption," the term for adoption outside of agency auspices, usually by individual professionals (doctors, lawyers, and social workers). This development has raised concern that private individuals, who stand to gain financially from adoption, may not be in the best position to help a pregnant woman make a decision to relinquish her child for adoption or to assess adoptive parents.

Adoption Today: Special Needs Adoption

At the same time that adoptive parents were unable to find infants, another trend was creating a different kind of mismatch: the increasing number of children without permanent families who were thought to be "unadoptable," particularly older children, children of color, and those with medical, emotional, or other handicapping conditions. Several developments led to an increase in the number of these children available for adoption. The abuse and neglect reporting laws, implemented in the 1960s and 1970s, resulted in many more abused and neglected children entering the child welfare system. Teenage pregnancy, the drug epidemic, racism, and poverty have also contributed to their growing numbers.

By the 1990s, adoption had split into two practice arenas: adoption for children with special needs, and adoption of healthy infants. Special needs adoption has become primarily the concern of public child and family agencies and is often linked programmatically to foster care programs. Attention has turned to finding adoptive homes for these "special needs" children. (See Adoption of Children with Special Needs and Adoption of Children of Color.)

Outmoded ideas about screening adoptive applicants gave way to a collaborative approach between applicants and agencies in developing applicants' readiness for adoption of special needs children. Modern screening techniques for adoptive applicants for special needs children and other children now rely on factors such as these: (1) applicants' abilities to participate in the study process and to evaluate their own capacities to be adopting parents; (2) the fact that before most adoptive couples approach an agency, they already have thoughtfully considered their motives and other aspects of their desire to seek adoption; (3) the readiness of many adoptive applicants to accept "aspects of parenthood" once regarded as "unjustifiable risks"; (4) open acknowledgment by the agency of its hope that the applicants will be able to receive a child, rather than projection of a more guarded attitude associated with "screening out"; and (5) interviews for the purpose of helping applicants achieve satisfaction in their forthcoming adoptive parenthood, with less emphasis on information gathering per se and judging that information.

Adoption Today: The Cooperative Adoption Movement

In the 1970s and 1980s, a change of great significance entered the social agency adoptive process. Traditional practice, termed *closed* (or *confidential*) adoption began to give way to a new *open* (or *cooperative*) adoption model. The notion that confidentiality was preferable for all three members of the adoptive triad—birth parents, adoptive parents, and children—came into question through the changes that have occurred in adoption during the last half of the twentieth century. As fewer infants became available for adoption, the birth mother found more leverage in the process of relinquishment and preferences about adoptive parents. Agencies learned that mothers might be less concerned with confidentiality than with helping to select the adoptive parents and with maintaining some kind of connection with the child after the adoption. Adults who had been adopted as infants, for their part, began assertively seeking to have their sealed records opened and demanded the right to know about their biological origins.

The movement to place children with special needs in adoption changed adoption practice dramatically. If older, these children have memories of their birth parents and siblings, and their foster, adoptive, and birth parents often have met one another. Adoptive applicants of children of color and of special needs children expressed the need for a shared partnership with the agency regarding selection and matching processes, leading to a trend toward open sharing of information with the prospective adoptive applicants so they could make an informed decision.

Many adoption agencies today have revised their traditional practices toward varying degrees of "openness" in the adoptive process. These changes take the form of planned communication between the adoptive parents and the biological parents prior to finalization of the adoption. All the parents may have face-to-face

meetings before the birth of the child, at agreement for placement, or at various times after the birth of the child. At such meetings the birth mother and the adopting parents may share first names, photographs, addresses, letters, or phone numbers. The range of information that is exchanged may include ethnic and religious backgrounds, level of education, aspects of personality and interest, physical characteristics, genetic background, or other matters of common interest. These options are arrived at when birth parents and adoptive parents, with the help of an agency social worker, have agreed on the extent of "openness" in the present and future. Some agencies may be more specific about the possibility of a continuing relationship after the legal adoption, with the birth parent playing an active role in the adoptive family (McRoy, Grotevant, & Ayers-Lopez, 1994; Pannor & Baran, 1984).

The move to cooperative adoption, though supported by many, has created concern that the field is moving too quickly to abandon a traditional form of adoption that worked well for many children and families, and taking largely untested new methods of arranging adoption. The issues in this controversy are discussed in a later section of this chapter.

SOME ADOPTION FACTS AND PATTERNS

Scope of Adoption in the United States

It is estimated that 1 million children in the United States live with adopted parents, and from 2 to 4 percent of all American families include an adopted child (Stolley, 1993). According to a report of the Evan P. Donaldson Adoption Institute (1998), which drew data from a variety of sources, "In 1992, the last year for which statistics are available, 127,441 children of all races and nationalities were adopted in the United States. Of the adoptions that occurred in 1992: 42% were stepparent or relative adoptions; 15.5% were adoptions of children in foster care; 5% were adoptions of children from other countries by U.S. families; 37.5% were adoptions handled by private agencies or independent practitioners such as lawyers" (p. 1).

Adoptions of children who are U.S. citizens (domestic adoptions) can be divided into two categories: related adoptions and nonrelated adoptions. Related adoptions include adoptions by stepparents and by relatives, such as grandparents, and usually formalize a preexisting family relationship. Unrelated adoptions are those in which a nonrelative adopts the child. The adopting family may be familiar to the child—for example, as foster parents—or it may be a new family and represent a real change in family relationships for the child.

Several changes have taken place over time in the number of adoptions. In regard to adoptions of relatives, the numbers increased each year from the 1950s until 1982, but dropped precipitously from a high of 91,000 in 1982 to about 53,000 in 1986. As these are mainly stepparent adoptions, the explanation for the drop may be a reflection of a decline in the marriage rate. Other factors noted by the National Committee for Adoption (1989) include changes in state and fed-

eral support benefits, court awards of support payments by the noncustodial parent in divorce, and more effectiveness in the collection of support payments in recent years. Since 1986, the number of related adoptions has remained steady at about 53,000 (Evan P. Donaldson Institute, 1998).

The number of unrelated adoptions increased every year until 1971, when about 89,000 children were adopted by nonrelatives. It declined to about 50,000 in 1974 and has remained at a lower number ever since. The decline in unrelated adoptions is explained mainly by the decrease in infant adoptions that has occurred over this period, a finding that underscores the effect of legalization of abortion in the early 1970s and increased use of contraceptives, and the current prevailing choice among unwed mothers to keep and parent their babies. Figure 10.1 shows

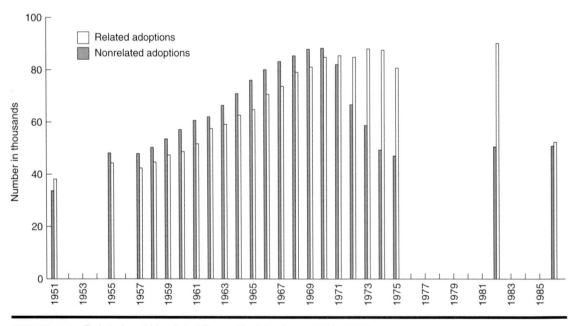

FIGURE 10.1   Related and Unrelated Domestic Adoptions, 1951–1986

Source: For 1951–1975 data, see Maza, P. (1984) *Adoption trends: 1944–1975.* Child Welfare Research Notes #9. Washington, DC: Administration for Children, Youth, and Families. For 1982 and 1986 data, see National Committee for Adoption. (1989). *1989 Adoption Factbook.* Washington, DC: Author. Table compiled by K. S. Stolley. (1993). Statistics on adoption in the United States. *The Future of Children, 3*(1), Figure 2. A publication of the Center for the Future of Children, the David and Lucile Packard Foundation.

these adoption patterns from 1951 through 1985. For difficulties in the collection of data since 1985, see Problems in Collection of National Data.

Problems in Collection of National Data

There is no aspect of child welfare practice in which, over time, accurate statistics have been in such short supply as in adoption. The National Center for Social Statistics (NCSS) collected annual national statistics on adoption from 1951 to 1975, when the NCSS was disbanded. The Department of Health and Human Services gathered limited data on adoption in two surveys of the substitute care population in the 1980s. To address the critical need for national adoption statistics, the American Public Welfare Association in 1983 established a Voluntary Cooperative Information System (VCIS), a significant undertaking but limited by the provision that data were submitted only by states that chose to cooperate and were limited to adoptions made by public agencies.

In 1993 the U.S. Department of Health and Human Services issued regulations to states requiring them to submit data on their foster care programs and also on the number of children adopted through the public child welfare agency or agencies under contract to it. States are also encouraged to report data on all other adoptions in the state. To date, preliminary data on adoptions for a six-month period in 1996 is available, with only about half the states reporting. This data collection system, called the Adoption and Foster Care Analysis and Reporting System (AFCARS), may provide reliable data on adoption in the future, depending on the extent of state compliance to reporting requirements.

Other sources of data are national surveys of families, such as the National Survey of Family Growth (NSFG), the National Survey of Families and Households (NSFH), and the National Health Interview Survey (NHIS), which ask respondents questions about adoption in their families.

Agency and Independent Placements

In the earlier years of adoption as a social service, voluntary agencies arranged the majority of agency adop-

tions. This pattern has changed. As public agencies have assumed increasing responsibility for social services to children, public welfare departments have substantially extended their adoption services, particularly for children with special needs—those with physical or mental handicaps, adjustment problems due to abuse, and older children and sibling groups. Children of color are often also included in the category of "special needs" because, like other children in this category, special efforts are required to recruit adoptive homes for them.

Placements by private individuals, termed *independent,* are of three types. *Direct placements* are those made by legal parents to someone known to them. Sometimes parents may gradually and informally relinquish more and more of their responsibilities for a child to a family friend or neighbor, and eventually adoption takes place. These placements are arranged within the state's legal framework and tend to work out satisfactorily for the child. Direct placements of this kind are legal except in three states.

Intermediary placements not for profit are arranged by a third person who is usually not seeking profit and may be well intentioned. Usually the adopting parents are unknown to the birth parents initially, though they may become acquainted if the adoption has some degree of "openness." An exchange of money may take place—for example, a standard fee for legal services or payment of the mother's medical or other living expenses during pregnancy—but the money exchanged is not disproportionate to real expenses and the placement is not motivated by a desire for profit. Such adoptions are legal in all but three states. A danger in this kind of independent placement is that the dividing line between paying legitimate expenses and paying for a child may be hard to distinguish and may facilitate "black market" adoptions (Hardin & Shalleck, 1984; U.S. Senate Committee on Children and Youth, 1975).

Intermediary placements for profit put children at great risk. These children are sold for adoption on the black market—that is, children are moved for profit, often across state lines. The intermediary in these instances usually charges what the traffic will bear.

Sometimes these operations are carried out in connection with abortion counseling services where vulnerable women or young adolescents are identified—those ambivalent about abortion or too far along in pregnancy for termination, or those who appear likely to give up the idea of abortion for an assurance of profit. In all instances of black market placement, the best interests of the child are given little or no consideration; the profit motive is primary. Such placements are illegal in all states, making it difficult to obtain accurate figures on the incidence. Reports suggest that such illegal placements are increasing because of the current shortage of white infants for adoption.

UNDERLYING PRINCIPLES OF THE AGENCY ADOPTIVE PROCESS

The social work profession relies on certain principles or generalizations in planning and extending adoption service. These are similar to guidelines for foster care but reflect greater attention to the permanency in the new parent-child relationship.

1. If a child has no long-term home and is legally free of parental ties (or could become so), society bears responsibility for action in his or her behalf; it is not a private matter. The formation of a new family unit, once an original one is broken, carries social responsibility and requires social and legal safeguards.

2. In most instances such homeless children should be provided with family life. Children of all ages need affection, security, continuity in relationships, and other kinds of care and guidance that are most feasibly and effectively provided within the family setting.

3. When adoption is contemplated, society has responsibility to give protection and service to three parties: the child, the biological parents, and the adopting parents. The child must be guarded against unnecessary loss of the biological parents and protected by the selection of new parents who give evidence that they can reasonably be expected to fulfill parental responsibilities. The child's first parents merit society's early help so they can utilize their strengths to establish and maintain a satisfactory home. When they cannot do so, they require protection from hurried decisions made under duress and sympathetic attention as individuals facing a critical life experience. Adoptive parents are entitled to counseling or guidance that may enhance the formation of a healthy parent-child relationship and an adequate assumption of parental duties.

4. Early placement of children who need adoption is desirable. Earlier placements generally are less complicated to carry out and offer a greater chance for success.

5. Adoptive parents must be selected with care; their personal qualities and the kind of home they create are of first importance to the child. The social worker's primary task is to assess and enhance the applicants' capacities for parenthood, and enable them to assess and understand their own readiness to be parents of a particular child.

6. Despite the many basic similarities between biological parenthood and adoptive parenthood, and the fundamental needs shared by all children, adopting is different from having children by birth. For example, some adopting parents have been unable to have children biologically and lack the experience of pregnancy and childbirth. All adoptive parents face the necessity of accepting the child's background and the adopted child's curiosity about her or his origins.

7. For the safe development of their identity, children must be told that they are adopted and be helped to understand the concept of adoption. This prescription is universally endorsed by social agencies. Adult adoptees need access to information about their biological parents, including the possibility of reunions in many cases.

8. Children lacking their own permanent homes constitute the primary service group in an adoption program. Although understanding help is offered to birth parents and adoptive applicants, children and their need for family must be paramount in planning and extending adoption services. Social workers are increasingly committed to children who need permanent homes but who are denied them because they have certain less "marketable" characteristics.

9. Adoption services must be linked to other community social services and offered in ways that reflect cognizance of community attitudes and resources.

THE EXPERIENCE OF ADOPTION

The Birth Parents

Birth parents interested in adoption are typically young, frightened, and confused about resolving an unplanned pregnancy. Most are unmarried, with varying levels of involvement of family, the father of the child, and friends. Agencies offering counseling to these young women, and sometimes the prospective fathers and other family members as well, follow the general social work precepts of client self-determination and nonjudgmental attitudes. The decision on whether to place a child for adoption is fateful for the birth parents, and they need an environment in which they can make a voluntary and informed choice.

Agency services to help birth parents plan for the child should be comprehensive. They should be available to everyone in the community, regardless of whether the parent is interested in adoption. In agencies operating from the principles presented above, the parents are informed of all options available to them in a nonjudgmental setting. They also receive information on all relevant community resources and are helped in accessing those resources. They receive a clear statement of their legal rights and responsibilities, and information on the legal process of relinquishment. Should they decide on adoption, the agency helps them through the relinquishment process, and, very importantly, offers counseling and support to them as they cope with the grief, feelings of loss, and emotional conflicts that are inevitably aroused by permanent relinquishment of parental rights (Gritter, 1997).

The transfer of parental rights of a child should not be accepted until the birth parents have considered all alternatives, are sure of their decision, and are emotionally prepared to transfer these rights. (E. Jean Emery, former director of the Child Welfare League of America Adoption Program, in Emery, 1993, p. 141)

Social workers counseling teenage, unmarried birth parents need to communicate that the final decision is the parents' and at the same time help them face the reality of their situation and reflect on what will be in the best interests of the child. Some parents, through their young age, drug use, economic situation, lack of support from family, or other reasons, are unlikely to be able to provide a minimally sufficient standard of care for the child. The reality of an infant's incessant demands for care and the level of commitment he or she requires from competent caretakers need to be presented in concrete terms. Parents may be helped to see that in their current life situation they are unable to provide for the child the kind of care that they would like him or her to receive, and that relinquishment in such circumstances is an act of responsible parenting. Parents who face possible involuntary termination of parental rights in court may be helped to relinquish voluntarily, an option that preserves their dignity and sense of control.

With changing laws regarding privacy in adoption, it is important that agencies give complete and accurate information to birth parents concerning the limits to confidentiality of the adoption as well as their options regarding future exchanges of information with the child and the adoptive parents. Agencies vary widely in their policies regarding openness, with some arranging ongoing, personal contact between all parties in the adoption and others providing nonidentifying information only as necessary; most agencies fall between the two ends of the spectrum.

There is controversy on whether openness in adoption helps or hinders birth parents resolve their grief over the loss of their child. Proponents of confidential adoption suggest that openness hinders this resolution: "The increased knowledge and contact available through open adoption may encourage birth parents to avoid experiencing the loss, to postpone or prolong the separation and grieving process. Ongoing contact may serve as a continuous reminder of the loss, or as a stimulus for the fantasy that relinquishing a child is not really a loss at all" (Byrd, 1988, p. 20).

An opposing view is taken by those believing that openness promotes the resolution of grief, pointing out that loss of a child through relinquishment is different from loss through death. In death, "one can be certain that the lost person will never be encountered in earthly form again. In adoption, a parent knows that somewhere out there the child who has been relinquished still exists" (Watson, 1988, p. 27). Watson (1988) takes the position that "any attempt to make the adoption relinquishment a clean and total break denies the possibility of further contact and restricts the grief process from following its natural sequence. Openness, on the other hand, accepts the possibility of ongoing or subsequent contact and allows the relinquishing parent to face the real loss, the loss of the role of nurturing parent" (p. 27).

McRoy, Grotevant, and Ayers-Lopez (1994) interviewed 720 individuals, including 169 birth mothers, between 1987 and 1992 to ascertain their experiences with adoption. Those interviewed represented the full spectrum of adoption openness, including confidential adoptions, mediated adoptions, and adoptions with ongoing contact between birth mothers and children. The researchers found that mothers who were in adoptions in which information was shared with the adoptive parents generally felt positive about the experience. One mother stated: "Once she [the child] gets older, she won't think I just totally abandoned her, I didn't just give her up. She's gonna know I just did what I thought was best. . . . I didn't back out. . . . I'm just glad we keep in touch. It will help me I guess later, because I know she's gonna one day look me up" (p. 9). Some mothers expressed concern about ongoing contact with the child. For example, one mother with ongoing, mediated contact said: "I'm not sure how it will affect my other children. I haven't told them about Kerry. I'm not ready for them to know that I had a child as a teenager. I may have to stop seeing my birthchild when she gets old enough to ask to see my other children" (p. 9).

Whatever its policy on openness, the adoption agency has an obligation to remain available for grief counseling to parents whenever requested to do so, including after the adoption is finalized. A continuum of agency services may provide intermediary aids such as exchange of updated information with the adoptive family, open-ended support group meetings, individual or family problem-solving counseling, and counseling and go-between services in the event that contact of birth parent and child comes about through a "search" (Spencer, 1987; Roles, 1989).

The Child

Agencies have an obligation to arrange adoptions for children that are in their best interest. "The goal is to place children in families that will meet their needs" (Emery, 1993, p. 142). To this end, agencies undertake assessments of the child to ascertain her or his needs and attempt to find adoptive parents who are likely to meet those needs. They work to arrange adoptions as quickly as possible so that children are not left in the limbo of being without any family. Using strategies appropriate to the child's age, agencies also prepare children for adoption and support them through the placement process and afterward.

The adoption worker undertakes a sensitive assessment of the child's readiness for adoption. Most children will benefit from adoption with well-prepared, appropriate adoptive parents. However, older children may experience loyalty conflicts or fantasies about the future ability of the birth parent to care for them, which may hinder their ability to form new family relationships. Other children have been so severely traumatized by earlier experiences of harmful or inadequate parenting that they are not able to make an emotional attachment to a family. Information on the child's physical, social, cognitive, and emotional functioning, academic progress and school adjustment, and the kind of emotional traumas that she or he has experienced are important for assessment (McNamara, 1994; Edelstein, 1995). In making a thorough assessment of the child's readiness to use adoption, workers collect information from a variety of sources. Reports from teachers, previous foster parents, birth parents, and others who have known the child are very helpful. The child's view of these experiences must also be considered (Brown, 1989).

Preparation for adoption involves supporting children as they experience the grief of permanently leaving their birth family, a process that can be wrenching to all parties, including the social worker. For example, one worker recalled two preschool-age brothers who clung together and sobbed over a picture of their mother, trying to stroke her long hair in the photograph. Much skill is required to create an atmosphere in which grieving is safe and acceptable without forcing a "grief agenda" on children who are not yet prepared to acknowledge their feelings.

Life books have become a popular way to help older children make the transition to adoption. They consist of materials that help the child understand the narrative sequence of his or her life, such as photographs, school records, birth certificates, letters, and other memorabilia. Foster parents, birth parents, and workers can contribute valuable items to life books. Worksheets are available to help older children organize and make sense of their experiences of separation, loss, and attachment through a journey that may have included placements with foster families as well as birth parents and relatives (Schroen, n.d.).

In the case example at the beginning of this chapter, the social worker, Ms. Franklin, helped Grant to prepare for adoption in several ways. She collected extensive information about his past, including his birth family, the circumstances of his relinquishment, and his previous, failed adoptive placement. Analysis of the information led her to an assessment that Grant needed a home with a father, as he had experienced rejection from two mothers, and that he needed adults with realistic expectations for school achievement. Then she set out to find an adoptive family who would meet these criteria.

Once Grant was placed, she helped him and the adoptive family address Grant's loyalty conflicts by introducing the possibility that, to some extent, the birth family could be included in his new life as an adopted son, and by helping him see that the adoptive family "would not replace the birth family" but could provide him with the home and nurturing he needed now. She also helped the adoptive family to see that Grant's acting out was not a rejection of them or of the adoption, but was a reaction to the earlier family breakups. Together they were able to devise a strategy that helped Grant control his behavior and deescalated the situation so that the adoption process could move forward.

The Adoptive Family

In contrast to earlier years, the process of selecting adoptive parents has become more open, engaging the applicants themselves much more in the process. In the past, the focus was on "screening" adoptive applicants through an investigative procedure. The screening inevitably led to comparing the adoptive applicants to "ideal" homes, a process that often involved the worker's own unexamined biases and assumptions about family life. Hartman (1979) observed that "perhaps no area of adoption practice has been more obviously an expression of the value positions of the time than the assessment process or 'the home study' " (p. 17).

With today's new thrust to find adoptive homes for older children in foster care, social workers have been compelled to reassess and modify their previous pattern of perceptions and evaluation of applicants for adoption. A less rigid set of requirements exists, partly because of the difficulties in finding enough homes for children with special needs, clearly a market factor, but also because social workers came to recognize and value particular characteristics (previously considered marginal for purposes of adoption) that enable selected adults to succeed in providing safe and caring family experiences for children with special needs.

Today, agencies actively recruit adoptive parents for special needs children rather than wait for prospective families to approach the agency. Families interested in adoption are treated from the start as potential partners with the agency in the work of caring for children. Lakin (1992) describes the change in perception: "Agencies began to see adoptive parents as resources to be taught the skills necessary to meet the needs of these children, rather than to be ruled out if they did not meet certain age, income, housing, or other arbitrary criteria established to handle the supply and demand issues faced when couples approached the agency for healthy European American infants" (p. 4). When foster parents seek to adopt children in their care, considerable weight is given to the extent to which they have come to feel and act as *psychological parents* to the child and are in turn regarded with love and trust by the child who needs a permanent home through adoption.

Prospective adoptive parents are given much more information than in the past on the child's background. The current trend is toward full disclosure. The matching of a child to the home is no longer simply a worker decision. Rather, responsibility for the decision is shared with the adoptive parents, who will ultimately have full responsibility for the child. Drenda Lakin, director on Special Needs Adoption, explains:

> The worker does not abdicate responsibility. The worker has experiences, skills and knowledge to share with the family. It is the worker's job to share the child's history completely, explaining what happened, how the child may have interpreted what happened, and how earlier experiences are likely to affect the future. For example, if a child has a history of being moved every two years, the adoptive parents might anticipate the child having a reaction of some kind after being with them for two years (known as an "anniversary reaction"). No one can predict the future, but the worker can help the prospective adoptive parents anticipate challenges. Then the parents can decide if they can handle these situations or not. The worker can help the family develop plans to handle these anticipated challenges or identify those challenges they feel they cannot handle. (Lakin, 1994)

For adoptive parents, the issue of openness in adoption is related somewhat to the age of the child. Older children usually have memories of their birth families and possibly foster families as well. If the adoptive parents were also the child's foster family, it is quite likely that they have a great deal of information about the birth parents and may have met them. The decision about how much contact there will be between the two families needs to be resolved sensitively and with the help of a skilled agency worker, in light of the individual circumstances of the case. In the case example that introduced this chapter, the worker supported the adoptive mother's decision to meet with the birth mother and brother to help her adopted child resolve his loyalty conflicts over leaving the birth family for the adoptive one.

If the child to be adopted is an infant, the adoption may be contingent on the birth mother's requests regarding ongoing contact. Adoptive parents are challenged to consider the extent to which they feel comfortable in ongoing acknowledgment of the infant's original affiliation with the birth family (Gritter, 1997). Limited research to date indicates that most adoptive parents have misgivings initially. In a

study by Siegel (1993) of 21 adoptive parents, one mother reported:

> A year or so ago, the idea of a birthmother was so threatening to me. It was just some terrible obstacle between me and getting a baby. At that point, I didn't want to deal with birthmothers at all. I wanted my own baby. And if I couldn't have that, I wanted the closest thing I could get to it. (p. 17)

However, when interviewed several months to a year later, most adoptive parents in the study reported that openness helped them "prepare for their role as parents and would help them parent more effectively." Interviewing the birth mother directly on genetic and medical issues and on information they would need later to share with their child about the birth family gave adoptive parents a feeling of control.

> Those parents who knew the birthparents' last names and addresses felt relieved that the information was not controlled by an agency or law, but could be freely handed over to the children when the parents deemed it appropriate. . . . Most stated that it was more humane and compassionate to enable the birthparents to choose the children's families. As one father put it, open adoption "empowers both sides. Both sides hold the cards. They're informed and knowledgeable." (p. 19)

Adoptive parents also noted some disadvantages, particularly in the area of controlling the amount of contact between the birth mother and the family. "Two respondents mentioned that if they were in the birth mother's hometown, they might feel some tension and anxiety over the prospect of accidentally bumping into her" (p. 19). Others were concerned about how to set limits on the frequency and type of contact without hurting the birth mother's feelings.

Social workers can help birth parents and adoptive parents in the process of arranging and carrying out an adoption involving some degree of openness. Siegel (1993) offers the following guidelines for practice:

1. The social worker can help the birth parent–adoptive parent set choose an arrangement with which they are comfortable.

2. "It may be wise for the birth parent–adoptive parent match to delineate, in writing, before placement, how often and what form of postplacement contact will occur. Because people's needs change over time, they should have an agreed-on mechanism for renegotiating their plan. For instance, they may agree that the person who wants a different arrangement will communicate that wish to the social worker, who will then contact the other party to begin formulating a new agreement" (p. 21).

3. Adoptive parents who take on the role of primary nurturer of the birth parent during pregnancy and delivery may have difficulty relinquishing that role later on. The social worker can serve as confidant and crisis manager to both sets of parents, to help them negotiate role changes.

4. Ongoing supportive, educational, and therapeutic services should be available to each member of the adoption triad throughout the life cycle.

THE LEGAL FRAMEWORK FOR ADOPTION

The legal process of adoption is regulated by a myriad of state, federal, and international laws. For the most part, adoption law, like other laws dealing with families and children, is a state rather than a federal matter. The adoption laws in the states are not uniform and have not been applied consistently in the courts. Federal legislation exists in some areas, particularly the Indian Child Welfare Act, regarding the adoption of Native American children; federal immigration and naturalization laws affecting international adoptions; and the Adoption Assistance and Child Welfare Act, providing for federal subsidies for families adopting special needs children. Other federal laws affect Social Security and taxes as they relate to adoptive families. A number of U.S. Supreme Court decisions have implications for adoption law. Depending on the legislation in a particular state, jurisdiction over adoption may be vested in juvenile courts, probate courts, or family courts within a district or circuit court system. The complexity of laws and jurisdictions has created great variation over even the most basic legal procedures such as obtaining parental consent and ensuring

confidentiality. Hollinger (1993) has identified the legal framework for several related areas of adoption: parental consent or termination of parental rights; serving the child's best interests in making an adoptive placement, financial aspects of adoption; confidentiality; and permanence of adoption.

Parental Consent

An essential condition for adoption is the consent of the biological parents or a judicial termination of parental rights so that the child is legally free for adoption. Courts will not grant adoption petitions unless the rights of the biological parents have been terminated either by consent or through involuntary termination, based on a finding that they have failed to exercise their parental responsibilities. This requirement is based on traditions of American law that give primacy to parental autonomy and privacy in rearing their children.

Parental rights are not dependent on marital status. The U.S. Supreme Court has indicated that unmarried fathers who have established a parental relationship with their child have rights that cannot be terminated without clear and convincing evidence of unfitness. (See Chapters 2 and 6.)

The need for parental consent or judicial termination of parental rights is well established in American law. However, a number of areas of uncertainty currently exist regarding parental consent, which may call into question whether a particular child is in fact "free" for adoption. For example, do the rights of the birth mother to relinquish her child and of the child to remain with adoptive parents outweigh the rights of a birth father who has been unjustly thwarted in exercising parental duties through the actions of the birth mother or adoptive parents? Once consent has been given, should it be revocable, and if so, for how long? Another area of uncertainty concerns which parents have the right to consent to or block the child's adoption when the child has been created through artificial insemination or surrogate parenting.

Frequently a state statute specifies that when children to be adopted are of a certain age, perhaps 10, 12, or 14, their consent must also be given to the adoption. Children even younger than this age may have the opportunity to express their wishes. Should the children's wishes override those of the birth parent? (Hollinger, 1993).

Serving the Child's Best Interests

There is agreement that the prospective adopters should be suitable parents and that the primary purpose of adoption is to provide children with permanent homes rather than to provide parents with adopted children. Traditionally, this has been accomplished by requiring that a social agency make the placement, except in adoptions by close relatives, or, if the adoption is done outside an agency, that the agency at least be involved to the extent of completing a home study of the adoptive family. Whether the adoption is arranged by an agency or independently, the completion of a home study and the judge's consideration of it are essential to adoption practice. The report should include a summary and evaluation of the social data relevant to the pending adoption and a written recommendation regarding the suitability of the proposed adoption.

It is of current concern that the proportion of nonrelative adoptions arranged independently of a licensed child placing agency has increased. All but five states permit birth parents to make direct private placements of children, with varying levels of supervision by a state-authorized agency over these placements. Where placements are made outside licensed adoption agencies, there is concern that the door is open for unscrupulous or misguided third parties to cooperate with or influence a mother to place her child for adoption. The third party may be a lawyer who stands to profit through a fee for legal adoption services even though he or she may technically stand free of the charge of procuring an adoption for profit. Physicians, nurses, clergy, or other persons in contact with unwed mothers may also participate in placements arranged independently of child welfare agencies (Hollinger, 1993).

Financial Aspects of Adoption

Adoptions are not supposed to involve profit. Laws prohibiting "baby selling" were passed earlier in this century to curtail trafficking in children or soliciting birth mothers to influence their decision to relinquish. These laws are considered essential safeguards to protect birth parents and children in the adoptive process.

Although the principle of "gratuitous transfer" is clear, financial arrangements are inevitably involved in many adoptions. In infant adoptions, birth mothers often receive financial help for living expenses and medical costs. Social agencies and private practitioners may charge legal and service fees to prospective adoptive parents as long as they are in amounts reflecting reasonable compensation for professional services. In these situations, it is important that the prospective adoptive parents accept the risk that the birth mother, though originally planning to consent to adoption, may change her mind and decide not to consent. They must pay expenses as originally agreed on, such as the birth mother's expenses and professional fees, whether or not the birth parent eventually consents to the adoption. Adoptions arranged by private agencies or by third parties (independent adoptions) may range in cost from a few hundred dollars to $15,000 or more (Evan P. Donaldson Institute, 1998). Adoptions arranged by public agencies are usually without cost to the adoptive parent, except possibly for attorney fees to finalize the adoption.

In special needs adoption, adoptive parents are frequently the recipients of payment, through state subsidies and medical insurance, to help them with the costs of caring for children who may have emotional or physical handicaps or be members of a sibling group (Hollinger, 1993). Many adoption advocates believe that the practice of charging fees should be abolished entirely for families adopting children with special needs, in order to reduce barriers to timely permanency planning for these children.

Confidentiality

Legally, the adoptive parents replace completely the birth parents regarding all aspects of the parent-child relationship. This differentiates adoption from foster care and guardianship, which are intended to be temporary; in these latter situations, the birth parents retain the right to petition the court for the return of the child to them. If the court's decision is to approve the adoption, entry of its decree should endow the child and the adopting parents with all the legal rights and obligations that exist between a child and his or her birth parents. (Citizenship is not transferred to the child, however. This factor requires special attention in intercountry adoptions.) Adoptive parents have all the same rights to family privacy and freedom from state interference that biologically created families have. Traditionally, this principle of totally and irrevocably transferring parental rights and responsibilities from birth to adoptive parents has been reflected in the practices of maintaining a rigid boundary between the birth family and the adoptive family, such as sealing adoption records and issuing new birth certificates following the issuance of adoption decrees. These practices have limited the amount of information that is passed between the two families.

With current recognition that children in the adoptive triad remain linked in fundamental ways to both birth and adoptive families, traditional practices in these areas are changing. Since the 1970s, most states have required that agencies share with adoptive parents all nonidentifying information that is "reasonably available" to them about the child they are adopting. The statutes in these states also provide for the release of nonidentifying information to adoptees who request it after they reach adulthood. Some courts have held that agencies may be liable "for intentionally withholding or negligently misrepresenting information about a child's physical or mental condition" (Hollinger, 1993, p. 50). Confusion still exists, however, about what kinds of information agencies or other intermediaries are required to collect on the child. For example, most child welfare agencies and lawyers are not qualified to gather extensive genetic histories.

Regarding confidentiality of adoption records, there is general agreement that the records should be kept separate and withheld from public inspection, and that persons and agencies having a legitimate interest in the case should be able to have access to them. However, there is little agreement on how much access they should have or under what circumstances. Hollinger (1993) identifies two aspects of confidentiality now coming into question: the legal status of "open adop-

tion" agreements whereby adoptive parents permit the birth parents to maintain contact with the child after the adoption is finalized; and the circumstances under which members of the adoption triad may have access to identifying information about one another.

In open adoption, the adoptive parents may agree to ongoing contact with the birth parents. According to Hollinger (1993), some courts have upheld the right of adoptive parents to breach these agreements while others have enforced the agreements, over the objections of adoptive parents. At this time, the legal standing of such agreements is open to question.

As indicated above, nonidentifying information is generally available to adoptive parents and adult adoptees. However, identifying information is usually not available, except for "good cause" or in situations where the birth parents and the child have mutually consented to share it. Most adoptions of current adult adoptees took place under laws guaranteeing anonymity of all parties. Recognizing that over time anonymity may be less desirable to both adult adoptees and birth parents, states are changing their statutes regarding circumstances under which interested parties may have identifying information on one another. The Evan P. Donaldson Institute (1998), using information from Hollinger (1998), offers the following survey of state statutes regarding confidentiality:

> *Only three states, Kansas, Alaska, and Tennessee, allow the adult adoptee to have the original birth certificate on request. In all other states, some form of mutual consent between the birth parents and the adult adoptee is required. Oklahoma allows access to birth certificates for individuals whose adoptions were completed after November 1, 1997. Washington allows access to birth certificates for individuals whose adoptions were completed after October 1, 1993.*
>
> *As of February 1998, mutual consent registries were in place in at least twenty-four states. Mutual consent registries permit parties to an adoption to register their willingness to meet at some point in the future, but they allow the release of identifying information only when a birth parent and an adult adoptee both file formal consents to the disclosure of their identities.*
>
> *As of February 1998, "search and consent" statutes were in place in at least twenty-four states. These statutes provide that when a birth parent, upon being*

contacted by an individual or agency acting as a "confidential intermediary", consents to the disclosure of his or her identity to the adoptee, the disclosure may then be authorized by a court.

As of February 1998, several states allow access to adoption information only for "good cause" shown to a court: New Jersey, Nevada, Iowa, and North Carolina in addition to the District of Columbia.

States vary in how they obtain mutual consent. Seventeen states have a process involving "confidential intermediaries," though they vary in the specific arrangements the intermediaries are authorized to make. For example, if waivers of confidentiality are on record from both the adult adoptee and the birth parent, a state-appointed intermediary may undertake to arrange a reunion. If the adult adoptee requests it, the intermediary may try to locate the birth parents, even if there is no waiver of confidentiality on file, to learn whether they wish a reunion. Some states allow members of the birth family to initiate a reunion request; in other states, only an adult adoptee may do so. The intermediary approach is intended to facilitate reunions when both parties wish them, without violating the privacy of those who wish to retain anonymity. The approach is criticized both by those who believe that it can become intrusive and confrontational, and by those who believe that it maintains the state as an interfering presence in a relationship between persons who have the alleged right to contact one another directly (Hollinger, 1993).

Permanence of Adoption

States require a period of time for the child to live within the proposed adoptive home under the guidance of a social welfare agency before the adoption is finalized. In some states the required period is six months; in others, twelve. Waiver provisions give flexibility so that the court can shorten the time if doing so is in the best interests of the child. Once the adoption is finalized, it is "for keeps" and cannot be abrogated because the birth parents wish to revoke their consent or because the adoptive parents decide that they do not want the child. Adoptive parents may lose their adopted children in exactly the same ways that pertain to biologi-

cal parents: They may relinquish their rights to the child, and the state may remove the child from the home if it is found that the parents have abused or neglected the child. With the increase of adoption of children with special needs, more adoptions are dissolving, causing some persons to advocate the creation of humane ways to legally undo these placements so that the children can move on to more appropriate placements without feelings of failure (Hollinger, 1993).

Legal-Risk Adoptions

Children who are not legally free for adoption are sometimes placed with families committed to permanent placement as foster parents or as adoptive parents in the event of termination of biological parental rights. Legal-risk adoption differs from foster parent adoption in that the commitment to permanency takes place before placement rather than after a long-term relationship with the child has been formed. In that respect, legal-risk adoption varies from traditional adoption in that adoption is not the sole goal of the prospective parents, nor is there any certainty that the child will become legally available for adoption. Such families are assessed as "potential adoptive families, as well as for their ability to tolerate short-term care and separation from the child under agency supervision, if adoption does not eventuate" (Proch, 1981, p. 623). This form of adoption provides another alternative in planning permanency for neglected and abused children who are at risk of multiple foster placements. (See Concurrent Planning.)

POSTADOPTION SERVICES

The purpose and rationale for postlegal adoption services has been expressed thus:

Adoption is both a legal event that occurs at a particular moment and a lifelong condition with continuing impact on the lives of the individuals involved. Postlegal adoption services are those available to all the participants in the adoption process (adopted person, adoptive parents, and birth parents) beyond the point when an adoption is legally finalized. (North American Council, 1984, p. 3)

Postadoptive services have been developed in recognition that "normally, adoptive families from time to time will need help with some of the complex changes in their lives. Such difficulties do not represent failure or a serious problem—only an understandable part of a special life situation" (Hartman, 1984, p. 2). Prior to the development of openness in adoption, contact between adoptive parents and the placing agency was time limited, ending when the legal adoption decree was issued. Although termed "postplacement supervision," a worker's visits to the home, particularly in infant adoptions, were often superficial, with the worker hesitant to appear interfering and the adoptive parents unable to mention any problems through fear of losing the child. The agency, having done an extensive homestudy prior to placement, did not expect problems and tended to assume that all would go well. Families who needed services after adoption were encouraged to use community services available to any family.

Yet families maintained that "the professionals from whom they sought service did not understand the unique needs of their family or their child." Families adopting children with special needs, particularly those who are older and have had painful life experiences, recognized that it takes more than "love and permanency" to heal their traumatized children (Lakin, 1992, p. 7). The movement toward openness in adoption prompted the realization that at different times in the developmental cycle of family life, issues related to adoption will emerge.

The Jenkins Siblings: An Example of Postadoption Services

The following case illustrates several of the central issues in adoption that characterize the development of adoptive families and also the postadoption services offered by the agency social worker.

Ms. Phillips first met the three Jenkins brothers when Antoine was 4, Samuel was 3, and Kareem was 2. They had been in the child welfare system for two years, having been picked up by the police because of the mother's absence from the home. The mother was a teenager who had a history of neglect. All the boys

had different fathers. The mother continued to have five more children, all of whom where removed from her care shortly after birth because of her inability to provide a minimally acceptable level of care.

While in the child welfare system, both Antoine and Samuel had had six or more separate foster placements; Kareem had been in one foster home. The foster mother who eventually took all three boys was in her early sixties, and the agency decided that she was too old to adopt them. They were placed in an adoptive home but were removed soon after when the agency discovered that the parents were using extreme physical discipline and not meeting the children's medical needs. Antoine had scoliosis. Samuel was a failure-to-thrive baby and was discovered to have a learning disability. Among them, they had a number of other developmental and medical problems as well.

Ms. Phillips found an adoptive parent for the boys—a single, middle-aged mother, Ms. Martin, who had two teenage sons at home and two older sons who had left the home. The sons were all helpful with the young adoptive brothers; they were gentle with them and took the responsibility of socializing them to the family.

Unfortunately, the placement got off to a bad start when on the first day, the boys destroyed the bedroom that the adoptive mother had prepared for them.

Ms. Phillips worked closely with the adoptive mother. She helped her plan activities and devise strategies to manage the boys' behavior and set limits for them. Ms. Martin was a grandmother but she had to learn how to be a mother of young children all over again. Samuel required a great deal of medical attention. All the children needed help in school. Samuel needed special education and Kareem needed to be admitted to an early intervention program. The adoptive mother needed coaching on how to deal with the medical and educational systems, since the problems of these children were very different from the ones she had experienced with her own children. Even with Ms. Phillips's help, she had difficulty organizing a medical schedule and maintaining collaboration with the schools.

Ms. Phillips began to wonder if this home was an appropriate setting for these children. Because the placement was still officially a foster home, she started looking for a new adoptive family. However, very few families expressed interest in three sibling boys, all of whom had special medical and educational needs.

Finally, another family did come forward who seemed appropriate.

The advent of this new family seemed to mobilize Ms. Martin and helped her to clarify that she really wanted these children. Ms. Phillips had to make an agonizing choice: whether to place the children with the new family, who had a proven track record as capable adoptive parents, or whether to continue to work to strengthen the current placement and avoid another separation for the boys. To help her decide, Ms. Phillips worked with Ms. Martin to explore in detail her strengths and to understand where the gaps were. After this process, both Ms. Phillips and Ms. Martin came to the decision that she would be able to meet the needs of the children.

At about this time, Antoine had surgery for scoliosis. Ms. Martin, his adoptive mother, rose to the occasion and became aware of how much she had bonded with this boy. She organized her schedule and the family's so they could help Antoine. Ms. Phillips felt that she showed commitment to the children and decided to proceed with the adoption.

Ms. Phillips also worked to help the boys recover their past. They had been in so many foster homes that much of their history was missing. The adoptive mother developed a relationship with the foster mother who had had all three of them; the foster mother became a "grandma" for the boys. This foster mother was now caring for the younger siblings of the boys, born after they had gone into care. She had pictures to share of the boys when they were very young and knew more about the birth family than was contained in the agency's records. She arranged for the boys to visit their siblings who were in her care.

Antoine, Samuel, and Kareem are now 9, 8, and 7 and are doing well. The adoptive mother calls occasionally to let Ms. Phillips know how they are faring.

Dynamics in Adoptive Family Development

Child welfare practice was long in acknowledging that most adoptive families are different from other families in at least three ways: adoptive parents go through a unique process, often without the kinds of supports and sanctions that accrue to biological parents; adopted children come into the family by means of a unique set of circumstances; and family dynamics are affected dif-

ferently by adoption than by childbirth (Bourguignon & Watson, 1987; Silin, 1996).

These differences between adoptive and biological families are apparent when the central issues of adoption are considered. Lakin (1992) has identified the following themes that characterize the adoption experience: entitlement; unmatched expectations; separation, loss, and grief; bonding and attachment; and identity formation.

Entitlement is a process that occurs before and during the time the child enters the family. It refers to the sense of the adoptive parent and child that they have a "right" to each other. Legal entitlement is granted with a court decree, but emotional entitlement is more complex and may take more time to appear. Until it develops, adoptive parents and children may hold back on their commitment to each other. In the Jenkins case, the entitlement issues are illustrated dramatically. The adoptive mother, who had been struggling with three special needs brothers, found when Antoine had surgery that she had become more attached to Antoine than she had realized. She told the social worker that she became aware that "This is my kid" when she saw him in the hospital. Recognizing that she had "claimed" the boys, she mobilized resources effectively to help him recover.

When adoptive children enter the family, both the parents and the children may be confronted with a discrepancy between the *expectations* they had and the reality of the situation. This can be especially troublesome for adoptive parents at the beginning of the placement. In the Jenkins case, the adoptive mother experienced disillusionment when the carefully prepared bedroom was trashed by the boys during their first day in the home. The process of giving up one's expectations and accepting other, alternative sources of satisfaction may take a long time. Another source of stress can occur around adapting to changed *patterns of everyday life*. Birth children may feel resentful about having to develop new family roles and modifying their family routines. Older adoptive children may resist adapting to the family's life patterns.

Feelings of *loss* are pervasive in adoption. Adopted children wonder, "Why did my parent give me up?" Infertile adoptive parents may need to grieve the loss of children they will never have. Before children and parents can make a commitment to the adoptive relationship, they must have resolved, to some extent, these earlier losses (Gritter, 1997).

Attachment refers to an emotional connectedness between two people. Infants and children who are denied the opportunity to form attachments with consistent, nurturing, parental figures may not learn how to make meaningful attachments. Symptoms commonly seen in children with attachment problems are in the areas of conscience development, impulse control, self-esteem, interpersonal interactions, expression and recognition of their own and others' feelings, and a variety of developmental difficulties (Fahlberg, 1991; Lakin, 1992). The Jenkins siblings had experienced many losses in their young lives. Learning more about their past and having contact with their siblings who were in another home helped them resolve some of their feelings about having been given up by their mother and by other families, so that they could invest emotionally in their new adoptive family.

Forming one's sense of self as a unique and valuable individual with boundaries is an essential developmental task of adolescence and beyond. *Identity* is rooted in the family history, nurtured through the natural processes of development, and shaped by individual and family dynamics (Bourguignon & Watson, 1987; Lakin, 1992). Adopted children may feel that something is wrong with them or their birth parents would not have given them up, which lowers their self-esteem and affects their evolving sense of personal identity. An important step for some adopted children is to learn about their birth family and to incorporate that heritage into their sense of self. Incorporating the adoption into one's sense of self is a process that may go on well into young adulthood. Adolescent and young adult adoptees may benefit from support groups to process their evolving sense of personal identity (Grotevant, 1997).

When I die, I want my birth name on my tombstone, underneath the adoptive name I lived with all my life. I never met my birth parents; I never chose to "search." But I feel I have this phantom self, with my birth name, who has gone through life with me. I wonder what his *life might have been if he had stayed with his birth parents.* (A 60-year-old adult adoptee)

Survival Behavior

When adoptive families need help, it is essential to arrive at a good understanding of the nature of the problem, based on a thorough assessment of the situation. In addition to gathering information on the child and each adoptive parent, the social worker needs to clarify her or his own expectations about families. Families may have characteristics that are highly functional for adopting older children who have behavioral difficulties, but these same characteristics may not match the worker's unexamined expectations about "ideal" families. When working cross-culturally, social workers must be particularly aware of their own culture and how it may influence their interpretation of the family dynamics (Bourguignon & Watson, 1987; Lakin, 1992).

With older children, the problem may revolve around the child's "survival behaviors," which are rooted in earlier, traumatic experiences. For some children, the main issue is that they have "unfinished business" with their earlier family; they may experience loyalty conflicts or unresolved grief. For others, the problem may be difficulty in forming attachments to caring adults. A goal of the intervention in these situations is to increase the parents' competence and reduce anxiety by helping them understand the child's behavior in terms of the child's past experiences, and to show them strategies for how to anticipate the child's reactions to particular situations and then prepare appropriate responses. For the child, the goals are to help him or her feel secure and to establish trust with the adoptive family, and then help the child mourn past losses so that he or she can make a commitment to the present (Lakin, 1992).

It is not uncommon for postadoption services to occur during a crisis, when the family is not sure that it will actually stay together. Adoptive parents may be angry at the child, at themselves for perceived failure, and at the agency, which the family may see as not having fully disclosed information about the child. Child welfare workers may blame themselves for having made the placement. Experience has shown that successful crisis intervention with adoptive families should be quick and responsive, with clear lines of communication between family and worker, so that the family can reach help whenever it is needed. At the same time that the help should be timely and supportive, it is important that the worker not "overreact" and move the child precipitously.

Clearly recognized in today's practice is that adoption is a family-building process. The development of postlegal adoption services simply represents "an orderly extension of the quest to make adoption a positive experience for all those involved, an attempt to meet the needs of the individuals concerned at whatever point in their lives these may occur" (North American Council, 1984, p. 2).

Adoption Disruption

Although the large majority of adoptive placements prove to be successful for both children and adopted parents, in some instances and for various reasons the inability to establish stable family relationships may result in disruption of the placement. Adoption disruption refers to placements that end with the return of the child to the agency before legal finalization has occurred. The extent of current adoption disruption is of concern in view of the inherent risk that accompanies the present-day commitment to finding adoptive homes for older and special needs children. Rosenthal (1993) estimates that from 10 to 15 percent of the adoptions of older children disrupt, in comparison with 1 or 2 percent for infants. A study of children adopted as adolescents showed a disruption rate of about 24 percent, over twice as high as that of other special needs children (Berry & Barth, 1990).

From his own research and a review of other major studies, Rosenthal (1993) has identified a number of factors that affect the success of special needs adoption placements. The older the child, particularly past age 7 or 8, the more likely it is that the adoption will disrupt. Some studies show that boys are slightly more susceptible to having disrupted adoptions than girls. Developmental and serious medical disabilities do not appear to be major factors in disruption. However,

emotional disabilities are strong predictors, especially aggressive, acting-out behavior. Other child behaviors that place a child at risk for disruption are sexual acting out (a characteristic of children who have been sexually abused), stealing, vandalizing, threatening or attempting suicide, and wetting or soiling.

Research has also identified certain qualities in adoptive parents that may influence the success of the adoption (Rosenthal & Groze, 1992). Although the evidence is somewhat contradictory, it appears that lower socioeconomic status is associated with increased success, perhaps because the parents' expectations, particularly in regard to academic achievement, are more congruent with the child's ability to perform in school. "What would once have been barriers to adoption—low income and education, minority ethnicity, single-parent family structure—do not increase risk and . . . may be modest predictors of increased success in special needs adoption" (p. 82). Barth and Brooks (1997) report that adoptions in families with a mix of biological and adopted children tend to be less successful than those in families with only adopted children.

Various dimensions of adoptive family life can reduce or increase the risk of disruption. Families in which the adoptive parents expect and are prepared to accept behavioral and emotional problems resulting from the stress the child has already experienced and who can be flexible in family roles and rules have a better chance of succeeding than others. The degree of adequacy in family system supports and the parents' skill in adaptive problem solving in some instances can be crucial. Unpredicted events in family life can severely affect the chance of disruption—for example, marital stress, financial difficulties, or serious illness of an adoptive parent or of another family member that brings long-term demands on the adoptive family. In such instances, if the new family stability has not yet been established or is tentative, the risk of disruption is keen.

Adoptions by former foster parents are less likely to disrupt than those by new families, a finding that underscores the importance of thoroughly familiarizing the prospective adoptive parent with the child's situation. Research and the reports of adoptive parents have consistently shown that providing adequate background information on the child is an extremely important task that agencies must undertake to increase the chances that an adoption will be successful. Rosenthal (1993) quotes a parent who experienced a disrupted adoption: " 'We were told [about his problems], but we really thought we could handle this and anyway, our child would never act that way.' Such a comment emphasizes the need for realistic, detailed preparation and good background information" (p. 81).

In their work, Barth and Berry (1988) addressed some of the ways the children's and the parents' experiences in the child welfare system influenced adoptive outcomes. Long time lags between entrance into care and a referral for adoption, followed by another long lag between referral and placement, were counterproductive to successful adoption. Disrupting families were found to have sought the agency's help later than was true for stable families, leading to provision of services that were "too little too late." Adoptive parents were not always given adequate preparation for the changes to come. Children, in turn, were sometimes not allowed a valid opportunity to express their feelings about a continuing desire for reunification with their biological parents or to examine the ambivalence they felt. These omissions contributed to the failure of child and adoptive parents to develop reciprocal positive personal exchanges. Significantly, the benefits of adoption subsidies is very clear. Disruption rates are higher for unsubsidized than for subsidized children.

According to Bourguignon and Watson (1987), the reasons adoptions do not succeed are these: the adoptive parents lack the capacity to be adoptive parents to any child; the child lacks the capacity to function in any adoptive placement; the particular child and parents involved in the adoption are mismatched and the adoption cannot work out for them; or the child and parents were not ready for the adoptive experience. If the reasons for the disruption are either of the latter two (mismatch or unreadiness), it may be possible for both to move forward into another adoption. Such a decision should be made only after enough time has elapsed for resolution of the earlier failure and for a thorough assessment of the factors in the disruption.

To expect that disruptions in the adoptive placements of special needs children will not sometimes happen can unjustly leave adoption workers with a sense of failure. An adoptive disruption does not necessarily result in continuing impermanence for the child. Many of these children are placed later in other adoptive homes (Barth & Berry, 1988). Pursuing homes for children through adoption requires that agencies be ready to take risks. Despite delay in permanency for children after a disrupted adoption placement, "in the long run most of these children do get adopted. . . . Giving all children the opportunity to grow up in families they can call their own necessarily involves an element of calculated risk" (Festinger, 1986, p. 44).

Searches and Reunions

Some of the complex identity issues adopted children must resolve are now receiving more attention as adult adoptees in greater numbers have sought access to sealed court records or have returned to adoption agencies for information about their origins. In the past, agencies received inquiries from time to time, but these seemed to be only occasional happenings and little attention was given in the literature to adult adoptees' rights to information about their origins. In the past three decades, however, a national movement was initiated by adult adoptees that has gained support from many social workers, lawyers, and other professionals.

Among adult adoptees who embark on a search of their past, some want only information—for example, the personal, social, or physical characteristics of their biological parents. They may believe such information will add to an understanding of themselves and their sense of identity. Practical considerations, such as obtaining security clearance for a job or obtaining medical history, may also cause adopted persons to seek more information about themselves than they have. Some others want to locate their birth parents, meet them, and attempt to establish a relationship with them.

Initially, agencies thought that only people who had unsatisfactory experiences in adoption wanted to seek out their birth parents. However, it is now recognized that many people from successful adoptions return to agencies to initiate a search. Lakin (1992) has identified several "triggers" that may impel an adult adoptee to initiate a search; the need for medical information; the birth of a child, which, particularly for women, raises issues of genetic connection; the death or illness of an adoptive parent; and media accounts of others who have had successful reunions with birth parents and siblings. Motivations for all those searching are the need to find out why the birth parents gave them up and to bring together pieces of their identity so that they can feel more whole.

The following case vignette shows how important it was for one young woman to find the missing family from her past.

> When Melissa was three days old she was adopted by a family who offered her ample care and affection throughout her growing up years. However, questions about her birth family were always at the back of her mind. Birthdays were particularly difficult, and she tended to become moody and unresponsive each year around that time. As she became older, on her birthday she checked the personal columns of the city where she had been born, to see if there was a message from her birth mother. Finally, when she was 21, she decided to undertake a search for her birth mother. Above all she wanted to ask her the question that is on the minds of all adoptees, "Why did you give me up?"

When adult adoptees first began to return to agencies requesting information, agencies often viewed the issue as a major challenge to their practice, even though individual social workers were sympathetic to the desire of adult adoptees to search for their past. More recently, however, agency practices have been reexamined. Despite confidentiality laws and regulations (discussed in the section on the legal framework for adoption), most adult adoptees are successful in their efforts to seek out information on their past. Social workers, in addition to knowing the laws in their state regarding confidentiality, should have information about the various regional and national networks for adoption searches. They may refer adult adoptees to support groups or to individuals who conduct searches, and they may also engage actively in the search. Some agencies offer "intermediary services," contacting the birth mother to see if she wishes a reunion with her adult child who has initiated a search. The following case vignette illustrates the way an agency helped a young man initiate a search for his birth family.

Ramon was 19 and in an agency-sponsored independent living situation when he telephoned the agency that had placed him for adoption when he was three years old. His relationship with his adoptive parents became conflictual as he grew older, and he was eventually placed in a residential setting. He now was interested in learning about his birth family and particularly about two siblings, a brother and a sister, whom he had heard were a part of his original family. He wanted to know if they had also been adopted and if he could find them. The agency representative made an appointment to see him, and, after checking the records, was able to give him information about his birth family. He actually had three younger siblings, two of whom had been adopted by one family; the youngest child had remained with the mother. Ramon was overwhelmed to meet the agency worker who had actually arranged the adoption. Through an intermediary, who contacted the other siblings and the mother, Ramon was able to reconnect with his family of origin.

Bourguignon and Watson (1987; summarized in Lakin, 1992) suggest that social workers have an important supportive role in helping adult adoptees or birth parents who are seeking reunions. Those searching may need help in preparing for the myriad of emotions they face as they undertake the search process. Often effective intervention is aimed at supporting the individual through the many starts and stops, ups and downs of this process. Persons searching also often need assistance in creating realistic expectations about the type of relationship they envision once a reunion is effected. Searchers need to be aware that the person being found may have very different feelings from those of the searcher over the prospect of personal contact. A very real aspect of a successful reunion is that those involved are faced with negotiating a relationship with a stranger with whom they have a genetic tie, a bond, past issues to resolve, and current lives that are not usually congruent.

ADOPTION OF CHILDREN WITH SPECIAL NEEDS

As long as the definition of an adoptable child was focused on favorable heredity and good physical development, children with various mental or physical handicaps were viewed as unwarranted risks for successful adoption. During the latter half of the twentieth century, concern grew among leaders in adoption about children who needed permanent homes and were denied them because of instabilities within the foster care system and the limitations and restrictions of adoption services. Attention turned to searching out factors that led some children to be termed *unadoptable* and to discovering whether there were adoptive applicants who would accept these children.

Today, the term *special needs adoption* refers to children who require special efforts to be placed in adoptive homes. They may have physical, mental, or emotional disabilities, but their primary shared characteristic is that they are wards of the public child welfare system and need planning services to be placed in permanent homes. Special agency services are needed to recruit, train, and support families who undertake adoption of these children (see Survival Behavior).

Children Who Wait

From the time special needs adoption programs began in the 1960s until the early 1980s, special needs adoption programs in many states were able to keep pace with the number of foster children becoming free for adoption each year. Public agencies had formed partnerships with the developmental disabilities service systems and had begun to plan adoption for children with disabilities. However, in the mid-1980s, the public child welfare system came under increased strain because of the drug epidemic, which left thousands of children in extremely dangerous home situations. The drug problem created a new population of vulnerable infants who had suffered developmental damage prenatally as a result of their mothers' drug usage during pregnancy. Some were abandoned or mistreated by their substance-addicted parents. The HIV virus created infants who were, or soon would be, orphaned as their parents died of AIDS, or who had the virus themselves. Foster care caseloads rose steeply in most major cities in the United States, where the drug epidemic hit hardest. Planning for children who have lost their families because of drug abuse presents a host of extremely complex problems for the public child welfare system, which is challenged to the utmost to find effective responses (McKenzie, 1993).

State adoption program statistics document the increase in the numbers of children coming into the child welfare system who can never go home and for whom adoption planning is indicated. The number of children who had a permanency plan for adoption reached a low of 37,000 in 1985; it increased to 86,000 in 1993, the most recent year for which statistics are available. In 1997, the Department of Health and Human Services estimated that as many as 100,000 children currently in foster care needed adoptive families (Evan P. Donaldson Institute, 1998). The child welfare system is losing ground in its efforts to place these children in adoption. In spite of the fact that the numbers awaiting adoption continue to grow, the number of adoptive placements made for foster children awaiting adoption have remained stable at about 18,000 to 20,000 a year. In 1993, these 18,000 adoptions represented only about 4 percent of the total number of children in care that year and only about 27 percent of the children whose plan was adoption. In that year, there were 17,000 children residing in nonfinalized adoptive homes and 21,000 children were still waiting to be adopted (Tatara, 1993).

Children in need of adoption planning by public child welfare agencies share certain characteristics. Most are categorized as having one or more "special need" (e.g., age, disability, minority ethnicity, or sibling group status). Only about one-third have been in foster care for less than a year, and many have waited for an adoptive placement for two years or more. The children are of all races and cultural backgrounds; a little over 40 percent are white, and a similar percentage are African-American. Another 7 percent are Latino, and the rest are of other ethnicities. The younger the child, the more likely he or she is to be adopted from foster care. In 1990, for example almost 55 percent of all finalized adoptions were of children between birth and 5 years of age. About a third of the adoptions were of children between the ages of 6 and 12 and only 8 percent of the adoptions were of children between 13 and 18 years of age (Evan P. Donaldson Institute, 1998). Of those who do get adopted, nearly half are adopted by their former foster parents, and another 7 percent are adopted by relatives. For the rest, adoption involves adjustment to a new family (Tatara, 1993).

Foster Parent Adoption

Major system barriers to adoption of special needs children exist, which account to some extent for the great backlog of children awaiting adoptive homes. However, two barriers have been overcome in recent decades: policies prohibiting foster parents from adopting the foster children in their home, and the potential loss of foster care payments if the foster parent adopted. Before the 1960s, the idea of adoption by foster parents was little explored, even after foster parents had shown their commitment to a child and an ability to provide a reliable and caring home. However, as permanency planning efforts freed foster children for adoption, the foster parents became key candidates for the role of adoptive parents, in order to maintain continuity of family relationships. Another advantage of foster parent adoptions is that the foster parent's familiarity with the child makes adoption disruption less likely.

The possibility of foster parent adoption makes it all the more important that agencies make careful placement decisions from the time the child first comes into care. Some foster parents are not able to meet the long-term needs of the child, because of age or other factors—a situation that can cause pain to all concerned later on if the child needs to be moved to another, permanent home. Siblings placed apart initially, a practice often seen as a necessity if no home is available for a sibling group, may not be easily reunified into a single home when adoptive planning begins.

Adoption Subsidies

In earlier decades, a major barrier to the adoption of special needs children was the financial strain they placed on adoptive parents. Depending on the disability, children might require alterations to the home, special equipment, specialized educational services, and help for emotional difficulties. Medical insurance was an additional burden that could be quite expensive if the child had extensive medical problems. In 1980, Congress passed the Adoption Assistance and Child Welfare Act (PL 96-272), which for the first time provided federal funds for adoption subsidies and Medicaid insurance for special needs children. The subsidies are particularly helpful in allowing many foster placements to achieve permanent, legal status through adoption, as they make it possible for the foster parents to give up foster payments in return for adoption subsidy and Medicaid.

System Barriers to Timely Adoptions

In spite of increased foster parent adoption, children in the child welfare system still wait too long for adoption. Waits of three to seven years are not uncommon. Many children enter foster care as infants or preschoolers and reach grade school before they are referred to the adoption unit for planning. During their years in foster care, they may have experienced traumas that compounded whatever problems they had coming into care and make them even more challenging to adopt.

McKenzie's (1993) analysis of system barriers to timely adoption identified three planning phases: the reunification phase; preparation for adoption planning, including termination of parental rights; and adoption planning. Excessive delays occur in each phase, cumulatively causing children to wait excessively long periods of time for adoption. For example, a common bottleneck in the family reunification phase involves delays in court determination that the agency has made reasonable efforts to reunify the family, a necessary precondition for moving to the second phase of adoption planning.

Only after the agency and juvenile court have decided that adoption is the appropriate plan can work begin on freeing the child for adoption. This is an unnecessarily complicated process. The issue of whether adoption is the appropriate plan may be reopened, requiring a return to phase one. In some states, an adoptive family must be found before planning can continue. Other roadblocks include "inadequate legal resources for child welfare cases; crowded court dockets, continuances and nonappearance hearings without procedural documentation; judicial biases or inaction" (McKenzie, 1993, p. 68).

Once a child is legally free, adoption planning begins. The tasks of this phase include preparing the child for adoption, recruiting an adoptive family if no foster parents or relatives are available, arranging preplacement visits, and, finally, placing the child. For some children, more than one family will need to be recruited before the right match is found. In addition to the casework, there is extensive technical work to be done. Arranging adoption subsidies can be a time-consuming process. After a child moves into the adoptive home, an additional waiting period of six to twelve months occurs before the adoption is finalized. Figure 10.2 shows the stages in moving a child from foster care into an adoptive home, and the time delays of each stage.

McKenzie (1993) has summarized the factors causing a growing backlog in adoption caseloads as follows:

- Increases in numbers of children coming into foster care, especially infants and/or children of color.
- Increased emphasis on timelines and permanency procedures as a result of Public Law 96-272 and

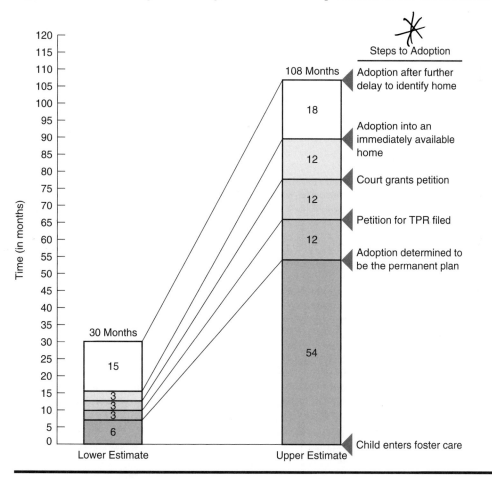

FIGURE 10.2   Time Spent in Foster Care by Children with Adoption Plans

Source: Kusserow, R. P. (1990). *Barriers to freeing children for adoption.* U.S. Department of Health and Human Services, Office of the Inspector General. Washington, DC: U.S. Government Printing Office.

state legislation. Thus, more children are legally free and/or have a plan for adoption.

- Limited capacity in adoption programs to process the increasing numbers and complexities of cases.
- Lack of coordination between family preservation, foster care, adoption, and legal services, which contributes to duplication of efforts and prolongs a child's stay in foster care.
- Lack of sufficient number of workers who are culturally competent and adequately trained in permanency planning and adoption. (p. 69).

The Adoption and Safe Families Act

In 1997, the U.S. Congress passed and President Clinton signed into law new legislation designed to expedite the progress of foster children who cannot return home into adoptive placements. Called the Adoption and Safe Families Act, the legislation addresses several of the barriers identified in McKenzie's analysis. Specifically, the law states that:

- In certain very serious situations, the courts do not need to require agencies to make "reasonable efforts" to reunify the family, but instead can move forward immediately with termination of parental rights and adoption. A permanency planning hearing must be held within thirty days.
- Agencies must make reasonable efforts to place the child in a timely manner, including completion of all steps needed to finalize the plan and recruitment of adoptive parents.
- The federal government will make incentive payments to states to increase the number of adoptions made, in accord with the proposals in President Clinton's "Adoption 2002" initiative. States must ensure that children eligible for adoption have full Medicaid or other health coverage, including coverage for mental health services.
- Termination of parental rights hearings must be held for children under the responsibility of the state for fifteen months out of the most recent twenty-two months, although exceptions can be made if the child is living with a relative.

Concurrent Planning

The law also permits states to conduct "concurrent planning," which means that a state may plan to place a child for adoption or with a legal guardian at the same time that it is making "reasonable efforts" to reunify the child with his/her parents (Children's Defense Fund, 1997). Thus, concurrent planning provides for the simultaneous planning of both reunifcation services and, as a contingency, the preparation of an alternative permanent plan if reunification should fail. Concurrent planning requires that agencies and workers prepare for different outcomes all at the same time, instead of sequentially (Katz, Spoonemore, & Robinson, 1994).

Adoption of children with special needs has proved to be a successful child welfare program. Although the placement of children who are challenging to parent has inherent risks and the disruption rates for special needs children, not surprisingly, are higher than those for healthy infants, adoption offers thousands of children an opportunity for a permanent family when they would otherwise lack the security and accepted social status of legally sanctioned, permanent family relationships. More effort is needed to systematically identify and reduce system barriers to adoption so that children can move more quickly into adoptive homes.

Adoption Resource Exchanges

A development in adoption practice designed to increase the likelihood of permanent homes for children who need them is that of national "clearinghouses" by which agencies can cooperate more effectively in the location and use of adoption resources. Agencies having few contacts outside their own locality tend to be limited in the range of prospective adopters and children to be adopted. If agencies can be helped to communicate effectively, regional prejudices that prevent homeless children from being adopted can sometimes be surmounted.

In 1967 the Child Welfare League of America formed the Adoption Resource Exchange of North America (ARENA), designed to serve agencies in the United States and Canada. By 1989, there were fifty-one such exchanges in the two countries. The primary purpose of ARENA was to mobilize national efforts to find more homes for children with special needs, particularly those who were physically or mentally disabled or who belonged to minority groups or were of mixed racial background. ARENA provided a model for developing and publicizing a large-scale picture of the needs of the adoption field—that is, an identification of regions and localities where there was a surplus or shortage of homes and of children, the kind of homes available, and the kinds of children waiting for homes. Additional efforts were directed toward promoting better interagency relationships, raising adoption standards and practices among agencies, and identifying and breaking down agency and state barriers to adoption, for example, state laws blocking or hindering interstate placements.

Exchange functions are now performed by the federally sponsored National Adoption Exchange, based in Philadelphia and administered by the National Adoption Center. In its "match-referral" service, the Exchange coordinators search the computerized national registry to identify families who have expressed interest in adopting the kinds of children registered. Among the criteria used to determine appropriate match-referrals are the age of the child, sex, race, sibling status, and type of disability. Based on a review of this information, referrals are made to agencies and families. In 1988, which marked the completion of a full-scale network of all states, the Exchange facilitated eighty-two special needs adoptions (Lawrence, 1989). This number appears small unless one considers the highly significant individual and collective benefits of a permanent home to each child and to society.

KINSHIP ADOPTION

Children in kinship care are currently less likely to be adopted than children who are in nonrelative placement settings. Tatara (1993) estimates that only 7 percent of adoptions within the child welfare field are by relatives. Although kinship caregivers usually express a commitment and sense of permanency with the child, they may not see the need for adoption of someone with whom they already have an existing relationship (Hegar & Scannapieco, 1994; Thornton,

1991). Kinship caregiver barriers to adoption include fears of disrupting existing familial roles and relationships, unwillingness to pursue termination of parental rights of a family member, and the hope that the children's parents will be able to resume parenting at some point in the future.

Systems barriers to kinship adoption include a residual reluctance by some workers to consider kinfolk as a resource; a lower level of resourcing for family than for nonfamily subsidized adoption; and lack of effective policy concerning kinship care in general (Child Welfare League of America, 1994; Takas, 1993). Magruder (1994) found that kinship adoption parents are different from nonkin adoptive parents. They are more likely to be single parents, to be older, and to have lower levels of income and fewer years of education.

Adoption by kin is becoming an increasingly favored permanency planning option. Kinship care has many advantages over family foster care and may be viewed as a form of family preservation (Berrick & Barth, 1994). Kinship adoption promotes family continuity, maintaining children within the potentially rich resources of an extended kinship network. The child adopted by kin has access to family history, a variety of familiar relationships, and a shared biological and cultural heritage. Questions of identity are more easily resolved within the context of family. Remaining within the extended family network reduces the effects of separation on children and minimizes the risk of "foster care drift" with multiple placements.

Case One: Family Continuity Decision-Making Model

The following case example illustrates positive aspects of kinship adoption and demonstrates the importance of examining the extended kinship network for permanency options.

> Jametta and Kemal, ages 3 and 5 respectively, had been placed with their grandmother when their mother had left them unattended and they were found by a CPS worker in a filthy apartment with no food and no electricity. Their mother had been in a crack house for several days. Although substance abuse treatment

services had been offered to their mother, she continued to use drugs. On several earlier occasions she had left the children alone when she was high.

Supports were offered to the grandmother to assist her in working with the children. They had a variety of needs for developmental services, including speech therapy for Kemal's elective mutism and a play group for socialization. Ms. Jones, the grandmother, also lacked day care so that she could continue employment, and needed beds and dressers for the children, which the agency helped her to obtain. With support from the kinship care worker, the children had responded well to their grandmother's nurturing and the wraparound supports put in place.

When it became evident that Keisha, the children's mother, had not responded to treatment for her addiction and was unable to stabilize her living situation, a permanency planning hearing was held. The plan was for termination of parental rights followed by adoption planning. Ms. Jones was distraught, as she felt that her health problems (arthritis and a heart condition) might preclude her from raising the children to adulthood, but she was insistent that the children should not be placed for adoption outside the family.

The kinship care worker met with Ms. Jones to set up a family group meeting to plan for the children. They contacted Ms. Jones's sister, known to the family as Auntie Grace. Auntie Grace was the family communicator, who had the names and addresses of the kinship network, and was a central figure in "holding the family together." With the help of Auntie Grace, the kinship care worker and Ms. Jones invited a number of members from the kinship network and the pastor of their church to a family meeting. At the meeting, which was held in the social hall of the church, ten extended family members met to plan for the children. The social worker explained the family situation and the need of Jametta and Kemal for a permanent home. She commended Ms. Jones for the excellent care given to the children while the agency had tried to work with their mother toward reunification. Pastor Robertson then led the entire group in a prayer, asking for a blessing on the children and their deliberations about the future plans for the children. From this meeting, two families—one, a cousin and her husband; the other, an aunt who had several adolescent children—volunteered interest in providing a long-term home for the children.

Following the family group meeting, the kinship care worker visited and studied both families as possible kinship adoption resources. The cousin and her husband were childless and eager to take the children. However, they had serious concerns about possible interference from the children's mother. The aunt, a resourceful single parent, was not concerned about dealing with the children's mother, but had reservations about being able to provide adequately for the children as she was feeling financially stretched by the needs of her own teenagers. Both homes seemed suitable to the kinship worker. She reconvened another meeting in which the grandmother, the mother, and the two prospective adoptive families discussed the next steps. They arrived at a mutually satisfactory solution. The children would be placed with the cousin and her husband after a series of family visits by the grandmother and the children. Both the grandmother and the aunt's family would be involved in supporting the adoptive placement with respite care, family outings, and setting boundaries with the children's mother. If the children and their mother wanted to see each other, visits would occur at the aunt's home with the grandmother present. They made it clear to the mother that she was not to try to visit at the adoptive home, and that she would not see the children if she was high. The children's mother was pleased that the children would remain within the family and gave them a positive message about the adoptive plan.

Case Two: Helping Grandparents Accept Adoption

For many kinship caregivers, particularly grandparents, adoption is not a preferred solution because they do not want to see parental rights terminated. Termination of parental rights may represent "giving up on" the children's parents. It is difficult to give up hope on one's adult child, no matter how serious the problems may appear. The following case illustrates the adoption worker's ability to help the grandparents through this process of grieving and letting go:

Mr. and Mrs. Harper had been caring for their grandchildren for several years while their adopted daughter sought treatment for manic depression and substance abuse. The Harpers had called CPS in desperation when they discovered that the children had been sexually abused by several of their mother's boyfriends. They continued to hope that their daughter would improve enough to resume caring for the children, with support from them. They felt that, especially because their daughter had been adopted herself, it was important not to take the children from her permanently. They kept in close contact with their daughter, supported a reunification plan by taking the children to visit her in the treatment facility, and even helped her by setting her up in an apartment near their home. They attended Al-Anon support groups and tried to learn as much as they could about how to help her. When the first reunification attempt did not work out, despite their support, they pleaded with the caseworker to try again, as they felt that termination of parental rights would destroy their daughter. They wanted to work more closely with their daughter in monitoring and supporting her use of medication.

However, when their daughter took the children out for ice cream and disappeared with them and a new boyfriend, the grandparents were distraught. The worker supported them through the difficult time when the children were missing. Several weeks later their daughter returned the children saying that they were "too hard to handle." The children revealed that they had once again been sexually abused while their mother was partying.

When the grandparents contacted the worker to report the children had been returned, they said, "Okay, now we need to talk about doing whatever we have to do to keep them safe," realizing that their daughter's problems continued to place the children at risk. The worker spent several visits listening to their grief and feelings of failure with their daughter as they struggled to let go of their hopes and unrealistic expectations for their daughter and to focus instead on planning a future for the children. While the worker had some initial concerns about the grandparents' ability to protect the children and to maintain realistic boundaries with the mother, she could see the strong attachment between grandparents and grandchildren. She felt another move would only place the children further at risk emotionally. The Harpers sought counseling for themselves and worked closely with the children's therapist on treatment of the sexual abuse traumatization. As the reformed family began to stabilize, adoption proceedings were initiated. The Harpers began attending a community-based support group for grandparents raising grandchildren and continued with the treatment plan for the children.

Case Three: Returning Children to Kin from Foster Care

Adoption by kin is also an important option for children who have been in family foster care or group care. Children are often placed in foster homes without an adequate exploration of placement resources in the family's kinship network. Some workers are still biased against kinship placements, fearing that the problems of the parents will be endemic in their extended families. With high caseload turnover, later workers may not be aware of the interest of relatives. At the point when adoption planning is appropriate, it is good practice to reexamine the kinship network for resources. The following case illustrates the successful reconnection of separated siblings through a kinship adoption:

Natasha, age 10, had been in three foster homes in three years. Her older brother Danny had been placed with Natasha initially, but when the first foster placement disrupted they had been separated, with Danny going into group care because of his angry acting-out behavior. The siblings saw each other sporadically and expressed a wish to be together. When parental rights had been terminated, the adoption worker looked for an adoptive home that could take Natasha and Danny together and would work to help them rebuild their sibling bond. When it became clear that several homes would be willing to take Natasha but were ambivalent about taking Danny, the worker reevaluated the situation, wondering if it was best to ensure a permanent home for Natasha, perhaps with the current foster home in which she appeared to be adjusting satisfactorily. The worker talked with a consultant from a special needs adoption agency who suggested reexamining the children's kinship network for an adoptive home.

The worker located in a nearby city a paternal uncle who had been Danny's godfather. He had sent cards to Danny while he was in care and had visited him several times, but had been discouraged from visiting after Danny tried to run away from the group home to see him. The uncle and his wife agreed to take Danny for a series of trial visits and were interested in the possibility of reuniting him with Natasha. The worker decided to leave Natasha temporarily with her foster parents while assessing Danny's attachment to his uncle and aunt, and his adjustment in their home. Danny settled in with his relatives, and Natasha began visiting on weekends.

In one turbulent session in the new home, Danny expressed his feeling that his behavior had not only caused his parents to abuse him but had also caused the separation from Natasha. His uncle was able to remind him that the original separation was caused by his parents' problems, not by anything Danny had done. Danny asked why his uncle had not stepped in at that point to offer him a home. The uncle said, "I would have liked to take both of you, but you were put in a foster home, and the worker said that was best for you. I didn't know how to get you, and the plan was for you to go back to your parents. I just felt like I was interfering when I tried to talk to your worker." The worker explained that at the time he was separated from Natasha there had not been a foster home available that could meet his needs, and there was a new worker who wasn't really aware of his uncle's interest in him. Natasha said that she blamed herself for the separation from Danny. "Whenever he picked on me I'd tattle to the foster mom. If I hadn't said anything they wouldn't have felt like there was such a problem, and we could have stayed there together."

The worker and the aunt and uncle worked together for several sessions with the siblings, helping them to correct their distortions about the placement experience, reassuring them that siblings do pick on each other and that they were not to blame for the separations. The aunt and uncle used old family photographs and reminiscences about their family to help them reconnect with each other and with their memories of earlier life in their family. Soon Natasha joined the family, and the adoptions took place.

Case Commentary. The three cases above illustrate the importance of working with kin when planning adoption. In each case the strengths of the extended family network were tapped for problem solving and ensuring permanence for the children. The important principle of family continuity was honored by the adoption worker's sensitive work with children and their relatives to promote healing and connection in the process of ensuring a permanent home and secure legal status. In each situation the process of adoptive plan-

ning enabled the children and their relatives to examine what it meant to be kin, and to integrate their earlier experiences of family into the new adoptive status.

ADOPTION OF CHILDREN OF COLOR

Children of color awaiting adoption are often included in the category of "special needs children," and, indeed, many children with special needs are also children of color. Racism in the larger society and within the child welfare system and the acute crisis of the drug epidemic in urban areas have contributed to the increasing numbers of African-American and other children of color awaiting adoption who have special needs characteristics (older, members of sibling group; behavioral, medical, or developmental disabilities). However, the relationship of children of color to the adoption system has its own history and practice and policy issues that need to be addressed separately from the special needs adoption movement.

Native American Children

Transracial adoption of Indian children occurred in the 1950s and 1960s. In the late 1950s, the Bureau of Indian Affairs and the Child Welfare League of America sponsored the Indian Adoption Project to find inracial and transracial homes for Native American children needing adoptive placement. About 400 children were placed, mainly transracially, during these years (Silverman, 1993).

By the 1970s, it is estimated that a quarter of all Indian children were not living with their families but were in boarding schools, or foster or adoptive homes (Johnson, 1981). This great loss to Indian children of their cultural heritage gave impetus to the passage of the Indian Child Welfare Act (ICWA) of 1978, federal legislation intended to restore and preserve Indian families.

The ICWA reaffirmed the right of tribal courts to assume jurisdiction over the placement of Native American children. Its intent is to preserve cultural and racial identity by reducing the number of Indian children placed in non-Indian homes. Preferences must be given to adoptive placements that are (1) a member of the child's extended family, (2) other members of the Indian child's tribe, or (3) other Indian families.

> *The state and federal government still have control over us. When is it going to end? When is it going to end? I think we will have to take the first steps. For the rest of our Indian children coming up, it is a shame that we cannot raise our head and say, "My home is ready for an Indian child!" (A graduate from an Indian boarding school and current adoptive father—Johnson, 1991, p. 208)*

Adherence to these preferences for adoptive placements is improving, according to a federally commissioned survey of the implementation of the act (Plantz, Hubbell, Barrett, & Dobrec, 1989). Compliance is enhanced by employment of Native American staff in child welfare programs. Barriers remain to inrace adoption of Native American children, however. Adoption agencies may not identify a child as Native American or they may not know how to comply with the ICWA, so children are still placed transracially. Children adopted on-reservation may not be eligible for adoption subsidies. Many Indian families accept the child without subsidy but, lacking Medicaid, find that access to medical care off-reservation can be a problem. The Native American Resource Exchange lists waiting adoptive families from every state but Hawaii, offers assistance in helping families and children establish Indian identity, and provides technical assistance to tribal courts that are making custody decisions about children (Woods, 1989).

African-American Children

Traditionally, African-American families have informally adopted children in their kin networks. The absorption of children who cannot live with their own parents into extended family systems has been a major strength of black families (Hill, 1972; Prater, 1992). It has offered security and status as a member of a family to large numbers of children who otherwise would have been completely destitute.

No formal protections were available to children needing homes under slavery. After emancipation,

very few adoption services were available to African-American children. Until the 1970s, adoption agencies served mainly white, middle-class families, and, for a number of reasons, African-American parents seeking to adopt did not use these services (Neal & Stumph, 1993).

The past several decades have brought vast social changes that influence African-American families. African Americans are now included in child welfare programs both as recipients and providers of service. African-American children needing adoption planning during the 1960s and early 1970s were often placed with white families, a practice that set off a controversy over the merits of transracial adoption. More recently, adoption programs have reached out to the African-American community to recruit adoptive parents of the same race as the child. Kinship adoption is a developing area of practice, in which the child's absorption into the family of a grandparent or other extended family member is formalized through court action.

Transracial Adoption of African-American Children

Transracial adoption of children of color with white families occurred primarily in the 1960s and 1970s, inspired primarily by the shortage of healthy white infants and by social activism emanating from the civil rights movements of the 1960s. As with Native American children, the adoption of African-American children by white families has created great controversy as leaders of these ethnic groups have objected to the practice on a number of grounds, including the loss of children as "culture bearers" in these communities, and concerns about racism and identity formation for the children being adopted.

A nationwide survey on transracial adoption in 1972 indicated that since 1967, when agencies began to increase substantially their efforts to make such placements, about 10,000 African-American children had been placed in white homes across the country. In 1970, more than one-third of the adopted African-American children went into white homes (Klemesrud, 1972). Social workers, although not unanimous in their approval, for the most part seemed to endorse the practice as a means of providing homes for children who were otherwise likely to grow up in foster homes and institutions.

In the early 1970s, however, the climate of opinion about the appropriateness of transracial adoption began to change sharply as communities of color stressed the fostering of racial and cultural identity. At their 1972 meeting, the National Association of Black Social Workers came out "in vehement opposition" to the practice of placing black children with white families, and called on the public and voluntary agencies to "cease and desist" transracial placements, which were termed "a growing threat to the preservation of the black family." The Association directed much of its attack toward the Child Welfare League of America for sanctioning placement of children across racial lines in its standards and for undertaking research on transracial adoption. The practice of transracial placement of black children fell off sharply and in some agencies virtually ended. No comprehensive statistics exist on the number of children of all races transracially adopted today, but the Child Welfare League of America (1995) estimates that transracial adoptions constitute about 4 percent of all public child welfare agency adoptions of foster children.

A major concern of those who opposed transracial adoption was that as children became adolescents they would face increasing difficulties in two areas:

- That adolescents would experience severe identity problems, as they would be estranged (it was feared) from the black community and yet not be fully accepted into the white community
- That they would be vulnerable to attacks on their self-respect because they wouldn't have learned coping mechanisms to deal with racism in the larger society

A number of studies have addressed these concerns (Courtney, 1997). Studies have tracked adopted children over time, since they were first transracially adopted in the 1960s and 1970s (Feigelman & Silverman, 1984; Shireman, 1988; Simon, Alstein, & Melli, 1994). Other studies have used a retrospective design, collecting data during adolescence or young adulthood of children transracially adopted at a young age (McRoy & Zurcher, 1983). The results of these studies

are quite similar. They show that, overall, there are no significant differences in outcomes of children adopted transracially from those adopted inracially. However, some studies do show that transracially adopted children experience conflict over their racial identity and prefer Caucasian friends (McRoy & Zurcher, 1983).

A study by Rosenthal and Groze (1992) illustrates the nuances in the research findings that point toward overall positive outcomes of transracial adoptions but at the same time give evidence of the somewhat stronger outcomes of inracial adoption. The researchers studied the adoption of transracially adopted special needs children as part of a larger study of special needs adoption (see Adoption Disruption). Sixty-three children in their sample were African-American children with special needs who had been placed in white families. These children were compared to larger samples of special needs children of color and white children who had been adopted inracially. The average age of adoption was 5 years for the transracially adopted group, 4.6 years for the children of color adopted inracially, and 6 years for the white inracial group. At the time of the survey study, the children were 10 to 11 years old.

Basically good outcomes were observed for all three groups. The percentages of parents reporting that the adoption's impact was very positive was 58 percent for the minority, inracial group; 41 percent for the white, inracial group; and 53 percent for the transracial group. Nearly all the children in all three groups were attending school, over half had a B average or better, and about two-thirds of the parents reported that the children enjoyed school. Adoption outcomes were most positive for the inracial, minority children on various measures of parent satisfaction and child adjustment. The authors explain this finding partly with reference to the observation that the children in this group were the least "damaged" at the time of adoption, in that they were least likely "to have experienced sexual abuse or group home or psychiatric placement prior to adoption. They were least likely to be handicapped and to evidence behavioral problems" (Rosenthal & Groze, 1992, p. 143). Another possible reason for the somewhat better outcomes of inracial, minority placements lie in the qualities of the minority adoptive families. The authors observe that *minority, inracial placements were distinguished from the other subgroups by the fact that problems with behavior and in school appear less damaging to the quality of parent-child relationship. Study findings suggest that many parents and children in minority, inracial families maintain close parent-child relationships even when the children experience serious problems in behavior or school. This resilience of parent-child relationship conveys a strong acceptance of the child as a valued family member and is a distinct asset in special-needs adoption. (p. 145)*

The results of this study, in line with thirty years of research on this issue, support both the viability of transracial adoption and the advantages of inracial adoption for African-American children.

Culturally Competent Adoption Practice

While the controversy over transracial adoption continues, substantial efforts have been made to increase the number of same-race adoptive families available to children. Although many agencies have successfully developed their ability to recruit African-American families and place children with them, the continuing backlog of African-American children awaiting an adoptive home has impelled a redoubling of efforts. In 1990, the North American Council on Adoptable Children (NACAC) conducted a national survey to identify barriers to same-race adoption of children of color (Gilles & Kroll, 1991). The researchers conducted telephone surveys of sixty-four private and twenty-three public child-placing agencies in twenty-five states. Of the sixty-four private agencies, seventeen specialized in placing children of color and the rest were traditional adoption agencies placing white as well as minority children.

In hiring staff I look for good clinical skills, a sense of family, dependability, maturity, competence, and responsibility. . . . I want workers to know the strengths of black families, have pride in being black, appreciate cultural values, and love and appreciate black people and their differences. (Adoption agency director)

The findings reveal that barriers still exist that were first identified thirty years ago (Billingsley & Giovannoni, 1972). Most (83 percent) of those interviewed said that they were aware of organizational or institutional barriers preventing or discouraging families of color seeking to adopt. The most frequently mentioned barriers were these:

- *Institutional/systematic racism.* Virtually all procedures and guidelines impacting standard agency adoption are developed from white middle-class perspectives. Whether conscious of this or not, agencies have come to espouse—and cater to those holding—distinctly middle-class views. Unfortunately, many families of color aren't familiar with or don't have a mindset that allows them to access "middle-class agencies."
- *Lack of people of color in managerial positions.* Boards of directors and agency heads remain predominantly white.
- *"Adoption as business" mentality/reality.* Heavy dependence on fee income, coupled with the fact that supplies of healthy white infants are decreasing drastically, force many agencies to place transracially to ensure survival.
- *Historical tendencies of communities of color toward informal adoption.* Potential adopters of color question the relevance of formalized adoption procedures, many times wondering why such procedures are needed at all.
- *Negative perceptions of agencies and their practices.* Families of color often possess negative perceptions of public and private agencies and their underlying motives.
- *Lack of minority staff.* Minority workers "in the trenches" are crucial in building trust among families of color. Consequently, their relative scarcity impedes minority families hoping to adopt.
- *Inflexible standards.* Insistence on young, two-parent, materially-endowed families eliminates many potentially viable minority homes.
- *General lack of recruitment activity and poor recruitment techniques.* Agencies are unable to set aside financial and human resources required for effective recruitment.
- *Word not out.* Communities of color remain largely unaware of the need for their services.

A very promising development over the past decades has been the effort by African-American communities to recruit families, such as the One Church, One Child project located in many cities. A number of "specialist" African-American adoption agencies located in African-American communities have been created to emphasize their accessibility to African-American potential adoptive applicants (Gant, 1984). The NACAC survey found that these "minority specializing" agencies were much more successful in finding same-race adoptive parents than were traditional private agencies; specializing agencies placed 94 percent of their African-American children in same-race homes, compared to 51 percent for traditional private agencies and 91 percent for public agencies.

The specializing agencies had found ways to overcome the barriers listed above by instituting policies and procedures reflecting a commitment to same-race placement. They conduct ongoing recruitment and screen families in rather than screen families out. They respond to inquiries very quickly and arrange meetings at times that are convenient for the family. The home-study process is less investigative than it is informative, a process of sharing information and mutually exploring the family's needs and interests in adoption. The survey found that specializing agencies are much less likely than traditional agencies to charge fees (41 percent compared to 91 percent), and when fees are charged, they are much lower (average of $1,439 among minority placement specialist agencies, compared to an average of $5,789 in traditional agencies).

We only place black kids in black families, so the community has to be a key resource for the agency's work. This goes far beyond being a source of homes for our children. The people in the community are the most effective links to resources that Homes for Black Children needs in this work. (Adoption agency director)

The transracial adoption controversy has caused deep rifts of resentment and misunderstanding among groups who should be natural allies in acting as advocates for meeting the needs of children (Neal & Stumph, 1997). In a historic presentation, Sydney Duncan (1988), a national leader in the development of African-American adoption agencies, put the controversy in historical perspective and called for a "healing of wounds":

When Homes for Black Children . . . opened its doors in 1969 it was the energy of the black consciousness movement that engulfed and moved us forward. And, for the first time the fuel and energy of our history was brought to the fore on behalf of black children in the child welfare system. . . . Black children were being placed in record numbers with black families. But more than the numbers, the success of Homes for Black Children affirmed our history of being able to care for the children. Through slavery, when our families were torn apart and sold away from each other, whoever was available took care of the children, and this included children who were any part black. Through the period following slavery, when family members were unable to find each other, the children were cared for. Throughout our struggles in this country black people always took care of the children. . . .

[T]here is real fear, in the hearts of some of us who are black, as to whether a child who is black can be protected in this society, without the protection of families who are most like him. In our hearts, there is the fear, of what he will think of himself if he believes that his own kind did not want him, or did not have the resources to take him in. In our hearts, there is the fear, that his images of black people will not be those which we as black people know ourselves to be, both the good and the bad, but, rather will be the images that white folks have of black folks. Images that may have been developed out of the media, or limited and confusing contact with black people. . . .

The white families who had adopted black children were unprepared for the attack from black social workers. What had happened to the dreams and ideals of the early 60's civil rights movement? Only a few years earlier these families had been commended by a black national leader. I believe these families expected and were prepared for the bigotry and rejection from whites but not from blacks. I believe they felt a kinship to us through the children and sincerely believed that together we could reach the highest ideals for which this country stands. . . .

[E]ven if my dream of a network of black child welfare agencies were to come true tomorrow, there still would be some children who would fall through the cracks and whose need would not be met. . . . Through understanding we can free ourselves of the struggles about the rightness of transracial adoption. Out of the hope, that through understanding each other, and for the sake of the children who are caught in the middle, we can build a bridge that will allow us to transcend

our differences; allow us to renew our dreams, and work together on behalf of the children. (Duncan, 1988. Reprinted with permission.)

Latino Children

For many years, Latino children needing substitute care were "matched" not by placement with families of Latino culture but along color lines; dark-skinned Latino children with African-American families and lighter-skinned children with white families. About 10 percent of children adopted each year are Latino (Jones, 1993), yet little research has been conducted to understand their needs in adoption or the extent to which they are being placed in Latino families. The evidence that is available suggests that many Latino children are adopted by white families (Benson, Sharma, & Roehlkepartain, 1994; Gilles & Kroll, 1991).

The Latino community has expressed concern about interethnic placement of Mexican-American children with non-Mexican–American parents. A recent survey of over 1,000 persons with Hispanic surnames in California revealed that around half of those surveyed agreed with one or more of the following statements: "(1) the child may have an ethnic identity conflict, (2) the child may forget his or her Latino background, (3) the child's participation in Latino cultural events may be limited, and (4) the child may not acquire the skills to cope with racism" (Bausch & Serpe, 1997, p. 136).

Elba Montalvo (1994), Executive Director of the Committee for Hispanic Children and Families, has identified a need for more Latino adoptive homes. She points out that Latinos are not monolithic; the major Spanish-speaking groups in the United States are Mexican American, Puerto Rican, and Cuban. These groups differ from one another culturally in many ways. She recommends the following to increase cultural competency in placement of Latino children:

- Welcome Latino families into adoption agencies with posters and handouts conveying the message "Bienvenidos Latinos." Recruitment efforts should make use of radio, particularly Spanish language stations. All written materials should be conceptualized and written in Spanish first, then translated into English.

- Hire Spanish-speaking staff, with attention to cultural congruence with the various Spanish speaking groups in the area.
- Place Latino children, in order of preference: with relatives, with someone of his or her culture (i.e., Puerto Rican children in a Puerto Rican home), with a family of another Latino background.
- If a non-Latino home must be used, it should be evaluated for the family's ability to help the child learn about Latino culture and have contact with other Latinos.
- We agree with other child advocates that is preferable to provide a child the opportunity of a loving permanent home of any race or cultural background than to allow him or her to grow up without a permanent home and parents who care.
- Build the necessary bridges. Latinos are not asking adoption specialists to change their own values, but rather to understand the values of Latinos and to incorporate them into their practice.
- Collect data to reflect ethnic breakdown in all categories, programs, and services, which will enable everyone to better understand the needs of Latino children and will assist in designing programs that have a cultural fit. (pp. 1–5).

Strengthening Multiethnic Placements

Many children continue to be placed transracially, even though it is generally considered that, all things being equal, same-race adoptions are preferable. Several factors influence the continuing use of transracial adoptions. Multiethnic placements are needed to accommodate the increasing numbers of children who are damaged survivors of the drug epidemic or have other special needs; their number and challenging condition appear to exceed the capacity of any one ethnic group to provide permanent homes. In multiethnic foster placements that last a long time, children and foster parents may form strong attachments that all parties wish to see formalized in a permanent adoption. A troubling trend is the unknown number of transracial placements made by "independent vendors"—doctors, lawyers, ministers, and others unaffiliated with public or private agencies. Few records are kept or oversight done in this adoption arena, but some observers believe that the number of transracial adoptions in this largely unregulated field are "much higher than in general" (Gilles & Kroll, 1991, p. 26).

Federal and state legislation addresses the issue of transracial adoption. The Multiethnic Placement Act of 1994 represented a compromise among the various constituencies of transracial adoption (Curtis & Alexander, 1996). In an effort to speed up adoption for children in foster care by reducing race as a barrier to adoption, it required that agencies receiving federal assistance could not "categorically deny to any person the opportunity to become an adoptive or foster parent, solely on the basis of the race, color, or national origin of the adoptive or foster parent, or the child, involved." However, in recognition of the probable psychosocial advantages to the child of same-race placement, the law also stated that agencies could "consider the cultural, ethnic, or racial background of the child and the capacity of the prospective foster or adoptive parents to meet the needs of a child of such background as one of a number of factors used to determine the best interests of the child" (North American Council on Adoptable Children, 1995, p. 3).

In 1997, the U.S. Congress amended the Multiethnic Placement Act to prohibit agencies receiving federal funds from delaying or denying adoptions on the basis of race, color, or national origin of the child or the foster or adoptive parent. The reason for the amendment was the belief in Congress that the 1994 Act had been ineffective in decreasing the length of time children wait for adoption. At the time this book is being written, it is too soon to tell the effects of the new law. However, a report by the Government Accounting Office to the U.S. Congress shows it has not been widely implemented (U.S. Government Accounting Office, 1998). (See Chapter 9). The National Association of Social Workers has expressed concern about the law's implementation. The law does not appear to allow professional social workers the needed room for judgment and discretion in making placement decisions, which should include an assessment of the adoptive parent's ability to help the child understand her or his cultural heritage (NASW News, 1997). Courtney (1997) and Hollingsworth (1998) argue strongly that easing barriers to transracial adop-

tion will not significantly improve the adoption prospects of many children in long-term foster care, who may have stable kinship placements that should not be disrupted or have multiple disabilities that make recruitment of adoptive families extremely difficult.

Agencies, adoptive parents, and leaders of communities of color have developed assessment tools and guidelines for families regarding their role in helping the child achieve a positive racial or ethnic identity. Prospective transracial adoptive parents need to have positive views about the ethnicity of the child they are adopting and be willing to involve themselves and the child in the child's ethnic community, such as a church or community center. They should be willing to help the child learn about his or her race's history and leaders, and in other ways proactively address the child's need for positive ethnic affiliation (Neal & Stumph, 1997).

Communities of color can also reach out to help families in multiethnic placements. "How do we help each other? For those of you who are white and whose children carry our color and the warmth of the sun in their genes, I believe we as black people can be of help . . . as you seek to give your children of color answers about their heritage, answers about the craziness of our world in relation to color, and, as you seek to give them answers to the questions of why [was I given up by my mother]" (Duncan, 1988, p. 4).

INTERCOUNTRY ADOPTIONS

Since World War II there has been a substantial movement into the United States of children who are adopted across national boundaries. During 1997, 13,620 such children found adoptive homes in this country, up from 9,000 children in 1991. Intercountry adoptions account for about 5 percent of all adoptions in the United States. The primary sending countries for children adopted internationally in 1997 were China (3,318 children), the Russian Federation (2,531 children), Korea (1,580 children), and Romania (554 children). South and Central America are also represented among countries sending children to the United States (U.S. Immigration and Naturalization Service, 1991; Evan P. Donaldson Institute, 1998).

South Korea has sent more than half the children who have ever come to this country for adoption. As a result of the continuing population of Americans in Asia since World War II, many children were born who were "virtually unadoptable within Korean society because of certain cultural and moral factors" (Haring, 1976). One such factor was the Korean cultural ideal of ethnic homogeneity and the rejection of children who are products of admixture with other races or nations, even in the midst of foreign occupation. Another factor was the strong disapproval of extramarital sexual relationships in Korea, as well as legislation that discriminated against those classified as illegitimate. In addition, historically, adoption in Korean family life has served mainly to facilitate inheritance and establish a lineal relationship with a male offspring of a relative in the adoptive parents' maternal or paternal line (Kim & Carroll, 1975).

Recently Korea has begun to develop a strong domestic adoption program that is enabling it to reduce international placements. The trend in Korea is matched by similar movements in other countries that have traditionally been sources of children for international adoption. According to Bartholet (1993), "The notion that there is, today, something shameful in sending homeless children abroad rather than taking care of 'one's own' has gained widespread acceptance" (p. 91). This view may result in fewer international adoptions from some countries, although others, such as Russia and China, counter this trend by sending more children than formerly.

Agency reports suggest that, to some extent, intercountry adoptions are a means for matching the "surplus" of white homes in the U.S. seeking to adopt with the corresponding "surplus" of orphaned, nonmarital children in other countries for whom no families are available. Other factors contributing to intercountry adoptions include the mobility of families around the world; the greater ease of communication between countries; the continuing large numbers of American servicemen stationed abroad, many of whom seek to adopt children during their residence in another country or who father children out of wedlock with no means to care for them; and a humanitarian concern by many persons for the plight of refugee and other homeless children, many of whom are grossly neglected or discriminated against in their own country because of illegitimacy or mixed racial background.

Persons in this country become interested in adopting a child from another country in various ways. Widely televised stories of the plight of Romanian orphans has created enormous interest in adopting children from the former Soviet bloc. Some adoption agencies have ties to foreign countries and are able to offer infertile couples the option of adopting internationally. Some adopters are related to the child whom they want to bring to this country. Sometimes they seek to adopt a child with an ethnic background and cultural ties like their own. In some instances they have met a child during a temporary stay abroad and want to adopt him or her.

The legal adoption of children from other countries requires compliance with laws in two or more countries. Foreign countries have laws and policies governing adoption. Islamic countries prohibit all adoption, foreign and domestic. Other countries prohibit or severely restrict international adoption. Many countries require that foreign adoptions follow the same procedures as domestic adoptions, which may necessitate that the adoptive parents come to the country to be screened. The United States has immigration rules that must be satisfied; and each state also has procedures governing adoption. The bureaucratic complexities are a significant barrier to international adoption, though adopters who work through established international adoption agencies may find that the procedures are no more complicated than those for domestic adoption. It may, however, be more expensive. Bartholet (1993) estimates that the costs "generally range upwards of $10,000, with many international adoptions costing $15,000 to $25,000" (p. 93).

Geographical distances and national boundaries create additional hazards to an adoption service:

> *Because there are few adoption or other social service agencies in the countries with children needing homes . . . it is difficult to have the same assurances, as an adoptive parent, as one would have with an adoption arranged within the United States.*

First, since there are frequently no medical or other records on the child, it is difficult to know how old or how sick the child is.

In addition, because of the extreme poverty of some families, as well as because of the social disruptions taking place, it is difficult to be sure that the child is legally free for adoption. Sometimes a child is abandoned—but sometimes, as press reports from Colombia have shown, children are stolen for "adoption" in other countries. (National Committee for Adoption, 1982, pp. 2–3)

Sociolegal aspects of intercountry adoptions require special attention to parental consent (Bell, 1985), the child's status in matters of guardianship, citizenship, birth certificate, and assurance that the adoption is legally valid in both countries.

A sound intercountry adoption plan requires collaboration between child welfare agencies in both countries. Child Welfare League of America standards state that intercountry adoption of children should be considered only when suitable arrangements cannot be made in their own country. When family or ethnic-cultural background prevent their acceptance and optimum care in their native land, international adoption should be considered. In all instances, parents should be helped to consider alternatives within their own country and to understand the finality of the adoption process (Child Welfare League of America, 1988).

The same safeguards should apply in intercountry adoption plans as exist in this country for native-born adopted children. Observing this standard requires pertinent information about the child's background and development, active involvement of older children in the planning and preparation for their new relationships and way of life, a study of the adoptive parents' suitability, and counseling with them about the needs of the particular child they are receiving, including what it means to a child to leave a familiar environment and enter a new culture. The agency is responsible for postplacement supervision until the adoption is legally finalized and for supplying postlegal adoption services when they are requested (Child Welfare League of America, 1988).

Researchers have been interested in how children from foreign countries fare in adoptive placements in the United States. A recent study compared 199 Asian adoptees with 579 white adopted children and small numbers of American children adopted transracially. The sample of families was randomly selected from the records of forty-five public and private adoption agencies in the four states of Colorado, Illinois, Minnesota, and Wisconsin. The study participants, including adopted children who were adolescents at the time the study was conducted and their adoptive parents, completed extensive and confidential survey instruments containing a wide range of psychological and family measures. The study compared the Asian adoptions with same-race adoptions in regard to identity, attachment, family, and psychological health. The findings indicate that the Asian adopted adolescents were doing as well as their white counterparts in same-race families. In the important and controversial dimension of racial identity, 79 percent of the Asian children reported that "my parents want me to be proud of my racial background," and 66 percent stated that their parents actively try to promote racial pride. The study also found that most (80 percent) of the Asian children agreed with the statement that "I get along equally well with people of my own racial background and people of other racial backgrounds" (Benson et al., 1994, pp. 97–111). Other studies have also shown mainly positive outcomes for children of international adoptions, a surprisingly optimistic result considering that many of these children had negative experiences prior to adoption that might have been expected to affect their later adjustment (Tizard, 1991).

Benson and colleagues (1994) expressed some concern that most families who adopted Asian children "could do more to connect their children to same-race role models" (p. 8). In an effort to meet this need, some international adoption organizations have organized "culture camps" for Korean adopted children, where they can spend time in the summer learning about their country of origin and interacting with Korean adults.

TRENDS AND ISSUES

Open Adoption Controversy

The last three decades have seen the emergence of a controversy around the "search" phenomenon and the development of "openness" in present-day adoption practice. One result has been a recognition that the adoption experience has dimensions that were not acknowledged in closed adoption practice. Two main reasons for the growing controversy have been cited: "First, there is no consensus among adoptive professionals as to what openness or open placement means. Second, the practice of open placement is relatively new and its impact on members of the adoptive triad . . . has not been adequately addressed by research" (McRoy, Grotevant, & White, 1988, p. 18).

The interest in various degrees of openness is in sharp contrast to the traditional viewpoint that normal well-adjusted individuals, although adopted, would not need nor want to know about their birth parents; the adoptive parents, the ones who raised them and brought them to maturity, would be sufficient. But we have learned that adoptees may at some point want access to a wider range of information that will give them a better understanding of themselves. These adoptees are not motivated by idle curiosity; they have specific questions related to their personal identity. Most searches stem from a lack of needed information (Gritter, 1997).

Dukette (1984) identified some of the changing values in the 1960s that influenced adoptees toward searches and made inevitable the expectation of change in adoption policies and practices:

1. As abortion became more widely used, and as marriage was no longer an absolute condition for an out-of-wedlock mother to keep her child, fewer infants became available for adoption. The birth mother found more leverage in the process of relinquishment and preferences about adoptive parents.

2. The civil rights movement of the 1960s brought about openness in varied ways. Access to one's school records, medical records, and information in other institutions was achieved. Secrecy was associated with discrimination: Individuals claimed their civil right to know fully about matters concerning them that others knew. "A lack of trust in institutions and a devaluing of expertise became more prevalent" (p. 237).

3. Individuals who felt different and isolated in their personal life—gay and lesbian individuals,

as well as others who struggled with serious problems that were hard to acknowledge, such as drug addiction—began to let their situation be known. Assertiveness training and self-help groups became a means to obtain individual rights. Not unexpectedly, some adopted adults felt the increased openness in society that allowed them to seek information about their birth origins. " 'Entitlement' came to be a word used in private lives as well as in public policy" (p. 238).

4. In addition, advances in communication technology simplified the task of finding persons in adoptee searches.

There is considerable acknowledgment that for birth parents and adoptive parents who freely and fully agree to ongoing contact, open adoption has the potential to bring about genuinely satisfying relationships for all concerned (Baran & Pannor, 1993). At the same time, questions have been raised as to the problems open adoption can bring and the need for various degrees of openness, and for some birth parents and adoptive parents, availability of some degree of closed adoption. Fears about too-rapid policy changes include these: Some families have more than one adopted child; what will it mean in family relationships if one has continuing contact with the birth mother and another does not? What of the risk of birth parents dropping out of the child's life after contacts have been in place? Young birth parents, however conscientiously they try to make the right decisions affecting their child at the time of adoptive planning, cannot foresee or judge future demands on their yet undeveloped capacities and the opportunities or disappointments that may follow. How will the task of helping children to understand the concept of adoption be further complicated by an active role of the birth mother in the child's life? Clearly the problem of role ambiguity is a serious and unresolved one in open adoption (McRoy et al., 1988).

Some professionals have observed that in discussions of open adoption, few benefits to the adopting parents are mentioned. There are concerns that because of a deeply felt need for a child, and the stated or unstated requirement in open adoption to satisfy the needs of the birth parents, the adoptive applicants may agree too quickly to proposed arrangements that may be to the detriment of their own needs and right to privacy. In addition, to the extent that aspects of "openness" affect adoptive parents' decisions about child rearing, to what extent will normal difficulties in parenting be made more complex in serious and subtle ways? (Kraft, Palombo, Mitchell, Woods, & Schmidt, 1985).

These and other questions require research to assess the effects on adoption and its outcomes for children and families (Berry, 1993). It is troubling that much of the discussion of open adoption is based on ideology, anecdotes, and untested presumptions. Whatever the shortcomings of the traditional model of adoption with its emphasis on confidentiality and family privacy, several decades of research have found that adoption has been "tremendously advantageous" for children, with benefits to all parties to adoption that should not be lost (Dukette, 1984, p. 241). Admittedly, traditional adoption was faulty in the limited choices it afforded to adoptees who might want to know more about their birth and biological parents, as well as the limitations in the role assigned the birth parents during the adoptive process. However, Dukette (1984) warns of "a tendency now to repeat the mistake of a rigid policy that offered few variations by being equally rigid in the opposite direction" (p. 241).

There are repeated suggestions in the literature that adopting parents and birth parents should be allowed to choose participation in either open or closed adoption. The degree of acceptable and workable openness in any adoption plan is a highly individual matter, reason enough for caution about making drastic policy changes before research has been done.

Still untested but of considerable interest is this observation: "Over time and between groups of children placed through open versus closed adoption procedures, there may be no substantive differences in the eventual adjustments of the children. This appears to be the outcome of earlier dialectical arguments such as within-race versus transracial adoption and two-parent versus single-parent adoptions. . . . There may be no single characteristic that predicts success in adoptions" (Curtis, 1986, p. 443).

Independent Adoption

Whether independent placements provide sufficient protection for children, compared with agency placements, has not yet been fully answered (McDermott, 1993). In the 1950s and 1960s, independent adoption became a matter of keen concern in the child welfare community and prompted several follow-up studies. The rate of success among independently arranged adoptions was found to be greater than had been claimed by critics of nonagency placements. A 1978 study by the Child Welfare League of America also found that most independent adoptions seemed to fare well, but that there was evidence that the traditional concerns about independent adoptions—exceptionally high costs to adoptive parents and lack of counseling for birth mothers—were justified in some cases (Meezan, Katz, & Russo, 1978).

New attention to placement of children for adoption that are arranged apart from a recognized public or private adoption agency has accelerated with a claim that independent adoptions have become "part of an increasingly self-protective institution with its own advocacy groups, its own protocol and its own lawyers" (Mansnerus, 1989, p. 1). Children placed in independent adoptions are most often infants who are sought by urban, college-educated couples accustomed to directing their own lives. Frequently they have already approached an adoption agency and looked into foreign adoptions. Disappointed by the lack of assurance of a certain and early infant placement, they see advantages associated with bypassing adoption agencies. By going to a lawyer who is known to arrange adoptive placements, they expect to find a more acceptable reception and to avoid rejection and a long waiting list. In addition, lawyers who specialize in helping prospective parents often give clear instructions as to efforts they can make themselves to find a healthy baby—writing and distributing resumes that include descriptions of their characteristics, interests, and values, as well as photographs of themselves and their homes (a practice used often in open adoptions). The lawyer may also provide a list of newspapers across the country that will accept adoption advertising—illegal in nineteen states (Mansnerus, 1989).

Birth mothers may prefer not to work with an agency out of fear of too much questioning. Or they may seek more financial compensation for expenses than they would receive from an agency. Child welfare professionals, in turn, cite the drawbacks for the birth mother in the lack of counseling and other safeguards that agencies provide. The National Committee for Adoption (1989) cites the hazards to some children who are "transferred or actually 'sold' for high fees . . . a black market that actually exists" (p. 170).

The opposition to independent adoptions by many social work and legal professionals who seek better protection for children has led to proposals that all nonrelative adoptions, by use of regulatory power, should be processed by licensed adoption agencies or be accredited by the Council on Accreditation for Services to Children and Families (COA). The Child Welfare League of America and the National Committee for Adoption take that position.

Brieland (1984) cautions, however, that

before one responds enthusiastically, it is important to be aware that child welfare staffs are already increasingly overburdened as a result of the passage of child abuse statutes in every state and of the increased urgency in investigating neglect. Protective services have a higher priority than the selection of adoptive parents. If all nonrelative adoptions had to be processed by an agency, many placements would still be made in advance of the home study, and lack of adequate staff could easily lead to superficial adoptive studies. To provide advantages over the status quo, mandatory adoptions though agencies must involve more personnel to do the larger job effectively—a requirement that is not feasible in most states. (p. 77)

The Controversial Uniform Adoption Act

Adding a new dimension to debates on open versus closed adoption and on the rights of all members of the adoption triad is the Uniform Adoption Act, developed by the National Conference of Commissioners on Uniform State Laws (NCCUSL), an influential group of judges, lawyers, and law professors. The act is intended for state legislatures to consider as a model in revising their state's adoption laws. The act has laudable goals: to provide consistency in state laws re-

garding adoption and to ensure that adoptions, once made, remain final (The Adoptive Family Rights Council, 1996). However, the act as currently written has several controversial provisions; concerned advocacy organizations such as the Child Welfare League of America, Adoptive Families of America, the National Council of Juvenile and Family Court Judges, the North American Council on Adoptable Children, and the National Association of Social Workers are publicly opposed to it.

One hotly debated area concerns the rights of the birth father in adoption; these rights are at the center of such widely publicized cases as Baby Richard in Illinois and Baby Jessica in Michigan. In the Baby Richard case, a judge revoked the adoption of a 3-year-old boy and gave custody to the birth father, whom the child had never known. The birth mother had falsely told the father that the child had died. In the situation of Baby Jessica, the birth mother falsely named the wrong man as the birth father. Both the birth father and mother, who later married, challenged the nonfinalized adoption of the child, a process that took several years and finally resulted in their being awarded custody of their child. Birth fathers are successfully challenging adoptions of their offspring in court, on the grounds that they were not told of the child's existence and had not relinquished their rights. Most state courts do not have clear guidelines for these cases.

The Uniform Act would require that birth fathers receive notice that their children were being placed for adoption and set a strict time limit (thirty days) on their ability to make a claim for the child. If the father could not be found, his rights would be terminated. He could appeal within six months, but after that, he would have no further legal recourse.

Critics of the model law point out that in both the Baby Richard and the Baby Jessica cases, the birth fathers did appeal within six months. However, the appeals were delayed by the courts for over two years, accounting for the long period of uncertainty in the children's living situation and culminating in a wrenching move for them away from the families they had been part of since their infancy. The model law encourages judges to speed up such cases but does not impose deadlines.

The model act goes too far in limiting birth parents' rights, according to some critics. Birth parents would have only eight days in which to revoke their signed consent for an adoption unless they could show that the consent was obtained by "fraud or duress." The act largely ignores the need of birth parents for counseling. According to the North American Council on Adoptable Children, "Between the abbreviated revocation period and lack of counseling, a birth mother in the throes of postpartum blues may easily make a hasty, uninformed decision that will later lead to litigation." In other provisions, "the act grants the court broad powers to allow termination of parental rights and adoption in spite of a father's opposition or a procedural violation of the Act itself." There is concern that judge's decisions may "be based upon economic or class differences" which often exist between birth parents and adoptive parents (Vick, 1995, p. 4).

The act also would appear to turn back the clock on openness in adoption. Although it allows birth and adoptive parents to make early arrangements so that the child can make contact when turning 18, it closes the option of seeking information for children whose birth parents or adoptive parents resist it. In these situations, "the adoptee is condemned to a life without history; the act mandates secrecy for 99 years and deters illicit disclosure through a system of significant fines and other legal penalties" (Vick, 1995, p. 5).

Critics believe that, overall, the act caters to the needs and wishes of adoptive parents at the expense of children (Sullivan, 1995). It focuses mainly on infant adoption and does not deal with issues for older and special needs children in search of adoptive homes. A uniform law for states to follow in adoption is needed, but the current model act has not found wide acceptance among adoption experts. A consensus has yet to emerge on how adoptions are to be arranged so as to protect the rights of children as well as those of birth and adoptive parents.

CHAPTER SUMMARY

Adoption is a social and legal process whereby the parent-child relationship is established between persons not so related at birth. By this means a child born to one set of parents becomes, legally and socially, the child of other parent and a member of another family, and assumes the same rights and duties as those that obtain between children and their biological parents.

Adoption of children is an ancient practice, whose original purpose was to provide an heir for a family. In the United States, adoption became common in the twentieth century, to resolve the problem of out-of-wedlock pregnancies and to meet the demands of infertile couples for a child. More recently, the adoption of infants has declined, as abortion has become available and single parenthood has become more economically feasible and socially acceptable. At the same time, the adoption of children formerly considered unadoptable, including older children and those with special needs, has become more common. Today, adoption practice has split into two arenas, with private agencies and third parties such as lawyers handling most of the adoptions of healthy infants, and public agencies maintaining responsibility for the placement of special needs children who have become free for adoption after entering the child welfare system.

Adoption practice today faces many changes. During the last 30 years, the secrecy which surrounded both the legal and social aspects of adoption has been challenged by adult adoptees, who demand as a birthright information about their biological origins. Searching for biological family members separated by adoption has become common. Many agencies are now practicing various levels of openness in adoption, in which some measure of contact is maintained between the biological family and the adoptive family.

Protecting the right of unmarried fathers to be involved in adoption planning has required adjustments in adoption practice. As a result of U.S. Supreme Court decisions in the 1970s, the rights of unmarried fathers to their children cannot be disregarded in adoption planning. A problem arises when a father is not informed of his paternity until after the child has been adopted and then challenges the adoption. States are currently developing legislation to try to protect the rights of fathers while also ensuring the stability of the adoption.

Permanency planning, the policy of moving children out of long-term foster care and into permanent homes, has increased the number of older and special needs children who require adoption planning. This movement has challenged the child welfare system in several ways. Many children have waited for a long time in the child welfare system before being placed in a permanent, adoptive home, because of numerous delays in the system. The need to give biological parents every chance to demonstrate their ability to resume care of their children and the difficulties in finding suitable adoptive homes for children who present special difficulties to caregivers have prevented the timely adoption of children. Bureaucratic stagnation in child welfare agencies and the courts have also slowed the process. Many states have discouraged transracial adoption, on the grounds that children are better served in same-race families, and this, too, has had the effect of delaying adoption for some children. Recently, new legislation, the Adoption and Safe Families Act, and amendments to the Multiethnic Placement Act, have been created to reduce barriers to the timely adoption of children in the child welfare system. Increased recruitment efforts for adoptive parents in communities of color and more attention to kinship adoption have provided additional adoption resources.

In response to the challenges presented by the troubled histories of many children adopted after years in the child welfare system, postadoption services to children and families have expanded and developed a specialized knowledge base. Understanding children's survival behavior, anticipating anniversary reactions, and accepting that children may have ambivalent feelings about permanently separating from their biological family and becoming attached to a new family, have helped social workers and adoptive parents better meet the needs of adopted children. Inevitably, some of the placements of older, emotionally troubled children break down, requiring agencies to develop sensitive practices to help the child recover from the disruption and move on to another placement.

In summary, adoption is a dynamic field of practice, which is evolving due to the expectations of the parties primarily involved—adopted children, biological parents, and adoptive parents—changing legal requirements, and the needs of children in the child welfare system.

FOR STUDY AND DISCUSSION

1. Watch a movie with an adoption theme, such as "Secrets and Lies" or "Raising Isaiah." Identify ways in which the movie illustrates and expands concepts in this chapter, such as transracial adoption, open adoption, postadoption services, and psychosocial adjustment to adoption.

2. Review the section on postadoption services and then answer the question: Are there issues in adoptive family development so specific that they must be dealt with only by specialists in adoption? Or can they be adequately addressed by generalist family and individual therapists?

3. Consider the merits of the position taken by the National Committee for Adoption and the one taken by Brieland with respect to the issue of independent adoptions. Should all nonrelative adoptions be processed by an adoption agency? If so, how could the obstacles to implementing the policy be overcome? If not, how could the risks that are said to attach to independent placements be reduced?

4. What position do you take on the issue of transracial placement as an alternative adoption practice? State your reasoning on the question and compare it with that of others.

5. Consider and debate with others what you see as the benefits and the risks to open adoptions. On the assumption that some degree of "openness" in adoption practice is here to stay, state and describe a flexible policy that could best serve the needs and preferences of the three parties to the adoption triad.

6. Discover whether innovative programs exist in your area to recruit adoptive parents for special needs children. How are they working? Do they offer ongoing support to the family after the adoption?

7. Interview a family involved in kinship adoption. What kinds of supports and resources do they need from the child welfare agency? Do they have needs different from those of nonrelative adopters?

8. Read the novels *The Bean Tree* and *Pigs in Heaven* by Barbara Kingsolver, and analyze them in terms of the Indian Child Welfare Act. In what ways does the ICWA affect the adopted child, the biological mother, the adoptive mother, and the tribal nation involved?

FOR ADDITIONAL STUDY

Benson, P. L., Sharma, A. R., & Roehlkepartain, E. C. (1994). *Growing up adopted: A portrait of adolescents and their families.* Minneapolis, MN: The Search Institute.

Courtney, M. E. (1997). The politics and realities of transracial adoption. *Child Welfare, 76*(6), 749–779.

Edelstein, S. B. (1995). *Children with prenatal alcohol and/or other drug exposure: Weighing the risks of adoption.* Washington, DC: Child Welfare League of America Press.

Lakin, D. (1992). *Empowering adoptive families: Issues in postadoption services, reference and resource guide.* Southfield, MI: National Resource Center for Special Needs Adoption; and Baltimore: Baltimore City Department of Social Services.

McRoy, R. G., Grotevant, H. D., & White, K. L. (1988). *Openness in adoption: New practices, new issues.* New York: Praeger.

Reitz, M., & Watson, K. W. (1992). *Adoption and the family system: Strategies for treatment.* New York: Guilford Press.

Rosenthal, J. A., & Groze, V. K. (1992). *Special Needs Adoption.* New York: Praeger.

Sorosky, A. D., Baran, A., & Pannor, R. (1989). *The adoption triangle: Sealed or opened records: How they affect adoptees, birth parents, and adoptive parents.* San Antonio: Corona Publishing.

INTERNET SITES

The Evan P. Donaldson Adoption Institute. Provides up-to-date information on research, policy, and practice in adoption. http://www.adoptioninstitute.org [June, 1998]

National Adoption Information Clearinghouse. Established by the U.S. Congress to provide information on all aspects of adoption, including infant and intercountry adoption and adopting children with special needs. http://www.calib.com/naic [June, 1998]

Welfare Information Network. A comprehensive Web site on national and state policies, with one section devoted to child welfare, including a subsection on adoption and foster care publications. http://www.welfareinfo.org/childwelf.htm [June, 1998]

REFERENCES

Abbott, G. (1938). *The child and the state* (Vol. 1). Chicago: University of Chicago Press.

Adoptive Family Rights Council. (1996, April 3). Seminar on the Uniform Adoption Act. Harrisburg, PA: Author.

Baran, A., & Pannor, R. (1993). Perspectives on open adoption. *The Future of Children, 3*(1), 119–124 (a publication of the Center for the Future of Children, the David and Lucile Packard Foundation).

Barth, R. P., & Berry, M. (1988). *Adoption and disruption: Rates, risks, and responses.* New York: Aldine De Gruyter.

Barth, R. P., & Brooks, D. (1997). A longitudinal study of family structure and size and adoption outcomes. *Adoption Quarterly, 1*(1), 29–56.

Bartholet, E. (1993). International adoption: Current status and future prospects. *The Future of Children, 3*(1), 89–103 (a publication of the Center for the Future of Children, the David and Lucile Packard Foundation).

Bausch, R. S., & Serpe, R. T. (1997). Negative outcomes of interethnic adoption of Mexican American children. *Social Work, 42*(2), 136–143.

Bell, C. J. (1985). Consent issues in inter-country adoption. *Children's Legal Rights Journal, 6*(3), 2–8.

Benson, P. L., Sharma, A. R., & Roehlkepartain, E. C. (1994). *Growing up adopted: A portrait of adolescents and their families.* Minneapolis, MN: Search Institute.

Berrick, J., & Barth, R. (1994). Research of kinship foster care: What do we know? Where do we go from here? *Children and Youth Services Review, 16*(1–2), 1–5.

Berry, M. (1993). Risks and benefits of open adoption. *The Future of Children, 3*(1), 125–138 (a publication of the Center for the Future of Children, the David and Lucile Packard Foundation).

Berry, M., & Barth, R. P. (1990). A study of disrupted adoptive placements of adolescents. *Child Welfare, 69*(3), 209–225.

Billinsgley, A., & Giovannoni, J. M. (1972). *Children of the storm: Black children and American child welfare.* New York: Harcourt Brace Jovanovich.

Bourguignon, J. P., & Watson, K. W. (1987). *After adoption: A manual for professionals working with adoptive families.* Post-Placement Post-Legal Adoption Services Project for Special Needs Children and Their Families: Federal Grant #90-CKO-02871. Chicago: Illinois Department of Children and Family Services.

Brieland, D. (1984). Selection of adoptive parents. In P. Sachdev (Ed.), *Adoption: Issues and trends* (pp. 65–85). Toronto: Butterworth.

Brown, S. L. (1989). *Profile: Permanency planning assessment for children with developmental disabilities and special health needs.* Southfield, MI: Spaulding for Children.

Byrd, A. D. (1988). The case for confidential adoption. *Public Welfare, 46*(4), 20–23.

Carp, E. W. (1995). Adoption and disclosure of family information: A historical perspective. *Child Welfare, 74,*(1), 217–239.

Child Welfare League of America. (1988). *Standards for adoption services.* Washington, DC: Author.

Child Welfare League of America. (1994). *Kinship care: A natural bridge.* Washington, DC: Child Welfare League of America Press.

Child Welfare League of America. (1995). *Child abuse and neglect: A look at the states.* Washington, DC: Child Welfare League of America Press.

Children's Defense Fund. (1997, November). Summary of the Adoption and Safe Families Act of 1997. Available online at http://www.childrensdefense.org/safestart

Courtney, M. E. (1997). The politics and realities of transracial adoption. *Child Welfare, 76*(6), 749–779.

Curtis, C. M., & Alexander, R. (1996) The Multiethnic Placement Act: Implications for social work practice. *Child and Adolescent Social Work Journal, 13*(5), 401–410.

Curtis, P. A. (1986). The dialectics of open versus closed adoption of infants. *Child Welfare, 65*(5), 437–445.

Dukette, R.(1984). Value issues in present-day adoption. *Child Welfare, 63*(3), 233–244.

Duncan, S. (1988). *Healing old wounds.* Paper presented at the North American Conference on Adoptable Children, St. Louis, MO.

Edelstein, S. B. (1995). *Children with prenatal alcohol and/or other drug exposure: Weighing the risks of adoption.* Washington, DC: Child Welfare League of America Press.

Emery, L. J. (1993). The case for agency adoption. *The Future of Children, 3*(1), 139–145 (a publication of the Center for the Future of Children, the David and Lucile Packard Foundation).

Evan P. Donaldson Adoption Institute. (1998). *Adoption in the United States.* Chicago: Author. Also available at: http://www.adoptioninstitute.org/research/ressta.html [June, 1998].

Fahlberg, V. (1991). *A child's journey through placement.* Indianapolis: Perspectives Press.

Feigelman, W., & Silverman, A. R. (1984). The long-term effects of transracial adoption. *Social Service Review, 58,* 588–602.

Festinger, T. B. (1986). *Necessary risk—A study of adoptions and disrupted adoptive placements.* Washington, DC: Child Welfare League of America.

Gant, L. M. (1984). *Black adoption programs: Pacesetters in practice.* Ann Arbor: National Child Welfare Training Center, University of Michigan School of Social Work.

Gilles, T., & Kroll, J. (1991). *Barriers to same race placement.* St. Paul, MN: North American Council on Adoptable Children.

Gritter, J. L. (1997). *The spirit of open adoption.* Washington, DC: Child Welfare League of America Press.

Grotevant, H. D. (1997). Coming to terms with adoption: The construction of identity from adolescence into adulthood. *Adoption Quarterly, 1*(1), 3–28.

Hardin, M. A., & Shalleck, A. (1984). Children living apart from their parents. In R. M. Horowitz & H. A. Davidson (Eds.), *Legal rights of children* (pp. 353–421). Colorado Springs: McGraw-Hill.

Haring, B. L. (1976). *Adoption statistics: Annual data, January 1–December 31, 1975: Submitted by 41 voluntary and 16 public agencies*(Publication No. X-9). New York: Child Welfare League of America.

Hartman, A. (1979). *Finding families: An ecological approach to family assessment in adoption.* Beverly Hills, CA: Sage.

Hartman, A. (1984). *Working with adoptive families beyond placement.* New York: Child Welfare League of America.

Hegar, R., & Scannapieco, M. (1994). From family duty to family policy: The evolution of kinship care. *Child Welfare, 74*(1), 200–216.

Hill, R. (1972). *The strengths of black families.* New York: Emerson Hall.

Hollinger, J. H. (1991). *Adoption law and practice.* New York: Matthew Bender.

Hollinger, J. H. (1993). Adoption law. *The Future of Children, 3*(1), 43–61 (a publication of the Center for the Future of Children, the David and Lucile Packard Foundation).

Hollinger, J. H. (1998). *Adoption law and practice* (Vol. I, 1998 supplement). New York: Matthew Bender.

Hollingsworth, L. D. (1998). Promoting same-race adoption for children of color. *Social Work, 43,*(2), 104–116.

Jones, C. (1993, October 24). Role of race in adoptions: Old debate is being reborn. *New York Times,* 1.

Katz, L., Spoonemore, N., & Robinson, C. (1994). *Concurrent planning: From permanency planning to permanency action.* Seattle: Lutheran Social Services of Washington and Idaho.

Kim, C., & Carroll, T. G. (1975). Intercountry adoption of South Korean orphans: A lawyer's guide. *Journal of Family Law, 14*(2), 223–253.

Klemesrud, J. (1972, April 12). Furor over whites adopting blacks. *New York Times.*

Kraft, A. D., Palombo, J., Mitchell, D. L., Woods, P. K., & Schmidt, A. W. (1985). Some theoretical considerations on confidential adoptions. Pt. 1: The birth mother. *Child and Adolescent Social Work, 2*(1).

Lakin, D. (1992). *Empowering adoptive families: Issues in post adoption services.* Baltimore: Baltimore City Department of Social Services.

Lakin, D. (1994). *Personal communication.* Southfield, Michigan.

Lawrence, S. (1989, July 17). Personal communication. Philadelphia: Exchange Services, National Adoption Center.

Lewin, T. (1997). U.S. is divided on adoption, survey of attitudes asserts. *New York Times,* November 9, p. 10.

Magruder, J. (1994). Characteristics of relative and nonrelative adoptions by California public agencies. *Children and Youth Services Review, 16,* 123–132.

Mansnerus, L. (1989, October 5). Private adoptions aided by expanding network. *New York Times,* 1.

McDermott, M. T. (1993). The case for independent adoption. *The Future of Children, 3*(1), 146–152.

McKenzie, J. K. (1993). Adoption of children with special needs. *The Future of Children, 3*(1), 62–76 (a publication of the Center for the Future of Children, the David and Lucile Packard Foundation).

McNamara, J. (Ed.). (1994). *Sexually reactive children in adoption and foster care.* Grennsboro, NC: Family Resources.

McRoy, R. G., Grotevant, H. D., & Ayers-Lopez, S. (1994). *Changing practices in adoption.* Austin, TX: The Hogg Foundation for Mental Health, University of Texas.

McRoy, R. G., Grotevant, H. D., & White, K. L. (1988). *Openness in adoption: New practices, new issues.* New York: Praeger.

McRoy, R. G., & Zurcher, L. A. (1983). *Transracial and inracial adoptees. The adolescent years.* Springfield, IL: Charles C. Thomas.

Meezan, W., Katz, S., & Russo, E. M. (1978). Independent adoptions. *Child Welfare, 57*(7).

Michaels, R.(1947). Casework considerations in rejecting the adoption application. *Journal of Social Casework, 28*(10), 370–375.

Montalvo, E. (1994). Against all odds: The challenges faced by Latino families and children in the United States. *The Roundtable: Journal of the National Resource Center for Special Needs Adoption, 8*(2), 1–5.

Mosher, W. D., & Bachrach, C. A. (1996). Understanding U.S. fertility: Continuity and change in the National Survey of Family Growth. *Family Planning Perspectives, 28*(1), 4–12.

National Association of Social Workers News. (1997, September). Adoption law raises questions. *NASW News,* 15.

National Committee for Adoption. (1982). *Children from other lands.* Unpublished mimeographed draft. Washington, DC: Author.

National Committee for Adoption. (1989). *Adoption factbook. United States data, issues, regulations and resources.* Washington, DC: Author.

Neal, L., & Stumph, A. (1993). *Transracial adoptive parenting: A black/white community issue.* Bronx, NY: Haskett-Neal Publications.

North American Council on Adoptable Children. (1995, Winter). The Multiethnic Placement Act. *Adoptalk,* p. 3.

Pannor, R., & Baran, A. (1984). Open adopton as standard practice. *Child Welfare, 63*(3), 245–250.

Plantz, M. C., Hubbell, R., Barrett, B. J., & Dobrec, A. (1989). Indian child welfare: A status report. *Children Today, 18*(1), 24–29.

Prater, G. S. (1992). Child welfare and African-American families. In N. A. Cohen (Ed.), *Child welfare: A multicultural focus.* Boston: Allyn & Bacon.

Proch, K. (1981). Foster parents as preferred adoptive parents: Practice implications. *Child Welfare, 60*(9), 617–626.

Reitz, M., & Watson, K. (1992). *Adoption and the family system: Strategies for treatment.* New York: Guilford Press.

Roles, P. E. (1989). *Saying goodbye to a baby.* Washington, DC: Child Welfare League of America.

Rosenthal, J. A. (1993). Outcomes of adoption of children with special needs. *The Future of Children, 3*(1), 77–88 (a publication of the Center for the Future of Children, the David and Lucile Packard Foundation).

Rosenthal, J. A., & Groze, V. K. (1992). *Special-needs adoption: A study of intact families.* New York: Praeger.

Schroen, S. (n.d.) *Here I am: A lifebook kit for use with children with developmental disabilities.* Southfield, MI: Spaulding for Children.

Shireman, J. F. (1988). *Growing up adopted: An examination of major issues.* Chicago: Chicago Child Care Society.

Siegel, D. H. (1993). Open adoption of infants: Adoptive parents' perceptions of advantages and disadvantages. *Social Work, 38*(1), 15–23.

Silverman, A. R. (1993). Outcomes of transracial adoption. *The Future of Children, 3*(1), 104–118 (a publication of the Center for the Future of Children, the David and Lucile Packard Foundation).

Simon, A., Alstein, H., & Melli, M. S. (1994). *The case for transracial adoption.* Washington, DC: American University Press.

Silin, M. W. (1996). The vicissitudes of adoption for parents and children. *Child and Adolescent Social Work Journal, 13*(3), 255–269.

Sokoloff, B. Z. (1993). Antecedents of American adoption. *The Future of Children, 3*(1), 17–25 (a publication of the Center for the Future of Children, the David and Lucille Packard Foundation).

Spencer, M. E. (1987). Post-legal adoption services: A lifelong commitment. *Journal of Social Work and Human Sexuality, 6*(1), 155–167.

Stolley, K. S. (1993). Statistics on adoption in the United States. *The Future of Children, 3*(1), 26–42 (a publication of the Center for the Future of Children, the David and Lucile Packard Foundation).

Sullivan, A. (1995, Winter). The uniform adoption act: What price uniformity? *The Children's Voice, 4*(2), 25–26.

Takas, M. (1993). *Kinship care and family preservation: A guide for states in legal and policy development.* Washington, DC: American Bar Association Center on Children and the Law.

Tatara, T. (1993). *Characteristics of children in substitute and adoptive care: A statistical summary of the VCIS national child welfare data base.* Washington, DC: American Public Welfare Association.

Thornton, J. (1991). Permanency planning for children in kinship foster homes. *Child Welfare, 70*(5), 593–601.

Tizard, B. (1991). Intercountry adoption: A review of the evidence. *Journal of Child Psychology and Psychiatry, 32*(5), 43–56.

U.S. Department of Health and Human Services. (1997, February). *Adoption 2002: A response to the Presidential executive memorandum on adoption.* Washington, DC: Author. Also available at: http://www.acf.dhhs.gov/programs/cb/special/2002toc. [February, 1997]

U.S. General Accounting Office, HEHS Division. (1998). *Foster care implementation of the Multiethnic Placement Act poses difficult challenges.* Washington, DC: U.S. Government Printing Office.

U.S. Immigration and Naturalization Service. (1991). *Statistical yearbook of the Immigration and Naturalization Service, 1991.* Washington, DC: U.S. Government Printing Office.

U.S. Senate Committee on Children and Youth. (1975). Hearings before the Subcommittee on Labor and Public Welfare. *Adoption and foster care.* Washington, DC: U.S. Senate, 94th Congress, First Session.

Vick, C. (1995, Winter). The 1994 Uniform Adoption Act: The wrong model for positive change. *Adoptalk,* 4–5.

Watson, K. W. (1988). The case for open adoption. *Public Welfare, 46* (4), 24–28.

Witmer, H., Herzog, E., Weinstein, E. A., & Sullivan, M. E. (1963). *Independent adoptions: A follow-up study.* New York: Russell Sage Foundation.

Woods, M. (1989). Adoptive planning for American Indian children. *The Roundtable: Journal of the National Resource Center for Special Needs Adoption, 4*(2), 3.

CHAPTER 11

Juvenile Delinquents
The Community's Dilemma

*But the Constitution does not mandate elimination of all differences in
the treatment of juveniles.*
—*Shall v. Martin* 1984 p. 269

CHAPTER OUTLINE:

CASE EXAMPLE

Peter is 15 years old. He became a temporary ward of the court when he was 4 years old. His mother had repeatedly beaten him with an extension cord. The last time he was beaten, he ran out of the house and into the street. His mother, in a drunken stupor, chased after him with the extension cord in her hands. Neighbors kept him from her and called the police. After being taken to the hospital, he was placed in a foster home. Over the next two years, his mother visited twice. When the foster parents sought to adopt him after he had been with them for two years, the agency told them that they were working on placing him with an aunt. The foster parents questioned this plan, since no family member had visited the child and he had not mentioned an aunt. The agency told the foster parents that they had located the aunt in another state. A homestudy had been completed and she would be coming to meet Peter in the next month. The aunt came and took Peter home with her.

Peter began to wet the bed immediately. The aunt thought he was having some initial adjustment problems, so attempted to console him when it happened. About eight months into the placement, he began to urinate on and hit other children at home and at school. The aunt became worried. The school social worker recommended that she get counseling for him. He was seen by the child guidance agency for two years. The urinating behavior stopped and the hitting behaviors were significantly reduced. Services were terminated.

At ten years of age, Peter stole a bicycle from a garage. His aunt made him return it, spanked him with a belt, and told him he would not be allowed to play outside for a week. The next day, Peter told the teacher that his aunt had beaten him with a belt and he did not want to go back to her house. The teacher called child protective services. Child protective services talked with Peter and the aunt. Both confirmed that the aunt had hit him with a belt. The aunt said she would just as soon he not come back to her house because he had been a constant problem since he was placed with her. He was placed in a shelter.

The home state was contacted to arrange for Peter's return. After two weeks, a worker came to pick him up and took him to a shelter in the home state. The agency sought a foster home placement. As they were preparing to move him to a foster home, the shelter reported that he had been found having sexual intercourse with an 8-year-old girl in the shelter. The agency told the prospective foster parents of this incident, and they declined to have him placed in the home since they had younger children. He remained in shelter for six months and was eventually placed in a small group home for children with sexually aggressive behaviors. He remained in this placement for two years.

Peter had to leave the group home because it could only keep children until their twelfth birthday. He moved from one group home to another. A fight with another youth that Peter had allegedly started precipitated each move. No delinquency charges were filed in any of these incidents. He is now in the juvenile detention facility charged with forcible rape of a 12-year-old girl.

This case example highlights an issue of great concern in child welfare, that children who originally come to the attention of the child welfare system because of neglect, abuse, or abandonment later appear in the juvenile justice system (Kelley, Thornberry, & Smith, 1997). Their reappearance as juvenile delinquents suggests that the earlier interventions of the child welfare system were not successful in reversing the negative effects of their maltreatment.

JUVENILE OFFENDER CATEGORIES

Juvenile delinquency policy and practice addresses two distinctly different categories of juvenile offenders: the juvenile who commits an act that violates a criminal statute, and the juvenile who commits an act that violates a law or ordinance designed to regulate his or her behavior because of his or her age or status.

Within the first category of delinquents, those who commit violations of criminal statutes, there are two subgroups. The first are those who commit violent crimes, including murder; forcible rape; robbery, and aggravated assault. These are the juvenile offenses that receive the most media attention and public discussion. Yet these offenses accounted for less than 5 percent of all juvenile offenses reported in 1995. For example, the total number of violent crimes by juveniles reported (147,700) was much less than the number of juvenile runaways (249,500). (Office of Juvenile Justice and Delinquency Prevention, 1997). In spite of the relatively small number of violent juvenile offenders, the failure of the juvenile justice system to effectively address them has sparked the "adult crime—adult time" movement, which holds that the juvenile who commits certain categories of offenses should be tried and sentenced as an adult.

The second subgroup of delinquents who commit violations of criminal statutes, are minors whose offenses include property crimes such as burglary, larceny-theft, motor vehicle theft, arson, receiving or possessing stolen property, embezzlement, fraud, drug manufacture, possession, or sale, and the nonviolent personal crimes such as sexual offenses and nonaggravated assault.

Within the second category of delinquents are those who commit acts that are deemed status offenses, such as truancy from home, truancy from school, failure to obey the reasonable commands of the parent or guardian, and violating curfew. In some states, these juveniles are called children in need of supervision, persons in need of services, status offenders, or wayward minors. A status offense is an act that is an offense only when committed by a juvenile. A continuing controversy among policy makers is whether status offenders should be removed from juvenile court jurisdiction and their problems dealt with by noncoercive, community-based services. Those who hold this view are concerned that the traditional responsibility of the family to control children's misbehavior is being seriously weakened by a too-ready transfer of responsibility to bureaucratic discretion. There is also concern that the juvenile justice system is being forced to treat delinquents and status offenders alike, without distinction for their different statuses, in an increasingly adversarial and bureaucratic context (Howell, 1997).

This chapter explores the historical development of a separate system of justice for juveniles, the current trend toward treating juveniles who commit the more serious offenses in the adult criminal system, the risk factors for delinquency, and the range of prevention and treatment strategies used to address the multiple problems of juvenile delinquents and their families.

SCOPE OF THE PROBLEM

The data inform us that, in spite of negative publicity, relatively few children come before the juvenile court. Of the 29.9 million youths aged 10 through 17 in the United States in 1995, only 2.7 million, or less than 10 percent, were arrested for delinquent acts, including status offenses. Violent crimes (murder, forcible rape, robbery, and aggravated assault) accounted for 5 percent of all juvenile arrests. The ages of youths at the time of arrest for all crimes were as follows: 23 percent were 17 years of age; 68 percent were 13 through 16 years of age, and 9 percent were less than 13 years of age. The racial composition was 69 percent white, 28 percent black, 1 percent Native American, and 2 percent Asian. Males make up about 75 percent of all delinquency arrests (Office of Juvenile Justice and Delinquency Prevention, 1997). Table 11.1 presents these statistics in detail.

Butts and Snyder completed an analysis of the arrests and juvenile court dispositions for crimes committed by juveniles under the age of 15 years in response to the perception that younger juveniles are committing more serious offenses and in increasing numbers. This perception is, in part, the basis for the push to lower the age at which juveniles can be tried as adults and for more serious punishment for juvenile offenders. They concluded:

This study suggests that today's serious and violent juvenile offenders are not significantly younger than those of 10 or 15 years ago. Yet many juvenile justice professionals, as well as the public, would assert the opposite. What explains this discrepancy? The authors of this study believe several factors are at work.

First, overall growth in the number of violent juvenile offenders has drawn increased attention to the problem of young offenders in general. . . . Second, the nature of delinquency cases involving juveniles age 12 or younger has changed. Person offenses, which once constituted 16% of the total court cases for this age group, now constitute 25%. . . . Third, delinquency caseloads have doubled nationwide since 1970. . . . Fourth, justice professionals tend to accumulate memories of exceptional cases. . . . Finally, the news media have increased their reporting of crime, especially violent crimes by the very young. . . . The

TABLE 11.1   Juvenile Arrests in 1995

This table is based on the authors' analysis of data presented in the FBI's Crime in the United States 1995. National estimates of juvenile arrests were developed using FBI estimates of total arrests and juvenile arrest proportions in the reporting sample.

In 1995 law enforcement agencies made more than 2.7 million arrests of persons under the age of 18. In 23 percent of these arrests the person was age 17 and in 69 percent the youth was white.

Most Serious Offense Charged	Estimated Number of Juvenile Arrests	PERCENT OF TOTAL JUVENILE ARRESTS					
		Age 12 & Younger	Age 17	White	Black	Native American	Asian
Total	**2,745,000**	**9%**	**23%**	**69%**	**28%**	**1%**	**2%**
Crime Index total	885,100	12	20	66	31	1	2
Violent Crime Index	147,700	8	26	48	49	1	1
Murder and nonneglient manslaughter	3,300	3	39	39	58	1	2
Forcible rape	5,500	11	24	54	45	1	1
Robbery	55,500	6	26	38	60	1	2
Aggravated assault	83,500	9	25	56	42	1	1
Property Crime Index	737,400	13	19	69	27	1	2
Burglary	135,800	12	20	73	24	1	1
Larceny-theft	510,600	15	18	70	27	1	2
Motor vehicle theft	80,500	4	21	58	38	2	2
Arson	10,500	35	9	79	18	1	1
Nonindex offenses							
Other assaults	215,700	13	20	62	35	1	2
Forgery and counterfeiting	8,800	3	45	79	19	1	2
Fraud	25,100	4	29	55	42	1	3
Embezzlement	1,300	3	56	65	32	1	2
Stolen property buying, receiving, possessing	42,800	6	27	60	37	1	2
Vandalism	139,600	19	17	80	17	1	2
Weapons carrying, possessing, etc.	56,300	8	27	63	34	1	2
Prostitution and commercialized vice	1,300	5	44	64	33	1	2
Sex offense (except forcible rape and prostitution)	16,100	18	15	70	28	1	1
Drug abuse violations	189,800	2	36	64	35	1	1
Gambling	1,600	3	39	21	77	0	2
Offenses against the family and children	6,900	8	24	71	26	1	2
Driving under the influence	14,900	2	66	91	6	2	1
Liquor laws	120,000	1	45	91	5	3	1
Drunkeness	20,600	2	46	87	10	2	1

continued

TABLE 11.1   continued

	PERCENT OF TOTAL JUVENILE ARRESTS						
Most Serious Offense Charged	Estimated Number of Juvenile Arrests	Age 12 & Younger	Age 17	White	Black	Native American	Asian
Disorderly conduct	173,900	9%	22%	64%	35%	1%	1
Vagrancy	3,500	4	33	64	35	1	1
All other offenses (except traffic)	420,300	7	29	69	28	1	2
Suspicion	2,000	6	28	80	19	0	0
Curfew and loitering law violations	149,800	5	20	76	21	1	2
Runaways	249,500	8	9	77	19	1	3
U.S. population ages 10–17	29,929,000	38	12	79	15	1	4

Source: Sigmund, M., Snyder, H. N., & Poe-Yamagata, E. (1997). *Juvenile offenders and victims: 1997 update on violence.* Pittsburgh, PA: National Center on Juvenile Justice.

- About 1 in 8 juvenile arrests in 1995 was for either an alcohol or drug offense, with arrests roughly evenly spread over these two categories.
- While juveniles below age 13 were involved in 9% of all juvenile arrests (i.e., persons below age 18), these young juveniles were involved in greater proportions of arrests for arson (35%), vandalism (19%), nonviolent sex offense (18%), larceny-theft (15%), simple assault (13%), burglary (12%), and forcible rape (11%).
- Black youth were 15% of the juvenile population in 1995 and involved in 28% of all juvenile arrests. Black youth were most disproportionately involved in arrests for murder (58%), forcible rape (45%,) robbery (60%), aggravated assault (42%), motor vehicle theft (38%), fraud (42%), and gambling (77%).

growing publicity about these cases may suggest to the public that they are occurring more frequently, even if juvenile crime trends indicate otherwise. (1997, p. 11)

A National Center on Juvenile Justice study found that female arrests had increased by 50 percent and juvenile court cases involving females had increased by 54 percent between 1986 and 1995. Once in the juvenile court system, cases involving females were more likely to receive probation than those involving males charged with the same offenses (Poe-Yamagata & Butts, 1996).

The Office of Juvenile Justice and Delinquency Prevention is the best source of data on juvenile crime. Its most recent comprehensive report, *Juvenile Offenders and Victims: 1997 Update on Violence (1997),* provides the following trend data:

- "The juvenile crime arrest rate declined in 1995 following a ten-year period of constant increases." (p. 18)
- "The number of juvenile murderers increased steadily from 1984 through 1994 and dropped by 17 percent in 1995." (p. 13)
- "The juvenile murderer was likely to be co-defendant with an adult in 32 percent of the murders." (p. 12)
- "The victims of juvenile murderers were predominately family members and acquaintances (64 percent) as opposed to strangers (36 percent)." (p. 12)
- "Juvenile murderers used a gun in 79 percent of all murders." (p. 12)
- "The issue of school-related crime is growing in significance—10 percent of high school students

completing the 1995 Youth Risk Behavior Survey stated that they had carried a gun, knife, or club to school within the last thirty days; 8 percent reported that they had been threatened or injured at school by a student using a weapon, and 5 percent stated that they had not gone to school because they were afraid either at school or traveling between home and school." (pp. 14–15)

- "Official records indicate that there are more chronic (defined as four or more juvenile justice system referrals) offenders and that they are proportionately responsible for more of the juvenile offenses." (p. 25)
- "Fifty-seven percent of all juvenile crimes are committed on school days." (p. 26)

Regarding the processing of juvenile cases, the report found that:

juveniles in all states can be tried as adults in criminal courts. The states vary as to the procedure used to effect these transfers—judicial waiver; prosecutor dis-

cretion or legislative exclusion covers the categories. In juvenile waiver states, the juvenile court must decide to transfer the case to the criminal court. In prosecutor discretion states, the prosecutor chooses to file in juvenile or criminal court. In legislative exclusion states, the state statute specifically identifies the offense categories that are excluded from juvenile court jurisdiction. (p. 29)

There has been a trend toward increasing the proportion of cases waived to adult court. The National Center on Juvenile Justice (1997) reports that the number of waived cases grew 71 percent between 1985 and 1994. In 1994, according to Butts (1997), of the 15 million cases handled by the juvenile courts, 55 percent were processed by formal petition in juvenile court, with 33 percent of those handled by waiver of jurisdiction to the criminal court. It is important to note that the data are not conclusive, but are estimates based on information supplied by 1,800 jurisdictions to the National Juvenile Court Data Archive. These reporting jurisdictions represent 67 percent of the juvenile

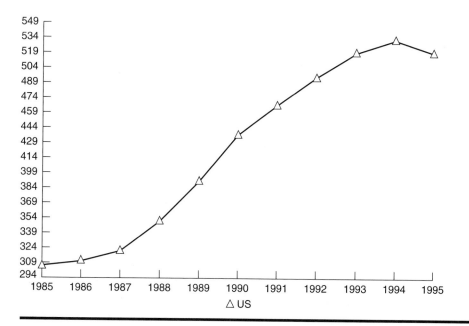

FIGURE 11.1   Juvenile Violent Crime Arrest Rate in 1995

Source: Annie E. Casey Foundation, 1998 Kids Count Data Online. Available online at http://www.aecf.org

population. These figures support some policy and practice perspectives and not others.

HISTORICAL DEVELOPMENT OF JUVENILE DELINQUENCY SERVICES

From Adult Criminal Court to Juvenile Court

Historically, juveniles over the age of 7 years—the age recognized under Common Law as the age at which one could form criminal intent—who committed crimes enjoyed no special privileges due to their age. They were arrested, detained, tried, and sentenced in the same manner as an adult would be for the same crime. The Society for the Reformation of Juvenile Delinquents (the Society), organized in 1823, called for removing juveniles from adult jails. Their organizers saw this removal as a way to save these youth from the negative influences of adult criminals. Their basic belief was that prisons did not reform adult criminals, and by exposing juvenile offenders to adult criminals, the juveniles would most likely develop into better criminals (Finestone, 1976).

In 1825, the Society opened the New York House of Refuge, designed to provide an environment that would ensure the positive development of youth by focusing on meeting their basic needs, instilling in them the value of work, providing education, and overseeing their moral development. Finestone (1976) commented, "So certain were its founders of the righteousness of their mission that they showed little concern with the civil rights of the children they institutionalized: admissions included homeless children and convicted juvenile offenders indiscriminately" (p. 7).

Nonetheless, this movement caught on and spread throughout the United States (Dean & Reppucci, 1974). During the period from 1825 until the founding of the juvenile court system at the end of the century, these reform, industrial, or training schools (as they were known in various localities) continued to increase in number. Unfortunately they became sources of constant scandals rather than the incubators of positive youth development as first envisioned. They were overcrowded, used excessive disciplinary methods, experienced significant violence, and provided a custodial rather than a treatment environment (Howell, 1997).

Charles Lording Brace at the New York Children's Aid Society challenged the institutionalization of children and youth in reform schools. He promoted relocating children from the inner cities to families in the Midwest and West. (See Chapter 9.) Concurrently, Jane Addams, Julia Lathrop, and Lucy Flower were undertaking a movement in Chicago to establish settlement houses to address the impact of increasing urbanization and poverty on families and children. They chose to work with the family and child within the neighborhood. Both initiatives focused on helping the child develop within the context of a family environment rather than an institutional one.

Out of this grew the interest of the Chicago Women's Club in improving the conditions of juveniles who were institutionalized. Their work resulted in the establishment of the first juvenile court. Their vision was that this court would treat those who committed delinquent acts as children in need of firm direction and support, not as criminals deserving of punishment. The judge was given full discretion to determine what was the best course of intervention for the child, with the input of social workers and others. It is interesting to note that the Illinois statute, while precluding placing juveniles in adult prisons and providing for alternatives in dispositions such as family placement and probation, did not preclude placing them in the same reform schools that were the source of significant scandal at the time (Jacobs, 1997).

A complete discussion of the juvenile court's operation and the subsequent attacks on it is described in Chapter 6. The reader is reminded that the challenge to the juvenile courts' operations was that its "benevolence" often took precedence over the due process rights of the juvenile. These attacks on the juvenile court system operation emanated out of its informal, individualized handling of juvenile delinquency matters. Specifically, the U.S. Supreme Court decisions *In re Gault* and *Kent v. United States,* decided in 1967, marked the beginning of the juveniles' right to due process. (Kramer, 1994). What had been designed as a benevolent system to handle child abuse, neglect, and delinquency and to protect children from the trauma of the adult legal system was found to be constitutionally deficient.

In the Kent case, the law of the District of Columbia provided that a person 16 years of age or older charged with an offense that would be a felony if committed by an adult could be waived to the adult court for trial after a full investigation by the juvenile judge. Kent, who was charged with robbery, rape, and breaking and entering, was waived. He challenged the waiver on the grounds that he was not afforded a hearing, no reasons for the waiver were provided to him, and his lawyer was denied access to his records. The Court held that under the due process clause, a juvenile was entitled to a hearing, full access to records and reports used by the court in arriving at its decision, and a statement of the reason for the juvenile court's decision (*Kent v. United States,* 1966).

Gault was a 15-year-old Arizona teenager charged with making a lewd telephone call to a neighbor. He was on probation at the time of the call. He was arrested without notification to his parents, detained, not provided counsel, and never afforded a formal hearing. He was found delinquent and committed to the state training school until the age of majority. He challenged the proceedings. The Court, in reversing the decision of the Arizona Supreme Court, established the due process requirements for juvenile delinquency hearings: (1) notice of sufficient detail to mount a defense; (2) right to be represented by counsel and, if necessary, right to court appointed and paid counsel if child and parents could not afford counsel; (3) privilege against self-incrimination; and (4) right to review evidence and cross-examine witnesses. Justice Fortas made two statements in this decision that challenged the basic foundation of the juvenile court system and signaled the scope of Constitutional protections for juveniles

> ... *neither the Fourteenth Amendment nor the Bill of Rights is for adults alone. (In re Gault,* 1967, p. 13); and
>
> ... *juvenile court history has again demonstrated that unbridled discretion, however benevolently motivated, is frequently a poor substitute for principle and procedure. (Id, p. 18)*

Subsequent U.S. Supreme Court decisions went on to place the rights of juveniles in the juvenile court system on par with the rights granted adults in the criminal system in most respects. It held that the standard of proof in a delinquency case is "beyond a reasonable doubt," the same standard required in adult criminal proceedings (*In re Winship,* 1970). It held that a transfer to adult court for prosecution after an adjudication of delinquency in the juvenile court violates the 5th Amendment protection against double jeopardy (*Breed v. Jones,* 1975).

The Supreme Court has not required that the juvenile court operate like the adult criminal courts in all respects. It has supported variations in the treatment of juveniles in the juvenile court system. In *McKeiver v. Pennsylvania* (1971) it held that the fundamental fairness standard in fact-finding procedures for juvenile proceedings as developed by *Gault* and *Winship* did not require a jury trial. The 1984 *Schall v. Martin* decision, in which the Supreme Court upheld a New York statute that provided for pretrial detention, reflects the continuing balancing of juvenile rights and differential treatment provided by the juvenile courts. The Court stated

> *There is no doubt that the Due Process Clause is applicable in juvenile proceedings. "The problem," we have stressed, "is to ascertain the precise impact of the due process requirement upon such proceedings. . ." We have held that certain basic constitutional protections enjoyed by adults accused of crimes also apply to juveniles. . . . But the Constitution does not mandate elimination of all differences in the treatment of juveniles. . . . The State has "a parens patriae interest in preserving and promoting the welfare of the child," . . . which makes a juvenile proceeding fundamentally different from an adult criminal trial. We have tried, therefore, to strike a balance—to respect the "informality" and "flexibility" that characterize juvenile proceedings, . . . , and yet ensure that such proceedings comport with the "fundamental fairness" demanded by the Due Process Clause.*

In summary, then, for juveniles charged with delinquent or criminal offenses, the Court has clearly established that they must be afforded due process rights equal to those afforded adults and that the states can, provided the fundamental fairness tests are met, maintain some flexibility and informality in its juvenile court processes to ensure the benevolent treatment of juveniles.

Federal Government Leadership

The federal government began an active involvement in juvenile justice policy in the 1960s. As is the norm, it established policies and influenced state action, acceptance, and implementation of these policies by linking federal funding to adoption and implementation of the federal policies.

The White House Conference on Children and Youth of 1960 was followed by the 1961 establishment of the Crime Committee on Juvenile Delinquency and Youth Crime. The Crime Committee combined the efforts of several federal departments to focus on delinquency prevention projects. The Juvenile Delinquency and Youth Offenses Control Act of 1961 funded demonstration projects for delinquency prevention.

The Juvenile Delinquency Prevention and Control Act of 1968, which was renamed the Juvenile Delinquency Prevention Act in 1971, provided federal support to states for delinquency services.

In 1974, the Juvenile Justice and Delinquency Prevention Act (JJDPA) signaled the beginning of a new era in juvenile justice policy reform at the federal level. This act was the result of several reports articulating juvenile court failures, namely lack of due process for juveniles before the court, crowded training schools, excessive use of detention of children in jails, increasing juvenile crime rates, and ineffective interventions. (Empey & Stafford, 1991). The act called for, among other things, diversion of minor offenders from the juvenile court, separation of juvenile offenders from adult offenders in detention, the removal of status offenders from secure detention facilities and the establishment of nonsecure alternatives for them, and the establishment of the Office of Juvenile Justice and Delinquency Prevention (OJJDP). The act was especially significant in that it required compliance with these provisions as a condition for states to receive federal funding. (Howell, 1997 p. 33)

Over the course of the twenty-five years since its initial passage, the act has been amended several times. These amendments have provided exceptions to some of the original mandates and expanded others. For example, the adult-juvenile separation mandate progressed from total sight and sound separation to total removal of juveniles from adult jails to delineation of specific instances in which juveniles can be detained with adults. Additionally, status offenders can be ordered into secure facilities if there is sufficient evidence to show that they have violated a court order and secure detention is found to be the only way to contain them. This option can be used for a limited period of time. The 1988 amendment called for states to pursue reductions in the disproportionate representation of minorities in the system. This provision was made a mandate in 1992 (Howell, 1997).

As the Juvenile Justice and Delinquency Act approaches its twenty-fifth anniversary, monitoring reports suggest that all eligible states and territories are participating, with fifty-five of the fifty-seven governmental bodies in full compliance with the mandates. Howell (1997) states, "These accomplishments are unprecedented in the history of federal social legislation. . . . Excepting the creation of reform schools and juvenile courts, these are the most significant changes in the history of juvenile justice in the United States" (p. 38). The reasons he gives for this success are

- professionals and advocacy organizations joined together
- required infrastructure to monitor compliance at the state level
- prevention and intervention program focus
- Department of Justice legal support for compliance
- JJDP Act's promotion of progressive programming (pp. 39–41).

Back to the Criminal Court

Despite the successes of the Juvenile Justice Delinquency Prevention Act and the Office of Juvenile Delinquency Prevention in administering it, the juvenile justice system is being challenged with the "just desserts" or "adult crime—adult time" punishment approach. This approach rests on the assumption that the juvenile court system has not been effective in deterring juvenile crime nor correcting juvenile offenders' behaviors. Clearly the data supports that conclusion and has been used by those who wish to eliminate the juvenile court system. According to the proposed reform, juveniles would be adjudicated by the criminal courts and incarcerated in adult prisons if the crimes were serious enough. Howell (1997) notes: "Once again, punishing the offense rather than the offender is the object of current crime policy" (p. 23).

RISK FACTORS FOR DELINQUENCY

Many factors contribute to delinquency. Catalano and Hawkins (1995) have summarized the research findings from longitudinal studies which have identified risk factors within the community, the family, the school, and the individual that contribute to adolescent problem behaviors of substance abuse, delinquency, teenage pregnancy, school dropout, and violence. Figure 11.2 summarizes those risk factors and the adolescent problem behaviors likely to result from those risk factors.

This conceptualization of the risk factors of delinquency has influenced the development of a model of delinquency prevention and intervention

FIGURE 11.2   Communities that Care: Risk Factors for Adolescent Problem Behaviors

RISK FACTORS	ADOLESCENT PROBLEM BEHAVIORS				
	Substance Abuse	Delinquency	Teen Pregnancy	School Drop-Out	Violence
Community					
Availability of drugs	✔				
Availability of firearms		✔			✔
Community law and norms favorable toward drug use, firearms, and crime	✔	✔			✔
Media portrayals of violence					✔
Transitions and mobility	✔	✔		✔	
Low neighborhood attachment and community disorganization	✔	✔			✔
Extreme economic deprivation	✔	✔	✔	✔	✔
Family					
Family history of the problem behavior	✔	✔	✔	✔	✔
Family management problems	✔	✔	✔	✔	✔
Family conflict	✔	✔	✔	✔	✔
Favorable parental attitudes and involvement in the behavior	✔	✔			✔
School					
Early and persistent antisocial behavior	✔	✔	✔	✔	✔
Academic failure in elementary school	✔	✔	✔	✔	✔
Lack of commitment to school	✔	✔	✔	✔	✔
Individual/Peer					
Alienation and rebelliousness	✔	✔		✔	
Friends who engage in a problem behavior	✔	✔	✔	✔	✔
Favorable attitudes toward the problem behavior	✔	✔	✔	✔	
Early initiation of the problem behavior	✔	✔	✔	✔	✔
Constitutional factors	✔	✔			✔

Source: DRP, Inc. (1994). *Risk and Resource Assessment.* San Francisco, CA: Jossey-Bass.
© 1996–1997, Developmental Resource and Research Programs, Inc. All rights reserved. Online at http://www.DRP.org

called Communities That Care, which is being implemented in many communities. Essentially, the conceptualization and model suggest the following (Hawkins & Catalano, 1992; Howell, 1995):

- The greater the number of exposures to risks, the higher the likelihood of the juvenile engaging in the undesired behaviors.
- Because risks are found in multiple domains, multiple strategies must be used concurrently to reduce the risks.
- There is consistency in risk factors across races and cultures, although the levels of risk vary.
- Some common risk factors are predictive of the different problem behaviors, which indicates implementation of prevention strategies that can address multiple problems.
- Protective factors can reduce the impact of exposure to risk factors.
- Communities have a significant number of resources that can provide the protective factors.
- Communities must take charge of the prevention and intervention of juvenile delinquency by engagement in a strategic process that identifies the risks and resources within the community and targets intervention with specific programs which have been proven to be effective in reducing or eliminating the identified risks.

THE JUVENILE OFFENDER IN THE JUVENILE COURT SYSTEM

The juvenile court's jurisdiction over juvenile offenders, while threatened, remains the primary legal intervention for juveniles. The juvenile court, legislative mandate, or prosecutorial discretion statutes continue to waive only a small number of juvenile offenders to adult court; most cases are still handled by the juvenile court system (National Center for Juvenile Justice, 1997, 4)

Jurisdiction

The jurisdiction of a court (that is, its legal authority to hear and decide a particular matter) is determined by state statutes. The judge's authority in decision-making is limited to those situations authorized by the statute. In juvenile matters, the primary factors enumerated in the statutes are the subject matter; the maximum age of the children for original jurisdiction, the geographic boundaries of the court, and the matters in which the court has exclusive, shared, or concurrent jurisdictions.

The **age** of the young person under question is a primary factor in deciding whether a juvenile court or the criminal court has jurisdiction. For delinquency matters, in thirty-seven states the maximum age for original jurisdiction is 17 years; in ten states the maximum age is 16 years; and in three states the maximum age is 15 years (Office of Juvenile Justice and Delinquency Prevention, 1997). Most states allow the juvenile court to continue jurisdiction over juvenile offenders once they are adjudicated, beyond the maximum age of original jurisdiction (1995, 1997)

The delinquency **subject matter** jurisdiction of the juvenile courts includes those juveniles who commit violations of criminal statutes as well as wayward minors, status offenders, and minors in need of supervision. The specific facts of the case determine the appropriate jurisdictional basis. Jurisdictional elements are state-specific. Refer to the specific statutes and court rules for the state in which you are practicing.

Once the complaint or petition is filed, the court must follow specific procedures outlined in state statute and court rules to ensure that the rights of the juvenile are protected. As discussed in Chapter 6, juveniles have the following rights:

- the right to remain silent, that is, to not give information to the police or the court and not to be presumed guilty because they refuse to give information
- the right to have an attorney
- the right to know the charges against them, who is making those charges, the evidence the charging party has, and when and where the hearing will be held
- the right to examine and cross-examine witnesses and documents
- the right to proof beyond a reasonable doubt that they committed the offense. A standard of proof

is the degree of evidence required for the party who has the burden of proof to present to the court in order to sustain its burden, that is, prove what the party asserts (Jacobs, 1995, 1997).

The adjudicatory phase requires a fact-finding procedure by the judge or the jury. This entails reaching a conclusion that the evidence presented at trial proved beyond a reasonable doubt that the juvenile committed the offense or that the evidence was insufficient. If the evidence was insufficient, the case must be dismissed and the juvenile released if he or she has been in custody. If the evidence was sufficient, then the dispositional phase is required.

The dispositional phase requires an order by the court for the sanctions the juvenile is to endure for the offense and the selection of alternative placements and rehabilitative interventions.

Processing a Delinquency Case

Courts do not go out and seek cases. Someone must file a complaint or petition for the courts to become involved. Processes vary from state to state. In many states, law enforcement agencies have the authority to divert a juvenile from the juvenile court process and refer him or her to a community agency for intervention voluntarily or to turn the juvenile over to the parent with no intervention. In general, the process of juvenile court intervention includes the following steps:

- the filing of a complaint and/or petition by law enforcement/prosecutor or, in some cases, the parent, school, victim or social agency;
- the determination by the court that it has jurisdiction to hear the complaint and/or petition;
- a series of pretrial hearings—such as a custody hearing to determine whether there is basis to retain the juvenile in custody if he or she was taken into custody by the police or to take him or her into custody or to determine whether the juvenile should be waived to criminal court—motions, production, and sharing of evidence;
- a trial or adjudicatory hearing where the evidence is presented and the judge or jury makes a finding of the guilt or innocence of the accused;

- a dispositional hearing where the judge receives evidence and determines the punishment and treatment alternatives;
- a series of postdispositional review hearings to assess the progress the juvenile is making in rehabilitation and/or modify placement (Jacobs, 1995, 1997; Kramer, 1994).

Complaint or Petition and Detention

In delinquency matters, law enforcement and prosecutors usually file the complaint or petition. The complaint or petition is filed after investigation and determination that there is evidence to believe that a crime was committed and the person charged with the crime was likely to have committed it.

Juveniles may be placed in a detention facility by the court at various points between intake and case disposition. In 1994 about 21 percent, or 321,200 juveniles charged with delinquency, were held in detention at some point during the court process. The percentage has historically been around 20 percent annually (Poe-Yamagata, 1997). Detention may be deemed necessary to protect the community, to protect the youth, or both. Detention may also be ordered to ensure the youth's appearance at an upcoming hearing or to evaluate the youth for the purpose of planning treatment. Youths charged with drug-related offenses and violent crimes are the most likely to be held in detention; those charged with offenses against property are least likely to be detained. However, because of the large volume of property cases, nearly half of all detained youth are there for property offenses (Poe-Yamagata, 1997).

Court Review of Complaint or Petition

The court reviews the complaint or petition to determine that it has jurisdiction. That is, it is looking into whether there was a violation of a criminal statute or a status offense committed by a person who at the time of the commission of the act was within the age jurisdiction of the court. If so, the court can authorize the complaint or petition, or it can divert the case from the formal court process. Overall, about half the intake cases are diverted. Most of these cases are dismissed, but others are referred to another agency, or the juvenile is given informal probation or required to pay fines or restitution (Office for Juvenile Justice and Delinquency Prevention 1997).

For cases that are handled formally, a petition is filed and the case placed on the court calendar for a hearing. At a waiver hearing, the court decides whether to keep jurisdiction or to transfer jurisdiction to adult criminal court. The waiver decision is based on the seriousness of the offense, on whether the youth appears to be amenable to rehabilitation through programs available to the juvenile court, and on state statutes governing waivers. As indicated earlier, only a small proportion of all delinquency cases are waived to adult court, although the percentage is increasing in response to the increase in violent crimes committed by juveniles.

The Adjudicatory Hearing

For youths not diverted at intake or waived to adult court, the court holds an adjudicatory hearing, at which time the judge decides whether the youth should be adjudicated delinquent. The adjudicatory phase requires a fact-finding by the judge or the jury. This entails reaching a conclusion that the evidence presented at trial proved beyond a reasonable doubt that the juvenile committed the offense or that the evidence was insufficient. If the evidence was insufficient, the case must be dismissed and the juvenile released if he or she has been in custody. If the evidence was sufficient, then the dispositional phase is required.

The Dispositional Hearing

The dispositional phase requires an order by the court for the sanctions the juvenile is to endure for the offense, and the selection of alternative placements and rehabilitative interventions. Dispositional options may include commitment to a residential facility, probation, referral to another agency or treatment program, fines, restitution, or community service. The most common disposition is probation, though about 30 percent of ad-

judicated delinquents are placed outside the home. Everything that the court does on a delinquency case after the adjudication is dispositional, unless a new charge is brought that requires a new adjudication.

The Changing Philosophy of the Juvenile Court

The juvenile court appears to be abandoning its historical tradition of basing its dispositional decisions on the individual characteristics of the juvenile and his or her need for rehabilitation, and moving toward a system of making dispositional decisions based on punishment, accountability and public safety or offense-based dispositions (Office of Juvenile Justice and Delinquency Prevention, 1997, p. 32). The goals appear to be retribution and deterrence (Howell, 1997).

This change in the juvenile court processing of juvenile offenders is its acknowledgement of the increasing presence of serious, chronic juvenile offenders, the increasing use of drugs and alcohol by juvenile offenders within the system, and the need to hold juveniles accountable for their actions earlier in their delinquency careers in order to deter more effectively the tendency to continue and escalate their delinquent behaviors. The National Council of Juvenile and Family Court Judges endorsed a number of recommendations relating to the problem of serious juvenile crime in 1984, the first of which was this: "*Serious juvenile offenders should be held accountable by the courts.* Dispositions of such offenders should be proportionate to the injury done and the culpability of the juvenile and to the prior record of adjudication, if any" (National Council of Juvenile and Family Court Judges, 1984, p. x) The Council added that "the principal purpose of the juvenile justice court system is to protect the public," and qualified this position only by the statement, "Although rehabilitation is a primary goal of the court, it is not the sole objective and not always appropriate" (Heck et al., 1985, p. 29).

In recognition of the sometimes inappropriate efforts of the juvenile court to rehabilitate the juvenile offender, the Council further recommended that "*offenders unamenable to juvenile treatment should be transferred."* In other words, "if a juvenile commits a crime which is, for one reason or another, beyond the limits of juvenile court, that juvenile should be waived to criminal court" (Heck et al., 1985, p. 31).

The Council recommended as well that *"Substance abuse programs should be provided for juveniles* and . . . made part of the dispositional plan for those offenders whose criminal conduct is determined to be related to substance abuse" (Heck et al., 19985, p. 34). A difficulty in developing such programs was cited as the limited data available in the juvenile justice system on this type of juvenile who is drug or alcohol involved.

THE JUVENILE IN THE CRIMINAL COURT SYSTEM

The number of juveniles in the criminal court system is comparatively small. At the same time, there is increasing activity in federal and state legislatures to lower the jurisdictional age and offense types within the juvenile court system and reserve the more serious juvenile offenses to the criminal court system.

Types of Offenses

Although states vary, in general youths from age 14 to 17 may be tried as adults for the following types of offenses (Jacobs, 1995, 1997; Kramer, 1994):

- burning a dwelling
- assault with intent to commit murder
- assault with intent to commit great bodily harm less than murder
- assault with intent to rob, unarmed
- assault with intent to rob, armed
- attempted murder
- first-degree murder
- second-degree murder
- kidnapping
- criminal sexual conduct
- assault with intent to commit criminal sexual conduct
- armed robbery

- unarmed robbery
- possession, manufacture, or delivery of a controlled substance

How a Juvenile Offender Comes Before the Criminal Court

The states vary as to the procedure used to effect these transfers—judicial waiver, prosecutor discretion, or legislative exclusion. In the judicial waiver situation, the case originates in the juvenile court and, prior to holding an adjudicatory hearing, the juvenile court, consistent with state statutory guidelines, determines that the nature of the offense, the age of the juvenile, and the juvenile's past history are such that the juvenile is unlikely to benefit from juvenile court intervention. Then the case is waived to criminal court.

In the prosecutorial discretion situation, the prosecutor—the official who brings the charge on behalf of the people of the state—has full authority to decide, consistent with the state statutory requirements, whether or not he or she will prosecute the juvenile in the juvenile court or in the criminal court.

If he or she originates the action in juvenile court, the juvenile judge has authority to waive the case. However, if he or she chooses to originate the action in criminal court, the criminal court does not have authority to return the case to the juvenile court in most states. In the legislative exclusion situation, certain crimes committed by juveniles of certain ages are automatically within the exclusive jurisdiction of the criminal courts, meaning only the criminal court can hear the case.

While the names of the different phases differ, the substantive processes are similar and the rights granted the juvenile are the same.

Processing a Juvenile Offender in Criminal Court

Again, the courts do not seek out cases. Cases are brought to them. In criminal offenses, the police usually receive a complaint from a victim or are called to the scene of a crime by an individual in the community. They investigate and apprehend or arrest the suspected offender. After investigation, they can choose not to file charges to divert the juvenile for other services. If they choose to go forward, the police submit their information to the prosecutor, who determines the specific crime to charge, based on the evidence submitted by the police, and files a complaint with the court.

Once it is determined that a juvenile offense is to be prosecuted in the criminal courts, the prosecutor must file a complaint. The matter is then scheduled for preliminary examination or probable cause hearing. When probable cause is found, it is scheduled for arraignment or bail hearing if these matters are not scheduled as part of the preliminary examination or probable cause hearing, and a date is set for trial. If the juvenile is found guilty at trial or pleads guilty, a sentencing hearing is scheduled.

The Complaint

This complaint is similar to the complaint or petition filed in juvenile court in that it contains specifics about the offense, the law it violates, and the name, age, and address of the person alleged to have committed the offense. The prosecutor is given discretion to charge a crime less than the one supported by the evidence.

The Preliminary Examination or Probable Cause Hearing

This procedure is a review of the evidence against the juvenile by the judge and results in a determination as to whether or not the evidence is sufficient to believe that this juvenile committed the charged offense, should be charged with a lesser offense, or should be diverted.

The Arraignment or Bail Hearing

If the person has been arrested, he or she must be arraigned on the charges, that is, given an opportunity to appear in court and hear the charges and the evidence, enter a plea (guilty or not guilty), and have bail set (an amount of money to be posted with the court to guarantee appearance at the trial). Many states do not permit bail to be set if a serious crime such as murder or rape is charged. There is no proscription as to the maximum amount of bail that can be set. Thus many courts set high bails for juvenile offenders as a way of keeping them in custody until the trial. If the juvenile cannot post bail, he or she is held in jail. There is some debate as to whether or not a juvenile charged as an adult must be confined separately from adults.

The Trial

The trial in criminal court is similar in form and process to the adjudication in juvenile court. The juvenile has a right to have the facts determined by a judge or jury. During the trial the evidence is presented in accordance with the state's rules of evidence. If the evidence does not prove beyond a reasonable doubt that the juvenile committed the crimes charged, he or she must be found not guilty and released. If the evidence proves beyond a reasonable doubt that the juvenile committed the crimes charged, he or she must be found guilty and the matter set for sentencing.

The Sentencing

The sentencing is the phase where the punishment is rendered. In some states sentencing guidelines require the judge to issue certain sentences for certain offenses. In other states, it is totally within the judge's discretion to determine the sentence. Most sentencing decisions are based on the crime, the juvenile's participation in the crime, the juvenile's past history, and any unique factors made known to the court in the sentencing report or by the juvenile.

Traditional sentences include

- probation
- suspended sentence
- fine
- community service
- restitution
- jail and probation
- periodic imprisonment (to permit the juvenile to continue employment while serving sentence)

- confinement in jail or prison
- death (Saltzman & Proch, 1990; Kramer, 1994; Jacobs, 1995, 1997)

JUVENILE DELINQUENCY PREVENTION AND INTERVENTION STRATEGIES

Juvenile delinquency prevention and intervention strategies developed and implemented over the last twenty-five years with federal funding assistance include parenting training, early education, school behavior management, conflict resolution and violence prevention, mentoring, intensive family preservation services, gang prevention, recreation and leisure activities, vocational training, community services, policing strategies, out-of-home placement continuum, and incarceration. All of these strategies have been shown to be effective with some juveniles and not with others.

Figure 11.2 identifies the risk factors for adolescent problem behaviors as documented by Catalano and Hawkins. In the two sections below, the research findings for the types of interventions that work to prevent and treat juvenile delinquency are presented. It is divided into prevention and early intervention strategies effective with non-chronic offenders and strategies effective with chronic and serious juvenile offenders. A chronic or serious offender is one who commits four or more crimes and/or who commits at least one violent offense (Butts, 1997).

Prevention and Early Intervention with Non-Chronic Offender

The objective of prevention and early intervention programs is to reduce risk factors, increase protective factors, and achieve prosocial behavior. While no intervention has proven to be completely successful with all children and youth, in the last twenty years, many programs have been implemented that are designed to reduce the number of youth who engage in delinquent behaviors and/or reduce the number of youth who have been adjudicated delinquent who commit subsequent offenses (recidivate). The prevention programs are aimed at populations identified as at-risk because of the presence of risk factors discussed above. Early intervention programs are aimed at children who have had a non-serious offense contact with the police or who have exhibited problem behaviors which, if not corrected, could lead to delinquent behaviors.

Parenting Programs. Provide parents with developmental information, so that they are better able to direct the behaviors of their child and themselves in relation to the child. Most focus on both parent and child factors. For example, a program provides education and training for the mother's employment as well as information of developmental needs of the child and modeling parental approaches to problem behaviors. These programs have proven successful for general prevention in at-risk populations and with the non-chronic status offender and non-violent offender.

Early education programs. Academic achievement or lack thereof is a significant risk factor for problem behaviors. Early education programs focus on providing the child with a head start cognitively and socially. If children enter school ready to learn and knowing how to interact with others in a socially appropriate non-aggressive way, they are more likely to succeed. These programs are targeted to at-risk populations.

Early Elementary School Programs. Focus additional training in social development for children identified as at-risk because they engage in anti-social behaviors. In addition, many school districts provide general health promotion instruction for all children to encourage positive development. Mentoring and after school leisure and recreation programs are added interventions.

Middle and High School Programs. Focus specifically on substance abuse education and alternatives; sex education; gang prevention; social conduct and peer relations, e.g. peer mediation and counseling. Mentoring and after-school leisure and education programs continue in importance.

Specific Interventions.   Focus on juveniles who have committed non-serious offenses. They are designed to specifically address the underlying issues which precipitated the offense with the expectation of "turning the juvenile around". Interventions include mental health counseling, substance abuse treatment, teen issues groups focused on providing general awareness and alternative approaches, intensive family preservation services, placement outside the parental home if that environment is found to contribute to the youth's problem behaviors, remedial education, vocational training and supported employment.

Intervention with chronic or serious juvenile offenders

As stated previously, although the number of chronic or serious juvenile offenders is relatively small, they have been and continue to be the focus of both the public's and the policymakers' discourse. In 1993, OJJDP proposed a graduated sanctions model to address this issue. Specifically, this model combines treatment and rehabilitation with reasonable, fair, humane, and appropriate sanctions, and offers a continuum of care consisting of diverse programs. The continuum includes the following:

- immediate sanctions within the community for first-time, nonviolent offenders.
- intermediate sanctions within the community for more serious offenders.
- secure care programs for the most violent offenders.
- aftercare programs that provide high levels of social control and treatment services. (Howell, 1995)

In implementing the graduated sanctions philosophy over the last five years, practitioners have focused on risk assessments and interventions based on the juvenile's likelihood to reoffend based on the risk assessments. It is too early in the process to provide conclusive statements as to the effectiveness of this approach. To support graduated sanctions philosophy, several new program interventions have been added to the traditional group homes or institutions/training schools. They include boot camps, wilderness/survival programs, intensive community supervision, work-study-home detention, and individual mentoring. These programs are designed to give immediately more severe consequences to the youth with the hope that the youth will see that all behaviors have consequences (graduated sanctions). Some commentators suggest that the system was out of control because juveniles did not see any immediate consequences for their behaviors and continued to escalate until they had to be incarcerated because of the nature of the offense. If the behaviors receive progressively more severe consequences, then escalation might not occur. (Torbet, 1996). The prevention and early intervention programs discussed above are critical to the continued decrease in the number of youth who commit serious or violent offenses because early antisocial behavior is generally documented in case histories of youth who commit these acts. Increasingly, interventions at the later childhood years are recognizing the need for multidimensional, integrated interventions instead of simply targeting the children and youth with school-based programs (Wasserman & Miller, 1998).

TRENDS AND ISSUES

Although the juvenile justice system has changed greatly since passage of the Juvenile Justice Delinquency Prevention Act in 1974, the issues that have plagued it since the early 1970s continue to remain of concern. Specifically, the nation's provisions for juvenile offenders have not yet resolved the following issues: the legitimate designation and service system for status offenders; services designed for the unique needs of female offenders; overrepresentation of minorities; alternatives to secure detention; and the community's readiness to support alternative programs. These concerns reflect the increasing severity of mental health and substance abuse problems of juvenile offenders.

Status Offenders

Status offenses are acts that are only an offense because of the juvenile's age; they would not be offenses if committed by an adult. Examples of status offenses are truancy from home, truancy from school, failure to obey the reasonable commands of the parent or guardian, violating curfew, and underaged drinking. In some states, juveniles who commit these acts are also classified as juvenile delinquents. In other states, these juveniles are called children in need of supervision, persons in need of services, status offenders, or wayward minors (Kramer, 1994). According to the U.S. Department of Justice, juvenile courts process about 100,000 status offense cases a year (Office of Juvenile Justice and Delinquency Prevention, 1997). About one-third of these involve underage drinking; about a quarter relate to truancy; the remaining cases include "ungovernability" or incorrigibility (19 percent), runaway cases (20 percent), and other offenses such as curfew violations (10 percent). More than half of all status offenders are 15 or younger. The ratio of males to females is about six to five. Males and females are equally likely to be involved in cases involving truancy or incorrigibility. Males are more likely to be charged with liquor law violations, while females make up the majority of runaways.

Fewer than 5 percent of status offenders are held in secure detention facilities. For the most part, those in secure detention are placed there after a hearing in which it was determined that secure detention was necessary for the youth's safety until appropriate placement could be arranged.

A continuing controversy among policy makers is whether status offenders should be removed from juvenile court jurisdiction and their problems dealt with by noncoercive community-based services. "It has been urged that only juveniles whose acts would result in criminal prosecutions if they were adults be handled in the juvenile justice system and that status offenders should be kept from contact with the juvenile justice system and cared for by alternative agencies" (Simonsen, 1991, p. 449).

The issue of jurisdiction over status offenders is complicated by research findings on the question of whether status offenders are more similar than different from delinquent youth. So far, the weight of evidence strongly suggests that youth tend to be concurrently involved in both delinquent and status offense behavior. Such findings imply that it is not possible at this time to differentiate involvement in status offenses from involvement in delinquency, at least in less serious delinquency. "There seem to be two major categories of illegal involvement . . . one is petty illegal behavior which includes status offenses and less serious delinquency, and the other is serious delinquency" (Weis, Sakumato, Sederstrom, & Seiss, 1980, p. 99; OJJDPS, 1997).

Such findings suggest that the juvenile justice system should treat the two categories of petty and serious offenders differently. Some recommend that jurisdiction over status offenders, as well as over less serious delinquents, should be restricted or perhaps abandoned. Appropriate dispositional decisions by the court and treatment alternatives in the community for status offenders and for less seriously delinquent youth may well be the same (Weis et al., 1980).

The status offender concept can be traced back to colonial America, where the family was held strictly responsible for serving as the primary socializing agent of children. Parents were held accountable for training the child into patterns of life acceptable to the community, and children, in turn, were expected to obey their parents. These prescriptions were written into laws that became the archetypes of modern status offense laws. The homogeneous colonial culture underwent social change in the face of immigration and urbanization. Skepticism began to be expressed about the family as the traditional agency of socialization and social control. Creation of the juvenile court was only one movement by the state, although a powerful one, to assume the role of surrogate parent.

As the juvenile court approaches its one hundredth anniversary, youth policy planners are questioning whether any quasi-legal means of regulating childhood can take the place of the family as the primary source of nurture and support for the child. The juvenile justice system, many contend, has been vested with overwhelming and sometimes quite unrealistic expectations. Its institutional limitations must be acknowledged and efforts made to reeducate the public about the responsibilities the family and the community must accept, particularly in relation to children in need of supervision (Smith, Berkman, Fraser, & Sutton, 1980, p. 160; Schwartz, 1989; Ayers, 1997).

For the most part, status offenders commit no offenses except against themselves. Their actions are often a response to neglect, abuse, alcohol and substance abuse, or other family dysfunctions, but they are treated as if they were guilty of some very serious wrongdoing. Some of them do come within the province of the delinquency system; however, their offense is more likely to be running away, truancy, substance abuse, or being beyond control. Children who run away from home, for the most part, can cite credible reasons. Some understand that their lives would be in danger if they stayed at home. Many have been rejected by their families and thrown out of their homes. Unhappily, many have had bad experiences with social welfare agencies and other would-be helpers who wished to help but unwittingly made matters worse. In such cases, the activities of these children should be seen as urgent signals to look into the causes. For some advocates this suggests that the family is not the caring and supporting environment that others contend, and, in those situations where the parental actions do not rise to the level of abuse or neglect under the statute, status offenders should have a quasi-legal system to protect them from the actions of their parents.

Arguments cited in support of doing so usually focus on the misapplication of judicial power and the injustice that often results when the punishment is out of proportion to the offense—for example, truancy or being on the streets after curfew. The proponents of policy change also cite the harm done to youths by the stigma of having participated in the judicial process. They maintain as well that the juvenile justice system clearly lacks the capability to resolve individual behavior problems typical of minors in need of supervision. On the other hand, juvenile court judges in many states strongly oppose the proposal to remove status offenders from their authority and have lobbied effectively against it.

The status offender problem is persistent despite the efforts of the National Institute of Juvenile Justice and Delinquency Prevention (NIJJDP) and the various states to improve the handling of minors in need of supervision. An assessment by the NIJJDP of the current state of knowledge concerning status offenders found that they continue to be involved in a significant portion of juvenile arrests, intake and court procedures, and detention homes and other institutional placements. Wide variation in state status offense legislation exists, negating any assumption that decisions are being made on uniform principles and procedures. Dealing with noncriminal adolescent behavior is a significant issue in most states (Smith et al, 1980; Kramer, 1994; Jacobs, 1995 supp. 1997; Howell, 1997; Davis, 1998).

Overrepresentation of Minorities

African-American and Latino youth are overrepresented in every phase of the juvenile justice system. A recent study found that, compared to white youth who commit the same type of offense, they are more likely to be arrested and less likely to be released while awaiting trial. A Florida study found that "Florida courts were three times as likely to transfer an African-American or Native American charged with delinquency to adult court than they were to transfer his or her white counterpart. The impact on African Americans was particularly disproportionate, and they were far more likely to be sentenced to detention by a juvenile court" (American Bar Association, 1993, p. 62). The Florida Supreme Court Race and Ethnic Bias Commission (1990) has described the compounding effect on minority youth of being less likely to be diverted out of the system:

> Unlike the non-minority youth, the minority youth develops a prior record that he or she carries as a liability into the future. The presence of that prior record is likely to increase the severity of treatment which that youth will receive should he or she reoffend. . . . Thus bias has a 'snowball' effect—one which leads to a characterization of habitualization for that minority youth which may not be fully warranted by the circumstances. (p. 73)

As stated previously, a 1992 amendment to the Juvenile Justice and Delinquency Prevention Act requires states to reduce the number of minority youth in detention, but the federal government has not enforced this provision in the law. The ABA Presidential Working Group on the Unmet Legal Needs of Children and Their Families (1993) recommended that communities develop culturally sensitive training for police and judges and increase the representation of minority staff at the juvenile court. They also recommended that effective grievance procedures be instituted for situations in which the police use excessive force or other situations relating to ethnic, racial, or gender bias.

In 1997, the Office of Juvenile Justice and Delinquency Prevention reported that African-American juveniles, who comprise 15 percent of the juvenile population in 1995, account for 28 percent of all juvenile arrests; 58 percent of murder arrests; 45 percent of forcible rape arrests; 60 percent of robbery arrests; 42 percent of aggravated assault arrests; 38 percent of motor vehicle theft arrests; 42 percent of fraud arrests; and 77 percent of gambling arrests (Office of Juvenile Justice and Delinquency Prevention, 1997). Additionally minority youth, including African Americans, Hispanics, Asian/Pacific Islanders, and Native Americans, who were 32 percent of the youth population in 1995, made up 68 percent of the detention center population on the day in time chosen, February 15, 1995. Further, they represented 68 percent of the juveniles in public long-term facilities (Office of Juvenile Justice and Delinquency Prevention, 1997).

Gender Issues

In the 1996 edition of this text, we stated juvenile delinquency in the United States is largely a male phenomenon: "Males under the age of 18 account for the overwhelming majority of arrests, the bulk of the referrals to juvenile courts, and the largest proportion of young people in detention centers and training schools across the country." Nevertheless, large numbers of girls enter the juvenile justice system each year, and some are inappropriately sent into institutions because few if any community-based programs have been provided for delinquent females. For the most part, these girls have been confined because of relatively minor delinquent acts. Follow-up studies have not produced clear evidence that locking girls into institutions has been helpful to them in any clear way. Instead, it appears that "most young female offenders can be managed and treated in their own community without

compromising public safety." Nevertheless, troubled and delinquent girls continue to be neglected amidst policy-maker preoccupation and public concern about violent juvenile crime, primarily committed by male adolescents (Schwartz & Orlando, 1991).

While that statement remains substantially true, a 1996 study by Poe-Yamagata and Butts, *Female Offenders in the Juvenile Justice System,* found that juvenile female arrests for violent crimes increased 131 percent compared to juvenile male arrests for violent crimes, which increased by 66 percent between 1986 and 1995. Furthermore, juvenile female arrests for property crimes increased 38 percent while juvenile male arrests for property crimes increased only 1 percent. With these increases, females accounted for 20 percent of the juvenile violent crime arrest growth and 89 percent of the growth in property crime arrests. Since that report was issued, NCJJ has issued these additional findings:

- 702,200 juvenile females were arrested in 1995
- By 1995, the ratio of male to female arrests for violent crimes was 6 to 1 and for property crimes was 3 to 1, down from 8 to 1 and 4 to 1, respectively, in 1986.
- The female proportion of all juvenile court cases increased from 19 percent to 21 percent between 1985 and 1995.
- In 1994 delinquency cases involving females were less likely to be adjudicated once petitioned (52 percent versus 56 percent) and females whose cases were processed formally were more likely to receive probation and less likely to be in detention or out-of-home placement. (National Center for Juvenile Justice, 1997).

The potential for change is contained in the Juvenile Justice and Delinquency Prevention Act. Federal funds are available for developing alternative programs for juvenile offenders. The act states specifically that assistance must be made available to "all disadvantaged youth, including . . . females" (1974). Young female offenders have some special needs that, for the most part, are not addressed in the juvenile justice system. They are frequently victims of sexual abuse and can see only one way to safety—to run away. In such instances they soon learn that there is no safety for them on the street. Access to crisis intervention services, shelter care, day treatment, therapeutic foster care, independent living arrangements, and, not to be overlooked, access to continued education are much needed.

Alternatives to the Use of Secure Detention

Criteria established by the National Council on Crime and Delinquency for admission of children and youth into secure detention emphasize that detention should not be used "unless failure to do so would be likely to place the child or the community in danger" (Pappenfort & Young, 1980, p. 99). In all jurisdictions, courts are faced at times with children who, after arrest or some other form of intake, cannot be returned home. In such instances, secure detention is often misused. The reasons given in justification are numerous: (1) a child's psychiatric and neurological problems require attention, and no alternative to detention is available; (2) neglected and dependent children are sometimes classified as children in need of supervision and detained, pointing up in another way the common characteristics of status offenders and other children before the court; (3) some youth must be detained to prevent the chance of their committing a delinquent act or engaging in incorrigible behavior while awaiting adjudication; (4) some children go into secure detention only because there is no other place for them to stay; and (5) some children who present little or no danger to themselves or the community go into detention so that they can be readily referred into services that otherwise would not be available to them (Pappenfort & Young, 1980).

Many jurisdictions are attempting to avoid inappropriate use of detention by developing strict criteria for its use, by reviewing early the detention decisions by a juvenile court judge, and by developing nonresidential and residential alternatives. Home detention is one such alternative. Youths are released to their parents to await court hearings with supervision by a youth worker attached to the court's probation department (Howell, 1997). Residential group homes also are used as alternatives to detention and are fre-

quently directed toward runaway children, a type of status offender generally considered to be troublesome to deal with effectively. Another alternative to detention is found in some jurisdictions in which foster parents are paid an annual salary to make their homes available for youths on a short-term basis. The foster parent role is to provide care and supervision as well as companionship to troubled youth awaiting court hearings.

Community Readiness to Support Alternative Programs

The term *community-based* implies an intention to enable troubled youth to retain their ties to persons in the community, to move about and communicate freely within the community, and to experience some degree of acceptance from others in the community. Yet community residents often object to plans for alternative programs. Such proposals, especially for residential programs, often bring prompt and vigorous opposition on the assumption that the kind of youth served would be a danger to the surrounding neighborhood. Somewhat paradoxically, professional interests and federal guidelines that favor community-based alternatives came at a time when many citizens were expressing intense fear about delinquency and crime, and state legislatures were enacting more restrictive laws affecting the handling of law offenders generally. Those statements are as accurate today as when stated by citizens in 1996. There is some hope of community support, as evidenced by the expansion of diversion and early intervention programs for less serious offenders. But, as to the serious and chronic offender, community support for community-based alternatives does not exist (Howell, 1995; Howell, 1997).

CHAPTER SUMMARY

This chapter has focused on juvenile delinquency. It is the first time that we have included this topic as a separate chapter in this text. Heretofore, we addressed the topic within the discussion of the child in the courts. As we thought of the revision, we were struck by the need to give voice to juveniles involved in delinquency activities, and to do so within the scope of child welfare and family services. Historically, U.S. society has addressed these youth separately from abuse, neglected, and abandoned youth. Increasingly, society is seeing that they are the same or that some children in the same family carry abuse or neglect labels while others carry juvenile delinquent labels. If society is to develop effective child, family, and community interventions to prevent and treat child abuse, neglect, and delinquency, we must begin to look at children and families holistically.

This chapter provided an overview of the scope of the problem, the types of offenses committed by juveniles, the processing of juveniles in the juvenile court and criminal court systems, some persistent issues, and some promising interventions.

FOR STUDY AND DISCUSSION

1. Explain and evaluate the aims of the juvenile justice system. How do they differ from those of the adult corrections system?

2. Give arguments to support either the traditional benevolent-rehabilitative model of the juvenile court or a model based on constitutional guarantees of due process and legal justice.

3. Obtain a copy of the juvenile court act in your state or some other. Evaluate it in these terms:

    a. What is the expressed intent of the act? How well does this intent reflect a modern juvenile court philosophy?

    b. Compare its definitions of classes of children who come under its jurisdiction to the categories discussed in this chapter.

    c. What indications are there in the statute that the child's and parent's constitutional rights shall be respected?

    d. How adequate are the act's provisions in regard to personnel and services of the court?

4. What are some of the principal differences between children and youth who are (a) neglected or abused, (b) delinquent, or (c) guilty of a status offense? What are some of their similarities?

5. How would you design an "ideal" juvenile delinquency program? What would be its features? Why? How could stigma be averted?

6. Review the data discussed in the Scope of the Problem section. Is delinquent behavior as serious as the media projects? Explain your answer.

FOR ADDITIONAL STUDY

Butt, J. A., & Harre, A. V. (1998). *Delinquents or criminals: Policy options for young offenders.* Washington, DC: The Urban Institute.

Breckenridge, S. & Abbott, E. (1912). *The delinquent child and the home.* New York: Russell Sage Foundation.

Heide, M. (1999). *Young Killers—The challenge of juvenile homicide.* Thousand Oaks, CA: Sage Publications, Inc.

Humm, S. R., Ort, B. A., Anbari, M. M., Lader, W. S., & Biel, W. S. (1994). *Child, parent, and state: Law and policy reader.* Philadelphia: Temple University Press.

Kelly, B. T., Huizinga, D., Thornberry, T. P., & Loeber, R. (1997, June). *Epidemiology of serious violence.* Washington, DC: Office of Juvenile Justice and Delinquency Prevention.

Loeber, R., & Farrington, D. P., Eds. (1998) *Serious and violent offenders: Risk factors and successful interventions.* Thousand Oaks, CA: Sage Publications, Inc.

National Juvenile Court Data Archive, Juvenile Justice Clearinghouse, Rockville, MD.

Nelson, K. E. (1990). Family based services for juvenile offenders. *Children and Youth Services Review, 12*(3), 193–212.

Scalia, J. (1997, January). *Juvenile delinquents in the federal criminal justice system.* Washington, DC: Office of Juvenile Justice and Delinquency Prevention.

INTERNET SITES

These internet sites offer a broad range of legal, statistical, program, and policy information.

American Bar Association Juvenile Justice Center.
http://www.abanet.org

National Council of Juvenile and Family Court Judges, Inc.   http://www.ncjfcjunr.edu

National Center for Juvenile Justice.   http://www.ncjj.org

Office of Juvenile Justice Delinquency Prevention.
http://www.ncjrs.org/ojjhome.html

U.S. Department of Justice, Bureau of Justice Statistics.   http://www.ojp.usdoj.gov/bjs

REFERENCES

American Bar Association (1993). *Unmet legal needs of children and their families.* Chicago: American Bar Association.

Ayers, W. (1997). *A kind and just parent: The children of the juvenile court.* Boston: Beacon Press.

Breed v. Jones, 421 U.S. 519 (1975).

Butts, J. A. (1997, April). Prosecuting juveniles in criminal court. *National Center for Juvenile Justice in brief,* (Vol. 1, No. 4). Pittsburgh, PA: National Center for Juvenile Justice.

Dean, C. W., & Reppucci, N. D. (1974). Juvenile correctional institutions. In Glasser, D. (Ed.) Handbook of criminology. (pp. 865–894). Chicago: Rand-McNally.

Empey, L. T., & Stafford, M. C. (1991). *American delinquency: Its meaning and construction* (3rd ed.). Belomont, CA: Wadsworth.

Finestone, H. (1996). *Victims of change.* Westport, CT: Greenwood.

Flexner, B., & Baldwin, R. N. (1914). *Juvenile courts and probation.* New York: Century.

Heck, R. O., Pindur, W., & Wells, D. K. (1985). The juvenile serious habitual offender/drug involved program: A means to implement recommendations of the National Council of Juvenile and Family Court Judges. *Juvenile and Family Court Journal, 36,* 27–37.

Howell, J. C. (1995). *Guide for implementing the comprehensive strategy for serious, violent, and chronic juvenile offenders.* Washington, DC: Office of Juvenile Justice and Delinquency Prevention.

Howell, J. C. (1997). *Juvenile justice and youth policy.* Thousand Oaks, CA: Sage.

In re Gault, 387 U.S. 1 (1967).

In re Winship, 397 U.S. 358 (1970).

Jacobs, T. A. (1995, supp 1997). *Children and the law: Rights and obligations.* St. Paul, MN: West Publishing.

Kramer, D. T. (1994). *Legal rights of children. 2nd Ed.* Colorado Springs: Shepards/McGraw Hill.

Kelley, B. T., Thornberry, T. P., & Smith, C. A. (August, 1997). *In the wake of childhood maltreatment.* Washington, DC: Office of Juvenile Justice and Delinquency Prevention.

Kent v. United States, 383 U.S. 541 (1966).

McKeiver v. Pennsylvania, 403 U.S. 538 (1971).

Office of Juvenile Justice and Delinquency Prevention. (1997). *Juvenile offenders and victims: 1997 update on violence: Statistics summary.* Pittsburgh, PA: National Center for Juvenile Justice.

Pappenfort, D. M., & Young, T. W. (1980, December). *Use of secure detention for juveniles and alternatives to its use: A national study of juvenile detention.* Office of Juvenile Justice and Delinquency Prevention. Washington, DC: U.S. Government Printing Office.

Poe-Yamagata, E. (1997, March). *Detention and delinquency cases, 1985–1995* (Office of Juvenile Justice and Delinquency Prevention Fact Sheet #56). Washington, DC: Office of Juvenile Justice and Delinquency Prevention.

Poe-Yamagata, E. (1997, February). *Female participation in delinquent behavior is on the rise.* NCJJ in Brief, Vol. 1, No. 2. Pittsburgh, PA: National Center for Juvenile Justice.

Poe-Yamagata, E., & Butts, J. A. (1996). *Female offenders in the juvenile justice system.* Washington, DC: U.S. Department of Justice, Office of Juvenile Justice and Delinquency Prevention.

Saltzman, A., & Proch, K. (1990). *Law in social work practice.* Chicago: Nelson-Hall

Schall v. Martin, 467 U.S. 253 (1984).

Schwartz. I., & Orlando, F. (1991). *Programming for young women in the juvenile justice system.* Ann Arbor: University of Michigan, Center for the Study of Youth Policy.

Simonsen, C. (1991) *Status offenders: An attempt to clarify the system. Juvenile justice in America.* New York: Macmillan.

Smith, C. P., Berkman, D. J., Fraser, W. M., & Sutton, J. (1980). *Jurisdiction and the elusive status offender: A comparison of involvement in delinquent behavior and status offenses.* U.S. Department of Justice, Law Enforcement Assistance Administration, Office of Juvenile Justice and Delinquency Prevention. Washington, DC: U.S. Government Printing Office.

Torbet, Patricia, et al. (1996). *State responses to serious and violent juvenile crime.* Washington, DC: Office of Juvenile Justice and Delinquency Prevention.

Wasserman, G. A., & Miller, L. S. (1998). The prevention of serious and violent juvenile offending. In Loeber, R., & Farrington, D. P. (Eds.) *Serious and violent juvenile offenders: Risk factors and successful interventions.* Thousand Oaks, CA: Sage Publications, Inc.

Weis, J. G., Sakumato, K., Sederstrom, J., & Seiss, C. (1980). *Reports of the national juvenile justice assessment centers: Jurisdiction and the elusive status offender: A comparison of involvement in delinquent behavior and status offenses.* U.S. Department of Justice, Law Enforcement Assistance Administration, Office of Juvenile Justice and Delinquency Prevention. Washington, DC: U.S. Government Printing Office.

CHAPTER 12

Professional Responsibilities
Ethics and Advocacy

*Vision without action is merely a dream. Action without vision just
passes the time. Vision with action can change the world.*
—Joel Arthur Barker, *The Power of Vision*

CHAPTER OUTLINE

CASE EXAMPLE: BALANCING CLIENT ADVOCACY AND ETHICAL REQUIREMENTS

Susan Smith is a child welfare worker for the Big County Children's Services Agency (BCCSA). She has worked in child welfare for two years after receiving her MSW from Big State University. She has had approximately eight days of program-specific training and attended a one-day conference on permanency planning since employment. She is a member of the National Association of Social Workers (NASW). She began employment in BCCSA in the protective services program and moved into the foster care program approximately six months ago.

Last week Susan received the Blue case. There are three children, Mary (4 years old), Michael (2 years old), and Joseph (2 weeks old). The case came to protective services on a complaint from the hospital that Joseph was born drug addicted. The protective services worker recommended that a petition be filed and all children be removed from the home.

Susan's initial assessment, based on the materials in the files, was that the children should not have been removed from the home. The case file stated that the mother denied using cocaine on an ongoing basis. She stated that she went to a party about two weeks before Joseph's birth and smoked cocaine for the first time. Susan confronted the protective services worker in the staff lunchroom and they engaged in a loud, heated argument about their different assessments of the case. Her final statement to the protective services worker was "You are so ignorant! I'm going to bring this case to the attention of the administration. You ought to be fired."

Susan proceeded to tell her supervisor that this was the third case that she had received from this protective services worker. In all three cases, there had been inadequate documentation to justify a removal under the agency's policies. It appeared to her that this protective services worker and her supervisor did not accept the agency's family preservation policies and were intentionally harming children and families because of this bias. She stated that, in one of the cases, after she gave her testimony, the judge stated that BCCSA administration needed to "do something" with this worker and supervisor. She forgot to pass the information on to administration at the time.

Susan is concerned that other workers might not be as vigilant as she in defending families against the misjudgments of this worker. She wants administration to intervene so that no family has to suffer the trauma of separation due to worker bias, inadequate and incomplete investigations, and the general incompetence of the worker.

After this communication with her supervisor, Susan interviewed the mother. She told the mother that the file did not contain sufficient documentation to warrant removal of the children from the home. Susan told her that she wanted to work with her to get the children returned as soon as possible. To help her determine the approach to presenting her recommendation, Susan asked Ms. Blue to tell her everything she needed to know about the one instance of drug use. Ms. Blue stated that she had used cocaine during the entire pregnancy and that she had used cocaine for

about three years. The downstairs neighbor would check on them several times a day and would take Mary and Michael to her flat when she found Ms. Blue too high to care for them. The neighbor had called protective services once when she did not come home for two days, but Ms. Blue arrived before protective services came out, and the neighbor had called protective services back and told them she made a mistake.

Ms. Blue had been in a substance abuse treatment program, but services were terminated because she had received the full thirty days of services for which she was eligible under Medicaid. Ms. Blue stated that she loved her children and that she knew it was stupid to continue to use cocaine while she was pregnant. She knew it was stupid to deny to the protective services worker that she was an ongoing user, but she did so because she knew the protective services worker was against her from the beginning.

Ms. Blue said she would like the children returned to her as soon as possible and she would do whatever Susan required because she felt Susan understood her. Susan became concerned and asked her to talk more about her drug use. As the story unfolded, Susan told Ms. Blue that she would have to reconsider her recommendation due to Ms. Blue's admissions of long-term and continuing drug use. Susan needed to discuss the matter with her supervisor. Ms. Blue became enraged that Susan would "worm her way into her confidence with false promises." She asked Susan to leave immediately.

DISCUSSION OF CASE EXAMPLE

While Susan Smith seems to have the right credentials for child welfare practice—several years of child welfare experience, the appropriate advanced degree, membership in the professional organization, and some training—she has apparently had a lapse in judgment and then committed an ethical violation in the course of her work on the Blue case. One wonders why her credentials did not better prepare Susan in the area of sensitivity to ethical practice. The most obvious ethical violation was her public criticism of a colleague. But the lapse in judgment was potentially more problematic. Without having interviewed the new client, Susan decided, based only on materials in the file, that the children should not have been removed from the home. This placed her in the awkward position of appearing to promise to return the children from foster care soon. On discovering that the parent did have a long-standing history of substance abuse, Susan had to re-evaluate her earlier position, which was now completely invalidated by her new knowledge.

In all likelihood Susan is a conscientious professional who would be shocked and upset to think that she had violated part of the NASW Code of Ethics and that she did not use sound professional judgment in her interactions with her client. If she is as busy as most foster care workers are, she may not even have time to reflect on her actions. Yet if she is to develop her professional potential, it is imperative that she understand the implications of her actions. Failure to do so could result in damaged relationships with clients, an ethics complaint, or even, at some point, litigation. Child welfare workers operate under difficult conditions. Many are not as well prepared as Susan.

This chapter addresses several issues which on the surface appear disparate: professional responsibility, liability and malpractice, confidentiality and privileges, forensic interviewing, risk management and duty to warn, the client's right to treatment in a managed care environment, testimony, and advocacy. The common thread is the social work profession's mission, ethics, and values. "The primary mission of the social work profession is to enhance human well-being and help meet the basic human needs of all people, with particular attention to the needs and empowerment of people who are vulnerable, oppressed, and living in poverty (National Association of Social Workers, 1996, p. 1).

Child welfare practice presents many ethical dilemmas. These dilemmas result from the challenges of serving multiple clients—parents and children—in multiple organizational environments (public and private child welfare, mental health, substance abuse agencies, schools, hospitals, mental health facilities, and juvenile and family courts) subject to multiple legal and regulatory requirements that are not consistent and/or compatible. In previous chapters, we have discussed legal and regulatory issues. In this chapter, we raise and discuss several common dilemmas within the context of the NASW Code of Ethics (the Code). The Code is liberally cited and case examples are used to help you recognise some of the dilemmas and the

alternate considerations. Reamer (1995) states "there is no precise formula available for resolving ethical dilemmas. Reasonable thoughtful social workers can disagree about the ethical principles and criteria that ought to guide ethical decisions in any given case" (p. 64). He suggests a seven-step process in resolving these dilemmas:

1. Identify the ethical issues and the conflicts.
2. Identify individuals, groups, and organizations who might be affected by the decision.
3. Identify all courses of action and benefits and harms to each party.
4. Examine the reasons supporting or negating a particular course of action.
5. Consult with supervisors, administrators, and attorneys.
6. Decide and document how you came to that decision.
7. Monitor impact of decision. (Id., pp. 64–65).

PROFESSIONAL RESPONSIBILITY

Professional responsibility is an ominous term. It embraces the concept that a person who has attained the education and training necessary for entry into a profession has a responsibility to maintain the integrity of that profession. The integrity of the profession is maintained if its individual members are accountable to the general public for individual execution of the values and standards that the profession has established for itself or that have been established by various state statutes and regulatory schemes.

National Association of Social Workers Code of Ethics

The National Association of Social Workers (NASW) is the largest professional organization of social workers in the United States. It adopted its first code of ethics in 1960 (Reamer, 1995). There have been several revisions, the latest in 1996. Codes of ethics are adopted by professional organizations to establish norms and standards for the operation of the profession. If the professions themselves adopt these norms and standards, then it is less likely that outside administrative organizations will find the need to do so. In addition, these codes provide objective criteria for adjudicating misconduct (Reamer, 1995). Operationally, they are not as black and white as this might lead you to believe. The NASW Code of Ethics has been revised several times since its original adoption in 1960. Those revisions have occurred in response to developments in the profession and in the NASW. In this chapter, we use the latest revision, adopted in 1996.

The Code sets out the mission, values, ethical principles, and ethical standards for social work professionals in the United States. Other countries have different codes, which reflect the interplay of the social work profession within the context of their societies. The Code identifies six purposes to be served: to identify the core values of the profession; to provide a summary of the core values and standards to guide practice; to assist in resolving professional conflicts or ethical uncertainties; to provide notice to the general public of the expectations of the profession; to socialize new practitioners to the profession; and to give standards by which the profession can regulate itself (NASW, 1996).

The challenge to the professional is found in this statement:

> *The Code offers a set of values, principles, and standards to guide decision making and conduct when ethical issues arise. It does not provide a set of rules that prescribe how social workers should act in all situations. Specific application of the Code must take into account the context in which it is being considered and the possibility of conflicts among the Code's values, principles, and standards. (NASW, 1996, pp. 2–3)*

Space does not permit us to discuss all the principles and standards stated in the Code. We discuss only those principles that raise ethical dilemmas for child welfare practitioners most often: that social workers should respect the inherent dignity and worth of the person; that social workers should recognize the central importance of human relationships; that social workers should behave in a trustworthy manner; that social workers should practice within their areas of competence, and develop and enhance their

professional expertise; and that social workers should challenge social injustice.

It should be noted that the National Association of Social Workers has an established procedure for dealing with violations of the Code of Ethics—the Committee on Inquiry, a professional peer review process. When a request for review (formerly known as a complaint) is filed with a state chapter or the national office, it is screened to determine whether the issue involved would constitute an ethical violation if it had actually occurred. If so, the matter is reviewed by a Committee on Inquiry, which hears the requester or complainant and the social work respondent. There are a number of sanctions for social workers who have been found to have breached ethics, ranging from a recommendation by NASW for professional supervision to publication of the offense and suspension of membership. This process is used only for ethical violations—actions that go against the professional code of conduct—and is different from the legal process set in motion through the courts when a social worker has committed bad practice and violated professional standards of practice—malpractice.

Professional Malpractice and Liability

Malpractice is the failure to meet the standards of the profession in the provision of professional services. A person is held legally responsible for the consequences of her or his actions or inactions if the suing party has sufficient evidence to prove all of the following factors:

- The person against whom the suit is brought owed the suing party a duty.
- The person breached that duty.
- The person's breach was unreasonable—that is, a reasonable person of like education and training, under the same or similar circumstances, would not have acted in the same way.
- The suing person suffered injury or damages.
- The breach was the proximate cause of the injury or damages.

In child welfare practice, federal and state laws, administrative policies, rules, and regulations create duties, case decisions, and standards adopted by the profession. Previous chapters addressed the duties created in decisional and statutory law and administrative policies, rules, and regulations. Such issues as who can consent to entry into the home, interviewing children without parental permission, visual inspections of children's bodies, medical examinations without parental permission, failure to adequately monitor care provided in parental homes after abuse or neglect has been found, failure to adequately monitor care provided in foster homes and institutions, and failure to ensure permanency have been litigated. In this chapter we focus on the ethical duties created by the Code. The question becomes whether or nor the social worker's behaviors were within the ethical standards of the profession.

The first section of the Code of Ethics addresses the ethical responsibility for competent practice. This may feel problematic to child welfare workers, who often feel overwhelmed by the responsibilities of being entrusted with decisions that can affect children's lives. Like Susan Smith in the case study at the beginning of this chapter, child welfare social workers may have the right credentials but still have difficulty learning the fine points of child welfare practice. Code Section 1.04 states

(a) *Social workers should provide services and represent themselves as competent only within the boundaries of their education, training, license, certification, consultation received, supervised experience, or other relevant experience.*

(b) *Social workers should provide services in substantive areas or use intervention techniques or approaches that are new to them only after engaging in appropriate study, training, consultation, and supervision from people who are competent in those interventions or techniques.*

(c) *When generally recognized standards do not exist with respect to an emerging area of practice, social workers should exercise careful judgment and take responsible steps (including appropriate education, research, training, consultation, and supervision) to ensure the competency of their work and to protect clients from harm. (NASW, 1996, pp. 8–9)*

Section 4.01 states

(a) *Social workers should accept responsibility or employment only on the basis of existing competence or the intention to acquire the necessary competence.*

(b) *Social workers should strive to become and remain proficient in professional practice and the performance of professional functions. Social workers should critically examine and keep current with emerging knowledge relevant to social work. Social workers should routinely review the professional literature and participate in continuing education relevant to social work practice and social work ethics.*

(c) *Social workers should base practice on recognized knowledge, including empirically based knowledge, relevant to social work and social work ethics. (NASW, 1996, pp. 22–23)*

Child welfare, as a field of practice, is one of the most complex in the field of social work. Its complexity lies in the multiplicity of the knowledge base and intervention techniques required, as well as the ever-changing public attitudes that translate into federal and state policies. Child welfare practitioners, as a whole, do not hold degrees in social work, yet are characterized as social workers or caseworkers in the minds of the general public. Those who have degrees in social work frequently are in need of supplemental education and training specific to child welfare practice. The demands on child welfare workers are such that frequently they lack the time to engage in the further education and training necessary. Thus the dilemma. See Figure 12.1 for specific activities of child welfare work that may raise liability issues.

Child welfare practice is, for the most part, an involuntary service. Even where there is no court intervention, the parents' general belief is that they must do what the worker and the agency expects or risk having their children removed from their custody. It is the rare parent who comes to a child protection agency requesting assistance. Many parents seek assistance from mental health agencies or juvenile or family courts when their children are exhibiting behavioral difficulties. Some receive this assistance and some do not or do not receive it in the manner necessary to resolve the difficulties. The latter group generally receives involuntary services through the abuse or neglect or delinquency systems. The involuntary nature of the system, coupled with the dual client problem, raises many ethical issues. Code Section 1.03 states

(a) *Social workers should provide services to clients only in the context of a professional relationship*

FIGURE 12.1   Areas of Risk of Liability*

ACTIVITY	LEVEL OF RISK
Failure to report	Moderate
Failure to accept report for investigation	Moderate
Failure to adequately investigate report	Moderate**
Failure to remove child from home	High**
Failure to protect child once returned home	Moderate-High**
Wrongful reporting	Low
Defamation/slanderous investigation	Low
Negligent, overintrusive investigation	Low-Moderate
Malicious initiation of a child abuse or neglect proceeding	Low
Breach of confidentiality	Low
Wrongful removal	Moderate
Failure to adequately protect child from harm in foster care (e.g., due to inappropriate placement, inadequate supervision, failure to revoke license, etc.)	High**
Negligent diagnosis or treatment	Moderate
Sexual impropriety	Moderate
Failure to provide services leading to return of child	Moderate
Failure to warn of child's dangerousness	Moderate-High
Fraud (e.g., in adoptive placement)	Moderate

Source: American Bar Association. *Liability in child welfare and protection work.* (1991). Washington, DC: Author.

*This list was developed as a starting point for evaluating levels of risks nationwide. It is unlikely that it will reflect accurately the situation in a particular jurisdiction but serves instead as a model for the process of identification and evaluation of the risks of liability.

**The level of risk in federal court actions may be different.

based, when appropriate, on valid informed consent. Social workers should use clear and understandable language to inform clients of the purpose of the services, risks related to the services, limits to services because of the requirements of a third-party payer, relevant costs, reasonable alternatives, clients' right to refuse or withdraw consent, and the time frame covered by the consent. Social workers should provide clients with an opportunity to ask questions. . . .

(b) . . .

(c) In instances when clients lack the capacity to provide informed consent, social workers should protect clients' interests by seeking permission from an appropriate third party, informing clients consistent with the clients' level of understanding. In such instances social workers should seek to ensure that the third party acts in a manner consistent with clients' wishes and interests. Social workers should take reasonable steps to enhance such clients' ability to give informed consent.

(d) In instances when the clients are receiving services involuntarily, social workers should provide information about the nature and extent of services and about the extent of clients' right to refuse service.

(e) . . .

(f) Social workers should obtain clients' informed consent before audiotaping or videotaping clients or permitting observation of services to clients by a third party. (NASW, 1996, pp. 7–8)

In general, children lack the capacity to give informed consent. In general, it is the role of the parent or guardian to give consent on behalf of the child. In child welfare practice, however, the interests of the parent and child may conflict. Should the social worker inform the parent that he or she will request court intervention in those situations where, in the social worker's judgment, the parent's decision is not in the child's best interests? Should the social worker inform the parent that he or she will report statements made by the client to the court? What does the social worker tell the child client? Consider this case situation.

> David, an autistic child with extremely self-injurious behaviors, has not been helped by a number of behavioral programs designed to control head banging and self-mutilation. An expert that the parents consulted independently recommends that the child be sent out of state to a private treatment setting that uses electric shocks as a deterrent to the behavior. This treatment center claims outstanding results in reduction of self-injurious behavior and maintenance of the non–self-injurious state, through an ongoing program of intermittent shocks when the child first begins to display the undesired behavior.
>
> Understandably, the parents feel quite desperate. They have stated to you that their marriage is in jeopardy due to the stress from this child. The mother is not willing to have the child placed in group care or an institutional setting. The father is stating that his wife's constant preoccupation with David's needs is damaging the well-being of their other two children. Jenny, the younger sister, appears depressed. Donny, the eldest child, has been failing in school. Clearly the whole family is in a lot of pain. Their minister has counseled them to take the advice of the expert, who seems to be highly regarded within their denomination.
>
> In order to be admitted to the program, the family must be recommended by their minister, and by a child and family therapist. They plead with you to make the referral for them. They believe it is David's last chance, and the family's last chance to remain intact.

Confidentiality and Privileges

Confidentiality and *privilege* are frequently used interchangably, but they do not mean the same thing. *Confidentiality* refers to the statements made by a client with the expectation that they will not be shared with persons other than those to whom they are spoken unless the client authorizes otherwise. *Privilege* refers to confidential communications that are protected by statute from being disclosed in legal proceedings. The rationale for privilege statutes is that confidentiality is necessary to ensure and establish a trusting relation-

ship so that the client divulges information necessary in the intervention process which he or she might not otherwise divulge if he or she thought the information might be passed on to someone else without her or his knowledge or consent (Gothard, 1995).

Child welfare communications may or may not be privileged, depending on individual state statutes and the specific evidence contained in the confidential communication. Even where states provide for social worker–client privilege, there are generally exceptions to absolute privilege—that is, disclosure only with client consent—which provide that confidential information can be disclosed by order of the court under certain circumstances delineated in the statutes. Remember that the confidence and the privilege belong to the client and not the professional. While the professional can state that the communication is confidential and/or privileged, the client is the one who must assert the privilege—that is, consent or not consent to the release of the information—and in the final analysis, the court will determine if it should overrule the client's decision not to consent.

You should review the privilege statute for the state(s) in which you are currently practicing or intend to practice.

The Code provides direction and dilemma on this issue. Section 1.07 states

> (a) *Social workers should respect clients' right to privacy. Social workers should not solicit private information from clients unless it is essential to providing services or conducting social work evaluation or research. Once private information is shared, standards of confidentiality apply.*
>
> (b) *Social workers may disclose confidential information when appropriate with valid consent from a client or a person legally authorized to consent on behalf of a client.*
>
> (c) *Social workers should protect the confidentiality of all information obtained in the course of professional service, except for compelling professional reasons. The general expectation that social workers will keep information confidential does not apply when disclosure is necessary to prevent serious, foreseeable, and imminent harm to a client or other identifiable person or when laws or regulations require disclosure without a client's*

consent. In all instances, social workers should disclose the least amount of confidential information necessary to achieve the desired purpose; only information that is directly relevant to the purpose for which the disclosure is made should be revealed.

(d) . . .

(e) Social workers should discuss with clients and other interested parties the nature of confidentiality and limitations of clients' right to confidentiality. Social workers should review with clients circumstances where confidential information may be requested and where disclosure of confidential information may be legally required. This discussion should occur as soon as possible in the social worker–client relationship and as needed throughout the course of the relationship.

(f) . . .

(g) . . .

(h) . . .

(i) Social workers should not disclose confidential information in any setting unless privacy can be ensured. Social workers should not discuss confidential information in public or semipublic areas such as hallways, waiting rooms, elevators, and restaurants.

(j) Social workers should protect the confidentiality of clients during legal proceedings to the extent permitted by law. When a court of law or other legally authorized body orders social workers to disclose confidential or privileged information without a client's consent and such disclosure could cause harm to the client, social workers should request that the court withdraw the order or limit the order as narrowly as possible or maintain the records under seal, unavailable for public inspection.

(k) Social workers should protect the confidentiality of clients when responding to requests from members of the media.

(l) Social workers should protect the confidentiality of clients' written and electronic records and other sensitive information. Social workers should take reasonable steps to ensure that clients' records are stored in a secure location and that clients' records are not available to others who are not authorized to have access.

(m) . . .

(n) . . .

(o) . . .

(p) Social workers should not disclose identifying information when discussing clients for teaching or training purposes unless the client has consented to disclosure of confidential information.

(q) Social workers should not disclose identifying information when discussing clients with consultants unless the client has consented to disclosure of confidential information or there is a compelling need for such disclosure. (NASW, 1996, pp. 10–12)

Section 1.08 states

(a) Social workers should provide clients with reasonable access to records concerning the clients. . . . Social workers should limit clients' access to their records, or portions of their records, only in exceptional circumstances when there is compelling evidence that such access would cause serious harm to the client. Both clients' requests and the rationale for withholding some or all of the record should be documented in the clients' files.

(b) When providing clients with access to their records, social workers should take steps to protect the confidentiality of other individuals identified or discussed in such records. (NASW, p. 12)

Section 3.04 states

(a) Social workers should take reasonable steps to ensure that documentation in records is accurate and reflects the services provided.

(b) Social workers should include sufficient and timely documentation in records to facilitate the delivery of services and to ensure continuity of services provided to clients in the future.

(c) Social workers' documentation should protect clients' privacy to the extent that is possible and appropriate and should include only information that is directly relevant to the delivery of services. (NASW, p. 20)

The Code encourages protection of client's privacy while at the same time acknowledging that there are instances in which the client's privacy must give way to the sharing of the information with or without client consent. In child welfare practice, there are many instances in which the confidentiality of clients may be compromised. For example, when a child with HIV is placed in a foster home, the foster parents will probably need to know about the child's medical condition in order to work as part of a health care team. Or if a parent, believing that he has a confidential relationship with a child welfare worker, confides in the worker that he did indeed molest his child, this information could be used in criminal proceedings against that parent.

Under the law, social workers are required to report abuse and neglect. Yet in doing so, the social worker may face angry accusations of betrayal from a parent or other client who dared to trust. Social workers also have an affirmative responsibility to act to prevent murder or suicide. It is important in all professional relationships to discuss the limits of confidentiality when first engaging a client.

Child Client Confidentiality.   The ever-present questions for the child welfare practitioners is what information provided by the child the social worker may share and with whom. The social worker also faces the dilemma of needing to confirm the child's information without revealing the source. Consider the following case situation.

> Hank, age 13, was in a residential treatment setting. His foster care worker was making a routine visit to monitor Hank's progress, when Hank confided that he was being "beat up" by other youths in the program who made fun of him and harassed him after lights out. Hank said he had a secret that he would only share if his worker promised not to tell anyone. Janice, his worker said, "I won't tell anyone unless it is absolutely necessary to protect you." After some hesitation, Hank confided that he couldn't take it any more and had developed a plan to commit suicide.
>
> Janice moved quickly to inform child care staff and Hank's therapist of the suicide threat, and to put necessary precautions in place. Hank was very angry, and told Janice he couldn't trust her any more. Janice reminded him that she had said she would not tell anyone unless it was necessary to protect Hank. "Hank, this time it was necessary. It could have been a matter of life and death. Your well-being is my first concern."

Working with Other Professionals

Child welfare practice involves engagement with many different professionals. Given the diversity of

professionals, it is not atypical for professional disagreements to arise. Code Section 2.01 provides guidance to the social worker on how to handle referrals and the disagreements that may result from these referrals. It states

> (b) *Social workers should avoid unwarranted negative criticism of colleagues in communications with clients or with other professionals. (National Association of Social Workers, 1996, p. 15)*

Section 2.04 states

> (a) *Social workers should not exploit clients in disputes with colleagues or engage clients in any inappropriate discussion of conflicts between social workers and their colleagues. (Id., p.16)*

Section 2.06 states

> (a) *Social workers should refer clients to other professionals when the other professionals' specialized knowledge or expertise is needed to serve clients fully or when social workers believe that they are not being effective or making reasonable progress with clients and that additional service is required.*
>
> (b) *Social workers who refer clients to other professionals should take appropriate steps to facilitate an orderly transfer of responsibility. Social workers who refer clients to other professionals should disclose, with clients' consent, all pertinent information to the new service providers. (Id., p. 17)*

SPECIAL ISSUES IN CHILD WELFARE PRACTICE

Treatment in a Managed Care Environment

Managed care is gaining momentum in child welfare practice. It became a standard in mental health and substance abuse services during the 1990s. For many of the parents, and increasingly for many of the children, these services are critical to successful outcomes in child welfare. Historically, the lack of availability of appropriate mental health and substance abuse services in the appropriate "dosage" have been identified as barriers to permanency for children in out-of-home care and as underlying conditions for referrals to children's protective services and juvenile justice services. Managed care practice exacerbates the problem (US General Accounting Office, 1998; Stroul, Pires, Armstrong, & Meyers, 1998; Field, 1996; Kowal, 1996; Institute for Human Services Management, 1996).

In addition, managed care potentially raises ethical dilemmas for the social worker. Section 1.16 of the Code states

> (a) *Social workers should terminate services to clients and professional relationships with them when such services and relationships are no longer required or no longer serve the clients' needs or interests.*
>
> (b) *Social workers should take reasonable steps to avoid abandoning clients who are still in need of services. Social workers should withdraw services precipitously only under unusual circumstances, giving careful consideration to all factors in the situation and taking care to minimize possible adverse effects. Social workers should assist in making appropriate arrangements for continuation of services when necessary. (National Association of Social Workers, 1996, pp. 14–15)*

Given the complexity of child welfare cases, it is highly unlikely that they will be conducive to a managed care model that limits the number of sessions provided or the time period in which service eligibility exists. Several states are experimenting with the concept of managed care in the child welfare environment to determine its applicability to child welfare practice and any necessary modifications to the model for implementation to child welfare practice (National Community Mental Healthcare Council, 1997).

A related ethical problem is raised within the policy and financing context demonstrated in the following case situation.

> You are employed by a foster care agency to provide treatment for abused and neglected children and adolescents. You have been working with an 8-year-old girl who, after six months of treatment, has begun to trust you enough to disclose sexual abuse by both her parents. She has been placed in a kinship care situation with an aunt, who is due to receive guardianship as a permanence plan. (Parental rights were terminated earlier.) Because the permanence plan is about to be completed, the agency is preparing to close the case.

> The agency's service contract, which funds you, provides funding for treatment of foster children. It does not, however, provide funds for children in guardianship situations. This means that you as therapist will no longer be funded to provide treatment. Thus you have been advised by agency management to terminate treatment within the next two weeks.

> You have seen the child's reaction as she began to play out sexual abuse themes. You can honestly describe the child as having been in a state of terror at that time. You are also aware of her dissociative episodes and are beginning to speculate as to whether the child may have a multiple personality disorder. You are of course concerned about the possible potential of the child to perpetrate against other children. You have strong clinical indications that it is essential for you to continue treatment at this critical point.

> You have suggested that the agency continue the child's foster care status so as not to disrupt treatment. The agency management is not willing to do so, as such an action would violate their funding contract by prolonging foster care when a permanence option was available. Your supervisor suggests that the aunt could take the child to the local community mental health agency, or even that she could bring the child to your agency's private-pay family counseling branch, and pay the sliding scale fee herself. The problem as you see it is that changing therapists at this point would jeopardize the child's progress in treatment at the most critical point, when the child's defenses are down and she has just started to trust.

> The supervisor has suggested tactfully to you that you may perhaps be emotionally over-involved with the child, as you are having problems "letting go." The supervisor is also concerned that if you press your point with the aunt she may be reluctant to assume guardianship. She feels her niece is "a normal kid who just needs a lot of love." You think that to terminate prematurely for reasons related to agency funding patterns constitutes the ethical violation of client abandonment.

Child welfare practice is inherently a process of risk-evaluation and risk-taking. Advocates have long argued that to be effective, child welfare practitioners need to have a comprehensive knowledge and skills base coupled with a range of supportive resources and interventions that could be utilized, based on their comprehensive initial assessment and continuous reassessment of the family, its individuals and its environment. Managed care is a system based on the principle that the majority of cases and conditions fall within a prescriptive intervention which can be delivered in a certain time period or number of sessions. Child welfare policy has advanced the concept of permanency through the adoption of specific time frames, although not absolute time frames, for returning the child to the home or termination of parental rights. This policy is based on research addressing the child's needs for stability in relationships, not on research on the effectiveness of service delivery systems in meeting the complex needs of multiproblem child welfare cases.

Duty to Warn and Report

All states now have statutes that require certain professionals to warn third parties, generally through law enforcement agencies, of threats to their physical safety made by clients receiving treatment from the professional which the professional believes the client has the intent and means to carry out (Dickson, 1995). In addition, all states require social workers, as well as other specifically identified professionals, to report instances of suspected child abuse and neglect (National Clearinghouse on Child Abuse and Neglect Information, 1998). Code Section 1.07 (e) states

> Social workers should discuss with clients and other interested parties the nature of confidentiality and limitations of clients' right to confidentiality. Social workers should review with clients the circumstances where confidential information may be legally required. This discussion should occur as soon as possible in the social worker–client relationship and as needed throughout the course of the relationship. (p. 11)

Forensic Social Work Practice

Child welfare matters, including juvenile delinquency, frequently result in court intervention. *Forensic* means "belonging to or connected with a court" (Black, 1992). Juvenile court procedures have changed substantially since their inception as a court of benevolent and discretionary decision-making. Court decisions, discussed in Chapter 2, have resulted in greater for-

malities in the decision-making processes to ensure constitutional safeguards for children, juveniles, and their parents. These formalities have resulted in the need to conduct child welfare investigations in ways that preserve the evidence and limit the attack by opposing attorneys on the child welfare worker's methodology in the collection of the evidence.

The goal of a forensic interview with a child "is to obtain a statement from the child, in a developmentally-sensitive, unbiased and truthseeking manner, that will support accurate and fair decision-making in the criminal justice and child welfare systems" (Michigan Governor's Task Force on Children's Justice, 1998, p. 1). The process of forensic interviewing has been discussed in Chapter 6. Here we are concerned with the ethical dilemmas raised when you know that you are interviewing to gather information for use in a legal proceeding. Section 1.07 of the Code states

> (a) Social workers should inform clients, to the extent possible, about the disclosure of confidential information and the potential consequences, when feasible before the disclosure is made. This applies whether social workers disclose confidential information on the basis of a legal requirement or client consent. . . .
>
> (e) Social workers should discuss with clients and other interested parties the nature of confidentiality and limitations of clients' right to confidentiality. Social workers should review with clients circumstances where confidential information might be legally required. This discussion should occur as soon as possible in the social worker–client relationship and as needed throughout the course of the relationship. . . .
>
> (j) Social workers should protect confidentiality of clients during legal proceedings to the extent permitted by law. When a court of law or other legally authorized body orders social workers to disclose confidential or privileged information without a client's consent and such disclosure could cause harm to the client, social workers should request that the court withdraw the order or limit the order as narrowly as possible or maintain the records under seal, unavailable for public inspection.

The dilemma is that, by informing the client of the possible uses and consequences of disclosures in advance of those disclosures, you limit the information available for assessment and intervention. This could result in improper intervention and decision-making. On the other hand, if you do not inform the client in advance, you are not complying with your ethical duty.

Testifying in Administrative and Judicial Proceedings

The principles of testifying were discussed in Chapter 6. Here the focus is the dilemmas raised by Section 1.07 (j) of the Code:

> *Social workers should protect confidentiality of clients during legal proceedings to the extent permitted by law. When a court of law or other legally authorized body orders social workers to disclose confidential or privileged information without a client's consent and such disclosure could cause harm to the client, social workers should request that the court withdraw the order or limit the order as narrowly as possible or maintain the records under seal, unavailable for public inspection.*

How do the terms "to the extent permitted by law" and "could cause harm to the client" apply in child welfare practice? The social worker is engaged with the child and family to carry out a public function, that is, the protection of vulnerable children and/or the protection of society from the actions of wayward or delinquent children. Which client do you protect—the adult or the child? Perhaps even society is your client. Whose interests are paramount? Should you consider the potential harms to yourself and your agency? The child welfare worker must be aware of federal laws, such as strict confidentiality with respect to federally funded recipients of substance abuse services, that supercede state laws with respect to what information the court can order divulged.

CHILD ADVOCACY

The history of the social work profession is rich with initiatives focused on advocacy for the poor and vulnerable. Over the years, the profession has shifted focus to individual, group and community practice and, in the view of some commentators, has lost sight of its roots in social reform (Fink, Anderson, &

Conover, 1968; Bailey & Brake, 1975; Netting, Kettner, & McMurtry, 1998; Richan, 1991). While advocacy efforts for some disadvantaged groups may have diminished, it is clear that child advocacy efforts continue to grow and achieve significant gains at the federal, state, and local levels.

Responsibility for Advancing Social and Economic Justice

The social worker's ethical responsibility to engage in advocacy efforts is delineated in Section 6 of the Code. The responsibilities are broad-based and rooted in the concept of advancing social and economic justice. Section 6.01 states

> *Social workers should promote the general welfare of society, from local to global levels, and the development of people, their communities, and their environments. Social workers should advocate for living conditions conducive to the fulfillment of basic human needs and should promote social, economic, political, and cultural values and institutions that are compatible with the realization of social justice.* (National Association of Social Workers, 1996, pp. 26–27)

Section 6.02 states, "Social workers should facilitate informed participation by the public in shaping social policies and institutions" (Id., p. 27). Section 6.04 states

> (a) *Social workers should engage in social and political action that seeks to ensure that all people have equal access to the resources, employment, services, and opportunities they require to meet their basic human needs and to develop fully. Social workers should be aware of the impact of the political arena on practice and should advocate for changes in policy and legislation to improve social conditions in order to meet basic human needs and promote social justice.*
>
> (b) *Social workers should act to expand choice and opportunity for all people, with special regard for vulnerable, disadvantaged, oppressed, and exploited people and groups.* (Id., p. 27)

What Is Advocacy?

In 1981, the Child Welfare League of America defined child advocacy as "the process of sensitizing individuals and groups to the unmet needs of children and to society's obligation to provide positive response to these needs" (p. ix). This definition emphasizes the educational role inherent in all advocacy efforts. But the League also recognized the definitional dilemma by stating: "Whether one talks in terms of advocacy, or influencing public social policy, or engaging in social action or promoting institutional change makes no essential difference" (p. 1). It is interesting to note that persons who viewed advocacy as a large part of their work defined it as "intervention on behalf of a client or client groups with an unresponsive system" (Epstein, 1981, p. 8). Mickelson (1995) has advanced the following definition: "In social work, advocacy can be defined as the act of directly representing, defending, intervening, supporting, or recommending a course of action on behalf of one or more individuals, groups, or communities with the goal of securing or retaining social justice" (p. 27).

Historical Background.   The practice of child advocacy takes different forms as the needs of children and the organizational environments responding to those needs change. Present-day child advocacy has its origins in 1899 with the juvenile court movement, the 1910 White House Conference on Children, and the establishment in 1912 of the Children's Bureau at the federal level. Among the forces that helped to produce interest in child advocacy in more recent times were the new visibility given to poverty and delinquency in the 1960s and the government programs intended to reduce the number of children and families living under seriously inadequate economic conditions.

From the Mobilization for Youth project came the concept of "client advocacy," defined as intervention "on behalf of a client with a public agency to secure an entitlement or right which has been obscured or denied" (Cloward & Elman, 1967, p. 267). Mobilization for Youth was an inner-city youth project developed by a multidisciplinary social agency on New York City's Lower East Side. Its focus was on the need for broad social, economic, and institutional reform. Delinquency was viewed as the result of a lack of congruence between a young person's aspirations and opportunities. A range of services was offered—employment, legal, educational, psychological, and

social. The community action programs under the Economic Opportunity Act were largely modeled on the Mobilization for Youth experience. The "War on Poverty" launched by the Economic Opportunity Act produced the principle of "maximum feasible participation" on the part of clients affected by the new antipoverty programs, challenged the conventional and sometimes complacent service delivery methods, and persistently questioned the processes that led to institutional decisions about poor families and children.

Another set of influences that moved the idea of child advocacy forward came from attention to problems in public school education. The 1960s brought a stream of studies, evaluations, and opinions with provocative titles, such as *Death at an Early Age, How Children Fail,* and *Crisis in the Classroom,* about inadequate educational facilities and the failure of the schools to educate children, especially children of the poor and children with special needs—for example, physically and mentally handicapped children and children in need of bilingual education (Holt, 1964; Kozol, 1967; Silberman, 1971). Out of the controversy came attempts to create new approaches to education by modifying school conditions and practices.

Successful demonstrations in the late 1960s of the gains to be made for children through the use of the judicial system constituted another influence on the development of the child advocacy movement. The *Kent* and *Gault* decisions affirmed due process rights of juveniles alleged to be delinquent. A significant court case in Pennsylvania questioned the constitutionality of school policies that resulted in the exclusion of handicapped children (*Pennsylvania Association,* 1971). Similar suits followed and eventually played an important part in congressional enactment of the Education for All Handicapped Children Act of 1975. Another major litigation challenged conditions in juvenile correctional institutions and resulted not only in an order for changes in such institutions but also in the creation of a community-based system of alternative forms of care and treatment (*Morales v. Turman,* 1974). These and other demonstrations of ways in which litigation can be used to advance child rights not only led to change in service procedures and methods but also helped to establish important principles inherent in the concept and practice of child advocacy.

Another development begun in the 1960s was also related to the emergence of interest in child advocacy. Ralph Nader's consumer advocacy efforts have been focused on the obligations of corporations to respond to consumer interests and on the failure of government regulatory authorities to monitor the activities of industry adequately. Knitzer (1976) pointed out that, unlike the participatory model of antipoverty activists, Nader's strategies are "overtly elitist, both in choice of staff and in the processes by which issues are selected" (p. 207). Nevertheless, she acknowledged, Nader and his staff have been highly successful in researching and focusing attention on systemic problems—an accomplishment that has not been lost on proponents of child advocacy.

Illustrations of avant-garde child advocacy programs are found in the records of the U.S. Children's Bureau in the years between the progressive era and the enactment of the Social Security Act in 1935 and in the contemporary Children's Defense Fund. In each instance far-thinking and daring women committed to social justice for women, children, and young families are credited with successful leadership. Julia Lathrop was the first and Grace Abbott the second chief of the Children's Bureau; Marian Wright Edelman is the founder and president of the Children's Defense Fund. All three have records that encompass the following:

- effective definition of problems that require social action
- development and maintenance of diverse constituencies
- building and supporting coalitions
- conceptualizing and implementing systematic studies of the problem and the forces affecting it
- disseminating findings in strategic forums
- astutely recognizing political factors that control the targeted problem
- applying sound judgment as to where and when pressure can be effective.

Children's Defense Fund. Following the new surge of advocacy in the 1960s, attempts were made to develop national child advocacy organizations, most of

which had limited success (Steiner, 1976). One that has survived as an effective and dynamic advocacy unit is the Children's Defense Fund, a nonprofit organization committed to long-range systematic advocacy to bring about reforms in behalf of children. Marian Wright Edelman, who founded the organization in 1973 and has provided its leadership since then, is recognized as a dynamic and highly effective advocate for children in the complex and competitive arena where social policies and legislation are influenced. Through her work in Mississippi in the 1960s, Edelman recognized that it was necessary to find a way to affect not only state policy but federal policy as well. She sought and obtained a Field Foundation grant and in 1968 established an organization based in Washington, D.C.—the Washington Research Project—with an intent to monitor a variety of federal-level activities and influence change by research and dissemination of findings.

This experience demonstrated the need to set priorities and specific goals if one sought the attention of policy makers. "The country was tired of the concerns of the sixties. When you talked about poor people or black people, you faced a shrinking audience" (Tomkins, 1989, p. 67). Carefully defined goals in relation to children and their unmet needs seemed to Edelman an effective focus for broadening the base and building a coalition for social change. Edelman sought to cut through race and class barriers by addressing the needs of children throughout the country. In 1973 Edelman founded the Children's Defense Fund (CDF).

What scares me is that today people don't have the sense that they can struggle and change things. In the sixties, in Mississippi, it just never occurred to us that we weren't going to win. We always had the feeling that there was something we could do, and that there was hope. (Marian Wright Edelman—Tomkins, 1989, p. 74)

The CDF set out to protect effective programs already in existence and work for new programs that would emphasize parental involvement and community change. The selection of targets for reform activity was made on the premise that effective advocacy must be specialized, not global, in its approach to change, and that the issues should be ones that affect large numbers of children, that are easily understood by the public, that are subject to attacks at local, state, and federal levels, and that give promise of being affected by a combination of strategies. The early issues the CDF chose to pursue included the following:

- the exclusion of children from school
- classification and treatment of children with special needs
- the use of children in medical (particularly drug) research and experimentation
- the child's right to privacy in the face of computerization and data banks
- reform of the juvenile justice system
- child development and child care
- children in foster care (Beck & Butler, 1974).

Over time, CDF has broadened its areas of interests to include other child neglect and abuse, children's health care, early education/Head Start, homelessness, poverty, youth violence, and teenage pregnancy and parenting. The wide dissemination of findings from CDF studies by means of publications, testimony before congressional committees, and presentations in a variety of public forums has been highly effective in securing interest and action for change.

Even though the success of the CDF has rested in large measure on the particular talents of Edelman, its staffing pattern and its in-depth strength are also crucial. Staff members from various disciplines have been able to use their specialized knowledge in a unified approach to change. They serve as litigators, researchers, and federal administrative monitors. Community liaison people are also important in maintaining a constituency and in helping to bridge the gap between people in local communities and advocates at the federal level.

On the assumption that some groups that may not support a general effort may come together around a children's issue that affects their special interests, the CDF relies on specialized coalition-building as a primary strategy. Issues for reform activity are selected not only for their importance to children and families but also for their potential for building coalitions and constituencies. Other specialized strategies and activities include litigation, drafting and pushing legislation, monitoring administrative agencies, providing

public education, and organizing local groups who work with children and offering them technical support (*CDF Reports,* 1998).

Case and Class Advocacy

The types of situations and issues that indicate the need for child advocacy have been discussed in each chapter of this book: poverty; poor nutrition; inadequate housing; homelessness; lack of proper health care; and the failure to provide educational programs that succeed in preparing young people for the basic skills that are required for entry into the world of work. Specific to the field of child welfare are issues of the application of due process guarantees in the juvenile courts; the definitions of child abuse and neglect; the meanings of reasonable efforts, permanency, family preservation, and child protection; the jailing or secure detention of youth prior to adjudication; sexism and racism in the dispositional decisions of child welfare agencies and the courts; the provision of legal representation for children and parents in adjudications directly affecting them; and the question of the scope of constitutional protections for children.

Advocacy on behalf of children is needed now as much as it has been in the past. All of these situations, and others as well, call attention to the necessity of monitoring legislative, administrative, and budgetary processes and, at times, the professional behavior of persons charged by society to act in behalf of children. The approach to advocacy for a specific issue can include techniques focused on resolution of the issue for an individual client or techniques focused on resolution of the issue for all persons now affected or who may be affected in the future. The former is *case advocacy* and the latter is *class advocacy.*

Case advocacy is focused on an individual child in order to bring about resolution of some barrier to the child's receiving a needed service or concrete benefit. A child may need a service that is not available in the community, or is in such short supply as to be unavailable to this particular child. Sometimes the service exists, but parents do not know how to find and use it, and sometimes children are denied service without any defensible rationale. In other instances, services may be given, but in a form that is seriously inadequate or inappropriate. In situations like these, someone directly concerned usually initiates advocacy action for the child—a social worker or other professional, or a paraprofessional, such as a health aide or teacher's aide.

Other situations that invite case advocacy are readily illustrated—a child is unfairly detained in jail; a child is inappropriately or unfairly placed outside the mainstream of the school learning structure; a child is denied an adoptive home because no one in the foster care system has initiated or followed through on a positively oriented review of his or her suitability for adoption; or a child is repeatedly suspended from school without a hearing by school personnel to determine whether the child is persisting in the offending behavior for reasons over which he or she has little or no control.

If these individual case advocacy issues appear over time to involve the same policy, practice, or agency, then the effective advocate will shift to class advocacy techniques. This approach is more efficient where the problem is widespread, in that class advocacy maximizes the current benefit to all children who should receive the benefit or who should not be subjected to the sanction. When successful, it results in changes in policies, practices, or agency administration. For example, the advocate may involve a citizen's group in examining the conditions that lead to children's being held in the community's jails, or, with a group of parents, the advocate may endeavor to bring change in school practices in relation to suspensions or placement of children in special education classes. These actions may not be adversarial nor require legal action. They may rather be aimed at supporting school or court personnel in the development of corrective measures to advance generally approved goals for children.

If there is a need for litigation, Rule 23 of the Federal Rules of Civil Procedure (1998) provide that a class action can be advanced if these four conditions exist:

- The class membership is so numerous that to join all members in the court action is impracticable.
- The legal issue or problem common to the class predominates over any legal issue or problem affecting members as individuals.

- Claims of the representative members are typical of the claims of the class.
- The representative members will fairly and adequately protect the interests of the class.

Action on behalf of a class of persons is done primarily for the purpose of efficiency. Progress on a case-by-case basis takes too long and does not necessarily bring change for others. Nor does case advocacy provide the political leverage that helps to bring change for children generally in related problem areas.

Nevertheless, efficiency and political leverage are by no means the central reason for child advocacy. Protecting the rights of the individual child is the central purpose of all child advocacy efforts. Although for child advocacy to be successful individual needs must often be grouped and classified, the needs and the rights of the individual are the heart of advocacy at any level and for any group of persons. Advocacy of the individual and class advocacy are inseparably related.

Writing from the perspective of the highly effective advocacy programs of the Children's Defense Fund, Knitzer (1976) identified some underlying assumptions common to all forms of advocacy:

1. Advocacy assumes that people have, or ought to have, certain basic rights.
2. Advocacy assumes that rights are enforceable by statutes, administration, or judicial procedures.
3. Advocacy efforts are focused on institutional failures that produce or aggravate individual problems.
4. Advocacy is inherently political.
5. Advocacy is most effective when it is focused on specific issues.
6. Advocacy is different from the provision of direct services. (p. 205)

Child advocacy, then, is primarily concerned with seeing that existing organizations and services work for children rather than with undertaking to provide another special service. In contrast to the professional service role, the role of a child advocate is partisan. The advocate is first and foremost for the child. The professional, in contrast, is to a large extent for all the persons concerned with the problem situation—even the target agency—and tries to bring about a constructive balance in the varying and sometimes conflicting characteristics and needs of the different parties. This does not mean that a professional social worker in a children's service agency cannot take an advocacy stance in behalf of children or groups of children, and sometimes go beyond role expectations and conventional procedures to enable individual children or families to secure a necessary service or the observance of their rights. In addition, some child welfare services have added an advocacy unit that performs a separate administrative function.

For too long professionals have been locked into a point of view that tells them that "trouble" or "problems" are the exclusive property of a child or of his or her parents. Far less frequently has attention been given to the social process of interaction between a child and his or her environment. _Environment_ includes the aggregate of external conditions and influences that affect or control a child's life and development. In addition to the family, such determinants include schools, courts, neighborhoods, hospitals and clinics, and the mass media. Advocacy intervention is focused on the events that have taken place or are taking place between the child and his or her environment and that are causing trouble—perhaps even to the point of expulsion from the family or peer group.

Child advocacy objectives are not attained by defining the job to be done in terms of either the problems of children or the problems of the environment of children. Instead, advocacy tasks must be defined in terms of problems that are generated by the interaction between children and their environments—in the exchanges or transactions that take place in those interactions (Paul, 1977).

Components of Child Advocacy

Child advocacy projects vary in significant ways. Within the diversity, however, there appear to be features that are fundamental to all projects: auspices, sanction for intervention, target selection, and basic tasks, strategies, and techniques.

Auspices.   The question of auspices for a child advocacy program is a significant one. Auspices determine certain basic characteristics of a project: Who authorizes it, who pays for it, and who runs it—that is, the balance between citizen and professional participation.

Early debate about who should authorize and fund child advocacy centered on the question of whether child advocacy should be separate from any governmental system to avoid the inhibitions that might result from risks in challenging high-level officials. But private funding can also pose constraints. Consider this example cited by Knitzer—that of a child advocacy program run by a local voluntary agency receiving funds from the United Way: "The child advocates may have difficulty focusing community attention on children excluded from schools if the United Way Board includes several school officials who have publicly denied the problem" (Knitzer, 1976, pp. 213–214). In practice, the necessity of locating and competing for funds has meant that both public and private funds have been used for child advocacy projects.

As child advocacy has developed, advocacy projects have come to include these types, classified according to their auspices: (1) projects authorized and paid for by a governmental body—for example, county councils or commissions made up of citizens and mandated by a county government to serve as an adviser on children's needs; (2) projects authorized and operated within a governmental body, often at the state level, with staff members who are employees of government—for example, the South Carolina Office of Child Advocacy, which is responsible to the governor; (3) projects independent of governmental auspices and supported by, and part of, preexisting private organizations; and (4) projects independent of any government or preexisting private organization and often funded by private foundations—for example, the Children's Defense Fund—or projects funded by memberships or other forms of individual contributions.

The auspices of a project can be a crucial determinant of what can be undertaken and accomplished by child advocacy. But, as Knitzer (1976) pointed out, any advocacy effort involves risks, and important as the auspices are, the energy, commitment, and political know-how of the advocates are equally important.

Who Is the Advocate?   The question of who is best equipped to be an advocate for children continues to be debated. The last twenty years have witnessed proposals for a wide range of professionals to be involved, including lawyers, social workers, psychologists, physicians, and urban planners. Some have argued for a more limited role for professionals. In fact, the renewed interest in child advocacy was largely based on a mistrust of professionals and the organizations they operate. The fear was that professionally directed advocacy efforts would be weighted more toward professional self-interest than toward the needs of children. This has led to a demand for a significant degree of citizen and paraprofessional participation in advocacy projects.

In many cases, an effective advocacy effort involves multiple groups of professionals, scholars, citizens, and the youth themselves. Many advocacy efforts are complex, requiring a variety of roles to be filled, depending on the situation. Successful child advocacy programs have employed, in various configurations, different kinds of personnel, including college students, social scientists, parents, citizens, lawyers, and other professionals. There is obviously not a single answer. What is most clear, however, is that the welfare of children is best served when increased numbers of people from all stations of life become actively involved.

Sanction for the Right to Intervene.   Child advocacy requires sanction. Responsible child advocacy means that persons who attempt to intervene in society's institutions must be sure that their assertive or adversarial stance is justified.

In view of all that has been said about the injustice to children and the unmet needs for social services, one may well question why individuals should be required to justify their right to try to improve the status of children. But when an advocacy group decides that an individual agency or institution is not responding adequately to the children for whom it carries responsibility, then that advocacy group is usually attempting to bring about some significant change in an institution or agency, such as making the target agency more flexible in its approach to child needs, increasing budget allocations, undertaking new programs, or reassigning control of programs.

But on what basis can child advocates establish their right to intervene? Kahn, Kamerman, &

McGowan (1972) gave the following guidelines for validating the right to advocate:

1. *A sanction for child advocacy exists when children have justifiable rights, that is, "legislatively specified benefits for which administrative discretion is quite circumscribed and which can be adjudicated in the courts when administrative agencies do not deliver." In such instances there is a clear-cut entitlement to a benefit or a specific service, such as survivors' benefits under Social Security, or an appropriate educational program in the least-restrictive environment for a handicapped child. In such cases, the child advocate's sanction to act is clear-cut. Other instances in which the right to advocate is easily recognized include those where there is strong indication that some children or families are being treated differently from others in a similar situation, perhaps because agencies and personnel are ignoring their own policies and procedures or are acting carelessly or in a discriminatory way. For example, the right to advocate is clear if a children's agency mandated by law to receive and investigate all reports of child abuse and neglect attempts to manage a heavy workload by deciding to respond to reports of neglect only when those reports carry an indication of physical abuse as well, or if a juvenile court makes sure that middle- and upper-income parents are present and informed of their right to counsel when hearings affecting them and their children are held, but fails to do the same for parents who are very poor.*

2. *A sanction for child advocacy exists when the effort is intended to expand the boundaries of legally governed child rights. For example, it is generally held that the parent-child relationship remains intact, with parental rights primary, unless serious abuse, neglect, or unfitness on the part of parents is established. But a question arises as to whether continued state intervention is justified if it is merely an exchange of governmental neglect for parental neglect. If a child's parents make the difficult but often necessary decision to institutionalize their child and only a simple regime of enforced custodial care is given—not treatment that is appropriate and adequate in light of present knowledge—then the issue of a right to treatment emerges.*

   In situations like these, advocates for children may choose to work for an extension of child rights beyond what is already clearly established in law.

Sometimes the sanction to do so rests on a series of lower court decisions or inconclusive actions, or simply on statements of some authoritative body that has spoken out on the issue.

3. *A sanction for child advocacy may exist even when no specific right or statement of principle appears in law. The right to intervene may be validated in a number of ways, which Kahn et al. (1972) identified:*

   1. *Available professional knowledge and expertise about dangers to child development may provide backing for child advocacy.*
   2. *The joining of knowledge and values may bring about agreement on a "social minimum" that finds support in professional and community norms and thus gives validity to the child advocacy effort.*
   3. *Sometimes groups such as parents of disadvantaged or handicapped children articulate their own needs, and in doing so provide a sanction for child advocacy. Even though this sanction rests on self-definition and personal experience, it is often enough for advocacy to proceed.*
   4. *Sometimes the view people have of society, social justice, and acceptable priorities in the use of resources leads them to study social indicators of the status of children and to collect data about families and children in relation to such critical factors as school attendance and achievement, health and illness, and nutrition. Their analysis of such data then becomes a sanction for child advocacy (pp. 70–75).*

Selecting the Target for Advocacy.   In some child advocacy projects, the target is only one system—for example, the school system—and the advocacy group attempts to deal with a range of school-related problems such as suspension, corporal punishment, education for children with disabilities, and the use of drugs for control of pupil behavior. Other projects may at various times attack issues involving a number of agencies or institutions that impinge on children's lives. Often a project that starts out with only one institution as the target begins to uncover negative effects of other institutions on children, and so its advocacy efforts are expanded. For example, dealing with advocacy issues in a public school often raises questions about the mental health system, and atten-

tion to the mental health system may lead in turn to concern about the juvenile justice system.

Tasks, Strategies, and Techniques.   Child advocacy sometimes is an adversarial process, but, as Knitzer (1976) reminds us, "it is also a problem solving process that requires keen attention to problem definition and analysis" (p. 208). Once a constituency is settled on, whether that constituency be mentally ill children, teenage parents, children adrift in foster care, children waiting throughout their childhood for a permanent home, children given corporal punishment at school, or some other group of special concern, then the advocacy group must turn its energies to fact finding. Both client-centered and institution-centered data that are relevant to the need for advocacy must be collected, organized, studied, and assessed—data such as the identified characteristics, needs, and legal rights of clients; societal and institutional perceptions of the client group; the responsibilities and resources of the institution; the location of the sources of power in the institution; and the nature of the decision-making processes in the institution. Gaps in services and obstacles to the utilization of services must be identified, such as barriers posed by insufficient or inappropriate allocation of staff resources, or failure to develop alternative practices—for example, alternatives to the use of jails for children or to "banishment" into distant states of children in need of foster care. The problem that is causing the trouble—the difficulty in the child-environment transactions—must be documented and analyzed before remedies can be developed and effective intervention can take place. Frequently this procedure requires becoming informed on substantive matters that affect the workings of the target institution: the nature of law and the judicial process, the knowledge about foster care that has been verified through research, the curriculum content of a public school program and what school administrators and teachers consider to be major curriculum issues, or the institution's sources of funding and the legal constraints on its budgeting processes.

Political factors that affect or control the situation of concern must be assessed. These could include the positions taken earlier by key persons in the institutional target or the points at which pressure is likely to be effective or to intensify resistance.

Once the problem has been defined and analyzed, then comes attention to what Knitzer terms "the heart of advocacy," that is, *the development of strategies and remedies.* "Without attention to strategies and remedies, fact-finding alone would be nothing more than an exposé" (Knitzer, 1976, p. 208). The advocate may rely on a single strategy or a range of interventions. The strategy may be adversarial, perhaps the use of a class action litigation. Courts are often the target system for advocacy, but they are also important instruments of advocacy. The strategy selected may also be benign, such as one that relies on support from consensus about values or from widely accepted knowledge and ideas about human rights. Whether the strategy is adversarial or benign, the advocate must be a person or group of recognized status and must possess influence that can be expended. Enthusiasm, compassion, and a sense of mission are not enough.

The advocate's influence can derive from coalitions of different groups of people, sometimes quite diverse, who have an interest in the problem or the proposed remedy. Steiner (1976) has emphasized the significance of involving groups with a self-interest and joining them with social altruists as a driving force in the children's cause. As an example he cites the national school lunch program. A powerful coalition of political forces came together to produce a greatly expanded national school lunch program. Lobbyists for agricultural interests and congressmen from rural states wanted to maintain an outlet for surplus farm products. Welfare-oriented congressmen were responsive to the nutritional problems of children in poor families. The school lunch program was a convenience for middle-income groups, and the middle-income subsidy it provided was popular with some lawmakers in Washington. Lobbyists for various nutrition groups and others interested in children's learning problems saw hungry children as unable to learn at school. Proponents of the War on Poverty viewed school lunches as an acceptable relief program. The American School Food Services Association, an association that exists in all fifty states, had a self-interest in an expanded uni-

versal program rather than one for poor children only. The association is made up of school lunch directors, supervisors, and line workers, and their organizational intent is to maintain job opportunities and improve wages and working conditions. A group of social altruists—an ad hoc Committee on School Lunch Participation—made up of five women's organizations, each with a religious orientation, set out to learn why relatively few children were participating in the school lunch program and why it was failing to meet the needs of poor children. As a result of their inquiry, they came out on the side of a universal program. An expanded program also had the support of another lobby, the Children's Foundation, an antihunger organization made up of social altruists and functioning independently of governmental funds. The result was a social benefit that is almost universally available in schools. Aside from public education itself, Steiner noted, no social welfare program provides public benefits to more children than the national school lunch program (Steiner, 1976).

As important as coalition building is, so is the *maintenance of coalitions.* Keeping a coalition together can be difficult and sometimes impossible, particularly when advocacy efforts at the peak of their consensus and influence meet powerful opposition. The congressional enactment of comprehensive child development legislation in 1971 provides an example. An unusually effective coalition had been put together (despite far from identical goals among the groups) by the advocacy talents of Marian Wright Edelman and her Children's Defense Fund. The coalition reflected the interests of these major segments: (1) professionals and citizens interested in child care for children as a program of care and protection; (2) similar groups whose interest in child care was focused on early childhood education with an emphasis on cognitive development; and (3) activists interested in community change, such as those in the movement to enlarge the input of parents and citizens into the use of public funds and into program design. Edelman's emphasis was on child development as an instrument for civil rights and community change. She was able to put together a coalition of groups such as the National Association for the Education of Young

Children, the League of Women Voters, the AFL-CIO, the Day Care and Child Development Council of America, the National Committee of Negro Women, the National League of Cities, the U.S. Conference of Mayors, and the National Welfare Rights Organization. The appearance of support from organized labor was important. The bill that passed Congress was far from perfect, but it stood as a significant effort in child advocacy. President Nixon's veto, however, halted the drive for child development legislation. The coalition began to weaken as the differences among its three main segments became clearer. Child development as an issue in Congress went into a "holding action"—meaning "maintaining Head Start without growth while waiting for a political climate more favorable to new legislation" (Steiner, 1976, p. 90).

Supporters of federal legislation for child care began again to rebuild the coalition and succeeded in influencing significantly higher appropriations for Head Start during the Carter administration. With child care becoming a white, middle-class issue, as Edelman went around the country she found growing public support for federal child care legislation. A comprehensive child care bill became the legislative goal of the CDF in 1988. The reconstructed coalition was larger than the one put together in 1971. Outreach to the business community corrected an earlier omission and strengthened the coalition (Tomkins, 1989).

A strategy that has been used successfully by advocacy groups as a way to increase the cadre of advocates and give them a self-interest in bringing about reform is to *reach out to and co-opt groups of volunteers.* "The volunteer-as-participant invariably becomes the volunteer-as-partisan" (Steiner, 1976, p. 249).

Advocates use the technique of *articulating findings in appropriate forums,* such as among persons or groups who have potential power to affect the problem—the governor, city councils, school boards, regional and county officials, civic organizations, federal officials, state department heads, or mayors. In such instances advocates must have a repertoire of technical knowledge about government structures, budgeting, legislatures, and official program guidelines as well as skill in political negotiation. It is not enough to know how to reach and even influence

major officials; the advocate must also be well informed on substantive issues.

Child advocacy groups may also engage in *lobbying* in an effort to persuade legislators to introduce certain bills or to influence the passage or defeat of bills under debate.

Advocates use a range of *other specific techniques*—suggestion, negotiation, education, persuasion, pressure, demands, confrontation, and legal action. Another important part of successful advocacy is *monitoring*—maintaining contact with persons in a position to watch over the conduct of those who serve children. Monitoring, or follow-through, is essential if advocacy is to be more than a one-time exposé. Monitoring is a way to assure continuous community awareness and presence. It is particularly important in class action litigation in order to make sure that the process of implementing court decisions gets under way. It has also been used successfully in assuring that federal agencies implement legislation or that state agencies observe federal program guidelines.

TRENDS AND ISSUES

Media attention to problems of children, youth, and their families will continue to play a significant role in elevating the needs of children to public exposure, discussion, and debate. Television, newspapers, opinion journals, popular magazines, and films publicize in different ways the problems of poverty, teenage pregnancy, juvenile crime, youth drug use and sales, increased HIV infection and AIDS in children and adolescents, multiple foster care placements, sibling separations, adoption drift (legally available children languishing in foster care because adoptive homes are not available), inadequate mental health services, and homelessness. Much of the publicity has drawn attention to the inadequacies of the child welfare system, among others. Currently, and historically, media publicity often focuses on the inadequacies of the systems and individuals charged with the responsibility to provide services to these children. Effective use of these media stories as advocacy tools requires, in the author's opinion, less defensiveness on the part of the systems and individuals attacked and greater readiness to objectively analyze the weaknesses and strengths of the system and make constructive changes. The College of Journalism at the University of Maryland has established the Casey Journalism Center for Children and Families as a national resource for journalists who cover children and their parents. It promotes careful and thorough examination of issues by reporters and supports this with conferences that expose journalists to national policy and research experts on a range of issues affecting disadvantaged children. This type of engagement promotes, within the journalism profession as a whole, reporting that provides more "good news" stories where the systems or individuals are effective and more evidence based, specific target stories where the systems or individuals are ineffective (Casey Journalism Center for Families and Children, 1998).

Federal and state legislation in behalf of children does not come easily. The 1990s saw continued shrinking of resources and a concomitant increase in competition for those that are available. Without doubt, many decisions in the next decade will be reached on the basis of finances. Specifically, we are moving into an age of managed care. In such a milieu, the need for case and class action on behalf of children (illustrated repeatedly throughout this text) will be critical. An essential piece of advocacy in the 2000s will be data. Outcome data on organizations and programs currently serving the population will be a requisite to enter the executive and legislative hallways. Once in the doors, advocates must clearly articulate how their proposals will enhance those outcomes. Suggesting and monitoring legislation, building coalitions, testifying in Congress and state capitals, securing and maintaining presence on executive agency policy-making and advisory committees, and becoming active in political campaigns will be necessary. Parents, youth, and other citizens need encouragement to express their views about the status of child and family life, the risks they see, and the changes they want in order to strengthen and maintain strong family life and maximum opportunity for children and youth.

The qualifications and training of child welfare workers continues to receive public scrutiny. Most child welfare workers are not professionally trained in social work. Few receive the depth and breadth of in-service or on-the-job training and supervision necessary to effectively manage the responsibilities of their positions. Many professionally trained social workers do not have child welfare–specific expertise. This presents challenges to the profession as well as to the individual worker. The community as a whole views all child welfare workers as "social workers." Bad practice is attributed to the profession, irrespective of the training of the child welfare worker involved. The National Association of Social Workers has undertaken the professionalization of child welfare workers as a strategy to alleviate the current situation (National Association of Social Workers, 1997). Liability exposures with resultant legal judgments or settlements in cases involving "bad practice" could persuade public officials to join with NASW in this effort.

CHAPTER SUMMARY

In discussing professional responsibility, this chapter has provided a broad set of issues to consider as you undertake child welfare practice: confidentiality and privacy; liability and malpractice; confidentiality and privileges; forensic interviewing; risk management and duty to warn; clients' rights to treatment in a managed care environment; testimony; and advocacy. Its purpose was to show the range of responsibilities attributed to the professional and the dilemmas inherent in these responsibilities. Many of the dilemmas have no conclusive answer that the child welfare worker can rely on in every case. Decisions require balancing interests and consequences as applied to the current case situation. On the other hand, some are clearly resolved by statutory requirements that supercede ethical principles and standards, such as reporting suspected child abuse or neglect. A methodology has been provided to assist the worker in resolving the dilemmas.

FOR STUDY AND DISCUSSION _____

1. Apply Reamer's seven steps for resolving ethical dilemmas to the following case situation. Kevin,

age 16, has run away from his adoptive home. You have been working with the adoptive parents and Kevin concerning his adjustment to the family's expectations (he was adopted two years ago), his poor academic performance and acting out behaviors in school (he was recently expelled for bringing a knife to school), and his sometimes explosive anger. You have identified several critical issues in your individual work with Kevin. He has never processed his grief over the termination of parental rights prior to his adoption. He yearns to find his birth family and has threatened to run away to look for them. He is frightened of some of the other male students at his high school and has verbalized that they might do "terrible things" to him, although he refuses to say more on the topic. His self-esteem is, as Kevin himself says, "so down in the pits it couldn't be lower." Kevin's perception is that he will never fit into his adoptive family because they are "so good and so religious."

You are awakened from a deep sleep at 2 A.M. by your agency on-call service. Kevin is in crisis and needs to talk to you immediately. You call the number given. Kevin is so upset that the conversation is disjointed and rambling, and it takes your best skills to keep him talking and get the facts: Kevin ran away in search of his birth parents, whom he could not locate. He is calling from the home of his (biological) uncle. While at his uncle's house he used some drugs (he does not specify what) and allowed his uncle to have anal intercourse with him, hoping to please his uncle so that he could find out what happened to his parents. He has been having what he describes as "flashbacks" about "nasty things that I did when I was a kid." He is afraid that he is gay and is in a panic. He wants to meet with you to talk, but won't do it unless you promise that you won't tell his adoptive parents you have had contact with him. If you try to contact his parents (or the police) he says he will either run away and never come back, or kill himself. He won't tell you where his uncle's house is or what his uncle's name is. He offers to come to your house to see you now or to meet you in some place away from the agency in the morning.

2. Which should take precedence when the needs of the child, the family, the agency or society in general are in conflict? Are we ever justified in violating the law to help a client?

3. Joe is a 10-year-old child who entered foster care after his mother had broken his arm for the third time. He wants to go home with his mother. Does he have a right to self-determination? Why or why not? How do you explain your answer to him?

4. Joan is the 8-year-old daughter of the mayor of Big City. She has been referred to you by her teacher because she appears unusually anxious. Joan told you that her father has been rubbing the inside of her leg next to her vagina each night since school started. She thinks he shouldn't be doing this and she wants to tell her mother, but she doesn't want her mother to get mad at her. You tell her that her father should not be doing this and you will help her. You report this to your supervisor and tell her that you will make the mandated report to the child protective services agency. She tells you not to make the report. She will make the report after she has discussed the situation with "administration". What do you say?

5. How can children and youth be given an opportunity to help define the problems and issues that are advocated in their behalf?

6. Select a problem facing a group of children or youth in your state or community. Apply the steps of advocacy described in this chapter to the problem.

7. Debate the merits of a variety of persons acting as children's advocates. Include lawyers, social workers, college students, parents, and teachers. A list of qualifications for advocates should emanate from such a discussion.

8. Discuss the limits on the extent to which agency child welfare workers can act as advocates for children on their caseloads and children not on their caseloads who are served by the agency.

9. Responsibility for the neglect of today's youth is broadly shared. Discuss ways in which society could reshape its attitudes and priorities to help children and youth with their problems.

INTERNET SITES

There are several sites that provide competently re-searched policy and data for child welfare advocacy use.

Administration for Children & Families. http://www.acf.dhhs.gov/programs/acyf

American Public Human Services Association. http://www.apwa.org

Center for Law and Social Policy. http://www.epn.org/clasp.html

Child Trends. http://www.childtrends.org

Child Welfare League of America. http://www.cwla.org

Children, Youth and Family Education and Re-search Network. http://www.cyfernet.mes.umn.edu/index.html

Children's Defense Fund. http://www.childrensdefense.org/index.html

Families & Work Institute. http://www.familiesandworkinst.org

Family Life Development Center. http://child.cornell.edu/fldc.home.html

US General Accounting Office. http://www.gao.gov

Kids Count. http://www.aecf.org

National Association of Social Workers. http://www.nasw.org

National Center on Child Abuse and Neglect Clear-inghouse. http://www.calib.com/nccanch/

National Center for Children in Poverty. http://www.cpmcnet.columbia.edu/dept/nccp

Office of Juvenile Justice and Delinquency Pre-vention. http://www.ncjrs.org/ojjhome.html

The Juvenile Justice Clearinghouse. http://www.fsu.edu/~crimdo/jjclearinghouse/jjclearinghouse.html

Urban Institute. http://www.urban.org

United States Congress. http://thomas.loc.gov

FOR ADDITIONAL STUDY

Barker, R., & Branson, D. (1993). When laws and ethics col-lide. In *Forensic social work.* New York: Haworth Press.

Gustavsson, N. S., & Segal, E. A. (1994). *Critical issues in child welfare.* Thousand Oaks: Sage.

Jansson, B. (1994). Social policy: From theory to policy practice. Pacific Grove, CA: Brooks Cole.

Myers, J. E. B. (1992). *Legal issues in child abuse and ne-glect.* Newbury Park, CA: Sage.

Myers, J. E. B. (1994). *The backlash—child protection under fire.* Thousand Oaks, CA: Sage.

Rothman, J., Erlich, J. L., & Tropman, J. E. (1995). Strate-gies of community intervention (5th ed.). Itaska, IL: F. E. Peacock.

Thomas, J. C. (1995). *Public participation in public deci-sions.* San Francisco, CA: Jossey-Bass.

REFERENCES

American Bar Association (1991). *Liability in child wel-fare and protection work.* Chicago: Author.

Bailey, R., & Brake, M. (Eds.) (1975). In *Introduction: Social work in the welfare state.* New York: Pantheon Books.

Beck, R., & Butler, J. (1974). An interview with Marian Wright Edelman. *Harvard Educational Review, 44*(1), pp. 1–12.

Black, H. C. (1992). *Black's law dictionary* (8th ed.). St. Paul, MN: West Publishing.

Child Welfare League of America. (1981). *Statement on child advocacy.* New York: Author.

Cloward, R. A., & Elman, R. M. (1967). The storefront on Stanton Street: Advocacy in the ghetto. In G. Brager & F. P. Purcell (Eds.), *Community action against poverty.* New Haven, CT: College and University Press.

Dickson, D. T. (1995). *Law in the health and human services—a guide for social workers, psychologists, psychiatrists and related professionals.* New York: Free Press.

Epstein, I. (1981, Summer). Advocates on advocacy: An exploratory study. *Social Work Research & Abstracts.*

Field, T. (1996). Managed care and child welfare—will it work? In *Public Welfare/Summer 1996.* Washington, DC: American Public Welfare Association.

Fink, A. E., Anderson, C. W., & Conover, M. B. (1968). *The field of social work.* New York: Holt, Rinehart and Winston.

Gothard, S. (1995). Legal issues: Confidentiality and privileged communication. In *Encyclopedia of social work* (19th ed., 2:1579–1584). Washington, DC: National Association of Social Workers.

Holt, J. (1964). *How children fail.* New York: Pitman.

Institute for Human Services Management. (1996). *Managed care and child welfare: are they compatible? Design issues in managed care for child welfare.* Bethesda, MD: Author.

Kahn, A. J., Kamerman, S. B., & McGowan, B. G. (1972). *Child advocacy: Report of a national baseline study.* New York: Columbia University Press.

Knitzer, J. E. (1976). Child advocacy: A perspective. *American Journal of Orthopsychiatry, 46*(2), 200–16.

Kowal, L. W. (1996). *Keeping the focus on kids: Outcomes, ethics and partnerships in a managed care environment.* Paper presented at the American Humane Association's roundtable in Vail, Colorado.

Kozol, J. (1967). *Death at an early age.* Boston: Houghton Mifflin.

Michigan Governor's Task Force on Children's Justice and Family Independence Agency. (1998). *Forensic interviewing protocol.* Lansing, MI: Family Independence Agency.

Morales v. Thurman 380 F. Supp. 53 E. D. Tex. (1974).

National Association of Social Workers. (1996). *Code of ethics.* Washington, DC: Author.

National Clearinghouse on Child Abuse and Neglect Information. (1998). *State statute series.* Washington, DC: Author.

National Community Mental Healthcare Council. (1997). *Child welfare and managed care briefing.* Rockville, MD: Author.

Netting, F. E., Kettner, P. M., & McMurtry, S. L. (1998). *Social work macro practice* (2nd ed.). New York: Addison Wesley Longman.

Paul, J. L. (1977). *Child advocacy within the system.* Syracuse, NY: Syracuse University Press.

Pennsylvania Association for Retarded Citizens v. Commonwealth of Pennsylvania, 334 F. Supp. 1257, E. D. Pa. (1971).

Reamer, F. G. (1995). *Social work values and ethics.* New York: Columbia University Press.

Richan, W. C. (1991). *Lobbying for social change.* New York: Haworth Press.

Rule 23 Federal Rules of Civil Procedure.

Silberman, C. E. (1971). *Crisis in the classroom.* New York: Random House.

Steiner, G. Y. (1976). *The children's cause.* Washington, DC: Brookings Institution.

Stroul, B. A., Pires, S. A., Armstrong, M. I., & Meyers, J. C. (1998). The impact of managed care on mental health services for children and their families. *The future of children: Children and managed mental health care.* Los Altos, CA: The David and Lucille Packard Foundation.

Tompkins, C. (1989, March 27). Profiles: Marian Wright Edelman: A sense of urgency. *New Yorker,* 48–50.

Curriculum Competencies for Social Work Education in Family and Children's Services

In 1986, the Administration for Children, Youth and Families and the National Association of Social Workers issued an *Agenda for Action* for meeting the crisis in public child welfare. (See Chapter 1, Trends and Issues.) Social work education has responded to the call for the reprofessionalization of public child welfare by developing partnerships with state agencies to counter the shortage of social work professionals. Changes in federal legislation have also furthered this collaborative effort.

The following curriculum competencies were developed by the six graduate schools of social work in Michigan (Eastern Michigan University, Grand Valley State University, Michigan State University, University of Michigan, Wayne State University, and Western Michigan University) in partnership with the Michigan Department of Social Services. The Michigan chapter of the National Association of Social Workers convened a partnership committee, which included social work educators plus line staff, union representatives, and administrators from the Department of Social Services. The task was to develop a set of competencies that would be used consistently in all graduate social work programs in the state.

Underlying Principles

In preparing the competencies, the partnership committee was guided by the mission, philosophy, and operating principles of the Michigan Department of Social Services. These principles include:

- Every child should have a safe, stable, and permanent family relationship to help the child reach his or her potential.

- The focus for human service programs should be on prevention and early intervention to prepare children for future success.

- Programs and services for children and families should be community-oriented, home-based, and family-centered. Services also should be accessible, comprehensive, coordinated, culturally sensitive, and of high quality.

- Social work practice in family and children's services requires specialized knowledge, awareness, and skill in working with issues of child abuse, neglect, and other maltreatment in a family-centered manner.

Competencies for Family and Child Services in Child Welfare Settings

The following competencies, which comprise one section of the complete set of Michigan competencies, address the specialized subject matter in family and child services needed to prepare students for practice in child welfare agencies. We have endeavored to make this textbook responsive to the scope and intent of these competencies.

The curriculum in schools of social work which prepares students for advanced practice in child and family welfare settings builds on a general knowledge base found in the curricula of undergraduate social work programs and the core curriculum of graduate schools. The complete set of Michigan competencies address the general knowledge base as well as the specialized curriculum in family and child services and are available in the instructor's manual that accompanies this text.

The competencies can be a helpful tool for schools of social work attempting to adapt their curriculum to the needs of potential social workers in the field of family and child welfare and for training departments of state public agencies. They have also demonstrated their usefulness as a self-assessment instrument for students, who can use the assessment to focus their choice of courses and of assignments.

Students will gain **knowledge** in the following areas:

1. The state's legal definitions of physical abuse, sexual abuse, neglect, dependency, and endangerment

2. The proper role of the court system in family and children's services practice; how the court system is used to protect children; and the role of social workers in relation to the courts

3. The proper responsibilities of the child protection agency and workers, including investigating complaints of maltreatment, providing ongoing in-home services, providing temporary substitute care placements, and facilitating permanent homes for children

4. The importance of maintaining continuity of relationships for the child or youth in placement and working with family, kinfolk, friends, and foster and adoptive parents to ensure that placement or status changes do not sever important emotional bonds

5. The potential negative effects of child abuse, neglect, and sexual abuse on a child's development; how children's behavior problems maybe symptoms of underlying developmental delays or emotional disturbance, and the indicators of developmental problems in abused and neglected children

6. The value of teamwork for providing support and fulfilling job-related responsibilities and principles of collaboration

7. The policy issues and legal requirements affecting family and children's services practice, including confidentiality, worker liability, reasonable effort requirements, and permanency planning

8. The present structure and organization of service delivery systems to children and families, and major studies relevant to these systems

9. The history of child and family welfare and factors that influence change over time

10. The importance of judicial decisions on state and federal policies issued, affecting families and children, such as *in re Gault; Stanley v. Illinois;* and *DeShaney*

11. How the well-being of families and children is affected by social and economic factors such as poverty, sexism, racism, unemployment, and the demands of employment

12. Significant state and federal legislation affecting families and children

13. The function of family support and prevention programs in the continuum of family and children's services, the values and theories on which they are based, the services they provide, and the role of the social worker in accessing these services

Students will develop **understanding and awareness** of the following:

14. Their own emotional responses to clients, especially in areas where their values are challenged, as they relate to violence, substance abuse, neglect, physical, sexual and emotional abuse, and strategies to deal with these responses

15. The dual roles of the family and children's services workers to protect children from maltreatment and to provide services that enable and empower families, as well as the legal, ethical, and practical dilemmas inherent in fulfilling these sometimes conflicting responsibilities

16. The dynamics of resistance and other barriers to the development of the helping relationship, and techniques for overcoming the resistance that is the natural consequence of involuntary services and situations that are threatening to clients

17. How ethnocultural backgrounds affect the way adults rear and discipline their children

18. The principles of permanency planning and the importance of family continuity, the negative effects on children of changing and inconsistent living arrangements, the importance of permanency planning throughout the life of a case, and the importance of achieving permanence and continuity of relationships

19. The process and dynamics of normal attachment of children to their parents, their significant caregivers, and substitute caregivers, and the situational and emotional barriers to such attachment

20. The physical, emotional, and behavioral indicators of placement-induced stress in children of varying ages

21. The importance of home visiting and other out-of-office contacts with families and children and how to conduct interviews under these circumstances

22. The medical, legal, and social management needs of the child with HIV, and the importance of working with kinfolk, foster, adoptive, and birth families in meeting these needs, and in coping with the stresses of such care

23. The importance of conducting routine and timely case reviews; and the reassessment of case goals, plans, and service interventions to make needed modifications in a family case plan

24. The appropriate use of termination of parental rights and initiation of adoption planning and family continuity when return of a child to his or her family or to relatives can no longer be considered

25. The issues related to the adoption of older children or children with special needs, including family recruitment, assessment, and preparation, post-placement supportive services, and strategies for preparing children and families for adoptive placement

26. The signs of institutional abuse in foster care, residential care, and other institutions in which children are placed and the methods to refer child abuse and neglect to the appropriate family and children's services agency personnel

27. Ritual, cult, and satanic abuse

Students will develop the **practice skills** to:

28. Incorporate into practice the values of the social work profession, including respect for the client's dignity, individuality, and the right to self-determination

29. Work cooperatively with other disciplines routinely involved in the investigation, prosecution, and treatment of family and children's services cases

30. Assess the individual, family, and environmental factors and dynamics that contribute to child maltreatment (including physical abuse, emotional abuse, sexual abuse, and neglect) and delinquency

31. Recognize and assess the primary manifestations of adult/parental dysfunction, such as substance abuse, mental illness, and domestic violence, and their impact on children, including the assessment of risk to the child

32. Recognize specific physical and behavioral indicators of child neglect, physical abuse, sexual abuse, and psychological maltreatment

33. Evaluate the level of risk for abused or neglected children in the family, assess the level of continuing risk for abused or neglected children within the family, and weigh it against the trauma of separation and other risks of out-of-home placement and its possible impact on the child and family

34. Assess and implement treatment plans that view the whole child and family across major areas of functioning, including family and children's services, health education, psychological functioning, income maintenance, housing, strengths of the family, and other relevant factors

35. Develop an intervention plan specific to the needs and strengths of the child and family that addresses the specific treatment needs for sexual abuse, failure to thrive, physical abuse, educational neglect, and so forth

36. Structure the placement of a child to prevent crisis and its consequences, including using preplacement preparation and visits and other strategies that minimize stress and provide support to the child

37. Work collaboratively with foster families, kinship caregivers, adoptive families, and other caregivers, involving them in assessment and planning and supporting them in coping with special stresses and difficulties

38. Develop intervention and treatment plans to improve a child's or adolescent's capacity for attachment to parents and others, and a parent's capacity for reciprocal bonding

39. Teach appropriate parenting, including behavior management and setting realistic expectations, and explain and demonstrate parenting techniques

40. Advise parents and other caregivers on age-appropriate expectations for children and how to help set realistic expectations for children by demonstrating parenting techniques or referring parents to formal training classes or groups when needed

41. Assist the teenage parent in understanding his or her developmental needs and in assuming adult responsibilities

42. Promote family preservation, family continuity, and permanence for children in foster care by involving parents in all aspects of placement planning, by promoting regular parental visiting with the placed child, by working with foster parents, kinship caregivers, and other foster care providers as part of the professional team, and by providing services toward timely reunification

43. Assess the behavior of children and youth in relation to delinquency policy and intervene appropriately

44. Understand the organizational structure of the public child welfare agency, and the ability to work within that structure to improve services for children and families

45. Use differential diagnosis, that is, the different levels of risk to children, different strengths and weaknesses in family members, and variability in types of child and family problems. Differential diagnosis should dictate different interventions, including when necessary the placement of a child in an alternate care setting

46. Evaluate various child welfare interventions and what the interventions indicate about the efficacy of child welfare practice

Students will use this knowledge in their practice.